Critical Thinking and Learning

Critical Thinking and Learning

An Encyclopedia for Parents and Teachers

Edited by Joe L. Kincheloe and Danny Weil

Greenwood Press
Westport, Connecticut · London

Library of Congress Cataloging-in Publication Data

Critical thinking and learning : an encyclopedia for parents and teachers /
edited by Joe L. Kincheloe and Danny Weil.
    p. cm.
  Includes bibliographical references and index.
  ISBN 0-313-32389-5 (alk. paper)
    1. Critical thinking—Study and teaching—Encyclopedias. 2. Cognitive
learning— Encyclopedias. I. Kincheloe, Joe L. II. Weil, Danny K.
  LB1590.3.C735   2004
  370.15′2—dc21   2003052848

British Library Cataloguing in Publication Data is available.

Library of Congress Catalog Card Number: 2003052848
ISBN: 0-313-32389-5

First published in 2004

Greenwood Press, 88 Post Road West, Westport, CT 06881
An imprint of Greenwood Publishing Group, Inc.
www.greenwood.com

Printed in the United States of America

∞™

The paper used in this book complies with the
Permanent Paper Standard issued by the National
Information Standards Organization (Z39.48-1984).

10 9 8 7 6 5 4 3 2 1

Contents

Preface

We live in a turbulent time, especially when it comes to issues surrounding education, schooling, and definitions of success within educational institutions. *Critical Thinking and Learning: An Encyclopedia for Parents and Teachers* sets itself in the middle of this turbulence, asserting that in the description of what constitutes critical thinking, the conversation surrounding it, and its implementation in classrooms rest some important insights into the social and educational contexts of the early twenty-first century. We cannot describe critical thinking without revealing our values and political affiliations; our perspectives on the educational reforms of an era that prescribes an ideologically charged, standardized curriculum; and our view of teachers as functionaries who implement what they are told by administrative superiors.

As I visit schools in New York City and talk to teachers working in this system, I detect a sense of despair. Such a feeling emanates from the implicit message of the reforms with which they are faced: teachers are assumed to be incapable of self-directed professional behavior marked by curriculum development and implementation. They are viewed as incompetents who are unable to assess individual student needs and prescribe particular pedagogical experiences. It is a sad time for the advocates of a rigorous and just education.

This encyclopedia develops a conception of critical thinking that respects the intellectual abilities of teachers and assumes that educational practitioners are capable of developing sophisticated cognitive abilities and passing such rigorous modes of thinking along to their students in every curricular domain. With this in mind, the encyclopedia lays out a new theory of critical thinking that is informed by a variety of innovations in social, political, philosophical, pedagogical, and cognitive scholarship. The introduction grounds this work and points to entries in the encyclopedia that further develop the theory or delineate ways teachers can implement this articulation of critical thinking in their classrooms. Thus, the encyclopedia attempts to be both conceptually challenging and pragmatic. In this context, it serves as both a source for rethinking critical thinking and for providing teachers with specific examples of how such ideas can be practically employed. It is our hope as editors that the encyclopedia helps open a new conversation about the very concept of what constitutes critical thinking and higher-level cognition in general.

The encyclopedia is organized around the introduction, which not only develops the new notion of critical thinking but also conceptually ties together the various entries. The editors suggest that you begin your exploration of the encyclopedia by reading this conceptual introduction and then go to specific entries that interest you or are directly related to your teaching. In this way, the conceptual background that we have tried to construct will help guide your use of the encyclopedia. Of course, some readers will use the encyclopedia for a quick reference to a particular educational domain. The encyclopedia's 84 entries, which are arranged by broad topics, are all usable in this way.

Either a quick or a deeper examination of this encyclopedia will grant the reader a new experience in thinking about educational purpose, the nature of higher-order cognition, new ways to arrange classrooms, or the relationship between school and the larger society. Some of these ideas may be quite different from concepts gleaned from prevailing modes of teacher education and college and university curricula. We hope that these unique perspectives will grab your interest and lead you to explore some of the references and additional readings listed at the end of each entry, or some of the important works listed in the general bibliography at the back of the book. Of course, what we really want is for the encyclopedia to open a new world of scholarship for you that helps you reconceptualize what you want to do with your professional life.

Obviously, we are writing for people who are interested in changing education for the better, whether they be teachers, parents, educational leaders, scholars of education and psychology, students, or participants in community organizations. From our perspective, the more readers from diverse social locations, the better. Realistically, we know that many of our readers will be teachers and teacher education students. For such readers, we believe that this book can provide both mind-altering and practical suggestions for your professional life. From whatever domain you come, we hope that the encyclopedia engages your interest and catalyzes your pedagogical and cognitive imagination. Unfortunately, in this era, there are many forces operating in the world of education and schooling that are designed to move individuals in an opposite direction.

Joe L. Kincheloe

Into the Great Wide Open: Introducing Critical Thinking

Joe L. Kincheloe

This introduction is designed to orient readers to *Critical Thinking and Learning: An Encyclopedia,* and to help make sense of what we're attempting to accomplish in this volume. My co-editor, Danny Weil, and I have envisioned two simple goals for the encyclopedia: (1) a reconceptualization of what is called critical thinking that includes the dramatic social and academic changes that occurred over the last few decades, and (2) an innovative analysis of the implications of this new mode of critical thinking for the classroom. We are especially interested in reaching the teachers and other scholars, teacher education students, and elementary, secondary, and college students who will make use of these ideas in their academic, vocational, and everyday lives. In this introduction I will describe the dominant types of critical thinking, then carefully develop a critical complex postformal mode of critical thinking.

Danny and I are very interested in the construction of critical thinking, its foundations, its assumptions, and its educa-tional use. We have no trouble with tradi-tional critical thinking's attempt to avoid unexamined living. We profoundly respect the tradition's emphasis on logic, concep-tual analysis, and epistemological insight, but we suspect that we can go farther. We believe that there are unexplored domains of human consciousness and cognition. While we make no claim that we have achieved some transcendent mind space, we do believe that some of the ideas and concepts explored here may lead the wis-est among us to new domains of human thinking, being, and doing.

It is in this context that we gave birth to *Critical Thinking and Learning.* We constructed it as a starting point for some-thing much greater than ourselves. Our book explores new, exciting ways of un-derstanding; new ways to be a student of the world; and ways to change those as-pects of human civilization that cause in-justice, pain, and suffering. We hope we can share our excitement about this pro-cess with you.

GROUNDING THE CONCEPT

We want to emphasize our indebtedness to those who have preceded us in the traditional field of critical thinking, including John McPeck, Robert Ennis, Matthew Lipman, Richard Paul, Israel Sheffler, and Harvey Siegel. Since we want to make sure critical thinking is not just a boys' club, we also wish to thank Barbara Thayer-Bacon, Sandra Harding, bell hooks, Patricia Hill Collins, Jane Flax, Judith Butler, Jane Roland Martin, and many others. These analysts have used their diverse racial, ethnic, and gender backgrounds to bring new insights and understanding to critical thinking.

In particular, we want to express our debt to John Dewey and his visionary insights, which we drew from Kathy Hytten's essay "Democracy and John Dewey." After delineating the nature of careful and reflective thinking, Dewey outlines the dispositions necessary for critical thinking to occur, then links critical thinking with the development of a moral sensibility and the process of social reform. The reconceptualization of critical thinking proposed here takes Dewey's ideas into account.

The encyclopedia also includes material that represents the intersection of the Frankfurt School critical theory with the hermeneutic work of Hans-Georg Gadamer. Gadamer's hermeneutics (the study of the art and process of interpretation and meaning making) maintains that mainstream and scientific modes of knowledge production take their meaning from unexamined assumptions and disguised ideologies. Knowing this, teachers and other scholars who understand hermeneutics realize that meaning making is more complex than previously realized. Max Horkheimer, Theodor Adorno, and Herbert Marcuse, members of the Frankfurt School during the 1920s, posited that the

world they were witnessing was in dire need of reinterpretation. Emerging from a deep knowledge of German philosophy and social and pedagogical science, the scholars of the Frankfurt School explored the ways injustice and subjugation shaped everyday life in post–World War I Germany. Directing their attention to the changing nature of market capitalism, these early critical theorists analyzed the mutating forms of domination that occurred in their environment.

Understanding these mutating forms of domination is the key to understanding what we are attempting to do in this book. Danny Weil and myself, as well as the numerous authors involved in the project, are attempting to develop new ways of thinking and teaching that help us deal with the complexities of domination. We have developed new concepts of human agency (how human beings direct their own fate and the fate of society—see Danny Weil's essay "Dialectical Thinking" for profound insight into this process), and write with the belief that individuals can shape their own existence and learn to operate in ways that resist oppression and the imposition of dominant ideologies (ways of making meaning of the world that support existing unequal power relationships). We cannot conceive of critical thinking outside such a sociocultural and political context.

We have forged the hermeneutic and the critical theoretical traditions to create a critical hermeneutics, which grounds our notion of critical thinking in the complexity of human existence, and connects everyday life to public issues of power, justice, and democracy. Classroom teaching can never be the same once teachers appreciate the influence of such concerns on knowledge production, curriculum development, and the formation of educational goals. We use a combination of critical hermeneutics, women's understandings of the power of patriarchy, complexity theory, African American socio-cultural insights, situated/enactivist cognitive theories, and indigenous knowledges to push the boundaries of cognition and create a better understanding of social justice. Our critical hermeneutics provides insight into the diverse academic and cultural texts that reinforce the ideology of privilege and entitlement for empowered members of society. We make the argument that critical thinking can be profoundly enhanced via an interaction with these ideas, and the power of such new and improved critical thinking can reform schools in ways never before imagined.

CRITICAL THINKING AS A NEW TERRAIN OF COGNITION

When critical thinkers started using diverse ways of seeing and making meaning, they began to discern interconnections between texts, ideas, physical objects, social circumstances, and the educational process that had previously been ignored. Complex critical thinking involves many different perspectives, diverse disciplines of knowledge (e.g., history, philosophy, sociology), and trans-disciplinary methods of cultural study. Complex critical thinkers, informed by these multiple perspectives, understand the relations between values and different interpretations of the world (Weinstein, 1995). They understand the way one's location in the world or position in the web of reality (which is determined by race, class, gender, sexuality, religion, etc.) shapes how one sees oneself and the world. In his essay "Critical Multicultural Literacy: Problematizing a Multicultural Curriculum Based on Reasoning," Danny Weil provides concrete classroom examples of ways to help students understand multiple perspectives and the influence of their own location in the web of reality on their world view.

These are the basic skills the critical thinkers we would like to graduate from our schools will need. We want them to recognize the benefits of using diverse ways of thinking to understand the world. Such critical thinkers become students of the different forms of intelligence to be found around the globe. They explore the world looking for and constructing new forms of critical thinking. In their essay on bilingual education, Hermán García and Teresa Valenzuela highlight this point when they say that critical thinkers have to find diverse ways of seeing in an educational system "that has produced historical and social analyses that are devoid of the Others' experience."

While we respect those who came before us, we are ambitious—we want to go farther. While benefits have come from teaching critical thinking as logic, we think this approach is inadequate. Critical thinking that teaches only how to discern the political inscriptions of texts and academic practices is also not enough. There is more to learn, more to be addressed, more to do. We need to question the nature of criticality more deeply and determine what it means to be critical in many different ways. We must question our assumptions, our notions of self, and our comfortable views of everyday life (Burbules & Beck, 1999).

In this mode, critical thinkers possess a radical humility, fallibility, and an awareness of complexity. We view ourselves and our ways of seeing in the light of new horizons and new contexts, and in the process make previously unnoticed connections. Such connections alert us to new dimensions of ourselves and our capabilities. We break through the cognitive confines of

Western ways of thinking into the great wide open.

In our attempt to move critical thinking to a new level, we do not tie our cognitive horses to the hitching post of hyperrationality and the instrumental rationality that characterizes it. Such a rationality involves an obsession with means rather than ends, method, procedure, and efficiency rather than human purpose and well being. Danny Weil illustrates the power of such rationalism in the early childhood curriculum in "Reasoning Readiness for Primary School Students: Critical Thinking As Developmentally Appropriate," in which he refutes the argument that learning is a rationalistic linear process that demands a set of prescribed locksteps.

Hyperrationality limits questions to how rather than why. This approach is illustrated by the Nazi medical researcher who meticulously recorded and analyzed the cephalic index (the shape of the head) of people entering Hitler's death camps but ignored the moral implications of genocide. To resist such rationalism, we do not need to go to the other extreme of nihilism and relativism that offer no hope for cognitive improvement or moral action. The answer lies in avoiding both extremes and searching for new and higher forms of thinking that allow us to engage in empowered action for our individual and social good.

Such alternative cognitive practices are often grounded in cooperative interaction and interrelatedness, even among very diverse populations. When connections are discovered, individuals come to see order instead of chaos in diversity. Humberto Maturana and Francisco Varela's cognitive theory of enactivism highlights interconnectedness and is an important part of our critical thinking melange. Varela wrote:

Lots of simple agents having simple properties may be brought together, even in a haphazard way, to give rise to what appears to be a purposeful and integrated whole, without the need for central supervision. (Varela 1999, p. 52)

This simple statement reveals a whole new dimension of both higher-order cognition and the character of the self. Using this concept, we blaze new trails into the domains of epistemology (the branch of philosophy that deals with knowledge) and ontology (the branch of philosophy that deals with the nature of being in the world). When we apply Varela to the epistemological domain, we realize that knowledge is stripped of its meaning when it stands alone. This holds profound implications for education and research because European science has studied the world in a way that isolates the object of study and abstracts it from the contexts and interrelationships that give it meaning. A critical thinker in Varela's enactivist mode studies the world in context, searches for the interrelationships that give knowledge meaning, and avoids decontextualized study.

In the ontological realm, a critical thinker influenced by Varela realizes that to be in the world is to operate in context, in relation to other entities. Western science, which originates from the scientific method delineated by Rene Descartes in the 1600s, sees the basic building blocks of the universe as things-in-themselves. What much recent research in physics, biology, social science, the humanities, and cognitive science posits is that relationships, not things-in-themselves, are the world's building blocks. To *be* in the world is to be in relationship.

People are not abstract individuals who live as fragments, in isolation from one another. Human beings become who they are and change who they are as a result of their connections to the social sphere. We learn to think and talk via socially constructed languages, behave in ways sanctioned by the cultural norms of our communities, and take care of ourselves by imitating significant others in our immediate environment. Race, class, gender, religion, and geographical place affiliations exert powerful influences on how we see ourselves and our relation to the world. To be human means to exist in a web of interrelationships and to possess the power to change, to be better, to be smarter, and to become a critical thinker.

According to Varela and the enactivists, human selfhood and consciousness emerge and evolve from the relationships of a variety of simple systems in human and social organisms, without the need for central supervision. We cannot find a seat of consciousness, a part of the mind that directs everything else, because it does not exist. The self is a virtual concept and changes in response to relationships in particular circumstances. Varela refers to it as the "selfless self: a coherent whole that is nowhere to be found and yet can provide an occasion for the coordinated activity of neural ensembles" (Varela 1999, p. 60). This virtual self holds profound implications for the future of human beings. If we have a socially constructed, humble consciousness, we can abandon egocentric, narcissistic ways of being and restructure ourselves around an awareness of the social forces at work in our world. This is a powerful starting place for a quest to become a more rigorous and empowered critical thinker. As we become more able to discern the connections between ourselves and other social, cultural, historical, physical, and human dimensions of the world, we become complex critical thinkers who view that world with humility and awe. This is the foundation on which we begin our quest to reconceptualize critical thinking and learn to teach critical thinking in a smarter way.

THE RECONCEPTUALIZATION OF CRITICAL THINKING

Critical thinking is not a new concept. It has been used throughout the history of western education, especially at the more advanced levels. The early critical thinking movement in North America was focused on developing Cartesian rationality among students and using critical thinking to ground the entire curriculum and all aspects of teaching and learning. The Frankfurt School would find such a perspective ideologically limited because it fails to discern the ideological, status quo-supporting, dimensions of pedagogy—features that teach ideological conformity, subservience to the regulatory goals of schools, and an unquestioning approach to oppressive social norms.

Stated in different terms, much critical thinking pedagogy unquestionably promoted certain patriarchal and Eurocentric modes of thinking as superior to all others. Much to the credit of some of our critical-thinking forebears, this implied debasement of other ways of thinking was recognized. Richard Paul called such a form of critical thinking and critical-thinking pedagogy sociocentric flawed thinking. Paul argues that we must respectfully understand the thinking of others and be more hesitant to reject other modes of knowledge production and meaning making.

Feminist scholars have extended these critiques, arguing that the mainstream critical thinking tradition as well as the Frankfurt School position have too often been domains populated and ruled by men and have excluded the contributions of women and non-white people (Burbules & Beck, 1999). A central dimension of *Critical Thinking and Learning: An Encyclopedia for Parents and Teachers* involves addressing these exclusionary practices on numerous levels. Barbara Thayer-Bacon, a leading scholar in the field, expands these ideas in her chapter, "Feminism and Critical Thinking."

Many different cultural groups have felt no sense of identification with the different articulations of critical thinking, because they do not address the needs of marginalized social groups. How can this reality be changed? Is it possible to articulate an accessible, race-, class-, gender-, sexual-, religious-, geographical, place-sensitive form of critical thinking that moves us to rethink who we are and where we are going? The editors and authors of this encyclopedia believe it is.

Thinking is always political. It is never detached from the world, its people, and their emotional needs. Advocates of complex critical thinking must be aware of the power implications of who sits at the negotiating table and who does not. Teresa Valenzuela and Hermán García expand this issue in "Gaining Access to Critical Literacy: Rethinking the Role of Reading Programs." No matter how loudly we proclaim our fidelity to inclusion and egalitarianism, we must prove it over and over again by asking who designs our curriculums, whose voices do they include, whose work do they draw upon, and what role do they assign cultural, social, and economic others when they are included?

THE TEACHER AS CRITICAL THINKER

Central to our conception of this encyclopedia is the idea that, in order to teach critical thinking, teachers must be critical thinkers. They must become scholar-practitioners. "Most would agree that teaching is a very complex process," Brenda Edgerton Conley writes in her entry on the reflective practitioner, "and that the development of competence and expertise in the profession is tied to critical learning." Conley goes on to make one of the encyclopedia's main points: teachers as critical thinkers must be exposed to alternate rationalities, or different ways of making sense of the world. Of course, this sets up one of the most important battles in contemporary educational politics: the role of teachers in the educational process. Should teachers be empowered critical thinkers who develop curriculums and direct their own professional lives or, as right-wing reformers would have it, should teachers be rule followers who simply execute standardized curricular materials and instructional practices developed by experts? John Smyth writes about this issue in "Teachers' Work: What Is Happening to It?" as does Jaime Grinberg, who imagines more complex and respectful roles for teachers in his "Only the 'Facts'?"

Teachers are consistently represented as incapable functionaries who simply don't have the ability to think critically (see Nancy Kraft's essay on "Students As Scholar Practitioners"). Brilliant teachers continue to teach, despite attempts to control their work and represent them as incompetent. If they are critical thinkers, they analyze their dilemma in the larger socio-political context and explore the ways it affects the profession and the teaching and learning process. Critical thinking teachers, as Kenneth Teitelbaum writes in his essay "Curriculum Theorizing," overcome restrictions and become theorizers—teachers who engage in inquiry along with action. Teitelbaum thinks that such an orientation connects teachers with the original meaning of the Greek word, *theoria,* or "wakefulness of mind," and helps teachers realize that schools usually do not view teachers or students as empowered democratic citizens. As Paul Brawdy and Juan-Miguel Fernández-Balboa put it in "Becoming a 'Good Teacher': Thinking Critically about Teaching," in many circles a good teacher is someone who enforces rules devised by outsiders to the teaching process. In such a context, critical thinking by both teachers and students is crushed.

The subject of critical thinking in education is complicated because teachers must think in action and must instantaneously account for hundreds of considerations, including differing individual viewpoints and irrational behavior. Critical thinking in education is an art form and goes beyond a Cartesian notion of reasoned choices among available logical alternatives or a Piagetian notion of formal operations where the linear procedures of the scientific method are followed by individuals seeking higher forms of cognitive activity. It is what we call postformal thinking—a form of cognition that contends that Piaget's Cartesian-based formal stages do not represent the apex of human cognitive ability.

Postformalists carefully attend to the work of Francisco Varela of the Santiago enactivist school. Varela argues that higher-order thinking occurs when individuals take knowledge, feelings, and actions that are considered smart in one set of circumstances and transfer them to more complex circumstances where smart thinking and actions are harder to identify. Thus, intelligent behavior does not involve a form of reasoning where universal rules are followed, but an ability to adjust knowledge to different sets of circumstances. In this context, intelligent and even ethical action may seem logically

contradictory to people operating at a formal level of critical thinking. Varela uses the Vajrayana Buddhist tradition's notion of "crazy wisdom" to describe the process of operating well in complex and ambiguous circumstances. At another point in his work, Varela refers to such abilities as "intelligent awareness" (Varela, 1999). The critical-thinking teachers referred to in this encyclopedia use crazy wisdom and intelligent awareness in their work. We are dedicated to a vision of highly professional, empowered, critical-thinking teachers.

Obviously, our definition of critical thinking is only one of many perspectives on the subject. Any student of critical thinking can find a wide variety of visions, including theories focused on the social context, political reality, or psychology, plus pedagogically and cognitively savvy theories and rationalized, or test-driven formulations. Unfortunately, the latter still thrive in the teacher-unfriendly, top-down, technical standards movement of the twenty-first century. (See Valerie Janesick's "Standards and Critical Thinking" for a compelling insight into the consequences of this hyperrational movement.) Everyone agrees that it is important to teach students and teachers to think critically; but often teachers are taught about critical thinking in workshops that are only a few hours long and cannot possibly address the unique, complex, dynamic process of the classroom. Friends of complex critical thinking must expose such educational charlatanism when we find it and inform the field of its dangerous oversights. Such commodified, packaged versions of critical thinking have become so common that they have besmirched the very concept of critical thinking.

Complex critical thinkers also reject authoritarian or rationalistic concepts of critical thinking. No final version of criti-cal thinking is offered in their place; criti-cal thinkers have simply committed them-selves to diversifying the meaning of critical thinking and finding new ways to apply it. Concurrently, critical-thinking teachers are trying to democratize the pro-cess and admit more marginalized people into the intellectual community.

In part, this call is an admission that we don't know exactly what critical think-ing is and never will. Once it is finally de-fined, it may die. The editors and authors of the encyclopedia realize that our only alternative is to simply keep searching for the unexpected and the unprecedented.

QUESTIONS FROM THE FIELD OF CRITICAL THINKING

Over the last several decades, numer-ous authors, theorists, and educators have asked a variety of questions about the study and use of critical thinking:

- Is critical thinking a separate subject that can be taught as an isolated discipline?

- Is critical thinking a particular set of skills or more an orientation toward, and valuing of, the process of thinking crit-ically?

- Is there a specific unchanging definition of critical thinking or is it context- and subject-specific?

- Is there a difference between critical thinking and rational thinking?

- Does a businessperson employ the same forms of critical thinking as a philoso-pher?

- Can we design a way to test critical thinking aptitude?

- Is critical thinking transferable from one domain to another?

Such questions give us a general sense of what students of critical thinking have been discussing. Francisco Varela (1999) raises some important issues in his work in cognitivism that help us take the con-versation further. Varela maintains that, whenever we create normative rules and procedures for engaging in activities such as critical thinking, we then face the di-lemma of applying these general rules to the complexity of everyday life. General-ized critical thinking that cannot be mod-ified to address the difficulties of a specific situation will become an inert and scho-lastic impediment to human ingenuity. This is where the "enaction" occurs in the Santiago notion of enactivism. Critical thinking must be enacted and not scholas-ticized.

Our concept of critical thinking joins Varela with Paulo Freire and compares and contrasts the Santiago notion of enaction with Freire's critical praxis (activity that combines theory and practice for demo-cratic and liberating outcomes). Good things happen in this South American in-teraction.

One of these good things involves the challenge our concept poses to positivistic definitions of critical thinking (the episte-mological orientation that claims to pro-duce objective, verifiable, and universal data by rigorously following the proce-dures of the scientific method). Our view of critical thinking questions positivistic critical thinking's claims that it can pro-vide answers to our questions, solutions to our problems, final truth to quell our anx-ieties, and a universal set of procedures for evaluating our ideas. These basic episte-mological issues are generally ignored, even in the foundational debates over criti-cal thinking that involve questions such as whether critical thinking is better concep-tualized as a set of skills or as a mental tendency or disposition. Also neglected are questions about the nature of the self, which is so important in our critical thinking concept.

Nicholas Burbules and Rupert Beck query the effect of social relationships on critical thinking and critical thinking pedagogy (Burbules & Beck, 1999). Does critical thinking demand particular social conditions before it can take place? Burbules and Beck alter the traditional conversation about critical thinking by contending that an important aspect of being a critical thinker is being able to create particular social circumstances in which particular types of conversations take place and certain interpersonal relationships develop.

Another question that refocuses the discourse of critical thinking and is central to our complex theory involves whether or not particular traditional definitions of the concept are Eurocentric and patriarchal. The more positivistic the articulation, the more Eurocentric and patriarchal critical thinking becomes. Danny Weil and I argue that too much critical thinking literature does indeed fall into the Eurocentric and patriarchal quagmire, which results in a tendency to devalue modes of thought that fall outside these narrow confines and to quell efforts to investigate new forms of intelligence emerging from non-European or non-patriarchal populations. Such narrow modes of critical thinking promote a cultural arrogance that blinds proponents to a number of profound moral, ethical, cognitive, and pedagogical insights.

Complex critical thinkers develop the ability to ask questions that expand the boundaries of the field. In a globalized, postcolonial world, we must move beyond monocultural standards of reason and become detectives of intelligence, finding cognitive forms that can make complex critical thinking more elastic.

AVOIDING UNCRITICAL CRITICAL THINKING

Our concept of complex critical thinking takes into account a wide variety of social, cultural, political, cognitive, and pedagogical discourses that may not play well in some quarters of the critical thinking cosmos. Some reductionistic articulations—labeled here as uncritical forms of critical thinking—view critical thinking as a puzzle-solving process. Advocates of such forms cut through the purple haze of complexity to find set solutions to neatly outlined problems. The critical thinker enters a virtual world without rough edges where all relationships are in place and easily discerned. The assumptions behind such a virtual world are beyond question, and inquiries into the disjunction between the virtual world and complex lived experience are ignored. In this uncritical model of critical thinking, a macho element prevails and doubters must assume a combative stance to ensure clarity and hone argumentation.

The work of Harvey Siegel represents this tradition. Siegel ties his vision of critical thinking to the rugged cross of rationality—the traditional cognitive/pedagogical dimension of the white man's burden. Viewing rationality as a monocultural, monolithic domain, Siegel fights off those who would defile the sanctity of Western reason.

In this corner of the critical thinking world, rationalists can't imagine why anyone would want to call the sanctity of science and reason into question. They speak with outrage about the use of phrases such as "regimes of truth," "conceptual frames," "the power dimensions of rationality," and "the normal science of a paradigm." Science and rationality are universal concepts, they argue, that do not need historicization or cultural contextualization—

they are above all that. Critical thinking based on these notions, they assert, occupies a transcendent location (Hatcher, 1995), so what more could we want? We have a mode of understanding the world that is objective, value-free, efficient, and to the point. But all views of rationality and critical thinking make assumptions about the world, human beings, the nature of knowledge, and values using the language of cosmological, ontological, epistemological, and axiological philosophic presuppositions. As John Covaleskie points out in his piece "Philosophical Instruction," all teaching and all definitions of critical thinking make these assumptions.

Complex critical thinkers use these insights to determine what assumptions are being made in their own and other analysts' versions of critical thinking. Ian Steinberg, in "Consumer Culture and Critical Thinking," provides an example of what happens when uncritical critical thinkers fail to examine assumptions about their own modes of social analysis. He suggests that questions of power and social justice are covered up and the status quo is upheld via the omission of important knowledge forms.

Positivistic, uncritical thinkers do not seek out and analyze their basic assumptions because they are comfortable with their conception of what does and does not constitute rational behavior and believe it is the truth. Forget, they entreat, all this critical theoretical blather about emancipatory social change and modes of critical thinking that reveal the fingerprints of power and the dominant ideology's support of an unjust status quo. True social change will occur, they insist, only when the world is Westernized/rationalized and sufficient numbers of individuals employ

Cartesian forms of critical thinking. This will lead to critical thinking at the social level, which leads to human progress.

Complex critical thinking values these Cartesian abilities and contends that all students and teachers should understand this tradition's historical and cultural development, its contributions to the world, and its contemporary benefits. But complex critical thinkers also believe that teachers and students should understand the Cartesian tradition's limitations and exclusions as well as the tacit social interests it often serves. Kathleen Berry has some very helpful insights about how to discover what interests critical thinking serves in her essay "Radical Critical Thinking: Part 1: Theoretical Background." She maintains that corporate power wielders have appropriated the term "critical thinking" to serve their own political agendas.

A central debate in the field of critical thinking that also reflects a larger conflict in contemporary academic life, involves the value of exposing the limitations, blindnesses, and political implications of traditional modes of Western Cartesian rationalistic thinking. There are many scholars, educators, and proponents of critical thinking who take great offense at this idea. The gap between the two camps has polarized the ranks of those associated with the critical thinking movement.

Complex critical thinking's questioning of the benefits of rationalistic critical thinking is often characterized as a postmodern rejection of reason. Shaped by rationalistic philosophers and supported by mainstream articulations of psychology, what we call uncritical critical thinking is based on the Western Enlightenment (the scientific revolution that occurred between c.1650 and c.1800), when people searched for meaning in a post-medieval, post-theocentric age. As traditional religious views of truth as divine revelation fell like bamboo huts in the wake of the intellectual tsunami produced by Enlightenment scholars such as Rene Descartes, Isaac Newton, and Francis Bacon, modern disciplines of knowledge began to emerge that reestablished certainty and stability. These modernist social and behavioral sciences offered the hope that humans could escape religious dogmatism and oppressive authority by pursuing rational, neutral, and objective science. Of course, such ways of thinking produced successes, but flaws in the structure began to appear as the decades passed. These included:

- efficiency at the expense of human well being,

- environmental destruction,

- male-centeredness,

- a tendency to view humans like variables in an equation,

- the devaluation of feeling and emotion,

- an overemphasis on dynamics that lend themselves to mathematical measurement, and

- a de-emphasis of those profound human qualities that do not.

All of these flaws and many others gradually began to reveal themselves as the nineteenth and twentieth centuries passed (see Juan-Miguel Fernández-Balboa's essay, "Emancipatory Critical Thinking").

The social, scientific, and psychological disciplines that arose in the nineteenth century employed an epistemology that assumed the world was perceived similarly by everyone. Complex critical thinkers see this epistemological dynamic as one of the fatal flaws of the rationalistic tradition, and one that finds contemporary expression in uncritical critical thinking. In this encyclopedia, the editors and authors argue that what we know is always tied to the context that shapes us as humans. Indeed, different people will perceive and interpret the meaning of the same event quite differently. The recognition of this phenomenon holds dramatic implications for teachers working in elementary and secondary classrooms.

Students with divergent frames of reference will understand not only particular lessons in different ways but will conceptualize the entire school experience in profoundly contrasting manners. In childhood education and developmental psychology, for example, this concept is especially important for the creation of lesson plans that use language and materials appropriate to students' developmental age. The assumption that everyone perceives schooling in a similar manner and that all students are operating on a level playing field is false, but many developmental appropriateness practitioners employ it and the field is riddled with monocultural, gender, and class-based presuppositions about behavioral norms, cognitive styles, and educational goals. When students operating outside of white, middle/upper middle-class norms do not match these culturally inscribed expectations, they are deemed incompetent, incapable of critical thinking, and are shunted to remedial classes designed to make them more orderly and structured people. Teachers of all subjects at all levels must employ critical thinking and be on the lookout for this type of hidden assumption, which has caused so much harm.

THE TROUBLE WITH RATIONALITY: CRITICAL THINKING IN CRISIS

In their essay "Becoming a 'Good Teacher': Thinking Critically about Teaching," Paul Brawdy and Juan-Miguel Fernández-Balboa argue that special situations occur in classrooms immersed in uncritical critical thinking. If the meaning of rationality is unquestioned, students' questions are designed not to gain understanding about the world but to clarify their teacher's edicts about what they are supposed to do. Brawdy and Fernández-Balboa ask, "of what practical use are such compliant response-providers in a vital democracy?"

Rationalistic definitions of critical thinking and pedagogy fail to examine rationality as the cultural artifact of a particular place and time. A central feature of uncritical critical thinking is this reluctance to study the trouble with rationality.

Many educators argue that to raise questions about the origin, nature, strengths, and weaknesses of traditional forms of western rationality opens a Pandora's box of values and subjective opinion. They want us to stick to hard evidence. This sort of attitude suggests that an intellectual tradition's efforts to examine itself, its development, and its assumptions somehow fall outside of the tradition of scientific rationality. Of course, all traditions need to be questioned about their development and assumptions. Our notion of complex critical thinking demands it.

We should constantly ask ourselves:

- How is our evidence evaluated?
- Is our tradition comfortable calling its sacred beliefs into question?
- Does our tradition allow its students to reject its guiding principles?

- What socio-cultural forces influenced our tradition's development?

Any tradition that refuses to ask such questions cannot make a contribution to the literature and pedagogy of its topic.

Complex critical thinkers must understand the concept of rationality in its larger historical context. There were numerous responses to the birth of scientific reason in the Western Enlightenment of the seventeenth and eighteenth centuries, and many analysts maintain that a large number of these positions can be relegated to two poles of a continuum of responses. The first pole, operating within what we are referring to as the positivistic/rationalistic domain, contends that faith in Cartesian rationality leads to freedom, intellectual development, progress, and even human happiness. The second pole of the continuum associates Western rationality with terror, regulation, and oppression. The first pole falls apart when it encounters the gulf between neutral, objective reason and moral questions about what should be. The second pole fails because it offers no alternative to positivistic reason. Those of us involved with this encyclopedia seek a middle ground that avoids the oppressive nature of positivistic reason while developing alternative rationalities that move us to new intellectual plateaus.

Complex critical thinking is based on a knowledge of the trouble with prevailing concepts of rationality, which has been referred to as the crisis of rationality. Juan-Miguel Fernández-Balboa reminds us in his "Emancipatory Critical Thinking," that complex critical thinking is as concerned with why we should solve a problem as it is with how we solve it. Rationalistic forms of critical thinking, he tells us, "are viewed as value-free and objective, thus contributing to the universalization of dominant norms, relations of power, values, and practices."

Documenting the trouble with rationality is an important step in the continuing effort to establish social justice and democracy. We are very interested in combining an understanding of the mind as a socially constructed entity that is realized through interaction in a variety of social contexts with social, cultural, and political insights into the ways the world operates—a theory of mind integrated with a social theory. The relationship between these complex processes, within which critical thinking must operate, is a key dimension in our concept of *complex* critical thinking.

What pedagogical tools and resources does a culture provide to help its members confront this complex interaction? Such resources are hard to find in contemporary U.S. society, especially for its least-privileged members.

THINKING ABOUT COMPLEXITY IN COMPLEX CRITICAL THINKING

Over the last several decades, many observers have come to the conclusion that the simplicity of Cartesian rationalism and mainstream forms of knowledge production do not meet our needs. The web of reality is composed of too many variables to be controlled. Scientist Illya Prigogene calls this multitude of variables extraneous perturbations, meaning that one extraneous variable (i.e., in an educational experiment) can produce an expanding, exponential effect. So-called inconsequential entities can have a profound effect in a complex, nonlinear universe. The shape of the physical and social world depends on its smallest part. The part, in a sense, is the whole, for the action of any particular part can produce transformative change in the entire entity. To exclude such considerations is to miss the nature of the interactions that constitute reality.

The development of a counter-Cartesian reconceptualization of critical thinking does not mean that we simplistically reject all empirical science, it means that we see the scientific view as only one perspective on the complex web we refer to as reality.

Reality is too complex to lend itself to fixed views and reductionistic descriptions. Koshi Dhingra's essay "Critical Thinking and the Teaching of Science" contains helpful explanations of these complex dynamics. Kenneth Teitelbaum, in his essay on curriculum, extends Dhingra's attempt to transcend simplistic models of curriculum development and says that positivistic views of theorizing have subverted the effort to create a relationship-oriented perspective on the activity of teaching. In Teitelbaum's estimation, such a relational perspective would connect our knowledge of individuals to their social and historical backgrounds, which would create a deeper and more helpful context for the teacher.

This theme of complexity reverberates throughout the encyclopedia, as other authors address the development of a critical thinking process that avoids reductionism. Consider Stephen Fleury's assertions in his entry "Critical Consciousness through a Critical Constructivist Pedagogy." Critical thinkers who take complexity seriously, he writes, challenge reductionistic, bipolar, true or false epistemologies. As complex critical thinkers come to recognize the complexity of the lived world—with its maze of uncontrollable variables, irrationality, non-linearity, and unpredictable interactions of wholes and parts—they also begin to see the interpretative dimension of reality. We are bamboozled by a science that offers only one way to make sense of the world.

Complex critical thinkers maintain that we must possess, and be able to use, multiple methods of producing knowledge about reality. Such methods create a variety of perspectives on similar events and alert us to relationships between events. In this complex context we understand that, even when we use diverse methods and produce multiple perspectives on the world, different observers will perceive these perspectives differently, which will add to the variables we must address.

As Charles Bingham argues in his essay "Knowledge Acquisition," we must understand this complexity in order to appreciate how complicated it is to learn. Humans, Bingham maintains, are not atomistic in their ability to acquire knowledge—they must receive help from others to engage in learning.

Bingham's ideas about the relationship between the knower and the known changes the way we approach knowledge, learning, teaching, and, of course, critical thinking. Critical thinking is not something engaged in by solitary critical thinkers operating on their own. Critical thinkers use language developed by others, live in specific contexts that have produced particular ways of being and ways of thinking about thinking, have access to some knowledges and not others, and live and operate in circumstances shaped by particular dominant ideological perspectives. Any critical thinking that attempts to deal with the lived world must address contextual dynamics. Our method of critical thinking both appreciates these contextual factors and accounts for them.

Complex critical thinkers are not isolated individuals but people who understand the nature of their sociocultural context and their overt and occluded relationships with others. If people cannot understand their own contextual embeddedness, they will not be able to identify the origins of their prejudices and predispositions. Patricia Hinchey, in her essay "Diversity and Critical Thinking," illustrates this point using racial and ethnic prejudices.

COGNITIVE FOG CUTTERS: CRITICAL THINKING AND THE THEORETICAL DOMAIN

Cognitive, social, and pedagogical theories are essential to the development of rigorous and complex critical thinking that can move us to new intellectual domains. When educators ask about the purpose of schools, how to organize schools for maximum learning, how to conceptualize curricula, and the relationship between schools and society, they are asking questions that cannot be answered without the help of a variety of theoretical constructs. In the social theoretical domain, for example, we might ask how the existence of socioeconomic inequality that arises from race, class, gender, sexuality, religion, or language influences our answers to these questions. What happens to our answers when we bring an understanding of power to the analytical table? What is the effect of social theoretical insight on the subjectivity and context-dependency of knowledge production? Might the knowledge emerging here help shape the way we answer questions about the curriculum? (See David Hursch's chapter "Critical Theory" for more insights into these ideas.)

Rationalism and science cannot help us determine the purpose of schools, and contribute little to such a discussion. Combining social and educational theory is helpful, and can enhance the ability of critical-thinking educators to evaluate educational goals, curriculum ideas, and evaluation practices. Such theories help teachers and students escape the well regulated world that unbridled rationalism tries to construct. Complex critical thinkers as critical thinkers use these theoretical tools to sidestep new models of social control that put a chokehold on individual and social freedom.

Peter Appelbaum's essay "Mathematics Education" critiques prevailing views of math education in the U.S. over the last several decades. In it, Appelbaum challenges the educational establishment's assumption that democracy in the U.S. already exists. The author states that, because of this underlying assumption, math educators develop democratic teaching methods that attempt to include all students in the math learning community as equals. Applebaum thinks that democracy is not complete in America and that this is reason students come into math and all other branches of education with vastly unequal resources and tools. He suggests that all of these differences must be taken into account when curricula are designed.

In his essay "Cultural Studies in Education," Handel Wright describes theoretically informed teacher activists who understand and act on the contextual realities of inequality. David Hursh contends in "Critical Theory," that all of us are theorists because we develop and hold particular views about how things work that shape our actions as lovers, parents, citizens, students, and teachers. Complex critical thinkers say that these social, cognitive, and educational theories we hold and act on must be made conscious so we can explore their origins in our lives, reflect on them, consider how they may have unconsciously shaped our actions in the world, and change them when needed.

This ability to change our own theories is an indispensable dimension of the complex critical thinking in this encyclopedia.

If we reject the rationalistic Cartesian notion that there is a monolithic knowable world that can be explained by Western science, an epistemology of complexity views the cosmos as a human and social construction. The world is what dominant groups of humans perceive it to be. This complicates theory-making. Positivistic/rationalistic theories were simple because proponents claimed that their theories corresponded to *true* reality. More complex, post-positivistic theories are a collection of philosophical and social viewpoints, and the makers have learned about the social construction of them all. Our theory of complex critical thinking includes hermeneutical, feminist, and fallibalist dimensions and is pluralistic and multiperspectival (or, as I have termed it elsewhere, bricolage).

In other work, I have used the term critical constructivism to describe my epistemological perspective, and postformalism to describe my cognitive theoretical orientation. Constructivism maintains that nothing represents a neutral perspective and no truly objective way of seeing exists. Nothing exists before consciousness shapes it into something we can perceive. What appears to be objective reality is merely what our mind constructs and what we are accustomed to seeing. The structures and phenomena we observe in the physical world are nothing more than the creations of our own measuring and categorizing minds, and the world has to be interpreted by the human beings who are part of that world. The theory of perspective developed by fifteenth-century artists was simply one way of portraying space and held no *absolute* validity.

Whether we are attempting to understand the music of West Africa, the art of Marcel Duchamp, the pedagogical theory of Michael Apple, or the insights into critical thinking of Barbara Thayer-Bacon, the constructivist principle is the same and shakes the epistemological foundations of modernist Cartesian grand narratives.

In constructivist theory, individuals that come from different backgrounds see the world in different ways. Imagine, for example, how a German, a member of the Ibo tribe in Africa, a Texan, and a woman from a small village in China might describe a major league baseball game. It is safe to assume that the descriptions would be quite different and even humorous to individuals who understand the intricacies of the game. The point is, of course, that background and expectations shape perception. Consider how a classroom is perceived by a class clown, a traditionally good student, a burnt-out teacher, a standardized test maker, an anti-standards activist, a bureaucratic supervisor, a disgruntled parent, and a nostalgic alumnus.

The fact that our psychosocial dispositions shape how we perceive the world has important implications for teaching and critical thinking. Each of our students and each teacher brings a unique disposition into the classroom. Stephen Fain and Mary Anne Ullery's description of xenophobia in their essay in this volume demonstrates the ways our backgrounds shape how we see the other.

Students of critical thinking might ask:

- What shaped how I see the world and what does this construction have to do with critical thinking?
- Is my psychosocial orientation beyond my conscious control?
- Do we simply surrender our perceptions to the determinations of our environ-

ment and our social and cultural context?

Because people are often unable to discern the ways their environments shape their perception and construct their consciousness, critical thinking motifs that expose this complex process are very important to our new theory of critical thinking. This is where theoretically informed complex critical thinking collides with constructivism. Critical theory is concerned with extending people's consciousness of themselves as social beings. Critical thinkers with such a consciousness understand how their political opinions, religious beliefs, gender roles, racial self-concepts, or view of the goals of education are influenced by both the dominant culture and subcultures.

In many of the undergraduate teacher education courses I've taught over the last few decades, I have attempted to help students cultivate a theoretically grounded view of the way their consciousness as prospective teachers was constructed. I encourage them to ask themselves why they have decided to teach, what forces in their lives shaped this decision, and how they think those forces will contribute to the type of teacher they become. These questions and many others, combined with an introduction to complex critical theory, initiate an introspective process that results not only in self-knowledge, but in a critique of the student's own culture and educational system. As we study major issues in education, the students are also analyzing themselves, and the combination of these two processes produces some interesting perspectives. If a student finds a part of their consciousness that is counterproductive, they can correct it once they understand the psychological, ethical, moral, and political origins of the problem.

In addition, students see various educational goals and reform movements play out on the terrain of their own lives as educators.

This ability to step back from the way we normally see the world and discover the ways our perceptions are constructed by linguistic codes, cultural signs, race, class, gender, sexual ideologies, and embedded modes of power is a giant step towards becoming a complex critical thinker, an emancipatory teacher, and a knowledge producer.

Critical constructivism is a theoretically grounded form of world-making. We ask penetrating questions, such as how did that which has come to be, come to be and whose interests do particular institutional arrangements serve? As complex critical thinkers remake and rename their world, they are constantly guided by their critical theoretical system of meaning, which provides an emancipatory source of authority. (Shirley Steinberg provides insight to these questions in "Popular Culture." I raise similar questions in "The New Childhood and Critical Thinking.") The development of a theoretical facility is one of the most neglected dimensions in traditional modes of critical thinking, but indispensable to our paradigm.

Teachers with training in theoretical critical thinking ask typically ignored questions about the sociopolitical purposes of schooling because they understand how education can either reproduce or challenge dominant sociopolitical and economic structures. As my co-editor, Danny Weil, has often argued in his scholarship, this kind of theoretical understanding is profoundly important to learning to think, teach, and live democratically. Educational purpose cannot be separated from social justice, human liberation, self-direction, resistance to regulation, and the fight for freedom. When educators fail to see this, he argues, schools inexorably become sorting machines for the new corporate order and reinforce patriarchal structures, Eurocentric educational practices, homophobia, and racism. The struggle for the soul of critical thinking will be played out on the road before us.

CRITICAL THINKING, THE IMPORTANCE OF THEORY, AND THE SELF

Complex critical thinkers learn to understand the oppressive forces that shape them so they can become less self-absorbed and individually oriented. They learn to situate themselves historically and socially, and are therefore far better equipped to make conscious decisions about who they want to be and how they will deal with the ideological socialization processes of twenty-first century electronic societies. This effort to gain insight into personal identity is not a call to narcissism; indeed, it is quite the opposite.

In what we call uncritical critical thinking, students and teachers are not encouraged to confront why they think as they do about themselves, the world around them, and their relationship to that world. This part of the critical thinking movement is also virtually unconcerned with the consequences of thinking, since it views cognition as a process that takes place in a vacuum. Thinking in new ways always necessitates personal transformation, and if enough people think in new ways, social transformation is inevitable. Social and personal change is not especially important to uncritical critical thinking advocates. I describe and critique this problem in my essay, "Educational Psychology and Critical Thinking."

I believe that one reason an exploration of the self in the world does not take place in uncritical critical thinking programs is that the proponents of these programs do not have the background in historical, philosophical, sociological, and cultural studies that would allow them to understand what such an act might entail, or to identify the ways that dominant power structures have subverted democratic impulses in the fields of politics, epistemology, psychology, and education. These fields have become increasingly dominated by private interests, which want individual identities to be constructed in ways that meet the needs of the dominant wielders of power. In the past, these private interests have made concerted attempts to create individuals who are more compliant with the need of corporations and are more accepting of government by the market, globalized capitalism, free market ideologies, the irrelevance of the political domain, etc. Schools became sorting mechanisms for the new corporate order, and the way the self might fit into these power-driven dynamics, was, of course, irrelevant.

The concept of an abstract individual formed outside the boundaries of the social and cultural world is common in uncritical forms of critical thinking. In her analysis of traditional critical thinking modes, Barbara Thayer-Bacon (2000) asserts that most of the major figures in the field have described critical thinkers as "individual, disembodied minds" (p. 64). A central tenet of our concept of complex critical thinking is that thinking and consciousness itself cannot be separated from history. All thinking and action take place in the continuum of history, and the role of complex critical thinking is to bring this recognition to the front burner of consciousness. With such awareness, critical thinkers begin to realize that consciousness is constructed by individual agency, individual will, and the ideological, discursive, and regulatory influences of society. Who we are is not deterministically constructed by sociohistorical forces that totally shape our ways of seeing; nor is consciousness and selfhood autonomously constructed by free and independent individuals unhindered by the burden of history.

Human efforts to make sense of the self and the world are challenged by ideological forces—free market economics, an abstract individualism which removes human beings from historical and social contexts, an epistemology of positivism that devalues human existence, and hegemonic political perspectives that win our consent to "moral" and "patriotic" policies that serve the interests of the privileged few—that thwart our pursuit of individual goals, but genuine motivation can transcend the confines of existing social forces. Social theorists have traditionally been guilty of not recognizing this dynamic in consciousness construction, identity production, and social action.

For instance, it was not until the 1980s, with the influx of new theories of language analysis and cultural understanding, that scholars appreciated the way power was embedded in language and the implications of such inscriptions on the production of the self. Human beings are initiated into language communities where people share bodies of knowledge, epistemologies, and the cognitive styles that accompany them. These are powerful forces that shape who we are. How we think about critical thinking and the modes of critical thinking we devise are inseparable from these language communities. Current complex critical thinking understands that the sociohistorical dimensions of self-production are often manifested on the terrain of language.

American students may find these concepts strange and unfamiliar. Unfortunately, because linguistic and ideological factors are hidden from many of us, we find ourselves unaware of how our consciousness has been constructed. American educational experience has focused on the mastery (read memorization) of many bits and pieces of unrelated data for standardized tests—not on the forces that have made us who we are.

The schemas that guide a culture are rarely part of an individual's conscious mind. They are usually part of an individual's worldview and are taken for granted in most versions of critical thinking. It was these ideas that the great Italian social theorist Antonio Gramsci had in mind when he argued that philosophy should be viewed as a form of self-criticism. Gramsci asserted that the starting point for any higher understanding of self involves the consciousness of oneself as a product of sociohistorical forces. A critical philosophy, he wrote, involves the ability of its adherents to criticize the ideological frames that they use to make sense of the world. My colleagues and myself find it difficult to get our students to engage with Gramsci's ideas. Teachers of complex critical thinking must be patient and empathetic to their twenty-first century students, who have had very few opportunities in the contemporary world of media and corporately influenced schooling to gain the skills that would equip them to undertake such an individual and cultural analysis.

Complex critical thinking is profoundly concerned with how the production of self is influenced by the power blocs of contemporary society. The social, cultural, political, economic, epistemological, and linguistic structures that shape human consciousness, as well as the historical contexts that gave birth to these structures, are questioned by complex critical thinking, which helps people explore the sociohistorical and political dimensions of schooling, the kind of meanings that are constructed in classrooms, and how these meaning are translated into student consciousness.

Advocates of uncritical critical thinking often speak of student and teacher empowerment as if it were a simple process that could be accomplished by a couple of creative learning activities. One thing our ideological critique of self-production tells us is that the self is a complex, ambiguous, and contradictory entity pushed and pulled by a potpourri of forces. The idea that the self can be reconstructed and empowered without historical study, linguistic analysis, and an understanding of social forces is a trivialization of the goals of critical thinking.

Complex critical thinking asks the question: how do we move beyond simply uncovering the sources of consciousness construction and reconstruct the self in a critical manner? To engage in this self-reconstruction, students and teachers must transcend the modernist conception of the static and unified self that goes through life with a genetically fixed I.Q. While freeing ourselves from this prison of the intellect is urgent, the first step towards changing our reality should be to develop our social and aesthetic imaginations and search for alternate discourses in literature, history, popular culture, the community, and especially in previously devalued, subjugated knowledges. We must imagine what we might become by recovering and reinterpreting what we once were.

THE CENTRALITY OF COGNITIVE THEORY IN CRITICAL THINKING: THE WORLD OF ENACTIVISM

As we continue our journey through the fog, the pedagogical and social theoretical realms provide insight into our effort to reconceptualize critical thinking. The cognitive domain is a central and neglected feature of the theoretical base on which a new complex critical thinking might be constructed. Enactivism and the Santiago School address the cognitive domain, and pick up where the epistemology of constructivism leaves off. Humberto Maturana and Francisco Varela argue in a constructivist vein that the world we know is not pre-given but enacted. The act of cognition in this context does not involve the Cartesian effort to commit to memory *mental* reflections of the real world. Cognition is more complex than this—an insight educational reformers and standards devisors should try to grasp. Instead of attempting to reconstruct true mental reflections of the real world, learners should focus on how our actions *in relation* to the world create it.

The idea that cognition and learning reflect or represent reality is a key dimension of the history of Western cognitive psychology. In this Cartesian cognitivism, sensory input is reconstituted by the brain into internal representations of the exterior world, and these fixed perspectives are considered reality itself. In this view of cognition, canons replace conversation and, contrary to Allen Bloom's argument, minds are closed. Critical thinkers using Cartesian cognitivism can announce that they have deduced the truth and are representing reality correctly. Curricula can be constructed around this truth, and once they are formulated both students and teachers should take their truth-based curriculum home and learn it without asking questions.

Enactivism throws a monkey wrench into such cognitive arrogance, forcing us to account for the profoundly different constructions of reality that emerge when the world is encountered in different times and places. Critical thinking that does not take such cognitive complexity into account is inadequate.

The problems of the physical, social, psychological, and educational domains rarely present themselves in well-structured, puzzle-like ways. Rationalistic technical thinking does not work very well when it confronts complex, ill-structured, lived world problems. Analysts must understand a range of tacit knowledges, the multiple contexts in which the problem is situated, and thinking processes that may or may not be of value in order to solve such problems. Complex critical thinkers understand that the step-by-step procedures laid down by rationalists and the rules of rigorous research specified by positivists can hinder rather than help people understand the complications of the lived world. Enactivists maintain that such rules must give way to the specificity and improvisation of immediate experience. In my chapter "Multiple Intelligences and Critical Thinking," I use this enactivist perspective combined with a critical perspective to critique the rationalistic dimensions of Howard Gardner's theory of multiple intelligences.

In order to repair the Western rationalistic reduction and fragmentation of the world, enactivists turn to the concepts of mind produced by biology and psychology. We have used these concepts to ground our theoretical bricolage of critical theory, complexity theory, feminism, and postformalism. In the spirit of Lev Vygotsky, over the last two decades Jean Lave,

Valerie Walkerdine, James Werstch, Etienne Wenger, Roy Pea, and numerous other cognitive theorists have argued that cognition and the knowledge it produces are socially situated activities that take place in concrete historical situations. Varela maintains that our particular concrete historical circumstances help us realize who we are and what we can become.

Let's pause at this point and collect our thoughts. It is important to ask what these theories say to those of us in the teaching profession who want to teach critical thinking. The social, pedagogical, political, and cognitive theories we have explored say that the world in general, and the educational realm in particular, may be more complex than we have been taught. If this is true, teaching critical thinking in simple workshops will not be successful. Teachers must become scholars who understand the multiple dimensions of the cognitive act and the reasons that it has been conceptualized so differently by different analysts at different times. Critical thinking has to be both theoretically understood and enacted in particular circumstances.

Teachers and students who are trying to understand a specific, lived situation must learn to be questioners-in-action and examine all the viewpoints the situation involves. They must examine the consequences of their actions from interpersonal, political, moral, and ethical perspectives. They must ask from where the definition of what they are calling critical thinking emanates and how they might have acted differently in the situation if they had used a different kind of critical thinking. They must question whether critical thinkers could disagree about what the informed actions of a critical thinker might be in the circumstances being considered and, finally, they must ask them-selves whether they personally agree with the definitions of critical thinking that are being used to analyze the situation.

MINING ENACTIVIST INSIGHTS: EXPANDING THE BOUNDARIES OF CRITICAL THINKING

Using the enactivist model, we crawl outside the conceptual window and move into our post-Cartesian great wide open. From biology we learn that all animals possess knowledge they have gathered from concrete situations. I have often marveled at how my dogs, Celtic and Ozzy, will negotiate a difficult physical maneuver in a way that is cognitively sophisticated and was improvised in only a few split seconds. This is Varela's point, that "what we call general and abstract are aggregates of readiness-for-action" (Varela 1999, p. 18). This means that complex critical thinkers don't manifest their intelligence by developing efficient mental file cabinets for storing data. Intelligence is manifested by discerning the meanings of and relationships between pieces of knowledge and being able to put them together improvisationally in new and effective ways to solve the problems produced by particular circumstances. In an academic setting, the particular circumstances might involve making an argument, defending a position, figuring out how to use the knowledge of oppression to help an individual who is suffering, or figuring out how to help a student who is having difficulty in a math class. Danny Weil uses his understanding of the classroom to directly address this enactivist readiness-for-action in "Educational Relevance, Personalized Education, and Critical Thinking," arguing that an active critical thinking curriculum engages students in thinking about the world so they can act on it.

The next cognitive theoretical step involves the profoundly important and complex process of how the self is produced and how this process shapes the way we construct the world. At times in the recent history of cognitive psychology—in behaviorism, for example—scientists insisted that consciousness did not exist because it did not lend itself to empirical measurement. Other cognitive perspectives, while not denying the existence of consciousness three times before the cock crowed, simply ignored it. Obviously, such approaches to consciousness, immediate experience, and the awareness of selfhood left an unfillable theoretical hole in their wake.

Rather than ignoring this hole, Varela attempts to fill it and examine the disjunction between scientifically validated cognitive theory and our experience of consciousness. Why, Varela asks, do humans experience the self so profoundly? His answer is that the self is a virtual entity that emerges from a maze of relationships. It has no definable central processing mechanism and no command center in the brain where control is coordinated. Such a process creates new social, cultural, political, and economic relationships between the self and the world, and produces new and more market-compliant selves. According to Varela, the self is infinitely more malleable, more open to change than we had previously imagined, and can be mobilized for great benefit or manipulated for great harm.

Using this theory, complex critical thinkers know that, (1) despite the power of generations of cognitive determinists operating under the flag of I.Q., human beings can learn to become more intelligent, (2) selfhood is even more of a miraculous phenomenon than many had imagined, and (3) to live is to have a point of view.

Varela writes of a moment-to-moment monitoring of the nature of our selfhood that produces a meta-awareness of the connections we make to the socio-physical world around us. To monitor ourselves this way, we must let go of our egocentrism that blinds us to the virtual and relational nature of our selfhood and defines critical thinking as a manifestation of the combative proponent of rationality. If we can do so, we will avoid the cultural and gender restrictions such perspectives drag along with them.

THE ORE OF ENACTIVISM: CONNECTING ABSTRACT THINKING TO THE COGNITION OF IMPROVISATION

Digging deeper in the enactivist mine, we encounter a new vein of insight into the nature of abstract thought that holds profound implications for critical thinking.

Although the symbolic and abstract dimensions of human thought are very important, enactivists maintain that they constitute only one dimension of cognition. In everyday decision-making, abstract and symbolic thinking are joined by emotional considerations and gut feelings (sensations from the body). Of course, cognitive science, pedagogy, and the discourse of critical thinking have typically ignored the non-rational aspects of the thinking process. Varela's moment-by-moment monitoring includes all of these dynamics. The traditional Cartesian emphasis on rationality dismisses such considerations from the domain of critical thinking, even though this narrowing of focus limits what is seen and constricts the horizon on which cognition is conceptualized.

This is exactly what has happened in the study of artificial intelligence (AI). It was not long until AI scholars realized that

their computer programs could not dupli-
cate the non-rational dimensions of human
thinking. Some of these scholars understood that one of the central feature of human intelligence (and critical thinking) is
its ability to solve ill-defined problems using solutions that are not obvious, and to
identify multiple solutions to problems,
depending on the values the human beings
involved bring to a situation. In the latter
case, rationality actually works to blind
computers and AI researchers to other possibilities in the cognitive realm.

The same rational blindness afflicted
Jean Piaget when he focused on the ra-
tional-cognitive domain of human thought
most prized by Western science and rationalistic traditions. The idea that critical
thinking may involve a number of human
capabilities outside the rational domain
has been lost in the Cartesian snowdrift.
Cognitive science has been asleep at the
wheel, focusing on types of thinking that
operate in isolation from everyday life.

Complex critical thinkers are careful
not to draw the wrong lessons from these
insights. The point is not to abandon rationality in favor of workshops about getting in touch with our feelings. The moral
of the story from our perspective is that we
search for alternative rationalities (more
rigorous, smarter rationalities) that take
into account the unique capacities of the
body, the emotions, and the intuition that
only human beings bring to the thinking
process. As complex critical thinkers, we
immerse ourselves in the specifics of how
these rigorous rationalities operate in the
specific domain of immediate action and
the improvisation of living in concrete circumstances. Such circumstances demand
we understand:

- Previously constructed cultural meanings, as Gadamer and the hermeneuts
  have contended,

- Epistemes (the ways truth is produced
  and knowledge is constructed), as Foucault and many poststructuralists have
  argued,

- The deployment of rationality for irrational and oppressive goals, as presented
  by Horkheimer and Adorno,

- How larger political issues show up in
  concrete personal interactions, as Judith
  Butler and critical feminist theorists
  have maintained,

- The ways language practices set tacit
  rules that regulate what can and cannot
  be said, who can speak and who must
  listen, and whose pronouncements are
  valid and learned and whose are ignorant in everyday conversation, as James
  Paul Gee and discourse analysts in pedagogy have posited,

- The socially embedded dimensions of
  all forms of cognitive activity, as Vygotsky, Lave, and the sociocognitivists
  have pointed out, and

- The ways that all acts of teaching and
  learning are shaped by an individual's
  relationship with power and domination,
  as explained by Paulo Freire and other
  critical pedagogues.

- All of these understandings help us deal
  with sophisticated cognition in the concrete situations of everyday life.

In this encyclopedia we maintain that
the next step forward in the discourse of
critical thinking is viewing critical thinking as intelligent awareness shaped by the
intersection of abstract and concrete
modes of thinking. When moral and ethical concerns are injected into this intersection, new modes of being human and new
concepts of thoughtful living begin to
emerge that produce a non-egocentric, interconnected, *intentionless* state of virtual

selfhood that becomes second nature to us, a central aspect of who we are.

Drawing upon Buddhist insights, Varela implores us to develop a self devoid of self-nature. Such a position opens us to a wide range of new self-understandings that bring about ever-expanding forms of intelligent awareness. If this process results in a reinforcement of the all-too-common egocentrism of the critical scholar, then complex critical thinking has failed. Unless such a position induces a mode of letting go that moves us to new forms of interconnection and compassion, then complex critical thinking is a sham and we are no more than inside traders of intellectual commodities.

DEFINING WISDOM: ENACTIVISM, EMERGENCE, AND THE CULTIVATION OF IMMEDIATE INSIGHT

In the ill-structured problems of the lived world, enactivist critical thinking proves its value. Until the cognitive, political, cultural, and pedagogical assumptions embedded in the everyday life of classroom are exposed to the light of analysis, educational practice and perspectives toward critical thinking will not change (see Tom Nelson's essay "Formulating Best Practices for Teaching and Learning" for an expansion of this idea). Everyday classroom teaching and the thinking of teachers in practice provide excellent examples of the types of immediate coping in concrete situations that so concern enactivists. In this situation we can appreciate Varela's complaint about cognitive science's emphasis on abstract reasoning over the power of immediate insight.

As we know, great teachers don't browse among relevant educational theories and pick the correct one for applica-tion in a particular context. Masterful teachers are not merely information processors—the phrase used in the cognitivist lexicon. At one end of a continuum of practical wisdom, Varela posits, there are those who maintain that the ability to act intelligently in immediate situations is an intuitive act of spontaneity that has no connection to reason. At the other end of the continuum are those who argue that such spontaneous action should be avoided and individuals should follow the rules of rational action. The enactivist wisdom that Varela promotes claims the middle ground between the two poles of the continuum, which he describes as immediate action that harmonizes with the lived context while refusing to follow a set of procedures or steps to rational action.

Varela's type of improvisational action is especially important in an educational system that is highly rationalistic and beset by the fragmentation of standardized testing and content standards. It is not unusual for educators to encounter honor students with high-test scores who are unable to identify or solve problems in unusual contexts. When math, chemistry, history, or language and literacy students have to deal with ill-defined problems presented in a format that differs from the test questions to which they are accustomed, many are lost. They have not been taught to *enact intelligence*, but to store knowledge and procedures. Enacting intelligence in a way that harmonizes with lived contexts and cultivates improvisational ability based on multiple knowledge bases is not a part of the normal learning experience. Critical thinking informed by enactivism is especially needed in the education of the first decade of the twenty-first century, where schools are being rationalized into irrationality.

Complex critical thinkers pursue a type of wisdom that might be characterized as readiness-for-action. It produces compelling modes of educational practice. Handel Wright puts it well in his essay "Cultural Studies in Education," maintaining that cultural studies promote a form of critical thinking that manifests as action or even activism. Wright's focus on action connects directly to the enactivist concern with the larger organic flow of activity in which consciousness is a player.

Looking back from a twenty-first century perspective, we can discern a forty-year movement in cognitive science that took the field from cognitivism to connectionism/constructivism (the emphasis on the social embedding of the mind) to enactivism. No longer can the mind be viewed as a computer, a mechanical information-processing device. Enactivism invites us to discern a new complexity in the study of the mind, which is seen as a socially constructed emergent network that achieves its highest expression in interaction with the complications of the lived world. One way that Varela learned about the emergent, self-organizing properties of the mind was by studying ant and bee behavior. Varela noted that in ant colonies, when the most efficient nurses were removed to form a new sub-colony, these specialists changed their behavior. Instead of performing an exclusive nursing function they became foragers for food and needed materials. In the original colony, formerly low-level nurses became more active and increased their nursing activities. In Varela's words, "the whole colony . . . showed evidence of both configurational identity and memory." In this example, the ants' relationship to the colony shaped individual behavior. Even though the ants were individuals, the colony behaved as a cohesive whole. It operated as if there was a coordinating consciousness directing group behavior. Such a group

consciousness was autopoietic—self-produced. It emerged as a macro-pattern from the actions and relationships of simple individual components (Varela, 1999). It was virtual—like the virtual self—because it was *not a thing*. It did not exist as a substance, only as a set of relationships.

This concept reminds us that we are constructing a theory of complex critical thinking based on what we can become, both in an individual and a social sense, as well as on the basis of the emergent nature of relationships. Something profound happens when we take knowledge, thought systems, and theories from diverse contexts and bring them together to form new relationships, new patterns of interaction, and new imperatives for intellectual and ethical action.

Michael Dumas puts it well in "Black Existence As Critical Thinking" when he argues that knowledge must be "felt in the flesh" and acted upon in light of our individual and collective struggles. Without this dimension, learning to become a critical thinker is a rather shallow enterprise. Nothing new *emerges* because knowledge and concepts are contained rather than related and enacted.

I believe that our concept of critical thinking, because of our theoretical bricolage and the cognitive enactivist principles (especially readiness-for-action) we bring to the conversation, will change critical thinking forever.

"CRITICAL CRITICAL THINKING" IN THE TWENTY-FIRST CENTURY

Before going into detail about critical critical thinking or critical thinking informed by critical theory, I wanted to introduce several theoretical ideas—

especially the cognitivist concerns of enactivism. Let us put the notion of critical theory, and the concept of criticality that it produces, into context.

Many analysts begin their description of Frankfurt School critical theory by stating that Theodor Adorno, Max Horkheimer, and Herbert Marcuse based their notion of criticality on the theoretical fusion of Marx and Freud. Such an approach helped them understand the relationship between the psyche and socioeconomic and political forces. In our theoretical construction of complex critical thinking, we are attempting to carry this project forward, delving deeply into the concept of mind vis-à-vis sociocultural and political structures, and incorporating the new insights developed since the inception of critical theory.

The scholars of the Frankfurt School were fascinated by the ways this mind-society relationship operated to impede popular support for political movements dedicated to freedom, democracy, and justice. No emancipatory politics, they argued, is complete without a political psychology that traces the effects of particular political arrangements on human consciousness and vice versa. In the course of their analysis, the critical theorists came to the conclusion that the growth of the traditional disciplines of academia has not led to a profound understanding of consciousness, moral growth, or human happiness. Indeed, this irrational rationality has often served the interests of dominant power blocs by repressing human self-direction and undermining critical critical thinking.

Of course, the Frankfurt School did not achieve final success in their efforts to reveal the connections between the psyche and the political. They did, however, establish a line of inquiry and mode of theorizing that remains extremely valuable to the development of critical critical thinking and the complex critical thinking referenced in this introduction.

As advocates of complex critical thinking followed the paths blazed by the Frankfurt School, they came to the stark realization that educational psychology was isolated from both the political realm and the process of critical consciousness formation. The study of the complexity that characterizes the production of subjectivity seemed to be lost in mainstream educational psychology to the point that such issues could not even be discussed in the discipline's conferences and literature.

While the Frankfurt School was concerned primarily with the insights of psychoanalysis in the marriage of the political and the psychological, complex critical thinking attempts to reintroduce the psychological into the critical domain and into the contemporary conversation about critical thinking. This re-emphasizes the importance of enactivism in our analysis and in the reconceptualization of critical thinking. From a psychological point of view, power helps shape the choices that determine the types of aptitudes and cognitive abilities individuals develop. Not only do humans become the sort of beings they are, as a consequence of their location in the web of power relations, but such political dynamics even define the characteristics educational psychologists designate as higher-order thinking. What is labeled critical thinking is not only influenced by society, it is politically inscribed and constructed in part by the nature of one's relationship to power.

Though grounded on the work of the Frankfurt School, critical theory and its educational offspring, critical pedagogy, have evolved beyond their beginnings. Buoyed by the rediscovery of Italian social theorist Antonio Gramsci and his hegemony theory, the critical tradition has also profited from its encounter with feminism and poststructuralism during the last quarter of the twentieth century.

It is important to recognize these transitions in critical theory and pedagogy. Social theory in the mid-1970s embraced new ideologies and the formation of subjectivity (identity). The idea that power/ ideology produced a distorted version of true reality (if it was viewed by an authentic undistorted consciousness) was dropped. Since the evolving social theory challenged the possibility of critical scholars ever telling the whole truth, critical critical thinking sought a new humility.

Advocates of complex critical thinking and other scholars in the new paradigm had to be content with providing partial explanations of phenomena because they recognized that they were restricted by their particular vantage points in the web of reality. Although postformalists critiqued the authoritative pronouncements of positivistic educational psychology about higher-order thinking, they offered no objective, final revelation about the eternal nature of such a mode of thinking in its stead. Their call to democratize the beast is open-ended, motivated by an effort to diversify meaning and admit more marginalized people into the intellectual community. In part, the call is an admission that we don't exactly know what critical thinking is and never will; our only alternative is to simply keep looking for and collecting manifestations of it that meet the standards of our historically constructed value judgments. Such uncertainty is preferable to the antidemocratic, ethnocentric tyranny of positivistic certainty. Complex critical thinking in this context tries to get beyond such reductionism.

A central dimension of theoretically informed critical critical thinking is, of course, its concern with power and oppression and its understanding of the insidious work of hegemony. Richard Cary, in his entry "Art and Aesthetics," describes hegemony as the oppression of particular groups of people who unconsciously perpetuate their own oppression by cooperating with the dominant power structure. Cary discusses the ways individuals consent to oppression when they accept the authority and knowledge of people designated as experts.

In his essay, John Smyth points out that students and teachers who are critical critical thinkers always see knowledge as contestable. Such questioning involves asking if the knowledge provided is hegemonic. Does it attempt to win our consent to a dominating power, and if so, how? Often these persuasions are promoted under the banner of neutrality, objectivity and rationality. Modes of critical thinking that do not take hegemonic factors into account can seriously harm those who adopt them.

Ian Steinberg, in "Advertising and Ideology," examines the ways ideology turns ideas that support the status quo into common sense. Steinberg thinks understanding this process is crucial to becoming a complex critical thinker. Kathleen Berry, in "Radical Critical Thinking: Part 2: The Practice," argues that critical teachers dare their colleagues and students to challenge textbooks and the official nature of pre-packaged sources of knowledge. Berry's insights remind us why complex critical thinkers try to bring individuals from diverse backgrounds into the conversation about critical thinking. Often such individuals can point out hegemonic dimensions of common knowledge or the school curriculum not seen by those who live in the mainstream of society. Priya

Parmar's "Rap Music: The Critical Pedagogy of KRS-One" contains a good example of how individuals from different
backgrounds can point out unseen hegemonic dynamics.

UNDERMINING COMFORT: CHALLENGING CRITICALITY AND ITS VERSION OF CRITICAL THINKING

Any tradition can grow lazy and complacent and stop examining its underlying
assumptions and modes of operation. In
critical theory, critical pedagogy, and critical critical thinking we want to push accepted conceptual boundaries. We attempt
to do so in this encyclopedia by bringing
feminist theory, poststructuralism, postformalism, complexity theory, hermeneutics,
and enactivism to the conceptual table of
critical critical thinking.

We request that those within the traditions of such work keep it fresh and keep
trying to conceptually expand the field's
basic tenets. Complex critical thinkers
want criticality to step outside the frame
and question its own assumptions. Does
critical critical thinking involve more than
understanding the way we are hoodwinked
by power? Does critical understanding
provide us with a clear picture of reality?
Do we have to talk in particular ways to
claim criticality? If we ask questions of
this type, critical analysts will achieve a
better grasp of the complexity of everyday
life. Such insights undermine fundamentalism in the field and prevent an unthinking adherence to a previously formulated
set of tenets.

How do the paradigm shifts in knowledge production, the questioning of colonialist Eurocentrism and patriarchy, the
challenge to cognitive science, and other

domains affect our concept of critical critical thinking? As Gadamer argued in his
hermeneutics, the effort to interpret and
make meaning is never complete and must
always be open to rethinking. Such a perspective profoundly subverts tendencies
toward the authoritarianism of fundamentalism. Complex critical thinkers are ever
vigilant in their effort to expose and analyze unnamed assumptions. We study how
power works, but we also become aware of
our *understanding* of how power works.
As complex critical thinkers we develop a
multi-layered consciousness of the hegemonic, ideological, discursive, and regulatory dimensions of power. Concurrently,
we explore the assumptions behind power
theory and how our particular theoretical
assumptions may blind us to hidden power
dynamics and mutating forms of power in
new socioeconomic, political, and cultural
conditions.

When analysts explore how excluding
intuition and emotion from particular
modes of rationality affects rationality theories, they expose cultural and gender biases that have never been questioned. Male
Europeans often prided themselves on
their ability to employ critical reasoning
untainted by emotion or intuition. Now we
can include caring, empathy, and emotional connection in discussions about
critical thinking. By taking these factors
into account, European males can redefine
not only critical thinking but their own
ways of being men. Critical thinking then
moves into the ontological realm since it
helps us rethink who we are and what it
means to be human.

In this ontological realm, our rethinking of criticality takes us back to the enactivist imperative to let go of egocentrism
and focus on forging new connections to
the world around us. Using the language

of the Santiago School, complex critical thinkers enact this critical ontology in the specificity of lived situations.

One of the questions complex critical thinkers ask of the critical tradition is why gaining an understanding of critical critical thinking tends to exacerbate egoistic tendencies instead of purging them. Of course, human beings take pride in their knowledge and their ability to see what others do not. If criticality doesn't help us transcend egocentrism and produce an ethic of compassion and humility, then *it has failed.* So important is this dimension of rethinking critical thinking that I would label the egocentrism referred to here as the ideology of egocentrism.

A central activity in critical critical thinking is asking who benefits from particular power relationships. In my own work, I often ask who benefits from the status quo or from the certification of this or that body of knowledge. Gadamer argued that there is always an evaluative dimension to research and analysis and, as a result, we must always ask whose interests are served by this tacit orientation. Freire spoke frequently of "reading the world." He was referring to power dynamics, and tried to help his students make the connection between social and educational knowledge and the political forces that shape them.

In our complex questioning of criticality, we maintain that critical thinkers must always ask who benefits from a particular action or way of thinking. Who benefits from my knowing this? How do I personally gain from possessing and enacting such knowledge? What is my relationship with those who do not possess it? What is my responsibility to such individuals? Complex critical thinkers understand that in groups and out groups can develop

around the possession and deployment of critical theoretical knowledge. We must guard against the pathologies emerging from such hierarchies. (See Kathleen Berry's "Radical Critical Thinking: Part 1: Theoretical Background.")

NEW WAYS OF SEEING: THE EXPANDING DOMAIN OF COMPLEX CRITICAL THINKING

Central to the reconceptualization of critical thinking is the quest for different perspectives and new ways of seeing. Postformal thinking, with its effort to see the world from as many vantage points as possible, is important to the development of complex critical thinking. A valuable feature of postformalism's expansion of reason is its ability to uncover new perspectives, new angles on the world, everyday life, and self. In a postformal classroom, for example, students of critical thinking studying the Gulf War of 1991 would explore not only U.S. accounts of the conflict, but Iraqi perspectives as well. They would interview gung-ho U.S. Army veterans, opponents of the war, Iraqi victims, and observers from Africa and Latin America. Students would analyze the war in a geopolitical context, a multinational economic context, an environmental context, and a medical context. The role of the postformal teacher would involve devising new perspectives from which to explore the meaning of the war. Moral and ethical questions would be raised, and student interpretations of the event and analyses of its personal meaning in their lives would be encouraged.

In her essay "Democracy and John Dewey," Kathy Hytten expands postformalism's and complex critical thinking's efforts to exploit difference, as she explores Dewey's concern with seeing what is supposedly already known in a different light. Carol Korn picks up on this idea in her essay "Art Education, Young Children, and Critical Thinking," and describes the ways the arts can help even very young children extend their "capacity for imagining or playing with possibilities." Of course, different schools of complex critical thinking often meet with great hostility, with proponents of traditional rationality claiming that the search for diverse ways of seeing constitutes an assault on reason and a form of educational indoctrination. The model of complex critical thinking promoted in this encyclopedia demands that students always be allowed to pursue their own conclusions. Many versions of traditional education *are* guilty of indoctrination because they offer students no alternatives to the point of view that is being taught.

Complex critical thinking seeks to explore that which has been excluded (see Pat Williams-Boyd's "Empowerment: A Transformative Process" for an expansion of this idea). As Marjorie Mayers and Jim Field put it in their "Hermeneutics in the Classroom," critical thinking pedagogy involves helping students "explore meanings that were . . . invisible to them in their taken-for-grantedness." Complex critical thinking's search for differences profoundly shapes the process of developing curriculum and helps teachers and educational leaders reflect on the purpose of schooling and what it means to be an educated person. Zeus Leonardo, in his essay "Race," expands our understanding of difference and its uses in critical thinking and developing a profound sense of educational purpose. Since no aspect of society remains unaffected by race, teachers need to listen carefully to, read, and interact with those who are racially different from

themselves. The insights about thinking, education, politics, and self-construction one picks up in this manner are invaluable to personal and social growth.

New ways of seeing help critical thinkers achieve higher levels of self-awareness, and liberate them from stale convention. Teachers who can see from a variety of often forbidden perspectives become aware of the construction of their own professional consciousness and the ways that social and institutional forces try to undermine their autonomy as educators. Self-images, inherited dogmas, and absolute beliefs are called into question, and teachers begin to perceive the school as a piece of a larger mosaic. The inseparable relationship between thinking and acting becomes obvious as the boundary between feeling and logic begins to fade from the cognitive map.

To value different ways of seeing is on some level to acknowledge the interconnectedness of human beings and to reject the isolated, logical individual of Cartesianism. Kenneth Teitelbaum breathes life into this concept in "Curriculum Theorizing" when he writes, "critical thinking about curriculum means taking into account the actual human environment involved, the individual and collective biographies of students and teachers, and 'the wider society' of which schools are a part."

This emphasis on difference, biography, and self moves students of critical thinking to explore how we evolve and develop new ways of being human. Complex critical thinking focuses on these differences as central to human evolution. Complex critical thinkers pay close attention to the conditions in which humans confront knowledge, learn, grow, and develop. Obviously, these conditions are socially constructed, as is the language used in them. Individuals, no matter how brilliant, can't create the conditions in which they learn and develop. Our social interconnectedness is pre-given; but as we grow we gain the ability to choose how to extend and nurture the interconnections we make. We can avoid the exclusions that race, class, gender, sexuality, geographical place, and religion often create for us, and can ignore the sociocultural no trespassing signs that segregate us from one another.

Francisco Varela describes this ontological dynamic when he discusses the nature of the relationship between the self and the environment. Everyday life, he asserts, can be described as the domain of situated agents continuously dealing with unexpected events. They cannot create a master plan to guide them step-by-step through the wilderness, but must develop the wisdom and reflective ability to respond to the ill-defined and contextually specific conditions they encounter. Individuals can either embrace and expand their interactions or they can retreat and limit such connections.

Complex critical thinkers thirst for new interactions and connections. They see themselves as cognitive adventurers who get a rush from the process of exploring new ways of seeing. As teachers, they can hardly wait to get to their classrooms to help their students experience the excitement and insight that come from this process.

THE CRITICAL CONCEPT OF IMMANENCE: CRITICAL THINKING ABOUT WHAT COULD BE

Complex critical thinking is always concerned with what could be and what is immanent in various ways of thinking. It should move beyond the contemplative realm and lead to concrete social reform.

Paulo Freire thought complex critical thinking possessed immanence when it explored new ways to ease human suffering and produce psychological health. Critical immanence helps us get beyond egocentrism and ethnocentrism and work to build new forms of relationships with a variety of different people. Leila Villaverde extends this point about immanence in her entry "Developing Curriculum and Critical Pedagogy," when she says we need to help students "retain a vision of the not yet."

We find this concern with immanence in the work of the Frankfurt School and the hermeneutics of Hans-Georg Gadamer. Gadamer argues that our efforts to determine "what is" must be more cautious because they hold such dramatic consequences for how we explore "what ought to be." In Gadamer's view, the process of understanding involves interpreting meaning *and* applying the concepts realized to the historical moment that faces us. Another author in this encyclopedia, Michael Dumas, writes in his essay "Black Existence As Critical Thinking" about the "engagement of yearning" and "crossing the River Jordan and going to the mountaintop to see the Promised Land."

Immanence in complex critical thinking involves the use of human wisdom to bring about a better and more just world, less suffering, and more individual fulfillment instead of helping students and teachers adapt to the world as it is. In the context of immanence, complex critical thinking is profoundly concerned with who we are, how we got this way, and where we go from here. To answer these questions, we have to understand the ways we produce knowledge and the hidden assumptions about knowledge embedded within what we call the truth. These explorations move us to a new cognitive plateau where we can gain a far better look at what forces are shaping us—forces that have for so long traveled undetected under our cognitive radar. We are creatures of history who are both shaped by it and have the capacity to change it. What we are able to discern today about the historical forces that form us may be very different from what we were able to see ten years ago or what we may be able to see ten years from now.

In the language of complexity and enactivism, human beings are systems that are open to the flow of energy and matter. Though the human system maintains a stable biological form, the social world it encounters is constantly changing. In a cognitive sense, human beings have the capacity to both create and recreate their processes of knowing, the nature of their interactions with their environment(s), and the relationships they develop between mind and matter. All matter has immanence because there are infinite ways humans can relate to it. In every new encounter, we can develop a new relationship and become something more than we are. Since the self is a historical construction and not an immaterial transcultural ghost, it can be remade and remolded through critical thinking to become something better.

JUSTICE, IMMANENCE, AND CRITICAL THINKING

Jerome Bruner has contended that native intelligence may be more a product of one's relationship to the symbol systems used in schools than the distribution of genes (Bruner, 1996). Bruner's point is profoundly important to our notion of complex critical thinking because it states that the limitations on human ability that psychometricians attributed to congenital inferiority are only the misguided pronouncements of an ethnocentric and blind science unequipped to stand back from its own assumptions and recognize the pathological ways it has shaped so-called truths about human capacity. While there are numerous ideological tools for producing and justifying the inequality between human beings, this is one of the most important ones for the twenty-first century. (See Danny Weil's essay "Values and Dispositions of Critical Thinking: Developing Habits of Mind As Moral Commitments to Thought" for insight into these value-related questions.)

New cognitive theories, including sociocognition and enactivism, must always take these questions of justice into account. It is important for students of critical thinking to understand that (1) there are social dynamics in the cognitive process and, (2) cognition reaches its fullest expression in enactment; but such understandings are hollow if they fail to account for issues of race, class, and gender oppression that are embedded in unexamined dimensions of cognitive theory. Subjugated communities do not have access to Bruner's symbol systems and other social tools used for cognitive advancement, and they often challenge communities of learners who are exclusive in who they admit to their social conversation. Do such acts constitute manifestations of cognitive sophistication? Although the deliberations and actions of subjugated communities may be automatically excluded from the dominant intellectual community, the immanence and possibility of their cognitive activities may have relevance for more privileged communities and individuals.

Complex critical thinking is always concerned with a variety of contexts, including cognitive theory and its implications for social justice. Such an orientation makes complex critical thinkers very sensitive to cognitive theorists who claim progressive social intentions but continue to produce ways of seeing and pedagogies that foster oppression through race, class, and gender. Too often the seeds of such oppression can be found in knowledge that is taken for granted.

These are dangerous questions in the early twenty-first century. Such questions about the attacks of September 11, 2001, on New York and Washington, D.C., have been pronounced anti-American and unpatriotic by some political and educational leaders. If we are not careful, some cognitive scientists maintain, we may produce students who refuse to accept particular Western values.

What exactly do such analysts fear? Critical complex thinkers encourage students to question Western (and other cultural) values and see students who point out hypocrisies and contradictions in Western values as thoughtful young people, not undesirables. The editors and authors of this encyclopedia are not frightened by such students—we embrace them. In a globalized society where many different forms of colonial oppression have scarred the world's cultural and social landscape over the last 500 years, questions of cultural values become very complex and open to diverse interpretations. Complex critical thinkers hope that those who would suppress thinking informed by these dynamics do not win the ideological struggles of our era.

Judi Hirsch, in her entry "Teaching Current Events Using a Constructivist Critical Thinking Paradigm: A Model for Teachers," writes of the ways the fight against terrorism has been represented as a fight of good versus evil and asks how teachers of critical thinking can help students "know what is true and who is good? Are there circumstances under which it might be OK to nuke a country?"

Complex critical thinkers are amazed by the ways traditional psychology and cognitive science consistently underestimate the abilities of those who do not have upper middle class European ancestry. We can't talk about the issues Judi Hirsch raises with students, many maintain, because students are not ready for such topics. We can't deal with complexity and criticality in the elementary and secondary curriculum because it would stir up nothing but trouble. Questions of justice are too controversial for such students and the schools are not the place for them, others contend. Students, especially young people marginalized by race, class, or gender, are consistently more capable than psychology gives them credit for being. With the recent moves to increase the deskilling of teachers that John Smyth documents in his essay in this encyclopedia, even educational practitioners are viewed as incapable of monitoring student progress, diagnosing educational situations, or developing curriculum and instructional practices.

The vast majority of students and teachers are capable of becoming complex critical thinkers. When we assume otherwise we are not only making an erroneous supposition, we are setting the stage for unjust and undemocratic actions.

CRITICAL THINKING AS TEACHER KNOWLEDGE: EXAMINING THE REGULATORY POWER OF PSYCHOLOGY

One of the central goals of our encyclopedia is to produce an innovative analysis of the implications of a reconceptualized critical thinking for the classroom. An important dimension of that goal is making complex critical thinking an integral aspect of the teacher knowledge base.

A key concept that we think teachers need to grasp is that cognition is always a political and ideological act, not an individual psychological activity, and can lead to higher orders of thinking when it can expand into its full power. As both a psychological and a sociopolitical activity, complex critical thinking is never static but always in process, ever in a state of being constructed.

Teachers are induced by rationalistic management systems to think of the curriculum outside of its social context. The people who create the curriculum and those who distribute it pretend that the knowledge it contains is politically neutral—a body of agreed-upon information being systematically passed on to students by an ever-evolving, but always impartial, instructional process. Complex critical thinkers are not seduced by the sirens of political neutrality. The curriculum is always a formal transmission of *particular* aspects of a culture's knowledge. Do we teach women's history and African American history in eleventh-grade social studies? Do we read Toni Morrison and Alice Walker in twelfth-grade literature? The psychological domain involves the same political concepts. The power-related assumptions and practices that characterize contemporary psychology act at a level invisible to many observers and inscribe the interests of dominant power on the cognitive terrain.

Teachers who are complex critical thinkers study the subtle ways power is a part of psychology. They are not conspiracy buffs who see psychologists as evil villains, covertly operating to control our minds. Some readers will interpret such analyses of the politics and disciplines of knowledge as efforts to uncover conspiracies. While not denying that some power

wielders undertake covert actions, the analysis of power in the psychological domain is much less romantic than such a view would imply. Power typically operates here under the flag of common sense, which is the unconscious inscription of dominant cultural norms and values on the human psyche and psychological knowledge production. For example, psychology has constructed a model of what our society considers the mind to be, and this model has been used by the society to shape social organizations, politics, schools, curricula, and the role of the teacher.

Complex critical thinkers urge psychologists to be more aware of the profession's power—as a discipline that categorizes, classifies, and assesses cognition—to proclaim normality, pathology, or a lack of intelligence. (See my essay "Educational Psychology and Critical Thinking.") Tanya Brown's two essays on Bloom's Taxonomy and higher-order thinking shed light on this subject. Any attempt to reconceptualize critical thinking must involve tracing the imprint of unexamined sociopolitical assumptions on how psychology determines an individual's aptitude and how these determinations maintain dominant power relations. Far too often it is the socioeconomically well-to-do who are deemed intelligent and the poor and racially marginalized who are deemed incapable by the psychological establishment. In this context, reconceptualizing critical thinking becomes an act of resistance: a counter-hegemonic struggle to challenge psychological authority.

If the political aspects of educational psychology are not identified, educational psychology can become a vehicle for the dominant power structure to oppress particular individuals instead of the liberating, humanistic force it was intended to be. The positivistic, hyperrational articulation of the discipline (with its standardized methods, narrow linear thinking, distance from a natural context, and universal application of techniques and assumptions) sets psychology up for failure. Because this articulation refuses to consider the sociopolitical role of psychological activities, it produces a bureaucracy of rule-following technocrats.

These functionaries study the mechanical parts of the watch but have never thought about the nature of time. Psychology did not come out of nowhere but emerged in a particular time and place—the Western hemisphere in the nineteenth century—with particular assumptions and cultural ways of seeing. It has been described many times as a technology of power that affects the lives of different people in diverse ways—some for better, some for worse. These dynamics cannot be fully understood without the help of social, cultural, political, economic, discursive, and even psychoanalytical analyses.

The cultural inscription on psychology and the ways it contributes to how we conceptualize thinking in general and critical thinking in particular is palpable. As a creation of power, psychology develops special political relations with particular groups of people. Michael Dumas speaks in this volume about psychology and black existence in America. Black people, he writes, were never meant to think in the United States. They were positioned outside of meaning making and deemed to have no relation to meaning other than the meaning imposed on them.

Dumas is alluding to the ways psychology and education leave African Americans out of the scholarly picture. Informed by Dumas and countless other scholars who fall outside the European upper middle class circle, complex critical thinkers understand that such exclusions are a manifestation of neo-colonial power that invalidates the cultural production, cognition, and worth of the vast majority of the people who currently inhabit the planet. Complex critical thinkers cannot stomach such ethnocentric scholarship, and consistently address these regulatory and exclusionary practices. Many psychologists' pernicious use of African American IQ scores to illustrate black inferiority to whites is an obvious use of psychology as a technology of power. Of course, when such assertions are made, analysts find that tough questions about the nature of intelligence, cultural factors that affect a student's ability to understand the test, the motives of the psychologists involved, or the perspectives of dissenting psychologists are often repressed.

Complex critical thinkers are profoundly interested in these dynamics and what they tell us about the politics of knowledge production. They argue that such understandings should be a central dimension of what teachers need to know.

CRITICAL THINKING AS THE RESISTANCE OF REGULATION

Teachers who are complex critical thinkers are constantly watching for the ways Western elitist vantage points are normalized in education. We see them at work in the world of art and art education, as Richard Cary points out in his chapter in this volume, when dominant power supports certain modes of representing the world and excludes others. We also see dominant modes of perceiving in history, government, literature, and scientific curricula. Students study Western history and are told that the history of other parts of the world are not as important, are exposed to little criticism of the structure of their nation's government, read the white male canon with only a few tokenistic additions, and are shielded from a view of science as a human construction put together by a particular cultural group at a specific time in history.

The promulgation of such ways of seeing is an attempt to regulate the population and reduce resistance to the interests of dominant groups. Regulated individuals, including teachers, are more likely to accept their role in the workplace of global capitalism.

The electronic world of the twenty-first century is vulnerable to power in ways never before imagined. Dominant power now has 24-hour access to people in their most private spaces, and can use television, the Internet, and other methods of communication, as well as schooling, to produce more compliant forms of consciousness and identity that allow it more freedom to operate. In both workplaces and schools, power wielders offer a debased view of those they seek to regulate (including incompetent workers who need to be controlled by top-down management schemes, unprepared teachers who need scripts and lessons planned by experts, and undisciplined students who are capable of little more than the regurgitation of unconnected facts on standardized tests).

Complex critical thinkers understand that the ways these different groups are represented by dominant power is part of a larger struggle on the landscape of twenty-first century cultural politics. If dominant power wins the battle, the op-

pressive modes of top-down regulation it has devised will be seen as necessary measures to deal with the sea of incompetents that plague our nation. I often listen to individuals speak who parrot the pronouncements of power as mere common sense. ("Somebody's got to do something about all these bad teachers. If they're left to their own devices they'll destroy our children.") The cultural struggle over such representations is daunting, since dominant power wielders are the only ones with the financial resources to shape the content of the mass media.

This makes media literacy (see Steinberg, "Popular Culture") an extremely important aspect of complex critical thinking and the rigorous educational curriculum it demands. Teachers and students must be able to identify and analyze the politics of knowledge production and information access in the twenty-first century. They must understand the inseparability of knowledge and power and the relationship between what dominant power wants us to know and the content of television, radio, movies, and school curricula.

This discussion brings us back to complex critical thinking's persistent concern with ideology. Dominant power produces ideologies in the contemporary electronic world that appeal to our hearts as well as our minds. The emotional appeal of loyalty to country, for example, despite the ill-advised and violent paths the nation might take, often works as an ideological tool to quell dissent. "I can't speak out against the invasion of Indonesia," many might someday assert, "because people will think I'm not a patriotic American." Complex critical thinking invites us to embrace civic courage, to face accusations of disloyalty, and to challenge dominant ideological efforts to shape public consciousness. The seduction of a dominant ideology is powerful and hard to resist. Ideologies are the lifeblood of hegemonic power, which employs them to win the consent of the governed to dominant power wielders in government, corporations, and other sociopolitical locations.

Complex critical thinking is not afraid to confront these ideologies A central dimension of this confrontation involves tracing the social and historical processes that shaped dominant ideas and analyzing how common-sense doctrine achieved its status. In doing so, critical thinkers begin to understand whose interests are served by these social and educational structures and the ways of seeing they encourage. Complex critical thinkers study the way meaning is shaped in the social, political, and educational discourse of the day and the way cultural signs, such as patriotism, are deployed in the interests of power. They become able to discern hidden meanings and exclusions in political discourse, media production, and school curricula, and become much more insightful about how the sociopolitical world operates and about our role in it. Such knowledge makes us far more capable of challenging and resisting the way power hurts disempowered individuals and regulates the society.

CRITICAL THINKING, POWER, AND THE UNCONSCIOUS

Complex critical thinkers dig deeper into the ways power operates by delving into the psychoanalytic realm, the domain of the unconscious. When we operate within the boundaries of rationality and consciousness, there are limits to our understanding of ideological and hegemonic processes. These limits can be overcome by a study of depth psychology. Psychoanalysis has traditionally been concerned with the forces of irrationality and the ways they shape both consciousness and behavior. Any force that shapes behavior in a manner that is contradictory to the ways in which we think of experience is important—even if the notion of self is not as stable and knowable as early psychoanalysts assumed.

Psychoanalysis allows us to view the formation of identity from unique vantage points not attainable via other methodologies. Psychoanalysts looks for the power-inscribed unconscious processes that create resistance to progressive change and induce self-destructive behavior. The tradition offers hope to complex critical thinkers concerned with social justice and the related attempt to admit presently marginalized people into the intellectual community, as well as to those who want to explore human potential. When psychoanalysis is reconceptualized in a way that rejects Freud's separation of the psychic from the social realm, it becomes a powerful tool in understanding the effects of power. The contributions of the field of depth psychology, an admittedly old-fashioned term associated with psychoanalysis, are important to the sociopolitical concerns of complex critical thinking.

I choose depth psychology as a tradition worthy of contribution to critical thinking because its concerns are directly relevant to educational psychology. Depth psychology is focused on the analysis of irrationality, the emotions, the complexity of personality, creativity, artistic endeavor, and morality. No educational psychology worthy of its important task can ignore these issues and their relationship to learning, motivation, school performance, and the nature of the teaching process. In addition, if depth psychology incorporates the insights of the social theoretical domain, it can motivate interest in the way an individual subjectively experiences power and allow us to view the effects of large social and political forces at the private level. Cartesian boundaries between the public and the personal, and regressive ideas that separate the social production of identity and intelligence, can be erased.

As we begin to grasp the importance of a socially situated unconscious in the production of identity and the learning process connected to it, teachers gain vital insights into the ways education might be reconfigured. Complex critical thinkers are quick to note that their appreciation of psychoanalysis and depth psychology is cautious and very selective. Following the lead of many feminist psychoanalysts, psychologists and educators in the complex critical tradition understand the patriarchal inscriptions of traditional psychoanalysis and struggle to avoid the hegemonic landmines hidden in the field. They understand that psychoanalysis and depth psychology possess progressive features that can be used in conjunction with a critical theoretical awareness to create a more just and better-educated world, a new sacred society where human beings are studied and appreciated in terms of their unique abilities and talents.

Complex critical thinkers develop a vision of psychoanalysis that is poststructural because it reveals how human problems are embedded in the sciences that emerged from Cartesianism and the structures it has created. Poststructuralist psychoanalysis presents a view of human beings that is quite different from the traditional psychological portrait. In the process, it challenges the modern Cartesian erasure of feeling, valuing, and caring in contemporary Western societies and attempts to rethink these features in light of power and the way it influences the construction of consciousness.

The poststructuralist impulse challenges Freud's positioning of the pleasure principle in opposition to the reality principle and traditional rationality as the goal of therapy. In many ways, such an oppositional construction places Freudianism squarely within the boundaries of Western logocentrism, which values rationality over irrationality, masculinity over femininity, civilization over primitivism, and logic over emotion. From this perspective, the psychoanalytic tradition is a tool of the regulatory objectives of modernist science.

In its effort to produce a healthy (read conformist) population, traditional psychoanalysis has, in the same manner as its modernist brother educational psychology, set out to repress desire. Poststructuralist psychoanalysis has often embraced unconscious desire as a positive entity with the social revolutionary potential to unfasten the hegemonic straitjacket of modernist psychology and education.

Modernist psychology, education, and the uncritical critical thinkers they produce must understand that rationalistic views of being human and faith in an unexamined rationality are poor tools for a successful contemporary life, where we are bombarded with power structure-produced information aimed directly at our emotions and libidinal desires. Humbled by the poststructuralist critique, traditional psychoanalysis has begun to discern the relationship between suppressed desire and political power, the affiliation between the fear of passion and the maintenance of the status quo. Complex critical thinkers use these insights to free themselves from the blinders of rationalism, its biases and ethnocentric exclusions, its fear of libidinal energy, and its inability to address the way contemporary power wielders use the media to colonize emotion for political gain.

CRITICAL THINKING, POWER, AND SCHOOLING

As complex critical thinking explores the cosmos of power and its efforts to regulate human beings, it turns its analytical gaze to schools and classrooms and asks questions about the socio-cultural role of schooling, the relationship between this role and dominant power blocs in the culture, and how this relationship affects the construction of the curriculum.

John Covaleskie, in his entry "Philosophical Instruction," writes "a pedagogy that commits to making children receptive and docile is also one that denies human dignity and freedom." When complex critical thinkers examine curriculum development and school operation, they find too often that the knowledge distributed to teachers and students feigns neutrality but covertly supports particular political interests. Students are not encouraged to study multiple points of view or learn that, both within U.S. society and around the planet, there are profoundly different interpretations of history, biology, literacy, and political, social, and economic issues than the ones offered in their textbooks and curriculum guides. Students are typically not taught about the complex nature of interpretation and the assumptions embedded in, and the power imprinted on, all knowledge.

Many political and educational leaders think these dramatically important dimensions of learning are inconsequential, and many power wielders view such insights as downright frightening. Knowledge production and curriculum development are always historically embedded and culturally inscribed processes, and the base on which school knowledge rests is slippery indeed. Complex critical thinkers are suspicious of any curriculum that presents itself as the truth if it does not include at least some differing perspectives.

Complex critical thinkers complain that American education has not been very interested in understanding the dynamics of knowledge production or exploring theories of knowledge, but tends to take knowledge at face value. Few people question how information got here and most discount the need to determine how this process takes place. Students either learn the subject matter or they don't. Complex critical thinkers maintain that the key to becoming a scholar resides at this level of interpretation—not in stuffing volumes of unproblematized data in mental filing cabinets.

The role schools play in the historical construction of the self is not an important topic of study in contemporary U.S. culture. The dominant culture's conversation about education simply ignores questions of power and justice in the development of educational policy and classroom practice.

Those who study these features of power have come to understand the ways it shapes a student's capacity to succeed in schooling. As a student from the rural southern Appalachian mountains, I ran into college professors who felt that someone from my background could not do well in school. My status as a member of a subculture determined my relationship to dominant power. I was an outsider seeking certification by the academy. I was told on numerous occasions, after handing in an essay or research paper, that the professor knew I had plagiarized the work because "someone like me" was not capable of producing such writing. For some reason that maybe only a psychoanalyst might understand, I chose to continue pursuing an academic career. I was lucky because I possessed the confidence that I could become a scholar. Most students who find themselves in such a disempowered situation don't have the confidence to continue.

Understanding this lack of confidence alerts complex critical thinkers to the many subtle ways that power wielders—through race, class, gender, geographical place, religion, and so on—rank students and sort them out. When technologies of power such as standardized testing and curricular standardization are in place, there is even less possibility that marginalized students will gain the confidence to reshape their relationship to power or even reshape power's relationship to them.

Critical educators have worked hard to try to get these understandings of power across to teachers, administrators, educational leaders, and the public. As Juan-Miguel Fernández-Balboa points out in his entry in this volume, "one of the first steps in the empowerment of people is to help them realize that their status is due, to a great extent, to systemic forces (e.g., institutional meritocracy) designed to keep them ignorant and resigned." Unfortunately, in the twenty-first century, seeing schools as locales for political struggle and resistance seems profoundly out of touch with the right-wing Zeitgeist, but complex critical thinkers are working diligently to develop new ways to make these points.

When I teach about power, schooling, and critical thinking, I often make use of Pierre Bourdieu's idea of cultural capital to illustrate these ideas. In the same way that money is a form of economic capital, members of the dominant culture develop ways of knowing, acting, and being (cultural capital) that can be cashed in in order to get ahead in the lived world. These ways of knowing, acting, and being include manners, deportment, taste, style, accent, grammar, level of affect, etc. Those like

myself, who come from social and cultural locations outside of the dominant culture, may possess excellent abilities but are marginalized because we don't understand the codes of dominant cultural capital. My students become more adept critical thinkers when they understand the ways cultural capital is deployed to keep the marginalized in a subordinate position and the privileged in a dominant one. This support of the status quo takes place within the boundaries of common sense: "We wouldn't want someone like her in our corporation, company, department." Teachers who are complex critical thinkers expose the power-related dynamics that prop up the status quo, undermine social mobility, and produce ideologies that justify these anti-democratic practices.

Marjorie Mayers and Jim Field have written about the phenomenon that the knowledge presented in textbooks is currently considered unassailable. Teachers who are complex critical thinkers demand that a variety of opinions and perspectives be brought to schools. Such a demand is not merely an affirmation of diversity and an insistence on fairness. While fairness is obviously important, the way curricular exclusions are executed is typically an insidious process that takes place under a flag of objectivity and can produce great harm. To eliminate this practice, we have to appeal to a broader and more complicated concept than fairness and understand the way Cartesian scientists quash dissent. (If an expert says that a body of sociological knowledge has been produced by objective social scientists and a complex critical thinker responds that there is no mention of the role of poor women in the social process being described, the scientist is likely to say that including women of lower socio-economic class was outside the purview of the research design.)

COMPLEX CRITICAL THINKING, POWER, AND HUMAN AGENCY: THE QUEST FOR SELF-DIRECTION AND CONNECTION

Complex critical thinking always takes into account the ways hegemonic, ideological, regulatory, and discursive forces shape human beings and their ways of perceiving themselves and the world, and also includes the ways human beings can critique and resist such malevolent forces. Knowledge can be used as a weapon of dominant power. To those who control its production, knowledge is a warm gun. When used as a gun, Cartesian knowledge can keep away those who fall outside the group anointed by the society's wielders of power. It is extremely important that critical thinkers understand the construction, use, and effects of knowledge production in the society at large and in schools in particular. We are what we know and our ability to act depends on what we know. Being able to identify the hidden forces that shape what we know is even more important than we originally thought.

Many analysts (Burbules & Beck, 1999, among others) have argued that large groups of individuals are aware that they are excluded from the discourses of the field of critical thinking. Complex critical thinkers understand that, in any movement, in-groups and hip lexicons develop, including in the field of critically grounded education. They recognize that these in-groups exclude people and find that fact unacceptable for the inclusivity-based struggle of complex critical thinking.

It is tragic that, when they address the search for self-direction and connection with other human beings, the pedagogical discourses of critical thinking are not more user friendly. Complex critical thinkers understand that many of the concepts central to these discourses are complex and sound strange to the uninitiated. Like good teachers in any domain, they are trying to understand the reasons that particular individuals find these concepts unintelligible or off-putting.

There are multiple reasons for this reaction, some related to educational background, some involved with ideological conditioning, and some a combination of both. During lessons on patriarchal forms of power, I have known angry students to stand up in class and proclaim, "Don't talk to me about patriarchy. I am more than happy to live in subjugation to my husband." Obviously, my attempt to engender what I considered complex critical thinking about power did not touch the lived emotions and needs of these particular students. Instead, I alienated these individuals from any interest in power, human agency, self-direction, and my version of connecting with other people. Teachers of complex critical thinking must learn from such failures.

If critical education reinvents the voice of the expert in a new package, students will not be motivated to undertake a critical quest for self-direction. I have often observed professors of complex critical thinking create the same distance between themselves and their students that plagued the pedagogy of the most traditional and canonical scholars. Almost everything is the same in the two situations—only the brand of orthodoxy has changed. Students in these conditions do nothing but reproduce the truths of the teachers, copying their vocabulary and writing style and even excluding the uninitiated groups the teacher indicates are inferior.

While complex critical thinking treasures the critical theoretical context and draws profound theoretical sustenance from it, the field is not blind to the problems of the tradition. A pedagogy and mode of thinking constructed on a foundation of justice and emancipation must *enact* these dynamics in its everyday operations. We hold complex critical thinkers to a higher standard than people from traditions that don't make this claim.

This is why enactivism is so important to complex critical thinking. If we are teaching people about the workings of power and how they shape the individual, we cannot just theorize about these complicated dynamics, we must demonstrate their antithesis in everyday life. Teachers of theoretically informed critical thinking must develop the crazy wisdom, the immediate coping abilities, the improvisational finesse, to show students how to live in accordance with complex critical thinking's ideals. This connection is a central dimension of the purpose of this encyclopedia—the development of a complex critical thinking that can change the tenor of educational goals and pedagogical practices, and the development of teachers who can model these practices in everyday life as well as teach abstract knowledge and theory.

Several authors in the encyclopedia deal with issues directly connected to this theme. Marjorie Mayers and Jim Field, in "The Anti-Textbook Textbook: Critical Thinking and Politics in the Apolitical Classroom," raise questions about "everyday consciousness" that rest at the heart of our concern with the theoretical emphasis of criticality. These authors maintain that we need to develop ways of dealing with "the kinds of things that we take for granted in our everyday lives." Judith Slater in her essay "Constructing Selfhood" also addresses this theme, saying that scholars and teachers of critical theoretical education must get beyond the habit of separating the theoretical dimension from the enactment of criticality. As Slater puts it, "To change assumptions there has to be an optimistic view that past behavior is no longer able to meet the reality of new demands." Ray Horn adds to these voices as he describes his insights into becoming a scholar/practitioner/leader of complex critical thinking. Horn's vision offers complex critical thinkers a way to talk about this connection between the critical theoretical domain and their own activities as teachers and pedagogical leaders.

Complex critical thinkers develop new modes of reflection and action that combine ideological analysis, rhetorical/linguistic insight, and socio-cultural and policy study with an awareness of self and its complex relationship to everyday life.

How can we avoid self-righteous, elitist proclamations of critical principles in schools, classrooms, and a multitude of other lived situations? The moment-to-moment monitoring proposed by Varela becomes indispensable in this context. Such monitoring alerts complex critical thinkers to how they make connections to both different contexts and other people, so they can uncover and eliminate the contradictions in their own psyches with which complex critical thinkers are so concerned.

COMPLEX CRITICAL THINKING VIS-À-VIS POSTFORMALISM

Regardless of what modernist education and the critical thinking it promoted have become, the idea behind the concepts involved the human attempt to move beyond the randomness of natural selection. As human beings developed the ability to think critically and choose, they came to believe that, through education, they could shape the nature of future evolution. No longer bound by instincts, humans use education to pose questions about the way things are, to understand what confuses them, and to change what impedes them. While doing so, they pay attention to the consequences of their actions, generate alternatives, and become increasingly aware of possibilities in their lives. This is the educational vision of critical thinking postformal teachers, who want to develop new ways of cultivating the intellect while they act upon their understanding of power's cooption of schooling.

Postformal critical thinkers are trying to shape the evolution of the species and move to a higher order of thinking. Such teachers refuse to naively accept or reject any body of knowledge until they determine where its information came from, what the dominant power structure allows to be officially transmitted and what is not, and who transmits it and who listens. This form of discursive meta-awareness is essential to postformal thinking and gives us a larger picture of the nature of the information that shapes our lives. See Colin Lankshear and Michele Knobel's essay "Literacy" for more insight into these discursive dynamics.

Unfortunately, research indicates that, at the present time, few teachers are able to operate at such a level of meta-awareness. Far too many people involved with education hold a monological view of knowledge and possess little awareness of the social dependence of knowledge construction. They are taught to view knowledge in terms of considering evidence for or against the truth of particular ideas, rather than determining where and from whom the knowledge comes and how it is validated. Postformalism as a mode of complex critical thinking seeks to upset this epistemological apple cart and expose the hidden processes that shape what we are supposed to know.

Critical thinking postformal teachers understand that the process of inquiring and reflecting is important. No text, no principle, no work of art, and no person should be beyond questioning, analysis, or criticism. Bertrand Russell wrote almost a century ago that philosophy's value has little to do with its ability to produce answers to our uncertainties. Individuals without philosophy, Russell wrote, travel through life imprisoned by the prejudices derived from everyday existence, which they call common sense. The habitual beliefs of an individual's time in history become tyrants to a mind unable to reflect upon their genesis. At its best, Russell concluded, philosophy expands our thoughts and liberates them from the prison of custom. Postformal critical thinkers release themselves from the prison of custom and convention and exist in the world of freedom on their own recognizance.

In order for postformal critical thinkers to expand their cognitive abilities, it is essential that they understand how they think and why they think that way. Cartesian scientific thinking (formal thinking) attempts to move people through a regulated progression of discrete stages to reach the goal of Cartesian thought. While traditional developmentalism may have understood that teaching is enhanced when the learner is surprised by the discrepancy between his or her expectations and reality, it failed to follow up on the implications embedded in that concept.

Expectation implies an awareness of one's own perceptions—but formal thinkers were uninterested in the nature of these perceptions or how they might have been constructed and forfeited their claim to meta-awareness and the self-knowledge that leads to emancipation. Because they did not study the production of self, formalists were not ready for the electronic, media-driven culture that emerged in the last half of the twentieth century. The ways that the world is covertly shaped by power and the ways this process operates at the levels of individual consciousness and unconsciousness are central to any study of cognition and critical thinking; but the formalists ignored these sociocultural processes as if they had nothing to do with selfhood, thinking, teaching, and learning. Postformalists do not make this mistake.

Postformalism is an important foundation for complex critical thinking. The way we define critical thinking exerts a profound impact on both our educational goals and the classroom activities of teachers. As a model for a higher-order form of thinking, postformalism can change the direction of pedagogical work. In a school shaped by educators who understand postformalism and the type of critical thinking that emerges from it, self-reflection would lead teachers to become detectives of intelligence, both inside and outside of academia. Such teachers would explore indigenous and other subjugated knowledges excluded by mainstream education and the mind-expanding insights of Santiago School enactivism and critical and complexity theories. (See Erik Malewski's "Organizational Change in Public Education: From Crucial to Critical Leadership" on the use of complexity theory in leadership.) The excitement of cultivating the intellect, expanding consciousness, promoting new ways of being human, and resisting the ways power distorts these processes as it punishes the marginalized would become a way of life for such pedagogues. Forgive my enthusiasm, but what wonderful places such schools could become.

BASIC CHARACTERISTICS OF POSTFORMALISM

I have written about postformalism and postformal education in a number of works (Kincheloe, 1993, 2001; Kincheloe & Steinberg, 1993). The following is an explanation of the main postformal categories of analysis and their relation to complex critical thinking. (Ray Horn contributes to this explanation in his essay in this volume.) I will conclude this introduction with some follow-up ideas about the intersection of postformalism and critical thinking.

I. *Etymology.* Etymology is the study of the origins and history of any subject under examination. Postformal etymology insists that critical thinking should always involve understanding how things came to be and an awareness of the dynamics of the world's social construction. This applies to knowledge, consciousness, educational folk wisdom, political common sense, etc. Postformal teachers, for example, explore the etymology of their views on the roles of teachers and students, their perspectives on the purpose of schools, and a variety of other subjects relevant to education.

Without a concept of etymology, critical thinkers do not understand the origins of their viewpoints, why they hold these viewpoints, and why they are not prepared to expose their viewpoints to rigorous scholarship.

A. *The Origins of Knowledge.* Exploring the origins of knowledge means understanding the complex process of how information gains the status of knowledge and truth. Postformalism challenges critical thinkers to question what they say they know, why they believe or reject what they know, and how they evaluate the credibility of evidence. Where did the epistemological and cultural forms that undergird our knowledge originate and gain social certification? In Gaile Cannella's entry "Early Childhood Education," readers see this process at work in her etymological examination of the construction of Western knowledges about childhood.

B. *Thinking about Thinking.* When people study the sociocultural and ideological forces that shaped their consciousness and the inner world of their psychological experience, they are thinking about thinking. There are many dimensions to postformal thinking about thinking, including activities such as developing the ability to understand the dominant narratives humans use to make sense of their lives and the world. Carol Mullen describes scholar-practitioners in her essay "Scholar Practitioners As Classroom Teachers," and Ray Horn speaks of scholar-practitioner postformal teachers. These scholar-practitioners become researchers who question the nature of their own thinking as they are teaching critical thinking to their students. (See also Danny Weil's entry "Metacognition: What Is Transformative Metacognition and Why Is It Important?")

Adults do not reach a final cognitive equilibrium beyond which no new levels of thought can emerge. There are modes of thinking that transcend the ability to formulate abstract conclusions, understand cause-effect relationships, and employ the traditional scientific method

to explain reality. Postformalists know too much to define formal Cartesian thinking as the zenith of human cognitive ability. These are some of the things we learn when we begin the process of thinking about thinking. Layla Suleiman Gonzalez in her entry "Youth Development: Critical Perspectives," expands these concepts in her critique of developmentalism.

C. *Asking Unique Questions and Problem Detection.* Postformalist critical thinkers discern problems where others see equilibrium and develop the ability to ask questions that reframe aspects of the cosmos that were previously missed. This type of critical thinker can trace the etymology of what is and is not deemed a problem in a particular cultural setting. Colin Lankshear and Michele Knobel, in their essay under *Literacy,* provide a compelling example of this postformal process. They offer a sample lesson on how to perform a linguistic analysis of the dominant Western ways of studying the historical role of Christopher Columbus, and they provide a list of postformal questions that allow teachers and students to understand problems that are buried in the text, such as the way most history books represent many indigenous peoples as passive and helpless. Danny Weil, in his entry "Socratic Questioning: Helping Students Figure Out What They Don't Know," provides an example of unique questioning by Leo Huberman, the former educational director for the National Maritime Union.

II. *Patterns.* Patterns are the connecting relationships that structure the physical and the social worlds. Knowledge, consciousness, and human beings are all created by invisible patterns of interlocking activities. From our vantage points as individuals operating in the middle of these patterns, we come to understand just how difficult patterns are to identify. Modernist science and education have typically focused on separate pieces of the patterns, many times missing the pattern itself. As a result, serious problems are ignored as experts focus on specific events in isolation. No matter how educated many modernist critical thinkers become, if they cannot escape the confinements of formal thinking, they will be held hostage by unseen patterns. Postformal critical thinkers work hard to uncover the patterns in the information and images with which they are confronted.

A. *Exploring Deep Patterns and Structures.* When we expose deep patterns and structures we expose the hidden forces, the below-the-radar assumptions, that construct our perceptions of the world and the forms the world takes. Without such insights, teachers and students see a reductionistic and fragmented view of the socio-cultural cosmos. Postformal critical thinkers recognize patterns of exclusion and identify socio-cultural and historical structures that have been eliminated from the curriculum.

John Gabriel, in his entry under *Language Arts,* provides a literary example of this concept. Writing about the importance of thinking about words, Gabriel posits that such analysis provides critical thinkers with a deeper understanding of language. Quoting Ralph Waldo Emerson, Gabriel tells his readers that every word originally emerged as a poem, as a part of a larger cosmic pattern. In Emerson's words, "whenever we are so finely organized that we can penetrate into that region where the air is music, we hear those primal warblings and attempt to write them down."

B. *Seeing Relationships between Ostensibly Different Things.* A metaphoric mode of cognition that involves the fusion of previously disparate concepts in unanticipated ways is created when we are able to see relationships between ostensibly different things. Einstein argued in his Special Theory of Relativity, for example, that gravity illustrated that the universe itself was better understood as a relationship than as separate objects—an understanding missed by Cartesian modes of physics and rationalistic modes of critical thinking. Einstein said that gravity was not a thing, a wave, or a particle as warring factions argued for a quarter of a millennium. Instead, he thought that gravity reflected the relationships between space, time, and mass—an insight that changed the way we conceptualize the universe.

Postformalists use the same key to change the way we think about cognition and education. In enactivist theory, the mind *emerges* in response to a variety of relationships between humans and the world. This changes the nature of *being*—both for humans and for things-in-the world. Postformal critical thinkers understand that patterns of connection are more important than sets of fragmented parts. In this metaphorical dimension of pattern, human beings construct relationships and build bridges between themselves and their circumstances by seeing the connections between ostensibly different things. When we act on such patterns of relationship, we move to new cognitive and behavioral levels.

C. *Uncovering Levels of Interconnection between Mind and Ecosystem.* When we discover interconnections between our minds and the ecosystem in which we live, we uncover larger patterns of life force. Postformalists begin to redefine life itself when they appreciate that life may have less to do with the parts of a living system than with patterns of information, the relationships among these patterns, and the interconnected dance of the living process. Such patterns make it virtually impossible to discern where living things end and nonliving things begin. In this context, one can discern why the enactivist notion of autopoiesis (self-creation) or emergence becomes so important in the discourse of complex critical thinking.

Cynthia McCallister, in her essay "Writing Education Practices within the Reconceptualized Curriculum," provides an example of a sophisticated elementary classroom pedagogy that includes the role of the emergent self and the pattern of relationships that help produce it. In a fifth-grade writing class, students learn to improve their writing by developing writing-based relationships with the teacher and other students in the class and listening to reactions to their written ideas. Students learn how they are perceived by others, and not only begin to think about their writing but their relationships with others and the nature of their own selfhood. An informed teacher can use such exercises in a way that nurtures the emergence of a positive self—one that is predisposed to understand the patterns that shape its own production and to intervene in reshaping them when necessary.

III. *Process.* Process means developing new modes of making sense of and researching the world that help us place ourselves in the web of reality. Postformalist thinkers go beyond the ideas of reason and scientific reductionism that are common in Western civilization and construct new ways of studying critical thinking, often including methods of seeing the world and evaluating the historical and social forces that shape our perception that Western science dismisses as primitive and irrelevant.

In my own work, I have used the concept of bricolage to help conceptualize these new processes of research and analysis. Bricolage is a French word for the work of bricoleurs (handymen or women who use the tools available to complete a task). I use it to denote processes of research and analysis that draw upon multiple methods of inquiry and interpretation. Such methods involve not only research but social, theoretical, epistemological, and ontological concerns.

Process is the most complicated category of postformalism because it is used in two ways. The first involves the processes of inquiry and analysis just described; the second involves the idea that all information and all understandings are in process and are part of larger streams of development. This second meaning can be illustrated by the action of a river. The river that flows by me today is a different river than the one I observed from the same point on the bank last year. Today it is at a different stage in its process.

A. *Deconstruction*. Scholars have defined deconstruction in numerous ways—as an interpretive process, a philosophical orientation, or viewing the cosmos as a text to be read. Postformalists employ all three of these definitions and apply them to critical thinking. From this perspective, the world is full of texts to be deconstructed or explored for unintended meanings. Critical thinkers who understand this dynamic engage in an active process of discerning the multiple meanings embedded in the various aspects of the world, and realize the impossibility of coming to a final understanding. Roymeico Carter, in his entry "Visual Literacy: Critical Thinking with the Visual Image," contends that, when viewing a visual image, students must go beyond traditional concerns with the formal components of composition. As critical thinkers using a deconstructive process, students should uncover the hidden contexts involved with the production of the visual image— the time it was produced, its cultural location, and the social assumptions embedded within it. Are such social norms different from those of the individuals currently viewing it, Carter asks?

How do these and other dynamics affect the way the image is seen, the influence it exerts, and its social and educational role? The deconstructive process allows critical thinkers to gain a much deeper view of the world and the way it operates—especially its hidden, power-driven dimensions.

B. *Connecting Logic and Emotion*. This postformal process focuses on the unity of logic and emotion and the interactive potential such a connection creates. The process of postformal thinking, involves emotional as well as cognitive states of mind and an awareness of unconscious as well as conscious processes. When logic and emotion are connected, the boundaries of consciousness and critical thinking stretch and critical thinking, teaching, and learning are seen as far more complex processes than previously understood. Michael Dumas demonstrates this dynamic in "Black Existence As Critical Thinking" when he argues that we should avoid the binarism of logical facts and emotion. Nothing, he concludes, is "known unless it is felt in the flesh." Lourdes Diaz Soto picks up on these postformal themes in "Critical Bilingual/Bicultural Pedagogy: Relying on a Postformal Lens." After the terrorist attacks in New York City, Soto and her students at Teachers College, Columbia University examined the complexity of the event with the multiple lenses of bricolage, and connected the logical and emotional dimensions of the tragedy. Postformal critical thinking combines the emotional domain of compassion with the logical domain of understanding.

C. *Nonlinear Holism.* Nonlinear holism allows us to move beyond the simplistic notion of cause and effect. Scientific formalism promotes the idea of linear causality in the social, educational, and cognitive world. Postformal critical thinking embraces a complex process of reciprocity and holism and sees cause-effect rationality as a modernist tendency towards reductionism that removes the subject under study from the context that shaped it. Postformal teachers who use critical thinking understand that involving contexts and relationships in study moves learning into a zone of complexity where it is both more dynamic and unpredictable than the educational experience produced by scientific formalism. When learning becomes a complex, changing, unstable process, it is impossible to make generalized pronouncements about it or create a series of universal steps that describe how it happens. Postformal teachers who are complex critical thinkers realize that these new pedagogical systems can be self-organizing and carry great potential for creative innovation. Each teaching and learning situation has unique dimensions that must be dealt with individually.

Unfortunately, the educational reforms of the twenty-first century have so far moved us in exactly the opposite direction. In this rationalistic era that seeks to leave no child behind, educational problems are solved by using rational-istic, universal, positivistic, linear, decontextualized, and scientifically validated correct practices that are uniformly applied to all educational situations. American political and educational leaders have learned little from the insights into and innovations in knowledge production of the last few decades. Educators who are postformal critical thinkers have their work cut out for them in the years to come.

D. *An Epistemology and Ontology of Process.* Process is a fundamental state of the physical, social, educational, and cognitive domains. Knowledge and human beings are always in process and always changing in relation to the multiple processes of which they are a part. Knowledge has a past and a future, although human beings only see it in a particular stage of its development. When knowledge is removed from its process(es) and frozen in that stage of development, it is stripped of its life force, it immanence, and its possibility. Such a move is an act of cognitive and pedagogical violence. Regressive educational leaders in the twenty-first century are transforming living knowledge that is fluid, evolving, and enchanted into lifeless, static, immobile entities that can be inserted into mental filing cabinets. Such a procedure is similar to a lobotomy and comes from the same desire to control and regulate. The magical process of learning is destroyed when pedagogy becomes standardized and procedural. Sheldon Woods, in his entry "Science Education," describes anti-process science pedagogy as "a cold body of facts to be memorized and regurgitated on tests."

IV. *Contextualization.* Information can never stand alone or be complete in and of itself. In everyday life, where we are bombarded with data, human beings must abstract information and take it out of its context to assimilate it, otherwise the information gets lost in a larger pattern. Postformal critical thinkers must be adept at such abstraction, but must never lose sight of the larger conceptual field, the context that provides these separate, abstracted entities with meaning. This is a complex and tricky act which complex critical thinkers must learn to perform adeptly.

Postformal critical thinkers place great importance on the idea of context and try to contextualize every aspect of their lives. When teachers who are postformal critical thinkers encounter problems at work, they always connect the difficulty to a wider frame of reference with a wide array of possible causes.

When pedagogical problems fail to meet the criteria of an archetype, postformalists explore unused sources and employ the information acquired to develop a better understanding of the how the contexts surrounding the problem interact. When teachers fail to contextualize a problem, students get hurt. Educators in these circumstances see each element of a socio-educational difficulty as separate, and never see the larger context of which each element is a part.

Postformal critical thinkers understand that data has meaning only in the context created by other data, and con-

text may be more important than content. These insights change the way researchers, educational professionals, policy analysts, and practitioners of all varieties conduct their work.

A. *Attending to the Setting.* When we acknowledge the setting of a fact or problem, the additional data we gather makes our observations richer. Cartesian formalism often fails to analyze setting. The extraneous circumstances so quickly dismissed by rationalism often prove to be the keys to new insights that change our view of education, society, or the cosmos itself. John Dewey maintained that an individual is a sophisticated thinker to the degree that he or she sees an event not as something isolated, but in its relation to the larger experience of human beings. When we fail to account for the setting—or as hermeneutics puts it, the horizon—in which an observation is made, we make a huge mistake. For example, "given the historical context in which Dr. Cartman was operating, we can understand how it was difficult for her to understand these processes. After all she did not have the benefit of knowing what happened in 1974 when she constructed her analysis in the mid-1950s" (fictional quote).

B. *Understanding the Subtle Interaction of Particularity and Generalization.* When critical thinking is captured by the Cartesian obsession with generalization, the nature of the particular is missed. The life force, the visceral dynamic that makes the general worth knowing, is supplied only when the particular circumstances contained within it are placed in their proper context. This insight is deepened by the concept of the hermeneutic circle, where analysts examine the parts in the context of the whole, and the whole in the context of the parts in a back and forth fashion. No final interpretation is demanded because the circle never ends. Since the lived world is process-oriented, the parts and the whole may change and a new interpretation of the relationship between the particular and general may be needed. Vicki Carter, in her entry under *Work,* illustrates the way workers become postformal critical thinkers who engage in the analysis of the interaction of particularity and generalization. When workers understand the larger context in which their particular task exists (that the chassis on which they are working will eventually become part of a car, for example), they understand their vocational lives better and gain the power to change them in more just and equitable ways.

C. *The Role of Power in Shaping the Way the World is Represented.* Understanding the world around us is not as much a product of our own efforts to master information as it is the capacity of power (in the forms of discourse, ideology, and hegemony) to create meanings that support its need to maintain the status quo. As dominant power produces subjectivity and knowledge, it concurrently blocks our ability to identify its fingerprints.

Postformal critical thinkers are always looking for the context in which power operates and develop a power literacy that helps them explain how things came to be. A central dimension of this encyclopedia's reconceptualization of critical thinking involves accounting for the role of power in shaping the world and the way we perceive the world. As Charles Bingham argues in his essay "Justice and Equity," these power dynamics shape the ways teachers and other students perceive particular students and their needs.

Postformal critical thinkers do not let these dynamics out of their sight. In her essay "Mass Media and Communication," Christine Quail provides a historical overview of how power shapes communication. If we do not understand these power dynamics, Quail tells readers, we will be unable to comprehend the way information is shaped by dominant power wielders in the larger society.

CONCLUSION

The chapters that follow extend the ideas developed here. Danny Weil and I are attempting to reconceptualize critical thinking and analyze how teachers might use such concepts in the classroom. The authors of the chapters have contributed some very sophisticated scholarship that takes the complexity of reconceptualized critical thinking and ties it to the complications of the lived classroom. Danny and I hope that this encyclopedia will speak to you and your relationship to educational practice. We hope you will enjoy and profit from your journey into the great wide open of complex critical thinking.

References

Bruner, J. (1996). *The Culture of Education.* Cambridge, MA: Harvard University Press.

Burbules, N., & Beck, R. (1999). Critical thinking and critical pedagogy: Relations, differences, and limits. In T. Popkewitz & L. Fendler (Eds.), *Critical Theories in Education.* New York: Routledge.

Hatcher, D. (1995). Critical thinking and the postmodern view of reality. http://www.bakera.edu/html/crit/literature/dlhctpostmodern.htm

Kincheloe, J. (1993). *Toward a critical politics of teacher thinking: Mapping the postmodern.* Westport, CT: Bergin and Garvey.

Kincheloe, J. (2001). Introduction: Hope in the shadows—Reconstructing the debate over educational standards. In J. Kincheloe & D. Weil (Eds.), *Standards and schooling in the United States: An encyclopedia.* Santa Barbara, CA: ABC-Clio.

Kincheloe, J., & Steinberg, S. (1993). A tentative description of postformal thinking: The critical confrontation with cognitive theory. *Harvard Educational Review, 63*(3), 296–320.

Thayer-Bacon, B. (2000). *Transforming critical thinking: Thinking constructively.* New York: Teachers College Press.

Varela, F. (1999). *Ethical know-how: Action, wisdom, and cognition.* Stanford, CA: Stanford University Press.

Weinstein, M. (1995). "Critical thinking? Expanding the paradigm." <http://www.chss.montclair.edu/inquiry/fall95/weinste.html>

Art

Art and Aesthetics

Richard Cary

What happens when a person encounters a work of art? There are no convincing final answers to this persistent question. Contextual factors such as time, place, and culture interact with the individual characteristics such as class, gender, education, perceptual and cognitive abilities, emotions, motivational considerations, and confidence in forming judgments. These interactions are complex, and there is significant interest in learning more about the role of cognition, (thinking) in art and aesthetic experience. Many scholars, artists, and teachers believe that thinking, particularly critical thinking, is crucial to the quality of one's experience with a work of art. Experience with a work of art refers to either active viewing or making art.

An encounter with a work of art can be an enriching human experience, especially if it is transformed by critical thinking from the liking/disliking judgment typical of first impressions. Critical thinking, the catalyst of such a change, is a set of acquirable skills and understandings. It is a process accessible to virtually everyone. The concept of what it means to think critically about art and aesthetics emerged from two sources: traditional approaches to art criticism and the not-so-traditional intellectual movement of the twentieth century called critical theory.

ART CRITICISM

There are many approaches to art criticism: formalism, contextualism, instrumentalism, deconstruction, Marxism, postmodernism, structuralism, feminism, semiotics, and others. The important point for critical thinking is that, regardless of the model, art criticism is a systematic process with a well-defined sequence of conceptual steps, which can involve critical thinking. Critical thinking about art involves neither received knowledge nor revelation; it is an active process engaged in by a person encountering a work of art.

Terry Barrett has succinctly summarized the traditional steps in art criticism as description, interpretation, and evaluation (Barrett, 2000). Barrett's several books on the subject contain many examples of the application of these steps to particular works of art. While Barrett's model generally describes a first layer of engagement with an artwork, it does not necessarily achieve the level of critical thinking that can enhance aesthetic experience. To add a dimension of critical thinking to an encounter with art requires that people describe, interpret, and evaluate the four components of a work of art: subject, form, content, and context (Cary, 1998).

Subject refers to what is depicted in the artwork. In artworks produced by aesthetic strategies of mimesis and abstraction, the subject is the thing or things depicted. The image of these things is on the canvas, but the things themselves exist elsewhere in reality. The subject is external to the work of art. In non-representational art, the surface or composition of the work, the work of art itself, is the subject.

The form of an artwork is determined by the design elements and principles of its composition, and the material and techniques used to produce it. Design elements include shape, line, texture, value, and color. Design principles include variety, harmony, balance, proportion, dominance, movement, economy (Ocvirk et al., 1998).

The content is the meaning of a work of art. Meaning is usually conveyed by the artist's use of symbols or, in some cases, through the emotive association suggested by its formal properties such as color. Symbols, of course, must be interpreted to convey meaning. Knowledge of what symbols signify may come from formal education or from informal acculturation arising from membership in a group or community. Content then, depends on context. The discernment of meaning that occurs during a critical aesthetic experience (again, either making or encountering an artwork) is an active process that the individual constructs through cognition and perception. These include such mental tasks as information processing, symbol processing, problem-solving, concept for-

mation, language use—all employed in a complex thinking process. Art criticism is an excellent model for critical thinking in art and aesthetics.

CRITICAL THEORY

Critical theory emerged in Germany in the early twentieth century with the group of philosophers called the Frankfurt School, and continues today as an idealistic and often-confrontational discourse about power, democracy, social justice, culture, and other contemporary issues, including art, aesthetics, and art pedagogy. The aim of critical thinking about art is to understand how art can promote and sustain critical consciousness and how art can encourage emancipatory action. Critical consciousness is the awareness of covert sources of oppression or injustice in peoples' lives. Emancipatory action is the informed resistance to such influences.

A critical understanding of art is concerned with the experience of art more than the art object on display in a gallery, museum, or public square. This distinction has broad implications and extends to the ways artists make art, the ways individuals engage with art, the ways our society values art, the ways art contributes to the intellectual and spiritual domains, and, of course, to the ways teachers teach and students learn art.

To think critically about art, one begins by examining the ways art becomes designated as art, the basis on which it is distinguished from other material artifacts such as airplanes, televisions, or toasters. A second critical task is to examine the means by which artistic value is conferred; that is, how good art is distinguished from bad. Critical theory adherents recognize that the designation of art as art and the discernment of artistic value are open issues to which absolute answers are neither possible nor desirable. An individual can only construct a provisional response in an experience with art.

To think critically and deeply about art, one must recognize that both the designation of art as art and the conferral of artistic value are heavily influenced by a teeming complex of cultural, social, political, economic, and historical processes, many of which operate in silent contradiction to the values and ideals espoused by our democratic society.

An individual experiences these influences on art as part of his or her lifeworld, which means all the lived personal experience of the individual—beliefs, actions, values, and thoughts. Individuals consciously construct their lifeworld in social and cultural interaction. The individual's artworld is an important part of the lifeworld. In the popular consciousness, art is associated with beauty; but the artworld is a landscape of struggle as well. Like the lifeworld, the artworld can be colonized by oppressive, distorting influences of dominant power interests seeking to control beliefs, values, practices, and actions. The authority to designate objects as art and to ascribe artistic value is controlled by such interests. In a colonized artworld, art remains an exclusive property for the privileged few to learn about or to own. Art is not a part of all lives in the same way or to the same degree. In the Renaissance, admission to apprenticeships was rare for women. Later in Europe, artistic standards and practices were strictly controlled by academies, which were established to serve the interests and tastes of the royal court.

In nineteenth-century American schools, training in painting and sculpture, if it existed at all, was reserved for the economic elite and was often provided by private tutors. Although artistic training was legislatively mandated in the public schools of Massachusetts in the late 1800s, such training was essentially composed of lessons in mechanical drawing and copying geometric figures. Promoters of this legislation were American capitalists who used the schools to produce designers and artists for their industries, hoping to compete with European goods. Even today, access to learning about art is often considered an enrichment activity or reward, not a basic, worthwhile human activity.

The artworld is vulnerable to colonization, yet to the critical thinker, art offers the promise of emancipation through its capacity to promote critical consciousness, which is one attribute of critical thinking. Critical consciousness accepts the duality of art: art itself is a force that shapes our lives and yet in turn, is shaped by all that influences our lives. For example, the genre of the equestrian statue, ubiquitous in town squares, reinforces dominant power by portraying leaders as heroes or mighty warriors on horseback able to fend off all threats and thus provide security to their grateful subjects. The critical thinker understands that such statues mythologize power to maintain social control and subservience to authority. A critical consciousness can enrich understanding and appreciation of art. Donatello based his 1443 bronze statue of General Erasmo da Narni in Padua, Italy, on a classical-era equestrian statue of the Emperor Marcus Aurelius, in order to associate the General with that great leader in the minds of passersby. The statue of General da Narni, in full battle armor, lance in hand, and astride a surging horse depicts at first glance a powerful figure. The critical viewer, however, sees a deeper meaning when considering Donatello's depiction di Narni's face: instead of the youthful, energetic features of a mighty soldier, the haggard, ravaged features of a war-weary old man attest with tragic irony to the personal price of power.

Hegemony is an important concept in critical thinking. It refers to the oppression of certain groups, who themselves maintain the circumstances of oppression by unconscious cooperation with the dominating power. Uncritical thinkers believe that experts furnish a level of knowledge that supercedes the layperson's knowledge and direct experience. Knowledge approved by experts becomes common sense. This is especially true in the artworld. Art experts retain exclusive authority to administer the archive, the list of established masterpieces and appropriate aesthetic responses to them. Non-experts feel unqualified to determine what is art or to evaluate its quality. Their individual artworlds are tacitly marginalized or rendered illegitimate. Emancipatory action begins with the critical realization that artworlds are colonized in these ways, but are also open to liberating action ignited by critical thinking.

A critical theory view of art and aesthetics includes the concept of art-as-praxis. Praxis is practice united with theory, the action of making or engaging with art in a context of human values. Praxis is knowing and valuing integrated with doing. In contrast, techne is a labor carried out for an external goal, often in a dehumanizing, assembly-line manner. And, techne can be a means of colonization of the lifeworld. Art-as-techne is concerned only with the efficient application of mechanical art skills and techniques. Virtuoso technical ability in art is often uncritically and mistakenly preferred over other values of an artwork. Art-as-techne approaches the art object as if its artistic value is a stable property physically inher-ent in the art object. For the critical thinker, art-as-praxis situates artistic value in aesthetic experience, not in the physical art object. The ancient shamans inscribing lines on the cave walls to represent bison, deer, and hunters were engaging in art-as-praxis by sharing meaningful symbols, knowledge, and values to create a living community. Critical artistic thinking places priority on such values as connectedness, integration, and meaning—qualities which transcend the beauty of the art object.

Critical theory argues that we have lived in a positivist culture that awards privilege to science and objectivity. Positivism's tenets include a belief in absolute, final truth; that facts are separate from values; and that objective knowledge is not only possible, but constitutes the best form of knowledge. However, the individual who thinks critically about art and aesthetic experience rejects these positivist assumptions and believes that art and artistic knowledge have erroneously been presumed inferior to positivist ways of knowing. Critical thinkers recognize that there is no independent, incontestable authority to designate art as art or to determine ultimate artistic value. Critical thinking about art is skeptical about claims that judgments about art and artistic value can be based on value-free, objective assessments of an artwork's formal properties that are evident for all to see. The positivist mindset leads to an uncritical form of art education. Through either formal instruction or the acculturation that takes place as people live their lives, positivist art education limits itself to the downloading of expert opinions of an artwork's artistic value. These opinions are regarded as indisputable facts, and the person who has memorized the greatest number of opinions has the greatest appreciation of art.

This process colonizes the individual's art-world.

Critical artistic thinking recognizes no final endpoint toward which art is developing (e.g., toward greater accuracy in the depiction of nature). Such endpoints are inevitably contingent upon and vulnerable to ideological and historical forces. Instead, art works are texts that, like all texts, can be read in multiple ways. Critical thinking incorporates the understanding that art shapes people's modes of knowing, perceiving, believing, and valuing in ways that can either promote a critical consciousness that can resist corrosive, oppressive influences, or a consciousness that acquiesces to these influences. Examples of the former abound in the European tradition of political posters, such as those produced during the recent Solidarity Movement in Poland. Examples of the latter are ubiquitous in the advertising and entertainment media, especially in fashion photography, which often constructs images of the human body that create desire and spectacle.

References and Further Reading

Barrett, T. (2000). *Criticizing art: Understanding the contemporary* (2nd ed.). Mountain View, CA: Mayfield.

Cary, R. (1998). *Critical art pedagogy: Foundations for postmodern art education.* New York: Garland.

Ocvirk, O. G., Stinson, R. E., Wigg, P. R., Bone, R. O., & Cayton, D. L. (1998). *Art fundamentals: Theory and practice.* New York: McGraw-Hill.

Art Education, Young Children, and Critical Thinking

Carol Korn

The early years are increasingly gaining recognition as a critical time when attitudes towards learning are shaped and the foundation for academic skill development is first laid down. It is also a time when intellectual curiosity and the cognitive skills that enable sustained inquiry begin to emerge. This makes young children prolific questioners who bring a compelling need to know to their everyday lives. Even the casual observer of young children will soon be struck by their desire to learn about the world, and by their intuitive understanding that one gets to the root of how and why the world works by asking questions, imagining possibilities, and by doing. These three characteristics—questioning, imagining, and doing—undergird the development of critical thinking in early childhood. Their order of presentation here is not intended to imply a particular sequence: all three are commonly witnessed in young children and occur in multiple configurations.

These characteristics are also foundational to the arts in early education. The arts draw on a young child's affinity for asking questions, exploring, and experimenting, an inquiry-based approach to learning that extends children's capacity for imagining and playing with possibilities. The arts are consonant with the need of young children to concretize or make material what they are exploring, learning and imagining.

The arts also offer the possibility of stimulating the creative impulse celebrated in the early childhood years, and grounding this within an approach to critical thinking that places curiosity and inquiry, experimentation and experiential learning, imagination and its expression at its core. The capacity to ask questions emerges from the recognition of the gap between what one knows and what one needs to know. Imagination in the early childhood years fills these gaps, and plays an important role in the development of young children's critical thinking processes. Imagining provides an opportunity to play with alternate responses to questions about the world, and presents children with multiple ways of expressing their current understanding of how the world works. For young children, imagination and creative acts are not flights of fancy or escapist entertainment, but the tools of choice they can use to step back from their experiences in the world and reflect on their meaning.

Imagination, and the creative acts that lend shape and form to its expression, provide the ground upon which the capacity to reflect upon personal experience first emerges.

Vygotsky observed that "imagination is a necessary, integral aspect of realistic thinking," and that complex forms of understanding call for more complex forms of imagining (Vygotsky, 1934/1987, p. 349). Too often, imagination and the kinds of creative activity that the arts call for exist on the margins of school life. Even in classrooms for young children, opportunities to play and to engage in the arts are relegated to recreation rather than forming an integral

part of the early childhood curriculum. Imagination is dismissed as daydreaming, peripheral to and at odds with the real purpose of school. It continues to be the stepchild of skills-based learning, despite its recognition as central to the development of thinking in children by such diverse writers as Sigmund Freud (1901/1980), Jean Piaget (1929/1973), Lev Vygotsky (1934/1987), and Donald Winnicott (1971).

The arts provide another function significant to the development of critical thinking in young children. They foster a multimodal and multiperspectival approach to reflection and to the creation of personal knowledge about the world. They do so by providing, first, a point of entry into reflection on one's own personal experience, which is a key component in the early development of critical thinking. The arts allow young children to reflect on their experiences in a multi-sensory and multimodal fashion. Opportunities to work with art materials, to hear and to make music, to be in the company of dancers and to dance, to witness storytellers and to create one's own story dramas are all means by which young children reflect-in-action on their own experience. By reflecting-in-action, children build personal ways of learning about and knowing the world, which is the first step in developing the capacity for critical thinking.

Reflection undergirds critical thinking. It provides the mechanism by which experience may be considered, first self-referentially and later from multiple vantage points. We see this for the first time in very young children's self-talk, in the murmurings of young children before they fall asleep, and in toddlers' early play. The child is the subject and the perspective is predominantly "me." During the preschool years, the observant listener will note the multiple roles and voices that have developed in the child's self-talk and play. The preschooler, engaging in imaginary conversations between several subjects, can now move gracefully between these voices, adopting the pitch, mannerisms, and perspectives of the different characters she represents. Echoes of a decentering process, a process that will continue throughout the child's life and that is critical to the lifelong development of not only the capacity to engage in critical thinking but also the capacity to sustain a critical thinking attitude, can be discerned here. In assuming multiple roles and adopting multiple voices, young children signal a growing capacity to step outside of their own vantage points and consider, albeit briefly, the perspectives of others.

Through the visual arts, music, dance, and drama, young children explore their own experiences and encounter the experiences, creative productions, and perspectives of others. When, for example, children engage in dialogue with their peers and teachers about a work of art—their own, another child's, or a work of art by an adult artist—they encounter other views that may or may not be similar to their own. Such dialogue provides a decentering experience for young children; an experience in which children are confronted with, and must make an adjustment to, the reality of other people's perspectives. Unlike the occasions when differences of viewpoint (i.e., who gets the tricycle first) result in playground tussles, the arts provide opportunities for children to encounter and to respond to different ways of seeing the world in an affect-rich, but less emotionally charged situation. When young children decenter, they move beyond their own impressions, making room for the possibility of other perspectives. Such experiences are invaluable for the development of critical thinking, which implies the ability to step outside of one's immediate impression to consider alternate ways of perceiving the world.

The arts also create a bridge between the representational and the semiotic; a way young children can move between representations of meaning in pictorial and linguistic forms and between the representational and the symbolic. Research in children's developing metaphoric thinking suggests that metaphoric understanding in the iconic or pictorial mode precedes linguistic understanding. Children's drawings, for example, may encapsulate an entire story and range of affect. Anger and frustration may be represented in stomping, dancing feet, and heavily marked drawings. The bridging function that the arts serve between the representational and the symbolic make the arts in the early years significant to the development of metaphoric thinking in young children.

Why is this important? Metaphoric thinking has another, related and significant educational effect. The capacity to understand and to use metaphor is related to children's ability to comprehend, or to think broadly and critically, about text. Fluency in metaphoric thinking that involves linguistic expression is essential to the development of higher-order reading comprehension abilities in children of the middle-childhood years. Metaphoric thinking informs and shapes reading comprehension, the most sophisticated of reading skills. Reading comprehension, in turn, draws directly on the capacity for critical thinking.

Understanding the basis for early metaphors is one of the first steps in comprehending the early foundations of meaning constructed by the individual and the group culture. Metaphoric thinking calls upon the capacity to step outside one's immediate experience of an event and to transfer that understanding to an entirely different set of circumstances. The arts provide an opportunity for young children to make connections between experiences by calling upon multiple modes of representation, including, but not limited to, the linguistic.

By engaging in, developing an appreciation for, and becoming familiar with the visual and the performing arts, children's expressive repertoire is extended and enhanced. The arts provide an opportunity for young children to move from the physical experience of gesture and movement to visual representation and language.

Immersion in the arts, including multiple opportunities to experiment with a range of art materials and art forms and become familiar with works of art from the adult world, encourages the development of the early foundations of critical thinking in young children. The arts provide a way for children to respond to and to create new experiences by giving form to their own ideas or the ideas generated by works of art already in existence. Through the act of creating, unformulated experience is given shape, form, and expression. Young children readily call upon their perceptual and physical experiences and translate them from visual to gestural representations, then link both with language. This process allows young children to formulate and flexibly express their early conceptual understandings, and allows them to play with these concepts across both art forms and learning modalities.

Despite the obvious connections between the arts and the development of critical thinking, and despite children's love of the arts, the arts are increasingly seen as superfluous to content learning. Even in early childhood education, where the arts have traditionally had greater presence than in the upper grades, the arts are being given an ever-shrinking amount of time and attention from teachers, administrators, and parents as the pressure for early exposure to formal academic work has increased. Increasingly viewed as only incidentally supportive of curricular aims, the arts are typically called upon to decorate early attempts at writing, or as a restful alternative to the stress of early academics and decreased opportunities for physical mobility in the classroom. In more and more early childhood settings, the arts have come to occupy a niche on the outskirts of classroom life, behind the tables and chairs that identify the site of formal academic instruction and on the themed bulletin board displays that line school corridors. Where the arts have been reintroduced in classrooms, they have been linked to attempts to enhance academic skills, or to render subject matter more interesting. Less frequently are the arts, even in classrooms for young children, secured for their well-known connection to children's sense of well-being and motivation to learn, or for their place within a more comprehensive philosophical approach to teaching and learning.

The arts in early education provide opportunities to extend teacher understanding and parental support for the early foundations of critical thinking. Work in the arts can contribute to teachers' ability to appreciate children's thinking when it diverges from the expected and to imagine new ways of working with curriculum. In this way, the arts support lifelong development of critical thinking, providing opportunities for teachers and parents to face and to reflect on the perspectives of their children and of the adult artists whose work they encounter.

For adults, engaging in the arts with children provides a way to join them in making meaning of the world, of their own experiences, and of the experiences of others. Significantly, the arts provide an opportunity for adults to reflect with children on the gaps between the known and the unknown that are filled by imagination and creativity. They provide an opportunity to formulate questions and to consider possible worlds and outlooks that might otherwise be missed. Imagination in teaching and in teacher education is germane to what Maxine Greene refers to as "wide awakeness," an orientation towards the world that leaves one open to the possibilities which observation, experience, and critical reflection may bring (Greene, 1978). Young children are, by nature, wide-awake in their approach to life. Like teachers, parents can appreciate and re-learn from their children a wide-awake approach to everyday life. Having survived the sleep deprivation of their children's infancy, being wide-awake should not prove too great a challenge.

References

Freud, S. (1901/1980). *On dreams.* New York: W.W. Norton & Co.

Greene, M. (1978). *Landscapes of Learning.* New York: Teachers College Press.

Piaget, J. (1929/1973). *The child's conception of the world.* St. Albans, NF: Granada Publishing.

Vygotsky, L. (1934/1987). Lecture 5: Imagination and its development in childhood. In R. W. Rieber, & A. S. Carlton (Eds.). *The collected works of L. S. Vygotsky, Vol. 1* (pp. 339–349). New York: Plenum Press.

Winnicott, D. W. (1971). *Playing and reality.* New York: Basic Books, Inc.

Further Reading

Eisner, E. (1992). The misunderstood role of the arts in human development. *Phi Delta Kappan, 73*(8), 591–595.

Jagla, V. M. (1994). *Teachers' everyday use of imagination and intuition: In pursuit of the elusive image.* Albany, NY: State University of New York Press.

Sarason, S. (1990). *The challenge of art to psychology.* New Haven, CT: Yale University Press.

Assumptions

Believing and Knowing

Danny Weil

Whenever humans think we make assumptions. Many of the assumptions we make are a result of habit, routine, or the unconscious adoption of a prevailing ideology. Because our assumptions are constructed by our history and our relationships to the material world in which we live, they are always involved with issues of gender, race, class, culture, and power and control. Critical thinking takes place when people become aware of and enamored with probing their habitual ways of perceiving of themselves and the world; it also takes place when people learn to enthusiastically and critically examine the assumptions of others and learn to question complex relationships of power and control on a sociopolitical level.

Assumptions are the beliefs we have—the ideas we have taken for granted—about ourselves, people, and the world around us. Assumptions are those things we think we know, and so we rarely question them. Our assumptions are often transparent to us precisely because they form part of our identity. Just like a fish that may take the water they swim in for granted, we as humans often have difficulty seeing our own assumptions and how

they operate to form our judgments on personal and social issues. The predicament arises in that we often take things for granted that we have no right to take for granted or that we have not critically examined. We often fail to distinguish between what *we know and what we merely believe*, and sometimes we think that our personal experience is the only basis of our knowledge. The result is that we frequently come to the wrong conclusions, make the wrong decisions, make incomplete or inaccurate predictions and assessments, and create useless solutions and false judgments regarding social and personal problems.

Critical thinking is interested in helping people develop the ability to identify assumptions so that they can be held under the microscope of critical scrutiny, rigorously tested, and challenged. Because assumptions are the foundations on which reasoning stands, they often form the basis for our stereotypical notions about human behavior. Identifying and challenging assumptions asks us to look at how we are behaving towards our colleagues, friends, families, and community, and why we chose those behaviors.

For many people, challenging assumptions is difficult mental labor. It is hard to identify assumptions by looking at the language we use and our non-verbal communication, and tremendously difficult to effect the attitudinal shift that allows us to suspend judgment and fair-mindedly examine points of view that are different than the beliefs we hold. We think that we personally constructed our value systems. It is difficult to accept the fact that what we learn is influenced by the history of our place of origin, our culture, our race, our economic status, and our gender. We must make a complete critical inventory of what we think we know and how we came to know it, and develop a new relationship with the world in terms of *what we don't know.*

Developing the empathy, intellectual courage, tolerance for ambiguity, imagination, curiosity, humility, and civility that accompany the willingness to examine what we think are our personally constructed truths is a central aspect of critical thinking. Learning to make sense of our assumptions, which are the building blocks we use to make sense of the world, and become skilled at deeply questioning these assumptions helps us genuinely appreciate other points of view and, when necessary, to reassemble our sense of the world. The fact that there are a variety of assumptions about how the world operates does not create problems. Problems arise when the mind dismissively judges ideas that deviate from its own assumptions as wrong. This refusal to consider other viewpoints as valid prevents people from seeing their own assumptions clearly; and when the mind confuses what it thinks it knows with *facts and truth,* both listening and learning suffer.

Critical thinking is born from the idea that constructive doubt is a good thing and complacent certitude is not useful. Constructive doubt, or critical thinking, asks one to become wary of universal claims to truth and to question beliefs and the world around one in the interest of personal and social improvement. When someone says they have the answer to the difficult problems of life, critical thinking demands that we examine this answer, not take it on faith, and refuse to accept the idea that we have always done something a certain way as proof that this habit is the best of all possible arrangements (Brookfield, 1987). Identifying and challenging the assumptions inherent in the social structures in which we live, and learning to see how these assumptions can become habits of the mind that guide our actions and determine how we perceive the world, asks that we question both our assumptions and the assumptions of others deeply.

Although recognizing and challenging the assumptions by which we live is the bedrock of critical thinking, it is also a very complex and ponderous activity that requires time and commitment. Admitting that their assumptions may be socially transcribed, distorted, or perhaps wrong can be extremely threatening for many people because it implies that the very fabric of our lives may have been sewn from faulty cloth. To take what we see as self-evident truths of our own making and subject these truths to critical examination means that we may have to change our lives, the way we think, our activities, and our relationships with others. The process calls our very identity into question. Add to this the fact that the material conditions of Western societies, especially as taught in its schools, do not allocate the time or create the collaborative opportunities needed to develop critical consciousness, and the task is even more daunting.

It is the familiarity of our ideas, the fact that we have internalized a large number of our assumptions as *fact*, that makes the identification of assumptions highly problematic. After all, it is the structure of our thought that organizes our perceptions of the world, and if these perceptions seem to work for us, then the mind will often resist critical thinking in favor of the strong vested interest the mind has in maintaining regularity and habit. Yet it is precisely our cherished personal beliefs and values that must be routinely examined to allow us to see why we believe what we believe and why we act as we act, if we are truly interested in exercising self-authored, independent thought.

For many students, as for many people in general, the process of critical thinking can be disturbing and even unnerving. To facilitate a close examination of assumptions, the teacher as facilitator must engage students in identifying and challenging their assumptions in a manner that is not immediately intimidating to them — one that calls upon them to use their own experience in the interest of engaging critical thinking. If teachers understand that we are often prisoners of our own histories and our own socialization processes, they will work slowly and compassionately with students as they learn to harvest and challenge their assumptions. Such a process is almost a foreign language in the quick-fix environment of rigid educational standards and accountability.

Developing the ability to identify assumptions requires that we pay significant attention to the use of language. It is through the vehicle of language that we exchange our perspectives of the world, and it is through the definition of terms that we become aware of what we are denoting or connoting when we use language to describe our lives. Attention to the use of language leads to active listening skills.

Learning to identify and challenge assumptions requires that students have al-

ternative points of view about the world available, especially marginalized points of view that are often left out of dominant narratives and the mainstream, and these points of view should be provided an atmosphere of collaborative inquiry and civility within which the exchange of controversial opinions on personal and social issues is safe. Helping students harvest their assumptions within multiple perspectives will therefore require a complete reexamination and reconstitution of the school curriculum and the educational assessment process, during which educators will identify and challenge the rigid paradigms of schooling.

Learning to identify and challenge the assumptions we have can only be accomplished through painstaking dialogue and dialectical questioning, which give us the opportunity to examine our thinking in relationship to the thinking of others. Constructive critical questioning is the best way to externalize assumptions within a dialogical and dialectical setting. Once assumptions are externalized, they can be critically examined, compared, and contrasted with the assumptions inherent in other points of view.

Central to this process is critical thinking's preoccupation with gathering and assessing multiple perspectives. Thoughtful, patient questioning designed to dialectically elicit assumptions is a specific and unique form of inquiry. The role of this type of questioning is not so much to seek out new information, but to help people critically reflect on what they *think they know* in light of what others *claim they know*. Facilitators of critical thinking must learn to use this form of robust questioning in a constructive rather than adversarial way, so that the process will not feel intimidating to the people being questioned.

There are many ways that one can design thoughtful questions that will *make conscious* the assumptions that often operate unconsciously. For example, one might ask a group of students to imagine they have been hired to judge the performance or abilities of someone to be a mother, a daycare worker, or a student. "What qualities would someone need to possess to fulfill these roles and why?" A question such as this goes right to the heart of critical thinking and helps students externalize their assumptions they have about what makes a good mother, daycare worker, or student. It asks students to reason based on assumptions they may not have known they had.

Becoming critical thinkers requires that members of a given society see the connection between their personal lives and the larger outside world within which they and others live. This is often difficult for people who see no direct relationship between sociopolitical events and their personal lives. Yet providing students with the opportunities to construct and ask difficult, if not awkward, questions of those in power, to define freedom as participation *in* power, is crucial or they will not see how power can operate oppressively to construct consciousness, design emotional states, and restrict freedom in the name of choice. Critical thinking is a crucial part of good citizenship and citizenship education, for it promotes an investigative attitude that frisks dominant ideas for truth and merit and acknowledges the history and reality of power relationships.

Without citizens who are able to ask difficult and often disturbing questions of those who claim to have power within a society, governments, their officials, and vested private interests will feel more justified in making their policies and commitments secret and will operate outside public scrutiny. If this occurs, citizens may find that their real freedom—their freedom to think—has become such a subversive and under-rewarded activity that challenging the often narrow paradigms of thought and action that construct our lives has become both dangerous and undesirable. As Paulo Freire, the great educator, noted, critical thinking requires competence, courage, risk-taking and humility and is at the heart of all mental growth and development. As we begin to develop critical self-reflection, we develop the ability to break free from distorting perspectives imposed upon us by oppressive relationships. In this way we can come to critically examine and see the hierarchical relationships in society more clearly and define our individuality more completely (Freire, 1986). To ensure the health of any democracy, society's members must become critical, democratic thinkers, and of course this translates into the necessity of teaching critical thinking.

Conflicting assumptions are the foundation of both our greatest dilemmas and our greatest sense of social and individual creativity and freedom. By working through the discomfort of identifying our assumptions through dialogue, the mind learns to feel comfortable and at ease with the creative abrasion produced by a healthy exchange of points of view. By critically learning to identify and scrutinize our assumptions, critical thinking promises that we can learn from history, see patterns of oppression as they are contained within our personal and social structures, and ferret out these distortions and move beyond them to create alternative ways of thinking and acting. In short, learning to identify and examine our assumptions allows us to continually analyze our existence and remake our lives in the interest of emancipation, freedom, democracy and independent thought.

References

Brookfield, S. (1987). *Developing critical thinkers: Challenging adults to explore alternative ways of thinking and acting.* San Francisco: Jossey-Bass.

Freire, P. (1986, January 8). Keynote address, presented at a workshop on worker education, City College of New York, Center for Worker Education.

Further Reading

Freire, P. (1970). *Pedagogy of the oppressed.* New York: Continuum.

Phillips, C. (2001). *Socrates café.* New York: Norton.

Bilingual Education

Bilingual Education: Toward a Critical Comprehension of Engaging an Emancipatory Paradigm

Hermán S. García and Teresa Valenzuela

Bilingual education has long battled for an equal position among, and often against, educational narratives that habitually disregard it as a viable pedagogy that can provide a vigorous education for linguistic minority children. Bilingual education proponents have fought long and challenging battles in their attempt to gain personal, social, cognitive, and economic recognition for their programs.

A principal concern critical bilingual pedagogues commonly express about the underpinnings of bilingual education is its connection to positivist directions among a significant number of prominent bilingual educators. For example, traditional bilingual educators seem unaware of their instrumentalist promotions of bilingual education. Traditional theories of learning dominate American social theory, and these have regulated educational theory, practice and philosophy for decades. There is great danger of bilingual education collapsing into neoconservative narratives, but various critical pedagogies have of-fered a way for bilingual education to exist as an emancipatory and democratic praxis that could help restructure education in this image.

Binary views of bilingual education place it within colonized middle-class notions of education. In essence, bilingual educators have failed to advance bilingual education as a form of democratic education for linguistic minority communities. As it is commonly practiced, bilingual education is considered mainstream education in two languages, and mainstream educators who address issues of bilingualism and bilingual education present it as compensatory and remedial. Bilingual educators have not challenged these assumptions.

What then is critical pedagogy and how might one relate it to bilingual education? Critical pedagogy can help bilingual education establish its power base and bring new knowledges, new questions, and new analyses from different cultures that can reconstitute bilingual education as an emancipatory and empowering pedagogy. Bilingual educators must address bilingual education as a transformative discourse, one that allows bilingual educators to re-examine their positivist notions of teaching and learning.

The language of critical pedagogy presupposes a notion of learning through lived experience. That lived experience has to reflect students' everyday lives and the communities in which they live. Pedagogy cannot afford to be removed from the livelihoods of the people it attempts to inform and liberate. Critical pedagogy needs to evoke a political vision of what a classroom needs to have for creating a healthy understanding of multiculturalism that limits the power and privilege that subordinates bilingual education. In other words, bilingual education needs to be organized around a pedagogical and political theory of freedom from parasitic narratives that make excuses for the overall failure of education in America.

Bilingual educators have not been successful in their struggle to undo the destruction of bilingual education prevalent in American educational institutions, and have failed to produce new knowledge bases that deconstruct bilingual education's colonized location within Eurocentric and sociocentric canons. This may be related to self-colonization in our belief about how education functions. For example, standardized testing that reflects mainstream culture continues to be used against students from marginalized communities, even though it is commonly known that knowledge is deeply rooted in cultural meanings that are socially produced and children from marginalized communities do not have the same knowledge referents as children from the mainstream culture. At the very least, bilingual educators need to speak boldly and cou-

rageously about the damage standardized tests do to all children.

Bilingual educators have also failed to show the historical and cultural relationship between race, ethnicity, language, class, and gender and the socially, economically, and psychologically conquered status of the people bilingual education was designed to serve, and have failed to reconstruct bilingual education into a form that can be used to create social change. The language of bilingual education should help educators position minority children in the mainstream on an equal footing.

Bilingual educators have been working in direct opposition to the development of a form of politics that represents the needs of linguistic minority children whose identities are not located within the schooling curricula. Bilingual educators have been left to fend for themselves as they struggle against a Eurocentric social science that has produced historical and social analyses devoid of the Others' experience.

Cultural power wielders dispense cultural privilege to specific groups that speak the right language, have the right social status inheritance, and possess other attributes that represent the cultural cash with which people map their way through life. This cultural currency distinguishes between mainstream and subordinate class norms and values and the everyday workings of cultural power. Bilingual education also needs to better address issues of race, class, ethnicity and gender in relation to American education through ethnic studies programs and multicultural education practices. Bilingual education was rarely an area of study in traditional education and was never offered by the educational system itself, but emerged through struggle by various ethnic, racial, and gender groups. Most dominant canons rejected multiculturalism and diversity and most current discussions about multicultural education center around ethnic minorities' inability to become versed in dominant cultural values and norms. Rarely is there a discourse focused on the issue of Euroethnics acquiring minority languages, values, and norms. Their Eurocentric status remains invisible and thus protected.

Most discourses on ethnicity are presented in nonpoliticized contexts that focus on the Other as a problem rather than as an enrichment opportunity for enhancing the learning process. The monolithic conceptions of ethnicity garner power from a capacity to mask the issue of whiteness and to masquerade the relationships of privilege and power as innocent. To counter this situation, critical multiculturalists and bilingual educators must embrace a transformative political plan that moves beyond the multicultural models of accommodation commonly used in educational circles.

The need to remap and advance our thinking about bilingual education and connect it to a critical perspective is significant. Critical pedagogy offers opportunities for bilingual educators to create a viable oppositional medium that can see beyond the dualistic vision of modernism. Language minority students can ill afford to continue experiencing educational failure and neglect in a system that views their identity in a deficit framework and does not see difference as a valuable way to transform history, culture, and meaning. Language minority students are the fastest-growing segregated group in American schools. Unless cultural diversity becomes a part of governing and organizing schools, little can be expected to change or improve in their schooling condition. Change entails working against the grain of dominant narratives that name, locate, and colonize poor and working-class communities as inferior to the mainstream culture.

Cultural diversity is still a challenge for American education, and the educational pipeline for people of color in America remains narrow and is frequently plugged. Issues of race, ethnicity, gender, and class will not go away simply because we want them to. They are a natural part of the American social landscape in which Otherness and Difference are lived out daily. To deny the pressing needs of people outside the mainstream culture is to risk the loss of our identity as a democratic government. Transformative educators must challenge our country to actively include its diverse populations. Democracy must be reconstituted as a radical social practice that allows and encourages everyone to engage in problematic discourse.

Finally, American educational institutions need to recognize that subordinated communities, like other communities, speak with multiple voices and identities and there is no singular notion of cultural identity within them. The issues that face subordinated communities do not lie solely within their custody but rather, within dominant cultural knowledges and educational discourses that tend to view subordinate communities through stereotypic lenses. Learning to value diversity is central to moving toward a more healthy direction in American education!

Further Reading

Darder, A. (Ed.). (1995). *Culture and difference: critical perspectives on the bicultural experience in the United States*. Critical Studies in Education Series. Westport, CT: Greenwood.

Darder, A., Torres, R., & Gutierrez, H. (Eds.). (1997). *Latinos and education: A critical reader*. New York: Routledge.

Edelsky, C. (1996). *With literacy and justice for all: Rethinking the social in language and education*. Bristol, PA: Taylor & Francis.

Watts, J. G. (1996). *Reclaiming our voices: Bilingual education critical pedagogy & praxis*. California Association for Bilingual Education.

Critical Bilingual/Bicultural Pedagogy: Relying on a Postformal Lens

Lourdes Diaz Soto

A critical bilingual/bicultural pedagogy that relies on postformal ideas about critical thinking, will help to guide an increasingly complex global arena. Kincheloe and Steinberg have said that, when we look at postformal thinking, we can see how psychology and education are "riddled with ethnocentric and class-biased conceptions and make no allowance for the ravages of poverty, racism and other forms of disadvantage in many children's lives" (Kincheloe & Steinberg, 1999, p.45).

The strength of a postformal lens allows teachers and children the opportunity to examine not only the emotional and the cultural, but to raise questions about power and pursue a path toward peace, freedom, and social equity. It is not just about language and it is not just about thinking; it is about the emotional, the cultural, the intergenerational, and the spiritual since these are important aspects of monolingual and bilingual/bicultural children's experiences. A bilingual pedagogical ethic enriches postformal critical thinking at the same time that postformal critical thinking enriches bilingual pedagogy.

In this piece, I propose that, in view of the complexities facing our society and our classrooms, a critical bilingual/bicultural pedagogy based on postformal critical thinking will pay attention to the multiple challenges facing learners and can greatly benefit our mutual concerns. A critical bilingual/bicultural pedagogy based on a postformal lens will produce education that goes beyond conservative notions of language learning, Cartesian rationalistic forms of critical thinking, and critical literacy. In this transformative context, learners are guided to not only "read the word and the world," (Freire, 1985; Freire & Macedo, 1987) but to transform and heal the world. It would provide unique opportunities to interface with critical analysis of power so that classrooms are exciting centers of learning about issues of justice at local, national, and international levels. This type of education can produce healing for all learners.

A universal postformal space would contain an equitable post-monolingual education and a society focused on social justice, equity, peace, and healing. The entire learning community can benefit from knowledge about multiple cultures, languages, power, identities, gender roles, and socioeconomic issues.

Why a universal bilingual model for all children? Most bilingual and non-privileged monolingual children are currently denied an equitable education. Teaching children to co-exist in a peaceful manner is a priority for the increasingly war torn global arena. In her book, "Oasis of Dreams," Grace Feuerverger (2001) offers such a program.

So how can you implement this model in your classroom? I will share how I teach from my own being, not as a recipe, but simply to provoke our pedagogical imagination and to push the critical thinking envelope. Your teaching style and context will vary since you will be teaching from your own being. Let me humbly share what I am finding works for my students in the classroom, based on Freire's idea of conscientization, critical pedagogy, and postformal critical thinking.

I like to start with the local and most immediate needs of my learners, keeping in mind the daily realities, the contemporary issues, and the community needs that face us. We walk and learn together in solidarity expressing courage even when we walk on tenuous ground.

First, we choose readings that will elicit interest and dialogue. Second, we begin to create an environment that encourages respect and an opportunity to learn about each other and from each other. Learners are the best experts about their own lived daily realities. Third, we begin to explore mutual concerns as co-learners. Fourth, we explore and critically analyze the complexities of the issues we have identified. Fifth, we consider ways that we might pursue an education as cultural workers in collaboration to begin to solve our concerns.

This is not a complete road map because we are often grappling with how best to proceed. What I am finding is that the issues vary for different groups and the concerns expressed are directly related to their sociohistorical lived daily realities. Sometimes my co-learners choose multiple projects and at other times we decide that we would like to work on one concern.

This allows for a very exciting and contemporary way of learning-teaching-learning, and problem solving-transformation-healing. Those of you who choose this path will find that all of your collective creativities will be truly challenged and all your assumptions and the critical possibilities you envision will be questioned.

Examples of the projects and activities we have shared include:

- responding to specific community based needs,
- analyzing museum exhibits relating to the topic at hand,
- media literacy projects that critically view issues of race, class, and gender,
- role-playing to help us think about how others perceive a situation,
- drama and mini-reader's theatre,
- mapping concepts and possibilities,
- keeping journals,
- group chart depictions,
- autobiographical writing,
- making quilts,
- media presentations,
- community visits,
- interviews,
- drawings,
- and lots and lots of dialogue leading to new forms of critical thinking and acting.

I will share just one example of a class I taught at Teachers College during the wake of the World Trade Center tragedy. The September 11, 2001, events left a legacy that continues to haunt many teachers, learners, and families. No one could have predicted the magnitude of the event, and yet some of the teachers in New York City were advised not to discuss it with their students. Imagine the struggle for the teacher and her students when every minute of the assault was replayed daily by the media and the children had to deal with funerals, people carrying pictures of their loved ones on their chests, smells, fears, silences, tears, huge trailers and construction equipment, and noisy trucks. Most schools asked children to draw pictures of the event and brought counselors and psychologists to spend time with the children.

At Teachers College (and other institutions of higher learning) there were moving teach-ins where people spoke about the tragedy and how it was affecting their life and their memories. Some faculty felt that the tragedy did not relate to their coursework, while many of us, including my students and myself, felt that we could not ignore an event that was affecting local, national, and international policies and activities.

My students and I struggled with the curriculum in a seminar I was teaching titled, "Language, Culture and Power." Freire's (1985; Freire & Macedo, 1987) idea of "reading the word and reading the world" and the types of thinking that concept elicits had been uppermost on our minds. After the World Trade Center tragedy, we decided to begin our discussions by conducting informal discourse analyses of the daily news coverage. We found the language of war prevalent with little discussion about peace. We knew our nation was headed for war.

We also examined our own experiences and discussed the multiple lenses available to us as well as the complexities of the event. We relied on hermeneutics (the art of interpreting reality) and bricolage (a variety of disciplines and traditions) to inform our critical thinking. In the spirit of postformal critical thinking, we explored multiple layers of experience including the emotional, the corporate, the racial, the political, the sociocultural, the feminist, worker exploitation, the silencing of immigrants, and how spiritual values intersected with ethics, solidarity, and public responsibility.

We found that a critical bilingual/bicultural lens centering on the complexities of power offered us the opportunity to examine how power regulates discourses and how the multiple realities of power construct our consciousness—central features of postformal critical thinking. The students designed a postmodern multimedia mini-reader's theatre representing a slice of our discussion that portrayed a critical analysis with a pedagogy of feminist hope and change. The students dramatized our therapeutic dialogue to members of the Teachers College community. As a background to the dramatization, several students designed a timed slide presentation depicting the events on a large overhead screen. We saw several audience members weeping and we knew that there was still need for additional dialogue and critical bilingual/bicultural pedagogy centering on the complexity of the issues the event provided. We were searching for a space of healing that we could pursue together. In the spirit of postformal critical thinking, we brought the rational together with the emotional.

A post-monolingual society would offer us the unique opportunity to universalize bilingual education so that our mutual interests of world peace and understanding could be pursued. It would offer us the opportunity to have an informed nation that could understand, critically analyze, and interpret the multiple issues before us—a nation of critical thinkers. If all of our learners are seen as contributors of wisdom, language, and culture, then a learning community could be created where issues of social justice and equity could be discussed, solved, and healed. How much easier would it be if young children were socialized to understand and befriend culturally and linguistically diverse people? Perhaps we could avoid global conflicts if our children could envision peaceful resolutions. These interpersonal, emotional issues of human connectedness are explicitly left out of Cartesian rationalistic models of critical thinking.

What are the qualities of a good critical bilingual/bicultural teacher? Tucker presents research conducted by the World Bank on the aspects of successful bilingual programs (Tucker, 1999). Among the findings are the importance of the home language and the importance of teachers who are well versed on issues of language and culture. In addition, strong ties to the community and to parents are important aspects of successful bilingual programs. The benefits reaped from such programs include children spending additional years in school and an enhanced earning power for learners. It seems to me that in our post-monolingual model of a critical bilingual/bicultural pedagogy we will need to raise the bar by making sure that our teachers are critical experts in the needed world languages and cultures. The breadth and depth of knowledge that our teachers gain will ultimately help to address the need for increased social justice, cross-cultural, and inter-cultural understanding. These are central dimensions of the postformal conception of critical thinking that Kincheloe writes about in the introduction to this encyclopedia.

There may be ways that you can adapt this model to your own classroom, keeping in mind your learners' needs and experiences. How might you integrate the unique voices and wisdom represented in your class? How can you, your students, and your community become co-learners? What are the most pressing issues that you and your learners are facing? If you teach in an urban setting, are there issues of environmental justice impacting your lives? If you teach in a privileged monocultural suburban setting, are there issues of white privilege that can be critically analyzed? How do power issues affect the children attending your school? How does the global arena enter your classroom? How are parents supporting your work and vice versa? What is the greatest fear that you and your learners can address? How can you reach for a space of transformation and healing in a collaborative manner? Is it possible to fill your classroom with projects and activities that will bring education closer to the needs of your learners while helping you to feel the joy that brought you into your chosen profession in the first place? How do you monitor the impact these experiences have on moving your students to a new mode of critical thinking?

I hope this piece has, in some small way, helped you to reflect (and perhaps critically analyze) future possibilities for you and your learners. The pedagogy that I envision is broad, includes multiple learners, relies on multiple lenses/theories, and helps to move us into spaces of transformation and healing. The notion of agape love demonstrated by altruistic bilingual children (Soto, 2002) is one we may want to pursue in this type of teaching and thinking. Indeed, in the transformative critical teaching and thinking imagined here, the values of caring and human connectedness are central to the process of democracy and social justice.

References

Feuerverger, G. (2001). *Oasis of dreams: Teaching and learning peace in a Jewish-Palestinian village in Israel*. New York: Routledge-Falmer.

Freire, P. (1985). *The politics of education: Culture, power, and liberation*. South Hadley, MA: Bergin & Garvey.

Freire, P., & Macedo, D. (1987). *Literacy: Reading the word and the world*. South Hadley, MA: Bergin & Garvey.

Hahn, T. N. (1992). *Peace is every step*. New York: Bantam Books.

Kincheloe, J. L. (1999). Trouble ahead, trouble behind: Grounding the post-formal critique of educational psychology. In J. L. Kincheloe, S. R. Steinberg, & P. H. Hinchey (Eds.), *The postformal reader: Cognition and education*. New York: Falmer Press.

Kincheloe, J. L., & Steinberg, S. R. (1999). A tentative description of post-formal thinking: The critical confrontation with cognitive theory. In J. L. Kincheloe, S. R. Steinberg, & P. H. Hinchey (Eds.), *The postformal reader: Cognition and education*. New York: Falmer Press.

Soto, L. D. (2002). *Making a difference in the lives of bilingual/bicultural children*. New York: Peter Lang Publishers.

Tucker, G. R. (1999). A global perspective on bilingualism and bilingual education. http://www.cal.org/ericcll/digestgloabal.html

Bloom's Taxonomy

Bloom's Taxonomy and Critical Thinking

Tanya Brown

This entry will analyze Bloom's Taxonomy in relation to critical thinking. Teachers concerned with critical thinking should be familiar with Bloom's Taxonomy and the skills and tasks that evolve from it. Critical thinking requires, among other things, discipline, structure, and depth. Bloom's Taxonomy provides us with a tool for getting all of those things. This entry will explore some of the strengths and weaknesses of this very useful and significant structure.

WHAT IS BLOOM'S TAXONOMY?

Bloom's Taxonomy of the Cognitive Domain is a tool that organizes critical thinking skills. While the tenets of critical thinking may be somewhat ambiguous or abstract when we try to apply them in the classroom, Bloom's Taxonomy provides a very concrete structure that helps to foster the development of critical thinking skills in the classroom in such a way that students should be able to apply critical thinking to any subject at hand and most importantly, to their own lives.

Created by Benjamin Bloom in 1956, Bloom's Taxonomy organizes the func-

tions of the cognitive domain, which is concerned with the knowledge and understanding of facts, into a sort of a pyramid. The outcome is a thinking hierarchy. Thinking and learning behaviors are classified from the simplest to the most complex. Utilization of this taxonomy should result in a classroom full of thinkers that are capable of establishing clarity and accuracy, of assessing relevance, and demonstrating the ability to think with depth, reach, and logic: skills that are fundamental to critical thinking.

The assumed context of the learning situation in which Bloom is useful is one of carefully planned and measured objectives. The learning environment is teacher-centered, and the teacher plays the active role of creating, guiding and measuring the learning process. The intended purpose of this tool is that it should help teachers to understand the learning process so they can plan learning objectives and lessons to help meet their objectives. These lessons should include the steps necessary to lead a learner from one place to the next. This tool is appropriate for situations that assume learning is extrinsic to the learner because it focuses on the teacher's role as learning constructor.

The fact that it is a *taxonomy* implies that there are natural, successive relationships between each level and that this classification represents the natural way that learners develop from one stage to the next. The taxonomy has six different levels: *knowledge, comprehension, application, analysis, synthesis* and *evaluation*. The first two levels, *knowledge and comprehension*, entail thinking that is convergent in nature. This means that the learning moves toward a common, pre-established point that is determined by the text that is being studied or by the teacher. The last four stages, *application, analysis, synthesis* and *evaluation*, entail thinking that is divergent, meaning that it differs or deviates from any pre-established point. This kind of thinking can go in different directions that are determined by the learner, not the book or the teacher.

We can assume that the taxonomy developed out of a need to address the many varieties of abilities and personalities in the average classroom. Indeed, it is important to bear in mind the differences among the students being taught when planning any lesson. The trouble is that such a rigid structure, while intended to be a means to help planning, makes many assumptions about the learner and can easily become a device used to name, measure, and evaluate instead. As with the use of any teaching tool, one must be mindful of the limitations and be sure to distinguish the tool from the actual individual being taught.

Perhaps the most important aspect of Bloom's Taxonomy is that it teaches thinkers to be critical of *their own* thinking. It reassures awareness and assessment of the thinking process itself, creating metacognition. Without this awareness and self assessment, students are not critical thinkers.

WHAT HAPPENS AT EACH LEVEL?

The *knowledge* level, the most basic of the six levels, is concerned with the memorization and recalling of facts. To understand this level, it is important to distinguish exactly what a *fact* is. For our purpose, we will define a fact as something that is accurate, true and has evidence to back it up. We can prove it. Sixteen and sixteen equals thirty-two. That can be proven. To arrive at that sum the two numbers must be added together. That can also be proven. But, what if someone says that Toni Morrison thought *The Bluest Eye* was her most important book? This is not a fact because we cannot prove what Toni Morrison thought. We could prove, however, that Toni Morrison was quoted as saying that *The Bluest Eye* was her most important book. Why is this important? Because, even at this basic level, it can be easy for the learner to get caught if care is not taken to distinguish fact from opinion, and this is often a trouble spot on standardized tests.

It is also important to point out that once something is established at the higher levels (i.e., on Monday a student is asked to evaluate two pieces of literature and choose the most effective piece and on Tuesday, the class is asked to recall which piece the student chose) it is no longer an evaluative question because the students are being asked to recall information, not evaluate it. So, it is not necessarily the nature of the question that defines the levels, but rather the thinking process involved in coming to an answer.

The *comprehension* level, the second level, is concerned with how well the learner understands the knowledge level. Can learners repeat the information in their own words? Can they explain or summarize it? Asking a child to write a book report or to review something that was presented in class earlier are operations on the second level. Often we use these kinds of tasks to help cement the information in the learner's head so it will be remembered when it is time to give a test.

Typically, a large percentage of classroom time is devoted to these first two levels, and since these levels are concerned with convergent knowledge, they are the levels that lend themselves most to standardized measuring devices such as multiple choice and true or false tests. Ultimately, standardized tests work by converting all knowledge into convergent knowledge, which is why it is important to understand this conversion works.

To demonstrate, let's look at some multiple choice test items based on a reading sample by Zora Neale Hurston.

She knew that the world was a stallion rolling in the blue pasture of ether. She knew that God tore down the old world every evening and built a new one by sun-up. It was wonderful to see it take form with the sun and emerge from the gray dust of its making. The familiar people and things had failed her so she hung over the gate and looked up the road towards way off. She knew now that marriage did not make love. Janie's first dream was dead, so she became a woman. (Hurston, 1937)

In this reading, Hurston refers to the character, Janie, as a:

A. familiar person
B. a traveler
C. a widow
D. a woman

Hurston uses the metaphor *the world was a stallion rolling in the blue pasture of ether* to symbolize

A. death
B. the passage of time

C. the loss of love
D. old age

In the first question, the knowledge level is clearly being tested because the correct answer is D, a woman, and can be proven by going back to the text. The B answer and the C answer can easily be eliminated because, although Hurston refers to a stallion rolling in the pasture, there is no direct reference to travelers or widows. The first choice, familiar person, can also be eliminated because, while Hurston refers to Janie's disappointment with the familiar people in her life who have failed her, a re-reading of the line makes it clear that the author is not referring to Janie. The last line makes it clear that D is the best choice. The only skill required to answer this question correctly is to pull a fact from the reading on which the questions are based.

The second question is more involved and forces the reader to do two things: interpret the meaning of the metaphor *the world was a stallion rolling in the blue pasture of ether,* and then convert that information into knowledge that most closely resembles one of the four given choices.

The test taker is expected to choose the best possible answer to the question from four stems. In this case the answer is B, *the passage of time.* We know this is correct because we go through a process of elimination. There is no information in the passage that points us to death, so letter A is not a good choice. While the reading does speak to the character's newfound knowledge about marriage, letter C is only designed to throw the reader off. While the reader may infer that Janie is older because she is married, D is not the best choice either. We choose B because the lines that follow are all concerned with the passing of time as well. In reality, the metaphor may have nothing at all to do with the passing of time, but in this case that is not what matters. What matters is choosing the most appropriate answer of the four the test gives. While higher order processes may be involved in determining the appropriateness of each answer, the act of determining the best answer of the four is convergent. One must move toward an already established point. Although readers may, based on their own context and experience of the reading, have an entirely different understanding, the skill required at this level is to ignore that information and choose the best of the four answers already presented. This can be a frustrating and destructive process for children because while they may want to rely on their own interpretation or understanding of what they read and instead they must disregard their own perception and rely on the choices the test gives them to pass. Anyone who has taught small children is familiar with the somewhat schizophrenic process of getting them to understand the workings of a standardized test.

As we can see, these levels are only deceptively simple. Unfortunately, they are the levels to which, we must devote the most time and energy. In many ways, they can be the most complicated. It is here we see the difference between teaching a child *how* to think and teaching a child *what* to think. It is also in the tender space between the convergent and divergent levels that critical thinking is rooted in a child. Of course it is necessary for a child to have information, especially when trying to survive a standardized test; but a truly critical thinker must be able to question and deconstruct that information, even if the information is provided by the teacher. That requires a learning environment that is based on trust as much as the pursuit of truth.

The next level, the *application* level, involves the transfer of already acquired knowledge to a new situation. A student may have learned the basic elements of poetry and the procedure for writing a standard five-paragraph essay. If this student can write a five paragraph essay about the elements of poetry, then successful application has been achieved. This level is dependent upon the student knowing and understanding the elements of poetry as well as the procedure for constructing a five paragraph essay. To apply the skills and information, higher order thinking skills must be used. At this level, while there will be generalities, each learner should produce a result that is individual to his or her own application of the skills and information.

The fourth level is the level of *analysis*. At this level, the learner should be able to reorganize the information, and must know the facts well enough to rearrange them. Comparing and contrasting requires an analysis of information. But simply listing the elements of poetry and the elements of a short story does not require higher order thinking skills; drawing a conclusion based on those elements and how they relate to one another does. If the student is able to conclude that poetry is more conducive to expressing feelings about love because of the use of figurative language and imagery, that is a successful analysis.

At this level, it is especially necessary for the learner to be able to question for himself or herself. Learners must first be able to pose questions, or they will have nothing upon which to base an analysis.

After analysis comes synthesis. At this level, the student should be able to create something of his or her own that expresses an understanding and internalization of the given skills and information. If the student has learned the elements of poetry, he or she should now be able to write a poem that uses these elements correctly.

The final level, the level of *evaluation*, requires the learner to make a judgment of a similar body of information and support this judgment using the information and skills acquired at the earlier levels. The learner should be able to explain a piece of poetry, offer an opinion about it, and give criteria for how it was assessed. In order to make a valid and successful evaluation, all of the previous skills and information should be employed.

It is in the final four steps of the taxonomy that we can see the practice of critical thinking at work. In the hands of a skillful and open-minded teacher, these steps can be quite useful tools. True exploration of these steps requires a reconceptualization of how we define knowledge in the classroom. Knowing is no longer possession and retention of certain information, it is the ability to tolerate the elastic and enigmatic nature of that information as well as the ability to question, turn, and push that information, questioning oneself in the process.

WHAT ARE THE BENEFITS OF USING BLOOM'S TAXONOMY?

It is always useful to have a vocabulary to articulate what our students are doing and what we would like them to be able to do. Bloom's Taxonomy gives us a working vocabulary that describes some of the things that happen while an individual is learning. When a teacher is planning a lesson, an awareness of these levels can be helpful in designing activities that will force the student to really work with the text or resources that are provided.

Some things must be taught with a clear set of learning objectives in mind.

Bloom's Taxonomy can give structure and direction to those objectives, acting as a kind of a road map that gets the learner to the prearranged destination. If we are brave enough to question our own assumptions about knowledge and to use Bloom's Taxonomy with an open mind, then it can provide a structured and organized way to promote critical thinking in our classroom.

WHAT ARE THE PROBLEMS WITH USING BLOOM'S TAXONOMY?

The structure is inflexible. Only certain kinds of learners and learning processes will fit within the six levels. Very few learners start at the bottom of the taxonomy and then proceed from one level to the next. In fact, it is entirely possible that a learner may come to a situation with a pre-existing analysis or evaluation and then pursue the facts to back up these assumptions. Students usually have opinions about the content of their classes. They may enter the pyramid at the very top and make several loops before they are satisfied with what they have learned.

Beyond this, the taxonomy forces a learning environment that is focused on the teacher and where the teacher wants to go rather than on the learner and how he or she constructs knowledge based on context and previous experiences.

Since the development of each level is dependent upon the mastery of the previous one, the assumption is that the learner needs the information available at the lower levels to operate at any of the higher levels. This knowledge becomes a sort of a passport, and the result is a segregation of knowledge, with the teacher or the text holding information and determining what is important and necessary to know. This creates an exclusion of anything except that which the teacher and text deem valid. It is never a good idea to assume our students come to us as blank slates, wanting to be filled, nor is it a good idea to exclude the prior knowledge, understanding, or experience of any student. In fact, the resources with the student are often the most powerful tool we have at our disposal.

HOW DO WE USE BLOOM'S TAXONOMY?

The most important thing is to remember that it is a tool intended to help structure learning, not to evaluate it. Play with it; have fun. Start from the end and move backwards to test the learner's assumptions. Create flexibility where there is none. Use it as a way to crack open a text or an idea, and then put the results into the learner's hands.

When considering Bloom's Taxonomy of the Cognitive Domain, it may be useful to think about the Taxonomy of the *Affective* Domain, that which concerns itself with emotions, attitudes and personal growth. This structure, created later in 1964, begins with *Receptivity,* meaning the student is open to learning. It moves on to *Responsiveness,* meaning that the student voluntarily participates in the learning process. The next step is *Valuing*, in which the learning process becomes important to the learners and so they remain committed to it. After this is *Organizing*, where the learner integrates the new knowledge and values into his or her own experience. It ends with *Characterizing by Value*. In this stage, the learner incorporates what he or she has learned into long-range experiences.

Here, we could never expect a student to proceed rigidly from one step to the next. Instead, learning is seen as a lifelong and variable process. This is the goal of critical teaching. We want the ultimate learning outcome of our teaching to be a student who can approach the entire world and all of his or her experiences as a critical thinker.

The outcomes of this domain cannot be assessed or measured with simplistic, reductionist methods like multiple-choice tests. Instead we must rely on the intrinsic concerns and motivations of the students to push them in the directions they choose. Learning really is about the learner.

Perhaps it is some intersection of the two domains that bring us closer to the ideal learning situation. This way, while the first can provide a map, the students are still able to chart their own journeys and choose their own destinations.

Reference

Hurston, Z. N. (1937). *Their eyes were watching God.* New York: Lippincott.

Further Reading

Anderson, L. W., & Krathwohl, D. R. (2000). *A taxonomy for learning, teaching, and assessing: A revision of Bloom's Taxonomy of Educational Objectives.* Boston: Longman Press.

Bloom, B. S. (Ed.). (1956). *Taxonomy of educational objectives. Handbook one: Cognitive domain.* New York: David McCay.

Hale, J. B. (1982). *Black children: Their roots, culture, and learning style.* Baltimore: Johns Hopkins University Press.

Childhood and Adolescence

Adolescence

Kaia Skaggs

Adolescence is a particularly important stage for the development of critical thinking. In adolescence, people become capable of the kinds of cognitive activities that allow them to engage in critical thinking in its full sense. Two primary theoretical perspectives are particularly important in examining these changes: Piaget's descriptions of the stages of concrete and formal operational thought and insights from information-processing theory.

Jean Piaget was a Swiss psychologist who was interested in how people acquire knowledge. He described the general processes of cognitive development and how cognitive activities (which he called mental operations) change developmentally from infancy through adulthood. From the ages of about 6 or 7 to 11 or 12, children engage in what Piaget termed concrete operational thought. During this period, children can begin to reason logically in many ways, but their reasoning is tied to concrete, observable reality. They are able to recognize that their thoughts are their own

and may differ from those of others, can reason about changes and their effects, can classify objects as belonging to multiple categories simultaneously, and can draw logical inferences from two or more pieces of information.

Beginning around the age of 12, adolescents enter what Piaget considered the ultimate stage of cognitive development, the formal operational stage. Formal operational thought is characterized by abstract, flexible, logical, and scientific thinking. Adolescents can apply mental operations not only to concrete objects and events but also to abstractions. They can think about thought itself and reason in terms of theories and possibilities, even those that are contradictory or contrary to fact. They are able to take a systematic approach to problem-solving, instead of the trial-and-error or semi-systematic methods employed by younger children. They can imagine endless possibilities and alternate realities and think deeply about questions of meaning, truth, justice, and ethics. They are able to perform transformations of transformations, think about the relationships of relationships, and form classes of classes. In other words, they are capable of the mental operations required for and suited to the demands of critical thinking.

Piaget's theory has been modified and refined by modern researchers. It is commonly believed that Piaget overestimated the level of thought used by most adults most of the time. Researchers now believe that formal operational thought is slower to develop and may appear later than Piaget believed. Research suggests that formal operational thought is applied with any consistency by only a minority of adolescents and adults and then inconsistently across contexts. In addition, while individuals seem to proceed through the earlier stages of cognitive development relatively consistently given adequate environmental stimuli and opportunities, the formal operational stage seems to be more related to formal schooling than are the previous stages, and are more influenced by variables other than purely intellectual capacity. For example, the ability to apply formal operational thought seems to be related to differences in prior knowledge in a domain, the amount of experience with the types of problems used to evaluate such reasoning, the ease with which an individual can draw analogies to better known or better understood problems when attempting to solve unfamiliar ones, and the complexity of the most advanced solutions that can be formed by a given individual. Rather than suggesting that Piaget's descriptions were wrong, this evidence can be taken to suggest that schools have an important role to play in ensuring that adolescents attain the highest level of cognitive skills of which they are capable.

Information processing theories attempt to explore human cognition from the perspective of its component parts. Early information processing theories used the computer as a metaphor for human cognition and built computer programs to test and compare various models to human performance. These theories have focused primarily on how information is attended to, perceived, stored, and retrieved from memory and on how information can be used to solve problems. There are typically three components to an information processing system: the information that is stored; the cognitive processes used to perceive, store, retrieve, transform, and act on information; and the control processes that operate to coordinate the system, often known as metacognition or executive control processes. All of these components are important in critical thinking and all show developmental changes that have implications for adolescent thought.

The human information processing system becomes more efficient from childhood to adulthood. Adolescents process information more quickly than younger children, can operate on more bits of information at a time, and have greater stores of information. Many of the basic skills have become automatized so that they can be recalled and used without much cognitive effort, allowing existing cognitive capacity to be used for other types of processing. In addition, adolescents possess a greater variety of strategies for learning, storing, and retrieving information than younger children and have more highly developed metacognitive processes that allow them to employ those strategies more appropriately, monitor their use, and better evaluate their effectiveness.

As an example, consider working memory, commonly thought of as the limiting factor in our information processing system. Working memory is the term used to describe the part of memory where active thinking occurs. Whereas the amount of information that can be stored in long-term memory is vast, the number of storage slots available in working memory at any given time is limited. Furthermore, unless it is rehearsed or refreshed, information only stays in working memory a short amount of time. Adolescents differ from younger children in that they can hold more information in working memory and refresh what is there more quickly so that it is not lost. Adolescents are able to use their available working memory more efficiently because they have automatized common mental operations. This means that working memory resources do not have to be used to figure out the operation, it happens relatively without conscious effort. If asked "What is 4 + 5?" an elementary school child might have to pause and count or retrieve the process of addition from memory, whereas an older child or adult may have the answer instantaneously without having to work it out.

More importantly for critical thinking, adolescents are able to use a greater variety of metacognitive strategies to enhance and monitor their thinking than younger children. This greater metacognitive awareness is crucial to the development of critical thinking skills. Adolescents can plan an approach to problem-solving, hypothesize, combine, and evaluate multiple sources of information, use effective strategies for carrying out and evaluating their problem-solving processes, and evaluate whether their thinking has been effective.

Although by virtue of their increased cognitive capacities, adolescents are theoretically capable of engaging in critical thinking, the proportion that do so regularly and competently is small. It is important for schools to teach, encourage, and stimulate the type of advanced thinking of which adolescents are capable, although many fail to do so. At one time it was thought that critical thinking skills were developed through the study of particular subjects, most notably science, math, and Latin. Some people believed (and unfortunately perhaps still do) that critical thinking can be learned only by a minority of adolescents or that it cannot be learned at all but that some individuals are simply born with an enhanced ability to think critically. However, it is now clear that critical thinking skills can be developed and taught and that explicit teaching and practice in a wide variety of contexts is necessary if we expect adolescents to acquire these skills and use them on a regular basis.

Several factors increase the likelihood that adolescents will develop into critical thinkers. The first of these is in-depth knowledge. Research has shown that individuals are more likely to think critically about areas in which they have more in-depth knowledge. Although this may be an area in which schools feel they excel, the emphasis here is on the depth of content knowledge and not just possession of a wide store of isolated facts. Prior knowledge influences what adolescents learn and how well they learn, but this knowledge must be organized, accessible, and meaningful to be used as a springboard for critical thinking. Instruction that promotes deep processing of subject matter will promote not only richer stores of knowledge but more efficient storage and retrieval of that knowledge. It is also important that the basic skills and tools of learning need to be practiced until they become automatic. Automatized skills free cognitive capacity for critical processing. The student who is struggling to sound out words will have difficulty critically evaluating the impact or veracity of the writing as a whole.

A second factor is explicit identification and instruction of the skills inherent in critical thinking, such as hypothesis testing, logic, recognition of bias, problem-solving strategies, and analysis to name a few, in multiple, meaningful, engaging contexts. The incorporation of critical thinking skills must become part of the culture of schools and not something that is addressed implicitly or haphazardly at best. Standards for quality in critical thinking also need to be explicitly and precisely identified. Students should be able to evaluate their own thinking and that of others with respect to those standards.

A third factor is the role of attitudes and dispositions involved in critical thinking. One of the reasons that so few adolescents engage in critical thinking on a regular basis has to do not with their capability but with their disposition to doing so. Critical thinking is hard work and requires purposeful and sustained effort. It is important that schools not only teach the thinking skills themselves but also develop the attitudes and dispositions that assure that these skills will be used.

Many approaches have been suggested to teach various thinking skills including problem-solving, decision-making, creativity, and critical thinking. These approaches differ in terms of their breadth or specificity, their theoretical and/or philosophical underpinnings, and the degree to which the thinking skills are taught separately and explicitly or embedded in the context of specific subject matter.

Several generalizations can be made regarding the selection of an approach to the teaching of critical thinking skills in adolescence. The first fundamental question to be addressed is whether critical thinking skills can be taught. On this point, the answer is clear, Critical thinking skills can be taught and they are unlikely to be acquired by the majority of adolescents without explicit teaching. A second question is whether critical thinking skills should be taught as independent entities or embedded in the instruction of specific content matter. This issue is more complex. Critical thinking skills should be taught explicitly but, like other types of skills and knowledge, are more likely to be learned in the context of rich, meaningful, active instructional content. Attempts to teach formal logical or reasoning skills devoid of particular content have not generally resulted in their generalized use. However, it is important to make explicit the thinking skills that are being taught rather than subsuming them to a particular content. Some critical thinking skills are general enough to be applied to a wide range of disciplines and adolescents need explicit instruction to do so. Others are more specific to particular content domains, but the majority of adolescents need guidance in recognizing, practicing, and applying them. Third, teaching critical thinking skills alone is unlikely to result in their widespread use unless adolescents have the attitudes that predispose them to use the skills. Attitudes and dispositions cannot generally be taught directly, but are more likely to be acquired through the modeling, values, and behavior of adults.

To design secondary education to produce more students who are effective, habitual critical thinkers, several challenges must be met. One challenge is the development of critical thinking skills in teachers. Many teachers are uncomfortable designing instruction to promote development of critical thinking skills in their students because they are unsure of their own adequacy as critical thinkers. Thus, teachers need training not only in the instruction of critical thinking skills, but need ongoing opportunities to develop and practice critical thinking skills themselves. Teachers must model the attitudes, dispositions, and skills they wish to teach their students.

High-stakes standardized testing that tends to emphasize rote and fragmented memorization of basic skills and facts presents another challenge to the redesign of instruction for critical thinking. Students need to be engaged with authentic, complex, interesting problems that require hypothesis testing, inquiry, reasoning, interpretation, evaluation, synthesis, and varying strategies and possible solutions. These are not the kinds of problems easily amenable to evaluation by standardized, multiple choice tests.

Standards of excellence should incorporate competence in critical thinking and not rely on test scores to make judgments about the quality of schools and students' attainments. How to choose a way to develop the skills and dispositions adolescents need to become critical thinkers is itself a problem in need of critical thought. There are excellent programs and approaches available, but none will succeed if implemented in an uncritical, didactic fashion. None will flourish in schools that value quiet, conformity, and correct answers. None will be effective unless teachers themselves take on the challenge of developing their own abilities and dispositions for critical thinking and truly honor and encourage such thought in their students. It is imperative that we take seriously the challenge of preparing adolescents to be critical thinkers, for this is one of the skills that will enable them to succeed in a world of exploding information, accelerating change, increasing challenge, and unprecedented new opportunity.

Further Reading

Barell, J. (1995). *Teaching for thoughtfulness: Classroom strategies to enhance intellectual development* (2nd ed.). White Plains, NY: Longman.

Costa, A. (Ed.). (2001). *Developing minds: A resource book for teaching thinking.* Arlington, VA: Association for Supervision and Curriculum Development.

Tishman, S., Perkins, D. N., & Jay, E. S. (1995). *The thinking classroom: Learning and teaching in the culture of thinking.* Boston: Allyn & Bacon.

Early Childhood Education

Gaile S. Cannella

Although there is much interest in those who are younger, conceptualizations of early childhood education vary. The meaning is not always clear and appears to be different dependent on location, context, time, and political agenda. The history and contemporary practices of early childhood education are rooted in a variety of disciplines, conceptualized in a variety of ways by different people, and have been examined from a range of philosophical perspectives. For some, early childhood education means the broad range of life and learning experiences possible for children from birth to seven or eight years. For others, it means teaching the first grade. For others early childhood education is child care, Head Start, and the range of services in support of a nation's children. For some, early education is a focus on the improved life conditions for children in contemporary societies as compared to the past. Finally, for some the education of young children involves a continuous critique of even the concepts of child and education, since males, whites, and adults in general are privileged and practice the separation of those who are younger from the adult world. This discussion provides a critical perspective on early childhood education and a postformal problematization of the present of the field by examining the past.

What is early childhood education (ECE) from a critical theoretical perspective? To address this question one must recognize that the dominant view of early childhood education is grounded in philosophies that originated in Europe and have been developed in the United States. Generally, the field has not included people of color from diverse locations around the world. The field has been profoundly influenced by the ways in which various disciplines have focused on and constructed childhood in practice. The traditional *history* begins with discussions of child-rearing in prehistoric times. According to the elitist assumptions of Europeans, prehistoric life was simple and primitive, the same for adults and children alike, so early childhood education occurred within the adult world. This discussion is followed by tracing the next steps of human progress that are believed to be hunting/ gathering, farming, and the construction of villages. Within this notion of progress, children are seen as increasingly more dependent on adults for both safety and skill development. This focus on child as dependent has resulted in continual debates between those who believe that infanticide and abandonment were common practices in ancient cultures (focusing mainly on

children) and the critical perspective used by those who would look at the life conditions of all human beings in their particular historical contexts, without making children the only emphasis.

The construction during the enlightenment period of beliefs in nature, truth, science, and reason set the stage for the unquestioned assumption that younger human beings (labeled children) could be studied as a vehicle for understanding the advanced truths about and ways of functioning displayed by enlightened older human beings (labeled adults). The field of *psychology* that emerged during the enlightenment/modern eras (that covered the past 500 years), focused on revealing what were believed to be scientific truths about how those who were younger understood and functioned in the world, how/what changes occurred over time, and how younger human beings came to think like adults. This attempt to create sciences of human beings resulted in fields like *psychology, sociology,* and *anthropology.* In a variety of ways, *psychology* was taken up by the field of education in general and the more specific field of early childhood education in particular. Over time, the broad field of education has used the range of theories constructed as psychological content as a major knowledge base to label, control, and claim salvation for children. Whether using Piagetian developmental stages of cognitive growth/change to describe how a child thinks, behaviorism to create methods of reinforcing behavior, or calls to meet the learning needs of children, psychology has been a major influence in education. More specifically, early childhood education has constructed beliefs about who young children are and how they function based on theories of developmental psychology. During the 1900s, there actually appeared to be two fields, or two perspectives, that dealt specifically with young children—the field of child development (usually found in home economics or human ecology and dealing with issues like child care, preschool, family relations, and sometimes public policy) and the field of early childhood education (usually found in colleges of education and dealing more specifically with learning theories and academic content). Both used content and knowledge bases generated in the work of such scholars as Plato, Comenius, Rousseau, Pestalozzi, Froebel, Freud, Darwin, Hall, Thorndike, Erikson, Gesell, and Piaget; philosophers and researchers who were male and European.

Beliefs about children have been and continue to be influenced by societal values and political agendas. Just as schooling historically emerged from somewhat contradictory attempts to (1) save privileged white male children from the sinful world and (2) create locations that would teach the poor appropriate ways to live their lives, early childhood education also emerged as the field of *sociology* and philanthropic activity gained power.

To address deficiencies that were believed to exist within the homes of immigrants, culturally diverse populations, and the poor, charity schools emerged in the 1800s in the United States. In addition to Sunday Schools and urban primary schools, infant schools were supported extensively by ladies charity organizations. Although espousing nurturing, the purpose was to guide poor and immigrant children toward a predefined normalcy. Although the support for infant schools declined, Froebelian kindergartens (using Froebel's gifts and occupations curriculum) emerged in the 1870s and 1880s as a form of mission work for young privileged women with the purpose of providing play and learning opportunities for poor chil-

dren (Bloch, 1987). By the end of the 1800s, middle-class social reformers and philanthropists had created day nurseries to provide child care for the children of poor working mothers. Throughout the construction of the various forms of early education and care, a middle- and upper-class bias dominated—the belief that those who were more economically privileged already knew how to provide for and raise their children. The environment and activities offered by the middle-class were considered best for children; immigrants and the poor were to attend early education and care to learn moral values, hygiene, and how to structure their lives to be normal like those who were more privileged (Wrigley, 1991).

During the early part of the twentieth century, child development knowledge was used to construct the idea of enrichment for the middle-class child. Experts in development, like psychologists and teachers, were considered the individuals who could provide curriculum that would enrich the life experiences of middle-class children. The middle-class home environment continued to be praised as the best place for children, so educational and care environments outside the home like nursery schools were offered as additions to already fulfilled lives for a short period each day.

Until the 1950s, the major purposes of care and education programs for young children were (1) the legitimation of human sciences like psychology and sociology, and (2) the control and regulation of immigrants and the poor. A third major influence on beliefs about young human beings, and the resultant development of early childhood education, is the patriarchal embeddedness of American and European philosophies and ways of functioning in the world. For example, the

Depression in the 1930s and WWII in the 1940s resulted in the development of more child care programs by both government and the private business sector. Although more privileged children continued to attend expensive enrichment programs, the absolute requirement that great numbers of women work (as males were away at war) resulted in the construction of child care programs to meet the needs of female workers and their children. Large child care centers were even constructed on the work site (e.g., at Kieser Nurseries).

During this brief period, women were accepted as workers and children were understood as benefiting from a range of life experiences. However, when males returned home from the war (and wanted the jobs), women were pressured to leave the work force. Media campaigns were even constructed showing false pictures of children taken to mental hospitals because their mothers would not leave the work force and take care of them at home. A child need was created to put women back in their place and to give men the jobs they wanted.

Historically, a variety of social movements that focused on the welfare of children can be traced to the fear that women or the poor were making gains toward equity or were not capable of understanding what is best for children. Examples include the focus on mother/infant bonding, the belief that the early years will determine the rest of a person's life, the conceptualization of Head Start as teaching poor parents how to raise their children, and recent repeated debates over child care and the demonizing of working mothers.

During the last part of the twentieth century, early childhood educators pushed to make sure that their psychologically oriented developmental philosophy was part of elementary schools and all types of programs for young children. They maintained that human growth was the foundation of what should be taught and should guide how to teach young children. Their hope was that the increasing number of kindergartens in elementary education would developmentally ground the five-year olds who made up their classes. This foundation would then spread to primary classrooms, grades one through three. A curriculum perspective was also constructed by a committee of early childhood educators through the National Association for the Education of Young Children that espoused developmentally appropriate practice (DAP). The document describes the types of learning experiences and teaching methods the committee members felt were most consistent with their view of development, especially the theories of Piaget. This document is still being distributed and the ideas are being imposed on educational systems all around the world.

The focus on the development of young children for the past 40 years has not been an isolated or unidirectional activity. It has had some significant repercussions. Since large numbers of early childhood educators have emphasized child development, a discourse of judgment, accountability, and control has been constructed by those who were not happy with the gains made in human rights by women, minorities, or children during the 1960s and early 1970s. This dissatisfaction has led to the labeling of teachers, especially child-care workers who are mostly women, as incompetent, and poor women as responsible for all of society's ills. There has been an increased acceptance of control over children through rampant legislated testing and drill-oriented learning. Early childhood educators in the United States have been placed in the position of espousing exploration, hypothesis testing, and child-initiated learning while facing a system that has interpreted people and thinking as measurable, simple, and needing moral control.

This discussion has been somewhat European and very American. In countries all over the world, the work of Piaget and ideas like developmentally appropriate practice are being imposed, but using a language of accountability and measurement. However, from both the United States and other countries around the world, feminist poststructural and postmodernist discourses are emerging that counter extremist, truth-oriented discourses of judgment and accountability as well as the traditional deterministic focus on developmental psychology found in early childhood education. Groups of early childhood educators are recognizing the importance of issues like diversity and respect for the broad range of ways that human beings construct their lives. Further, they point out that dominant thought in the United States and Europe has constructed and controlled the very notion that younger human beings are children, whether this determination has arisen from developmental or more narrow accountability orientations. They suggest that while we continue child care, preschool, primary education, and social welfare programs for children and their families, we must (1) always critique underlying biases and assumptions about children and their cultural groups, (2) recognize that the dominant view of child has both ignored and disqualified the lives of great numbers of children around the world, (3) recognize the political agendas and power structures within which we/they function, and (4) examine and reconceptualize beliefs and practices.

References

Bloch, M. N. (1987). Becoming scientific and professional: An historical perspective on the aims and effects of early education. In T. S. Popkewitz (Ed.), *The formation of school subjects* (pp. 25–62). Basingstoke, England: Falmer Press.

Wrigley, J. (1991). Different care for different kids: Social class and child care policy. In L. Weis, P. G. Altbach, G. P. Kelly, & H. G. Petrie (Eds.), *Critical perspectives on early childhood education* (pp. 189–209). Albany: State University of New York Press.

Further Reading

Burman, E. (1995). *Deconstructing developmental psychology.* New York: Routledge.

Cannella, G. S. (1997). *Deconstructing early childhood education.* New York: Peter Lang.

Dahlberg, G., Moss, P., & Pence, A. (1999). *Beyond quality in early childhood education and care: Postmodern perspectives.* London: Falmer Press.

Middle Schools: Curiosity and Critical Thinking

Pat Williams-Boyd

Let's take a look at two schools of seventh and eighth graders. In one, students sit quietly in rows, instructed by well-meaning teachers who lecture, expect their words to be written down, memorized, and rewritten on exams. The emphasis is on teachers covering material, getting through the curriculum, and transferring knowledge from their minds into the vacuous minds of students who must perform well on standardized tests. There is little room here for critical thinking or confronting problems with multiple solutions. In many ways, this is the education of disrespect for it sees young adolescents as receptacles into which current knowledge is placed. Often these schools are junior high schools whose focus is on discrete pieces of information and on preparing young adolescents for high school.

In the other school, students and teachers are engaged in the active creation of meaning, the challenge of posing problems, gathering data, critically analyzing potential solutions, and then thoughtfully reflecting on the process and the action which the posed solution suggests. Often these schools are middle schools, built on the developmental needs of young adolescents and designed to stimulate their natural curiosity through exploration driven by critical thinking, inquiry, and the connectedness of knowledge. At a time when young adolescents are beginning to sculpt their own identities and ways of understanding, critical thinking provides them with valuable tools that are focused on es-tablishing the why of their positions, on scrutinizing their own biases or unexamined prejudices, on the variety of possible choices and the likelihood of a particular choice being successful, on the analyzed viewpoints of others, on solving problems in a self-directed and critically-reflective manner, and on finding the truth rather than being dogmatically right. In other words, critical thinking provides the vehicle through which young adolescents begin to learn how to exercise control over their own thinking and beliefs.

Middle schools that develop the skills of critical thinking and problem-solving celebrate and nurture the young adolescent in the process of becoming. To think critically, young people must exist in an environment of curiosity, creativity, compassion, and safety. Middle schools are guided by the beliefs that the pursuit of truth and of reason based on rationalized and challenged assumption, of inference based on logical reasoning and transference of process, will help prepare young people for a future world about which we have little idea. The critical thinking middle school is a greenhouse where desks are grouped by learning needs and activities, where teachers and students explore and grow together, and where teachers ask open-ended questions and then respectfully allow time during which students may formulate responses. Middle grades teachers are aware of the necessity of equal wait time to respond to a question for both boys and girls. Because of the nature of open-ended or critical thinking questions, some students may need more time to formulate responses than others. This is a culture of exploration, interaction, flexibility, and total engagement by all participants. It is a culture built on the modeled behavior of inquiry, positive support, and problem-solving.

For young adolescents to become more thoughtful about their own learning, they must be challenged to think critically about the knowledge and the meaning they create across the middle grades curriculum. Teachers who teach for meaning provide opportunities for the construction of individual understanding by engaging themselves and their students in the suspension of belief until they experience reflective thinking, focused questioning, analyzed critique, clarification of perspective and possibility, and reasoned dialogue; in other words until they engage in critical thinking and problem-solving. If students are to participate in a world culture, if they are to expand knowledge as it is currently known, if they are to push the frontiers of what we know and what we ask, they must critically examine themselves and their world.

One of the most typical ways in which teachers engage students is through questioning. Although studies have continued to point out that the majority of questions a teacher asks tends to be low level (simple answer, recall, fill in the blank), critical thinking challenges all students to think on the higher levels of Bloom's cognitive taxonomy (analysis, synthesis and evaluation). It is here that authentic understanding connects to the student's perception of reality. Critical thinking questions challenge young adolescents to think creatively, divergently, intuitively, deductively, and hypothetically. These questions encourage students to draw inferences based

on their understandings and to make new applications of previously learned information.

A low level question in a language arts seventh-grade unit on The Diary of Anne Frank might ask students to simply list the names of the main characters and where the story took place. A higher order question for the same unit might ask in what ways did the diary convey the sense of the time in which she was writing. Extending the critical thinking, the students may be asked what they would write if they were living then and corresponding with Anne. In a mixed-ability eighth-grade class studying reproduction, lower level questions would ask the student to label the reproductive organs as shown on a worksheet, while a higher level critical thinking question would ask students what their analyzed positions were concerning cloning and why they believed as they did.

Lower level questions stimulate no real conceptual understanding for they tend to be discrete and concrete. They concern only information: lists of battles and dates of wars, verbatim definitions for geometric theorems, vocabulary word definitions, the identification of musical symbols. However, until each of these is applied to a situation in which the student must make critical judgments and think more abstractly, until they make connections to prior knowledge, authentic understanding has not taken place. Learning itself is an abidingly personal adventure. Critical thinking asks young adolescents to examine their view of a particular situation after they have connected with the issue, identified the problem, gathered and evaluated the evidence, considered the possible choices with their attendant implications and values, and reflected metacognitively (or thought about their thinking process). "That's not fair," the ever-popular adolescent mantra, is no longer applicable because each student has developed his or her own sense of the situation based on evaluative evidence.

A middle school interdisciplinary team is composed of a group of teachers who teach different subjects but share the same students and teach in a specific content area. Teachers from language arts, science, math, social studies, and music who were collaborating on a unit on endangered species would be an example of an interdisciplinary team. The critical thinking guiding question they might pose could be "Who will survive?" The language arts teacher could choose narrative accounts that reflect a variety of positions on how contemporary culture values some species rather than others. The social studies teacher might examine the *Endangered Species Act* from a political standpoint, while the math teacher could examine exponential rates of repopulation or decay in both plants and animals. The science teacher might initiate a discussion on ecological biodiversity while the music teacher could examine compositions which address nature and then ask teams of students to write a short composition reflecting their findings (Traver, 1998).

Teachers guide this culture of inquiry through questions such as what is the purpose, can you offer examples, where are the points of tension, what supports your statement, from what viewpoint is it coming, does your conclusion make sense given the data, what kinds of data did you use and from where and what may you infer? In a seventh-grade unit on the American frontier, the teacher uses leading questions and the students respond: Q: When settlers and cattlemen came to this country where did they live? A: In the West. Q: Did anyone live there when they arrived? A: Yes. Q: Who? A: Indians. Q: What happened to these people?

A: They were moved to reservations. Q: Did the settlers give anything to the indigenous people for their land? A: They traded trinkets for the land. A: They brought disease. Q: If the native people were driven from their own land, forced into relatively unwanted land, and if they suffered from diseases brought by the white man, why are the Indians portrayed in movies as the bad guys and the cavalry are seen as heroes? In all questions there are perspectives driven by values. (Traver, 1998)

If eighth-graders are studying core democratic principles, a teacher may frame a question regarding the common good rather than lecturing, such as: The day after the September 11th attack on the United States, a local Midwest gas station, owned and operated by a family from the Middle East, was pelted with rocks, breaking all the windows and injuring the owner. Why do you think this happened and what is your role or responsibility, if any, given this situation?

In the critical thinking paradigm, young minds are schooled to detect problems, to seek out possible causes, and to be curious about the problem and the conditions which generate possible solutions. They are affirmed in asking the source of information, the biases or silenced voices that may not be heard, and the challenge of determining whether a problem or solution is a fact or an opinion. They access multiple data sources, including case studies, primary documents, personal interviews, court records, the popular media, and the Internet at the very least. They discourse openly about the consequences of choices, the advantages and disadvantages of given positions, and the impediments to implementing the posed solution.

The construction of new knowledge occurs in the discomfort zone or disequilibrium that students experience through critical inquiry. When young adolescents are told to read the chapter and answer the questions, natural curiosity has been suppressed and imagination stamped into conformity. How often do we hear teachers say, "I covered that material. I don't know why students did so poorly on the state exams." They attribute failure to lack of family support, to lethargic or lazy students, or to the neighborhood because of its deficits which imperil kids, when in fact their students were simply bored. Knowledge and textbooks are not sacrosanct, immutable, or unchanging. They should be challenged, reshaped, and recreated as students grapple with connecting to them and making sense of their world as interpreted through their own life's experiences. "Knowledge Is Power" is the slogan of a KIP academy where knowledge wears the clothes of different kinds of power, is seen in multiple forms, and can be verified in a variety of ways.

Issues of cultural norms and biases, racial and ethnic prejudice, class stereotyping and bigotry, bullying, drug abuse, violence, and homophobia are often ignored by teachers for class discussion because of the controversy they may ignite, when these are some of the very issues middle grades kids need and want to examine and discuss.

Middle grades teachers must process two bottomless pools of knowledge—students' perceptions of their world and content knowledge. The reflective, critical thinking middle grades teacher views knowledge through the lens of inquiry and data gathering, a lens that sees content knowledge as the evidence, hints, suggestion, probes, or data students discover in the pursuit of a solution to a problem. You may ask what skills middle level students have to equip them for such inquiry, and the key response is curiosity. Can content knowledge born of a teacher's rich understanding be uncovered, explored, examined, and collaboratively and cooperatively constructed by students? The culture of critical thinking and curiosity says yes.

John Dewey contended that the most crucial need in American society was for students to be taught to reflect upon what they learned in schools. Knowledge is not valid because it is in print. A popular 1960s bumper sticker shouted, "Question Authority." Students of teachers with training in critical thinking are challenged to discover and create verifiable knowledge, even to the extent of finding answers to question that have yet to be asked (Shermis, 1992). This requires time for thoughtful deliberation, careful examination, and logical and deductive reasoning. Unfortunately, while school boards and policy papers sing the battle song of critical thinking and higher-order thinking skills, they rush to fill students' time with more testing and more standards, as if the classroom and students' minds were similar kinds of empty vessels. And the refrain is silence.

Knowledge is not transmission, it is the construct of the human imagination. Freire maintained that when anyone was prevented from engaging in the process of inquiry, an act of violence ensued (Freire, 1993). Middle grades students are beginning to develop their own moral persona (a set of values apart from their parents). If their values, beliefs, opinions, and dispositions are constructed through inquiry and critical thinking, they will become dynamic individuals rather than part of a collective unthinking mass. Critical thinking and inquiry reflect freedom, and Freire sagely suggests that freedom is the indispensable quest for human completion (1993).

References

Freire, P. (1993). *Pedagogy of the oppressed.* New York: Continuum Publishing.

Shermis, S. (1992). *Critical thinking: Helping students learn reflectively.* Bloomington, IN: ERIC Clearinghouse on Reading and Communication Skills.

Traver, R. (1998). What is a good guiding question? *Educational Leadership, 55*(6), 70–73.

Further Reading

Keating, D. (1988). *Adolescents' ability to engage in critical thinking.* Madison, WI: National Center for Effective Secondary Schools.

King, P. M., & Kitchener, K. S. (1994). *Developing reflective judgment: Understanding and promoting intellectual growth and critical thinking in adolescents and adults.* San Francisco: Jossey-Bass.

Lynch, C. L., Kitchener, K. S., & King, P. M. (1994). *Developing reflective judgment in the classroom: A manual for faculty.* New Concord, KY: Lynch.

The Nature of Childhood

Wayne A. Reed

As we enter a new century, those of us working in public education face the important question of whether pedagogies that promote critical thinking are good for kids. On one hand, the question seems almost ludicrous since prevailing winds in today's schools blow heavily in favor of classrooms brimming with children who are able to demonstrate critical thinking skills. The problem with this trend, however prevalent, is the fact that critical thinking as an educational paradigm does not have as its starting point the nature of childhood.

Fundamentally, thinking is not a childhood activity but is something that emerges in adolescence and matures in adulthood. Adults (who are already thinkers themselves) project the need for critical thinking upon children, although higher forms of consciousness do not come naturally to kids. In fact, if today's teachers and principals were not constantly pushing critical thinking, most children of elementary years would happily function in the worlds of their imagination, exploring their environment for new understandings and negotiating the intense feelings that come with childhood. The fact that childhood has little natural connection to critical thinking raises questions about a child's readiness for a regimen of pedagogies to make thinking occur, including the possibility that forcing a child to think prematurely may thwart development in a number of areas and impede the child's capacity to become a critical thinker later in life.

One aspect of today's elementary classrooms that seems especially hard hit by thinking-dominated approaches is the teaching of literacy. The purpose of this essay is to argue that the preponderance of thinking-based strategies in schools today fails to account for the nature of childhood and, as a consequence, harms a child's ability to mature into a passionate, energetic, imaginative, thinking adult.

During the last decade, critical thinking has been the watchword in virtually all aspects of education: curriculum development, instructional strategies, student assessment, and teacher evaluation. Most experienced classroom teachers will acknowledge that critical thinking has a more central role in elementary education than it did ten years ago. It is not uncommon in the schools where I circulate to hear teachers rattle off Bloom's Taxonomy as comfortably as a shopping list. One third-grade teacher with twenty-three years of classroom experience recently told me, "In the last five years, critical thinking has become the focus of all that I do with my kids. In years gone by, I was concerned to give my students a variety of things. Now, I want them to think."

A driving force in this shift toward critical thinking is the national movement towards standards-based education, which claims critical thinking as a primary goal. A review of most state standards reveals a commitment to the promotion of critical thinking in children. For example, in New York State (the state where I work) those of us involved in elementary education are working with four standards in English Language Arts (ELA). These standards are supported by thirty-five performance indicators. Of the thirty-five indicators, thirty-three call for children to complete tasks that require thinking skills. These indicators include such tasks as: interpret and categorize information, correlate ideas from one text to another, convey information such as cause and effect, distinguish literary genres, evaluate literary merit, and use inference and deduction to understand a text. The two that invite children to use other intelligences (creating a story or poem and writing a letter to friend or relative) seem strangely out of place in the list of indicators which are primarily focused on cognition.

I highlight the standards in English Language Arts because my observation is that the teaching of literacy in elementary schools is especially impacted by thinking-dominated pedagogies. Literacy has become the barometer by which teachers, administrators, parents, and policy makers measure a child's ability to think. Concerns with reading comprehension, phonetic awareness, spelling, and writing skills place literacy at the core of a school's mission. If society wants anything, it wants its children to read and write; but is becoming literate the same thing as becoming a critical thinker?

Gone are the days when the teacher read a story simply because narratives are an innate, exciting, spontaneous aspect of childhood. With critical thinking as the goal, teachers are now required to lead children in the deconstruction of stories, to challenge children to compare and contrast the components of narratives, and to critique, synthesize, and analyze stories as text. No longer can an author's colorful narrative about a snake that flips in the air from tree to tree while changing his skin from yellow to green spark the imagination of children, sending their minds in scores of directions as they fantasize, generate their own narratives, and make their own connections. Stories about animals behaving as humans, children doing superhuman things, adults struggling to overcome, and hundreds of other dramas, both real and fantastic, can no longer stand by themselves as testimonies to the joys and trials of human existence. In the critical thinking paradigm, narratives are instrumental, they have a purpose, a usefulness, and their ultimate reason for existence in the literacy classroom is to teach children to think.

The process of deconstructing narratives hits me most starkly when I observe elementary teachers doing literacy instruction. In the public schools where I supervise student teachers, the literacy curriculum is taught every morning in a ninety-minute block. It begins with the children reading aloud. The children gather on the floor around the teacher, the teacher opens a large, colorful storybook, and begins to read. Because few things are more wonderful to a child than a good story, this time almost always begins with the children listening attentively, waiting to learn about the lead character or to catch the opening indications of the plot.

At this point, one of two things generally happens. In the higher functioning classes (that is the classes that the school has designated as gifted) I can almost feel the kids' brains shift into gear and start taking mental notes as the teacher reads the story, preparing for the questions that are sure to follow. How is the story sequenced? How does the story demonstrate cause and effect? What is the author's point of view? Sure enough, just as the flow of the narrative is moving along nicely and the children would otherwise be entering the soul of the story, the teacher stops and asks the children questions meant to promote thinking about the text.

When I observe a read-aloud in a nongifted class, the entire process breaks down once the teacher breaks the flow of the narrative by asking questions. The teacher reads a few lines, stops to question the children, proceeds to read more, then stops for further inquiry. Within five minutes, only a few of the children remain involved. Others are off in their own imagination or bored, maintaining just enough mental connection to what's happening to respond to the teacher if called upon. In other cases, the children are completely distracted, away in themselves. (Maybe they are in their own make-believe world, creating their own stories!)

At the conclusion of the read-aloud, regardless of whether or not the children were able to stay with the story, the teacher concludes this opening section of the literacy block with another series of questions. This time the teacher is trying to move the children from one level of thinking to another. Here, the teachers often follows the taxonomy, asking simple, descriptive questions at the outset, before moving to questions that promote analysis, synthesis, and so forth.

The problem with this approach to literacy instruction is that it attempts to insert critical thinking into narrative, an art form that primarily connects to the feeling life of a child. The fact that the gifted students preempt the flow of the narrative by becoming conscious of the narrative's structure does not indicate the success of critical thinking in education, but it's failure. Children need to hear stories as stories. They do not need to always pick narratives apart, deconstructing the characters, the plots, and the author's intent. They do not need to be graphically organizing the narrative in their minds as the teacher reads. They don't always need to be making text to text, text to self, and text to world connections. Children need to enter into the emotional life of a story, to interact with the feelings of the characters, to become involved in the emotions emerging from the plot. Childhood is a time of intense emotional development, a period when kids are laying the groundwork for the emotional beings they will be for the remainder of their lives. To push them into thinking too early is to thwart the development of their feeling life, something that has enormous implications for the kind of thinkers they become later on.

A.C. Harwood, the twentieth-century educator who based his work in the philosophy of Rudolf Steiner, observed that a child's capacity for thinking begins to emerge at about age twelve and continues to gain strength through adolescence and into early adulthood. According to Harwood and others of this school, a child's growth travels through two phases in the years prior to adolescence. The first phase is in early childhood and lasts until a child is six or seven years old. During this phase the development of the will dominates. The will is the life force that propels all physical movement and is the energy source for all aspects of human activity, including emotional development and mental cognition. The will is grounded in the body and strengthened through physical activity such as play, rhythmic exercise, and freedom of movement.

The second phase is the period when feelings and imagination dominate. Harwood calls it "the heart of childhood." During this period, emotions and imagination fuel a child's experience of the world. It is a time when fairy tales, myths, and stories are alive, a period when make-believe is real and the world is perceived in picture images rather than abstractions. It is a time, as Douglas Sloan puts it, "when children delight in vivid sense experiences—colors, rich and strange sounds, textures, movements . . . a time when they sit spellbound to hear a favorite story again and again, or enthusiastically take the characters of the story into themselves and act them out" (Sloan, 1983).

Harwood and his colleagues understand child development as a process involving three phases, with the third and final phase being the emergence of critical consciousness. Is it possible that the pressure being placed on children to think critically during their childhood years will in some way keep them from developing into healthy, whole adults? Harwood suggests that "we weaken a child's thinking for later years" when we disrupt the willing-feeling-thinking sequence of child devel-opment. If a young person's capacity for thinking is built on the dual foundation of willing and feeling, then thinking must be adversely effected if the life of the will and the life of feeling are not nurtured during childhood years. Not only may the capacity for thinking be impacted by the imposition of critical thinking too soon, but the quality of later thinking is certain to be influenced. Since critical thinking is rooted in the imagination, a child who has been deprived of opportunities to develop imagination during its early years is unlikely to have the creativity needed to construct a truly critical consciousness.

I do not deny the existence of consciousness in children prior to adolescence, but believe that thinking is not the primary mode of learning in the pre-adolescent years and should not be the major focus of elementary classrooms. Instead of concentrating on the development of critical thinking, the teachers of kindergarten and young elementary children need to focus on physical activities, especially rhythmic ones that build the child's will. Teachers of older elementary children need to foster the emotional and imaginative life of kids, allowing children to create, feel, explore, communicate, and socialize. By providing this kind of space in elementary classrooms, teachers help their students develop the imagination required for critical thinking in adolescence and lay an emotional foundation so that the critical thinking of later years is morally grounded. If what Harwood calls the "three-fold nature of childhood" is the starting point for our work in classrooms, we will equip children to become strong critical thinkers. If, however, we continue to demand that they do something for which they are not ready, the consequence for our children, our schools, and ultimately ourselves will be a decrease in critical thinking capacities.

Three years ago I happened to be in a fourth grade classroom when the principal, as was his custom, dropped by for a few minutes of interaction with the children. The principal, a major advocate of literacy instruction, proceeded to interview the class with a series of questions about the school's book of the month. The principal's questions challenged the children to think critically about the book. He asked a series of questions, encouraging the children to think about the author's purpose in writing the book, the connection of the text to other books, the sequence of events in the plot. After ten minutes of rigorous questioning, during which more than one child proved inadequate to the task, the principal left, and the look on his face seemed to indicate a sense of satisfaction at his performance. He had called his students to a higher level of excellence and fulfilled his mandate to promote the state standards. He was making his kids think!

Once the principal was out of earshot, a child sitting next to me put his head down on his desk and whispered, "Can't we have fun anymore?"

This fourth-grader's question speaks volumes to me of the debilitating effects of critical thinking pedagogies on children. The principal thought he was doing this class a service by helping the students deconstruct the story, by getting the kids to think. From a child's viewpoint, the emphasis on critical thinking is disruptive, discouraging, and nonsensical. Surely one reason that so many children reach only part of their potential is because they are tired of being pushed, coerced, and manipulated into tasks for which they are not naturally equipped. While the needs of a technological and scientifically-oriented society create a context that makes it appear as though we need kids to think as early as possible in their development, the consequence of prompting a cognitive awakening among the young appears to be classrooms filled with dispirited, bored, and resentful children. The answer to the little boy's question is an unequivocal no. School, in its present configuration, is not fun; it's work. The idea of having fun in our classrooms, of catching a ride on the natural flow of educational exploration and experiential learning, seems strangely out of place in current educational conversations. Listening to the discourse of many teachers, principals, district administrators, policy-makers and teacher educators reveals the laborious climate of schools. Rather than references to anything playful, imaginative, or fantastic, the vocabulary of teaching today is full of words like accountability, assessment, performance, measurement, and standards.

The dominance of critical thinking as an educational paradigm and the passion of those who promote standards-based teaching suggest that most educators view critical thinking as a child's greatest learning need. Proponents of thinking-dominated classrooms appear to operate with a definition of childhood that emphasizes only the child's brain. While few of these advocates would suggest that the child's mind is the only aspect of a child, or even the only dimension of a child that deserves a teacher's attention, in practice it is the child's brain and ability to think that dominates today's educational landscape. While strategies to promote critical thinking dominate classrooms more than ever, the verdict is out on the effectiveness of such strategies, particularly since thinking does not come naturally to children before early adolescence and the collateral damage wrought by pushing kids to think too soon must be quite high. For educators who view schools as an important contributor to the shaping of society, the current dominance of critical thinking in classrooms cannot help but be a major concern. Educators must challenge the dominance of critical thinking in elementary school classrooms because it narrows the focus of teaching and restricts the development of the whole child. In the end, it may even fail to achieve its own goal—a critically thinking public.

Reference

Sloan, D. (1983). *Insight-imagination: The emancipation of thought and the modern world.* Westport, CT: Greenwood Publishing Group.

Further Reading

Harwood, A. C. (1958). *The recovery of man in childhood.* New York: Myrin Books.

Schwartz, E. (1999). *Millennial child: Transforming education in the twenty-first century.* Hudson, NY: Anthroposophic Press.

The New Childhood and Critical Thinking

Joe L. Kincheloe

In a variety of previous publications, Shirley Steinberg and I have made the argument that a new childhood has been emerging over the last several decades. In light of such a social transformation, complex critical thinkers gain insights on a variety of levels. This essay delineates some of those insights, as it ponders the relationship between critical thinking and this so-called new childhood.

Childhood is a social construction that is subject to change whenever major social transformations take place. The zenith of what many in the United States in the first decade of the twenty-first century call the traditional childhood lasted from about 1850 to 1950 in the middle and upper-middle classes of Western societies. Protected from the dangers of the adult world, children during this period were removed from factories and placed into schools. As the prototype of the modern family developed in the late nineteenth century, proper parental behavior toward children coalesced around notions of tenderness and adult accountability for children's welfare. By 1900, many believed that childhood was a birthright—a perspective that resulted in a biological rather than a cultural definition of childhood. Emerging during this era of the protected child, modern child psychology was inadvertently constructed on the tacit assumptions of the period. The great child psychologists, from Erik Erikson to Arnold Gesell to Jean Piaget, viewed child development as shaped by biological forces.

Piaget's brilliance was constrained by his nonhistorical, socially decontextualized scientific approach. Whatever he observed as the genetic expression of child behavior in the early twentieth century he generalized to all cultures and historical eras—an error that holds serious consequences for those concerned with children. Since they consider the biological stages of child development fixed and unchangeable, teachers, psychologists, parents, welfare workers, and the community view and judge children along a taxonomy of development that is fictional. Those children who don't measure up will be relegated to the land of low and self-fulfilling expectations. Those children who make the grade will find that their racial and economic privilege will be confused with ability. For all the sociocultural and epistemological reasons that they reject other forms of Cartesian knowledge production, complex critical thinkers question the biological assumptions of classical child psychology.

We live in a historical period of great change and social upheaval, and critical observers are just beginning to notice changing social and cultural conditions that relate to this view of childhood. Categories of child development appropriated from Cartesian psychology may hold little relevance for raising and educating contemporary children.

Childhood began to change in the 1950s, when eighty percent of all children lived in homes in which the two biological parents were married to one another. No one has to be told that families have changed during the last fifty years. Volumes could be written on the scope of the social transformation. Before the end of the twentieth century, only about one in ten children lived with their two biological parents. Children of divorced parents—a group that represents more than half of the U.S. adult population—are almost three times as likely to suffer emotional and behavioral difficulties as children raised in two-parent homes. Despite this understanding, social institutions have been slow to recognize different, nontraditional family configurations and the special needs they create. Without support, the postmodern family of the twenty-first century, often with its plethora of working and single mothers, is beset by problems emanating from the feminization of poverty and the vulnerable position of women in both the public and private spaces of our society.

DEFINING THE NEW CHILDHOOD

While a number of factors have contributed to the formation of a new childhood, two important realities are (1) changing economic conditions, and (2) children's access to information that once was the exclusive domain of adults. The traditional childhood genie is out of the bottle and is unable to return. Recent literature about childhood in both the popular and scholarly presses speaks of childhoods lost, children growing up too fast, and child terror in the isolation of the fragmented home and community. There is no doubt that childhood has changed, in part as a result of the information saturation of hyperreality and children's access to adult information. Since the 1950s, more and more of our children's experiences are produced by corporations rather than by parents or even children themselves. The media—TV shows, movies (now on pay or cable TV, tapes, and DVDs), video games, and music (with earphones that allow seclusion from adults)—are now the private domain of children. Traditional notions of childhood as a time of innocence and dependence on adults have been undermined by how easy it is for children to tap into adult information sources.

Children's access to the media culture has a variety of complex consequences that affect different children and different groups of children in different ways. Children are not only taught to be consumers, they are introduced to a world of adult concerns—concerns from which economically privileged and often white children were protected during the age of the traditional childhood.

Advocates of traditional family values and severe discipline for children know something has changed, that for some reason authority has broken down. Such advocates often attribute the breakdown of authority to feminism and its encouragement of mothers to pursue careers outside the home, and to permissive liberals who oppose corporal punishment and other harsh forms of child control. Of course, they are wrong. Adult authority over children has, no doubt, broken down, but not because of feminist mothers or wimpy liberals. Children's access to the adult world via the electronic media has subverted contemporary children's consciousness of themselves as incompetent and dependent entities. Such a self-perception does not mix well with institutions such as the traditional family or the authoritarian school that view children as incapable of making decisions for themselves.

IMPLICATIONS FOR SCHOOLING AND CRITICAL THINKING

This change in children's access to adult knowledge about the world and the changes in the nature of childhood that it produces have undermined the conceptual/curricular/managerial bases on which schooling has been organized. It is not hyperbolic to argue that, in light of these cultural changes, schools must be reconceived from the bottom up. Currently the school curriculum is organized as a continuum of experience developmentally sequenced as if children learned about the world in school in progressive increments. Conservative efforts to protect outmoded school organizations and the traditional notions of childhood that come with them are in some ways understandable, but are ultimately doomed to failure.

We cannot protect our children from the knowledge of the world that electronic hyperreality has made available to them. Such a task would demand a form of sequestration tantamount to incarceration. The task that faces complex critical-thinking educators is intimidating but essential. We must develop education, parenting skills, and social institutions that will address this cultural revolution in a way that teaches our children to make sense of the chaos of information in the contemporary mediascape. In this context school becomes not so much an institution of information delivery as a hermeneutical site; a place where meaning is made and where understanding and interpretation are engendered. The task is difficult, but road maps to negotiate it are already being produced in our notion of complex critical thinking.

CHILDREN'S ABILITIES AND COMPLEX CRITICAL THINKING

As we examine the changes in childhood, we begin to realize that traditional cognitive and developmentalist understandings of the abilities of children that were formed during the period of the traditional childhood consistently underestimated what children can do. Children's ability to derive unique meanings from the information saturation of the contemporary environment is profound. In fact, some scholars are beginning to maintain that the new childhood and the sophisticated cognitive abilities that develop within it make the argument that childhood is a preliminary and preparatory stage of development prior to a different, higher phase of adulthood invalid.

Children of the new childhood are far more capable of becoming complex critical thinkers than mainstream cognitive theorists and educational psychologists have assumed. The smarter our questions to children become and the more we take time to listen to them, the better we understand the sophistication of their efforts to seek self-direction and construct a unique identity. In light of the complexity of the contemporary world of information, children's ability to process it with great speed is remarkable. I am amazed when I watch an eight-year-old surf the Internet, watch television, listen to a music CD, and talk on the telephone while doing homework—and fully attend to all tasks. Such abilities push the boundaries of critical thinking. One of the goals of a critical complex pedagogy to help adults understand the implications of these phenome-

nal abilities. Children coming out of the new childhood will take our notions of critical thinking and push them to currently unimaginable levels. I hope I can be around long enough to go on the ride.

Further Reading

Cannella, G., & Kincheloe, J. L. (Eds.). (2002). *Kidworld: Childhood studies, global perspectives, and education.* New York: Peter Lang.

Du Bois-Reymond, M., Sunker, H., & Heinz-Herman, K. (Eds.). (2001). *Childhood in Europe.* New York: Peter Lang.

Steinberg, S. R., & Kincheloe, J. L. (Eds.). (1997). *Kinderculture: The corporate construction of childhood.* Boulder, CO: Westview Press.

Youth Development: Critical Perspectives

Layla P. Suleiman Gonzalez

A critical approach to youth development challenges the notion that development is an internal process taking place independent of a context and unfolding in a universal fashion. The idea that development is an individual process that everyone follows in the same sequence of stages towards the same endpoint has dominated developmental psychology. Until very recently, the prevailing view has been that children move through a common developmental pathway, going from one stage to the next until they reach adulthood.

Today, new perspectives on youth development view young people as profoundly influenced and transformed by their sociocultural contexts. Development is viewed as having multiple dimensions and taking place as youth negotiates the inherent tension between the self and its multiple contexts, not just being a result of

some biological imperative. Moreover, there is a growing understanding of the role of young people as agents of change, involved in shaping and creating their context, and this has important implications for education.

Critical perspectives also challenge the current emphasis on cognitive explanations of development. Not only are young people developing cognitively, they are also developing emotionally, socially, physically, sexually, morally, and spiritually within particular sociopolitical and historical contexts. They are developing their identity (gender, ethnic/racial, and vocational, among others) and their relationship with the world, including the classroom, the community, the society and, increasingly, the global context. Focusing only on intellectual ability is insufficient when there is so much going on influencing a young person's growth and development. A critical approach to youth calls for a greater understanding of the cultural, social, and historical influences on developmental processes.

In fact, the very idea of adolescence, of a transition stage between childhood and adulthood, is a cultural concept invented in the twentieth century. Not all cultures share the idea of adolescence as a distinct stage, and even those that do may not draw the same conclusions about youth as those made in Western cultures. Sociocultural considerations not only shape definitions of youth and the very concept of adolescence, they also influence the experiences of youth at a given point in time.

From a sociohistorical perspective, each generation of youth is characterized by its political and cultural circumstances. For example, youth in the 1960s had to negotiate a very different reality than the young people who are growing up in the first decade of the twenty-first century. Even though there is a shared experience of global instability and greater technological capacity across the world today, a young person in the United States has to deal with a sociopolitical structure that is very different from a young person in Afghanistan. Their unique experiences have a tremendous impact on development. Each cultural context represents a different set of circumstances and relationships that young people must navigate as they invent and reinvent themselves.

Moreover, the way we view youth is related to the characteristics associated with that particular generation. A good example is Generation X. Perhaps most useful as a consumer profile for marketing purposes (young people are a huge market for corporations) the Generation X designation quickly became part of our popular language and shared perspective. This la-

bel became a lens used to relate to young people, even if many of them do not fit the stereotype. Although we acknowledge that generations of young people might be different from one another because of their relationship to the cultural ideologies and social structures of their time, the science of human development has been slow to embrace this notion.

And yet, young people's development is strongly related to how they make sense of these cultural ideologies and structures in terms of their own identity, viewed as the central quest in adolescence. Developing an identity in a complex world is a complex process. As young people try to define themselves, they struggle with questions such as the meaning of adolescence in their society, what it means to be male or female within their sociopolitical context, whether an identity based on gender is even necessary, the consequences of sexuality and sexual orientation, and the placement of their particular ethnic group in their sociohistorical and cultural context. It is a time when a young person is testing different values and different ways of being and is on the way to becoming their own person. The commitment to a set of values and beliefs is a pathway to identity.

Although all young people need many opportunities to explore possibilities and new experiences, many community support systems and educational practices take a deficit approach and are structured around the prevention or treatment of problem behavior for at-risk youth. However, preventing problems does not mean development is taking place. Even if young people have avoided drugs, pregnancy, or violence, it does not guarantee that they are better prepared for dealing with life. A nondeficit, or strength-based, approach focuses on identifying assets and working from there to make sure that young people have ample opportunities to develop their talents and abilities.

Positive youth development views young people as resources to their community, builds on their assets, and establishes caring and supportive relationships between young people and adults. Relationships with adults are critical in the development of young people. Studies in resiliency have shown that a relationship with a caring adult is a protective factor in the lives of youth. For many young people, that caring adult is a teacher or a coach in the school. With the help of adults, young people can explore new ways of thinking about their world. As young people begin to feel that they are valued and that they can create change, a powerful transformation takes place. Youth can be successful in challenging practices and policies, engage in a critical analysis of their own experience within and in relationship to these contexts, and advocate for solutions. Young people become more confident and more connected to their communities and to their future.

Understanding youth development as a transformation negotiated by young people in relation to their sociocultural contexts has implications for how institutions function. Schools, social service agencies, communities, media, and even government policies, can be empowering or restrictive. In education, we see shifts in school-student-community relationships, a move towards critical pedagogy, and a reformulation of the goals of education from cognitive enrichment to more holistic youth development.

Education is a critical context of development and both learning and teaching are political, cultural, and relational activities. To establish new ways of working with youth, educators must reevaluate their role and mission. Since the teacher has a political role in the lives of children, the relationship between teacher and student must be altered. This is challenging in the classroom environment since the teacher-student relationship assumes there are differences in power between teacher and student. A positive youth development model requires a different approach to engaging students and asks whether students believe that young people and adults can work together and learn from one another, whether students feel they are valued by and have something to contribute to their school/community, whether students feel they can be a resource for each other and their community, and whether students feel capable of analyzing a situation critically and creating new solutions and strategies for action.

In addition to changing school relationships, learning activities can be structured so that students can critically analyze their context and their possibilities for action. From a critical pedagogy perspective, education offers an opportunity to learn about alternative viewpoints and to challenge current ideologies and practices.

In the classroom, any project that challenges youth to think critically about a particular issue can be used to help them develop critical thinking. For example, students could analyze marketing campaigns to identify how a particular company has targeted teens and what that reveals about how young people are viewed in society. A text could be analyzed to demonstrate how the characters were influenced by their sociocultural context and what they did to challenge the status quo. In a math or social science course, resource allocation per pupil per school or city spending for youth programs could be analyzed as a way to show the inequity of the investments made in youth.

These activities need not be limited to the classroom setting, but should connect to real world contexts in the community. If they decide to take direct action on an issue, young people should be supported in their organization and mobilization efforts. They may present the results of their analysis to other young people, to adults in the community, or even to City Hall. These opportunities help young people develop their ability to analyze, understand their sociopolitical context, form their own identity, and actively participate in challenging and transforming themselves and their circumstances. This transformation is what drives youth development.

Further Reading

Packer, M. J. & Tappan, M. B. (2001). (Eds.). *Cultural and critical perspectives on human development*. Albany: State University of New York Press.

Penuel, W., & Wertsch, J. (1995). Vygotsky and identity formation: A sociocultural approach. *Educational Psychologist, 30,* 83–92.

U.S. Department of Health and Human Services Web sites: http://www.acf.dhhs.gov/programs/fysb/youthinfo/coverpositveyouth.htm and http://www.acf.dhhs.gov/programs/fysb/Resources-YD.htm

Cultural Studies

Consumer Culture and Critical Thinking

Ian Steinberg

Critical thinking about consumer culture is important for teachers and students since consumerism largely shapes the products, styles, and human interactions in contemporary culture. The knowledge and consciousness created by people acting in concert with consumerism are powerful. If they are confronted critically, they can help us think critically about the relationship between the construction of our identities and larger social entities.

Is consumerism a way of life, a full-time job, an economic model, a blueprint for democracy, a form of fascism, the destruction of the environment, the epitome of a society with no morals, vacuous, spiritually fulfilling, a form of rebellion, or a political movement? The conceptualizations of consumerism are as diverse as the motives for studying consumer culture. To critically reevaluate what consumerism means, one must use all the different and intricate parts of complex critical theory to uncover the threadlike forces that weave the fabric of culture together. In terms of consumer culture, this fabric is 100 percent polyester.

During this article I will answer the central question, what is consumerism? It should be noted that a critical inquiry into consumerism does not involve comparing advertising methods or consumer behavior, but analyzing the concept on societal and structural levels. It is also important to be aware that the way one asks a question determines how the question can be answered. A complex critical inquiry into consumerism requires a multiperspectival approach that recognizes that consumerism is a process composed of multiple, mutually constructive forces and not a singular cause and effect phenomenon. Douglas Kellner defined this type of approach, and a further explanation of it can be found in Joe Kincheloe's introduction to this encyclopedia.

THE UNCRITICAL/TRADITIONAL VIEW OF CONSUMER CULTURE

One of the starting points of a complex critical study of consumerism is the idea that the Industrial Revolution and the development of mass media created a mass culture or consumer culture. Complex critical thinking about consumerism should begin with an examination of the uncritical or traditional economic approach to the subject, which is based on mainstream assumptions about the functional role of the marketplace, consumerism, and advertising. By critically evaluating this traditional approach, we can begin to uncover its foundations and assumptions and their potentially unjust and harmful ramifications for consciousness construction, knowledge production, and the creation of culture.

The traditional approach is very supportive of advertising and mass consumption as vital institutions of a functioning, democratic economy. The advertising industry and its supporters place consumerism right in the heart of American-style democracy. It is a story about the triumph of the consumer—the individual citizen—over the industrial producer. This is a very American myth reflected in many of our cultural and historical heroes, such as the pioneer, the cowboy, the entrepreneur, movie star-presidents.

When American-style democracy is discussed, it is usually in terms of an individual citizen who makes a rational, informed choice, or vote, from a variety of options. Participating in a consumer economy is no less significant, according to uncritical advertising pundits, than participating in democracy. They claim that advertising is vital to a functioning democracy for multiple reasons.

First, advertising serves to inform the consumer/voter. For American-style democracy to function, an informed citizenry is very important and is what separates our rational, democratic process from the irrational authoritarian or communist regimes that rely on personality cults. Therefore, the consumer economy is the *most democratic* system of distribution for social wealth. Consumers vote for the system, and for products, by spending their dollars (also known as marketplace de-

mocracy). According to this line of thinking, if a company is successful, it is primarily because of consumer choice. Critical thinking about consumerism as a democratic system of social distribution questions the links made between consumption/buying/shopping and democracy. Is the marketplace democratic? Why would this discourse circulate?

Second, supporters of the traditional view say that advertising is vital to a functioning democracy as a source of revenue for the media industries. Democracy necessitates information, so a strong and diverse mass media can serve the public interest. Without the revenue of advertising the media would be underfunded and have less resources put to the task of informing the consumers/voters. This account fails to critically consider the many media systems around the world that function just fine without advertising and receive revenues through other forms of funding, such as licenses (England) or fees (Japan) or state support (post-communist Russia). It also fails to consider ad-free media in the U.S., such as public broadcasting or ad-free magazines like *Ms.* or *Z.*

The third point of the traditional argument is that if the media is supported by advertising, it is editorially liberated from government control. The American definition of free speech is better served by a *laissez faire* (hands-free) arrangement between media content and the government. If the government sponsors or produces media, a system must be arranged that would limit the potential for censorship. Therefore, the less a government body is involved in media content the better democracy is served.

Thinking critically about the role of the government in relation to culture might produce a different conclusion. Since the government is already involved in cultural production by regulating cultural industries in ways that encourage big business, critical thinking about this statement would question the notion of censorship and ask whether censorship is necessarily a government-sponsored event or what happens when cultural production is left to big business, which typically ignores people of color, homosexuals, indigenous people, women, and the elderly because they are not usually a profitable market.

Fourth, a vital democracy, from the industry perspective, is better served by a prosperous economy. Advertising is integral to a wealthy society because it inspires market efficiency and competition. Advertising (especially price advertising) inspires competition among producers. This keeps prices low, and product quality high. Producers, to gain the competitive edge, are always seeking new ways to inspire efficiency in the production process, as well as producing better, more desirable products. Without advertising, consumers would not be informed and would not be able to make the most rational choice based on price and quality of a product. Therefore, producers would not be compelled to keep prices competitive, nor would they continue to invest in research and development. The economy would be stagnant, the consumer would suffer, and democracy would be less functional. Traditionalists also claim that advertising contributes to a successful economy by inspiring individual production. When a consumer can see all the market has to offer, then s/he is inspired to work harder and make more money to consume.

The research methodology employed to back up this industry perspective can be generously termed Aristotelian. There is essentially no rigorous or defined research methodology—only a manifest and logical conclusion based on the observation and worldly wisdom of the author. The United States is usually cited as both the supreme example and proof. Quite often decontextualized statistics, procured from a study conducted elsewhere, are incorporated into the argument. John Hood, a researcher who has published many articles about consumerism and advertising from the marketing industry perspective, is the president of the North Carolina–based independent think tank The John Locke Foundation. This type of research is typical of these conservative or libertarian think tanks: it relies more on the perceived credibility of the author or institution than on convincing and rigorous academic research. Think tanks are multimillion dollar nonprofit organizations that reap huge corporate donations and both ignore issues of power and social justice and try to hide or nullify them whenever critical scholars try to bring them up.

In conclusion, the social, cultural, political, and economic implications of the uncritical understanding of consumerism are numerous. According to the uncritical perspective, the greatest political act of an American citizen is shopping. This polemic was heightened after September 11, 2001, when many government and corporate leaders donned American flags and urged people to buy things, to shop—in effect, to consume—patriotism. These real-life calls to shopping were even imported into media culture. For example, in the 2002 season premiere of HBO's *Sex and the City,* the characters discuss supporting New York City after 9/11 by shopping in the city's stores. Why this connection? Critical thinking about the traditional view of consumer culture raises several possible answers.

Luckily, there are many other ways to critically consider consumerism. The three ways I will discuss in this article are an anthropological view, a political/economic view, and a critical cultural perspective. Any one of these approaches can be carried to ever finer and rigorous detail, but the real strength of this inquiry is in the big picture provided by a complex alliance of critical perspectives.

ANTHROPOLOGY OF CONSUMPTION

Critical thinking about consumerism can be furthered by asking anthropological questions about the phenomenon. The anthropological approach is characterized by the work of Mary Douglas and Baron Isherwood (Douglas & Isherwood, 1979). In some ways, their work is the most different from the other categories because their theory is not tied to an industrial, capitalist context. The authors contend that the prevailing economic theories of consumption artificially abstract it from the social scheme and analyze or criticize consumption as only a result or objective of work. They further posit that this abstraction makes it virtually impossible to even begin to understand consumption and have redefined the concept using what they call an anthropology of consumption.

In critically redefining consumption, Douglas and Isherwood examine the possibly deterministic role of commodities, or goods, in culture. They assert that "[c]onsumption is the very arena in which culture is fought over and licked into shape." The authors separate how they conceive of consumption from the traditional economic perspective that focuses on the individual, rational consumer. They argue that consumption exists within two boundaries: first, it is not compelled or coerced, it is an act of free will, and second, consumption takes place at the end of the exchange process. This framework is use-

ful because it fits within many historical contexts, not just the context of a market economy. Since the consumption of goods inhabits a social space relatively free of the necessities of production or commerce, the decisions about how one consumes is "the vital source of the culture of the moment". This is an integral concept in thinking critically about the anthropology of consumption.

According to the critical anthropological view, goods are an *information system*. Since the social function of accumulating and consuming goods is important to the social construction of reality, we literally construct our universe from commodities. This is an important concept that ties the complex critical analysis of consumption to the larger examination of discursive and material forces that constitute human reality. This fundamental assumption is based on the concept that goods "are needed for making visible and stable the categories of culture," and that all possessions are signifiers of meaning and therefore one of their critical functions is communication. One of the aspects of commodities is their use in defining and maintaining social relationships.

There are many instances of this in all cultures—wedding rings and cattle, for example, are both used as goods that signify a nuptial agreement. The use of goods, then, can take on *ritualistic* significance and is one of the "conventions that set up visible public definitions." Quite often the degree of the importance of the ritual is mirrored by the value of the goods representing that particular ritual. The use of goods in ritual is necessarily a social usage, and one that has, conversely, a socialization effect on the participants. By carrying on the traditions of consumption, future generations are acculturated, and thus a continuity of social reality and the creation of culture and tradition are achieved. This creative process is necessarily flexible, is influenced by material reality, and is recreated all the time. "Consumption is an active process in which all the social categories are continually redefined." In this critical light, consumption can be seen as a vital arena in which people make sense of themselves and their social relationships. Ultimately this is a process of making sense of and creating reality.

Critical thinking about consumer culture raises anthropological questions about cultural ritual and tradition, cultural symbolism, cultural performance, and cultural identity formation. When examined in contrast to the traditional view of consumer culture, critical anthropological thinking paints a different picture of consumer culture.

POLITICAL ECONOMY OF CONSUMPTION

Complex critical thinking about consumer culture can also be analyzed through critical political economy, which is based on Marxist theory. Rather than looking at the economy and capitalism as functional, like mainstream economists, political economists see capitalism as ultimately dysfunctional and incapable of creating a stable and just society. According to critical political economy, the basic nature of capitalism undermines democracy. Consumerism, therefore, is not seen as a glowing pinnacle of the golden age of the United States, but as a very problematic and exploitative phenomenon.

Political economy is useful because of the open and manifest nature of its agenda, which is committed to historical analysis, links concerns to a social whole, has a sense of justice and moral philosophy, and

a plan for praxis or social action. Vincent Mosco (1996) provides an excellent summary of the political economic approach.

Many of the concepts in my article in this encyclopedia are part of a political economic approach to consumer ideology on a societal or institutional level of analysis, and can also be used to think critically at the individual level of analysis. Sut Jhally's book *The Codes of Advertising* also brings the debate from an institutional to an individual level of critical analysis when it examines the consumer in a mass media culture (Jhally, 1990). Building on an institutional argument, Jhally looks at two important institutionalizing roles of advertising in the consciousness industry: the commodification of symbolic meaning and communication, and the commodification of audience consciousness. Let us think critically about these concepts.

Commodification means, essentially, the process by which something's importance is no longer determined by its use-value or inherent quality, but rather its exchange-value or what someone will pay for it. Critical political economic thinking about advertising, then, suggests that advertising commodifies communication and cultural artifacts. A television program is determined by its exchange-value, rather than its importance as a cultural expression. Understood critically, because the medium is commodified, the symbolic meaning of the medium is also subjugated to exchange-value. That is, the symbols that people use to make meaning and fulfill the need for cultural expression are not available based on how useful they are in making sense of the world, but in how well they inspire and manipulate the need to consume commodities (commodity fetishism). Jhally calls this phenomenon a "double subsumation of use-value to exchange value," which is a central concept in a complex critical conceptualization of the social role of advertising in consumer culture.

The other commodifying role of advertising is the valorization of audience consciousness, or turning the consciousness of an individual audience member into a commodity. This unusual concept draws upon Marxist labor/capital dialectics. It is a popular cultural belief that most media are, if not free, at least heavily subsidized by advertising revenue, and that this is a gift to the audience. In a Marxist universe there is no audience, there are workers and nothing is *ever* free. The labor/capital dialectic describes a constant struggle over who gets to keep surplus value. In this theory, labor is the only thing that can create any value. After a worker on a given work day has worked long enough to produce enough revenue to pay for his/her own labor (wage), anything produced on top of this is surplus value, or profit.

Applying this theory to an audience, Jhally argues that watching TV is actually a form of unpaid labor. The individual's job is to watch television commercials, and the wage is the pleasure or gratification gained from watching the content. There are two products of this work. First, there is a very tangible and valuable item known as ratings—the eyeballs of advertisers. The ratings help advertisers create the second product—commodity fetishism—or the manipulation of desire for the commodities being sold (defined by Jhally in terms of both Marxism and psychoanalysis).

Critical thinkers examining consumer culture from a political economic perspective ask questions about the relationship between cultural creators, cultural consumers, and cultural products and try to determine who benefits from consumer society and mass culture. Critical political economic thinking calls into question the innocence of consumer culture. If injustice exists, critical political economic thinkers ask us to challenge the relationship between producer, citizen, and content.

CRITICAL CULTURAL CONCEPTION OF CONSUMPTION

I call this final approach to critical thinking about consumer culture critical cultural thinking, since it is more concerned with the nature of culture in consumer society than the culture's origins and functions. Thomas Frank, in his 1997 book *The Conquest of Cool*, thinks mass media culture and advertising are a way of examining the nature of consumerism because they can be seen as both reflections of consumer culture and guiding forces in sustaining and developing consumerism.

The Conquest of Cool, according to Frank, has a double meaning. If one focuses on the word conquest and interprets the phrase as a taking over that which is cool or hip, Frank says that is an example of the co-optation theory, or the belief that when the Establishment is faced with dissent, it responds by absorbing or appropriating the emblems, symbols, and *style* of the dissent. This nullifies the political threat of rebellion by turning the dissent into "harmless consumer commodities, emptied of content, and sold to their very originators as substitutes for the real thing." Frank also asks the reader to also critically think about the second meaning, or the use of the word cool as a powerful agent in the equation. When looked at from this angle, the conquest was not necessarily the colonization of Hiplandia by the gray flannel-suited conquistadors of Madison Avenue; but the rise of the new social hegemony of Hip Consumerism. This new consumer ideology is "the public philosophy of the age of flexible accumulation [the post-Fordist economy]."

Frank's metaphor is focused on the machinery of the culture industry itself rather than the operators, what he calls the "cultural perpetual motion machine." This machine has two primary, binary components: a square cog and a hip cog. The square cog is the cultural myth of the conformity-obsessed consumerism of the past. A vision constructed in the popular memory (largely by mass media—especially advertising) of the idyllic, suburban, self-surveillance culture of Mr. and Mrs. Jones. It is a way of thinking that fears social ostracism more than anything else, and leads its subscribers to live in orthodox, commodity-centered conformity. Mr. and Mrs. Jones lead a crass and soulless existence that does not include authentic emotion. The concept of youthful rebellion, embodied in the twentieth century by the counterculture movement of the 1960s, is the hip cog in the machine. The sixties youth, like Prometheus of ancient Greek mythology, rescued themselves (and thus society) from the cold, unauthentic future of consumer suburbia by embracing the authentic existence of Hipness. Being Hip meant striving for instant personal gratification and dropping out of the Protestant work ethic value system of middle America. According to the theory, becoming Hip is the only way to save one's soul in the modern consumer world. The binary of Square versus Hip is the dialectical apparatus of the cultural, perpetual motion machine.

Being Hip does not necessarily mean acquiring all the trappings and styles of Hipness. For Hip consumer ideology to work, all that is required is the individual's identification with, or understanding of, Hipness. Through this understanding, people can experience a vicarious rebellion against Squareness. When critically understood, this cultural development is a windfall for capitalism. Essentially, by redefining leisure-time consumption as rebelling against the system, two major problems of late capitalism are resolved. The first is the belief in continual revolution that gives a renewed and strengthened meaning to planned obsolescence. The second is resolution of the contradiction between the conservative values that are necessary for maintaining the status quo of the capitalist production system versus the hedonistic values of consumption. The opportunity to consume one's dissent is a liberating experience for the individual that reinforces the dominance of the capitalist system. Transforming the energy of rebellion against the capitalist system into energy motivating consumption is the ultimate efficiency of capitalism.

Within this system, new dissent is co-opted, packaged, depoliticized, and sold. The latest instance is the commodification of the anti-globalization movement and protest through commercials for a variety of products, from tea (Lipton) to banking accounts (Washington Mutual). Future youth and activist movements should be aware of how the system operates.

Ultimately, Frank is saying that the cultural resonance of business culture and counterculture lead to the creation of a new hegemony of Hip consumerism. He critically conceptualizes this machine, built by unguided collaboration, as an entity unto itself, working by the very designs of capitalism and outside the ability of any particular group or individual to totally control.

TOWARD A COMPLEX CRITICAL UNDERSTANDING OF CONSUMERISM

In addition to the traditional economic approach, I have outlined several distinct critical approaches to consumerism that contradict each other. To make sense of these different concepts and be able to think in a critical and complex manner about consumerism, we should put these theories together.

In the traditional economic approach we ask whether the marketplace is slanted towards competition or monopoly. Imagine the ramifications for the rhetoric of democracy depending on how one answers that question! If we use the anthropological approach, we ask about an item's symbolic cultural meaning, or the shared interpretation of the object by the cultural group. This meaning is assigned by people—but people are also socialized to the meaning by the use of the good. If we use the critical political economic approach, there are several viewpoints from which to choose. We can use the Marxist dialectic of capital and labor or the theory of the agency of the individual within the institution, which leads to questions about ideology and hegemony (which are necessarily dialectical inquiries). In the critical cultural approach, we can use Frank's square/hip theory and whether popular culture is reflected by or guided by the mass media. Thinking critically about consumerism means thinking critically about what forces are at play in society and where the society's power bases are located.

COMPLEX CRITICAL THINKING ABOUT CONSUMER CULTURE: IN THE CLASSROOM

Thinking about consumer culture in a complex critical way is useful in the classroom for many reasons, but especially because the cultural world in which students and teachers live is largely shaped by consumer culture. Our consciousness and identities are constructed in relation to consumption.

Critical thinking about the consumer culture might begin by engaging students in dialogue about their desires in relation to the mass media and advertising. Students could also be asked to name aspects of their lives that are not consumer-driven or to imagine non-consumerist ways of existing. Research projects could be assigned that get students to think critically about a well-known commodity (like name brand clothing or fast food). They could read about the production of the item, the advertising, and could interview people that use the commodity. These projects could help them to start to think critically about advertising, commodities, and their impact on wider social relationships.

References

Douglas, M., & Isherwood, B. (1979). *The world of goods*. New York: Basic Books.

Frank, T. (1997). *The conquest of cool*. Chicago: University of Chicago Press.

Jhally, S. (1990). *The codes of advertising*. New York: Routledge.

Mosco, V. (1996). *The poltiical economy of communication: Rethinking and renewal*. London: Sage.

Further Reading

Schiller, H. (1989). *Culture inc: The corporate takeover of public expression*. New York: Oxford University Press.

Cultural Studies in Education

Handel Kashope Wright

CULTURAL STUDIES IN EDUCATION: THE NEW KID ON THE BLOCK?

Cultural studies in education is a progressive approach to education that is at once new and not so new; a continuation of critical education and a break from previous critical approaches, and a single approach that is a blend of two multifaceted approaches. Because it operates almost exclusively in higher education, it has untapped potential in the adult education and K-12 classroom.

This introduction introduces cultural studies, outlines the emergence of cultural studies in contemporary critical education, presents the concept of critical thinking that dovetails with cultural studies, and provides a few examples of what cultural studies in education looks like and how it can contribute to education that promotes and reflects critical thinking and social justice pedagogy.

There have been various versions of progressive and critical approaches to education developed and/or utilized in the United States and Canada, from the progressive education movement at the turn of the last century to the wide array of contemporary approaches (feminist, antiracist, queer, multicultural, and critical theory and pedagogies). This multiplicity of approaches is made more complex by the fact that they all incorporate each other, both in theory and classroom practice (i.e., critical approaches to multiculturalism deal not only with race and culture but also with gender, social class and sexual orientation).

One would be tempted to think critical educators would have their hands full theorizing about and putting into practice this multiple and intersecting set of approaches. Instead, dissatisfaction with existing forms has led to both the proliferation of new forms and the development of new approaches. For instance, in reaction to dominant liberal multiculturalism, critical educators in the United States have developed critical and revolutionary multiculturalism, while in Canada they have turned away from multiculturalism to develop anti-racism.

Cultural studies theory and cultural pedagogy emerged in North America in the mid-1990s and are fast becoming the approach of choice for critical educators in both Canada and the United States who find the theory and pedagogy of multiculturalism and critical pedagogy inadequate or inappropriate for their purposes. Since the turn to cultural studies in the mid-1990s, there have been developments such as the establishment of cultural studies focuses in the colleges of education of institutions like the Ontario Institute for Studies in Education at the University of Toronto and the University of California at Los Angeles, and actual departments and programs of cultural studies at the University of Tennessee and the Ohio State University. Also, exciting new journals such as the *Review of Education/Pedagogy/Cultural Studies* and *Taboo: The Journal of Education and Culture* have emerged. Finally, papers and panels on cultural studies issues appear with increasing frequency on the programs of major conferences such as the American Educational Research Association, the American Educational Studies Association, and the *Journal of Curriculum Theorizing* conference. It would appear that the introduction of cultural studies to K-12 classrooms and adult education courses is all but inevitable.

Although cultural studies in education is relatively new, the relationship between cultural studies and education started in the 1940s and 1950s, and was well established and firmly in place when cultural studies got its name and was first institutionalized at the University of Birmingham, England in the early 1960s. Although they were unsuccessful, it is interesting to note that there were attempts to introduce cultural studies into the secondary school curriculum in pre-Thatcherite Britain.

This introduction raises at least two important questions. First, why are cultural studies emerging as a critical education approach of choice, competing with and perhaps threatening to displace more established forms such as multiculturalism and critical pedagogy? Second, how can cultural studies be conceptualized and put into practice as an approach to education that promotes critical thinking and social justice pedagogy?

WHAT IS CULTURAL STUDIES?

The discourse of cultural studies being discussed here is not the general study of culture nor the study of intercultural relations nor the anthropological study of culture; it is a relatively new discourse that had its institutional origins at the Centre for Contemporary Cultural Studies (CCCS) at the University of Birmingham, England in the 1960s. The British intellectuals that gave cultural studies its name and set up the CCCS as the first named

center of cultural studies were interested in developing a discourse that would allow them to undertake progressive activism in an academic setting and pursue specific projects that addressed pressing issues of social justice in and through culture in ways that were not constrained by the limits of specific disciplines. They considered the project and its questions and issues to be more important than the limits disciplines tend to place on what one could ask or what one could bring to bear in attempting to answer questions from within an individual discipline.

What they developed as a consequence was a new academic field that was not merely interdisciplinary but also anti-disciplinary, one that examined how power operated in culture and society and represented and championed the oppressed and marginalized of society. They drew from various disciplines, undertook mainly qualitative studies, read and utilized the latest theory and created theories of their own, and generally worked for progressive social change. Initially this meant undertaking such projects as drawing on education and sociology to examine and critique the educational policies of both the post–Second World War Labour and consequent Thatcherite Conservative governments, using Neo-Marxist and race theory to address the police brutality towards Black and working class populations, retelling history from the perspective of the working class, living with and studying hippies and the hippie movement, and formulating theories on how media operated and blending these with political economy to understand how meaning in/of television shows and films was encoded (by the industry) and decoded (by the audience).

Once cultural studies was established as a discourse that dealt primarily with issues of social class, feminist and race theory and politics were used to strongly introduce women and gender issues, and Blacks and race issues, and thus intervene in cultural studies itself and change the field from within.

The discipline that emerged from that wide variety of work was hard to define. As the cultural studies movement has spread around the world, it has taken on additional topics and placed less emphasis on old ones, which has made arriving at a definitive description of the field even more challenging. Cultural studies is now so notoriously difficult to define that this characteristic has, interestingly, become the most frequently employed definition. It is important to note that cultural studies is not difficult to define because no one knows what it is, but because it is different things to different people. The following are eight (sometimes diverging, often converging) ways in which cultural studies can legitimately be defined:

1. It is a way of studying formerly neglected subjects (for example, working class people's perspectives on historical events).
2. It is a means of taking seriously what has been traditionally deemed unworthy of serious study by academia, such as pop music and concerts, hip-hop culture, movies and videos, television and the televisual, sports, advertising, shopping malls, shopping and the culture of consumption, and other elements of popular culture.
3. It is a way of bringing out and taking seriously the perspectives of previously marginalized groups in society, such as by writing herstories (history from women's perspectives).
4. It is the ethnographic study of culture (observing a rave) and participating in one's culture (playing and teaching baseball).
5. It is a way of taking up projects that will address issues of social justice and radical democracy, such as discrimination based on race, gender, social class, sexual orientation.
6. It is a way of dealing with culture in the so-called postmodern age, when the grand narratives (God, Truth, History) have either been abandoned or heavily revised.
7. It is using critical theory to design a sociopolitical project for social justice ends.
8. It is intellectual/political activism heavily informed by theory.
9. It is the study of identity (social, cultural, national, regional) and one's individual and group place in community, society, and the globe, especially in relation to the distribution of power.
10. It is the study of the production, reception, and use of texts wherever the culture perceives texts to be (e.g., studying how TV shows are made, how their meaning is produced, and how the audience makes use of them as texts).

While all these definitions are valid, they are quite disparate and far from cohesive. Different cultural studies theorists and workers would emphasize or reject different aspects of these definitions. As Stuart Hall concludes, "Cultural studies is not one thing. It has never been one thing" (Hall, 1990, p. 11). Also, definitions change as the field continues to evolve, so any definition should be put forward with extreme caution. A primary reason why most people avoid providing a definition of cultural studies is because they are afraid of limiting the openness which is the heart of the discipline.

CULTURAL STUDIES AND CRITICAL THINKING

How can the field of cultural studies be an approach to education that promotes and reflects critical thinking and social justice? The answer lies in how critical thinking is conceptualized, how teachers and students position themselves in relation to the pedagogical situation, and indeed what is seen to constitute the pedagogical situation.

The version of critical thinking that dovetails well with cultural studies is one that does not see thinking as separate from action but as both a form of action and as joined with action and even activism. It is a form of critical thinking that is open, that is about thinking things through, and teaching and learning beyond the prescribed curriculum and formal space of school and schooling. It is about teachers who think in terms of a critical pedagogy rather than teaching (the difference being that teaching is about the techniques for passing on knowledge to learners while critical pedagogy takes into account the larger goal of what that knowledge will be used for—maintaining the status quo or questioning the status quo and promoting progressive change). It is a form of critical thinking that has both teacher and students working with sociocultural differences progressively rather than denying these difference or using them negatively in the classroom to further marginalize those who are already marginalized in society.

Cultural studies works best with critical thinking when the latter is seen not as an individualized activity with personal growth and individual enlightenment as endpoints, but as individual growth for communal benefit—the individual's contribution to group, community, and societal strategies for societal freedom, social justice, and equality. Cultural studies both demands and supports a version of critical thinking that has both teachers and students constantly asking questions about equity, power, and social and cultural differences. In short, cultural studies works best with a concept of critical thinking that is praxis-oriented, both psychological and social, questions the status quo, and supports strategies for promoting social justice, equity, and a free society.

CULTURAL PEDAGOGY AND CRITICAL THINKING

Each of the ten definitions of cultural studies provided above can help develop the existing pedagogical strategies that are based on them. The following are a few concrete examples of what a cultural studies approach to pedagogy that dovetails with critical thinking would look like in the classroom.

One example is classroom pedagogy that involves new media. Most educational systems that use computers see computers as instruments located in the classroom (or some other physical space) that can be used to search for traditional knowledge (even if that knowledge is presented in a non-traditional form). A cultural studies approach would point out that computers also allow students an entryway into cyberspace as an alternative "space without space" and allow students to explore new identities and become part of cyber communities.

A second example draws on the cultural studies emphasis on praxis and the conception of critical thinking as a combination of thinking and action. These complementary notions mean that the teacher would try to find out-of-school praxis activities for students that would provide experiential learning and allow them to think about their social identities, the relationship between school and the community, and issues of social justice. One good way to do this would be to incorporate service learning for social justice into the curriculum, since service learning involves students going outside the classroom, learning by doing, addressing issues of social justice, and thinking about relations between the school and the community.

A third example would be to use a multidisciplinary approach to address cultural studies dilemmas. The cultural studies and critical thinking classroom would be one where the teacher and the students draw on different disciplines to solve complex problems. For example, a Murder Mystery could involve students dressing up and acting out the roles of the murder suspects (drama), drawing sketches of the suspects from eyewitness accounts (art), and taking (fake) blood samples from the scene for analysis (chemistry), etc. What would enhance critical thinking in such an environment is making this process transparent and having students reflect on it. They should be invited to consider how much more productive and richer this approach is than addressing the problem from one discipline alone.

THE FUTURE OF CULTURAL STUDIES IN EDUCATION

Most accounts of the origin of cultural studies assert that it started with a series of crises in the humanities and social sciences in the 1950s and 1960s. In part because of this conception, cultural studies has remained largely an interdisciplinary approach to studying culture at the level of higher education. Raymond Williams who is widely acknowledged to be one of the three founders of cultural studies (the others being Edward P. Thompson and

Richard Hoggart), has repeatedly acknowledged that cultural studies started, in fact, with work in the 1940s and 1950s in adult education classes on town planning, film, radio, and newspapers (Williams, 1989). Faced with the depressing instrumentalism that was being imposed by the Thatcher government on vocational education in the United Kingdom in the 1980s, Raymond Williams was surprisingly optimistic (Williams, 1989). He declared that this was precisely the time to stress a cultural studies approach to education. Perhaps even more surprisingly, he declared that the future of cultural studies lay not in the universities and purely theoretical work, but in the very place it started, in a politicized approach to adult and vocational education.

For those engaged or interested in critical approaches to education in North America, Williams' vision ought to provide considerable hope in the current depressing environment of calls to go back to basics and have standardized tests dictate the content of and our approach to education. In a broader version of Williams' vision, this is perhaps the ideal time for a turn to cultural studies in education to foster critical thinking and promote social justice in and through education.

References

Hall, S. (1990). The emergence of cultural studies and the crisis of the humanities. *October, 53,* 11–90.

Williams, R. (1989). *The future of cultural studies. The politics of modernism: Against the new conformists.* London: Verso.

Further Reading

CCCS Education Group 2. (1991). *Education limited: Schooling, training and the new right in England since 1979.* London: Unwin Hyman.

Giroux, H., & Shannon, P. (Eds.). (1997). *Education and cultural studies: Toward a performative practice*. New York: Routledge.

Gray, A., & McGuigan, J. (Eds.). (1993). *Studying culture: An introductory reader*. London: Edward Arnold.

Storey, J. (Ed.). (1996). *What is cultural studies?: A reader*. London: Edward Arnold.

Wright, H. (2000). "Pressing, promising, and paradoxical": Larry Grossberg on the relationship between cultural studies and education. *Review of Education/Pedagogy/Cultural Studies, 22* (1), 1–25.

Popular Culture

Shirley R. Steinberg

How do we think about popular culture? How do we make that which entertains us part of the critical contextualization of our world? Does the ever-changing nature of popular culture devalue its importance for critical thinking? In this chapter, I will discuss popular culture, its impact on our lives, and ways in which we can both enjoy and think critically about culture which is popular.

Culture may be the most ambiguous and complex term to define in the domain of the social sciences and humanities. Arthur Asa Berger estimates that anthropologists alone have offered more than one hundred definitions of culture. I use the term in this chapter to signify behavior patterns socially acquired and transmitted by the use of social symbols such as language, art, science, morals, values, belief systems, politics, and many more. Culture is transmitted by teaching and learning, whether formally (in schools) or informally by wider social processes like popular culture, and teachers should be directly involved in cultural analysis. This pedagogical dynamic within popular culture is a central concern in critical thinking. Culture is inseparable from the human ability to be acculturated, to learn, and to employ language and symbols.

Another usage of the term culture involves its deployment in connection with the arts. This is where we move into the social territory traditionally referred to as elite or high culture and that which is referred to as low, or popular culture. Individuals who attend symphonies, read great books, and enjoy traditional European ballet are thought of as being cultured individuals. Many scholars assert that entertainment forms that grow within a local or regional movement (such as square dancing and Celtic music) are examples of low culture. Mass culture does not fit into either category. Cultural theorists do not agree on any one definition for each type of culture. The following is D. MacDonald's summary of the difference between the three cultural types, and the propensity for all types of culture to become political:

Folk art grew from below. It was a spontaneous, autonomous expression of the people, shaped by themselves, pretty much without the benefit of High Culture, to suit their own needs. Mass Culture is imposed from above. It is fabricated by technicians hired by businessmen; its audiences are passive consumers, their participation limited to the choice between buying and not buying . . . Folk Art was the people's own institution, their private little garden walled off from the great formal park of their master's High Culture. But Mass Culture breaks down the wall, integrating the masses into a debased form of High Culture and thus becoming an instrument of political domination. (MacDonald, 1957)

Different culture scholars maintain that the difference between elite/high culture and popular/low culture is blurring. This holds important ramifications for those interested in critical thinking. Popular culture defies easy definition. The term can refer to the culture of ordinary people: TV shows, films, records/CD's, radio, food, fashion, magazines, and other artifacts that figure in our everyday lives. Often analysts say such artifacts are low culture and maintain that they are created by the mass media and consumed by large numbers of individuals on a continuing basis. Academicians view them as unworthy subjects of scholarly analysis.

This chapter is not designed to engage in the argument about where popular culture should be categorized, but to discuss how we incorporate the influence and knowledge from popular culture into our critical thinking about the world. It is the social, political, and pedagogical messages contained in popular culture, and the effects of these messages, that are viewed as some of the most important influences in the contemporary era. The study of popular culture is connected with the sociology of every day life and the interaction and interconnection of this micro-domain with macro-sociopolitical and structural forces. Thus, the popular domain—as ambiguous and ever-shifting as it may be—takes on unprecedented importance in the electronically saturated contemporary era.

Critically thinking about popular culture involves educating the public that what is being consumed as culture is, indeed, important and that it does influence us. One can only look to the millions of

dollars spent daily by corporations to advertise products to gauge this importance. If advertising were not successful, it would be eliminated, and if popular culture was not attended to, it would cease to exist.

Much of the time we do not think about the thinking involved in our consumption of popular culture. In today's society we meet popular culture as we wake up each day. We confront and absorb popular culture as we listen to the radio when we dress, as we read the advertisements on cereal boxes as we eat, as we put on name-brand label clothes, drive in well-advertised cars, view large billboards, walk past windows displaying merchandise, keyboard on a computer with a logo and specific programs, eat at well-known restaurants, and make plans for an evening to view a contemporary event. Our lives are surrounded by the culture of the popular. We should be educated to establish the same kind of critical consumption of popular culture as we have created to evaluate financial consumption.

Critically thinking about popular culture can be taught while the entertainment elements of the popular culture are retained. The point of thinking critically about popular culture is not to censor or eliminate the cultural artifact, but to allow the influence of popular culture to take a critical place within our lives. To do this, I propose a four-level way of critically reading and understanding popular culture. Teachers will be able to lead students through a critical discussion of different types of popular culture without leveling an aesthetic value judgment on the students. Often students are wary of discussions about the cultures they value and see teachers/parents as attempting to undermine what they enjoy. By approaching popular culture in a critical way, classrooms become critically based research centers where popular culture is shared, enjoyed, critically discussed, and evaluated.

We do not have to try to create a critical study of a popular culture artifact or movement since specific cultural, power-related, and pedagogical issues are always present in films, TV, music, art, and all other popular cultural objects. Along with discussing the affective nature and personal appeal of a popular culture artifact, we can also examine its ideological dimensions by studying it in relation to themes of social history and cultural theory.

Taking a popular film as our artifact of examination, we enter into the critical discussion with our students by first examining what is it that we saw and heard. This opening step is designed to look at the obvious, the surface, and to discuss exactly what it was we viewed and absorbed in the film. This discussion allows the students to act as experts as they retell the scenes and dialogue and remind each other about different situations. This is the step that will focus the discussion and make its subject matter clear.

The second step is research-oriented. The author or director and the history and creation of the film should be examined to take the discussion from the students and teacher to the movie's historical context. Why was it written and produced? Who were the key authors and players in the film? Who was the audience? Where was the film made? What were the financial agreements involved in the film? What studio backed the film? Were there unusual or extraordinary events in the creation of the film?

The third step is examining the audience. As we think critically about this film, we realize that it cannot be separated from who is watching it. We must ask questions about the viewers. Why was the film viewed? Where was it viewed? How was it released? Was the film advertised and promoted? How was it advertised and promoted and who was the target audience? How was the film received? Did the critics view the film differently than the audience? This step also involves research in popular media like the Internet, magazines, and newspapers.

The fourth and final step in thinking critically about a film is to take the three previous categories and discuss and analyze how they intersect and what thoughts and meanings they produce about the film's creation. By looking at who produced and acted in the film, we are able to make some observations about the assumptions studios are making about us, the viewers. We can continue these observations as we look at the promotion of the film and how it is received. How does this film shape our consciousness and our sense of self? As we discuss these thoughts with our students, we can critically deconstruct the intent of the film and its actual effect. Naturally, these discussions will change as we move through the critical journey with our students.

Thinking critically about popular culture is not designed to produce a final answer or judgment on the worthiness of the product: that discussion lies within the personal, within our own taste and desires. As teachers we can only hope to lead our students into critically examining the history of the artifact, the production of the artifact, the appeal of the artifact, the consumption of the artifact, and finally, the students' own critically-based and informed understanding of the artifact. If we attempt to change students' minds about the cultural product or to indoctrinate them, we will fail miserably. We must be acutely aware of the importance of popular culture to our students, aware of its impact, aware of how easy it is to access, and aware that many students are cautious of adult interpretations of anything they enjoy. We do not want to engage in a judgmental alienation of something that students see as worthy and essential to their daily lives.

As critical educators, our work should be to help students become informed consumers. Many times the ideological intentions of the creators of popular culture are less than worthy, and students fall victim to these intentions without the critical tools to question and combat them. Critical thinking about popular culture empowers our students to be educated and knowledgeable consumers, ready to make their own decisions about what it is that will entertain and engage them.

Reference

MacDonald, D. (1957). "A theory of mass culture." In B. Rosenberg, & D. White (Eds.), *Mass Culture*. Glencoe, IL: Free Press.

Further Reading

Berger, A. (1995). *Cultural criticism: A primer of key concepts*. Thousand Oaks, CA: Sage.
Grossberg, L. (1995). "What's in a name (one more time)." *Taboo: The Journal of Culture and Education,* Spring, 1–37.
Steinberg, S. R., & Kincheloe, J. L. (1997). *Kinderculture: The corporate construction of childhood*. Boulder, CO: Westview Press.

Curriculum

Curriculum Theorizing

Kenneth Teitelbaum

The fact that the universe of knowledge is ever-expanding but there is a relatively constant, limited amount of time (and capacity) available to learn it creates a central question for any society: what knowledge is most valuable and should be taught in its educational system? To answer this question, several other questions must be asked. What are the goals of education? Who should be involved in the selection of knowledge to be taught? Why teach X rather than Y, and what are the consequences of such choices? How should the knowledge chosen be organized to create a coherent whole? Who should have access to what knowledge? What principles should govern the teaching of what has been selected? Thoughtful decisions are not easy because they are always about which viable possibilities among many to choose and which to eliminate from consideration. Critical thinking about curriculum means taking into account the actual human environment involved, the individual and collective biographies of students and teachers, and the wider society of which schools are a part.

The curriculum is of great significance because in its everyday implementation it does not merely imply but actually teaches versions of the good society, and both who and what are good in life and who and what are not. It represents a kind of battleground for the hearts and minds of children and youth, in which contrasting messages of who we are and what we should become, both individually and as a society, are played out. Decisions about what to teach are inevitably based on theories and values about a host of interests, including usefulness, morality, fairness, imagination, freedom, and community. It is vital for knowledge and ways of knowing to be considered social as well as individual constructions, and always as partial and relational.

Curriculum always involves definition, re-definition, and negotiation. Educators who engage in critical thinking ask not just how to teach (do) X better, but also the reasons for, nature, and consequences of teaching X in the first place.

Curriculum theorizing is the process educators engage in when they consider the many different aspects of how to teach, what to teach, and why they should teach it. This is a complex process because the curriculum itself is a multifaceted phenomenon, influencing and influenced by important cultural and political dynamics. Focusing on the intersection and interaction of four commonplaces (the learner, the subject matter, the teacher, and the milieu in which education takes place), curriculum theorizing draws on various fields of study, such as philosophy, political and social theory, psychology, art and literature, and ecology.

Each educator's initial approach to curriculum probably stems from his or her identification of the most salient issues or problems to be addressed. Basic literacy skills, personal development, good citizenship, cultural competence, or critical thinking have all commanded considerable attention among competing educational interest groups during the last 100 years, including the classical humanists, social efficiency educators, child-centered progressives, and social reconstructionists (Kliebard, 1995). The fast pace, unpredictability, and uniqueness of school environments add to the complexity of curriculum theorizing, making it impossible to develop a foolproof curriculum that can be used for any and all educational settings; and yet without such theorizing we are prone to acting haphazardly and without reflection about educational concerns that are crucial to ourselves personally and to the larger social world.

Critical thinking about curriculum theorizing means being aware of at least three conceptual difficulties. There are, for example, longstanding disputes about the definition of *curriculum* itself. The term is notoriously ambiguous, with a lack of agreement marking the professional field from its very beginning in the early twentieth century. These disagreements, which are rich and complex and highlight the dynamic and fluid nature of curriculum work, have major implications for the study, im-

plementation, and assessment of educational practice. To define curriculum as "a structured series of intended learning outcomes," for example, leads to a different kind of deliberation than to define it as "what students have opportunities to learn under the auspices of schools." The first may lead to a more narrow focus on the specifics of what is organized for classroom teaching (the explicit or official curriculum); the second may include a wider range of school activities, including ones that are not consciously planned (the hidden curriculum) and that do not take place in the classroom itself.

There are also differences regarding the nature of *theorizing.* Some educators look to the natural sciences or mathematics for guidance, an approach that may place particular value on predictability and certainty. Others look to the social sciences, philosophy, or art and literature, placing more of an emphasis on teaching as an art or craft and the personal experience of theorizing. Indeed, curriculum theorists as a group have not come to a consensus about the precise nature of their theorizing, with striking differences taking place between the descriptive school that tries to explain and predict the events in a curriculum without concern for values, and the normative/prescriptive school that focuses on the articulation and justification of a set of values.

In the past, educators tended to adopt a positivistic view of theorizing, based on accumulated and precise observations and data collection, objective validation, and logical conclusions. But alternative approaches to theorizing—ones more compatible with the actual activities of teaching—have emerged more prominently during the last several decades. These theories embrace a more relational perspective, taking into greater account the individual circumstances of the observer and school participant and the larger social, political, economic, ideological, and historical contexts within which she or he observes and acts. The current situation is thus more fluid and fragmented, with influences of phenomenology, neo-Marxism, critical pragmatism, multiple feminisms, postmodernism, poststructuralism, critical race theory, postcolonial emphases, queer theory, theology, aesthetic theory, cultural studies, and other bodies of work adding to the mix once dominated by scientific curriculum making and the Tyler Rationale.

In addition to the lack of agreement about the definition of curriculum and the nature of theorizing, there are many educators, in both the university and the school settings, who challenge the value of curriculum theorizing. One secondary school English teacher, with doctorate in hand and plans to be a university educator, recently remarked, "I get lost very easily and bored," suggesting that in most cases such theorizing is too removed from educational practice to be worth the time and effort spent on it. To be sure, the structure of schooling that exists today tends to mitigate against such theorizing (and critical thinking in general). In response, perhaps, some scholars who embrace curriculum theorizing have referred to something else, such as curriculum work, inquiry, study, or wisdom. Perhaps renaming it will enable educators to engage in it more willingly, or otherwise transform its nature into something more appealing to practitioners, to inquiry taking place alongside action.

The word theory comes from the Greek word *theoria,* which means wakefulness of mind. It involves a continuing process of critical questioning and interpretation that one might argue is necessary for all teachers as they strive to identify

and deal with the problems and dilemmas of everyday school and classroom life. Indeed, for those who challenge the notion of teaching as a narrowly applied, technical activity—and who at the same time seek to reform the school culture to allow for and encourage more teacher reflection—theorizing (and research) is viewed as central to the art and craft of teaching itself. Moreover, as French mathematician and philosopher Blaise Pascal suggested, "to reject philosophy is already to philosophize."

Although embraced at different levels of self-awareness, theorizing of some kind cannot be absent from our deliberations. We are always trying to make sense of our world—always theorizing—and in so doing, we are already deeply positioned in some way. We simply cannot escape theory (and the values implicit in theories) in our work as educators.

Theorizing is no longer considered the sole province of intellectuals or even of universities: everyone has a set of theories that helps to explain the world and helps to discover and confirm our meanings of it. These theories are necessary to make sense of experience, to make and see connections between and among the events that define our lives, individually and collectively, and to represent practice. Theory can provide a kind of intellectual coherence, enabling us to probe more deeply and insightfully into the practice we observe and engage in. Theories are always evolving. They are never fixed or final and never an exact science, and therefore the extent to which they can explain and guide our practice is limited. Nevertheless, they can and do serve as a basis for choices and actions. It is important to be aware of how particular theories, in their inevitable incompleteness, obscure or blur the phenomena being addressed. The key is to be critical thinkers of curriculum theorizing. We need to be more self-aware, reflective, and knowledgeable about how theories contribute to our understanding and practice, and what they can and cannot explain.

Theoretical inquiry has a vital role to play within the domain of schooling, on all levels, for teachers as well as those more removed from classroom practice. Even the most practical among us are guided by theories. Theory (inquiry) and practice (action) are in fact interdependent; they interpenetrate in active ways and are embedded in one another. This is not to say that theorizing cannot exist apart from practice, that it cannot reside a distance away that allows us to step back from the immediacy of direct experience and critically interrogate the common-sense, taken-for-granted assumptions of our work. Indeed, this is one of the contributions that theory can make: it helps us to think more deeply, coherently, and contextually about, for example, the "it" of the common pronouncement, "It works." For this reason, and for the enhancement of democratic social relations, scholars need to acknowledge and facilitate theorizing on the part of teachers at the same time that teachers assert the need for scholars to address the practical implications of their inquiries.

While teachers need to be proficient in the technical skills of curriculum planning, development, and evaluation, curriculum theorizing—or coming to deeper insights and more powerful and coherent principles about what is and should be taught to whom—is a primary activity of the thoughtful, critical educator. It is certainly not worth teaching well what is not worth teaching. Dewey says that one should not teach what is mis-educative ("has the effect of arresting or distorting the growth of further experience") or non-educative

("having no significant effect on the individual one way or the other") (Dewey, 1938, p. 25). Educators influenced by critical theories extend that argument and say that school knowledge should be guided by the ideals of democracy, justice and equality, and one should examine all knowledge for its emancipatory or repressive potential and its opposition to racist, sexist, classist, and other biases and oppressions if one wants to improve the human condition.

Curriculum theorizing can be a difficult process that provokes more questions than it answers; but it is a crucial component of critical thinking about education because it provides a lens through which one can more comprehensively address the issues and problems of curriculum development. It helps the educator more self-consciously relate experience and observations not only to meaningful educational principles and goals, but also to the ethical values and social practices embedded within all forms of schooling. In the end, as Dewey suggested, curriculum theory is the most practical of things, enabling us to widen and deepen our reflections on the world of concrete experience, disrupting that which is taken for granted and opening up considerations and possibilities that might otherwise remain unknown.

References

Dewey, J. (1938). *Experience and education.* New York: Collier Books.
Kliebard, H. (1995). *The struggle for the American curriculum, 1893–1958.* New York: Routledge.

Further Reading

Beyer, L., & Apple, M. W. (Eds.). (1998). *The curriculum: Problems, politics, and possibilities.* Albany: State University of New York Press.

Flinders, D., & Thornton, S. (Eds.). (1997). *The curriculum studies reader.* New York: Routledge.

Pinar, W., Reynolds, W., Slattery, P., & Taubman, P. (1995). *Understanding curriculum: An introduction to the study of historical and contemporary curriculum discourses.* New York: Peter Lang.

Developing Curriculum and Critical Pedagogy

Leila E. Villaverde

What makes pedagogy critical? What are the tools you'll need and what do you need to think about? These questions are examples of some very common concerns teachers have as they think about critical pedagogy, critical thinking, and curriculum. To understand how critical pedagogy intersects with your discipline and/or grade level, we must first define critical pedagogy and critical thinking. This entry will define, explain, and provide possibilities for developing critical pedagogy in the classroom.

We tend to think curriculum is what we teach, the standards, the lesson plan, and the manuscript we follow in the classroom; but that is only one part of what constitutes curriculum, and when it is thought of in this way, the richness, creativity, and potential it can offer are unrealized. Curriculum is at the heart of your classroom. It is the choreography of knowledge that dictates or shapes how students learn and what they are evaluated on. Whether the teacher has complete autonomy in creating the curriculum or must follow an existing curriculum, what happens in the classroom is largely dependent on both the teacher and the student.

With the increased use of standardized testing, curriculum design is becoming an extinct practice. Curriculum is what will be on the test. Yet the way in which we employ our learning capacities to cope with standardized tests doesn't exclude critical thinking and the development of excellent lifelong learning habits. Even if, as teachers, we rely on the static and predictable nature of standardized content and as students, we detach from the dynamic uncertainty of learning and equate intelligence with the amount we can memorize and recall, we can still see curriculum in multiple ways and discuss the different ways in which critical pedagogy can be developed in the classroom. We will do so throughout this entry.

Lets start with curriculum. Curriculum can be anything that happens and is learned in the school, classroom, home, or street, individually or collectively, as well as in society at large. In the classroom it is what is taught, learned, tested, and what is considered official by state or local standards (Cuban, 1993). There are explicit, implicit, and null curricula (Eisner, 1985). Both of these frameworks allow a complexity to enter the way we conceptualize, practice, and evaluate curriculum. If we look and define curriculum through these frameworks, teachers have more jurisdiction over the curriculum created in their classroom and students have a wider range of learning experiences.

For example, what Cuban defines as official is what the grade level, department, content area, school, district, state, national organizations, and accrediting associations dictate needs to be taught at a particular grade. What is taught, however, is based on the decisions the teacher makes about the official curriculum, what the teacher chooses to prioritize, and the way the teacher decides to proceed with the content matter. Although some people say curriculum in this situation should not deviate from official recommendations, the teacher has the option to put a distinct spin on content. The teacher's passion, likes, dislikes, knowledge, and experience come through and the content is never neutral.

Understanding this reality is part of practicing a critical pedagogy. What is learned is what students can demonstrate that they know after a lesson or unit is over. What students learn encompasses not only what the administration intends them to learn, but what they inadvertently learn as they interact with peers, teachers, parents, TV, music, and life in general.

Students may not always express the extent of what they know. This is why evaluation is crucial. Even though formal evaluation with tests, essays, and projects is usually preferred, there are numerous informal ways (conversations, observations) for students' knowledge to be assessed as well as numerous other creative methods the teacher may design. The key is to provide a balance of informal and formal, traditional and creative ways of evaluating student knowledge, classroom practice, and curricular practice so that students have a varied experience and become more adept in transferring knowledge to multiple contexts. This will, in the long run, make them better problem-solvers and more skilled at discerning what is most useful or appropriate.

Another tenet of critical pedagogy is that teachers should want students to be independent learners with skills for inquiry and autonomy. The current system of schooling produces dependent learners, trained to choose the best answer from a preselected group. Society requires multiple skills, the answers aren't always provided, and people aren't always there to guide the process of finding those answers. Society expects its members to be both followers and leaders, yet if curriculum is only designed to create followers where are students going to practice leadership thinking and action?

Eisner offers a three-part framework for curriculum: the explicit, implicit, and null. The explicit is much like Cuban's official curriculum and focuses on what is actually stated and named. The implicit curriculum is similar to the numerous possibilities in Cuban's learned category. With the implicit there is no guarantee of what is learned. The implicit is the hidden curriculum, the unplanned content, the tangents in conversation that occur when students ask questions and/or teachers try to make curriculum relevant to student lives. The implicit is the unspoken but existent knowledge that permeates the classroom. The implicit can also be the consequences of the teacher's decisions, passions, and inclinations. The null curriculum is that which is excluded both purposefully and accidentally. In critical pedagogy, a lot of attention is given to the implicit and null curriculum. It is said that the curriculum and student knowledge are shaped both by what is there and what is not there. The role of the teacher is crucial here. If teachers are aware of the methods by which a curriculum can be analyzed, they will spot the omissions. The teacher must enhance/ repair/complicate/problematized/challenge the existing curriculum if it is not up to date or excludes important viewpoints. This curriculum negotiation is at the heart of critical pedagogy and developing critical thinking skills in your students. The same kind of questioning that I am imploring you to exercise is the kind of questioning I want your students to exercise.

Questioning is the core of a critical pedagogy, yet it is not promoted for the sake of just questioning, but as a way to deepen knowledge, engage and critique multiple discourses, and transform ideas and actions into more equitable experiences for those involved. The motivation for critical pedagogy stems from a recognition that schooling is an agent of social change and the learning students can gain through years and years of study can transform their lives and the lives of others. The struggle is to find democratic ways of accomplishing this in institutions that have priorities and operations that contradict these goals.

For students and teachers to endure the necessary struggle I've mentioned, curriculum, learning, skills, content, thinking, culture, people, and history must be understood as they relate to everything else and each other. Things don't occur or exist in a vacuum. Learning surges from understanding the interrelated nature of what we are studying and experiencing, what we know and what we don't. For both teachers and students, understanding the connection between the larger philosophical and political conversations in the school, district, and society, as well as how culture (lived experience) is defined and how power operates in their circles and outside is critical to the ways in which they negotiate who they are in that context and how learning is shaped and accepted.

The relationship between ideology, culture, and power is also important as it dictates particular definitions of intelli-

gence and success. Critical pedagogy analyzes and exposes the dominant value systems that undergird the way knowledge is defined and curricula are constructed and tested. Tradition is critiqued and what is familiar is made unfamiliar to gain new perspectives and insights and to initiate the development of a critical consciousness (which I'll explain later). Critical pedagogy sees learning everywhere, not just in school. It validates people's experiences as sources for a priori knowledge and lenses for understanding new knowledge.

Dialogue and reflection are two other key components of a critical pedagogy. For tradition or curriculum to be questioned, teachers must construct the space in their classrooms for dialogue and conversation. Students must be able to speak their minds, question each other, and expand their thinking as they are exposed to how others perceive and understand alleged similar things. Part of this conversation requires reflection when students are asked to think about how their ideas and beliefs were constructed throughout time. During this process, some ground rules are essential. Students and teacher must be willing to listen to each other through agreement and disagreement and must respect each other's viewpoints, not for the sake of politeness but for the sake of inclusivity and inquiry. The point is not to have the class reach a consensus about issues, but to create the space for individuality in the collective space. During this process, the teacher should provide historical, social, philosophical, and/or political grounding and information when possible so that students understand the larger picture, the present in terms of the past, and the situated chronology of knowledge as it affected real lives.

The teacher's work is immense, and the responsibility is heightened by understanding what is at stake: the learning potential of students. To prepare students not only to excel at skills tests but in their lives is a difficult task. Teachers must become avid lovers of knowledge and inquiry and be able to transfer that passion to their students. The skills of inquiry, analysis, questioning, reflection, and dialogue will be used throughout life, not just in the years of schooling.

Critical pedagogy will not provide a book or brochure that prescribes classroom practice in ways that universalize learning or that ignore what students and teachers bring to the schooling experience. Instead, the field will provide a theoretical/philosophical vision/guide that describes the need for specific experiences without dictating how or when these experiences should happen. The ulterior motive is to dismantle oppressive and exclusive classroom practices that affect students' self-efficacy and identity.

Lets now turn to how it might be possible to develop a critical consciousness and critical thinking in students (assuming teachers have already worked on this for themselves). The need to get students to question and analyze curriculum and knowledge in general has several facts. Students need to be engaged in the learning process, develop ownership of their knowledge, expand the ways they can use the knowledge they have gained, become producers of knowledge, and continue inquiries beyond the basics in the classroom. A critical thinker will not only question the nature and purpose of an issue, but consider different perspectives, do further research, and formulate an opinion. As a teacher, you can manipulate the classroom experience to utilize this critical inquiry, regardless of how prescribed or open the curriculum is. Flexibility is important in your teaching. You need to be able to take advantage of the windows for critical inquiry that will present themselves in your classroom.

As both teachers and students learn, their histories, identities, and beliefs come to the foreground. The new intersects with the old and creates possible sites of struggle, and resolution. In critical thinking and learning, which inevitably deconstructs both history and the present, it is essential to retain a vision of the not yet. The imagination must be fed with realistic, accessible possibilities, not empty euphemisms that sugarcoat the realities students must face. The objective of critical pedagogy is for students to develop a clear sense of self in the social context, to be able to negotiate who they are in multiple contexts, to demand access to knowledge otherwise denied, and to help others do the same.

Finally, let's get specific about what critical thinking really is and what it looks like in the classroom. Students and teachers should ask a variety of questions. From whose perspective is this written? What else was/is happening in the world at this time that can help me understand this differently? Was there opposition to this, from whom, why, where, and how? Who is this about and are their viewpoints included? What purpose does this serve, for whom, and at the expense of whom? Where can I find more information on this and what kind of source will it be? How can this be applied/used outside of school? What are the potential consequences of implementing this information? The list can go on and on. Both students and teachers must question whatever is taken for granted, and every question is valid. As an inquiry progresses, more areas that need to be questioned will be revealed. Questioning and inquiry can be endless if an individual truly has a desire to understand a phenomenon or issue better.

Critically questioning and thinking allows students to become more skilled at problem-solving and increase their common sense as they question what is so common about it, to whom it is common, and why. There is no longer only one way to view the world, and even if they prefer their own viewpoint, they will not exercise it at the expense of tolerance. As students are exposed to knowledge, on both horizontal and vertical axes, they learn to comprehend not only cause and effect but factors, variables, and contingencies. In its most fundamental form, critical thinking connects the parts with the whole. How this happens and what comes first depends on the teacher, the student, the subject matter, and the context.

References

Cuban, L. (1993). The lure of curricular reform and its pitiful history. *Phi Delta Kappan, 75,*182–185.

Eisner, E. (1985). *The educational imagination: On the design and evaluation of school programs.* New York: Macmillan.

Further Reading

Bolotin, J., Luster-Bravmann, S., Windschitl, M. A., Mikel, E. R., & Stewart Green, N. (2000). *Cultures of curriculum.* Mahway, NJ: Lawrence Erlbaum.

Kincheloe, J., & Steinberg, S. (Eds.). (1998). *Unauthorized methods: Strategies for critical teaching.* New York: Routledge.

Leistyna, P., & Woodrum, A. (1996). Context and culture: What is critical pedagogy? In P. Leistyna, A. Woodrum, & S. A. Sherblom (Eds.), *Breaking free: The transformative power of critical pedagogy.* Cambridge, MA: Harvard Educational Review.

The Hidden Curriculum: Helping Students Reflect Critically on Issues of Schools, Equity, and Justice

Bill Bigelow

Students are rarely invited to reflect critically on their own schooling and learn to accept inequality as normal. Textbooks and school curricula fail to encourage students to ask an assortment of critical questions, including which social groups pushed for the particular kinds of schools we have today and why; how does ethnic background, race, class, or gender contribute to the character of schooling one receives; who benefits from ability grouping and the myriad special programs in school districts; what are the mechanisms by which students are classified and sorted, and how can students resist school's regimentation effectively? When have you heard of students banding together to reflect on the character of their schooling and to work for greater equity?

These and other critical questions may be taken up in the occasional sociology class, but most students will never be encouraged to consider them. According to a recently published critique of high school U.S. history texts, none of the books reviewed prompts students to think critically about the history or politics of education (Lowen, 1992). What underlying lesson do students learn when they leave high school after 13 years of schooling and have never once been asked to question the institution within which they've spent so many thousands of hours? Probably that their role in society is to perform the work they're assigned, in the context in which it is assigned, and not to wonder whether anything is right or fair or worthwhile. Inequity grows nicely in this soil of suppressed doubt and unasked questions.

Several years ago my partner, Linda Christensen, and I began teaching a unit on the history and sociology of schooling. We stumbled into it. A friend of ours, Michele Miller, asked if she could bring her classes from a more privileged suburban school south of Portland, to Jefferson—located in a working class, predominantly African American neighborhood. In exchange, Michele offered to host our students. We accepted her offer, and decided to make the trip to the school in the wealthier community a centerpiece of a larger inquiry on the nature of public schooling. Over the years, we added and subtracted pieces of this curriculum, but it's remained a vital component of the history and literature courses we've taught together and separately. We've described several of these lessons in other articles (Christensen, 1989; Bigelow, 1990, 1994). I will offer a sketch of this unit. It's a high school class, but our approach could be adapted to lower grades.

We introduce the concept of a hidden curriculum—the values, habits, and beliefs that are imparted to students through the way schools are structured and the routines of school life. The Chilean writer Ar-

iel Dorfman uses the term secret education to describe the deep but unacknowledged messages in children's literature; it's also a useful expression for describing the beneath-the-surface totality of school life. With the students, we brainstorm aspects of the explicit and hidden curriculum at Jefferson, and analyze the secret education in one classroom described in the first few pages of David Storey's 1963 novel, *Radcliffe*.

The excerpt we use describes a teacher who singles out a working class student for humiliation as she tries to elicit correct answers about why buildings are constructed with slanted roofs and tall chimneys— "Just you stand there a moment, *Vic,* and let me see you paying attention and listening." The other youngsters in class sit passively as the teacher uses Victor to show the unpleasant consequences of failing to answer her questions satisfactorily. As we introduce the piece, we ask our students to consider what the nine-year-olds in the class are learning, not about roofs and chimneys, but about authority and power, where knowledge comes from and what is valuable knowledge, decision-making, resistance, and solidarity or people's capacity to stand up for one another. Before we discuss the reading, we ask students to write an interior monologue—the inner thoughts—of one of the characters in the story, to imagine that they are nine-year olds in the classroom described and to write from their own imagined points of view, or to write as if they are immigrant children whose first language is not English.

Jennifer, a student who dropped in and out of school throughout the year, wrote hers as a dialogue between Victor and his mother. She portrays a Victor both compliant and critical:

"So son, what did you do at school today?"

He thought, "I was separated from the others, humiliated. I wanted to stand up for myself but couldn't. Why didn't anyone else help me? Why do teachers always have to be like this? I'll try my best, maybe I'll try more. I'm not good for anything but to listen to another. I just don't want to get in trouble."

"Mom, I did my work, and had a good day at school."

Afterward, as students read aloud these thought portraits, the patterns of deep learning in the classroom begin to emerge. Before we discuss them, we ask students to take a few minutes to write a summary of what they see as the secret education occurring in this class. This may sound like write-this, write-that teaching, but I've found that asking students to collect thoughts on paper prior to talking about a topic democratizes discussion— not all students are equally glib and able to call out thoughts the moment a question is asked.

I'm always amazed at the diversity of student response when we begin to ask the class to think deeply about the processes of schooling. Some kids tend to focus on the powerlessness of the nine-year-olds in the Radcliffe class, others on the competition between students promoted by the teacher. Forest's secret education summary blended his long experience as a student with his interpretation of the classroom dynamics described in the short reading. It was simultaneously pithy and extensive:

HIDDEN CURRICULUM

Never question.

Plot against or compete with your peers.

Resistance is futile.

Hate authority, but always fear it.

Knowledge comes naturally.

Some people will always be better than you.

Tonia wrote that "The students learn to keep their feelings to themselves. They learn to live with their fears." And in response to my asking what students *weren't* learning in this classroom, she wrote that the students are "learning to not stand up for themselves. These students are also learning to not stick together as a big group and solve problems." I wanted my students to see "not learning" as a verb— that curriculum can be both a presence and an absence, and what is *not* taught can be as significant as what *is* taught.

Sometimes we follow these initial discussions of the hidden curriculum by asking students to think of instances in their school lives when they experienced inequality or unfairness—either as victim or beneficiary—and to write these up as first-person narratives. Other times, we've asked students to write about positive learning experiences, either in or out of school. These stories contribute to a year-long grassroots literature that allows students to know and appreciate each other's experiences. We ask them to share their writings in read-arounds—Linda and I write and share as well—and to listen for patterns that recur throughout the stories, to read the collective text of the class.

One year, before the inequality read-around, we asked students to listen for what the hidden curriculum taught about authority, decision-making, equality, and creating change. Daniel, then an 11th grader, marched down his list:

Schools teach children to bow down to authority and that no matter what, all authority is correct and you must listen to them . . . Schools teach kids that the kids can't make decisions in the world, that all the decisions are made for them in what they learn and how to act . . . The schools teach children that no one is equal to another, that there is always someone who is better than you, no matter what you do to change that . . . Schools teach kids that they can't make any change . . . any changes that are made will be by the teacher and only the person in authority, you don't have a say.

A pretty grim picture, but an accurate and astute reading of the collective text created by class members. (By the way, although Forest and Daniel arrived at similar insights, they were students in different years.)

One might argue that to unearth and to publicly acknowledge this cynicism also reinforces it. This is a potential hazard of any classroom examination of injustice. It's important to nudge students beyond description to attempt to *explain* the discouraging realities they uncover. Who decided that the school day would be regimented by bells? Who decided that students would be slotted into advanced and remedial classes? Who decided how power would be distributed between the different members of a school community and, more importantly, why? Strategies (and hope) for change can come only from careful diagnosis of problems.

Through role playing, we engage students in probing the social realities of the early twentieth century that led schools to adopt standardized testing, tracking, and a civics/history curriculum of flag-waving indoctrination. (See "Testing, Tracking, and Toeing the Line: A Role Play on the Origins of the Modern High School," in *Rethinking Our Classrooms: Teaching for Equity and Justice.*) Students portray Hungarian immigrants, corporate executives, members of the middle class, Black activists, and Industrial Workers of the World organizers, and respond to an energetic superintendent committed to bringing the typical but fictional northern Central City into the modern world. For example, the superintendent proposes administering intelligence tests to scientifically sort stu-

dents into four tracks: feeble minded, dull, average, and superior—categories suggested by an influential educator of the time. In their roles, students examine an actual test developed by Stanford University in 1920 to measure students' scholastic aptitudes. "Sirloin is a cut of: beef, mutton, pork, veal," asks one question. Exactly what kind of intelligence is measured by a question like that? The role play exposes students to the underlying politics of early twentieth century school reform. In the face of huge enrollment increases, especially of immigrants and working class children, schools were engineered to reproduce social class hierarchies—not to further social equality, but to guard against it. Compulsory mass education gave an appearance of equal opportunity, but there was nothing equal about the education encountered by different groups of students in stratified tracks.

We also look at a typical teachers' contract from 1923 that regulates every inch of a female teacher's life. For example, the contract enjoins an instructor "Not to loiter downtown in ice cream stores," and requires her "To wear at least two petticoats," and "Not to wear dresses more than two inches above the ankles." This was part of an ethos of decorum and regimentation, but it's also worth considering the impact of gender on the scientific sorting of students. Could it be that the virtually all-male school hierarchy could not trust women teachers to adequately slot students into the appropriate feeble minded, dull, average, and superior tracks? As the century wore on, fewer and fewer males could be found in the classroom. What impact did this feminization of the educational workforce have on school structure? How was it connected to decades of low teacher salaries?

We also probe the role of testing as a sorting mechanism of students and as an allocator—and justifier—of the unequal distribution of educational resources. An excerpt from David Owens' *None of the Above,* "The Cult of Mental Measurement" (Chapter 9), is a bit difficult, but prompts students to think critically about the meritocratic rationale of the first Scholastic Aptitude Tests, and provides some startling background about the individuals who developed them. For example, Carl Campbell Brigham, father of the SAT, was a passionate racist who worried about the "alarming" increase in people of mixed race, and called for an end to the "infiltration of white blood into the Negro." He once published an article in *Eugenical News,* a journal that later reprinted Adolf Hitler's "Text of the German Sterilization Statute."

In a talk back journal, students select quotes from the article and respond to them. Sekou chose, "In a nation without dukes or princes, 'native capacity' provided the basis for a sort of alternative aristocracy. Intelligence tests gave the nation's privileged a scientific-sounding justification for the advantages they enjoyed. The wealthy lived in nice houses because they were smart; the poor were hungry because they were stupid. American society was just after all." Her response was, "This quote jumped out at me, not only because of its content, but because of the fact that, although it's written in the past tense, if you were to go through and change it to be in the present tense, it could be readily applied to today's society. When written out like this, people tend to consciously object to it. But unconsciously, I think people tend to accept it as the way of life. . . ."

Linda and I administer parts of a contemporary SAT test to students, both to build their skills in taking tests like these, but also to critique the tests' legitimacy. Some of the items resemble the 1920 sir-

loin question on the Stanford test: "Heirloom is to inheritance as . . ." and "oarsman is to regatta as. . . ." Whose knowledge is this? What does correctly answering these questions have to do with succeeding in college? How can we account for why SAT scores correlate more closely to family income than to future success in college?

Throughout the unit, we weave together history, contemporary society, and students' lives. We ask people in class to recall a personal test-taking experience and to write it up as a story. Feelings about tests are often close to the surface for students, and they rarely have difficulty thinking of something to write about. Again, after the read-around we ask people to analyze the collective text they created. Cam wrote, "Tests seem to just stack ourselves against others." "How do I measure up?" "They're smarter than me!" "You feel low or high, insecure or too secure, not confident or too much confidence. . . . Sometimes people just feel completely worthless and empty . . ." Tara noted that "it seemed as if just because someone told us we were dumb, we became dumb." Kimberly wrote, "The test made me feel as if I wasn't as smart as I thought I was. . . . these tests are designed to make people feel bad about themselves." And Christine, a student who had spent much of her school life in low tracks, noticed that students in class had never thought critically about the psychological effects of tests themselves: "No one really thought of the test and what its powers are."

We had shared with students a 1920 survey indicating that young people's expectations were simply too high; the economy of the time offered mostly farm labor and industrial jobs, but almost all students wanted professional and creative jobs. According to William Proctor, author of the study, tests and proper guidance counseling would lower students' employment aspirations. "For their own best good and the best good of the nation a great many of them should be directed toward the agricultural, mechanical, and industrial fields." This quote frames students' diminished sense of self as an intended and necessary attitude adjustment—an adjustment required by the economy's incapacity to provide creative, fulfilling jobs for all its citizens.

Comparing the curriculum at Jefferson—both hidden and explicit—to schools serving different social populations is an important part of the unit.

We ask students to keep a log of the hidden curricula in their classes. We're careful to emphasize that we don't want students to use the names of specific teachers; this is not a "let's rag on Mr. or Ms. so-and-so" assignment. And we also ask students to analyze our own class because inevitably all classes impart lessons of which the teachers are unaware. And students consistently make incisive, sometimes troubling, observations about our class. In preparation for their research, we discuss the kinds of things they should look for that might indicate something important about the hidden curricula of their classes. Here are some questions we've raised in past years:

How are the desks arranged?

Who does most of the talking?

How are students made to feel either important or unimportant?

What kinds of questions are asked: thought and analysis questions or memory questions?

Do students seem to be encouraged to think critically or to accept school and society as they are?

Is most of the work individual or group?

Do some classrooms have better equipment or facilities than other classrooms? How can we account for this?

What ways do you see students resisting (e.g., skipping class, talking, being rude, not paying attention)?

Some students make classroom maps, others tell stories, or jot quotes from various class sessions. Monique noted the ways she was made to feel important and unimportant during one week at Jefferson:

UNIMPORTANT

1. By telling us that they have already received their diploma and that we have ours to get.
2. "Shut up."
3. Saying you should have learned this years ago.
4. "I shouldn't have to go over the same thing more than twice for this group."
5. "You need me more than I need you so listen up."
6. "Pay attention or don't come back into this classroom."
7. "Don't make me write a referral."
8. "I'm busy right now. I'll get to you in a minute."

IMPORTANT

1. When they encourage students to speak out in class.
2. Help students for a long time one on one.
3. When they are understanding about other pressing obligations concerning schoolwork.
4. When they submit a student's name for an award.
5. When they put a professional business-like attitude back into their pockets.

For some students, this assignment uncovers great bitterness and raises difficult ethical questions for us as teachers. J. wrote,

In sixth period my teacher again plays favorites. He sometimes follows girls, especially good looking ones . . . You may get a better grade if you shake your butt in front of the teacher, or say or do something to stroke his ego. Many of the females who realize that he is overly friendly and that this may affect their grade positively accept this. And thus are accepting the whole connotation that women are sex objects and it is fine to use this to our advantage. We don't have to use any of our intellect when we can use our bodies. This is where the sick ideas of society today are introduced.

Once we encourage students to examine their own school lives through a critical lens of justice, it's hard to predict where it will lead. What is our responsibility as teachers when we receive a paper like this? A vital aspect of the unit, which I'll touch on in a moment, is to prompt students themselves to ask what can be done.

This student detective work on the school's hidden curriculum obviously doesn't need to be limited to teacher behaviors. Students can engage in a broader equity check of the school. Is there tracking? What kinds of assessments are used to place people? Do the ethnic backgrounds of the teachers match those of the students? Which classes or programs get the best equipment? Do some programs have special privileges, like more field trips or smaller class sizes? One year, my ninth graders surveyed students on their attitudes about justice in the school.

The question of whether the nature of the curriculum at Jefferson have something to do with the social class of the community the school serves does not go away. When we travel to the wealthier suburb—let's call it Oakwood—we test this out for ourselves. Students carry with them the same questions that they used to analyze the hidden curriculum at Jefferson. Over the years, we've traveled to several different "Oakwoods," but wherever we go students are consistently astonished by the numerous differences between these more elite schools and Jefferson. About Oakwood, Nicole wrote,

The school smelled clean. That was the first impression it made on me and several other people standing by me . . . The desks being arranged in their sterile rows seemed to reinforce the idea that the student's mind is a clean chalkboard that needs to be filled with information . . . Overall, I liked the quieter bells, bigger lockers, and better equipment. I also though got the impression from the hidden curriculum and attitudes of the kids that they knew they are and will become the 'beautiful' people of our generation.

It was hard not to notice the quieter bells. The bells at Jeff are the loudest of any school I've ever been in. Their volume seems to underscore a hoped-for order and discipline—and have surely damaged my ears at least as much as Grateful Dead concerts.

In preparation for discussion after our return from Oakwood, we asked students to write two summary paragraphs that might begin, "At Oakwood, students are being trained for . . . " and, "At Jefferson, students are being trained for . . . " Dyan wrote,

At [Oakwood], the students are being prepared to be bosses and in positions of high pay. This was seen in the way they regarded the rules . . . For instance, a student walked in a little late and he was not penalized at all—in fact, the teacher didn't even look at him. Also students would leave their classrooms to retrieve a book from their locker and wouldn't take a pass. Simple rules, but complex messages. By not being penalized, the administrators and staff were saying, "It's your life, your responsibility. One day you'll be the head of a corporation—we're getting you prepared for that now."

At Jefferson, the hidden curriculum is different. We're learning to give way to authority and *be* bossed rather than be a boss. This is demonstrated by our tardy policy, required hall passes, and again classroom structure. Quantity not quality is important for many teachers here. Ditto after ditto is passed out in hopes that by repetition and rote memorization we'll be able to take our place in the "working world" efficiently.

Last year, Linda and I used the powerful poem "Two Women" as a prompt for students to write about the sharp class and race differences they perceived between Oakwood and Jefferson. It's a dialogue poem between two Chilean women—one wealthy, one working class—who experience life very differently. The back and forth structure of the poem allows students a way to imagine and express some of the implications of the different kinds of school experiences at Oakwood and Jefferson.

Riding home on the bus from Oakwood, Rochelle, an 11th grader, turned to me with a disgusted look. "Have you ever thought that you shouldn't do this unit with juniors? You know, *we* still have to come back here next year." What did we expect these 11th graders to do with their new critical awareness? Was it just academic? Did we expect them to spontaneously rise in revolution against the school? We didn't sufficiently appreciate how disempowering it can feel when knowledge is not linked to action, critique not linked to transformation.

In recent years, we've made more efforts to encourage students to reflect on

how they can *act* on their new awarenesses. Last year we asked students to draft proposals that they might choose to present to the administration or site council recommending a concrete change at Jefferson. In all honesty, most of these weren't very good. From the beginning of the year the class was fractured along lines of race, class, sexual orientation, musical taste, speech patterns, athletic pursuits, senses of humor . . . you name it. They were all deeply concerned about issues of justice, albeit in different ways and for different reasons. Linda and I waged a constant, usually less-than-successful, struggle to get them to take themselves seriously as people who could make a difference.

One student, a young woman who mid-way through the year came out to the class as a lesbian, wrote an eloquent appeal to the administration. It began,

We have classes, clubs, and organizations for African Americans, Hispanics, Asians, Native Americans and many other oppressed groups; but there is one group that was forgotten. They have been oppressed throughout all of history, used as kindling to burn people at the stake. They are the "Queers," "Dykes," "Faggots," "Queens," "Butches," and "Fairies." Where are their clubs to support them and their needs? Where is a class dedicated to the history of homosexuals? Why have they been forgotten?

In a deeply personal paper dripping with pain and rage, she argues for more curriculum addressing gay and lesbian issues and for a gay and lesbian club. She returned to Jefferson for this, her senior year, and with administrative tolerance, if not approval, organized her club, which continues to meet regularly.

Students in my U.S. history class last year preempted the proposal-writing with direct action. In a lesson which called for students to discuss—without teacher involvement—problems in the school and possible solutions, class members decided that the school's no-hat rule best symbolized their powerlessness. So they decided to call for a one-day student boycott of the no-hat rule. I had agreed to say nothing during the discussion and kept my promise as they turned the classroom into an organizing center. Together, they wrote a short leaflet:

We're tired of bowing down and taking our hats off to please the administration. So this Wednesday, June 1st, fight back and stand your ground by boycotting the hat rule. Don't have no fear, and on Wednesday wear your head gear. Hats, shower caps, do rags and Kangos. If you don't control what you wear, what do you control? It's time students take power.

One student volunteered his uncle's printing press, other students volunteered for leafleting brigades.

Abolition of the hat rule did not seem to me like the most significant school reform that students could secure. But I was inspired by the intensity of their engagement, how careful they were to involve everyone in class, and how seriously they took themselves. The final assignment of the year in my U.S. history class asked students to write about what or who in U.S. history made them feel hopeful about the future. Jeremy wrote in part:

The class actually left me with more hope than I had when I entered. I learned about several ways of resisting, and actually practiced resisting, organizing, and protesting, and made a difference thru our non-violent demonstration. We have developed leadership skills in here, and that is something we can use on jobs, in other classes, and in our community. It is important to know that you can make a difference thru non-violence, and if everyone knew that, then there wouldn't be riots, and wars. Slaves resisted, soldiers in the Vietnam War resisted, and we resisted. And everyone made a difference.

The Vietnam reference is to the U.S. soldiers who refused, at great personal risk, to participate in the My Lai massacre. Jeremy is African American; he knows all too well that his hat protest does not rank with the struggles of Black slaves. However, we need to respect his list. He draws hope from both history as well as his own accomplishment. The challenge for me as a teacher is to continue to search for curricula that can impart critical knowledge and a sense of hope for the future at the same time.

I am not trying to sketch out a curriculum on the politics of schooling and to say, "Here, teach it like Linda and I taught it." My aim is more limited. I want to suggest that it is a basic skill for students to reflect critically on issues of schools, equity, and social justice. When we neglect to invite students to critique their own school lives, we teach them habits of *not*-thinking critically and *not*-questioning— we teach them to be morally numb to their immediate surroundings.

If we're serious about educating students for democracy, then such an education needs to reach beyond teaching about the three branches of government or how a bill becomes a law. We need to equip students to enter society as *subjects,* as individuals who look around at the social architecture and ask why is it like this. Who benefits and who suffers and what will it take to make it better for everyone? Studying an institution with which they're intimately familiar seems a good place to start.

References

Bigelow, B. (1990). Inside the classroom: Social vision and critical pedagogy. *Teachers College Record,* Spring.

Bigelow, B. (1994). Getting off the track. In B. Bigelow et al. (Eds.), *Rethinking our classrooms:*

Teaching for equity and justice. Milwaukee, WI: ReThinking Schools Limited.

Bigelow, B. (1994). Testing, tracking, and toeing the line: A role play on the origins of the modern high school. In B. Bigelow et al. (Eds.), *Rethinking our classrooms: Teaching for equity and justice.* Milwaukee, WI: ReThinking Schools Limited.

Christensen, L. (1989). Writing the word and the world. *English Journal,* February, 1989.

Dorfman, A. (1983). *The empire's old clothes: What the Lone Ranger, Babar, and other innocent heroes do to our minds.* New York: Pantheon.

Lowen, J. (1992). *Lies my teacher told me: Everything your American history textbook got wrong.* New York: Simon & Schuster.

Storey, D. (1963). *Radcliffe.* New York: Avon.

Further Reading

Bigelow, B., et al. (Eds.). (1994). *ReThinking Our Classrooms: Teaching for Equity and Justice.* Milwaukee, WI: ReThinking Schools, Limited.

Bigelow, B., & Peterson, B. (Eds.). (2002). *ReThinking Globalization: Teaching for Justice in an Unjust World.* Milwaukee, WI: ReThinking Schools, Limited.

Writing Education Practices within the Reconceptualized Curriculum

Cynthia McCallister

In the novel *Hard Times,* Charles Dickens satirized the rigid practices of nineteenth century European schooling. In the introduction, the retired hardware merchant schoolmaster, Mr. Thomas Gradgrind, admonishes one of his teachers in training, appropriately named Mr. McChoakumchild, saying:

Now, what I want is Facts. Teach these boys and girls nothing but Facts. Facts alone are wanted in life. Plant nothing else, and root out everything else. You can only form the minds of reasoning animals upon Facts: nothing else will ever be of any service to them . . . Stick to the Facts, sir!

Gradgrind instilled in his students values that were the lifeblood of nineteenth century European culture when capitalist systems had given rise to schools and other social institutions that exerted power and influence over people. In Gradgrind's school, none but the traits of thrift, obe-

dience, order, and docility were tolerated. Schooling, a process that Dickens likened to "murdering the innocent," was designed to obliterate the awakenings of critical or creative thinking. Gradgrind was a product of his time, and the ethos of his school would have been considered by his contemporaries a right and proper preparation for life in the burgeoning industrial economy of Victorian England, where most adults were destined to become laborers with few political rights, economic opportunities, or personal freedoms.

It goes without saying that society has changed dramatically since Dickens' time; but old habits die hard and the residue of nineteenth century mores continues to find expression in the contemporary classroom. As they did in Dickens's day, schools continue to reward obedience, efficiency, speed, attentiveness, and memory; but in recent decades, the importance of these traits has waned under the force of emerging social expectations. In economically developed, democratic states, the massive unskilled labor force is a remnant of the past. Computers manage information and do the work of rote thinking and repetitive movement tasks. Technology enables warp-speed communication and brings together people from the farthest points on the globe, making the ability to communicate across the boundaries of local language groups and social networks a requirement for modern life. Knowledge develops at a staggering pace, and new ideas flood into public discourses where people must make sense of them and integrate them into existing schemes. Virtually every position in society requires quick thinking, competent communication, and an ability to resolve conflict and reconcile diverse perspectives.

Schools have begun to respond by designing learning outcomes and reconceptualizing curricula to align with these new societal expectations. The reconceptualized curriculum emphasizes novel and creative thinking and encourages questioning, connecting, and reflecting that resembles what the philosopher John Dewey referred to as "wide-awake thinking"—a quality of open-mindedness that harnesses the individual perspective made unique by social connections, personal experiences, beliefs and ideals. Quite unlike the common school of Gradgrind's time, which sought to "murder innocence," the contemporary reform-oriented school strives to *revive* the spirit of innocence in the curriculum as a positive force in the learning process.

Writing plays an important part in this process by giving the student an opportunity to exercise the distanced, reflective, wide-awake stance. For the teacher who would like to incorporate critical writing opportunities into the curriculum, what are the qualities of a writing pedagogy that align with the intentions of the reconceptualized curriculum? How can school activities be structured to invite students to become critically thinking and questioning individuals engaged in learning about, participating in, and changing the worlds in which they live?

WRITING AS A PROCESS

The curriculum treats writing as a process that is both cognitive and social. Writing is, of course, a process that is controlled by the brain. The brain dictates what pieces of knowledge will be retrieved, and grapples with the multiple demands of composition and transcription. Certainly the writing curriculum should concern itself with helping students hone cognitive skills that ease and enhance the writing process.

But if the brain controls how writing is produced, the purpose for writing—the aims, intentions and motives that beckon the writer to the page—is governed by the social world. The reason that writing exists in the reconceptualized curriculum at all is to give students a tool to more successfully engage their world. The reconceptualized writing curriculum positions the student squarely in the midst of the world of things, ideas, history, and people and invites him or her to use writing as a means to participate in that world.

A brief visit to Mrs. Kelly's fifth-grade classroom will illustrate the reconceptualized writing curriculum in action. It is independent writing time and children are scattered around the room. Most work in pairs or threes, and groups are self-selected. Groups in this classroom form around friendships, and at first glance they can be characterized as unisex and pleasure-oriented. The children are writing stories, personal narratives, and information pieces about three wheelers, Nintendo, and television personalities—important topics to these children.

Mrs. Kelly announces it is time to stop working and come together on the rug for sharing time. The children put away the two-pocket folders containing their writing notebooks and papers. All make their way to the rug, except for Miranda, who sits in Mrs. Kelly's chair that faces the rug. Miranda is today's author, which means she gets to read a piece of her writing to her classmates. Today she shares "The Story of Silk." This entry was the result of a research session in which students spent time scanning library resource books and reporting on what they learned. Miranda tackled this assignment by taking out the "S" volume of the encyclopedia and skimming through its pages.

Silk was said to have been invented with the help of a Chinese legend. It was discovered 2700 B.C. in the garden of the emperor Huang-Fi. The emperor told his wife, Si-Ling-Shi, to investigate the mulberry trees because something was damaging them. When she got there, she found some little white caterpillars on the leaves of the trees. Si Ling-Shi loved the way they looked and begged her husband to give her a patch of trees so she could grow them and take care of them. When she got the trees she found a few of the silken cocoons and that is the story of silk.

The routine of writing share dictates that members of the class get the opportunity to give comments and ask questions of the author after he or she has finished reading, so when Miranda finishes "The Story of Silk," several children raise their hands and Miranda calls on them, one by one, and answers their questions: How does silk come from cocoons? Where did you hear the story? What are you going to do with this piece? How did you get the

idea to write about silk? Miranda responds to these questions and they linger in her thinking as she continues to work on her piece.

Writing share time has an important function in this classroom: it serves as a powerful context for interpersonal learning. As ideas and insights move from one person to the next, students are witness to a process of expanding understanding, and when students hear the reactions to their ideas and experiences, they gain insight into how they are perceived by others. Our sense of who we are evolves through the many encounters we have with others in our social groups. Over time we begin to see ourselves as we are seen through the eyes of others. The self is built through a continuing process of social interaction. Interpersonal learning and personal insight are critical building blocks in the development of self and personal identity.

DAILY OPPORTUNITIES TO WRITE AND SHARE WRITING

The curriculum provides students with daily opportunities to write and share their writing. In Mrs. Kelly's class, one hour a day is dedicated to writing. Within this time block, Mrs. Kelly spends 10 minutes teaching the whole class some element of writing that she deems important. Students spend another 30–40 minutes working on individual writing projects. Sometimes students select their own topics, other times topics are assigned by the teacher as part of a curriculum unit in social studies, science, or language arts. The city requires students to complete several examples of writing, including poetry, a response to literature, a report, and/or a personal narrative. Writing time provides a place in the schedule where this work can be accomplished. The last 10–20 minutes are writing share time, like the session described above, where one student reads a piece of finished writing or a work in progress.

WRITING MODELS AND OPPORTUNITIES TO EXPERIMENT

The curriculum provides students with writing models and opportunities to experiment with a variety of forms. Writing is most successful when the form suits the message, so students need opportunities to learn about a range of writing forms and how to use them. Among the text genres students in Mrs. Kelly's class have surveyed are news stories and editorials, advertisements, books and movie reviews, letters to the editor, novels, short stories, poems, song lyrics, and business letters. After they learn about a new form of writing, it's common for students in Mrs. Kelly's classroom to experiment doing their own writing in that form. Students are encouraged to try new genres, because the ability to express oneself in multiple forms and the flexibility to know which form suits a particular purpose are important skills to master.

INDEPENDENT WORK AND PERSONAL CONNECTIONS

The writing curriculum emphasizes independent work, but incorporates assertive, explicit instruction. The writing curriculum is designed to engage students to write on topics that interest them. As they work on their projects, Mrs. Kelly offers large-group, small-group, or individualized instruction as needed.

The curriculum invites the student to use writing to make sense of the world by exploring personal connections to events, ideas, people, and things. Because the writing curriculum is bound to the world

outside the student, engaging in public discourse is at its heart. The writing that students do is related to a purpose that is larger than themselves, but the link to that purpose is made through the self.

I'll illustrate by way of a contrast. When one of Gradgrind's pupils, a girl named Sissy whom Gradgrind refers to as "girl number twenty," could not offer an accurate definition of a horse upon his command, Gradgrind publicly ridiculed her: "Girl number twenty possessed of no facts, in reference to one of the commonest of animals!" He called on another child who responded to his satisfaction: "Quadruped. Graminivorous. Forty teeth, namely, twenty-four grinders, four eye-teeth, and twelve incisive, Sheds coat in the spring; in marshy countries, sheds hoofs, too. Hoofs hard, but requiring to be shod with iron. Age known by marks in mouth."

"Now girl number twenty," Gradgrind remarked, "you know what a horse is." Sissy, whose father was a veterinary surgeon and horse trainer, was of course very familiar with horses. The meanings she attached to the animal were probably thickly layered with emotions and experiences so elaborate they eluded simple definition; but only the most literal, concise, and efficiently stated definition met with approval.

If Sissy were a student in Mrs. Kelly's class, she would be encouraged to write as a means to explore what she knows about horses and to record what she learns through print and non-print resources such as video, film, the Internet, encyclopedias, non-fiction books, and others. She would have an opportunity to share her knowledge with her classmates and help them expand their understanding of horses. Her classmates' questions and comments would help her create an audience in her mind, which would guide further revisions.

This social process would become the engine of her learning, provoking her to think deeply, critically, and creatively about how to present what she knows in her writing. Sissy's naïve and *innocent* perspective on horses would be the foundation for new learning.

Reference

Dickens, C. (1980). *Hard times*. New York: Signet Classic.

Further Reading

Atwell, N. (1998). *In the middle*. Portsmouth, NH: Heinemann.

Calkins, L. (1993). *The art of teaching writing*. Portsmouth, NH: Heinemann.

Harwayne, S. (2001). *Writing through childhood*. Portsmouth, NH: Heinemann.

Democracy

Democracy and John Dewey

Kathy Hytten

Imagine schooling where student-generated questions frame the curriculum, where children's senses of wonder and curiosity are deepened and expanded, where they are engaged and enthusiastic about inquiry, and where they learn to use their minds well. Sadly, we would describe few schools today in this manner. Even worse, the goal of getting students to use their minds well—that is, to think critically—is rarely at the forefront of our educational agenda. Instead, the familiar litany of educational reform proposals center on increased standardization and high stakes accountability. In practice, this means greater emphasis on content coverage, teaching to tests, and precious classroom time spent encouraging knowledge recall.

The consequences for students in such environments are grim. Not only has this increased attention on standardized assessment exacerbated student passivity and disengagement in schools, it has also dulled their ability to think critically about the world around them. Rather than giving students time and resources to deeply explore ideas, to make meaningful connections, and to imagine possibilities, we implore them to accumulate information and reward them for recalling it accurately on demand. Writing nearly seventy years ago in a voice that still speaks to us today, John Dewey critiques such an exaltation of external standards and information recall when he says, "no one thing, probably, works so fatally against focusing the attention of teachers upon training of mind as the domination of *their* minds by the idea that the chief thing is to get pupils to recite their lessons correctly" (Dewey, 1933/1998, p. 65). He consistently laments our misguided conflation of knowledge with information, arguing that our educational goal should be the cultivation of wisdom, or "knowledge operating in the direction of powers to the better living of life" (Dewey, 1933/1998, p. 64). Ultimately, he argues, what matters is that we learn to think critically, to learn how to access and use information to create a vision of a better world and act to bring it into existence.

Despite writing predominantly in the first half of the twentieth century, Dewey's large body of work offers many resources that educators can draw upon today. In particular, he provides us with a thoughtful description of how we can better cultivate critical thinking, a rationale for why it is so imperative that we do so, and a faith in our ability to create schools marked by intellectual inquisitiveness and student engagement.

Dewey's ideas contribute to enriching our understanding of critical thinking in three important ways. First, he provides us with a well-developed description of what it means to think carefully, reflectively, and critically. Second, he details the habits and dispositions most conducive to thinking critically and argues persuasively on why schools should cultivate them. Third, he connects thinking with the development of both moral sensibility and ongoing social reform.

Dewey's ideas about critical thinking are intimately related to his general vision of the role of philosophy and philosophers. Perhaps one of the unique features of Dewey's overall approach to philosophy is that he believes philosophical thinking should be relevant to our efforts to reform society and to create more meaningful and enriched lives. He criticizes philosophers for spending so much of their time pursuing lofty ideals and abstract certainties in lieu of addressing the everyday problems of men and women. In his view, philosophy should be operative, not simply contemplative. It should help us identify problems and act on them. He writes that "the task of future philosophy is to clarify men's (and women's) ideas as to the social and moral strifes of their own day. Its aim is to become so far as is humanly possible an organ for dealing with these conflicts" (Dewey, 1920, p. 26). It is through learning to think critically that we can best deal with problems that face us individually, as a nation, and as a global community.

In *How We Think* (1933/1998), Dewey outlines the process involved in thinking critically, which he typically refers to as reflective thinking. This process involves experimentation and the projection of potential outcomes of our actions and choices, closely mirroring what we often teach as the scientific method. Dewey is attracted to the methods of science because he feels that they avoid dogmatism and unthinking routine and are, instead, careful, systematic, and open-ended. For him, this appeal to science is both methodological and attitudinal. By using a logic of inquiry, he thinks individuals replace haphazard and impulsive attempts at understanding with more thoughtful and intelligent steps. Attitudinally, this involves the will to inquire, reflect, discriminate, examine, and draw conclusions only on the basis of evidence and only after every effort has been made to gather all possible evidence. He further maintains that the methods we use in scientific inquiry should be applied to social inquiry and social reconstruction as well, arguing that we need to apply the "intelligently conducted doing" characteristic of the experimental sciences to social problems (Dewey, 1920, p. 121). Thinking more critically about such "social and moral defects and troubles" would thus involve "clearing up the causes and exact nature of these evils and . . . developing a clear idea of better social possibilities" (Dewey, 1920, p. 124).

Dewey describes reflective thinking as involving five interconnected and often overlapping stages. In simple terms, we can characterize these stages as frustration, naming, hypothesizing, reasoning, and experimenting. First, he argues that we only think when we have problems, or when there is an indeterminate situation. Most of the time we go through our days somewhat thoughtlessly, relying on many routinized and habitual actions. It is when something happens to disrupt our routine that we truly begin to engage in thinking.

For example, while writing this essay, I may occasionally print out a draft of what

I have written to assess my progress. To do so, I simply press the printer icon and the pages emerge. Yet, one time when I press the icon, nothing happens. I am frustrated and perplexed. The next stage of inquiry comes out of this confusion, as I attempt to determine what is wrong or, as Dewey puts it, I turn the "difficulty or perplexity that has been *felt* (directly experienced) into a *problem* to be solved, a question for which the answer must be sought" (Dewey, 1933/1998, p. 107). This is when I name the problem and say "There is something wrong with my computer or printer." Now I begin to notice things that I normally do not have to think about, such as the potentially empty paper feed tray, the flashing lights on the printer, the cables connecting the printer to the computer and the outlet, or the mysterious software that enables the computer and printer to communicate. I begin to make connections, and to recognize that these things matter to the functioning of my printer.

Moving on to the third stage, I begin to think more deeply. I go beyond noticing that cables and software matter and start wondering why they matter. Here I begin to brainstorm possible solutions and hypothesize about how I might figure out what is wrong. For example, I may take out the user's manual and look for a trouble-shooting guide, or check whether cables are loose, or turn the computer on and off, or call a friend for help. This moves me into the fourth stage of inquiry, where I reason more systematically about the problem and construct ways that I might test my hypotheses more carefully. In this stage I would also imagine the possible consequences of tests that I could perform to find a solution before I actually try them in practice. This helps to ensure that I don't make the problem worse by trying something that may have undesirable or irrevocable consequences, like trying to take apart the printer itself.

The final stage of inquiry is where I actually test the most promising hypothetical solutions. For example, I may have narrowed the problem down to a malfunction of the print driver software, and so I reload the software and try to print again. If this works, great! If it doesn't, I will return to the hypothesis stage and act upon other promising ideas.

What Dewey so values about these often intimately interrelated steps is not the result of the inquiry, but the reasoned and systematic way the process helps us to approach problems. Too often we do not address problems in such a thoughtful way, nor do we think about thinking in terms of framing questions, especially in schools. Yet as Dewey maintains, thinking and questioning go hand and hand. "Thinking is inquiry, investigation, turning over, probing or delving into, so as to find something new or to see what is already known in a different light. In short, it is *questioning*" (Dewey, 1933/1998, p. 265). He is concerned, however, that schooling is frequently an affair of telling rather than questioning and that students' questions are muted as we worry about an ever-expanding breadth of content coverage. This results in a kind of passivity that is antithetical to thinking critically. Dewey is justly worried that this "passivity is the opposition of thought; that it is not only a sign of failure to call out judgment and personal understanding, but that it also dulls curiosity, generates mind-wandering, and causes learning to be a task instead of a delight" (Dewey, 1933/1998, p. 261).

While passivity in schools is certainly a problem, the larger concern is that we carry it over into our everyday lives and become, for example, apathetic in the face of pressing social concerns. We do not have to look far to see manifestations of this apathy. The turnout for elections is often dreadfully low, particularly on the local level. Adults are unabashedly ignorant about issues of politics, national affairs, and global relations. We all too often become immune to the suffering and injustice that occurs around us every day. In part, Dewey would argue that this seeming disinterest is a consequence of not having learned the attitudes and habits necessary for critical and reflective thinking, nor the disposition to see and act upon problems that affect us.

Among the most important attitudes that Dewey claims are integral to thinking critically are open-mindedness, wholeheartedness, and responsibility. Open-mindedness involves a genuine willingness to explore ideas and to question even our most fundamental assumptions. "It includes an active desire to listen to more sides than one; to give heed to facts from whatever source they come; to give full attention to alternative possibilities; to recognize the possibility of error even in the beliefs that are dearest to us" (Dewey, 1933/1998, p. 30). When we are wholehearted, we put all of our energy and enthusiasm behind learning something. We are earnest and absorbed because what we are investigating matters, and matters more than simply to pass a test, receive a certain grade, or to please others. Intellectual responsibility entails imagining the consequences of our thinking, and being accountable for these consequences when they logically result from the positions we have already taken. Furthermore, it means ensuring a consistency between our beliefs and our actions.

Dewey argues that these are attitudes that we could and should learn in schools, not only because they are conducive to individual growth but because they help us to more intelligently conduct communal affairs and thereby to bring about a more desirable future. In this sense, critical thinking is more than simply a skill or a technique. It is a moral sensibility or outlook that assumes that we can develop the habit of using our minds well to solve pressing problems, especially social ones, and thus reconstruct the world around us in more meaningful, life-affirming, and enhancing ways.

Ultimately, for Dewey, the reflective thinking process and attitudes that he describes, while important in the classroom, are even more essential habits for democratic citizenship. Experimenting, being open to new ideas, taking responsibility for our current state of affairs, and striving to bring about greater social justice are all at the heart of democratic living. As citizens, we should seek wisdom; that is, the ability to recognize dilemmas, inquire about their nature and causes, discriminate among possible courses of action, and use our intelligence to better solve the problems we face. We should not act without thinking, or do things because we have always done them in a certain way. Critical thinking is essentially a moral sensibility because it involves the ameliorative desire to make choices and act in ways that cultivate more fulfilling and enriching lives. It is also the path towards the development of a socially conscious and actively engaged public.

Acting with commitment and intelligence is what will allow individuals to change and, to a degree, control the course of the future. It is therefore imperative that we work much harder to teach the habits necessary for using our minds well, and the attitudes consistent with such thinking.

Practically, this vision of critical thinking means we have to challenge practices in schools that result in student passivity and apathy. We must encourage students to develop questions that are individually and socially meaningful, and to take initiative in answering them fully. We also must help them see the connections between classroom learning and a larger moral vision of social betterment. Dewey believes that the key to social progress is found in using our minds well. The only way we can do this as adults is if we practice thinking critically in schools. This necessarily involves creating educational practices that are based on social involvement, responsibility, engagement, critique, and an ethically committed sensitivity to others and to the world around us.

Though we often say we value these ideas, what we do in schools, particularly in a climate of high stakes testing and accountability, is not typically consistent. Consequently, student disengagement and passivity are all too prevalent. While Dewey's perspectives on the importance of thinking critically make practical sense,

and resonate with contemporary calls for more engaged learning, we have yet to take seriously his passionate call for a change in how we think about thinking. His works still provide a valuable, largely untapped resource for rethinking how we educate democratic citizens in an ever-changing world.

References

Dewey, J. (1920). *Reconstruction in philosophy.* Boston: Beacon Press.

Dewey, J. (1933/1998). *How we think.* New York: Houghton Mifflin.

Further Reading

Campbell, J. (1995). *Understanding John Dewey: Nature and cooperative intelligence.* Chicago: Open Court.

Dewey, J. (1938/1997). *Experience and education.* New York: Touchstone.

Fishman, S. M., & McCarthy, L. (1998). *John Dewey and the challenge of classroom practice.* New York: Teachers College Press.

Diversity

Black Existence As Critical Thinking

Michael J. Dumas

Here . . . in this here place, we flesh; flesh that weeps, laughs; flesh that dances on bare feet in grass. Love it. Love it hard. Yonder they do not love your flesh. They despise it. They don't love your eyes; they'd just as soon pick em out. No more do they love the skin on your back. Yonder they flay it. And O my people they do not love your hands. Those they only use, tie, bind, chop off and leave empty. Love your hands! Love them. Raise them up and kiss them. Touch others with them, pat them together, stroke them on your face 'cause they don't love that either. *You* got to love it, *you!*

Baby Suggs in *Beloved*
(Morrison, 1987, p. 88)

This flesh, this Black flesh that Baby Suggs seeks to save in this sermon to her people, is a flesh in question. That is, the bodies of Black people have been and continue to be subject to a whole host of terrors and subjugations, physical, political, and spiritual. The question, then, from even the most disinterested objective observer's point of view is, will this flesh survive? The more sympathetic observer might wonder, how is this flesh to survive? However, the questions which most haunt and most threaten Black flesh—the ones rarely spoken above a whisper but so loudly reverberant in the social psyche—are these: *Should* Blacks survive? Are their bodies worth saving? Would it not be better if they did not exist?

Baby Suggs' sermon, delivered in a wooded clearing "known only to deer and whoever cleared the land in the first place," offered a spiritual respite from the deafening sounds of these questions. Understanding in her own flesh the trauma of antiblack racism, she sought to provide new ways of thinking to help her people withstand the assault. As such, Baby Suggs could certainly be considered a critical-thinking educator, but not one simply interested in developing sharper cognitive and analytical skills or in teaching methods of argumentation. Baby Suggs used critical thinking as a way to make sense of being Black, of experiencing life in a Black body.

I am moved by the case of antiblack oppression, and by the questions (im)posed against black flesh, and (ex)posed by the presence of Black bodies, to think about the relationship between critical thinking and existential thought (Gordon, 2000). In this paper, I use Lewis Gordon's conceptualization of Africana existential thought to provide some framework for what might be conceptualized as *critical thinking as Black existence*. By this I mean the ways in which Black people produce ways of thinking, construct identities/consciousnesses, and formulate/transmit values with the explicit or implicit aim of preventing self-annihilation, meaninglessness, and individual or collective disembodiment (the separation of the spirit/soul from the body/flesh). Although I'm concerned primarily with black experience, I believe that what we learn by looking at critical thinking through the lens of Black struggle has broader implications, not only for the field of critical thinking, but also for how we move more closely towards realization of a democratic, humane global society.

Africana existential thought is primarily concerned with how Black people make meaning of their lives and assert their humanity in an antiblack world (Gordon, 2000). Antiblack racism, Fanonian scholar Lewis Gordon argues, "espouses a world that will ultimately be better off without Blacks" (Gordon, 2000, p. 15). He explains, "Negro problems often collapsed into *the* Negro Problem—the problem, in other words, of having Negroes around" (Gordon, 2000, p. 69). Thus, Black people face not simply questions of equity or justice, but challenges to their very humanity, their right to exist, and perhaps, even after grudging admission of such rights, nagging doubts about the value of their existence. What is a Black body worth?

The presence of this question around the globe necessitates an ontological and teleological response from Black people, which comes, once again, in the form of two questions identified by Gordon as "What are we?" and "What shall we do?" (Gordon, 2000, p. 7). A Black existential analysis views Black lived experience as a response to the question "Why go on?" One goes on, Gordon asserts, "because one wants to, and in so doing seeks grounds for *having* to go on. The wanting, however, signifies an intentional framework that has already militated against nihilism, for self-value also emerges from valuing one's desire to bring meaning to one's existence" (Gordon, 2000, p. 15). Critical thinking, I would argue, is not a skill or method to bring meaning to Black existence; it is a crucial form of Black existence. In the act of thinking critically, Black people affirm their own humanity, assert their right to self-determination, and develop individual and collective purpose.

What are the spheres of practice for critical thinking as Black existence? I would argue that critical-thinking educators should take their practice to every space in which black people struggle to find meaning and purpose, and to every space where contestation, cultural production, and emancipation (or at least emancipatory moments) are possible. It should be understood, however, that wherever educators might go within Black cultural spaces, they will find organic critical-thinking educators already doing valuable work. These would include hip hop artists, grandmothers, beauticians, and preachers. Critical-thinking educators need to be willing to be both practitioners of critical thinking and people upon whom critical thinking is practiced; cognizant that there is much to learn from the brother on the corner getting his hustle on and the sister who braids hair and takes in children to make ends meet. One can even witness the act of critical thinking in the everyday expression and movement of Black people. For example, simply seeing sisters or brothers walking with their heads up can serve simultaneously as both evidence of critical thinking and critical-thinking education that teaches the worth of Black existence. Thus, all are teachers and all are students, constantly posing and responding to the question "Why go on?"

THE PRACTICE OF CRITICAL THINKING AS BLACK EXISTENCE

The .practice of critical thinking as Black existence is informed by the postformal critique of educational psychology. This critique is framed by a concern about what Kincheloe has called the "sociopsychological schizophrenia" that results from the divorce of reason and emotion. Schools and, I would argue, work and sometimes social life are structured with no larger purpose other than achievement of tasks for the sake of achievement. Students' passions are dismissed as beside the point, and in some cases as an impediment to achieving the aims of schooling. Obsessed with the dissemination and recitation of facts, schools make little or no attempt to help students connect emotionally with what they are learning. In such a learning experience, "the relationship between the facts or their applications to the problems of the world is irrelevant. As such, meaning is undermined, and purpose is lost" (Kincheloe, 1999, p. 9).

To avoid creating such an ontological and teleological wasteland, a postformal critique argues that "schools in a democratic society should exist to help students locate themselves in history, obtain the ability to direct their own lives, understand the ways power influences the production of knowledge, appreciate the nature of good work, become smart workers, and connect with a cognitive revolution that leads to a deeper understanding of themselves and the world. In these ways, meaning is salvaged and spirit is protected" (Kincheloe, 1999, p. 10).

A postformal critique treats seriously the relationship between educating the spirit (passions, emotion, connectedness to life) and educating the mind (facts, information, texts). In fact, postformalists assert that meaning can only occur after achieving some synergy between intuition and reason.

It should be clear by now that it is impossible to practice critical thinking as Black existence by attending solely to either facts or emotions. In fact, we need to begin by resisting that binary. No concept, fact, or object is truly known unless it is felt in the flesh. Emotions alone offer us no path to act, no way to discern how to move with, through or against what is before us individually or collectively.

I'd like to propose three key interrelated dimensions of practice for critical thinking as Black existence, which I believe could serve as a model for all critical-thinking education. These dimensions are not so much learning objectives or skills areas as they are spaces of inquiry in which we dialectically and critically engage thought and emotion.

The first dimension is related to *engagement of the body*. How does one begin to think critically about existence in black? Black bodies are perceived simultaneously as savagely primitive and thus imperialistically coveted and a threat to the preservation of all that is right and safe and pure. Black people must live and breathe in these bodies, so often despised and yet desired for consumption or simply to satisfy some curiosity about the primitive Other. Critical engagement calls us to attend to the range of emotional responses to such objectification, from rage to fear to pain to hatred (of self and/or others). Through engagement of the body, we also understand the need to wrestle with how to make sense of representations of variously situated

Black bodies in popular culture and everyday life, and how to situate ourselves within the field of representation but against representations that signify the *unhumanity* of the Black body.

Second, we must embrace *engagement of yearning*. Critical thinking as Black existence necessarily entails an understanding of the significance of memory, vision, faith, and possibility in Black life. Desire for full acknowledgment of Black humanity figures large in Black culture, from the employment of biblical metaphors about crossing the river Jordan and going to the mountaintop to see the Promised Land to Carter G. Woodson's creation of what was to become Black History Month.

Black historical narratives are filled with stories of the freedoms we gained and the communal spirit we lost in the process. Some hints remain, and definitely some memories of "a time not long ago" (when any Black elder could command respect from any Black child; when Black people said hello to one another; when Black people didn't "put their business in the street" for white people to see). Of course, we risk a certain essentialized romanticization of the Black past when we speak of such memories; however, there is some truth that integration brought with it a new kind of colonization of the Black mind and spirit. Still, the belief in shared notions of Black existence and the feeling that such values and experiences are fading fast can contribute to a loss of meaning as Black people of a certain generation and political stance come to conclude that the teleology of Black identity is more uncertain than the unstable condition of the race can withstand. A practice of critical thinking as Black existence calls us to investigate such questions of history, identity, and desire.

The third dimension in the practice of critical thinking as Black existence calls for *engagement of power*. If we begin with an understanding that, as far as White people are concerned, Black people were never meant to think, let alone think critically, then we have to consider the educational implications of this exercise of power. If one is positioned outside the sphere of meaning-making, it becomes clear that one is intended to have no meaning other than that which is imposed. If one is not allowed to construct knowledge, one is not a subject. If one is not a subject, one is not human, and therefore has no reason to exist. Why go on?

Of course, as Gordon points out, Black people have never fully embraced such subjugation. In fact, there is ample evidence that power has been and continues to be resisted at every turn. Thus, it would be erroneous to conclude that Black people have not exercised agency in thinking critically about their own oppression. However, given the increasing subtlety and covert operationalization of power, there is a need for a critical thinking practice that takes into account how new forms of racial terror are practiced and experienced.

As noted above, these three dimensions are inextricably interrelated. For example, thinking about the Black body is only possible through consideration of relations of power. Yearning entails placing the Black body at risk in the struggle against domination. Critiquing power raises questions about what desires are implicit in our own thinking about what "ought to be." The critical question, as it pertains to Black existence, is how do we engage in a practice, and keep Black people engaged in a practice, that will affirm Black subjectivity, blunt the challenges to Black humanity, and perhaps most of all, find an emancipatory response to the question, Why go on?

The concept of critical thinking as Black existence connotes that the very survival of Black people depends on our ability to make meaning out of the raw ingredients of thought, experience, and emotion. For Baby Suggs, the lived experience of struggling for meaning in an antiblack world proved too much. In the end, she could find no more answers. "Those white things have taken all I had or dreamed . . . and broke my heartstrings too," she said. "There is no bad luck in the world but whitefolks" (Morrison, 1987, p. 89). One wonders how many others have come to this same sad conclusion, and the myriad ways this resignation is made manifest in the flesh. Conceptualizing critical thinking as a crucial form of Black existence opens a space for this inquiry and offers possibilities for transformative intervention.

References and Further Reading

Gordon, L. R. (2000). *Existentia Africana: Understanding Africana existential thought*. New York: Routledge.

Kincheloe, J. L. (1999). Trouble ahead, trouble behind: Grounding the postformal critique of educational psychology. In J. L. Kincheloe, S. R. Steinberg, & P. H. Hinchey (Eds.), *The postformal reader: Cognition and education*. New York: Falmer Press.

Kincheloe, J. L., Steinberg, S. R., & Hinchey, P. H. (Eds.). (1999). *The postformal reader: Cognition and education*. New York: Falmer Press.

Morrison, T. (1987). *Beloved*. New York: Knopf.

Diverse Learners and Special Education: A Critical Thinking Perspective

Alberto M. Bursztyn

The increasingly diverse backgrounds, cultures, and languages of children in public schools present new challenges for teachers. Faced with the requirement of preparing all children to meet stringent local and national educational standards, teachers often express concern about children who are culturally and linguistically diverse (CLD); particularly when their test performance is below grade and/or when they show difficulties adjusting to classroom routines. Acting on these concerns, many teachers refer children for psychological evaluation to determine if they qualify for special education services. National studies indicate that, in the great majority of these cases, children who are referred for evaluation are found to be disabled, and are subsequently placed in special education programs (Artiles & Trent, 1994). This pattern of identification, referral and placement is so prevalent that it has resulted in the disproportional placement of CLD children in programs for the mild to moderately disabled. CLD children are labeled learning-disabled, speech-impaired and emotionally handicapped in greater numbers than expected by the size of their populations (Figueroa & Garcia, 1994).

A critical thinking perspective can help educators reconsider and question this process. We may ask whether this is fair and if this pattern of identification and referral serves CLD children and society at large? Does special education offer the child access to support services and enriched learning experiences, even if the child is not disabled? A critical perspective would lead us to answer no to these questions. Special education services often lead to segregated placements, and the educational outcomes for such programs are notoriously poor for CLD children.

In practice, the expected benefits of special education placement rarely materialize. Special education services for CLD children labeled as mildly to moderately disabled are chronically hampered by lack of trained personnel and resources. But even when resources are available, the consequences of being labeled mentally retarded or being singled out for services tends to decrease students' motivation and puncture their sense of self-efficacy. The cost of special education services, which are mostly delivered through uncertified monolingual staffs, does not seem to compensate for the stigma of being called a student with special needs. Educational outcomes for these children are poor. Few of them ever graduate from high school and a disturbingly large proportion of them are arrested soon after they drop out (Osher, Sims, & Woodruff, 2002).

Child advocates have characterized special education placement practices for CLD children as discriminatory. Occasionally judges have agreed and asserted their authority on these educational practices by finding districts liable and by requiring corrective actions.

Reflecting critically on referral and evaluation practices for CLD children implies questioning the assumptions, traditions, and policies that support them. Teachers reasonably expect that professional evaluators will be able to assess if a CLD child suffers from a disabling condition or not. This assumption is grounded in the general acceptance of professional evaluators' knowledge and competence. However, the psychological testing model now in place fails to account for the unique strengths of CLD children and highlights their difficulties in mastering the English language and/or gaining proficiency in the dominant American culture. In fact, many tests of cognitive ability administered in the English language are, for these children, tests of their proficiency in English and the test results tend to confound limited English proficiency with limited cognitive ability or a language disability (Bursztyn, 2002). Even when assessment incorporates translated tests or utilizes translators, reliability and validity are inadequate for diagnostic purposes, leading to potentially biased conclusions.

A critical thinking stance leads us to further question the nature of prevalent assessment practices. Standardized tests used in assessment assume that differences in test results may be attributed to individual variation. But that conclusion can only be true if all children tested have similar life experiences prior to testing. If children have significantly different life experiences in the cognitive and emotional domains tested, differences in results cannot be interpreted as reflecting differences in abilities. Test results are just as likely to reflect limited exposure to the dominant culture and language. Unfortunately, the prevalent belief system regarding test performance leads both teachers and clinicians to look for the roots of academic difficulty exclusively within the child, and to interpret poor learning outcomes as symptoms of a disorder (Cummins, 1986). Without a critical understanding of language learning and acculturation, low scores are interpreted as low innate ability. Critical reassessment is needed to correct this method of identifying CLD children for special education classification.

Children's physical, cognitive and emotional growth may be best understood in the context of adaptation to formative environments. A critical thinking approach to understanding children's experiences in context implies that children are immersed in particular languages, families, and communities. It follows that the greater the distance between the expectations of home and the expectations of mainstream culture, the more difficult it will be to distinguish between a child's idiosyncrasies (including disabilities) and family/community cultural patterns. What may appear to be unusual behaviors may be a reflection of different linguistic and cultural norms unfamiliar to the educators in a particular school setting.

Critical thinkers use tools of analysis from different disciplines. Anthropologists, for example, differentiate between *emic* and *etic* criteria for evaluation. The emic perspective looks at within-group characteristics, the etic criteria refer to cross-cultural and more universal dimensions of human behaviors. Teachers and evaluators could apply the emic approach to gain a better understanding of CLD children. If a child's learning rate or behavioral patterns are unusual *within* her family and community, there is greater certainty that these characteristics are intrinsic to the child, rather than a reflection of family and/or community values and traditions.

By extension, evaluation methods and instruments that were designed to highlight differences among children in the dominant language and culture cannot be fairly applied to children from other cultures and languages. Evaluation practices emerge from and reflect a particular group and culture and these practices may not be valid across groups. Results of evaluation may not represent interpersonal variation, but intercultural and linguistic differences.

A critical thinking approach as applied to evaluation, or what I refer to here as a critical thinking evaluation model, requires that the method fit the child. In contrast, accepted assessment practice calls for indiscriminate application of a pre-existing assessment template. Children who encounter early academic failure, and who by virtue of linguistic and cultural characteristics are more vulnerable to labeling, can benefit from an evaluation approach that recognizes the limitations of standardized practices. When critical thinking is integrated with evaluation practices, the assessment paradigm is expanded to address contextual elements and interactions. In this new paradigm, evaluators would need to consider the following principles.

A. The nature of children's life experiences and the linguistic and sociocultural context in which we find them (the emic perspective),

B. The nature of the school environment as a receiving context for diverse children (how welcoming or rejecting is the school vis-à-vis CLD children?), and

C. The degree of congruence between children's prior learning, including life experiences, and the academic and social expectations of the school (e.g., are children held responsible for learning experiences they never had, or will the school assume responsibility for addressing gaps in learning and experience?)

Assessment decisions regarding CLD children take place under conditions of uncertainty. When children's learning patterns are not easily matched with existing diagnostic categories, the impulse to classify along existing but inadequate categories should be resisted. In these circumstances, teachers and evaluators need to transcend the standard model of practice and to be guided by a critical approach to evaluation. When critical thinking is applied to assessment practices, it can enrich problem-solving by expanding the analytic frame in which educators, including clinicians, understand children.

A critical thinking approach to the education and evaluation of CLD children requires that clinicians and teachers a) reassess the reasons for suspecting disability, and b) reconsider the putative benefits of alternative educational placements. Rather than identifying school failure as an expression of limitations within the child, clinicians and teachers need to explore the social, cultural, linguistic, and academic contexts that promote or inhibit learning. Only then will educators have the information necessary for informed judgments.

References

Artiles, A., & Trent, S. C. (1994). Overrepresentation of minority students in special education: A continuing debate. *The Journal of Special Education, 27* (4), 410–437.

Bursztyn, A. (2002). The path to academic disability: Javier's school experience. In C. Korn, & A. Bursztyn (Eds.), *Rethinking multicultural education: Case studies in cultural transition* (pp. 160–183). Westport, CT: Bergin & Garvey.

Cummins, J. (1986). Psychological assessment of minority students: Out of context, out of control? *Journal of Reading, Writing and Learning Disabilities International, 2,* 1–8.

Figueroa, R. A., & Garcia, E. (1994). Issues in testing students from culturally and linguistically diverse backgrounds. *Multicultural Education, 1,* 9–10.

Osher, D., Sims, A., & Woodruff, D. (2002). Schools make a difference: The overrepresentation of African American youth in special education and the juvenile justice system. In D. Losen, & G. Orfield (Eds.), *Racial inequity in special education* (pp. 93–116). Cambridge: Harvard Education Press.

Further Reading

Artiles, A., & Zamora-Duran, G. (1997*). Reducing the disproportionate representation of culturally diverse students in special and gifted education.* Reston, VA: The Council for Exceptional Children.

Kincheloe, J. L., Steinberg, S. R., & Hinchey, P. H. (Eds.). (1999) *The postformal reader: Cognition and education.* New York: Falmer Press.

Losen, D. L., & Orfield, G. (2002). *Racial inequity and special education.* Cambridge, MA: The Civil Rights Project at Harvard University and Harvard Education Press.

Ogbu, J. U. (1995). Understanding cultural adversity and learning. In J. A. Banks, & C. A. McGee-Banks (Eds.), *Handbook of research on multicultural education* (pp. 582–595). New York: Macmillan.

Skrtic, T. M. (1995). *Disability and democracy: Reconstructing (special) education for postmodernity.* New York: Teachers College Press.

Diversity and Critical Thinking

Patricia H. Hinchey

The act of thinking generally implies some kind of forward mental movement: making a decision, taking a stance, or solving a problem. In situations where there is a judgment or choice to be made, people who say they need to think about the situation often assume that thinking means figuring out a single correct response. Those who think critically understand that issues do not divide neatly into right/

wrong, black/white, yes/no, with every question having a single correct answer. Essentially, critical thinking replaces an intellectually simplistic search for one *right* or *best* option with a conscious effort to identify a variety of possibilities, alternatives, and choices. Critical thinkers take nothing for granted and examine every issue from multiple perspectives. They explore different ways a problem might be defined (*I don't have money to pay my bills. Is the problem that I'm spending too much, lending too much, or earning too little?*) and multiple possible responses (*Should I stop spending? Stop lending? Should I get a job?*). Before choosing among options, critical thinkers examine the benefits and drawbacks of each, understanding that while they gain something with any choice, they inevitably lose something with it as well (*I can work more, but then I'll have less time with my friends. I can spend less, but then I won't be able to do and buy all the things I really enjoy.*)

While this description of critical thinking sounds—and is—remarkably simple and straightforward, elements of human experience and human nature make it difficult for many to think critically, especially about diversity and the differences among people. Yet cultivating the habit of thinking critically about diversity is essential, both because democracy requires that many very different groups who call themselves Americans live together in peace, and because technology is erasing geographic borders and intertwining the fate of people throughout the world.

THE COMPLICATIONS OF FEELING NORMAL

As humans, we all share certain basic experiences. Everyone grows up in a particular environment—a family, a neigh-

borhood, a region, a country—where certain ways of talking, of eating, of worshipping, of playing—of living—are considered *normal*. For children who grow up in one neighborhood, pierogi and kielbasa are *normal* foods, while for children who grow up in another, grits and black-eyed peas, or perhaps goat and papaya, or matzo and borscht, are equally *normal*. In one neighborhood, being *normal* might mean being Baptist and in another it might mean being Muslim—or Jewish—or Catholic—or Mormon.

Feeling normal, or the same as everyone else in a community, offers important psychological benefits. Having a sense of home, of being just like many others, lets people feel they belong, gives them a sure sense of identify, provides them with a sense that their world has a stable foundation: *This is where I fit in. I look, sound and act like these people, and I am one of them. I am at home here.* But as beneficial as this sense of belonging and normalcy is, it also constitutes a formidable barrier to critical thinking and generates dangerous social problems.

While everyone needs to feel normal, to identify as a member of a particular home and community, people not skilled in thinking critically often unconsciously equate what they define as *normal* as the *right* or *best* way to be. People whose normal idea of meat includes beef, pork, and chicken, for example, find it abnormal—possibly even disgusting—that others routinely eat goat, dog, or monkey. People of one faith often describe those of other faiths as *infidels, non-believers,* or *pagans.* It is human nature for one group to think that whatever it considers normal is superior to any other group's way of living, talking, or believing. So common is this tendency that most audiences immediately identify with a joke about normalcy informally credited to George Carlin: "Anyone who drives slower than I do is a moron. Anyone who drives faster than I do is a lunatic." As the joke implies, every person tends to assume that his or her way of being is the perfect way of being and that anyone who does things differently is obviously defective.

Such assumptions, however, mean that multiple groups of people constantly judge other groups as inferior or wrong or bad simply because they define *normal* differently. Carlin uses the words *lunatic* and *moron,* for example, and the negativity of those words is echoed in the religious terms above (*infidels, non-believers, pagans*) and in many political terms as well. In the United States, for example, *communists* and *socialists* are generally perceived as negative terms, while in many parts of the world *capitalist* is an equally derogatory description. Skin color, of course, as well as sexual orientation, are other ways some groups mark themselves off, or are marked off by others, as either normal (good) or abnormal (bad or inferior).

A potential problem with feeling *normal,* then, is that it leads groups of people to believe they are automatically better than other groups of people. When they encounter a person who is different in some way, many people respond to the implied question *"What shall I make of this person who is different?"* with the automatic response *"They aren't like me, so there's something wrong with them."* So pervasive is the tendency to judge other groups by a personal sense of normal that theorists who write about diversity issues often refer to any group that is disrespected or denigrated by another as the Other (*You're not like me; you're some other kind of person.*) The term can apply to any group discriminated against by some other group because of some difference between them: women/men, Southern/Northern, gay/straight, Christian/Buddhist, American/Egyptian, Republican/Democrat, and on and on.

This habit of automatically assuming superiority over the Other is the antithesis of critical thinking. Even more importantly, it is a dangerous habit that threatens both democracy and world peace. Those who feel superior generally either try to force their ways on others, causing much violence and many wars, or care less about the fate of humans they think less valuable, allowing widespread tolerance of national and global poverty and suffering. A sense of superiority leads people to forget that all groups have an essential similarity that is far more important than any difference among them and every group is human. It is neither reasonable nor productive to react to difference, which is to be expected, by thoughtlessly assuming that one particular human group is inferior or less valuable than another.

LEARNING TO THINK CRITICALLY ABOUT DIVERSITY

When one group assumes superiority over another as described above, the assumption is usually unconscious and unexamined. Few Americans think it's better to eat cow than monkey or insects because they have studied and thought carefully about all possible foods. They react negatively to the idea of an alternative diet because they have absorbed from their families and home communities the sense that it is normal, and therefore right, to eat [cow or monkey or whatever they eat] and that eating [whatever they eat] is better than eating [anything else]. In short, when people assume superiority for whatever is normal in their world, it's not a judgment based on thoughtful and informed consideration—on critical thinking. Rather, their assumptions are based on the simplistic scale of *similar to me (good)* vs. *different from me (bad)*. They are trying to make the whole world a mirror of their own life experience.

Critical thinking means avoiding such unfounded judgments. People thinking critically remember that any person's *normal* is only one of countless definitions of *normal*, they make a habit of gathering information about differences with an open mind, and they explore causes and effects, costs and benefits, before drawing any conclusions. And, they never lose sight of the critical fact that all people share the essential trait of being human beings.

Step 1: Learn to Expect Difference

Because the habit of thoughtless judgment is so ingrained, changing that behavior requires working consciously to employ critical thinking when confronted with difference. The first step towards thinking critically is to make a conscious and constant effort to remember that, given the vast, world-wide differences in geography, religions, and other characteristics, difference is to be *expected* and is, in fact, a normal part of the world at large. There is no rational reason to expect children on the island of Barbados, for example, to dress and eat the same way as children in Alaska or France. Nor is there any rational reason to expect children who grow up in Nashville to sound, act, and dress like children who grow up in New York City.

Different climates require different clothing, different housing, and different definitions of neighbors and communities. Different geography produces different food sources and, therefore, different eating habits. Different histories—especially in terms of who once conquered whom—produce differences in wealth, values, politics, religion, and language. Thus, no matter how any one particular group defines *normal*, in the world at large the most normal characteristic is *difference*. The first step to thinking critically about diversity, then, is a conscious effort to turn off the switch that immediately equates *different* with *inferior* and to remember that difference is actually to be expected—or normal.

While this may sound like an easy task, it is actually formidable. Humans have a strong tendency to constantly and unconsciously make such value judgments. In fact, the tendency is so ingrained that eliminating it is a major goal of many Eastern philosophies and religions, a goal that many people pursue for entire lifetimes. Learning to stop making immediate value judgments when confronted with difference constitutes tremendous progress toward thinking critically about issues of diversity.

Step 2: Learn to Pursue Understanding

As crucial as it is to learn to control immediate negative responses to difference, that lesson is only a first step. Confronted with difference, people thinking critically not only avoid the tendency to dismiss anything different as inferior, but to understand difference so that the conclusions they eventually reach are based on information rather than ignorance and an unconscious sense of superiority. Instead of judging they focus on understanding, asking such questions such as "What explains the difference I am noticing here? Why have Others adopted this as something that is *normal* for them? What values or circumstances explain the difference between their situation and expectations and mine? What needs of theirs are being met here? Are my needs different? Or do I meet the same needs but in a different way? Are there reasons that make this option better for them, mine better for me? Is it possible their way might be better for me in any way?" Asking such questions leads to the understanding that everyone's sense of normalcy is tied tightly to, and makes sense in, a specific individual context.

Clothing and food, for example, are often tied to geography. Wearing minimal clothing reflects climate (rather than a lack of civilization), and all diets are related to what foods that are plentiful in a particular place. Sometimes choices in these areas are dictated by differences in religion, which may prescribe clothing or diet to followers. There is no point in trying to establish one climate as better or worse than another when people live nearly everywhere, and most people like where they live. There is no point in trying to force others to accept one religion as better than another when each religion knows itself to be the one true religion. It is infinitely more helpful and important to understand these differences and to remember that all human beings are human and meeting very human needs (for shelter, clothing, food, and security) in ways that make sense *for them.*

WHY CRITICAL THINKING ABOUT DIVERSITY IS *NOT* POLITICAL CORRECTNESS

Many people are upset by the suggestion that there is no single best way to live or to think. They believe that their religion *is* the best religion, that their politics *are* the best hope for a good country, and that their way of life *is* the best way of life.

They forget that what is normal or best for them is normal or best *only* for them, and so they become upset when others suggest that other religions, politics, or lifestyles might deserve equal respect. People who feel by such suggestions often characterize efforts to promote respect for diversity as *political correctness,* a phrase that generally means an effort to make only one way of thinking publicly acceptable. Incorrectly, they argue that efforts to increase respect for diversity means that every way of living and thinking must be respected equally and that no one should have personal preferences or make any value judgments.

This is a misunderstanding. Thinking critically doesn't mean never making a personal value judgment; it means never making an *uninformed* value judgment. It also means never forgetting that others have the right to make different value judgments based on their own standards. For example, some religions require women or men to keep their heads covered as a reflection of their faith. Critical thinking doesn't require those of different faiths to agree with or practice the custom, it simply means they should not consider religious headwear weird and should try to understand its symbolic importance to the wearers.

In relation to more controversial topics, critical thinking means taking an informed stance after having made serious efforts to understand the thinking and reasoning of those on the other side of an issue. More importantly, it means not demonizing people who hold different views and respecting their right to think differently. Politicians thinking critically would make speeches embodying the theme "*I will support [some action] because I believe this particular action would accom-*

plish [these good things]. I know others believe this is not the best action, but I disagree [because of these factors]." Unfortunately, politicians usually offer examples of the kind of value judgments critical thinkers avoid: *"I'm right and my opponent's wrong because, as anyone can see, s/he's [not very smart, careless, bad in some way]."* In contrast to such blatant disrespect, critical thinking means being fully informed about all options and then taking a stance based on informed reasoning without personally attacking those who think differently.

The respectful approach of critical thinking is the very opposite of political correctness, which involves replacing one sanctified version of *truth* or *normalcy* with another. People may disagree vehemently about issues and strategies because their reasoning and values differ, but disagreeing does not require forgetting that the Other is also human and also has values, however different they may be.

How people react when confronted with difference has an enormous impact on both individual and group relationships. Any progress that a person or group can make in developing the habit of thinking critically about and trying to understand Others—instead of automatically assuming cultural superiority over them, demonizing them, and using force to impose conformity on them—will be progress toward the goal of living together peacefully, both nationally and internationally.

Further Reading

Brooks, K. (1995). *Cultural diversity without prejudice: A guide for critical thinking in the 21st century*. Vallejo, CA: Amper Publishing.

Elder, L., & Paul, R. (2001). Critical thinking: Thinking to some purpose. *Journal of Developmental Education, 25,* 40–41.

Paul, R., & Elder, L. (2001). Critical thinking: Inert information, activated ignorance, and activated knowledge. *Journal of Developmental Education, 25,* 36–37.

Indigenous Ways of Knowing and Critical Thinking

Ladislaus M. Semali

Learning to think critically is one of the most significant activities of human life and it is not unique to people from only one particular region of the world. The ability to think critically is important for our lives in many different ways. When we become critical thinkers we develop an awareness of the assumptions under which we, and others, think and act. When we think critically, we come to our judgments, choices, and decisions by ourselves, instead of letting others do this for us. We refuse to relinquish the responsibility for making the choices that determine our individual and collective futures to those who presume to know what is in our own best interests. We become actively engaged in creating our personal and social worlds. In short, we reclaim ourselves and take the reality of democracy seriously.

In this essay, I discuss the epistemology surrounding critical thinking and indigenous ways of knowing, an epistemology that is different from the Euro-American positivistic rationality prevalent in Western domains of science and technology. Through this discussion and by exposing the oral narratives of indigenous peoples, I envision a new, indigenously informed education inspired by the learning styles of indigenous and minority students' lived experiences. I also envisage the cultural learning environments of diverse populations, including indigenous children, to take on more importance as teachers connect them to the larger epistemological and cultural dynamics they are helping the students analyze. I anticipate that, from this discussion, new definitions of intelligence, critical thinking, and critical education will emerge that are broadly defined to include minority and indigenous worldviews.

My objective is to illustrate critical thinking as transformative pedagogy and as a learning method along the lines of what Paulo Freire, the Brazilian educator, called "unity in diversity." The assumption is that, as learners read the word and the world critically through multiple lenses, they can decolonize knowledge production from the hierarchies and dynamics of power. In the sense used here, indigeneity, which includes the use of indigenous languages, points to the notion of specific locality that identifies people's ways of thinking and ways of knowing with their environment. Such identity gives people a sense of consciousness or awareness to perceive themselves and their local-level understandings of how things are and are done, including perceptions of problems and strategies to solve them. This local people's consciousness also includes a sense of pride in owning their past, culture, and traditions. A sense of pride motivates local peoples and their children to be able to critically use knowledge about their history, culture, and traditions as a basis for contributing to global knowledge systems about their social development, welfare, and survival.

The debates raging in academia between traditional philosophers and the postmodern approaches that critique cognitive psychology are at the center of understanding the tensions and contradictions that have undermined the link between critical thinking, the constructive knower, and indigenous ways of knowing. In this debate, teachers of indigenous children struggle over the prevailing distinction made between Western scientific knowledge and non-Western indigenous knowledge. For example, in the postcolonial worlds of Africa, Asia, and Latin America, different world-views are expressed through oral traditions, rites, and agrarian and health practices. These practices have endured locally over many centuries. The diversity of knowledge systems found in these indigenous groups is staggering—from groups such as the Indians of the Americas, the Inuits and Samis of the Artic, the Maori of New Zealand, the Koori of Australia, the Karins and Katchins of Burma, the Kurds of Persia, the Bedouins of the African/Middle Eastern desert, many African tribal communities, and even the Basques and Gaels of contemporary Europe. There are indigenous people all over the world, and knowledge of their particular way of solving problems and seeing the world (that existed before Western schooling) was viewed as a prerequisite for participation in the mainstream political and economic institutions of their day.

In academia, critical thinking has been adopted and framed as the tool to guide philosophers towards the Truth and Certainty. Scholars such as Thomas Kuhn have challenged this narrow view of critical thinking, saying it is more than facts, truth, and certainty (Kuhn, 1970). The criticism over these traditional notions of critical thinking goes well beyond the references that associate critical thinking with masculine mental activity while believing is considered feminine or childlike. These positivistic ways of characterizing thinking and knowing and the quest for knowledge, truth, and certainty have inserted a wedge between dominant groups and subjugated communities, between those who can think and those who cannot, those who can name the world and those who cannot, between Western countries and non-Western countries, between developed and under-developed, and between industrial and non-industrial societies. Like children, women, and poor people, indigenous folks have been framed as the Other and presented as gullible, primitive, simple-minded creatures, rather than intellectual skeptics or problem-solvers.

Kuhn reminds us that defining critical thinking in these limited ways ignores the fundamental fact that we are contextual knowers, regardless of age, time, history, or ethnicity. There is a subjective side to all the things we come to know, experience, or represent in oral language, writing, or in visual communication. We cannot decontextualize ourselves from time, place, or culture. On the basis of Kuhn's insights, I would insist that it is important to recognize that all knowledge is contextually situated, local, and indigenous. The project of assigning critical thinking to academia rather than the community, to Western nations rather than non-Western nations, to colonizers rather than to native peoples, is a futile endeavor. The lesson to

be derived from these postmodern approaches is that human language and language-based thinking is tentative, subjective, and relative, not that the universe or human life is relative.

When I was a child, I learned everything in relation to others. Even learning how to use language and developing thought happens because we are social beings in relationship with each other. There is no better place to start to question this contradiction than to examine how the intelligence of minority and indigenous children is measured in schools. Some schools consider intelligence the ability to reason, solve problems, think critically, and adapt to the environment. Although this notion appears logical, it breaks down when one carefully examines how intelligence is measured by IQ tests. Typically, IQ tests evaluate factual knowledge, knowledge of the definitions of words, memory recall, fine-motor coordination, and an individual's ability to use expressive language. They usually do not measure reasoning or problem-solving skills and assess only what a person has learned, not what he or she is capable of doing.

When intelligence is perceived this way and tests are constructed on this perception, they are useless for evaluating the minds of indigenous children growing up in Chaggaland. An IQ test is not culture-free because it is based on the background of the test makers, nor is it language-free if it requires a knowledge of English. In some subsets of an IQ test, for example, extra points are given for responding quickly, which puts a premium on speed and quick thinking. An individual with a culturally based slow, deliberate style may not achieve as high a score as an individual who responds more quickly. This is a problem that cannot be overcome by simply translating the test into a student's first language. In essence, IQ tests are based on the notion that scores do not represent a single entity but are a composite of many skills (see Siegel, 1988 and Gunderson & Siegel, 2001).

These ways of defining intelligence contradict the indigenous ways of knowing in which I was socialized. In my upbringing, speaking or responding to a question impulsively was discouraged. It was considered simple-minded, not serious thinking. The old adage has it: "Look before you leap." This sums up the wisdom that was imparted to me by my parents and teachers. Pausing before reacting to a question was highly commended and was seen as good indicator of deep and critical thinking.

Knowing, however, encompasses both the process of learning and the process of mastering what is learned so it can be used in one's world. In my own indigenous context, *Imanya* (knowing) is a complex concept. *Imanya* is to know intellectually and to be morally or spiritually motivated at the same time. According to Chagga sages, these two concepts within *Imanya* are inseparable. There is also the idea of *Ikusara* (thinking). The concept of *Ikusara* includes the broad parameters of critical thinking. For instance, in conversations with my grandparents and common folk in the village where I grew up in Africa, the word *kusare* was used a lot. Literally, it means think. But, *kusare* is taken from the root *Isara,* which means to consider all the possibilities of a topic, including its context, the assumptions it makes, and the conditions that gave it birth. When an elder or a sage in the community told a young man: *Kusare necha* (Think, consider all possibilities), such admonition was profound. In this context *kusare* means to ponder, to think deeply.

To emphasize the value of deep thinking, variations of the term *Isara* were also used as personal names for certain individuals. Names such as *Makusaro, Ndekusara, Ndesara, Kusare,* and *Nzarenau* are common names for both boys and girls. Furthermore, thinking deeply can be found in a number of wise sayings found in the culture and was often used by sages and elders who summed up their advice or admonitions with a saying, riddle, or proverb to capture the essence or context of the guidance they desired to impart. As noted by Sambuli Mosha, customarily sages or formators such as *Walosha, Wamangi,* indigenous doctors, and others, tell proverbs extensively to give inspiration and insight or to evoke profound thinking, and to ultimately mold the listener's moral fiber (Sambuli-Mosha, 2000).

Proverbs are therefore at the very heart of the indigenous thought process and critical thinking is part of this process. Throughout my youth I was constantly reminded of the local parables, riddles, oral narratives, proverbs, and sayings of the sages. These narrative practices point to the epistemological assumptions about thinking, knowledge, and how the Chagga community acquired knowledge. The ability to remember and apply these devices and other figures of speech was commended and rewarded as signs of intelligence and maturity towards adult life, particularly the ability to match present assumptions with the wisdom of sages over time.

Because of prevailing myths and persistent misconceptions about indigenous peoples and minorities in academia, it is not surprising that local knowledges, histories, cultures, and traditions are not valued as significant resources of critical listening, critical thinking, or critical authoring in public schools. Critical thinking is a lived activity, not an abstract academic pastime. Pondering these alternative ways of thinking about indigenous ways of knowing, we need to take a harder glance at some of the myths surrounding questions still found in school texts: Are indigenous peoples rational? Can they think? Can they solve problems on their own? We need to ask ourselves: How did indigenous peoples go about solving problems endemic to their local environment about diseases, food, animal husbandry, etc., before the invention of science labs and funded research?

These questions require extensive discussion. However, the process of decolonization explored in critical thinking and in indigenous ways of knowing maps out the discursive terrain of indigeneity, histories, cultures, and traditions, and how they collectively impact the way common folk in indigenous communities think and live their lives. This process of decolonization requires indigenous peoples everywhere to confront the arrogant idea that other folks know and understand them better than they understand themselves. We must recognize that indigenous peoples can theorize about and conceptualize their social and natural world in ways that are as deep and complex as any produced by Western traditions.

References

Gunderson, L., & Siegel, L. (2001). The evils of the use of IQ tests to define learning disabilities in first- and second-language learners. *The Reading Teacher, 55* (1), 48–55.

Kuhn, T. (1970). *The structure of scientific revolutions* (2nd ed.). Chicago: University of Chicago Press.

Sambuli-Mosha, R. (2000). *The heartbeat of indigenous Africa: A study of the Chagga educational system.* New York: Falmer Press.

Siegel, L. (1988). Evidence that IQ scores are irrelevant to the definition and analysis of reading disability. *Canadian Journal of Psychology, 42,* 201–215.

Further Reading

Dei, G., Hall, B., & Rosenberg, D. (2000). *Indigenous knowledge in global contexts.* Toronto: Toronto University Press.

Freire, P., & Macedo, D. (1987). *Literacy: Reading the word and the world.* South Hadley, MA: Bergin & Garvey.

Semali, L., & Kincheloe, J. L. (1999). *What is indigenous knowledge: Voices from the academy.* New York: Falmer Press.

Multicultural Education

Timothy Spraggins

What is multicultural education? Some say it's a specific educational reform as well as a method or process (Banks, 1999), some say it is an idealistic view of the world that can never work in the classroom, and still others say multicultural education "just happens" whenever students from different cultures are in the same class. Just discussing the topic can be overwhelming because there are so many different views.

To answer the question, perhaps we should examine what multicultural education is not and go from there.

Multicultural education is not some idealistic theory or concept that lacks educational meaning for teachers and students at all grade levels. It is not the teaching of romanticized melting pot stories or an ethnic pot-luck dinner, nor does it involve seating students who are from different cultures next to each other in a classroom. After all, nearly everyone eats Chinese carry-out, but how does merely consuming Chinese food help us consume Chinese history or Chinese-American history/culture?

CONTEXT AND DEFINITION

While multicultural education is much bigger than any of these definitions, it can begin with any one of them. Multicultural education is indeed a movement. It expands the classroom's traditional responsibility to and relationship with society. At the same time, it is also a philosophy that encourages teachers to explore ways of helping students better understand society through critical thinking. For an experience to be both multicultural and education, however, several specific things must occur. First of all, learning should unfold within the greater context of citizenship education and the desire to help students view their world through critical lenses. In addition to—or as a part of—traditional academic lessons, students must discuss complex, even unsolvable, social problems. Students must express their honest thoughts, and the teacher/facilitator must structure and guide the discussions, challenging students to question their own ideas and values. When possible, the teacher should also bridge the discussion and include historical events already discussed (the Civil War, antebellum slavery, etc.) and national/local current events (publicized hate-crimes, racial profiling, etc.).

All students (and teachers) bring beliefs and values to the classroom. Many of these values stigmatize certain groups, such as the homeless, residents of inner-city housing projects, or members of ethnic/cultural/religious groups. It is important to understand that the source of the students' values is their communities of practice: their families, neighbors, schools, churches, and civil/social groups, most of which are neither multicultural nor diverse (Cullinan, 2000). Children hear their parents, grandparents, and family friends openly using slurs against gays, Blacks, Jews, etc., and they overhear offensive ethnic/gender jokes. This constitutes many students' early exposure to differences, and they mirror the behaviors and internalize the values. As a result, they dislike, fear, and stereotype the groups of people their relatives dislike, fear, and stereotype. This principle applies to all students, not just students from middle-class, White suburbia.

Although students bring their communities of practice to class each day inside themselves, the classroom itself fortunately becomes a community of practice of its own. As such, it provides an opportunity for un-learning and re-teaching. It provides a place for multicultural education to unfold.

Understanding the power of such external influences on students, teachers should help them become more than just merit scholars. Teachers should strive to inspire critical thinkers who will use their scholarship and skills to advance democracy, and the educational system should support these efforts. Most of today's classroom communities are both diverse and homogeneous at the same time. The diversity is in the different communities the students represent, and the homogeneity is in the ideas, teaching, and emotions that have already pushed these students worlds apart, although they literally sit next to each other. These same students will become leaders in every aspect of society. Multicultural education can help them view each other differently and fear each other less while in school. It can also teach them to think critically, to question rather than accept status-quo prejudices, and can help them (as adults) reshape and produce more democratic policies in society.

EXAMPLES

During critical discussions, the teacher should encourage students to speak honestly, capitalize on the positive voices and use them to help challenge the negative voices, and de-segregate both the values and voices of each community. It is important to hear the students' ideas. When stereotypes arise, the teacher should question the idea by offering examples that differ from the prejudices it represents and help the entire class understand how it represents stereotypes. Other students will also provide experiences and images that weaken prejudiced beliefs.

Throughout the dialogue, the teacher must question the idea, not the student or the source of the idea. This point is important because it's easy for students to interpret the teacher's words to mean their parents—and other role models—are bad people. It's also important because the students can interpret this to mean he/she is a bad person. At certain levels of development, students' total identity is determined by what they know and who taught it to them. The teacher should understand

that multicultural education often impacts identity. Not only should the teacher offer to talk further with anyone after such discussions, but the teacher should also monitor the classroom for signs of difficulty during discussions. The teacher should watch students who seem to struggle with a comment, as well as those who seem emotional and/or disconnected. Multicultural education activities should never be left completely in the hands of the students.

Few traditional curricula provide a context for meaningful multicultural education. The "Dick-and-Jane" concept—whether or not their names are ever called—of teaching elementary-school classes and the Twain/Shakespeare, "don't-rock-the-boat" curriculum of the higher grades equate to status-quo teaching and produce a status-quo citizenry, society, and culture. This does not mean that Twain and Shakespeare should not be taught, it means that they should be taught along with something else less traditional and it means they should be taught critically. The teacher can question the wisdom of Romeo and Juliet's decisions to kill themselves and can compare these two lovers' backgrounds to those of an interracial or inter-religious love affair, fleshing out specific prejudices that face such couples face in today's society. With a "Dick and Jane" (or a comparable paradigm), the teacher should help students identify which types of people are missing from the books, ask how many students have friends or know people who seem to be missing from the books, and apply this conversation to other aspects of society.

Within this context, the pot-luck can become multicultural education, but only if it unfolds within a discussion of the significance of food to aspects of culture. The significance can be defined as the economic, political, and/or social forces of given time-periods. For example, soul food includes such items as pig ears, tails, feet, and intestines (chitlins), all of which evolved from African slave culture. The masters discarded these pieces of the kill and slaves used the scraps to supplement their diets. Students can learn more about the lives any ethnic or cultural group by studying their food.

Seating people from different backgrounds next to each other is not multicultural and it is not education. Many of us sit/stand next to people who are different from us each day—and sometimes even exchange friendly greetings. How much does sitting next to or even saying, "Good morning . . . nice weather. . . . What do you think about The Cubs this year?" teach us about each other's culture, history, and the oppressions that often accompany both? How much do such superficial exchanges reduce our prejudices and liberate us from internalized oppressions? If we're honest, we will say, "Very little, if any." The same is true in classroom communities where the teacher seats Black students, White students, Asian students, Latino students, students from low-income families, students from wealthy families, students from same-sex parents, students whose first language is not English, etc., next to each other and continues with business as usual. The teacher (or school) who promotes this scenario as multicultural education has completely missed the boat.

Multicultural education teaches students to critically analyze complex social issues and regards this ability as a basic skill that is just as important as skills in mathematics and language. The teacher develops lesson plans to teach critical thinking in the same way lesson plans for teaching math, English, and biology are developed. For instance, as part of social

studies or current events, the teacher can facilitate a discussion about homeless people. The class can discuss reasons people become homeless and explore difficulties homeless children must face. If possible, the teacher can connect the discussion to local issues, such as a housing project that's being demolished, and discuss how they contribute to homelessness. Such discussions show students of all ages how to critically explore all aspects of issues, rather than merely accept the convenient, superficial answers. It will also push some students beyond the simplistic and prejudiced values learned from their other communities of practice.

To take the analogy one step further: after such a discussion, the teacher can show students (at all levels) how to exercise activism and democracy. They can write a letter to the mayor or the governor requesting that children displaced by the gentrification of a neighborhood or made homeless for other reasons have affordable housing and a quality education. The teacher can use a similar approach to help students understand other social issues, including the publicized racial/religious tensions in certain communities or the closing of a nursing home.

RISKS

Teachers of multicultural education take risks. One of these is never knowing where the conversation might go. This means the teacher must be insightful enough to recognize warning signs and steer the dialogue back to a positive direction, all at a moment's notice. The teacher should be able to tactfully diffuse slurs and inflammatory statements without attacking either the child or the source and without validating the statement. Another risk is parents' reactions. Some parents might think their children are too young to discuss such complicated issues, and some might think it's their role to shape their child's values. Using the contexts of citizenship education and teaching students to navigate a changing society/workforce, the teacher should inform parents that such topics will be discussed at the beginning of and throughout the year. Invite the parents to share their concerns in one-on-one conversations at any time. These discussions also make parents nervous about having dirty laundry aired. Just as on Art Linkletter's 1960's television show, *Kids Say the Darndest Things,* where children often revealed the very things their parents asked them not to say, students in this setting can easily expose their parents. The teacher should be sensitive to this and remember that parents will mask embarrassment with anger.

Obtain the approval of your principal before you begin multicultural discussions. Give her/him the rationale of your syllabus, your learning goals and strategies, and examples of topics in advance. In addition, share projects and ideas with other teachers. Even think of bringing groups together—depending on the sizes of the classes—for a special discussion or field trip, followed by a discussion.

SUMMARY

Multicultural education can help tomorrow's leaders become critical thinkers who understand democracy, citizenship, and the responsibilities of having power and privilege. The world has become a global village and it shrinks more each day. Educators have an opportunity and a responsibility to help transform this global village into a global community that functions with minimal friction because of differences.

Further Reading

Banks, J. A., & Banks, C. A. M. (1999). *Multicultural education issues and perspectives* (4th ed.). New York: John Wiley & Sons.

Cullinan, C. (2000). *Institute for diversity trainers resource manual.* The 13th Annual National Conference on Race and Ethnicity in Higher Education. Santa Fe, NM.

Sleeter, C., & Grant, C. A. (1999). *Making choices for multicultural education. Five approaches to race, class, and gender* (3rd ed.). New York: John Wiley & Sons.

Rap Music: The Critical Pedagogy of KRS-One

Priya Parmar

We live in a society that is undoubtedly becoming more multicultural by the moment, yet individuals and groups still experience social inequalities, structural exclusion, and anti-democratic practices. Such experiences and practices pose a significant challenge for educators because schools have failed to empower students to think critically, question power relations, and develop the critical thinking skills necessary to make informed and effective choices about the worlds of work, politics, culture, personal relationships, and the economy. Critical thinking empowers students, enabling them to stand up for themselves and appreciate others different from themselves.

A critical thinking approach to education is crucial. It allows students to receive culturally relevant, meaningful content, as well as to participate in student-centered activities. The absence of critical thinking results in schools that tend to confirm or value certain cultures and disavow, devalue, and marginalize others. Particular forms of knowledge, language, and experience familiar only to certain (privileged) students are legitimized, thereby reproducing what critical theorists often refer to as cultural capital. Students from the lower or working-classes are not familiar with, nor do they possess, the same cultural capital as mainstream-class students.

Legitimizing certain cultures and devaluing others disempowers the students, their families, and the communities who are part of the devalued cultures because their personal histories and experiences are not affirmed. Research has shown that, if given the opportunity to do creative and critical thinking activities, working-class students are capable of achieving the same success as upper-class students. For students to achieve this kind of success, the teacher must transform the curriculum and help students map their relation to the social worlds around them, comprehend the connection between personal and social problems, and realize the complex ways in which they are connected to people both like themselves and radically different from themselves. When students' histories are connected and compared to the larger social context, it encourages them to question and analyze power relations, inequality, and social justice issues in society.

Racism, sexism, and discrimination are frequently explored and discussed in a safe learning environment in which different perspectives are valued, respected, and understood. In such a critical thinking classroom, all opinions, thoughts, and ideas from all students are welcomed and respected.

Educators must empower all of their students, in particular those from different ethnic and cultural backgrounds as well as working class backgrounds, by ensuring that they develop both a strong self-identity and a proud and knowledgeable group identity to withstand the attacks of racism. Educators can accomplish this by expanding their curriculum to include literacies and/or texts with which their students are already familiar. One such example is the inclusion of rap music as a form of cultural pedagogy and cultural literacy used in critical thinking activities. According to the Recording Industry Association of America (RIAA), rap's share of the popular music market doubled from the late eighties to the nineties. Rap and rhythm 'n' blues together accounted for 23 percent of music sales in 1990, up from 16 percent in 1989. Because the popularity and sales of rap music alone skyrocketed so much in 1998, the RIAA announced that rap was the best-selling musical genre in the United States. In fact, what had traditionally been known as Black music had crossed the color line. Interesting to note as well is the fact that in 2001 more than 70 percent of rap consumers were White suburban youth as reported by SoundScan, a company that tracks retail sales.

Given the increasing popularity of the music, rap can be used as a tool to help the dominant class understand its position compared to others who are different from them. Many rap songs make this difference painfully clear and problematize this system of racial inequality where Blacks (and other minority groups) are marginalized, silenced, and excluded from the cultural dialogue, and White cultural values are assumed to be the norm. Using rap music in critical thinking activities challenges students to question and expose dominant ideological discourses and hegemonic practices. Rap music, and any other form of popular culture studied in such a fashion, creates the need for teachers and students to engage in the critical thinking of multiple literacies.

As indicated earlier by RIAA and Soundscan, rap music in general embodies a postmodern aesthetic because it reaches a wide range of audiences at national and international levels, regardless of race, culture, and ethnicity. In a cultural context, rap is a powerful language, articulating the experiences and marginality that African American working-class and under-class people experience. Rap provides a voice and method of social protest for these groups because it spoke out against oppressive conditions, from everyday life in the neighborhood and workplace to institutions of learning. Because certain kinds of rap music challenge the social forces that contribute to the rappers' living conditions, especially more political and militant rap styles, its creators may be met with what Houston Baker calls moral panic.

There are many political or consciousness-raising rap artists, such as Chuck D and Public Enemy, The Roots, Mos Def, Dead Prez, and others, but they do not receive as much media recognition as the raps that are indeed misogynist, homophobic, and violent. I will focus on one particular rap artist, KRS-One, who has become widely known as The Teacher.

KRS-One, which stands for Knowledge Reigns Supreme Over Nearly Every-

one, began his career in the mid-1980's as a member of Boogie Down Productions, the politically-driven rap group he helped form. In 1993, KRS-One went on to perform as a solo artist, releasing more than seven albums to date and organizing several hip hop benefit projects to educate youth on the construction and understanding of knowledge in all realms of life (*Stop the Violence Movement; HEAL–Human Education Against Lies,* a project that explores the need for cultural education and family responsibility, and most recently *The Temple of Hip Hop*). KRS-One has argued that the goal of *The Temple of Hip Hop* is to achieve a balance between traditional hip hop, modern hip hop, and future hip hop. He further argued that if we, as a society, do not begin today to educate the youth of tomorrow with a continued systematic flow of knowledge and tradition, hip hop culture could become overly commercialized and absorbed into the American mainstream, where it would lose all its richness, authenticity, and history. (Hip hop culture is composed of four elements: graffiti art, deejaying, rhyming or rapping, and breaking or breakdancing. Rap music is only one element of hip hop culture.)

KRS-One's rap reflects a knowledge that is subjugated, but he serves as a spokesperson and teacher for the oppressed. KRS-One teaches from a perspective commonly found in the daily lives of marginalized inner-city Black male youth. He also raps from his own lived experience on the streets. His message is authentic and real and is easy for youth to relate to.

KRS-One's self-proclaimed role as The Teacher could be legitimized and/or seen as Paulo Freire's cultural worker, Antonio Gramsci's organic intellectual, and Henry Giroux's public intellectual. Although some may argue that KRS-One is not a certified mainstream teacher or educator, his self-proclaimed role as The Teacher has passed the test of time. He has proven that he is not just another arrogant rapper or a here today, gone tomorrow rapper with a short-lived career like many other artists in the changeable popular music industry. In fact, KRS-One's career has spanned 15 years, earning him the distinguished titles of teacher, instructor, and even philosopher, as many now call him. Certification does not make a qualified teacher. KRS-One embodies the qualities that make any teacher memorable and excellent.

KRS-One's purpose, regardless of his target audience, is to unveil the unofficial truths about the social, political, and cultural conditions in urban communities. He wants his audience to develop a critical-consciousness and self-consciousness so that they become aware of the conditions surrounding poverty-stricken and ghetto areas. More importantly, KRS-One's pedagogy encourages the oppressed to take social action against power institutions (specifically the media, the police, the government, and the educational system) that may be holding them down. He encourages his audience, and youth in particular, to take control of their destiny in a positive manner if they want to attain material wealth, and asks them not to participate in destructive activities (i.e., violence, gangs, drugs) that will undermine the goal of beginning a revolution.

Educators can incorporate KRS-One's rap and critique of society and major power institutions across the curriculum, especially in the social sciences and language arts areas. For example, "You Must Learn" (*Ghetto Music: The Blueprint of Hip Hop,* Jive Records, 1989) is a powerful critique of the established curriculum in current educational systems. The song challenges educators and students to re-think the traditional curriculum and consider issues of racial and cultural representation in an undoubtedly growing multicultural society. KRS-One accuses traditional, Western-European curriculum content of alienating Black students from society and schooling because these students' experiences, culture, voice, and beliefs are different from those of mainstream students and are not represented in their education. As a result, Black students are unable to make the connections between what is supposed to be learned and how it relates to their own experiences, which is an important component of critical thinking and critical pedagogy.

Analyzing and interpreting rap lyrics in a classroom that uses critical thinking and critical literacy helps students gain new insights, perspectives, and ideas and to reflect critically and thoughtfully on the social, cultural, political, and economic forces that help shape their identity. In addition, critical analysis and reflection helps to dispel stereotypes, misperceptions, and myths about certain youths and their communities that are commonly perpetuated by dominant ideologies. For example, in "You Must Learn," KRS-One offers his listeners a short Black history lesson, stressing the importance of learning about all peoples' cultures and histories. He introduces his audience to many famous Blacks that traditional textbooks leave out, such as Benjamin Banneker who created the almanac; Eli Whitney, the inventor of the cotton gin; Haile Selassie, Egyptian leader and social reformer; Granville Woods who created the walkie talkie; Lewis Latimer, who improved on Edison's inventions; Charles Drew, a pioneer in medicine; Garrett Morgan who invented traffic lights; Madame C. J. Walker, who developed a straightening comb, etc. In

"You Must Learn," KRS-One blames the traditional Western-European history curriculum for not expanding further on the cultures, histories, and contributions of Other peoples, and producing brainwashed youth who have no real concept of American history. KRS-One's critique of the curriculum is one example of the awareness that critical thinking and critical pedagogy hopes to achieve.

Critical thinking involves actively engaging students by including their personal experiences in the texts being studied. Students who have control and are put in charge of their own learning by having the power to choose areas of interest to study are ultimately engaged in an emancipatory, democratic education. For example, instead of (or in addition to) having students simply find the author's main idea, purpose, and conclusion when reading any form of literature or text, they can be encouraged to write their own stories, using their own experiences, ideas, feelings, and interests, and include some of these basic elements.

Students reading or listening to KRS-One's rap lyrics, for example, can learn to read them with a critical eye, questioning his point of view; asking which cultures are represented and which gender, racial, or class stereotypes are found; what the relationship is between the story plot and the students' own personal lives; what some of the possible causes that lead to poverty, inhumane living conditions, unemployment, and other economic disparities and inequalities are; what role major power institutions, such as the government, media, and educational systems play in influencing or perpetuating, directly or indirectly, such inequalities. Students can ask whether they interact with their friends and family as the characters do, how their living conditions are similar to or different from those of the characters and why, what some of the possible reasons are for economic disparities and inequalities, and how their time and society are different from or similar to those in the text. When viewing texts such as rap, or any other form of popular culture, students learn to critically examine issues such as race, class, culture, ethnicity, and identity, instead of passively allowing the text to unconsciously shape their values, thoughts, and beliefs.

KRS-One's song "The Racist" (*Edutainment,* Jive Records, 1990) for example, could be brought into a high school classroom so students could deconstruct the lyrics. The song, according to KRS-One, makes clear distinctions between five different types of racists. He introduces his listeners to the most prevailing form of racism in today's society by implying that everything that is taught, learned, and viewed comes from the dominant culture's perspective and/or point of view. Students can argue for or against KRS-One's position by critically analyzing and evaluating how the dominant culture imposes its beliefs and/or influences, especially by examining various mediums within popular culture (media representations, films, television programs, radio, television, public and/or billboard advertisements, and other genres of music, etc.). KRS-One's reference to the "Great White Way" in the song has the possibility of triggering a stimulating and informative discussion as students learn to question the meaning behind these words, opening doors to learning exciting lessons in economics, history and social studies.

The song continues with KRS-One describing the second type of racist, who is motivated by fear. KRS-One challenges listeners to confront their own fears, stereotypes, and perceptions of people different from themselves. Students and, perhaps more importantly, teachers addressing this type of racism force themselves to evaluate their own conscious and unconscious fears about difference. The notion that racism is born out of fear and ignorance is an important, relevant, and necessary topic for discussion since it lies at the heart of why people of color experience injustices, inequities, misperceptions, and stereotyping.

KRS-One goes on to explore the third and fourth types of racists: people who are unconscious of their racist ideologies and people who are racist purely for financial and economic gain. He again opens the door for students to re-examine past historical events, forcing them to question what they have learned in traditional history courses and compare it to the truth about how the nation was built.

Prior to reading the last verse of the song, students (particularly White students) may feel that KRS-One is the real racist, blaming all social injustices on Whites alone. However, in the conclusion of the song, KRS-One identifies ignorant Black men as being the fifth type of racist. He condemns those who blame the entire White race for the social inequalities and injustices that Black people had to endure, especially during the periods of slavery and the Civil Rights movement. KRS-One argues that power institutions such as the media, government, and education systems mislead people and provoke a feeling of us versus them or Black versus White. These dichotomies lead to hostility, resentment, and separatism. KRS-One argues that Blacks and Whites did indeed come together for the fight of freedom (the Civil Rights movement), and therefore once both races (in particular the working classes) recognize they suffer from similar social, political, and economic struggles,

they will again fight together to overcome their oppression.

White students who are able to understand the dynamics of being in a privileged position simply by being White, and who are able to see through the eyes and perspectives of non-Whites, may then be able to understand that racial inequalities and injustices exist for a range of reasons. It is particularly important to teach students from the dominant (White) classes, who are largely unconscious of the privilege they hold, to understand both the concept of class and the fact that they come from a specific class themselves.

Using critical thinking skills when deconstructing a text such as "The Racist" helps the individual student draw a range of possible meanings from the text that reflect their gender, race, class, cultural background, and personal experiences. The meaning of this particular text, or any text for that matter, is not something determined by the teacher or even the author but by a dynamic and changeable relationship between the reader and the text. The role of the teacher is to assist students in developing critical skills that will allow them to negotiate active readings—readings which recognize the range of possible meanings in a text, the values and biases implicit in those meanings, and which involve conscious choices rather than the unconscious acceptance of preferred readings.

Critical thinking teachers also encourage students to create their own scripts and/or videos after watching, reading, and/or listening to popular culture texts such as rap music. Writing scripts from their own perspective is a form of critical thinking and critical pedagogy because the students' creative, personal writing allows them to construct stories based on their own experiences and gives them the freedom to select which cultures, races, and classes will be represented. Students can also present their script to the class, and give other students the chance to ask questions about the choices they made as the author, or their choice of point of view.

If given the opportunity, students can critically view numerous other popular culture texts besides rap music, such as commercials, music videos, television and radio programs, movies, video games, news broadcasts, newspapers, magazines, and many, many others. Comparing, contrasting, and connecting popular culture with the required traditional curricula (required readings of particular novels, poems, and literature) can facilitate and foster critical thinking skills.

If students have expert knowledge in a specific area of interest, such as rap music, the teacher could empower the students by asking them to explain to the teacher and the class the rules for creating a new rap song. After learning these patterns, the teacher could use them as a foundation to teach basic skills, such as grammar and sentence structure. To approach teaching in such a manner allows the media forms that are important to students to be incorporated into the existing curriculum.

Another example of KRS-One challenging the educational power system is in the appropriately titled song "Why Is That?" (*Ghetto Music: The Blueprint of Hip Hop,* Jive Records, 1989) in which he asks why traditional curriculum content appears to center around the lives of White students (culture). KRS-One's philosophy is similar to that of John Dewey's philosophy of education, which postulated that schools tend to create and re-create the existing (dominant) culture's beliefs and practices (cultural hegemony). The song continues with KRS-One acting as a teacher presenting a lesson to Black listeners ("well Black kids follow me"). He goes on to describe the genealogy of famous biblical figures including Abraham, Isaac, Moses, and Jacob, using examples of Scripture ("Genesis Chapter 14, Verse 13"; "Genesis, Chapter 10") to support his theory that humans originated in Africa and evolved from the Black race. KRS-One's reframing of the past helps people understand the present construction of Black identity in a way that reaffirms and reserves their sense of self. In addition, his attack on the standard curriculum, and in particular the teaching of history and how it leads to the construction of (false) identity, is an important issue that should be addressed within the educational system.

The lyrics in "Why Is That?" urge listeners to confront oppressive issues through knowledge and not through violence alone. Anger, according to KRS-One, is acceptable if one uses it constructively (through the mind) and with the hope of achieving empowerment and social equity as the final outcome. The song encourages listeners to think critically, to make decisions, and to take action against situations and/or conditions that do not include them, rather than to passively receive and adopt canonized modes of thinking and living that serve to maintain the status quo.

Educators are cheating both themselves and their students by not working in and with the various mediums that speak loudest to their students. Excluding rap and other examples of popular culture from the curriculum keeps voices from being heard and denies the validity of the life experiences, languages, and cultural expression of many students. The refusal to incorporate popular culture texts such as rap supports the belief that the culture that students bring to the schools is not legitimate or valued. The inclusion of the students' views (subjugated knowledge) creates an awareness that all individuals can claim an identity of their own rather than one forced on them.

The kind of knowledge that KRS-One articulates in his rap resonates with a system of literacies that move beyond the traditional forms of literacy taught in today's schools. KRS-One's rap can be viewed as a kind of literacy that could be a significant means of social change because it encompasses cultural literacy, social literacy, political literacy, and eco-literacy. KRS-One's pedagogy is, in Freire's terms, unquiet, which makes it more critical, radical, and controversial in the eyes of the dominant culture.

The knowledge and message that KRS-One sends attempt to enhance the autonomy and control of powerless learners and their communities over their environment. The inclusion of rap music in the curriculum produces new forms of social interaction and cultural awareness that are much needed because they result in an appreciation, awareness, and celebration of differences, multiplicity, and diversity.

KRS-One's rap is a conscientious rap that provokes listeners to fight for a more democratic and emancipatory curriculum and education, and it pushes his listeners to question all texts, which is the first step in attaining necessary change and freedom (similar to Freire's consciousness-raising). KRS-One says in his music that Black people are slaves to a belief system that is an integral part of the dominant culture. According to critical theory, once the oppressed become aware of their oppression they can then critique it to determine what is wrong and how it should be corrected, and make decisions and take actions toward the perceived change.

KRS-One's philosophy of education is strikingly analogous to themes found in critical theory and critical thinking. His music situates itself within a critical theory/critical thinking framework, confronting power issues from a critical, theoretical perspective. KRS-One, as a teacher, philosopher, and/or critical educator, helps create a self-consciousness that allows listeners to be more aware of the social justice, racial, economic, political, moral, and ethical issues that mainstream, modernist education does not address. Furthermore, KRS-One's rap helps people question and challenge issues relating to power, authority, domination, justice, meaning, and social responsibility, which are all goals of critical thinking and critical theory. Contextualizing rap within a critical framework allows students to develop a critical consciousness that recognizes the effects of power in society and recognizes how that power is created, who has it, and who benefits from it. KRS-One's rap is a critical, liberating pedagogy that invites listeners to further explore the social, historic, economic, and political constructs of racism, discrimination, violence, and disempowerment.

Furthermore, KRS-One's rap challenges students not only to question hegemonic practices but also to take action toward social change, social justice, and social equality, all elements of critical thinking and critical pedagogy. KRS-One urges his listeners to take a proactive stand based on their own beliefs and not merely to be objective, passive followers guided by superficial and meaningless words. From a critical, theoretical framework, KRS-One urges listeners to use critical thinking skills when listening or studying his rap. His role as a teacher juxtaposes that of a critical teacher. He hopes to inspire his listeners to re-think their position in society and to question the truths and meanings behind any given text. In addition, he hopes to encourage listeners to create and use knowledge from their own life experiences and, most importantly, to take social action against oppressive conditions that stand in the way of liberation.

Incorporating critical thinking using literacies such as rap can transform the traditional, modernist classroom into a democratic, liberating, postmodern classroom, where reflective, empowering pedagogies are practiced. Rap music a) analyzes, critiques, and interprets the complex relationships among power, knowledge, identity, and politics, b) examines ways in which identity and knowledge are produced, c) validates and empowers subjugated and/ or indigenous bodies of knowledge, and d) creates critical-consciousness and self-consciousness by challenging hegemonic practices, which, ultimately, helps people recognize their position in the world.

Ultimately, for students to truly be-come empowered, the concept of empowerment and the teaching of critical thinking skills must be seen as a *philosophy* of education and not just as a strategy to increase academic success. One of KRS-One's objectives in his rap is for youth to realize the potential power [knowledge] they already possess and to take action against oppressive conditions. Students who develop critical thinking skills, which ultimately lead to social activism, are then truly engaging in an empowering, democratic process of education.

Further Reading

Best, S., & Kellner, D. (1999). Rap, black rage, and racial difference. *Enculturation, 2* (2), 1–20.

Chuck D., & Jah, Y. (1998). *Fight the power: Rap, race, and reality.* New York, NY: Dell.

Rose, T. (1994). *Black noise: Rap music and black culture in contemporary America.* Hanover, NH: University Press of New England.

Educational Psychology

Critical Consciousness through a Critical Constructivist Pedagogy

Stephen C. Fleury

I write as one involved with an international group of educators who have been focusing for a number of years on the topic of critical constructivism, which we think will help bring about a greater personal and social consciousness in our students. Different critical thinking approaches have quite different personal, social and cultural value. A risk in writing about critical constructivism is its possible misinterpretation as an alternative, or even a complementary, means toward the educational end of students achieving higher test scores on narrowly prescribed subject matter. Our conversations about critical constructivism, described here briefly and elsewhere more extensively, clearly refer to developing an understanding and disposition about knowledge that furthers democratic living (Larochelle, Bednarz & Garrison, 1998).

The underpinnings of a critical constructivist teaching stance are first, explicitly drawing student attention to the relationship between how one knows (*epistemology*) and how one lives in the world; second, developing students' understanding of the *contingency* of knowledge (the idea that even officially sanctioned knowledge is only true until further notice); and third, emphasizing the *value-laden basis* of all humanly created knowledge, demonstrating that all knowledge is, at root, culturally and politically responsive. These ideas have significant implications for teaching and learning. Rather than producing merely more knowledgeable or higher-order thinkers within traditionally bounded areas of school subject matter, a critical constructivist approach promotes intellectual tools and attitudes about the social basis of knowledge, enabling students to participate in making and remaking their own conceptual biographies as social conditions change.

School subject matter is important, of course, but no more so than the student's indigenous knowledge that has been constructed through their lived experiences. Students who learn critical constructivism will be able to understand the difference between their own knowledge and knowledge represented as formal subject matter, and will consequently develop a different "rapport au savoir"—loosely translated as a relationship with knowledge—that will make them both more liberated and more "response-able" for democracy (what Dewey refers to as a "mode of associated living").

A teacher's deliberate enhancement of the critical consciousness of students involves more than a decision to improve traditionally defined student intelligence. Such intentionality and behavior on the part of a teacher is an ethical and aesthetic choice, directed towards bringing about a more pleasing, humane, and democratically lived world.

The following are a few examples of how teachers employ critical constructivist ideas in the everyday classroom. Professional development workshops are not needed, nor are expensive materials or training; What is required is a greater reflection about how students build and test ideas conceptually, and a willingness to modify classroom practices for welcoming this type of thinking from students.

CODIFYING AND DEFINING

One seemingly simple but immensely important area of critical constructivism is to develop student awareness of how knowledge is defined. We have described elsewhere (Desautels, Garrison & Fleury, 1998) a common classifying exercise in science classes, where students are taught that all living things can be divided into two categories, plants and animals. Yet, not all children intuitively agree with this official classification scheme, arguing instead that people cannot be classified as animals. Typically, a teacher may allow a discussion to take place, but will soon impose the *right* answer on the basis of his or her expert authority, an authority reinforced by the sanction of a test. In critical constructivism, before imposing an answer on students, the teacher might decide to first use the discrepancy between the student's knowledge and the official knowledge of the curriculum to involve students in examining both the tentativeness and the usefulness of different methods of classification.

A teacher might ask students in small groups to classify living and non-living beings and to make a list of the reasons they put each being in its category in order to introduce them to the use of criteria. Subsequently, the students might be assigned to seek input from other people, not only peers in school but parents and others, about their list. The classroom reports of these discussions may serve to generate a lively intellectual discussion that in many ways will emulate the type of thinking the experts used in creating the category system. The discussion may take different paths as new angles are presented.

Both the curricular, official two-category classification system and the students' indigenous three-category system mentioned above are cultural artifacts. The student likely has more in mind than a technical or biological distinction between humans and animals. He or she may hold a higher role for humans on religious grounds, or on the secular vestige of religion in Western society, the exceptionality of Western Man. How could such a living being, conquering other living things, lands, space, even nature itself, be commonly included with animals? Some students may reason that humans are distinct because of their ability to think; but who defines what thinking is, and on what basis can we be certain that no other living being thinks? Recent research shows how some animals learn to solve problems, and if solving problems is an indication of intelligence, is not a multiple classification of living things now even more arguable? The teacher may point out the historical and cultural contingency of scientific knowledge. Are there other types of classification based on different cultural criteria? How does either a two- or three-classification system fit with one's views on human and animal rights? The questions can continue, but the important effect is that students come to understand the influence of culture and society on both the school's knowledge and their own indigenous knowledge. Perhaps some students will adhere to a multiple category system, because it functions well in their everyday life. It is important for the teacher to recognize the viability of the multiple classification system for students, but also to involve them in considering why biologists prefer a two-classification system, and where it is useful.

Science curricula abound with taxonomies and classification schemes that children, if they are encouraged to ask supportive, substantive questions, can construct and reconstruct through their observations and reasoning. Other areas of the school curriculum provide the same opportunities for critical constructivist learnings. Social studies, mathematics, language arts, and every subject taught in kindergarten through grade twelve, are composed of categories and concepts that organize its flow. As teachers make knowledge approachable for students, they come to see themselves as social reasoners, participants in constructing knowledge that is accountable to what makes sense to them. This is a step towards a more critical consciousness.

QUESTIONING: CHANGING ONE'S RELATIONSHIP TO KNOWLEDGE

A focus on the definition and classification of knowledge is a useful precursor for introducing students, even very young children, to the issues of power that prevail in school subject matter. The teacher can develop learning activities for students that allow them to build and test the viability of different knowledge claims. Through their involvement in these epistemological activities, students come to see how their view of the world is shaped and become increasingly sensitive to the power others hold over them through textbooks, tests, media, and advertising. With a teacher's careful guidance, students quickly learn to distinguish between knowledge presented to them for their interaction and response, and one-dimensional knowledge that is used on them by others. Changing the students' passive approach of simply receiving knowledge to one where they pose questions is a starting point for transforming their relationship to knowledge. This involves both developing their skills and changing their attitudes. The following description of an actual situation with seventh grade students exemplifies the educational potential of critical constructivist thinking.

The students were assigned the task of writing three questions that were not asked by the authors at the end of a story about the social conditions in an African country published in a weekly news magazine. The students were to assume they would have the opportunity to speak with the author, and were asked to design questions that would really make the author think. The teacher wrote down the questions from the class—about 60—and placed them on an overhead transparency for discussion. Out of well-formed habit, the students were eager to provide the correct response to each question, but instead were asked to figure out what *kind* of a response would work for each question. Would a single fact or answer suffice or were many responses possible? And where could the evidence be found to satisfactorily respond to the question?

The students enthusiastically determined that questions were either open type questions (many responses) or closed type questions (one response). As the idea caught on, they began to offer other applications. One of the students said they classify the teachers this way, and the supervising principal, overhearing this remark, was drawn into the room and listened intently to their reasons for placing different teachers in the open or closed category. He later shared his amazement about the students' accurate judgments and applauded the teacher's conceptual creativity, but asked how this type of learning could be assessed? The teacher explained that the subject of the discussion was interchangeable and the focus could be questions, teachers, or television shows. The lesson's objective concerned recognizing different types of communication, and could be assessed by devising a similar set of subjects for students to categorize according to the open and closed criteria.

VALUE LADENNESS AND OBJECTIVITY

Another aspect of critical constructivism involves examining the limits of objectivity in school knowledge. On what basis does the author of the textbook know what he or she is claiming? If it is a factual statement, do other sources support it? Do all experts agree upon this idea? This idea relates to helping students develop an understanding of the value-ladenness of knowledge. A situation with a middle school social studies textbook that contains the usual consensus view of history exemplifies this point.

Three lines in a middle school textbook about the 1783 Treaty of Paris led the teacher to ask how each of the European countries involved had been rewarded for their role in determining the fate of North America. The students correctly reported their book's account that each of the four countries received particular parcels of land. The students felt that each country was rewarded equally, since the textbook listed an almost equal number of parcels for each as a result of the treaty. Treaties, the students believed, are reached by compromise, and compromise means that everyone gives up something to reach agreement. From the parcels listed in the textbook, and from their reasoning about a treaty, the students thought that France, Britain, Spain, and Portugal must have left the treaty table equally satisfied with the results.

The teacher assigned one country to each of four small groups. Students were to compile data about their country's respective territories in North America before 1783. Current maps and information obscured the ancient territorial boundaries referred to in the textbook. Using current almanac information, and through cooperative extrapolation and negotiated reasoning, they reached agreement on defining the old territorial boundaries, and then computed modern day acreages and production records. On the final day, the four groups were able to compare their results and found that the Treaty of Paris gave Britain 95 percent of the property, with minimal amounts to the other three (France received one half of 1 percent)! Their finding that Britain gained the lion's share was important, but even more important was their evaluation about whether the textbook had lied. They reasoned that, although the textbook had not made a direct claim, the passage was written in such a way as to lead them to think that everyone involved came out equally well. Their tentative conclusion provided an opportunity for the teacher to raise further issues about why authors might write things in a certain way. Some of the students suggested the authors of the textbook may have favored the English unintentionally because we speak English and the other European countries do not. This involved the class in a discussion of the possible influences on historians and other writers. These students developed an increasingly healthy skepticism about textbook claims, showing the growth of their awareness of the value-laden aspect of knowledge.

SUMMARY

The above examples, although limited, suggest how a critical constructivist approach to education promotes the students' critical consciousness by changing how they learn to interact with, and relate to, subject matter. The ideas of critical constructivism typically challenge the world views of students and teachers who have come to believe through their formal education that knowledge is bi-polar (either true or false), that objective truth is discovered, and that experts accurately represent an absolute reality. Developing a more sophisticated understanding about each of these issues has a direct bearing on students' consideration of what is real and relevant in their worlds.

On a cautionary note, some critics fear that operating with critical constructivist premises will instill a sense of hopelessness and meaninglessness in students. To the contrary, we find that a teacher's academic honesty about the cultural relativity and contingency of knowledge dignifies student intelligence, gives them intellectual tools, and allows them to actively determine the social fate of themselves and others. For those of us concerned about our pluralist world, there are few other ways of getting these concepts across. Education that is deliberately critical and constructivist liberates knowledge from its epistemological context.

References and Further Reading

Desautels, J., Garrison, J., & Fleury, S.C. (1998). Critical-constructivism and the sociopolitical agenda. In M. Larochelle, N. Bednarz, & J. Garrison (Eds.), *Constructivism and education*. New York: Cambridge University Press.

Kincheloe, J. L. (1993). *Toward a critical politics of teacher thinking: Mapping the postmodern*. Westport, CT: Bergin & Garvey. See Chapter 6, Critical Constructivism.

Larochelle, M., Bednarz, N., & Garrison, J. (Eds.). (1998). *Constructivism and education*. New York: Cambridge University Press.

Educational Psychology and Critical Thinking

Joe L. Kincheloe

Often scholarship in educational psychology, especially the literature produced for undergraduate and graduate students in teacher education, has operated outside the dramatic paradigm changes that have rocked academia over the last three decades. Of course many authors have produced specific works that have challenged educational psychology's sub-fields, but as a whole, relatively few efforts have been made to challenge the underlying assumptions of the discipline. The contributions of educational psychology to critical thinking have been meager. Indeed, most educational psychologists have maintained a profound lack of interest in the conversation about critical thinking and its implications for classroom teaching.

COMPLEX CRITICAL THINKERS AS PROVOCATEURS: PROMOTING PARADIGMATIC CHANGE IN EDUCATIONAL PSYCHOLOGY

Before educational psychology can become a provocative resource for students of complex critical thinking, a paradigmatic revolution must occur in the field. Complex critical thinkers, noting the importance of the educational psychological domain to their concerns, must lay out a set of ideas on which to base the paradigmatic reconceptualization of the discipline.

To begin with, complex critical thinkers maintain that educational psychology must pay far more attention to ways of seeing produced by cultural anthropology, sociology, social theory, philosophy, situated cognitive studies, psychoanalysis, theology, literary studies, linguistics, social psychology, qualitative research, and critical pedagogies. As the study of learners, learning, and teaching, educational psychology has traditionally attempted to isolate these topics from larger psychosocial and cultural processes.

Using quantitative empirical methodologies exclusively, mainstream articulations of educational psychology have attempted to focus on the processes by which information, skills, values, and attitudes have been transmitted from teacher to student. Unaccustomed to discursive analysis on the rules of knowledge production in educational psychology, mainstream educational psychologists have often failed to examine the omissions and the blindness of their theoretical orientations. Since complex critical thinkers are dedicated to both scholarly advances and practical teaching concerns, their efforts to ferment paradigmatic change in educational psychology make use of a variety of disciplinary and pedagogical perspectives. Complex critical thinkers are dedicated to changing educational psychology, but not in some narrow fundamentalist sense that will produce a new educational psychological orthodoxy. Complex critical thinkers promote multiple educational psychologies.

COMPLEX CRITICAL THINKING AND THE FOUR DIMENSIONS OF THE PARADIGM SHIFT

Integrating Changes in Psychology into Educational Psychology

The disciplinary changes in psychology witnessed over the last couple of decades have encountered resistance in educational psychology. Numerous psychologists have raised profound questions about traditional understandings of psychological concepts such as the production of selfhood, interpersonal relations, cognition, emotion, individual development/maturation, aging and death, morality, etc. Complex critical thinkers have urged educational psychologists to explore and reconsider the meaning of psychological research in a cultural context and as a situated practice, and science itself as a discursive and rhetorical practice.

While mainstream psychology has listened to conversations about such conceptual dynamics over the last couple of decades, educational psychology has stood outside earshot. During this period, numerous psychologists have come to understand the limited ways their discipline has addressed complex questions about the mind and the self. Recognizing that these limitations are not simply the result of an unwillingness on the part of psychologists to consider such issues, many critics have realized that the discipline has not possessed adequate language for discussing these questions. Such language involves the theoretical and methodological discourses that insist that practitioners/researchers isolate phenomena in a manner that undermines efforts to communicate with experts from other disciplines. Such limitations subvert the attempts of psychologists to provide sophisticated, integrated perspectives on complex phenomena such as the mind and the self. Complex critical thinkers use the work of those psychologists who have recognized these disciplinary dynamics to raise questions about the relationship between psychology and the pedagogical domain.

Appreciating the Insights of Sociocultural Psychology

Complex critical thinkers understand that a socioculturally oriented approach to psychology leads to a whole series of interesting and educationally relevant issues that are currently ignored. Such questions range from general concerns about social interaction to issues of hierarchy and authority, organizational psychology, and sociocultural change. As emphasized in other parts of the encyclopedia, the Cartesian acceptance of an autonomous, rational, and bounded selfhood has undermined mainstream educational psychology's understanding of the discipline's omnipresent social dynamics.

Criticism of this abstract individualism holds dramatic implications for educational psychology, which sees individuals as non-problematic units in scientific analysis. Acceptance of an abstract socioculturally decontextualized self means that learning is a simple process of absorbing the given. In this context, pedagogy becomes a matter of direct transmission and assimilation. This is the educational psychological model on which early twentieth century educational reforms at the federal level have been constructed. Such a perspective establishes strict boundaries between the inside and outside of the mind, and says that students take *in* information from *out*side themselves. Such a psychological mindset, critics argue, builds fences between ourselves and other people and borders between our mutual needs. Fragmented knowledge fragments the community.

Cultural psychologists often argue that failure to understand the social structuring of the self leads to a variety of problems, especially for those who are in less powerful, marginalized social positions. Without such contextualization, individuals from dominant cultural backgrounds are unable to understand that the behaviors of socioeconomic subordinates may reflect the structural pressures under which they operate. In this paradigmatic context, education psychologists often believe that socioeconomic success is simply the result of individual merit and that social hierarchies and bell curves represent the *natural* dispersion of innate cognitive aptitude. Both critics of educational psychology and complex critical thinkers point out that such belief structures conveniently hide the benefits bestowed on more privileged members of society by dominant group membership.

Culturally oriented psychologists refer to this process as concealment by individualization and challenge the universal hierarchies that have been established in its wake by mainstream developmental and cognitive psychologists. The mind, mainstream cognitive scientists have contended, is a software program that can be studied in social isolation by fragmenting it and analyzing its parts. This computer/machine metaphor for the mind produces a quick and clean form of analysis that avoids the complications of messy and complex sociohistorical contextualization. Such messiness/complexity involves touchy issues, such as social values or politics and the intersection of the biological (individual) with the collective.

Individualized psychology studies the machine (mind) but not the uses to which the mind is put in the social cosmos of ideological conflict and political activity. As a result, educational psychologists—not to mention teachers—are taught to be technicians and must pursue a critical and contextualized view of the world through their own efforts outside of their professional education. Complex critical thinkers focus attention on these sociocultural psychological dynamics, viewing them as an important base for paradigmatic reconceptualization.

Employing Innovations in Social Theory

Over the last three decades, a renewed interest in social theory has developed that holds profound implications for educational psychology and critical thinking. This renaissance, while multidimensional, has focused on the reconsideration of the assumptions of Western enlightenment science, rationality, epistemology, and the representation of reality. The new social theories have questioned the concept of absolute knowledge and the theory that truth operates in a dimension unaffected by history and culture. The reigning conviction that knowledge is knowledge only if it reflects the world as it really exists has been confronted with a view that promotes a socially constructed reality. Moreover, agreement on what should constitute and guide scientific practice in psychology and other domains has become a source of continuing epistemological debate.

In this theoretical context, the concept of discursive analysis has emerged. Many of the challenges complex critical thinkers pose to educational psychology come from the discursive analysis of the theoretical structures of present psychological and educational psychological practice. A discourse is defined as a set of tacit rules that regulate linguistic practices, such as what can and cannot be said, who can speak with the blessing of authority and who must listen, and whose educational and psychological perspectives are scientific and valid and whose are unlearned and unimportant. Recent advances in social theory allow us the analytical space to expose the discursive rules hidden within any discipline or institutional practice. Thus, complex critical thinkers argue that the renaissance in social theory provides educational psychologists with insight into the rules of knowledge production—an understanding that facilitates our appreciation of the ways knowledge both misrepresents and reflects the sociopsychological world that envelops us.

Using These Insights to Reconceptualize Teaching and Learning

Complex critical thinkers use the rethinking of educational psychology as a base for reconceptualizing educational practice. The failure of teaching and learning grounded on the mainstream perspectives of educational psychology is apparent to many observers in the early twenty-first century, as teachers and school leaders struggle for a sense of purpose and a pedagogical direction. The reformulation of educational psychology provides a missing link to the discussion of social purposes, the nature of schooling in a democratic society, the manner in which human identity is shaped, and the ways students learn. A reinvigorated educational psychology will elicit new perspectives on everyday educational practices, including innovative sociopsychological insights into the formation of student consciousness and identity. Such knowledge will help form the groundwork for the larger effort to subvert the tendency of schooling to adjust students to an unjust status quo. Teachers and students will be better prepared to deconstruct taken-for-granted practices, beliefs, and the tacit assumptions of everyday school life, and as a result will be empowered to break through the fog of expert educational psychological dogma—belief structures that have stifled progressive changes in the schools in the name of neutrality.

Further Reading

Bruner, J. (1995). *The culture of education.* Cambridge, MA: Harvard University Press.

Kincheloe, J. L., Steinberg, S. R., & Hinchey, P. H. (1999). *The postformal reader: Cognition and education.* New York: Falmer Press.

Kincheloe, J. L., Steinberg, S. R., & Villaverde, L. (1999). *Rethinking intelligence: Confronting psychological assumptions about teaching and learning.* New York: Routledge.

Metacognition: What Is Transformative Metacognition and Why Is It Important?

Danny Weil

Intrapersonal intelligence conceived of as transformative metacognition allows us to see the thoughts underlying emotions and the emotions underlying thoughts. Transformative metacognition helps us isolate and define these thoughts and feelings relative to historical constructs and sensibilities. Developing this notion of an interpersonal intelligence entails a rethinking our thinking and individual experience as public creatures in the interest of personal and social change (Weil, 1998). It specifically asks that we understand our life and consciousness as history-made and history-making. Transformative metacognition meshes our past, present, and future into a journey of self-analysis, and asks that we learn to take a critical self-inventory of our thoughts and feelings so we can ferret out what is oppressive and non-liberating in our psychological assembly. Our feelings are the source of our epistemology, and we must uncover them before we can understand contemporary reality, especially its oppression and resistance.

Transformative metacognition can help us situate our consciousness within history and develop a sense of intellectual humility that beseeches us to replace self-righteousness with self-questioning as we develop a new humanness, a new way of being in the world with and for others. We develop a curious sense of self-confidence in our reasoning abilities when we can locate our individuality amidst, between, and within our socioeconomic and cultural awareness. Transformative metacognition also encourages us to orient our behavior towards liberatory ends, and it allows us to grapple with a sense of psychological purpose, devote attention to our own estrangement, wrestle with issues of power and authority, grasp a deeper awareness of oppression, and squarely engage issues of freedom, dignity, and personal and social responsibility.

Helping students re-think their thinking in an effort to improve their thinking is essential if they are to grasp the artful process of self-assessment and self-awareness, which promotes the development of interpersonal and intrapersonal in-depth understandings. Teaching metacognition in schools is a way to help both students and teachers develop the lifelong habit of utilizing their self-reflective abilities to improve the way they think, learn, and behave. Therefore, teachers as well as students need to take time to rethink their thinking, to slow their thinking down through thoughtful internal questioning, and to reflect on what they believe and what they think they know by using constructive doubt to enter into other points of view. Metacognition is a process of thinking about thinking that improves performance in both thinking and life.

Sports are a perfect example of where self-assessment is honored in the service of improving performance. Fighters shadow box in front of full-length mirrors to evaluate their performance and improve it. Figure skaters watch videos of their performance to assess their weaknesses and grow beyond them, When applied to the improvement of thinking, this process is commonly referred to as *metacognition,* or the development of a critical inner-Socratic spirit and personal process that places thinking itself under rigorous scrutiny in order to improve knowledge acquisition and empathic relations with others. Because it involves both a spirit and a mode of cognition, students and teachers must develop the values that will allow them to make critical self-inventories and engage in inner Socratic discourse.

Many teachers and students do not know what they do when they think and, unfortunately, far too often they don't care. It is also rare for teachers to understand the necessity of metacognition for both themselves and their students. Designing thoughtful questions that allow students to see the way they think and others think and where they might need to rethink their assumptions, concepts, or conclusions is essential if students are to take responsibility for their own learning. The process is of equal importance to teachers and all other thoughtful people. Using metacognition helps teachers become more aware of both how students might be conceiving of an issue or problem and how they might be perceiving the same issue or problem.

Metacognitive activities also allow teachers to rethink their own assumptions about what it means to teach and what it means to learn, especially as applied to issues of race, culture, sexual preference, gender, class, developmental readiness, and linguistic differences. In this thoughtful process of mental self-monitoring, both the teacher and student can become more aware of the process of thinking while developing the attitudes that allow them to take the journey toward a critical cognitive self-inventory. The process is one of *becoming*, and seeks to achieve the improvement of critical thinking and the development of moral and cognitive values and attitudes.

QUESTION PROMPTS

Listed below are some prompts for questions that teachers might use to stimulate inner Socratic discussion with students for metacognitive purposes. After engaging students in critical thinking activities, it is important that the teacher stop and begin to ask students what they have been doing, using questions such as the following:

What have we been doing?

What do we do when we compare and contrast?

What do you think about first or do you have any order or process you use?

Does the compare and contrast process differ from identifying similarities and differences or is it the same thing? How?

Did you see any patterns in the similarities or differences when you were thinking about them?

Did those patterns and similarities enable you to draw conclusions about what you were comparing and contrasting? How? Explain the patterns you saw and how they led you to certain conclusions.

How do you know that your conclusions are valid? What would you say to someone who may not agree with you?

Did you have to correct or alter the way you were thinking as you were thinking? How?

Do you think that comparing and contrasting is a useful activity? Why? When in your life do you compare and contrast?

It is advisable to record student responses on the board or on a transparency so that they can see the process of thinking that motivated them. The teacher should encourage as many students as possible to uncover their thinking so that all students in the class can profit from the diversity of thought.

When having students assess the reliability of sources, some questions the teacher might ask are

What kinds of things did you feel you needed to know to evaluate the reliability of the sources you were studying or receiving information from?

How did you decide on the questions you wrote and why did you think they were important? What questions do you think others might have?

Did it help to generate questions to determine the reliability of the sources you were studying? Why or why not?

What would you say to a friend who was attempting to evaluate the reliability of a source or point of view?

How are you going to gather reliable information for the next topic you might have to research? Why? What is reliable information?

When in your own life are you asked to examine the reliability of sources or points of view that you hear? What kinds of things do you think you would need to do to evaluate critically?

When asking students to think about the way that they make decisions the teacher might ask

What is a decision?

How would you begin to think about a decision you are going to make or decisions made in what you are studying? What are some of the things you do with your mind when you have to make a difficult decision?

How do you go about weighing the consequences of a decision or do you?

What factors do you consider when you make a decision?

What options do you consider when you make a decision, or do you, and why?

What evidence do you look for to support the options or decisions you make or those made in what you are studying? Can you give an example?

Do you think that studying how you and others make decisions is important? When in your own life do you think that thinking about your decisions might help you come to better conclusions or solve problems more effectively?

When discussing point of view the teacher might ask

What is a point of view? How do you develop a point of view?

How do you go about assessing a point of view you may be studying or a point of view you are exposed to on TV or in the news or with friends or family?

What are some of the things you look for?

Is it important to first be clear and concise as to what the point of view is? In other words, do you need to know what assumptions might inform the point of view, what conclusions it comes to, what evidence and reasons it may marshal for its frame of reference, and how it uses vocabulary and language? Why or why not? Can you give an example?

Has your own point of view ever changed after reading or listening to what you were studying or what others are thinking? How? Can you give an example?

When you listen to or read a point of view, do you think about your own point of view? Are you able to suspend your own judgment when attempting to understand a point of view?

Can you understand a point of view if you do not allow yourself to suspend your own point of view? Why or why not?

Could you evaluate a point of view if you didn't listen to it or read it critically? Why or why not? Can you give an example of what you mean?

How do you evaluate your own point of view or do you? How have you gotten some of your points of view on things you feel are important in life?

Give an example of when evaluating a point of view might be important in your life and what you might think about in developing and evaluating your own point of view?

These are just some elementary questions that teachers might ask students when they are trying to help students develop a process of transformative metacognition. With practice and immediate-transfer questions that are based on a problem-posing curriculum that is relevant and encourages respect for differences, students can begin to comb their own reality when they think about thinking. If students can get an insight into how examining the way they think can improve how they think and help them relate to the world in new ways, they can become their own thought provocateurs and thought detectives. Like physical fitness, the development of the mind requires perseverance, personal responsibility, and the ability to engage in critical constructive doubt in the interest of becoming human.

Reference

Weil, D. (1998). *Towards a critical multicultural literacy: Theory and practice for education for liberation.* New York: Peter Lang.

Further Reading

Gardner, H. (1991). *The unschooled mind.* New York: Basic Books.
Giroux, H. (1988). *Teachers as intellectuals.* New York: Bergin & Garvey.

Multiple Intelligences and Critical Thinking

Joe L. Kincheloe

Howard Gardner's *Frames of Mind* was received enthusiastically in 1983 by sectors of a public intuitively unhappy with the technocratic and rationalistic perspective on human ability produced by psychometrics. Within the narrow boundaries of the American culture of scholarship, Gardner became a celebrity with his delineation of the seven, and later eight, intelligences:

- Linguistic Intelligence
- Logical-Mathematical Intelligence
- Visual-Spatial Intelligence
- Kinesthetic Intelligence
- Musical Intelligence
- Interpersonal Intelligence
- Intrapersonal Intelligence
- Naturalist Intelligence

    Teachers emerging from a humanistic culture of caring and helping were particularly taken with the young scholar, and many traveled all over the country to hear him speak. Multiple intelligences (MI), such teachers maintained, provided them with a theoretical grounding to justify a pedagogy sensitive to individual differences and committed to equity. Though Gardner consistently denied the political dimension of MI, liberal teachers and teacher educators viewed it as a force to democratize intelligence. Living in a Eurocentric world, many interpreted Gardner to be arguing that cognitive gifts are more equally dispersed throughout diverse cultural populations than mainstream psychology believed. They took MI as a challenge to an inequitable system.

    Frames of Mind and its theory of multiple intelligences struck all the right chords when it claimed that:

- Learning is culturally situated.

- Different communities value different forms of intelligence.

- Cognitive development is complex, not simply a linear cause-effect process.
- Creativity is an important dimension of intelligence.
- Psychometrics does not measure all aspects of human ability.
- Teaching grounded on psychometrically inspired standardized testing is often deemed irrelevant and trivial by students.

Numerous teachers, students, parents, and everyday citizens thought these ideas were important, and they are—especially in light of the positivist reductionism and standardization of the twenty-first-century educational standards movement. As with most popular theories, the time was right. MI resonated with numerous progressive impulses that had not retreated in the face of the right-wing educational onslaught coalescing in the early 1980s. Many of us thought that MI held profound consequences for the future of critical thinking; but as we watched Gardner develop the theory and its applications to cognition and pedagogy, we felt compelled to conclude that, despite all its democratic promise, Gardner's theory has not met the expectations of its devotees. The reasons for this failure are multidimensional and complex and are directly connected to the same ideas that drive our critical complex conceptualization of critical thinking.

One aspect of the failure comes from Gardner's inability to grasp the social, cultural, and political forces that helped shape the initial reception of MI. Even when he has addressed what he describes as a "disease" in American society, Gardner fails to historicize the concept in a way that provides a larger perspective on the fascinating relationship between MI and American sociocultural, political, and epistemological dynamics during the last two decades.

Gardner is entangled in this sociocultural, political, and epistemological web, whether he wants to be or not. He maintains that he does not have to consider these issues because his position is psychological and pedagogical, not social, cultural, political, or epistemological. In a naïve decontextualized and psychologized way of operating, he asserts that the psychological and pedagogical domains are separate from all these other factors.

This is a profound analytical error on Gardner's part. The epistemology (way of knowing) traditionally employed by Gardner's psychometric predecessors and contemporaries is the epistemology of MI. It is the epistemology of rationalistic incarnations of critical thinking that our critical complex notion of critical thinking moves beyond. There is less difference between Gardner and the psychological establishment than we first believed. Gardner has been unwilling to criticize the power wielders, the gatekeepers of the psychological castle. Any use that advocates of complex critical thinking make of MI must be accompanied by a warning about these regressive dimensions of the concept.

THE POSTFORMAL CHALLENGE TO MI: IMPLICATIONS FOR CRITICAL THINKING

Postformalism (as delineated in the introduction) is especially interested in modes of cognition and critical thinking that recognize the complicity of various academic discourses in their construction. Focusing on psychology in particular, postformalists study discourses that justify and maintain an inequitable status quo and an ecological and cosmological alienation from the planet and the universe in which we reside. Gardner seems either unable or unwilling to trace the relationship of MI to these issues. We as postformalist critical thinkers must deploy our power literacy to reveal MI's ideological inscriptions and examine the multiple and complex ways power operates to shape psychological descriptions of human abilities and behaviors.

For example, what is labeled intelligence can never be separated from what dominant power groups designate it to be. Thus, what Gardner attributes solely to the authority of a Cartesian science always reveals the fingerprints of power. The concepts of intelligence and aptitude always hold political and moral significance. Designating anything as intelligence produces social, cultural, and political consequences. Recognizing the important difference between postformalism and Gardner's psychology has meant that postformalists have had to admit that these consequences exist and try to shape their definitions of intelligence as democratically, inclusively, and self-consciously as possible. Gardner dismisses the existence of such political and moral consequences and clings to the claim of scientific neutrality.

Complex critical thinkers take the political and moral consequences of both Gardner's work and the knowledge produced by his psychological tradition seriously. Indeed—surprising as it may be to some of his devotees—there are moments within Gardner's MI theory that are antidemocratic, support abstract individualism, are epistemologically naive, are subversive of community, are insensitive to racial and socioeconomic class issues, are patriarchal, and are Western colonialist and Eurocentric.

Despite all of these concerns, postformal critical thinkers still believe there is value in Gardner's work. Indeed, we seek the kinetic potential of Gardner's ideas in the sociopsychological and educational domain as we try to retain the original democratic optimism of Gardner's theories, confront him and his many supporters with powerful paradigmatic insights refined over the last 20 years, and produce a conversation with him and his supporters about the relationship of MI to critical thinking that is grounded in a vision of a complex, rigorous, and transformative pedagogy.

CRITICAL THINKING, TEACHING, AND MI

In an article in the *Phi Delta Kappan* in the mid-1990s, Gardner wrote about his dedication to one of our most important concerns in this encyclopedia—stimulating a conversation about the purposes of education and schooling. In this piece he emphasized the importance of this consideration in his work with MI and of his belief that MI has stimulated these types of inquiries. Such a focus on the purpose of education, he contended, will move schools to teach for understanding rather than the rote mastery of test-based isolated data—a concern we obviously share with Gardner. Intoxicated with the popularity of MI among so many educators, Gardner boasted that MI was concerned with understanding, educational purpose, and pedagogical personalization and was creating a revolution in schooling around the world. Answering a right-wing critic of *The Disciplined Mind* (1999), Gardner reiterated his commitment to the analysis of educational purpose, saying that insufficient conversation about American education "has focused on why we should educate students at all."

What is difficult for us to understand is that, after all this expression of concern, Gardner studiously avoids any discussion of the social, cultural, political, ideological, and economic purposes of schooling in a democratic society.

This issue is profoundly important to understanding what is missing in Gardner's psychoeducational analysis and its benefits for students of critical thinking. When we examine his concept of the purpose of schooling, the abstract individual again rears her socially decontextualized head. Gardner says that the purpose of education is to help individuals achieve their potential. While readers may find nothing wrong with this particular goal, it is what Gardner omits in this discussion that is so troubling. When we understand the self as contextually embedded and relational, we begin to discern the multitude of forces that impede particular individuals from attaining their potential—whatever exactly this means. A student's socioeconomic, cultural, and/or linguistic background must be addressed to even get to the starting line of this process. If it is not, then the student may be blamed for not having the mental ability—the potential—to learn what is taught.

Just as importantly, complex critical thinking's focus on educational purpose, while certainly concerned with individual development and the contextual factors shaping that process, also addresses larger civic, democratic, ecological, justice-related, and power-based issues. Gardner fails to question the ways schools are used to regulate students for the political needs of business and government. From the school crusades of the mid-nineteenth century to the present, power wielders have attempted to use schools to domesticate students and perpetuate the status quo. Such social regulation is a central feature of the twenty-first-century standards movement that Gardner so vehemently opposes—but for reasons other than this political one. Gardner seems unconcerned

with the ways these forces of power shape the field of psychology or the ways they structure what goes on in classrooms across the country.

Gardner seems callous about the construction of the curriculum and its discursive, ideological, and disciplinary dimensions. The concept of problematizing what we learn, asking where it comes from, and why we learn A but not B is irrelevant in Gardner's world. He displays disconcerting confidence in what has been established as the true, the beautiful, and the good in dominant Western culture, operating as if the concepts have not been saturated by the power relations of ethnocentric, patriarchal, and class-elitist ways of seeing. Does he not understand that the anger various groups around the world and within this society direct at high-status educators of his stripe emerges precisely from these types of assumptions and exclusions? After carefully studying his pronouncements on the purpose of MI-grounded schooling, we conclude that Gardner wants to educate obedient subjects for the American global empire. This goal is profoundly at odds with complex critical thinking.

Gardner couches his speculations on educational purposes within his fidelity to traditional academic disciplines. In his response to right-wing critiques of *The Disciplined Mind*, Gardner (1999) writes:

Formal schooling has several purposes, of course, but I believe its most fundamental purpose should be the inculcation of the major ways of thinking that have been crystallized in the disciplines.

Gardner makes this disciplinary argument in an era when the sanctity of disciplinarity has been successfully called into question. In my recent work on bricolage (Kincheloe & Berry, 2004), I have referred to the ruins of disciplinarity and the need to move to a more rigorous and challenging form of scholarship. Once the understanding of the limits of objective science and its universal knowledge escaped from the genie's bottle, there was no return to the confines of modernist scholarship. Gardner is part of a larger attempt of many politicos and scholars to recover what they perceived to be lost in the implosion of the disciplines, including the value-laden products that operate under the flag of objectivity, the avoidance of contextual specificities that subvert the stability of a discipline's structures, and the fragmenting impulse that moves the disciplines to stash their methodologies and the knowledge they produce in neat, disciplinary drawers.

My argument here is that complex critical thinkers must operate in the ruins of the disciplinary temple, in postapocalyptic social, cultural, psychological, and educational sciences where certainty and stability have departed for parts unknown.

Gardner accepts the way complex knowledges are compartmentalized in the traditional disciplines, creating in the process a sense that truth exists in disciplinary canons. This type of subdividing fragments important topics such as intelligence, rendering it the exclusive domain of psychology instead of a product of sociology, cultural studies, history, linguistics, literary studies, philosophy, anthropology, education, and psychoanalysis to name a few. Gardner's acceptance of disciplinary ways of thinking, researching, and validating knowledge is unshakable. He unequivocally accepts school curricula that teach such knowledge and standardized tests that measure how well students have memorized it. In *Intelligence Reframed,* Gardner reports research results that prove that standardized test scores improve in MI schools. Such educational im-

provement, Gardner argues, is beyond dispute because it is "based on empirical data, which an impartial party cannot dismiss." Gardner simply cannot imagine a critique that questions the value of schools teaching the unassailable empirical truths of disciplines to uncritical, passive students.

CONCLUSION

While the view that intelligence is not a monolithic, one-dimensional entity is an important contribution to the study of critical thinking, people who use complex critical thinking must be wary of MI's tacit assumptions. Students of critical thinking must carefully take what they can use from MI theory and leave behind the reinscriptions of rationalistic, Eurocentric ways of seeing it insidiously promotes.

References

Gardner, H. (2000). *Intelligence reframed: Multiple intelligences for the 21st century.* New York: Basic Books.

Gardner, H. (1999). *The disciplined mind: Beyond facts and standardized tests, the K-12 education that every child deserves.* New York: Penguin Press.

Kincheloe, J. L., & Berry, K. (2004). *Rigour and complexity in educational research: Constructing the bricolage.* London: Open University Press.

Further Reading

Kincheloe, J. L. (Ed.). (2004). *Multiple intelligences reconsidered: An expanded vision.* New York: Peter Lang.

Sempsey, J. (1993). The pedagogical implications of cognitive science and Howard Gardner's MI theory (a critique). Available online at http://www.netaxes.com/~jamesiii/gardner.htm.

Weil, D. (1998). *Towards a critical multi-cultural literacy: Theory and practice for education for liberation.* New York: Peter Lang.

Educational Relevance

Educational Relevance, Personalized Education, and Critical Thinking

Danny Weil

Educational relevance and personalized learning must be the cornerstone of any meaningful critical thinking curriculum concerned with equity. The objective of teachers shouldn't be to describe something that should be memorized, they should problematize situations and present the challenge of reality that learners confront each day.

This pedagogical position creates an active critical thinking curriculum that encourages students to think about reality for the purpose of acting upon it. This, of course, means critically writing about reality, critically reading about reality, critically speaking about reality, Socratically questioning reality, and critically listening to diverse narratives of reality. Educators should take advantage of all opportunities to stimulate their students, even by sharing their own doubts, viewpoints, and criticisms. They should seek to encourage active student involvement, not sedentary passivity.

One of the great problems today is that students suffer from information overload and boredom. They pass notes to each

other or doze in the heat of the afternoon, foreheads down on their desks. And even though their students show these signs of boredom, many teachers feel that if they have covered the material they have selected for their lecture and controlled the class, their teaching has been successful. Classroom management becomes the priority and relevance in education becomes marginalized.

Unfortunately, what typically disguises itself as education does little to encourage critical thinking and exploration of the self through reality or reality through the self. Nor do these studies provide meaningful opportunities for informed social action and transformation. As it is presently constructed, education is little more than obedience training that is non-transformative and intellectually domesticating. It is unable to offer active life and voice to the students it purports to serve. Relegating students to mere spectators of education, too many current educational programs not only fail to invite critical multicultural discourse through dialogue and dialectical thinking, but they reinforce schooling as a mere trivial pursuit divorced from the living realities of everyday life.

To overcome this, educators need to work with the lived experiences of their students. Many students today are experiencing a Dickensian life of nightmarish proportions, especially in our inner cities as they deal with drug addiction, unemployment, inadequate opportunities, racism, sexism, dysfunctional families, teenage pregnancies, and the status of being illegal. These realities have redefined what it means to be an educator, a student, and a citizen in today's society. Students bring legacies of oppression and resistance to our classrooms for which they seek and expect critical exploration, critical listening, and critical evaluation through radical discourse and rigorous critical analysis.

For many newly arriving immigrant students and students of color or lower socioeconomic class, schooling divorced from reality becomes an actual process of alienation as they develop two worlds and two identities. One world and one identity is their life outside of schooling, which many consider their real self. The second self is the one that copes with academia and tries to become academia's idea of a good student. Good students learn to meet the teacher's expectations, whether they are that all students speak standard English no matter what their ethnic background or that students must reproduce certain specified information on tests. Creating an *academic self* is a way to survive within school for a large number of students and is encouraged by teachers. Many teachers demand that students leave their cultural baggage outside the classroom and develop a form of *conformist schizophrenia* that causes them to lead two separate lives: one where self-actualization is possible and identity is honored and one of regimented passivity and raw prescription.

Far too often the uncritical thinking curriculum serves to silence dialogue about students' lived lives, imaginations, dreams, and social realities. Frequently, what constitutes the lives of newly arriving immigrants and people of color is deemed irrelevant to academic life. This separation between the lives and voices of students and the academic curriculum and ideology of silence promises to foster the idea of schooling as a compulsory obligation, much like military service. It can never produce a lifelong commitment to education and enlightenment. Making the lived experiences of our students the lively subject of public and private debate means legitimizing these experiences and giving those who live them affirmation and voice. It means offering critical educational opportunities for students to articulate their language, dreams, hopes, values, and encounters with others. It heralds reflection, metacognition, and insight into these experiences for both teachers and students, while offering the promise of countless opportunities for critical thinking about social and personal issues. Students need to see that the purpose and implications of schooling are something that go beyond the classroom. Education, as presently structured, remains so disconnected from the lived struggles that takes place in community, neighborhood, churches, and the workplace that students are deceived into thinking that being educated has nothing to do with social institutions or their daily life.

What goes on within the four walls of school life does little to address the needs, goals, and lives of our changing student demographics. Texts add to this failure by generally offering the narrative of the dominant culture on issues of contemporary and historical concern, offering little opportunity to see the world from alternative cultural points of view. Texts suggest lesson plans that require only rote dissemination and memorization opportunities alienated from the discourse of everyday life instead of the opportunity to think independently. This type of divorced instruction—-the instruction of accommodation and trivialization, of decontextualization and alienation, of subjugation and domination—can have no appreciable effect on human growth and potential, and can certainly never act as a catalyst for transforming the human mind or world in which we live.

This anesthetized approach to learning claims *social and political neutrality* as the playground of educational practice. This neutrality presumes that education is not a form of *political* expression but is *generic* or *value free*. The generic curriculum fraudulently pretends to widely appeal to most students while conveniently shunning controversy, depersonalizing learning, and trivializing reality. Educators would be better served by asking salient questions such as whether there is a relationship between the work that is done in class the lives students lead outside of class, whether it is possible to incorporate aspects of students' culture and daily lives into schoolwork without simply providing opportunities for them to confirm what they think they already know, and whether this can be done without trivializing the issues important to students.

Social, economic, and cultural conflict are issues begging for acknowledgment and recognition. They provide relevant, real-life venues for the development of independent thinking, democratic decision-making, and intellectual character. Unlike many popularly advocated pedagogical positions, current reality with all its complexities and contradictions should not be renounced as too controversial or intimi-

dating for classroom discourse. In one school a biology teacher, one of the few black teachers in his high school, actually attempted to integrate creative writing assignments, such as *"My Life as An Alcoholic"* and *"My Life as a Child of An Alcoholic,"* into the biology class curriculum. When this came to the attention of the principal of the school, the teacher was severely reprimanded for bringing in extraneous materials.

My own experience in a primary school in south central Los Angeles illustrates this same silencing of teachers by administrators. I had solicited the help of an independent filmmaker and wanted to work with a group of kids on anti-gang messages. I was told by the principal that this was not the role of a teacher and that students in my class could not participate in this type of activity.

Fixating on a curriculum devoid of conflict undermines the necessity to reason about issues of social and personal relevance. It reduces the role of education to that of disempowerment—a pedagogy divorced from the real world. The implications for the teacher laboring under this paradigm is that he/she works *on* students, never *with* them. Students are looked on as mere objects to be filled like receptacles with teacher-generated, pre-digested truth. On the other hand, teachers who critically understand the role of education and society as a whole tend to work *with* students—helping them explore the complexities of their personal and social existence relative to the social structures in their world. These educators typically provide profound opportunities for students to develop the values and dispositions of learning, encouraging them to see the relevance of learning and the value of transferring educational insights into other domains of life. The use of popular culture as a *text* in the classroom can empower students, have a profound effect on students' lives, and help students to read culture critically as they begin to see how their own self-interests are either manipulated and/or reproduced by cultural forms.

Educators concerned with relevance see education and learning as a political act, one that requires reasoning within diverse and often opposing points of view, reflective thought, theory, practice, transformation, interdisciplinary transfer of learning, and personal and social commitment. For these educators, the student and the teacher are seen not as objects, but as living subjects in the process of critically knowing and learning. Education is defined not as a vertical authoritarian imposition dictated from above, nor an alienating obligatory relationship that ends in annulment at 18 years of age, but as an empowering journey into humanity. Understanding that the human being is creative, thoughtful, and capable of knowing is paramount to offering honest and empowering educational opportunities. Teachers should develop high expectations for all of their students, listen to their personal narratives, enter into their subjective lives, and have confidence in their ability to develop fairminded critical thinking and reasoning while simultaneously maintaining a vision that they, too, are or can be gifted.

Further Reading

Gardner, H. (1991). *The unschooled mind: How children think and how schools should teach.* New York: Basic Books.

Giroux, H. (1988). *Teachers as intellectuals: Toward a critical pedagogy of learning.* New York: Bergin & Garvey.

Illich, I. (1970). *DeSchooling society.* New York: Harper & Row.

Empowerment

Empowerment: A Transformative Process

Pat Williams-Boyd

Empowerment is an ongoing and intentional process that demands mutual respect, critical thinking, group commitment and active participation. Through this process, people lacking an equal share of valued resources gain greater access to and control over those resources. This control may be critically conceptualized as either real control (the actual transfer of power and resources to the individual) or perceived control (the individual's self-efficacious belief that he has the ability to control important aspects of his life).

More generally, it is a process by which individuals who often lie at the borders of social participation gain a sense of mastery and control over their own lives, a control that lies at the heart of democratic participation in the life of groups and of communities. The empowerment process can be gauged by the degree of decision-making power founded on critical thinking that people exercise in an organization. In a school, the people who have been marginalized are the families of students. The resources are both access to and equitable allocation of educational opportunities, as well as participation in schools.

When we examine empowerment as a process, we must first ask some critical questions. They are not questions about how to increase the number of attendees at parent conferences, or whether professional educational conferences should be two days and one night or three days. We engage in critical thinking by asking "To whom do public schools belong?' and then openly and critically examining who has power in schools and who does not, whose voice is heard and whose is silenced, and who has access to resources and who has been denied.

Empowerment is a relational process. It begins with how one sees oneself and one's place in the world and builds upon that a kinship relationship with the student and with the family, with the immediate community through networking, with the larger society, and with the institution called school. The process is inclusive because families are directly and indirectly beneficiaries of the school programs they develop and use, it is participatory because there is open debate about the direction the school is going between families and the school staff, and it is educational because it fosters learning for both families and students. Empowerment is framed by critical thinking and tries to produce a more equitable and just society, and it is action-oriented for it rigorously strives to alter the way schools have ignored families they see as different or have silenced their voices.

Empowerment is not the hierarchical, top-down granting of power (i.e., a principal asking herself how to get more families to attend district-mandated parent breakfasts or asking what tasks parents might be able to do should they volunteer to help in the school); it *critically* analyzes school ownership and asks critical thinking questions, such as how the school can be returned to the people to whom it belongs and how the school can reengage people who have been deliberately excluded from the educational process.

Empowerment means acknowledging that which has been wrongfully denied. Schools belong to a variety of stakeholders, and if schools have excluded families from having a say in what happens in the school, they must now give that privilege back because local schools should belong to the people they serve. If teachers distanced themselves from students and proclaimed their content expertise in the past, now teachers and students must cooperate in a student-centered, reciprocal relationship of teaching and learning. This is a deliberate process continually shaped and reshaped through critical thinking.

How does this look in the classroom? Through active, problem-based learning or conceptual critical thinking, teachers facilitate the active learning of students. In a project on the Harlem Renaissance, rather than have students answer a true-false test on facts and dates, a coalition of teachers, students, and families critically ask how they might improve their neighborhoods. One such coalition in Detroit found an abandoned warehouse and painted murals on it representing the artists of the time, and students at Albuquerque High School interviewed senior citizens about their emigration from Mexico to the United States instead of memorizing information on the numbers of people who migrated, which areas of Mexico they migrated from, and when. The entire class, along with their families and teachers, then presented the collected histories to the local historical society.

Empowerment does not use the deficit model—seeing only what people are unable to do, it recognizes that all people have strengths. It assumes that families, particularly low socioeconomic status (SES) families, who have been denied power in the school, have the same ability to examine and determine their own needs as the teachers, administrators, and higher SES parents who are in power.

Empowerment does not require people to demonstrate inadequacy to become eligible for either support or necessary resources. In working with a former ninth-grade student who had called in the middle of a quiet spring night and asked for help to get off of drugs and out of gangs, I found that, until he had been convicted of some felony, he was ineligible for support from any of the county's treatment facilities. Rather than the lockstep provision of services, critical thinking challenges the school to discover what keeps students from learning, determine how these impediments can be removed, and help all students to achieve academic success.

Dunst and Deal (1988) cite three conditions that must be present in an empowering relationship: a proactive stance, which sees families as competent or as having the capacity to become competent; enabling experiences, because the failure to display competence at school is not due to learning deficits but to the school's failure to provide opportunities for successful participation; and empowerment, which means that families can exercise their rightful opportunity to participate in their child's education.

The process of empowerment involves moving through needing help to getting help and then applying help. It is the vigilant process of involvement, action, and advocacy by families whom schools have historically left out. How does this look in the school? Teachers complain that the very families they need to speak to never attend parent-teacher conferences. What they never consider is that conferences are not offered at times that fit the family's work schedule. In a single-parent household, there is no one at home to watch younger siblings while mother attends a conference. If parents did not have a good experience as students, they may be hesitant to come back to a school and hear how they have failed again, through their children. What the school does not take into account is that, when families send their children to school, they are sending their very best work.

Empowerment is a process of critical thinking that persistently frames questions on how to understand the life experiences of people who are not part of the dominant culture. Empowerment is the language of possibility that attempts to ameliorate inequality through the strength of critical thought and collective struggle. Families who feel powerless in the local school when they are alone can band together through parent projects and feel valued. Empowerment is the language of human dignity that, through critical thinking, mobilizes individuals, groups, and schools to build socially responsive and democratically patterned communities. It is not the language of mere representation, applauding itself for bringing two minority families to the monthly parent meetings. Empowerment is the language of awakened and acknowledged moral, civic, and political responsibility, not the language of acquiescence or muted adherence to what has already been done or the uninformed uniformity that seeks no significant participation in community life.

The school should aggressively seek out families and encourage them to be part of its daily work by helping a student read, assisting in a math lesson, listening to and problem-solving with an angry student, or contacting other parents to join in sponsoring student activities.

Empowerment is a process that is ongoing, evolving, recurring, and critical in thought. Those who participate are motivated to new levels of personal control, which produces a greater sense of effectiveness. The increased involvement with others, plus the additional responsibility and organizational problem-solving and critical thinking, strengthen and nurture people's personal sense of empowerment. Empowerment encourages the dialogue of common struggle and the acquisition of competencies in the service of mobilizing resources and solving problems, for it is the language of diverse and multiple solutions. On the historical level, it is the language of critique and possibility which recognizes that the way we have always done things is the rubble upon which to build a new school-family dynamic.

When one asks what qualities we want our youth to demonstrate, what kind of citizens our youth should become, and for what kind of future society should these young people be prepared, one asks the critical questions of moral direction and speaks the language of empowerment through a critical thinking education. Empowerment is the lens through which the school and local community can clarify their vision of the identities that the dominant culture creates. In other words, through empowerment the white middle-class institution of school critically examines the ways it understands families of color, families of varied cultural heritage, and particularly lower SES families. It then clearly and critically analyzes the alienation families may feel and students experience.

Unfortunately, schools and communities use sanctions to induce conformity and discourage deviation. They often back institutionalized, deeply habituated patterns that may reduce diversity and which are resistant to change. For example, the simple raising of one's hand to gain attention does not recognize the minority cultural norm of spontaneously offering an idea. We cannot cast all students in the same mould and ask them only for passive compliance. Native American students see Columbus Day as a scourge rather than as a celebration, and students from minority cultures or lower SES whose behavior does not match middle-class values are often wrongly tracked to ability groups below their real level of performance. We must explore our students' cultural mindscapes.

I have often heard these families say that they hesitate to speak up on behalf of their children because they fear reprisal from teachers or administrators. They remain silent and fire go unlit or are snuffed out, thoughts are extinguished, human potential is marginalized, and who we could become is compromised, because they were never engaged in critical thinking about their school.

Rather than promoting opportunities for self empowerment through critical thinking, schools act as perpetuators of class power. One has only to look at the faces in the lower track of any of the nation's ability-grouped schools to bear witness to this charge. Empowerment is not just an individual act or a community perspective, but a concept of social class critical thinking. It is the process of investigating the why of things, of wondering, of understanding ourselves as historical, political, social, and cultural beings. It is the language of liberation, set into motion by the belief that the present can be changed for the common good.

Some researchers argue empowerment is not a social process where the behavior of parents is changed, but a social transformation where the barriers to parent involvement are eliminated through critical thought. For example, social process contends the poor academic achievement of a child from a low income, ethnically diverse home is due to a deficiency within the child, the family, or the culture that must be corrected. When parents become active arbiters of critical thought, when they become change agents, transforming their school and homes into settings where there is support for developing the capacity for the success of all members, social transformation has begun. In a predominantly Hispanic school district, major areas of change resulted from a collective process of critical thought and reflection on the part of the community. Parents discussed their common histories and school experiences, spoke of their shared feelings of isolation within the community, acknowledged their lack of information about the school, and committed themselves to learning how schools operate and how parents could effectively participate. They confronted common stereotypes imposed on them that involved limitations in their involvement in school and constructed an egalitarian system of interaction for their meetings based on mutual respect for everyone's ideas. They realized that maximum support for their children's education meant mutual cooperation between families and schools, and they committed to organize activities to encourage frequent and meaningful interaction between teachers and families (Delgado-Gaitan, 1990).

While the empowerment process does not promise harmonious accord, it does provide a context for dialogue and critical thinking that makes negotiation possible. The empowerment model contends that all families have strengths and the most useful knowledge regarding the child is found in the family, and it celebrates the intrinsic worth of cultural differences that so richly shape students and their families. Empowerment is part of American culture, for it deals with the individual determination of one's life and participation in the community. Empowerment is integration rather than alienation, critical thought rather than passive acquiescence, coalition rather than polarization, interdependence rather than dependence, emancipation rather than submission. Empowerment like education is the very practice of freedom itself.

References

Delgado-Gaitan, C. (1990). *Involving parents in the schools: A process of empowerment.* Paper presented at the Symposium on Race, Ethnicity, and Schooling, University of California.

Dunst, C., & Deal, A. (1988). *Enabling and empowering families.* Cambridge, MA: Brookline Books.

Further Reading

Freire, P. (1970). *Pedagogy of the oppressed.* New York: Continuum.

Rappaport, J. (1987). Terms of empowerment/exemplars of prevention: Toward a theory for community psychology. *American Journal of Community Psychology, 9,* 1–25.

Shor, I. (1992). *Empowering education.* Chicago: University of Chicago Press.

Empowerment of Teachers and Students

Raymond A. Horn, Jr.

Have you ever questioned authority? Of course you have. What is your batting average for obtaining satisfaction? When you weren't successful, what were the reasons why you didn't achieve your goal? These questions deal with awareness and empowerment, or more directly with how much power you have and how well you understand a situation when you try to do something that really matters to you. More than likely, the degree of awareness and power that you have is related to your knowledge about the issue in question and the skills that you can employ when engaged in the act of questioning authority.

The term scholar-practitioner applies to those teachers and students who possess knowledge, know how to acquire knowledge, have the skills that promote the effective processing of knowledge, and have the courage to use the knowledge to promote social justice, caring, and democratic participation for themselves and others. The prerequisites to become a scholar-practitioner leader are curiosity, trust in your innate creativity, and the desire to become a critical researcher. Scholar-practitioner leaders are not just university professors but can be teachers, students, and adults who wish to make a difference in their life and in the lives of others. Scholar-practitioner leaders ask questions, seek knowledge about the questions, and critically reflect on that knowledge. They learn to use a variety of skills and methods to question more deeply, and to acquire knowledge that is usually restricted to and used by those who define what true knowledge and force others to adhere to their true view.

Over time, scholar-practitioner leaders fill their critical toolbox with any skills, methods, or ways of seeing the world, that will allow them to see the deep and hidden implications of that which they question and the information that they uncover, especially when they question authority. They use their understanding and skill to promote social justice, caring, and democratic participation. Often scholars understand a great deal but act very little. Concerned practitioners may take action without understanding the situation and the full implications of their action. Scholar-practitioner leaders, as critical citizens, both understand and act, and effectively share their understanding in public debates.

Why become a scholar-practitioner leader? First, there is the personal satisfaction that comes from penetrating beyond the simplistic and surface meanings that others use to mask their real intent. In any public or personal issue, there are always deep and hidden values, beliefs, and knowledge. To understand the complexity of an issue, instead of being controlled by simplistic and narrow explanations, is empowering and makes you impervious to the manipulation that others use to gain your compliance and conformity to achieve their ends. However, there is an even more important reason. Being a scholar-practitioner is a whole-life experience. The skills that you use in academic settings or in the pursuit of a public issue can also be used in all other aspects of your professional and personal life.

How does one become a scholar-practitioner leader? It's not a linear process. You do not complete step A, followed by step B and step C. Instead, the parts of this process are dynamically interrelated and occur again and again in your continuing effort to acquire and hone the skills, attitudes, and knowledge that are essential for scholar-practitioner leadership. Scholar-practitioner leaders must become critically literate and develop the skills, knowledge, and attitudes that facilitate their ability to ask and research questions However, it is not enough to just gain knowledge and skill.

Patrick M. Jenlink (1999) talks about the process of inquiry that is used to gain knowledge, skill, and an understanding of the different sources of knowledge. He distinguishes between three levels of knowledge and inquiry: knowledge and inquiry-*for*-practice, knowledge and inquiry-*in*-practice, and knowledge and inquiry-*of*-practice. Knowledge and how to attain that knowledge, which Jenlink calls knowledge and inquiry-for-practice, is necessary as the basis for a scholar-practitioner's practice or actions, and must be acquired. However, there is knowledge that is already embedded within actions and is based on intuition and experience. This embedded knowledge, or knowledge and inquiry-in-practice, needs to be scrutinized through the process of critical reflection. Finally, knowledge and inquiry-*of*-practice is achieved through critical reflection on how knowledge and inquiry are individually and collectively constructed by the self and others within the workplace. Scholar-practitioner leaders pay attention to all of the contexts in which knowledge and inquiry reside, and to be critically literate involves critically reflecting and understanding these contexts.

To be a scholar-practitioner leader is to become aware of the origins, context, and patterns of the knowledge related to an issue. This postformal way of knowing creates the deep understanding and facilitates the continuous formation of questions that are the essence of scholar-practitioner leadership (Kincheloe, Steinberg, & Hinchey, 1999). What being critical implies is that, while the research is occurring, the knowledge, values, and beliefs that are uncovered must be evaluated for the way they impact social justice, caring, and democracy. The research is embedded within a continuous stream of critical reflection, which looks at how the research findings connect with the power relationships between the individuals involved in the issue. In other words, you continually ask how does what you have uncovered create inequity, injustice, or uncaring activity? Are some individuals empowered by what is going on while others are marginalized and disempowered?

Critical reflection is not enough because it is essentially looking outward or away from the self. An additional and essential activity is critical reflexion. This involves redirecting your critical reflection to yourself. How does your own bias prevent a deeper understanding of the issue or situation? How are your values and beliefs complicitly contributing to that which you are against? Scholar-practitioner leaders apply the skills and methods in their toolbox to their own beliefs, values, and knowledge to gain a greater understanding of themselves and their relationship to what they uncover about the issue or the situation. Scholar-practitioners must know themselves as well as they know the issue and the positions of others on that issue. Finally, scholar-practitioners must acquire a healthy dose of skepticism that will facilitate their curiosity and creativity.

Scholar-practitioner leaders understand that things are always more complex than they seem, and that every action has critical implications for themselves and others. They also realize that reality is not something external to human consciousness that can be discovered through some scientific process. They are aware that people, individually and socially, construct reality. Because of the constructivist nature of learning, the learning process becomes more complex than the simple memorization of information or the following of prescribed formulas. Being a scholar-practitioner leader means knowing that knowledge, values, and beliefs cannot be given or transmitted to others. These other individuals must be allowed to participate in the construction of meaning, definition, knowledge, or action so they can achieve the same level of critical literacy as the scholar-practitioner leader. Scholar-practitioner leaders realize that they are life-long learners and promote the same stance in others.

Scholar-practitioner leaders realize that emotion is a vital component in the understanding of a situation, issue, or another's beliefs. Since emotion cannot be separated from human activity, scholar-practitioner leaders utilize the techniques of critical reflection and reflexion to uncover the emotional aspects of a situation. This recognition and valuing of emotion is also facilitated in others. Dealing with the complexity of a situation also involves paying attention to the consequences of the scholar-practitioner leader's actions. In this case, the scholar-practitioner leader does not merely focus on whether actions will achieve the desired outcome, but also weighs the critical implications of these consequences. A critical concern for justice, caring, and democracy becomes a yardstick that is used to evaluate intended actions and their subsequent consequences.

This critical focus on consequences does not imply that the scholar-practitioner leader should become frozen in an endless loop of reflection on an intended action without ever taking action. Quite the contrary. Scholar-practitioner leaders make their best plan, take action, critically reflect on that action, and continue the cycle. This cycle relates to the praxis proposed by Paulo Freire (1996), and the critical pragmatism proposed by Cleo Cherryholmes (1999). Unlike the scientific method that proposes that the variables that can affect an outcome can be controlled, scholar-practitioner leaders understand that, because of the complexity of reality, not all variables can even be identified, much less controlled. With this belief, they strive to gain the necessary knowledge to make an informed decision and then take action.

One key difference between a scholar-practitioner leader and others is that they know they must critically reflect on their action. Sometimes, the complexity of a situation is hard to discern. This is another reason why scholar-practitioner leaders find it essential to learn and use a diversity of research methods and theoretical views in their analysis of a situation.

To return to the original question about your ability to question authority, as a scholar-practitioner leader you are well positioned to increase your batting average and to help others deal with authority, but as a teacher, you are an authority. Therefore, should your students question your authority, the school's authority, or the authority of instructional materials such as textbooks? If you promote the skills, knowledge, and attitudes of a scholar-practitioner leader in your students, are you putting your own authority at risk? The answer to these questions deals with another essential aspect of scholar-practitioner leadership—that of collegiality and cooperation.

Scholar-practitioner leaders find that it is not enough to facilitate the development of related skills, knowledge, and questioning in their students. Two things are also necessary—the attempt to develop collegial and caring communities, and the attempt to encourage the recognition of difference and diversity as important elements in a participatory democracy. In some cases, scholars and practitioners attempt to establish collegial and caring communities, but the processes that they use and the philosophies that guide their actions actually marginalize those who are different and those who differ in their thinking from the majority. This drive to achieve sameness suppresses difference, and consequently fosters a contrived collegiality that diminishes the value of diversity. In their attempt to construct collegial communities, scholar-practitioners utilize critical reflection, critical reflexion, and their commitment to social justice, caring, and participatory democracy to guide their community building. However, they also promote these same attitudes, knowledge, and skill in those whom which they work.

In collegial communities where difference and diversity are valued, questioning authority is an expected and desired activity. In a collegial community, the questioner and those who are being questioned are personally and collectively responsible for how those questions are asked and how they are processed. In relation to questions and their subsequent discussion, knowledge about and skill in conversation becomes another critical aspect of scholar-practitioner leadership. Scholar-practitioner leaders understand the difference between adversarial conversations and other types of conversations that promote understanding and the equitable and caring resolution of problems. The ability to engage in dialogue and to teach others how to dialogue is an essential part of constructive questioning. To dialogue requires individuals to suspend their own mindsets about an issue or another's position, and actively and empathically listen and respond to what another says. Dialogue creates bridges that create an understanding of differences and also help other individuals construct answers to their questions that equitably accommodate these differences.

Another type of conversation from the idealized systems design community, design conversation, allows the scholar-practitioner leader to guide others in the construction of a system (classroom, school, or larger society) that is centered upon the equal ideals of efficiency and effectiveness, justice and caring. When questions and problems are posed, all types of conversation come into play at different times, and scholar-practitioner leaders need to be proficient in their use and in how to critically guide others in their use.

Therefore, to answer the question, yes, authority should be questioned, but the scholar-practitioner leader needs to foster a climate that views questioning authority as a necessary and generative process in the creation of critical citizens and just and caring communities.

In conclusion, the concept of scholar-practitioner leadership sounds awfully idealistic and radical; and in relation to how questioning and decision-making usually occur, it probably is. However, a critical pragmatist would argue that this is the best option for the creation of a critical citizenry and a just and caring society. Other options are a vulgar form of pragmatism that focuses on the attainment of self-interest through any means, or the fanatical adherence to narrow and exclusive beliefs. The concept of scholar-practitioner leadership is appropriate for any individual within any aspect of society. The basic elements of scholar-practitioner leadership apply to and can be used by students, teachers, and administrators of any age and level, and in any professional or personal situation. They are essential for any individual who desires to understand more deeply, to care, and to promote the welfare of all.

References

Cherryholmes, C. (1999). *Reading pragmatism.* New York: Teachers College Press.

Freire, P. (1996). *Pedagogy of the oppressed.* New York: Continuum.

Jenlink, P. M. (1999, August). *Educational leaders as scholarly practitioners: Considerations for preparation and practice.* Paper presented at the National Council of Professors of Educational Administration annual conference, Jackson Hole, WY.

Kincheloe, J. L., Steinberg, S. R., & Hinchey, P. H. (Eds.). (1999). *The postformal reader: Cognition and education.* New York: Falmer Press.

Further Reading

Horn, R. A. (2002). *Understanding educational reform: A reference handbook.* Santa Barbara, CA: ABC-CLIO.

Teachers' Work: What Is Happening to It?

John Smyth

At the outset I should explain what I believe critical thinking means. To think critically means to stand back, look at the world, and ask how it came to be the way it is. From the point of view of teachers, this requires a certain amount of courage because it involves challenging what are, on the surface, some pretty big assumptions about teaching. Some of these assumptions are that students only learn when they are passive and silent, that we can only know if learning has occurred by testing students, that good teaching can only be ascertained through teacher appraisal or evaluation, and that teachers have to always be in control of students' learning.

These are not universal truths—they have actually been constructed by sets of interests that want schools to exist in a particular way. Critical thinking, as applied to teaching, involves challenging what appear to be self-evident truths and replacing them with alternatives—alternatives that might be more deeply rooted in the way teachers actually think good teaching and learning occurs.

The starting point for critical thinking involves asking questions about teaching and classrooms, such as:

- Who is allowed to talk in this classroom?
- Who get the teacher's time?
- Who makes the rules?
- How are decisions made?
- How is conflict resolved?

- Are facts and answers valued more than questions?
- Who determines standards?
- How are inequalities recognized and dealt with?
- Is competition more important than cooperation and why? (Smyth, 2000, p. 498).

Unfortunately, there are some impediments to thinking critically about teaching, and many of the new reforms undermine teachers' abilities to engage in such thinking. We also need to remember that there has never been a 'golden age' in teaching. For those who work in schools and classrooms, teaching has always had elements that have been rewarding and satisfying, but at the same time the work has been complex and difficult. The difficulties confronting teachers have become exacerbated in recent times by widespread reforms and restructuring that have often failed to properly understand or be sympathetic to what it is that teachers are trying to do in the course of their everyday lives.

It is possible to trace the contours of what is happening to teachers' work by pursuing and thinking critically about two questions: (1) what are the changes occurring in teachers' work and how do we make sense of these changes, and (2) what are the alternatives? Both of these questions apply to the work of teachers worldwide.

THE NATURE OF THE CHANGES AND HOW TO MAKE SENSE OF THEM

At the heart of the reform process being imposed on teachers around the world is the view that teachers need to be controlled more closely by being made more accountable for student learning. On the surface, this may not appear to be altogether a bad thing. We hear a lot, for example, about accountability, measurable outcomes, performance standards, more intensive testing of students, and placing teachers under greater control and surveillance of one kind or another. In some places teachers are tested to maintain their accreditation.

Behind these changes lies a set of views that implicitly argues that teachers are not to be trusted and they need to be more tightly controlled. One of the main ways this is done is by requiring that the work of teaching be less in the hands of teachers and their professional judgments, and that it be more tightly calibrated or scripted to meet arbitrarily imposed standards and benchmarks. The consequence is that the focus falls much less on the actual process of teaching and the complexities and mysteries of learning, and more upon measurable outcomes. Teaching, therefore, becomes much more like the work of a technician who follows directions, agendas, frameworks, guidelines, or policies developed by others, rather than operating autonomously on the basis of a profound understanding of what it means to be a teacher. The work is thus made less of an intellectual and professional pursuit, and more the kind of job that is easily controllable by agencies outside of the classroom.

Added to this increasingly centralized control over teachers' work (in some countries it has occurred by instituting a National Curriculum that includes accountability measures), is an increasing tendency to regard schools and what goes on within them as being subject to market forces. In other words, further pressure of a different kind is placed on teachers and their work by positioning parents as consumers able to treat the schooling of their children as another commodity to be shopped for. Parents look around for schools that will provide them with the best deal for what they consider necessary to improve the life chances of their children. In this scheme, schools have to become more adept at how they market themselves and present the kind of image they need to survive. One of the effects can be a shift to superficial impression management—the use of glossy marketing materials, pushing the existence of strong discipline or behavior management policies, and an emphasis on what is overtly measurable. In some parts of the world where school uniforms are in vogue, whether a school is vigorous or not in policing whether students wear their uniforms can be an important criteria parents use in defining whether or not it is a good school.

In other places, how students perform on examinations and tests and comparisons between schools on the basis of league tables is another way in which schools (and eventually teachers) are controlled by the workings of the education market. The rationale is that schools that fail to meet parental expectations either change what they do to conform to these expectations or they will not attract students and hence cease to exist.

While there may superficially appear to be some merit in treating schools as if they were no different than supermarkets, there are significant dangers, particularly in terms of the tensions this attitude creates in teachers and the way they go about their work. Behind the prevailing reforms is a marked shift away from education and schooling as a public good, that is indispensable in a democracy bent on pursuing questions about what kind of society is being constructed, debated, and discussed. Thinking about schools, and by implication the work of teachers, in terms that predominantly feed into fostering privatized and individualized competencies and self-interest is ultimately detrimental to all of us. We certainly need schools and teachers in which knowledge and skills are imparted, but we also need schools in which teachers are able to fire the imagination of students around big ideas of social importance, and that go beyond narrow acquisitive self-interest. And herein lies the rub! If teachers and their work are being forced into a narrow and constricted set of utilitarian values, then there is a greater likelihood that wider questions of social justice and working for the needs of the least advantaged will either become marginalized, expunged, or obliterated.

Many teachers feel affronted and confronted by the notion that their work is about adding value, even though they are prepared to accept that improvement is always a key aspect of the work. They prefer instead to see teaching as more of a social practice in which forming, sustaining, and maintaining relationships lies at the heart of what they do. The defining characteristic of teaching, for many teachers, is the quality of the associations they are able to develop with students, other teachers, parents, and careers. This involves quite complex negotiations of open-ended difference, rather than the capacity to put definitive closure on predetermined ends. Viewed this way, the work of teaching is about creating a set of circumstances in which everyone feels they are able to speak and have their aspirations listened to, not a situation in which teaching and learning are collapsed down to adherence to a set of one-size-fits-all authoritarian standards. Relationships are not optional add-ons for many teachers—they lie at the very heart of everything a teacher does.

We can only really understand the changes mentioned above if we see them as part of a much more complex process of structural adjustment that occurs in most Western countries when governments retreat from their responsibility to provide public education. What goes on in the schools is seen as the responsibility of the parent, the school, the teacher, or the student. At all of these levels, individuals and institutions are increasingly being urged to operate in ways that best serve their individual self-interests by pursuing what they consider is best for themselves. Wider collective interests are either not addressed at all or are considered to be of secondary importance.

This way of thinking about schooling and what goes in inside schools is somewhat at variance with the way many teachers think. For many teachers, the defining attribute of teaching lies in the aspiration of wanting to make a difference to the life chances of students. This can mean a variety of things, but it often means working with students to try and counteract the worst effects of poverty, industrialization, gender discrimination, racism, harassment, homophobia, and other forms of social disfigurement. Teachers often see their work as an opportunity to create moments of enlightenment, not ramp up achievement scores. Teaching is seen as a moral and political activity, in which young people are provided with forms of knowledge that will equip them to both understand and act in the world to change it for the better.

WHAT ARE THE ALTERNATIVES AND HOW MIGHT TEACHING BE VIEWED DIFFERENTLY?

At another level, it is possible to understand the changes occurring in the work of teachers if we realize that teaching has shifted noticeably in recent years from being an activity that is about enabling children to learn in ways that are curiosity-driven, to becoming a vehicle for economic growth and the advancement of international competitiveness between countries. What is strange about this conception of teaching is that, while the focus has shifted to the means by which individuals can personally benefit from being educated, the orientation brings with it processes like testing, standards, and accountability that are a long way from the concept of expanding and growing children's habits of mind.

What seems to get lost here is the opportunity to take risks, encourage children to ask difficult and controversial questions, and to generally organize and conduct schools in ways that are conducive to critical thinking. In other words, what we have are the ingredients of conservative and safe approaches to teaching that are primarily defensive. Children should be kept busy, fill out worksheets, and satisfy their parents who want their offspring to outperform other students and schools that on the surface appear to be neater and tidier places. When schools and teachers respond to the forces operating on them in these ways, teachers are rewarded for engaging in safe practices.

Rather than courageously questioning what they do, teachers in these circumstances are encouraged to act in ways that foster image and impression management (i.e., in glossy brochures that promote the academic and sporting prowess of the school). What gets expunged are the experimental and risk-taking teaching behaviors that good teachers know are crucial to real learning. Policies that are aimed at producing compliant teachers are low trust policies, not at all conducive to the risk-taking actions that enable children to interrogate, question, and get access to other perspectives, or ask how things came to be the way they are.

Under these circumstances, pedagogical choices become constrained and teachers become increasingly scripted. They are required to operate within frameworks, guidelines, and policies and according to standards that may have little to do with a teacher's professional judgment of how best to capture the elusive moments in which learning is optimal. The further consequence of policies that are disrespectful of teachers and that try to corral them is that the lives, experiences, cultures, and aspirations of students are further marginalized and excluded. The spaces in which teachers can genuinely engage with the richness, diversity, and complexity of the lives that children bring with them to school are closed down in the pursuit of the banal, the trivial, or the down-right anti-educative. Critical thinking under these circumstances becomes a dangerous practice, and one many teachers pursue at considerable personal risk to their jobs and their careers. This is a sad state of affairs, but it is a realistic one confronted daily by very many highly committed teachers, and it is unnecessary.

There are certainly many instances where teachers have found ways of very creatively constructing their teaching differently to that envisaged by the reform processes described above. At the heart of such alternatives are the ways teachers think and act critically and what they believe it means to be a teacher.

Thinking critically about teaching and learning, when stripped to its essentials, means standing apart from what goes on in teaching and asking difficult questions about how it came to be the way it is, and whose interests are really being served by continuing to have teaching the way it is. This is a very challenging thing to do because it brings into question many of the cherished assumptions many people in the wider community hold about what it means to teach. Such people may believe that it is the role of the teacher to teach and students should be passive and acquiescent, that teaching is not a political activity, that it should avoid controversy and be mainly concerned with conveying information in an unproblematic manner, and that children succeed in school only if they make a sustained effort.

Teachers who think deeply about their work and the wider circumstances in which they do it, especially teachers in urban and socially disadvantaged communities, know that these beliefs are untrue. Teachers don't possess all wisdom about teaching; when provided with the opportunity to voice their views, students reveal that they know a lot about how they learn best. What gets included in (or excluded from) the curriculum, and whose views, knowledge, customs, traditions, and language forms are used are all highly political decisions, and not all children have the same level of access to learning because of their lives, family backgrounds, linguistic forms, and aspirations for the future. Some schools give out messages that certain children are more welcome than others.

All these are serious issues that can only be attended to if teachers think deeply, critically, and outside of the normal ways in which teaching is currently talked about.

In other words, teaching is not a set of universal techniques to be applied in any setting. While teachers are knowledgeable pedagogically, they are also continually in the process of interrogating and questioning what it is they do, why things are working in particular circumstances or for particular groups of students, or what might need to be done differently.

This capacity to think about the nature of the work of teaching and to continuously re-focus what happens in the light of experience, especially in terms of the least advantaged students, is the hallmark of the refined teacher who thinks critically.

The starting point for this way of thinking critically about teaching is the willingness to confront the foundations of what it means to be a teacher, especially the view that the teacher is supposed to be in charge, that the students are there to be compliant, and that students are supposed to compete with one another for grades and other rewards from the teacher.

Another of the shibboleths that needs to be robustly confronted is the largely unchallenged (even widely celebrated) assumption prevalent at the moment that the experience of schooling is like any other good or service—it is merely another product on offer for consumption in the marketplace.

Teachers who can find the space (with other teachers) to think critically about their teaching, confront these axioms and regard teaching and learning as a more cooperative, democratic, and dialogical activities. They are continually asking what works, for whom, in what circumstances, and why? For them, teaching is something that is always open to questioning, argument and debate. Above all, teachers who think critically about their teaching carry with them a crucial ideal—that schooling is about advancing the learning of all children, not just that of a select few.

Further Reading

Robertson, S. (2000). *A class act: Changing teachers' work, the state and globalisation.* New York and London: Falmer Press.

Smyth, J. (2000). Reclaiming social capital through critical teaching. *The Elementary School Journal, 100* (5), 491–511.

Smyth, J. (2001). *Critical politics of teachers' work: An Australian perspective.* New York: Peter Lang.

Woods, P., Jeffrey, B., Troman, G., & Boyle, M. (1997). *Restructuring schools, reconstructing teachers: Responding to change in the primary school.* Buckingham and Philadelphia: Open University Press.

Epistemology

Epistemology

Barbara J. Thayer-Bacon

As a philosopher and former elementary teacher who teaches in a college of education and has worked mainly with teachers and future teachers, I am always trying to translate abstract philosophical language and ideas into terms that make sense to non-philosophers. *Epistemology* is one of those terms. It is a big, fancy term that just means theories about knowledge. The favorite story I tell is about the time that I had a student who thought I was saying *episiotomy* when I said *epistemology*. As the mother of four children, I think of that misunderstanding every time I use the word now!

Philosophers have historically divided their field of study into various branches, based on the kinds of questions they ask. In general, philosophers have tried to make the case for what is true, good, just, and beautiful for all of us, across time and place. They have asked questions about the essence of life and they have tried to argue for how things *should be,* ideally, not how things are. Philosophical questions about virtue and goodness are the focus of the branch of philosophy known as ethics. Questions about what is beautiful represent the branch of aesthetics. Questions

about essential categories are metaphysical, and questions about truth are epistemological concerns.

I always tell my students that philosophy is the place where you can envision *how things should be* in education, what's the *best* way to offer schooling to children, for example, without any concern for resources and the other limitations that we normally face on a daily basis as teachers. Philosophy is the place where we can argue for what the ideal classroom size should be, or determine what the best way is to try to measure what students have learned if we are trying to be fair and just. Here is the place where we can dream and make the case for what should necessarily be to create a fair, just, beautiful, truthful, and good educational system.

Philosophy offers us ideals to strive for in our daily classroom practice, gives us a guide that will help us in our daily decision-making, and offers us ways to be able to critique what exists in education. While scientists wrestle with trying to figure out how things are, based on empirical evidence, and religious leaders make religious arguments based on faith, philosophers make arguments based on the use of logic and reasoning, or what we call today *critical thinking.*

I have argued elsewhere that philosophers use their intuition, emotions, and imagination as well as their reasoning and critical thinking to help them make their case (Thayer-Bacon, 2000). Still, for our purposes here, I think this distinction between philosophy, religion, and science will help readers make sense of the branch of study in philosophy known as *epistemology.*

When we look more closely at epistemology, we find that philosophers have historically defined epistemology as the field of study that concerns itself with knowledge. Epistemological theories are theories about how it is we know what we know. It's important to draw your attention to the use of the term *knowledge* because philosophers don't mean that knowledge is the same thing as what we learn, yet these two terms are often treated as if they were synonymous. In philosophy, knowledge has historically been defined as that which is absolutely True, whereas what we learn can turn out to be false. We can believe that something is true, and even have good reasons to believe that something is true, but only the things that are True in an absolute sense get to be counted as knowledge. If we are not sure that something is True, we must call it a *belief* instead of *knowledge.*

There are different categories of beliefs, which depend on how close the beliefs are to being declared Knowledge or True beliefs. *Mere beliefs,* or right opinions, are stated as "S believes that p," with "S" symbolizing the subject of the belief, and "p" signifying the object of the belief. *Rational beliefs* are beliefs that are supported by compelling reasons ("S has good reason to believe that p"). We only call "p" Knowledge if what S believes about p, and

S has compelling reasons to believe about p, is really True ("S knows that p"). It is similar to how scientists develop hypotheses, test them out, and even arrive at solutions, but very few scientific results become scientific laws.

Knowledge, as it has been historically defined in philosophy, is that which is True for all times. Epistemologists, in their efforts to determine what counts as knowledge, look at questions about the *justification* of people's beliefs and concern themselves with the normative status of knowledge claims. They attempt to *verify* claims that are made and to prove the *validity* of arguments. Epistemologists attempt to establish the criteria and standards necessary to prove validity and truth. They are concerned with what *warrants* the knowledge claims we make and therefore ask normative questions such as what counts as good evidence, not causal questions concerning how beliefs are developed.

Let me give some examples of famous epistemological theories (remember, just translate that to *theories about knowledge*) that philosophers have developed over time. Plato and Aristotle, Plato's student, offer us examples of two different theories of knowledge that have had a tremendous impact on Euro-western philosophy. The roots of more recent continental *and* North American epistemological theories can be traced back to Plato and Aristotle.

Plato's theory is that we know 'that p' because our souls are immortal and therefore know all knowledge. Knowing is an act of remembering what our souls already know. Aristotle argues that it is not enough to recollect Truth, we must rely on thought as reality and the origin of knowledge. Aristotle suggests that we must test out our ideas through our experiences to be sure they are true, thus asserting that material things are the reality and the origin of knowledge. If our ideas correspond to our experiences then we can conclude they are True. Aristotle's correspondence theory follows a path that leads us to present day science and the scientific method.

In a similar vein to Plato, Descartes argues that what we know is what is beyond doubt. By using Descartes' doubting method to dismiss everything we can doubt until we come to what we take to be self-evident, we can find Truth. Peirce follows Aristotle's path into the future, arguing that we will not know Truth until the end of time. Truth is something that we are getting closer to as we continue to test out our ideas with our experiences, but none of us can be guaranteed of certain knowledge in our own lifetimes. We find today that, while epistemologists still strive for clarity and coherence, most have rejected certainty as a condition of knowledge, following Peirce's lead.

Foundational epistemologists seek to establish that we can ultimately justify our claims by relying on foundational beliefs that are justified, but not in terms of other beliefs. Coherentists seek to establish that claims fit coherently into the existing body of knowledge. Some describe foundationalists as embracing a pyramid model, and coherentists as embracing a raft model. The pyramid model attempts to establish basic foundational beliefs (undisputed Truths) and builds upon these. The raft model says that specific truths may change over time, as we change in our understanding, so that individual logs on the raft may need repair or replacement yet the raft continues to hold us and support us down the river of Truth.

Now that I have explained what *epistemology* is, as it has been defined historically by philosophers, I must move to challenging this definition of epistemology, for current philosophers, including myself, are bringing serious criticisms to bear on the epistemological theories of the past.

There are some key metaphysical assumptions embedded in traditional philosophy's definition of epistemology, no matter which theory one embraces, that present day philosophers are proving to be problematic and dangerous. These assumptions are based on several dualisms, which we have already come across in my above description. We found out already that philosophy distinguishes itself from science, for example, because it separates theory from practice and universality from particularity. Remember, I said that philosophy tries to answer general questions that apply to all of us across time and place, and science tries to answer causal questions about what exists in a particular time and place. Philosophy has to do with theory, science with practice. Philosophy has to do with the general, science has to do with the particular.

We also found out that epistemology defines itself by drawing a sharp distinction between relative (individual) belief and absolute (universal) Truth. Epistemology has to do with absolute, universal Truth, and science has to do with hypotheses that are always being further tested. Did you notice that when I described epistemologists as talking about knowers and the known (subjects/objects, S and p), this definition assumes a separation between S and p, knowers and what is known? Philosophy cares about the known, Truth, and speaks very little about the knowers. Philosophy assumes knowers are autonomous individuals who seem to sprout out of the ground as mature adults, already able to think for themselves. It is very rare for philosophers to even discuss children. Philosophy has been willing to let psychology worry about knowers as subjects/objects of inquiry.

Epistemologists believed that they could find what is True for all times and all people. That belief has now been shown to have tremendous power, and although it looks like a neutral, harmless assumption, it isn't. It has the power to determine who is heard and who is not, who is considered knowledgeable and who is not, who gets published or hired and who does not, who is judged to be a good teacher and who is not. It has been shown that the criteria and standards we use to judge what is true are fallible and subject to change. They are not neutral and objective, but are based on particular values and beliefs and we need to be able to continually critique and readjust our criteria and standards. We have learned that we cannot separate people's influences from their work, the questions they ask, and the theories they develop. Whatever theory a philosopher offers has their fingerprints all over it. We have learned that philosophers cannot jump out of their skins and rid themselves of their own perspectives. They do not have what feminists have called "a God's eye view" of Truth (Haraway, 1988; Harding, 1993). Instead they are embedded within their own setting and time and are contextual beings with their own unique experiences of the world. They experience the world through their own eyes, ears, mouth, and skin. So, for example, Aristotle's arguments on how things should be depended on what he called natural causes. These natural causes were based on how things were in ancient Greece at the time of his writings. Ancient Greece was an elitist, racist, and sexist society where only property-owning males were allowed to be educated and live the contemplative life, while women and slaves did the laundry, cooking, and cleaning for those men. While Aristotle took this life to be the norm on which to base his philosophy, today we can critique it as

not being a just or good model of how society should be. Rousseau made his arguments for what is natural based on his disdain for French society at the time of his writings, and his desire to be independent of that corrupt civilization. However, Emile could only develop into a self-made man if Sophie learned how to be a homemaker and took care of Emile's every need so that he could be free and independent. Today we can easily see the contradictions in such a philosophy.

The controversial assumptions that current philosophers are criticizing and bringing into question have triggered heated debates. For example, if we let go of the assumption of absolute Truth, the basis for how philosophy and epistemology originally were defined, the death of Philosophy is sure to follow say postmodernists such as Lyotard (1984) and Rorty (1979) argue? Siegel (1987) says such a move will signal the end of epistemology and a reign of terror in which anything goes for there will be no way to argue about what is right/wrong, good/bad, just/unjust.

I don't think it is as bad as all that. In fact, I think the future looks bright for philosophy and epistemology, once we let go of the assumption of absolute Truth. After all, it is just an assumption, and it has not been able to stand up to the test of time and the critique of further philosophical arguments. This means we have already functioned for a long time without Truth, we just kept hoping and believing we had it to guide us. What we are left with to help us make decisions and solve problems is a naturalized theory of knowing that I call a relational (e)pistemology. I put brackets around the "e" to underscore that this theory is based on qualified truths, not absolute Truth. What we have is each other. We can argue and debate and defend what we think are the best descriptions of reality and truth until we settle on one we can live with, but the one we settle on is not a description we can be sure is Right or True. Indeed, there are a variety of descriptions we could settle on as Right or True, depending on what lens we choose to use and which focus we want to emphasize. We can never settle comfortably on a description for long, but must continually research our findings.

We will never find Certainty, but this does not mean we cannot make decisions and act. Whether we like it or not, we must act. Even to decide not to decide is still a decision, and the decision to not act is still an action. What is important in a relational (e)pistemology is that we seek to act in ways that are as informed as we are able to make them, realizing we can never get rid of ourselves and that we are always implicated in our research findings. Knowing is not objective, neutral, or certain, it is in a state of flux. What I point to here is a more humble theory of knowing that can never claim absolute knowledge. It is a theory of knowing that focuses on the process, not just the product, and recognizes that knowers and the known are directly connected. It is a pluralistic, inclusive theory that insists that we include others in our process of inquiry, for we can never find the answer to our problems on our own. Others contribute to our thinking right from the start, and they help to enlarge our views beyond our own limitations.

We still need philosophers as fallible social critics, for philosophers help us redescribe what has already been described and they help us recreate and envision anew. Through philosophy we learn how we can reform education, but we also learn that we need each other's help in this process. Not one of us, alone, knows the Answers. I invite your contributions to the conversation, for as Dewey points out, inquiry only ends when we have solved all of our problems and answered all of our questions, and we are a long way from there. Not only do I think we will never get to that point, I doubt if it is even a desirable point to which to get. Disharmony, discontent, and diversity help us continue to grow and further our knowing.

References

Haraway, D. (1988). Situated knowledges: The science question in feminism and the privilege of partial perspective. *Feminist Studies, 14*(3), 575–599.

Harding, S. (1993). Rethinking standpoint epistemology: What is 'strong objectivity'? In L. Alcoff, & E. Potter (Eds.), *Feminist epistemologies* (pp. 49–82). New York: Routledge.

Lyotard, J-F. (1984). *The postmodern condition: A report on knowledge.* Minneapolis: University of Minnesota Press.

Rorty, R. (1979). *Philosophy and the mirror of nature.* Princeton, NJ: Princeton University Press.

Siegel, H. (1987). *Relativism refuted: A critique of contemporary epistemological relativism.* Dordrecht: Reidel.

Thayer-Bacon, B. (2000). *Transforming critical thinking: Thinking constructively.* New York: Teachers College Press.

Further Reading

Cahn, S. (Ed.). (1997). *Classic and contemporary readings in the philosophy of education.* New York: McGraw-Hill.

Feminism

Feminism and Critical Thinking

Barbara J. Thayer-Bacon

There are many different feminist perspectives, but for all the variety that exits there are still some basic concerns all feminists share. These are concerns for the well being and equal treatment of women and girls, and a valuation of the study of women and girls as an important, worthwhile research topic. Feminism is committed to exploring gendered dimensions and the restrictive nature of sex roles, believing that women historically have been oppressed and unjustly treated by human institutions and social relationships.

Feminists view gender as a socially constructed category in need of continual critique. They argue that men in patriarchal societies have historically described themselves in contrast to women and have placed women in an inferior, secondary, Other role as the second sex (de Beauvoir, 1952). Feminism is concerned with the forms and functions of power and how power has been wielded against women. Elizabeth Minnich defines feminism, at its most basic level, as having "to do with a cast of mind; a way of thinking, and a movement of heart and spirit; a way of being and acting with and for others. The cast of mind is fundamentally one of cri-

tique; the movement of heart is toward friendship" (Minnich, 1983, p. 317).

When we look at critical thinking through the lens of feminism, the first thing we notice is how *male* the image of a critical thinker seems to be. When I think of an artistic image of a critical thinker, I think of Rodin's *Thinker,* a naked male sitting by himself, head on hand, brow furrowed, deep in thought. When I think of an example of a teacher who is famous for being a critical thinker, and for teaching his students to be critical thinkers, I think of Socrates in the marketplace in Athens, surrounded by youthful males who are engaged in a heated discussion with him.

It is no accident that critical thinking is associated with males. The maleness of critical thinking can be traced back to its roots in Euro-western philosophy. Ancient Greece was a society ruled by property-owning males, and these were the people who had the leisure and education that gave them the opportunity to think critically and deeply about such topics as philosophy. There is more to the association than wealth and leisure time though, for men became associated with the mind and reason, and women became linked to the body and emotions. Plato can be pointed to as a key source for the mind/body split, with his theory about knowledge that says we know all there is to know already because our souls are immortal. However, we forget what we know when our souls inhabit our bodies, thus we spend our lives trying to recollect what our souls already know.

Right from the start, in Euro-western philosophy, the mind is associated with knowledge and the body is viewed as something that gets in our way of knowing. Our bodies cause us to forget. Not only did Plato suggest a split between the mind and the body, he also associated the mind with reason, and the emotions with the body. The emotions are described by Plato as something we must learn how to tame and try to keep under control, like horses pulling a chariot, so that they will work for us and not against us.

The next step to consider is how women became associated with the body, and thus with emotions, and disassociated from the mind and thinking critically. Women became linked to the body because of their reproductive role in society. They are the ones who carry a baby inside their bodies for nine months, and then nurse their baby until the baby can eat solid food, usually between six months and two years of age. Two to three years of a woman's life is affected by each child she conceives. It has never been as easy for women to disassociate their minds from their bodies as it has been for men. Only today, when women can take control of the reproductive process through the use of very effective birth control, are women becoming free of their bodies' demands, and sure enough, because they can do so they are becoming more associated with their minds and reason.

Some feminists argue that this is good, for it finally allows women to break down the hierarchy that ranks women inferior to men in their thinking abilities. Now women can work side-by-side with men as equals and have their ideas taken seriously and treated with respect. Other feminists argue that this is not such a good thing after all, for women have just adopted the male valuing of mind over body, reason over emotions, instead of questioning and critiquing the dualisms. These feminists argue that the mind/body, reason/emotion splits are dangerous, for they ask us to split ourselves from ourselves. They argue that we cannot just "add women and stir" to this very androcentric view of critical thinking; we must redescribe ourselves as having bodyminds and learn to value reason *and* emotions.

My voice has added to the critique of the male model for critical thinking. As a feminist I have argued we must transform the way we think about critical thinking, and redescribe it so that it no longer represents the male image that is so pervasive. It is not enough to add breasts to Rodin's Thinker; we need to break away from that solitary, contemplative, male image altogether.

What I offer in contrast to Rodin's Thinker is the image of a quilting party. I suggest this image for many reasons, including the fact that quilting enjoys a rich history and can be found in cultures all over the world. I do not suggest this image because I long to reach back to the past and "the good 'ole days." I don't think those ever existed for women. I want to bring the rich heritage of quilting forward and draw our attention to its continuing artistry and practicality, to which men *and* women have always contributed, but especially women. I want to suggest a social image, with people interacting with each other in a variety of ways, and a quilting party offers us that image.

Imagine that some people are preparing food, some are watching the children, some are playing musical instruments, and some are sewing together pieces of material to make a quilt. Let's say the material we use for the quilt represents our ideas and the quilts that become our final products represent the knowledge we socially construct together. It is possible to go off and work on an individual pattern or even an entire quilt of knowledge by oneself. However, with a quilting party we still come together to discuss our plans for the quilt, and continually renegotiate these as well as we help sew the individual pieces together in the end. If the material represents our ideas and the finished quilt our knowledge, then we, the quilters, are the inquirers, the knowers who construct knowledge quilts. We are young and old, male and female, with varying sexual orientations, physically challenged and physically able, of various shapes, sizes and shades of color, from a variety of economic backgrounds, and from cultures around the world.

We use some important tools to help us in our quilting. One is reason, or critical thinking as it is commonly referred to. Our critical thinking is used to help us assess our thoughts and ideas and decide which ones fit together well and which ones are underdeveloped or too contrasting and contradictory and need to be eliminated. Our critical thinking tool enables us to judge and critique our quilt as we develop it. Critical thinking functions like a ruler and scissors and straight pins in quilting. It helps us measure our ideas and order and straighten them, as well as helping us fit them together and hold them in place so we can check them for their quality and make sure they go together well. We also use intuition in making quilts of knowledge. Our intuition is represented in the quilting metaphor by a needle and thread, used to move through the material and hold the material together. Our intuition helps us move through our ideas and select the ones we want to develop and use. Whereas critical thinking offers us a way to access our ideas, intuition helps us generate and put our ideas together. Both tools are vital to inquiry, and help us produce beautiful and useful quilts of knowledge.

However, even if we have a needle and thread, scissors, straight pins, and a ruler, we still can't make a quilt without the vital ingredient of the material itself, the ideas. Intuition and reason may do the invaluable jobs of generating and critiquing, but they rely of imagination and emotions to help them, for our emotions and imagination are what motivate us and inspire us to inquire. All inquiry begins with the emotions and our imagination. Our emotions and imagination are represented in our quilting metaphor by the quality and texture, color, and patterns of the material. The vibrant colors and textures in the material represent our emotions, and the designs and patterns in the material represent our imagination. Our emotions are vital to inquiry because they are what get us started and keep us going through the hard work of constructing knowledge.

Our inquiry begins with a felt need; something stirs us to action. We are moved by doubts or concerns, or excited by the hint of possibilities, and so we begin to inquire. Our imagination helps us open up new spaces so that we can see the world differently and helps us understand alternative realities so we can have empathy for others not like us. Our imagination helps us create new order as it helps us bring parts that seemed to be severed together and helps us see patterns where there appeared to be none.

What does this transformed critical thinking, which I call constructive thinking, help us understand about our classrooms? Does it change how we look at the curriculum and methods of teaching, how we describe the role of the teacher and the student? Does it help us see things in new ways? I think it does. While Rodin's *Thinker* gets us to focus on the individual and his accomplishments, such as his test scores, grades, and research papers, a quilting party image draws our attention to the *people* involved in the constructing of knowledge quilts. We are asked to pay attention to the *process* of inquiring, and not just the products. We find we have to worry about whether everyone in our classroom is getting a chance to help construct quilts of knowledge and whether we can open up more spaces and ways for students to make contributions. We have to worry about whether our students feel like our classroom is a warm, welcoming, safe environment where their voices will be heard and treated with respect, even as we encourage our students to develop their reasoning abilities and to use them to critique what others have to say.

The students in the classroom are not treated as isolated individuals, they are viewed as individuals-in-relations-with-others and we find we need to determine whether our students are able to work together or not. We begin to understand that the social interaction that takes place in the classroom is an extremely valuable part of the curriculum at many levels. We are reminded that a dialogical style of teaching not only encourages critical thinking skills, it also helps students develop their communication skills and relational skills, which are also vitally important in helping students be better thinkers. We start to see our students as teachers as well, who actively participate in the construction of knowledge quilts.

Through a constructive thinking model, we also realize that logical and problem-solving activities are not the only activities that help students become better thinkers. Artistic endeavors also help students learn how to use the tools they need to think constructively: reason, emotions, intuition, and imagination. Activities that we may have thought of as frills that were playful and fun tag ons to the serious academic curriculum, we can now begin to see as vital to helping our students develop their abilities to think constructively. An artistic curriculum is full of activities that require us to practice the use of our emotions, intuition, imagination, and reasoning.

I have traveled a great distance in this essay, for I began by defining feminism and establishing that critical thinking is historically associated with males in the Euro-western world. I moved from there to a feminist redescription of critical thinking as constructive thinking, relying on a quilting image. Recall that I defined feminism as having a critical mind and a heart of friendship. I hope the reader is able to see that the model of constructive thinking I offer, in contrast to traditional critical thinking, is a model that represents feminism's influence on critical thinking theory very well. When you add women to discussions on critical thinking you don't create a softer and kinder look for Rodin's *Thinker*, you get a transformation of critical thinking theory into constructive thinking, and a quilting party that is both friendly and critical at the same time.

References

de Beauvoir, S. (1989). *The second sex* (H. M. Parshley, Ed. and Trans.). New York: Vintage Books. (Original work published 1952)

Minnich, E. K. (1983). Friends and critics: The feminist academy. In C. Bunch, & S. Pollack

(Eds.), *Learning our way: Essays in feminist education*. Trumasburg, NY: The Crossing Press.

Thayer-Bacon, B. (2000). *Transforming critical thinking: Thinking constructively.* New York: Teachers College Press.

Further Reading

Grimshaw, J. (1986). *Philosophy and feminist thinking.* Minneapolis: University of Minnesota Press.

Okin, S. M. (1979). *Women in western political thought.* Princeton, NJ: Princeton University Press.

Hermeneutics

Hermeneutics for the Classroom

Marjorie Mayers and James C. Field

We begin this chapter with a few simple premises. The first is that critical thinking is a desired disposition for *both* teaching and learning and that focusing on existential questions, such as "How should we live together?" is an exemplary form of critical thinking. Second, that it is possible, without a great deal of effort on the part of the teacher, to have students inquire into the meaning of life, to help them think existentially. Third, that this kind of focus and impulse is not different from coming to understand subject matter deeply and developing "real world"[1] skill. Last, that this kind of focus is essential if students are to develop the ability to apply their knowledge in the real world appropriately and be able to respond wisely to the question "What should I do, in these particular circumstances?" In an increasingly complex and rapidly changing world, this is an extremely practical question for us all, irrespective of whether we are good with our heads or good with our hands. Risser (1997) puts it this way:

Application is not a simple matter of following a procedure as one follows a recipe in cooking, but a matter of perceiving what is at stake in the situation . . . What really delimits the notion of practice is its difference from technical skill . . . Practice involves leading a life in a particular way. This way of life of human beings, in distinction from animals, is not fixed by nature, but involves *prohairesis,* knowingly preferring one thing to another and choosing among possible alternatives . . . This means that practice, properly understood, is the form of human life that goes beyond the technical "choice" of the best means for a pre-given end. Practical reasoning in the actuality of life preeminently pertains to what is each individual's due as a citizen, and no technique can spare us from this deliberation and decision, for which there are no determinate rules. (p. 112)

To bring to light the significance of the above mentioned premises and to highlight how application/practice applies to living in the world thoughtfully, we offer the following narrative from a freshly graduated high school student as an illustration of what might be possible in classrooms between teachers and students. We also offer a reading of this narrative that highlights what we are calling *critical hermeneutics,* or an approach to teaching and dealing with the world in a particular way, with particular ends in mind (i.e., existential versus technical understanding).

I hated Social Studies, for 11 years I hated it. Labeling maps, coloring maps, making maps, memorizing names, dates, places, making charts—"Food" "Clothing" "Customs"—making Greek Salad when we studied Greece in Grade 6 was it? Or "list three causes of the Industrial Revolution" or "Why was the elephant important to Hannibal"? Who cares? What is it my poly-sci prof said, "History from the perspective of the winners"? What did any of that crap have to do with my life? Nothing, absolutely nothing.

But Social 30 was different, totally. I love Social Studies, now. That's why I'm in Management. You want to talk about the interaction of political and economic systems? That's it. That's Social 30. I'll never forget that first day in class—there we were, with our Discman's and our Nike hats, you know "the Gap kids," and that's where Mr. G. started. He goes, "Where did all this stuff come from?" China, Indonesia, Mexico we all started reading our labels. What is that about he asked? Are these Chinese shirts? Mexican running shoes? Indonesian Discman's? Can you tell? Why not? What's the point? And we got into this awesome discussion about the clothes we were wearing, about the stuff we were watching on TV, about what we did outside school, like most of us work for instance. A lot of that—what we like, what we buy, what we all want—is about the way economic systems operate in the real world. Mr. G made it real. I loved it, and his classes were packed always, even though it was the last class on Fridays. My best mark ever in school, even on the provincial exams, was in Social 30.

What strikes us immediately are the differences between the way this student reflects upon the better part of his social studies career in high school, and the way in which Mr. G. is able to engage this student in meaningful praxis—the intersection of theory and practice—by connecting his clothes to a world that both makes his clothes and positions people, places, and practices in relations of power and privilege. We believe that this is not simply about the qualities of the teacher. Although Mr. G made social studies interesting, we think that the class exemplifies the possibilities that erupt in pedagogic spaces when teachers pay attention to the lived world and the lived experiences of themselves and their students.[2,3] Mr. G.'s classroom, and the world he helps to open up, is about encouraging inquiry into the particular and opening up the possibilities for dialogue and deliberation. It is to this practice of opening up that critical hermeneutics invites the classroom teacher.

Critical hermeneutics, or inquiry-oriented teaching and learning, is concerned with two primary things: first, that an essential part of understanding is self-understanding, and second, that understanding is related to creating meaning in the world and is already a form of application. Critical hermeneutics is invested in a kind of attentiveness to things as they are in our experience, not as givens but as possibilities, provoking us to ask certain kinds of questions that require that we examine how things are as well as where we are in relation to how things are. It is the attentive, active participation in this kind of continual inquiry that propels inquirers in their ever-widening and deepening quest for meaning.

In the above narrative, the teacher begins to inquire into the lifeworld of his students by exploring and bringing to light the world of his students' experience and what they find meaningful. Students begin to question how they live, in what clothes they live, and why it might matter. They begin a process of self-understanding that helps them to come to know the world in a deeper, more complex, and more comprehensible way. They ask questions, inquire into their lived practices, and explore meanings that were, until then, invisible to them in their taken-for-grantedness. This self-understanding is indeed the way in which we come to make meaning of the world. Gallagher (1992) tells us:

By self understanding we do not mean a quiet and lonely reflective consciousness of the self. On the contrary, self understanding is always being tested out, challenged in the process of learning about the world. Self understanding is not an autarkic state; it is a process interdependent with other persons and things that define the situation. (p. 167)

Abram (1996) explains how self-understanding embeds us in the larger world.

[We need] not explain the world as if from outside, but to give voice to the world from our experienced situation *within* it, recalling us to our participation in the here-and-now, rejuvenating our sense of wonder at the fathomless things, events, and powers that surround us on every hand . . . this recuperation of the living landscape in which we are corporeally embedded is, of course, the "life world." (pp. 47, 65)

Critical hermeneutics orients the teacher and the students towards making meaning in the world as a connected, lived, and practical exercise.[4] Again, the narrative above illumines the critical possibilities that erupt in these kinds of educational spaces. As the student comments on his learning with Mr. G., he says "Mr. G. made it real." To that, the student repeats the questions that inspired him to consider the particularity of his clothes in a deeper and more existentially connected way. He says " . . . we all started reading our labels . . . and got into this awesome discussion about the clothes we were wearing . . . and [about the origin of our clothes we asked] Can you tell? Why not? What's the point?"

We read this classroom experience as an invocation and invitation into dialogic conversations that summon the participants to consider the following existential questions:

- How should I live?
- What conditions give rise to the things in my life, and in the world?
- What ought I to do, what ought we to do?

As examples, these practical questions are concerned with the lifeworld in which social studies and students are ostensibly connected. These questions are not severed from the places and practicalities of schools or subjects, they do not represent high theory nor are they *distractions* from the pressing schedules of the imminent standardized tests. They form what we believe to be the seminal questions of critical hermeneutics, the questions that give rise to critical, transformative, and meaningful opportunities in the classroom. The teacher and the students create the possibility for critical learning and reflection to transpire.

Notes

1. We have placed "real world" in scare quotes here because it is often used by ultra conservative curriculum makers to indicate the kind of learning that simply requires students to memorize and regurgitate information, or to learn what they need to know through fragmented skill and drill exercises, or to demonstrate competence through one-shot performances on standardized tests, or to represent knowledge and skill entirely through mathematical notation. In our work with corporations, we have found that the skills that such curriculums develop are not what is required by

"the real world." There isn't a shred of evidence in the research to suggest that students taught through inquiring into what is significant in their lives will not do at least as well, and in most cases better, on standardized tests than those taught through the "OK-you-guys-pay-attention-this-is-really-important-because-it-is-on–the-final-exam" approach. We seem to have forgotten that the subject disciplines were brought into being through wonderment and meaningful inquiry into what matters in life. The possibility of retrieving that wonderment inspires us to talk about "the real world."

2. Put another way, although Mr. G. is likely a wonderful teacher in his own right, we are positing that he is an example (or representative) of a particular pedagogic disposition and it is to that disposition, rather than to the cult of the personality to which we turn our focus.

3. We ask the reader to pause here, for a moment, to "tarry awhile in experience" as Heidegger might say, and consider what it means "to not go by things when they happen." We would like to bring attention to the pace of pedagogy and to the potential, prevalence, and abundance of critical opportunities that present themselves in every classroom, across all subjects, for all kind of teachers and students. Critical hermeneutics orients the teacher to pay careful attention to these openings, to these happenings in which critical, meaningful, and transformative participation (read inquiry, understanding, and application) can take place. Abram (1996) puts "not going by things when they happen" this way:

> As we reacquaint ourselves with our breathing bodies [i.e., paying careful attention to the world and our experiences in it], then the perceived world itself begins to shift and transform. When we begin to consciously frequent the wordless dimension of our sensory participations, certain phenomena that have habitually commanded our focus begin to lose their distinctive fascination and to slip toward the background, while hitherto unnoticed or overlooked presences begin to stand forth from the periphery and to engage our awareness. (p. 63)

Such is the case in the narrative above for the student, his clothes, and his experience in Mr. G.'s Social Studies classroom.

4. Again, we caution the reader not to see practical as a code for severed, instrumental, or technical approaches to understanding, but rather as embodied, lived, and existential openings for questions, inquiry, meaning-making, and thoughtful practice. As Risser (1997) notes, "Participation, like experience, is a dialectical growth. In a way it is simply experience 'writ large' as the constant process of transformation of what was previously held as valid. This is not to suggest that participation is simply a 'going along'; rather in participation, we become vigilant to the question" (p. 116). The questions we come back to again and again are the pivotal questions of critical hermeneutics for pedagogic practice: What shall I make of this particular experience? How shall I participate in the world? What ought I to do?

References

Abram, D. (1996). *The spell of the sensuous: Perception and language in a more-than-human world.* New York: Pantheon.

Gallagher, S. (1992). *Hermeneutics and education.* Albany, NY: SUNY Press.

Risser, J. (1997). *Hermeneutics and the voice of the other: Re-reading Gadamer's philosophical hermeneutics.* Albany, NY: SUNY Press.

Further Reading

Brookfield, S. (1995). *Becoming a critically reflective teacher.* San Francisco: Jossey-Bass.

Simon, K. (2001). *Moral questions in the classroom: How to get kids to think deeply about real life and their schoolwork.* New Haven, CT: Yale University Press.

Identity

Constructing Selfhood

Judith J. Slater

Identity is a complex term. It has its roots in psychology, sociology, and learning theory and is commonly referred to as "the condition of being some specific person or thing." For our purposes, identity refers to the way people view themselves and is a reflection of the ways in which they interact with the people in their extended community. This is especially important in school environments since teachers determine the instructional climate of their classrooms. Because students are in school for so much time, it is necessary for teachers to be aware of the potential they have to influence identity formation in students. The school environment and the classroom can shape how students see themselves and influence how they behave. Yet individual actions in any environment are not always consistent with personal identity since family values, educational limitations, and rules and regulations can limit the possibilities for action.

Teachers often shape behavior to be consistent with the acceptable rules and regulations that govern the climate of schools. However, they also have the opportunity to critically empower students to act in ways that open possibilities for ac-

tion that could form better school communities. They are able to do this through the reasoning opportunities they provide students. These possibilities can transform into dispositions that students can take with them into the larger world.

Everyone acts and reacts to their surroundings. People perceive their environment and the world in which they reside and then act in ways that lead them through that environment. Their actions are those visible behaviors that they engage in as responses to the environment. Their ability to respond is dependent on a sense of capability. It is what they feel, based on prior experience, that allows people to use the strategies they have acquired. If people want to involve themselves in an action for which they do not have the skill, they can acquire the strategies or skills that are needed through critical thinking. Capabilities are related to the assumptions and values people hold about themselves. Beliefs or assumptions are the emotional connections that motivate people to pursue a goal and acquire the skills necessary to accomplish that goal. Identity is the sum of all these lower parts of the puzzle (Dilts, 1990) and it is precisely this notion that must be kept in mind when designing reasoning activities for students.

The effect of each level of education is to organize and control information. The environment level involves the external conditions where the behavior takes place. Behaviors must have a guide and direction, and that is where capabilities come in. Capabilities are the strategies a person has that guide them to select, alter, and adapt their behaviors to each situation in which they might find themselves. Beliefs and values encourage, inhibit, or generalize particular strategies, plans, or ways of thinking. Identity consolidates the whole system of beliefs and values into a sense of self. Providing students with powerful opportunities to identify their assumptions and the assumptions of others, and critically reflect upon them should be a central goal of education. By critically reflecting on their beliefs and the beliefs of others, students can become the authors of their own subjectivity and identity instead of having this identity authored for them.

These are powerful forces that structure the way people see themselves and then act. Psychologists call this competence, or the regard a person holds for herself. Competence is an assessment of personal capabilities as determined by beliefs and identity, resulting from repeated interactions in an environment. Central to competence formation is the ability to think critically. Teachers should be reflecting on when have they been successful in providing educational opportunities and why, what strategies they used, whether these strategies relate to theory, and what behaviors they acted on that were successful and why?

For students in a classroom, interaction in a school environment results in either rewards and success or internal doubt about their own abilities and skills. Learning to reason effectively in classroom environments elicit responses that, over time, can build up a sense of competence and thus confirm beliefs that reinforce and enhance an identity that is able to meet new challenges. On the other hand, repeated failures also influence a person's sense of competence. If students are not successful in classrooms they tend to avoid situations where they feel less able, internalizing the belief and identity that they cannot succeed, perhaps concluding they are failures in academics. This may, in fact, not be true. They may be fully able, but they may believe they are not. The belief can become part of a student's identity and it influences how they feel about their own capabilities (Bandura, 1995). It is the responsibility of teachers to think critically and direct students into pedagogical situations where they can develop new strategies and experience success.

When there is a low sense of competence, conflict arises between behaviors, beliefs, and capabilities, and people tend to hold on to their beliefs long after they are useful in a particular environment. They learn helplessness because they do not see any other way to behave. Why is that? If you believe you are not able to snowboard, then you won't take lessons, won't try to acquire the skills, won't practice, and will ultimately fail for not trying. If you believe that you are poor in mathematics, you will not succeed because you will not acquire the skills necessary to succeed. This precipitates an endless cycle of failure. Beliefs also help people gain control, to explain the world to themselves and others, and to justify their actions, so, a student might say to herself, "Why should I bother to do the homework? Why should I study for the exam? I am not good in math and never was and never will be." This type of belief limits behavior to the familiar habits of everyday life. Motivation to make change is hard since identity and beliefs cement habits. For this reason, providing students with opportunities for critical self-reflection is crucial to a healthy pedagogical experience.

We can see why it is so hard for people to make changes when they have not been given the skills that would allow them to take a critical self-inventory of their value and belief systems. Most people make do and cope with their environment by acting in ways that don't rock the boat. Motivation to change behaviors requires that people see themselves acting in other possible ways related to the task, and it is precisely at this juncture that educational experience can provide robust and powerful opportunities for self-reflection. Students must recognize that the habits of the past and the beliefs that created them may not be useful today to accomplish current goals. One has to say to oneself, "I can do this." Teachers play a critical role by structuring classroom opportunities that are risk-free when trying to motivate students to act in ways that promote the rejection of old beliefs about capabilities. This requires that teachers also adopt the belief that they can take risks in their own classrooms—that they too can become critical thinkers.

How is this done? People who view themselves as lacking in capabilities must continually enhance their self-worth by acquiring new knowledge and competencies, and this development must take place in a classroom imbued with critical spirit. Both students and teachers must adopt a goal to learn new skills, seek challenges, and expand their knowledge. If they cannot actively play this role, their ability becomes fixed and with this comes threats to their sense of competence. In this situation, people pick tasks that minimize errors—readily displaying talents and skills that do not require the learning of new skills. In classrooms, this means cutting through the false assumptions of defeated students who need to have their sense of capability reinforced by experiences where they are successful.

At the same time, these students need to expand their desire to learn new skills and strategies. The teacher must be aware of what skills each student needs to experience success. They need to think critically about their own practice and how they go about designing activities for students. Teachers have to adapt their curriculum and instruction to provide a student-oriented environment.

It is very dangerous to remain fixed in past perceptions of ability and competence. The world changes too fast for anyone to remain stationary in thought and action. People need to risk taking part in the decisions of government, decisions about education, decisions in the workplace, and decisions in the life of their family to remain secure and safe in our changing environment. This requires viewing themselves in new ways and this is exactly where critical thinking enters the picture. What better setting is there than schools for students to have the opportunity to internalize the belief that they can acquire new skills, that they can participate fully in the ever-changing world, that they can engage in problem-solving and decision-making, and that they make a difference?

There is great resistance to change behavior, let alone beliefs, values, and identity. The mind does not habitually re-think its systems of thought. People become used to doing things the way they have been taught, unconsciously repeating processes and procedures over and over without being aware that there might be another way to accomplish the same goal.

Of course, when businesses or educational systems want people to change their behavior, they don't take into consideration that critically reflecting on one's beliefs is really what is necessary for lasting change. Instead they use methods that are fast and efficient but are not long-lasting. One way is to coerce people into performing the alternative behavior, wielding authority and threatening punishment so that people behave in different ways. This might work in the short run, but people always retain their assumptions and identity when they are coerced and comply only superficially. Another way is to educate them with evidence and reasoning that acting in different ways is scientifically better (much like the advertising commercials tell us when they want us to switch to their product), but neither coercion nor education get to the heart of a person. Neither makes a lasting impact at the level of belief and identity and people remain inert receivers of orders and follow or comply only for a time (Benne, 1990).

To change assumptions there has to be an optimistic view that past behavior is no longer able to meet the reality of new demands. Because these new demands on our lives are changing so fast, it is important to prepare students for an uncertain future by providing critical thinking activities that ask students to rethink their thinking. Students must be taught that it is crucial that they participate fully in the decisions that affect their lives and that they understand the power of inaction and old habits. Teachers have the responsibility to provide situations in the classroom where students participate fully in decision-making and are given the opportunity to change the way they perceive themselves and their abilities.

Societies, schools, and classrooms must be open for this type of change to occur. There should be open forums to

critically think about and discuss issues that touch upon how identity is constituted, and there has to be a climate of inquiry to discuss and disclose new ideas. There also has to be a recognized desire by teachers to play the game of innovation and reform. Teachers have to make an investment in the operation of schools. They must be willing to critically re-think their own ideas, beliefs, and assumptions about students and education—and they must be willing to re-forge their own identity as well. They cannot sit on the sidelines and leave it to others. They must push themselves and their students into critical action fueled by the belief that they can make a difference. Then they come armed with the beliefs, strategies, and reflections of competence to drive behaviors that are consistent with those beliefs, and they can transfer this belief into educational opportunities for their students to fully participate and grow. Instruction should focus on student strategies that reinforce beliefs in the ability to make an impact on their own lives and on their community through their actions.

Each person has to consciously decide whether they are content with their behavior in a changing environment. If teachers believe what worked before in classrooms is appropriate for the future, then the same solutions will be used to motivate students. Teachers need to critically examine, through metacognition, whether their own identity and feelings of self-worth and ability to participate are limiting to students. If they believe that functioning out of habit is not meeting the new challenges of teaching, they can increase the students' sense of competence and give them the skills and strategies to mediate their world. The choice is clear. New ways of promoting community with others, solving problems, and finding solutions promote a critical identity formation. Knowing where one fits into a changing world has to be the center of classroom life, and helping students form identities that are dynamic and growing should be a major goal of teaching.

References and Further Reading

Bandura, A. (Ed.). (1995). *Self-efficacy in changing societies.* Cambridge: Cambridge University Press.

Benne, K. D. (1990). *The task of post-contemporary education: Essays in behalf of a human future.* New York: Teachers College Press.

Dilts, R. (1990). *Changing belief systems with NLP.* Cupertino, CA: Meta Publications.

Ideology

Advertising and Ideology

Ian Steinberg

The ideas of the ruling class are in every epoch the ruling ideas: i.e., the class which is the ruling material force of society is at the same time its ruling intellectual force. The class which has the means of material production at its disposal has control at the same time over the means of mental production, so that thereby, generally speaking, the ideas of those who lack the means of mental production are subject to it. (Marx & Engels, 1947)

I would like to take this quote from *German Ideology* as my entry point into a complex critical rethinking of the ideas of ideology and advertising in late capitalist society. Specifically, I shall refer to American society; however, due to many factors, I believe my analysis has important bearing on global culture as well.

I hope to achieve two objectives in this article. First, I shall discuss what a complex critical conception of ideology entails; how in this complex critical rethinking of ideology, Marx and Engels can get away with saying "[t]he ideas of the ruling class are in every epoch the ruling ideas." Second, I will illustrate the complex critical rethinking of the dialectical processes

of ideology and consciousness formation by discussing the advent of advertising and consumer ideology in industrial capitalist society. It is an impossible task, in the few pages of this book dedicated to this topic, to achieve the rigor worthy of a complex critical inquiry into the subject. Essentially, what I would like the reader to take away from this article is that critical thinking about ideology, and thus a social or cultural hegemony, is a complex, dialectical, historical process, and that the core of contradictions cross over different levels of social relations, or social organizations. That ideology is a dialectical process of individuals and of institutions.

Critically rethinking the problem of ideology isn't like cracking open a can of worms, it is like setting up a can of worms factory! Ideology is not a concept that becomes easier for a complex critical thinker to understand by spending more time reading and thinking about it. The topic of ideology becomes more confusing, but also more complex and rich, the more one explores it.

To establish a critical conception of ideology, let us extract the concept of *ruling ideas* from the above quote and say that these ruling ideas are what comprise the dominant ideology of society. How, then, do ideas rule or establish a social hegemony (i.e., become common sense)? Turning back to *German Ideology* we find that "[t]he ruling ideas are nothing more than the ideal expression of the dominant material relationships grasped as ideas; hence of the relationships which make the one class the ruling one, therefore, the ideas of its dominance" (Marx & Engels, 1947, p. 64). Further, Marx and Engels state that these ruling ideas are put forward by a revolutionary class in the process of establishing a new social hegemony, as the universalized, and only, rational way of thinking. Thinking critically about this statement is important because it illustrates how the constitution of a dominant ideology is a dialectic: it is not one process leading to something else, it is the symbiotic energy of the processes working in concert. Thus, critical thinking about ideology suggests that material conditions must allow the ruling class to become the recipients of society's surplus. As these material conditions evolve, the class that is ascending to the top, the revolutionary class, must displace the previous dominant ideology with a new ideology that makes it justified and truthful for the revolutionary class to be in charge.

Thinking critically about ideology also brings the concept of ideology into question and extrapolates the epistemological and linguistic aspects of ideology. How society or individuals conceive of truth, justice, or a good deal on toilet paper at the grocery store involves the dialectical process of ideology. If we take this critical concept to the next level, and we understand that ideology includes the social process of ascribing things with meaning, then we see that language is ideological at its root. "[L]anguage is practical con-

sciousness," state Marx and Engels (1947, p. 51), and for them language arises from the necessity of social relations. Therefore a dominant ideology is a dominant practical consciousness, and we are back to a system of mutually constituted, or dialectic, processes. This may seem circular, if not tautological, reasoning, but if this rethought, complex critical concept of ideology as a dialectical process is deployed in a specific, historical moment, it produces heady insights into the nature of power in society.

THE DEVELOPMENT OF ADVERTISING AND CONSUMER IDEOLOGY

Critical thinking about current ideological concepts must take into account the phenomenal changes in U.S. society brought on by the Industrial Revolution, which set into motion the necessary societal conditions for a consumer economy and thus advertising. Fundamentally, the shift to an industrial production base from an agrarian/artisan production base was a foundational condition that led to other social changes. New domestic patterns of production, consumption, and familial relations developed. Prior to industrialization, the family unit was the production system and nearly everything consumed by the household was also produced by the household. Industrialization atomized the family unit and moved the production of household goods outside of the household.

We understand that the ever-increasing industrial production capability, efficiency, and scale created an ever-decreasing marginal cost. To guard against surplus and to increase revenue to pay for capital expansion, it was necessary for capitalists to establish national markets. This was possible due to new realities of time and space brought about by new communication technology, the railways, and the need of the newly formed proletarian household to purchase commodities.

Let us think critically about the ideologies that are related to this shift in production, since legitimizing ideologies often support material processes and vice versa. In this case, advertising and other marketing strategies were used to establish the identity of a product in the national market. A product's identity is, on one level, its function and use by a specific group of people, but it is also (more importantly) a memorable product image. Name brands and product image are vital in establishing product differentiation—making a product that is functionally the same as its competitors seem different and more desirable. For example, Pepsi is "the choice of the next generation," and also what Britney Spears drinks. But really, is it very different from Coke or RC Cola, or has a branded identity associated youth with Pepsi?

Critical thinking about branding suggests that establishing a successful public image for a product helps guarantee that there will be a consistent, if not increasing, consumer demand for that product. The potential to control and foster consumer demand was vital to the capitalists who sought a return on their enormous capital investments in production facilities. Advertising and branding made it possible for capitalists to function like price-setting monopolists, instead of letting competition in the marketplace determine the price of commodities. This rationale, once entrenched, made marketing and advertising indispensable to business. These two entities became important new institutions in the national market, which led to consumerism as a way of life in the post–World War II economic boom.

Thinking critically about branding and advertising asks us to question the identities crafted around a product and to dig deeper into the relationships a cultural product has in a larger political and economic context. Complex critical thinking about the ideologies used to create this identity would question who benefits from these ideologies, who is harmed, and how and why.

THE CORPORATE VOICE AND RULING IDEAS

Critical thinking about ideology must also include critical thinking about power. Not only is power situated in the economy, it also plays a significant part in the production of culture and ideologies. This role is amplified exponentially by technology in today's mass-media culture. American communications scholar Herbert Schiller, in his book *Culture, Inc.* (1989), is concerned about the appropriation of public expression by corporate interests. This concern is based on the critical observation of the ever-conglomerating corporate media system, exponentially increasing communications and information technology, and the protection of corporate speech, in particular advertising, under the First Amendment. He argues that, as a result of market forces, federal deregulation, and the defunding of public information sources, "[t]he corporate voice, not surprisingly, is the loudest in the land" (Schiller, 1989, p. 4).

Critical thinking examines the origins of circulating ideologies. Since the inception of the mass-media culture in the United States, the media have been supported by advertising revenue. This arrangement has the effect of subordinating the mass media to regulation by market forces, again aligning the power to create culture with economic imperatives.

Complex critical thinking about advertising includes the acknowledgement that the individual is not a dupe of the system, nor are we victims of a conspiracy. Ideological belief is not controlled by a hypodermic injection of false consciousness, it is a cultivating process. An individual's practical consciousness is obviously shaped by that individual's experience and position in the web of reality; but the social boundaries that define the self, history, culture, and economic and social relations are established outside the realm of individual agency. Critical thinking about the power of the mass media in this society is important in terms of delineating these boundaries. Subjecting the mass media to the dictates of an advertising-supported, capitalist system creates a mass consciousness. Individuals do have agency in the construction of their individual ideologies; but a critical thinker acknowledges that the ideology of the marketplace determines much of the environment in which one's personal ideology is created. In the words of Schiller, "the growth of private corporate power . . . [is] the prime contractor in the construction of contemporary boundaries to expression" (1989, p. 7).

Critical thinking about advertising and ideology requires another review of history. After World War II, the U.S. enjoyed an unprecedented economic boom and became the predominant industrial producer of the global economy. Because of the virulent anti-Communist propaganda of the 1950s, the rise of commercial mass media, and the fact that many working Americans also received a modest share of the booming economy, the social/cultural hegemony of the patriotic belief that capitalism and democracy were inseparable was recognized as the only rational, universally valid way of defining democratic society. This is one of the strongest and most enduring popular beliefs in the United States.

American workers often do not question the disparity between the goal of capital (the maximization of profit at the expense of surplus value produced by labor) and the goal of labor (to keep the surplus value to maintain a comfortable living), for they are no longer workers but patriotic consumers (Schiller, 1989, pp. 11–29). Critical thinking about this process would question these disparate goals and ask whose needs are being met.

According to scholar Armand Mattelart, critical thinking about advertising seeks to understand it as a new consensus-generator, a way for the capitalist class to institute a neoliberal—or market driven—ideology as the dominant ideology in countries across the globe. Mattelart repeatedly demonstrates, by case study, the changes in the national media structure of countries that allow the mass media to be supported by advertising revenue. These changes are not uniform and do reflect the specific historical context of a particular country; but the basic trend is increasing dependence on advertising revenue to fund mass media. In some countries there is an adoption of advertising, but in countries just developing a national media system, transnational media corporations move in and establish a commercial system from the start. This is the exportation of democracy of which advertising pundits are so proud. It is, however, a *marketplace* democracy, a liberalization of commerce, which is very different from a democracy of civil society. Again, critical thinkers lay bare the assumption that this system is natural, necessary, and desirable for society.

CONCLUSION

As critical thinking about advertising and ideology deepens to the level of the individual, it is important to make strong disclaimers that, just as ideology is historically specific to a certain time and place, an individual's ideology is specific to the context of the unique social relations of that individual. There isn't a pure human essence, just like there is no pure ideology—it is a matter of "an ensemble of human relations" (Marx & Engels, 1947, p. 122). There is, however, a given historical context that does have a structuring influence on the social relations and ideological mindset of everyone who shares that historical moment.

A complex critical conception of ideology is in no way a relativist conception of ideology. The class that has power at any given historical moment, has the power to shape how subjugated people view the worthiness of that class to hold power. If consumer ideology (a consumer practical consciousness, or consumerist common sense) defines working individuals as consumers, not workers, then the production process as a class struggle is mystified or hidden. People see themselves not as the producers of surplus value, but the recipients (albeit *paying* recipients, or indentured recipients) of surplus value. In my opinion, this is in stark contrast with the actual nature of work and the late capitalist system, and critical thinking about these processes questions such contradictions.

Critical thinking about advertising and ideology must inquire about social change; and at this time, as always, things are changing. The historical conditions that allowed the proliferation of consumer culture are slipping away. With the collapse of Enron, WorldCom, and other large corporations, the dissolution of millions of people's retirement pensions, and the loss of their jobs to overseas labor, more and more people are facing the contradictions of the system. Critical thinking about these larger trends leads us to ask about the possibility of new configurations of society from which new ideologies will become dominant. What are the established social hegemonies that will shape this historical process of material change? Critical thinkers are sometimes accused of making generalizations that put too much emphasis on ideologies and other abstract theories at the expense of the facts, but this is a straw argument. Complex critical thinkers may make general claims, but they are always made with historical specificity, and contingency.

The concept of ideology can serve the complex critical thinker only if it is thought of as a process of mutually constitutive forces. Ideology is not static, just like history is not static. Ideology is not distilled and then visited upon society's members. Ideology is not divorced from the machinations of the capitalist class, for propaganda (advertising and other forms of knowledge and culture production) is as relevant to the organization of the political and economic spheres of society as roads and factories. The individual in society is not free to pick and choose his or her social relations or experience of culture. We are all subject to the historical moment; but we may also struggle against the pervasive forces of dominant ideology, just as we can struggle against exploitive organization in the workplace.

Critical thinking about advertising and ideology in the classroom can produce many rich experiences. Students can be asked to critique advertisements with an eye for uncovering the image of a product as opposed to the reality of that product. Also, students can draw out themes and ideologies that advertisements ask us to buy into. For example, cosmetics advertisements can be used to think critically about socially constructed notions of femininity, beauty, and youth, as well as the cosmetics industry's attempts to perpetuate the idea of flaws that can be fixed by using cosmetics. Another culture-jamming activity is creatively constructing anti-advertisements that co-opt the advertising format and critique advertising, consumer culture, and unjust social practices. This tactic is used by the magazine Adbusters (www.adbusters.org) and can be fun as well as intellectually and critically stimulating.

References

Marx, K., & Engels, F. (1947). *The German ideology*. New York: International Publishers.

Schiller, H. (1989). *Culture, inc.: The corporate takeover of public expression*. New York: Oxford University Press.

Further Reading

Kincheloe, J. L., & Steinberg, S. R. (1997). *Changing multiculturalism*. London: Open University Press.

Mattelart, A. (1991). *Advertising international*. New York: Routledge & Kegan.

Schudson, M. (1986). *Advertising, the uneasy persuasion*. New York: Basic Books.

Knowledge in the Interest of Power

Zeus Leonardo

Critical thinking requires an engagement with the concept of ideology so that students understand the structures of human thought and action that either promote or challenge domination. Critical thinking is a form of ideology critique that teachers use to shed light on the social relations that are responsible for chronic problems, such as racism, class exploitation, and sexism in schools. In everyday language, critical thinking is a form of analytical thinking; but this does not take educators far enough towards a political understanding of education. As defined here, critical thinking is not only analytical, it is also politicized. It is a willingness to confront ideology through an in-depth interpretation of school and social phenomena.

Critical discussions about ideology are usually not one of the preferred topics between educators. By and large, people seem to turn away from them, either because we feel uncomfortable with some of their politically charged usage or we fear admitting that some things we do or say are ideological. We liken ideology to bad breath: it is what someone else has (Eagleton, 1991). Like bad breath, ideology is not something we want and it is quite embarrassing to reek of either one. In short, there is a general tendency for people to avoid any suggestion of ideology. There are costs to this, one of which is the cultivation of an uncritical form of thinking. The term *ideological* has become a descriptor reserved for doctrinaires and political zealots, or people perceived as advancing their own interests. In fact, Napoleon Bonaparte claims to have invented the term *ideologue* to describe people who went too far in their criticisms, especially with respect to authority and government. In common sense language, being ideological is an altogether bad thing.

As a concept, ideology was first studied by the French philosopher Destutt de Tracy. Patterned after the natural sciences and as a reaction to abstract ideas, de Tracy's study of ideology purported to be a science of ideas. Later, Karl Marx and Friedrich Engels (1970) announced that ideology was a form of false thinking that claimed that our ideas about the world determined the way we produced the materials we need to survive, such as housing, food, and clothing. Marx and Engels also proposed that critical thinking begins with the assumption that humans live in a social world of things. The idea is that, to think, we must have a world to think about and this world is made up of materials, such as steel, trees, or buildings. Critical thinkers who follow the Marxist perspective believe in a true world based on a scientific understanding of how materials are produced, distributed, and used in society.

Since Marx and Engels' writings, critical thinkers from the school of thought called *cultural studies* have redefined ideology to mean something akin to a worldview. Whereas Marxism claims that ideology distorts critical thinking, cultural studies considers ideology a necessary framework for consciousness. In other words, ideological thinking is unavoidable and does not negate our ability to think critically about the world. Humans need ideology to organize information about the world, make meaning out of it, and then act based on their ability to think critically. In this second sense, ideology is not something people need to overcome (as in the Marxist idea of false consciousness) but something that is necessary to consciousness itself. Consciousness and ideology go hand in hand.

When reading a novel or the newspaper, critical thinkers use ideology critique to interpret the underlying assumptions or worldview in the materials they read. In cultural studies, the role that language plays in our understanding of the world becomes central to critical thinking. It is through language that students arrive at the ideological message contained in a poem, a textbook, or a piece of art because we translate all images into a language that we can understand. The point, however, is not that we can get outside of ideology but that we are intimately inside it at all times.

Ideology has also been used as a positive or enabling concept. Seen this way, ideology is neither negative in the purely Marxist sense, nor necessary, as in the cultural studies framework. As a form of critical thinking, ideology could be a weapon in building a platform for change. For instance, a positive form of ideology teaches students the ability to question inequality, exploitation, or oppression and asks the critical thinker to dismantle them. It is in light of this third definition that ideology has come a long way since its inception by Destutt de Tracy.

First, let us discuss the negative, or pejorative, definition of ideology. In his critique of capitalism and the relations it produces, Marx was the first critical thinker to systematically study the effects of ideology on a whole society. In *The German Ideology,* Marx and Engels (1970) criticized the perspective of idealism, saying it inverted our true understanding of human life and calling it a *camera obscura.* Like the way the lens of our eyes inverts the images we perceive to process them in the brain, idealism turns the world upside down. It is a camera that obscures our ability to think critically about the world because it leads people to the false belief that studying ideas gives people an accurate picture of the way society works. Marx insisted instead that critical thinking begins by understanding people in the midst of their activity, or what he called labor.

Of course, Marx did not reject ideas outright, but he insisted that critical thinking must be concerned with the production of material life. For example, a critical understanding of teaching means we must observe what teachers do at work, the materials they use, and who controls the production of things like textbooks. Likewise, student work must be understood as a form of labor. Research has shown that a certain academic division of labor is enforced in school that prepares students for the social division of labor they will find in the workplace. Schooling prepares students to take part in the system of production, which in many nations means they are preparing to enter the economic system of capitalism. Often, critical thinking is not the goal.

The critical thinker's task becomes one of cutting through the distortions to clear understanding, a process that both idealism and capitalism make difficult. With respect to idealism, Marx and Engels wrote,

The ideologists, in spite of their allegedly "world-shattering" statements, are the staunchest conservatives. The most recent of them have found the correct expression for their activity when they declare they are only fighting against *"phrases."* They forget, however, that to these phrases they themselves are only opposing other phrases, and that they are in no way combating the real existing world when they are merely combating phrases of this world (1970, p. 41, italics in original).

Idealism is depicted here as an illusory, ideological perspective that is also uncritical. Rather than examine real people in the midst of their labor, idealists examine abstract words associated with abstract people. Rather than investigate concrete life situations, they are content with the world of ideas. Fighting words with words, and ideas with ideas, idealists produce neither real knowledge nor a proper understanding of history. Marx and the critical thinkers who follow his thoughts understand that words matter, but are not made up of matter.

If ideology is thought of as chronic bad breath but is also considered necessary, then it is like paying taxes: you can't seem to avoid it. Seen this way, there is no way out of ideology. It becomes a necessary network of sense-making strategies that enable people to establish meaning from their lives. If Marxism emphasizes the means of production (e.g., factories), then cultural studies makes meaning central to its analysis. Ideology is comprised of the everyday thoughts teachers and students have, first to create their worldview and second to make meaning from them. Ideology becomes an unavoidable medium of thought that organizes our experience. To the extent that we live in a material world, we must organize our experience within this world, otherwise, it makes very little sense to us. As a pedagogical tool, ideology critique leads to an understanding of how teachers and students negotiate everyday meanings.

So how does cultural studies describe critical thinking? Before branding a student's thoughts as false, the critical teacher must first gain access to a student's worldview, or how she makes sense of the world. Without this critical moment, teaching becomes a form of imposition or indoctrination, and prevents the student from critically engaging her world. With this moment, teaching becomes a dialogue, which does not prevent teachers from pointing out misguided beliefs or false perceptions.

Seen in this sense, ideology is a necessary organizing process that is central to the formation of critical thinking. Worldview is like an opinion: everyone has one. It is the way people mediate their social life and achieve meaning from it. In this process, they develop a view of the world in light of their experience. Yet a worldview can be a product of false consciousness and worldviews can certainly be distorted. We must avoid thinking of worldviews as neutral because they are always forged with people in mind and do not come from an empty box. Worldviews should be regarded as necessary because we depend on them for functional reasons. We would be quite lost without them. Because educators exist in a society characterized by asymmetrical relations of power, it makes little sense to call ideology neutral since power skews our worldview. A critical thinker recognizes that even making sense of the world is involved with issues of politics and power and therefore is a process implicated in ideological struggle.

Ideology can also be thought of as a positive form of thinking, although the writing in this area is not as well developed as that of the previous two perspectives. Exemplary thinkers, such as Lenin and Lukacs, consider the ideological struggle as a sign of possibilities. Lenin spoke of a society grounded on a socialist ideology and Lukacs hoped to build a working class ideology. They considered the possibility that social change required a positive, or utopian, ideology to work. Therefore, critical thinking is not just a search for truth, it is central to freedom. Through counter-social movements, such as a teaching unit on the Civil Rights Movement, ideological struggle offers hope for hitherto marginalized groups of people.

When teachers recognize that oppressed groups have an ideology, it is tantamount to saying that they are able to project themselves into history, that they embody forms of critical thinking. A positive engagement of ideology comes from learning how to critique social relations, like racism, class exploitation, and patriarchy. Critical thinkers understand that teaching is a part of this triad, and building an ideology against its dehumanizing tendencies transforms teachers' work into a political vocation.

In its positive sense, critical thinking about ideology is not merely an exercise in criticism. Traditionally, a critic represented authority and was not bashful about exercising this status. Traditional critics spoke with much confidence and did not exactly inspire dialogue. In contrast, critical thinking is an intersubjective analysis of the structures that affect our lives. Through dialogue, ideology critique sheds light on what teachers and students normally gloss over. Ideology critique is like putting together the pieces of a puzzle. It is the act of threading together a social life that currently appears fragmented. Critical thinking means puzzling over fundamental questions concerning the relationship between school and society; for just as society creates schooling in its own image, schooling also gives rise to a society it has played a part in creating. Positive ideology comes from teachers' ability to cultivate an appreciation of criticism in their students, to encourage them to be critical of the information they receive, and to recognize themselves as subjects, rather than objects, of history. To the extent that a teacher nurtures critical thinking in her classroom, we may call her an ideologue.

References

Eagleton, T. (1991). *Ideology.* New York: Routledge.

Marx, K., & Engels, F. (1970). *The German ideology.* New York: International Publishers.

Further Reading

Apple, M. (1990). *Ideology and curriculum.* New York: Routledge.

Giroux, H. (1981). *Ideology, culture, and the process of schooling.* Philadelphia: Temple University Press.

Thompson, J. (1984). *Studies in the theory of ideology.* Berkeley: University of California Press.

Only the "Facts"?

Jaime Grinberg

Now, what I want is, Facts. Teach these boys and girls nothing but Facts. Facts alone are wanted in life. Plant nothing else, and root out everything else. You can only form the minds of reasoning animals upon Facts: nothing else will ever be of any service to them.

Charles Dickens, Hard Times

The above words are those of a school-teacher, Mr. Thomas Gradgrind; the utilitarian character created by Charles Dickens in *Hard Times*, first published in 1854, in which the alienation of everyday life during the industrial revolution is masterfully illustrated. This view of teaching and curriculum, the one that purposely resembles the factory and prepares youngsters to fit in the cages of the assembly line, continues to be present in the schools, discourse, policies, and practices of what is considered a democratic society. It is represented in popular culture critiques, such as Pink Floyd's movie, *Another Brick in the Wall.* The movie has powerful images, such as children standing in line to jump into a giant meat-grinding machine. Pink Floyd's lyrics are a powerful expression of transgression and a call for resistance against Mr. Gradgrind's approach of planting only facts and rooting out everything else.

Facts and information fed to reasoning animals who are caged in the restricted and disciplinary walls of schools, factories, or prisons not only elicit resistance but also belittle the need for broad participation in civil society and the democratic process. As American philosopher John Dewey has argued, in his seminal essay "Why Reflective Thinking Must Be an Educational Aim," facts and information alone cannot sustain and improve democratic life. On the contrary, they are dangerous because they can be manipulated to fit and serve the needs of a few at the expense of the rest, a classic way of maintaining hegemonic power. E. D. Hirsch's arguments for cultural literacy, which are just a reiteration of Mr. Gradgrind's views, are a false promise of access to knowledge because information and facts do not open or close possibilities in a stratified society, even with the illusion that everyone can have access to the same knowledge (which rarely happens according to J. Grinberg and E. Saavedra or J. Oakes). This view is also supported by scholars such as Michael Apple or P. Bourdieu and J. Passeron in their book *Reproduction in Education, Society, and Culture.*

What is important to consider, then, are questions about how we use facts and information, how we judge facts, whose facts and information are presented, and who will benefit from knowing these facts and this information. Just think of the tremendous amount of information and facts that governments collect. At least two federal organizations in the United States, the FBI and the CIA, had facts and intelligence information about the terrorist plot that ended with the tragedy on September 11, 2001. Yet, neither the intelligence apparatus nor the government leadership knew how to put the pieces of the puzzle together (or so we are told). This is similar to the significant number of researchers in education who continuously collect huge amounts of data, but the data is incorrect or they do not know how to analyze it.

In contrast to Mr. Gradgrind's pedagogy, a tradition of democratic discourse and practice presents possibilities that could create, support, and nourish a critical democratic disposition in students. Such a tradition was also present during industrial revolution times, but in a rural setting in Russia (where the industrial revolution didn't take place until decades later). Leo Tolstoy's school in Yasnaya Polyana, which he created in the 1860s, fostered a pedagogy and curriculum where facts, information, and skills met the community, the child, and a critical outlook when children were encouraged to question data and present possible alternative interpretations of the same information. Just consider the title of one of Tolstoy's essays: "Are the Peasant Children to Learn to Write from Us? Or, are We to Learn from the Peasant Children?"

Coming from one of the most famous writers of all times in Western tradition, such questions are not mere rhetoric. They demonstrate an important worldview of what education could be, and he struggled in his teaching to be coherent with his commitment to educate free minds. Furthermore, it invites us to reconsider the sources of our knowledge and facts. The suggestion that we can also learn from our students is something that contemporary scholars, such as Shirley Steinberg and Joe Kincheloe, have also presented when they write about students doing research and producing knowledge.

In his *Pedagogy of the Oppressed* and his *Pedagogy of Freedom,* Freire writes that this type of commitment to educate free minds involves a type of pedagogy that not only engages the mind (thinking), but also engages the body (feelings, behaviors, and even an aesthetic dimension). In Freire's perspective, critical thinking is about a process of gaining awareness that starts by questioning and problematizing the given conditions of our own experience and existence, or what we are told are the facts. Such questioning leads to opposition to the type of schooling represented by Mr. Gradgrind, which Freire calls *banking education* and the *culture of silence.* Within these two practices, docilization, marginalization, and alienation flourish. Critical education and critical thinking encourage resistance to this oppressive form of schooling, and could lead to dismantling the non-democratic practices and discourses that are present in education today, where, according to Michael Apple, states foster high stakes testing or the federal government legislates and executes definitions of what counts as knowledge and how this knowledge has to be produced. Joe Kincheloe and Shirley Steinberg write that, if students use critical thinking to analyze the processes, practices, curricula, institutions, and power relations of modern education, they will be able to alter, improve, or change them.

Therefore, *critical* is used as a descriptor for a systematic practice grounded in inquiry, multiple perspectives on knowledge and knowledge creation, the validation of what knowledge is being taught in schools, and the discovery of why that particular knowledge is being taught. The term *critical* is also used as a construct in the analysis of the assumptions upon which we base curriculum and teaching and how we determine who has access to what knowledge. Thus, critical is also used as a tool to analyze power arrangements in teaching and learning, as well as connections with larger contextual issues such as gender, social class, and race. Thinking refers to both the cognitive processes of learning and to the social, emotional, physical, and spiritual contexts of learning. The purpose here is to examine practices that enable systematic and scrutinized thinking within a critical framework.

Critical thinking is a fundamental aspect of good teaching because we want students to learn the complexities of different subjects, the ways by which knowledge is produced and validated, alternative ways of knowing, and the connections among different disciplines. Last, but not least, critical thinking is necessary if we want to foster democratic and egalitarian practices for everybody's children.

The biggest challenge, as J. Grinberg argued, is that most educators have not experienced critical education and critical thinking themselves. This means that they must have opportunities to experience how they should teach if they are committed to sustain and improve democracy, to educate students who are able and willing to participate and take responsibility, know their rights and duties and those of others, and have the capacity to contribute to and improve society. John Dewey discussed this need in his book *Experience and Education*. Teachers must have opportunities to develop the habit of making their experiences a subject matter of study; something they can puzzle over, deconstruct, problematize, examine for patterns, verbalize feelings about, and learn how to reframe

in multiple diverse contexts. We need teachers who will stand up against Mr. Gradgrind and challenge the assumptions behind his statement, and who can understand and oppose the idea of caging our students. After all, even Mr. Gradgrind granted that students are reasoning beings. What, then, are they reasoning about and how are they reasoning? I propose to start with problematization.

The focus of problematization is on questioning, interrogating, and disturbing what is considered taken-for-granted in the dominant discourses of teacher education and professional development. This includes best practices, wisdom, commonsense knowledge, and desire. To problematize practices also implies that we ought to consider multiple possible alternatives. This is important because, as a Foucauldian perspective proposes, a practice by itself is neither oppressive nor liberating, and there is nothing inherently true about them outside their context. Mr. Gradgrind's practices exist in the context of the Industrial Revolution, while Tolstoy's practices exist in the context of his views on childhood and nature, influenced by Rousseau, and by his anarchistic inclinations to resist the czar's oppressive regime.

It is the context that explains how relationships are constituted. Liberating practices are surrendered within institutional contexts that constrain the critique and favor demarcation and compartmentalization; forcing a closer analysis of the particularities of the enactment, the operation, and conditions of these practices. In other words, as Foucault suggested, problematization invites us to play with what counts as facts by also considering multiple coexisting realities.

Critical thinking for teachers is the practice and discourse of looking from multiple perspectives, and the propensity to unpack, analyze, make connections, see relationships and patterns, and provide alternative explanations to the dominant definitions of experience and fact. To analyze and criticize contemporary proposals, practices, and curricular reforms, it is necessary to understand the context, background, and consequences of what has been done, the patterns and structural tensions of educational systems, and how power operates to benefit some and oppress others.

However, experiencing critical education cannot happen in isolation. It is not just an individual process, it involves social interaction where ideas are shared, explored, challenged, and scrutinized. It demands to be nurtured in an environment that is safe, respectful, supportive, and engaging. According to Goldfarb and Grinberg, critical education needs to be developed within egalitarian practices, with symmetric relationships as much as possible, with careful attention to modes of participation so multiple ways of expression are ensured and risk-taking is encouraged, and where attempts to overpower and dominate the conversation are neutralized by bringing these attempts to the attention of the participants and using them as pedagogical opportunities. These spaces are commonly called *learning communities* or, as Splitter and Sharp explain in their book *Teaching for Better Thinking*, these are communities of inquiry, which also foster the practice of metacognition (thinking about thinking).

This collective endeavor is not an easy task. In reality it creates tensions, conflicts, and contradictions. The challenge is to articulate these issues with honesty and to further problematize them to facilitate learning and growth, not to avoid them and create a false sense of niceness, which often develops into passive aggression. Learning happens in community, and in the process, participants learn to live in community.

An example of critical thinking that can be used as a learning experience might be found in a research methods class, where not on what is being researched and how it is being researched is scrutinized, but the process of scrutinizing itself is examined. Questions that could be asked in such a class might include:

- Who asks the research questions?
- What are the types of questions asked?
- For what purposes?
- For whom are the questions asked?
- Under which conditions are these questions asked?
- How are these questions asked?
- Where are these questions asked?
- How do we do this research and for what purposes?
- How do we represent results?
- What counts as meaningful, valuable, and valid research?
- In favor of whom are we doing research?
- Who benefits from this research?
- What are the consequences or who are the winners and losers?

Perspective is another issue the class could discuss. A story could be read to the class in a neutral voice, and the students could re-write the story from the perspectives of the different actors involved. Reading these rewrites aloud could reveal a number of assumptions about producing knowledge and constitutes a fact. Students could also read a research document from multiple points of view, as the feminist scholars Fonow and Cook have suggested in their book *Beyond Methodology*, or the critical pragmatist C. Cherryholmes explains in *Reading Research*. Reading research using alternative theoretical frameworks produces further debate over possible explanations and implications of what has been presented as facts.

Certainly, a research methods class also invites the problematization of who produces knowledge and facts about whom. Traditionally, teachers are not considered researchers and producers of knowledge, even about their own practices and/or the settings where they practice, as Kincheloe discusses in his book *Teachers As Researchers*. The division of labor between producers and consumers could be problematized, and this critical process could create opportunities for teachers to see themselves as knowledge producers, see teaching as a form of inquiry, and become researchers by carefully scrutinizing and analyzing their own contexts and experiences.

Teacher education programs and advanced programs for the preparation and development of school personnel are important spaces where critical education, critical thinking, problematization, inquiry, and alternative teaching possibilities must be fostered. Focusing on facts and information produces "another brick in the wall." Engaging in critique and analysis can prepare students for and improve democratic life by allowing them to experience participation, produce knowledge, and learn from one another as a process of conscientization.

Further Reading

Cherryholmes, C. (1999). *Reading pragmatism.* New York: Teachers College Press.

Dewey, J. (1938/1997). *Experience and education.* New York: Touchstone.

Fonow, M., & Cook, J. (Eds.) (1991). *Beyond methodology: Feminist scholarship as lived research.* Bloomington: Indiana University Press.

Freire, P. (1970). *Pedagogy of the oppressed.* New York: Continuum Press.

Freire, P. (1998). *Pedagogy of freedom: Ethics, democracy, and civic courage.* Lanham, MD: Rowman & Littlefield.

Kincheloe, J. L. (2003). *Teachers as researchers: ualitative paths to empowerment* (2nd ed.). London: Falmer Press.

Kincheloe, J. L., & Steinberg, S. R. (Eds.). (1998). *Unauthorized methods: Strategies for critical teaching.* New York: Routledge.

Splitter, L., & Sharp, A. (1995). *Teaching for better thinking: The classroom community of inquiry.* Melbourne: Australian Council for Educational Research.

Journal Writing

Journal Writing and Critical Thinking Skills in Classroom Settings

Valerie J. Janesick

I have found that the best way to teach my students to be critical thinkers is to model critical thinking skills. As a journal writer of over 20 years, I like to teach about and model journal writing. Keeping a journal, either a written journal in a notebook or an electronic journal on the computer, allows anyone to sharpen their critical thinking skills.

I would like to focus on keeping a classroom journal. A classroom journal is a journal that individual learners, as well as the teacher, construct and create on a daily basis. I have used this approach with student teachers, intern teachers, and doctoral students who wish to improve their classroom practice. My doctoral students who teach use these techniques with their students, who range from elementary to post-secondary age. I invite the reader to adapt any of these ideas to the level appropriate to their own classroom.

As a teacher, keeping a classroom journal as a tool for deepening critical thinking about classroom practice is most provocative. I will focus on the teacher in this paper, and will begin the journey with a brief overview of the history and importance of journal writing.

A BRIEF HISTORICAL OVERVIEW OF JOURNAL WRITING

Journal writing has a lengthy history in the Arts and Humanities, and has also been used in the Sciences. It is not by accident that artists, writers, dancers, musicians, physicians, poets, architects, saints, scientists, therapists, and educators use journal writing in their lives. Virtually every field has produced journal writers who kept detailed and lengthy journals regarding their everyday lives and their life work.

I view journal writing as a powerful heuristic tool and classroom research technique. Keeping a classroom journal may help to illuminate and refine thinking skills at all levels, and can be used as an interactive tool of communication between the teacher and the learner.

People have probably kept journals throughout recorded history for various reasons. Some of the first known journals were written in Greek and Roman times. St. Augustine and Blaise Pascal kept journals to chronicle moments in their lives as they tried to find out more about how the mind works. In the tenth century, ladies of the Japanese court wrote precise and candid description of everyday life and the inner workings of their beliefs and feelings. Often these writers hid their journals under their pillows, so they became known as pillow diaries. These documents went beyond the daily record of life; they were texts that recorded dreams, hopes, visions, fantasies, feelings, and innermost thoughts. The rebirth and awakening of the Renaissance brought with it an era of almost required journal and diary writing. There was an almost understood agreement that one must chronicle the spirit of rebirth and living in personal terms case by case.

The 1660s brought us Samuel Pepys, who for nine years described exactly and in astounding detail the people, politics, sorrows, and joys of life in London. His dense descriptions of the problems of the Church of England, the monarchy, the navy in which he served, various wars of the day, the great fire, and the plague are brilliant and illuminative records of literature and history. As luck would have it, the first published versions of his diary did not appear until 1825, followed by reissues and new editions well into the late 1890s. It was at this time that the Victorians focused on both letter writing and journals.

Prior to the Victorian era, members of a number of spiritual and religious groups kept spiritual journals. The Quakers, for example, beginning in the seventeenth century, often and regularly described their spiritual journeys, doubts, questions, and beliefs. John Wesley, founder of Methodism, kept volumes recording his symbolic relationship with his God. Many Puritans recorded their trust in God, doubt, uncertainty, miseries in their lives, sins, omissions of goodness, and so on. The voyage of the Mayflower is eloquently and curiously described in journal form. For people who were embarking on new adventures, the journal became an outlet for fears and moments of deep despair on the voyage. The use of the journal as a political record flourished as well. During the French Revolution, many writers produced journals-in-time that recorded arguments regarding the revolution and that revealed deep and passionate feelings of patriotism, nationalism and disgust for the corrupt monarchy. Remember, at these points in time, writing was a key and important means of communication. There were no telephones, pagers, computers, televisions, or news media.

In this country, during the Westward expansion movement, explorers like Lewis and Clark chronicled their journeys, describing relationships with the Native Americans and encounters with existing communities. Pioneer women not only cooked around campfires, but took the time to record personal impressions of the Westward movement. Later, these would be chronicled in the play, *Quilters*. This play powerfully documented a history of depression, sorrow, joy, misunderstanding and treachery. There was no sugar-coating of injustice and bigotry in these diaries.

An eloquent account of the brutality of slavery in this country is chronicled in the writings of Olaudah Equiano, Mary Prince, Frederick Douglass, and Harriet Jacobs, by now all classics of this genre. The suffering, and degradation described in these slave narratives inform our understanding of the Black Diaspora. Were it not for these detailed accounts, a critical piece of American history would certainly have been lost.

Literary and historical figures are not the only journal writers. The field of psychology has long made use of the cathartic function of journal writing as a therapeutic aid. Therapists view the journal as an attempt to bring order to one's experience and a sense of coherence to one's life.

Most recently, Ira Progoff developed a set of techniques that provide a structure for keeping a journal and a springboard for development (Progoff, 1992). As a therapist himself, he has conducted workshops, and trained a network of individuals to conduct workshops, on keeping an intensive journal in order to unlock one's creativity and come to terms with oneself. The intensive journal method is a reflective, in-depth process of writing, speaking what is written, and in some cases sharing what is written with others. Feedback is an important part of the Progoff method. Progoff thinks that people must draw upon inner resources to arrive at an understanding of themselves as whole beings and to reopen the possibilities of learning and living.

Progoff advocates:

A. Regular entries in the journal in the form of dialogue with oneself.
B. Maintaining the journal as an intensive psychological workbook to record all the encounters of one's existence.
C. Sharing this growth through journal writing with others.

The method makes use of a special bound notebook divided into categories, including dreams, stepping stones, dialogues with persons, events, work, and the body. The writer is asked to reflect, free associate, meditate, and imagine anything that relates to their immediate experience. The latest version of his text, published in 1992, is a definite testimonial to the solid benefits of keeping a journal.

Beyond the psychologists, perhaps the two most identifiable writers of journals in our memory are Anne Frank and Anais Nin. In fact, *The Diary of Anne Frank* and the many volumes of *The Diary of Anais Nin* are published in over 20 languages. Anne Frank's lived experience hiding from the Nazis not only details her feelings of growing up under these conditions, but offer a political and moral interpretation of humanity's failures. On the other side of the coin, Anais Nin used her journal to understand her self, her body, and her mind. She studied Ira Progoff's journal writing method before she died, and although she rejected its structure, she commented on the importance of its purpose and ultimate goal of self-actualization. This genre is alive and well, and teachers and learners should not be afraid of trying to keep a journal to deepen their critical thinking and to record their experiences and their meaning.

Journal writing is so prevalent now, that the Internet contains thousands of journal resources, examples, and personal histories. For example, there is an online course on journal writing offered by Via Creativa, a web site entirely devoted to Ira Progoff's Intensive Journal Workshop, chat rooms on journal writing, examples of diaries and journal writing, and literally thousands of resources. In general, the common thread that unites all these resources is the agreement that journal writing is a way of getting in touch with yourself using reflection, catharsis, remembrance, creation, exploration, problem-solving, problem-posing, and personal growth.

Basically, the art of journal writing produces meaning and understanding that are shaped by genre, the narrative form used, and personal cultural and paradigmatic conventions of the writer who is either the researcher, participant, and or co-researcher. As Progoff notes, journal writing is ultimately a way of getting feedback from ourselves, and in so doing, experiencing in a full and open-ended way, the movement of our lives as a whole and the meaning that follows from reflecting on that movement (Progoff, 1992).

WHY JOURNAL WRITING?

Students and colleagues have often asked me why should one invest the time in journal writing? To this I can only reply that journal writing allows one to reflect and to dig deeper into the heart of the words, beliefs, and behaviors we describe in our journals. Writing down our thoughts allows us to step into our inner mind and find interpretations of the behaviors, beliefs, and words we write.

How does one set time apart for journal writing? I recall the teacher who said she only had twenty minutes after school to write in her journal and that was it. She ultimately decided she needed to keep a journal at home as well since, once she started to write, she found she was staying at school and writing for at least an hour each day. She got up an hour earlier than anyone in her house and started writing in the early morning hours, a technique advocated by many writers. Great journal advocates like Progoff encourage daily writing as well and talk about keeping a daily log. Progoff suggests using the journal to conduct dialogues with key people in our lives, with our body, with our work, with our roads not taken, with events that were critical in our lives in society, and with our dreams. He thinks the dialogue form allows us to think in new ways and to be more critical and reflective.

FAVORITE BOOKS ABOUT JOURNAL WRITING

One of my favorite books on journal writing, after Progoff, is Thomas Mallon's *A Book of One's Own: People and Their Diaries.* In his overview of diarists and journal writers, he categorizes the writers as follows:

- **Chroniclers:** People who keep their diaries every single day as if recording the news.
- **Travelers:** People who keep a written record during a special time such as a vacation or a trip.
- **Pilgrims:** People who want to discover who they really are.
- **Creators:** People who write to sketch out ideas, and inventions in art or science.
- **Apologists:** People who write to justify something they have done and plead their case before all who read the journal.
- **Confessors:** People who direct ritual unburdenings, conducted with the promise of secrecy or anonymity.
- **Prisoners:** People who must live their lives in prisons or who may be invalids and as a result must live their lives through keeping a journal.

Of course, any writer might be a combination of any of these categories, but this list is a useful tool to understand different approaches to keeping a journal. Mallon gives numerous examples of individuals who fall into these categories to illustrate the importance of keeping a journal, and became interested in writing his book because he had kept a journal for over thirty years. I share that interest with him. I started writing a journal in high school and have written journals faithfully since then.

Writing down what we think and feel helps us improve our classroom practice, our lives, and our work. Progoff calls this the scope of personal renewal. Others call it reflection. Still others, myself included, see journal writing as a tangible way to evaluate our experience, improve and clarify our thinking, and become better writers and scholars. We examine our own thoughts, beliefs, and behaviors, which ensures that we conduct the continuing self-reflection that is the first step towards modeling critical thinking behaviors for our students.

References and Further Reading

Mallon, T. (1995). *A book of one's own: People and their diaries.* Saint Paul, MN: Hungry Mind Press.

Nin, A. (1976). *The diary of Anais Nin 1955–1966.* (Gunther Shulman, Ed.). New York: Harcort Brace Jovanovich.

Progoff, I. (1992). *At a journal workshop.* Los Angeles: J. P. Tarcher.

Justice

Justice and Equity

Charles Bingham

Justice and *equity*. What do they mean for education? Are they the same, or are they different? Will there be justice in education once there is equity? Will there be equity in education once there is justice? Is there either equity or justice in education at present? What must be done to work for both justice *and* equity in classrooms and beyond. The purpose of this entry is to bring a critical analysis to bear on these questions. A critical perspective on justice and equity helps us to flesh out the ways we can foster these important themes in educational settings.

To begin a critical discussion on justice and equity, it is important to realize that there is a difference between the two. We must not pre-suppose that these themes are self-evident. We must use a critical lens to scrutinize the nuances of each. Equity, as its Latin root *equi* implies, relates to the practice of equal distribution. In the context of education, then, we emphasize equity when we make sure that students and teachers are given equal educational goods. Within a particular high school, for example, it cannot be considered equitable if one group of students, say honor stu-

dents, are granted more access to educational goods than another group of students. Educational goods such as technology, excellent instructors, comfortable classrooms, library privileges, participation in band and choir, access to athletic facilities, and access to counseling cannot be reserved for one particular group of students and withheld from other, less privileged groups. Yet a variety of common educational practices (including tracking, gifted programs, remedial back-to-basic courses, and course scheduling that makes it impossible for some students to take courses in the arts) often produce a distinct lack of equity in today's schools.

To achieve equity, we must think about the random and nonrandom practices that skew access to educational goods. Inequity between well-funded school districts and under-funded school districts is rife. Jonathon Kozol's informative book, *Savage Inequalities,* explains this problem well. Teachers can easily tell stories about the different levels of access that various students experience *even within the boundaries of one school.* For instance, it is not uncommon for special education students to be housed in inferior classrooms, and this inequity is explained away by saying that there are too few special education students to warrant a full-sized classroom, that the students spend only part of their day in the pull-out classroom, or that special education is not in itself a discipline and thus does not warrant the advanced facilities required for, say, the study of science. It is also not uncommon for one teacher's room in an elementary school to contain an inadequate allotment of computers, furniture, textbooks, air conditioners, audio-visual equipment, and often even desks, while another teacher in the same elementary school has a fully equipped room because he or she has managed to be the first to claim scarce resources in a particular year, or has managed to accrue resources over the years. In all of the above cases, students experience a lack of equity.

Justice, on the other hand, is a more complex and personal educational concern than equity. For while justice in education depends on equity, a critical analysis of justice demonstrates that it is also something more. Take the example of justice for students. Justice is the application of educational resources to particular students who are, by definition, *different from one another.* So while it is absolutely necessary to ensure that educational goods are equally available to all students at all times, justice also demands that we think about the individual needs of particular students. Students are not generic units. They are African American, Latino, Asian, Middle Eastern, and White. They are straight, gay, poor, middle-class, rich, native speakers of the teacher's language, or native speakers of another language. Because students arrive at the school door with such different cultural, sexual, class, and linguistic identity positions, it cannot be said that equity, even if it is equally available, is as equally attainable by each and every student.

Justice involves something more than equity; it involves the educational responsibility to ensure that students can take advantage of educational goods in ways that are relevant to the rich lives that they bring with them to the classroom.

From a critical thinking perspective, justice demands that educators practice *recognition* of the various identity positions of their students. To practice recognition means both to recognize students who demand to be noticed in their particular identity positions and to look for ways to recognize students even if such a demand is not forthcoming. Some students will arrive at school and *ask,* either explicitly or implicitly, to be recognized for their racial, cultural, gendered, sexual, or class positions. In such cases, the demands of justice will follow the explicit demands of the students, and access to educational goods can be mapped onto the students' particular needs. In other cases, students will not wear their identity position on their sleeves and it is the educator's responsibility to recognize the circumstances in their lives that need justice. Justice demands that educators be attuned to the circumstances of particular students. It goes beyond the general ways that equity tends to be fostered, and requires that educators pay attention to the personal/cultural aspects of student identity rather than solely to general student needs. For a further, helpful analysis of this issue, see Charles Bingham's book, *Schools of Recognition.*

From a less than critical perspective, justice is seen to be at odds with equity, but such is not the case. An example is in order. Some educators will say that paying attention to the particular circumstances of particular students is too time consuming. They will say, for example, that since *all* students in a given school have the opportunity to visit the library after school hours to check out the books they need, then there is equity as far as library access goes. When confronted with a student who is not able to visit the library after school, perhaps because they must work after school to supplement their family's income, some will say that there are not enough resources available to keep the library open during lunch just for those students who work after school. If the library were to be kept open during lunch, then the librarian would have to be paid both lunchtime wages *and* after school wages and there is not enough money to do so. In this case, justice is sacrificed to equity.

Critical analysis prompts us to be suspicious of such a trade-off. Equity does not exist, except in a watered down sense, if equity does not exist for each particular student. So, while justice is indeed something more than equity, equity does not exist in any real sense without justice. Justice and equity are not at odds; they give each other meaning.

Equity is availability of access; but such availability must continually be challenged by the necessity of justice. Even while access can *seem* to be available to all, even if the library can *seem* to be available to all students after school, there is no general availability unless justice is served on an individual basis. To say that equity is at odds with justice is to say that equity isn't *really* equitable.

Critical analysis would claim that justice and equity are certainly different, and although one does not guarantee the other they depend on each other. Both must be struggled for time and again in our schools and in our classrooms. Schools in the United States and beyond strive, at least nominally, to prepare students for participation in a society that works toward justice and equity. Attention to justice and equity *together* make such striving more than superficial. In our schools, equity and justice are ignored and watered down at the peril of democratic aspirations. While it is common to separate justice from equity, such a separation would be a mistake in educational institutions because students would then separate them in the future. Practicing justice and equity, together and at large, are begun at the level of the school. Such a practice is realizable once we bring a critical analysis to bear on these crucial concepts.

Further Reading

Bingham, C. (2001). *Schools of recognition.* New York: Rowman & Littlefield.

Fraser, N. (1997). *Justice interruptus: Critical reflections on the "postsocialist" condition.* New York: Routledge.

Kozol, J. (1991). *Savage inequalities: Children in America's schools.* New York: HarperCollins.

Language Arts

Critical Thinking, Teaching, and Language

John Gabriel

Critical thinking. We often hear these two words in education. What about critical thinking in the English classroom? What does it mean? What activities promote critical thinking?

For the first stop in addressing our questions, we go to the *Oxford English Dictionary* (OED), to study the histories of both words; to gain a broader, deeper, and more nuanced understanding of the words critical and thinking. The OED is an essential stop in the teaching of English. Where do words and their meanings come from? How have the meanings of words developed and changed over the years, since we first began recording and defining them? We study the history of the words because words are the meat, potatoes, and caviar in the English classroom. Words are the touchstone of our understanding. And history, a core subject in classical humanism, is the spine of our knowledge.

But, it's not just knowing history that is important. As Montaigne reminds us, "Let him [the student] be taught not so much the histories as how to judge them. That is, in my opinion, of all matters the one to which we apply our minds in the

most varying degree." The key phrase here is "how to judge," as we shall see when we look at the meanings of critical and thinking.

Critical, from Latin and Greek, means to decide or judge. It originated as a medical term, still recognized today when we hear of somebody in the hospital "in critical condition."

Other definitions include judging captiously or severely, censorious, carping, and fault-finding. A second definition, and the one that applies more to an understanding of critical thinking in the English classroom, states that critical means skilful in judging, especially about literary or artistic work. One example, cited in the OED, reads, "A critical judgment is made by experience and prudence and reason or discourse." In both definitions, the word judge is present. Casting a cold eye, to paraphrase Yeats.

Think is an Old English word with a rich and complex history that goes back twelve centuries to Cynewulf in 800 a.d. (No, Cynewulf won't be on the test and we don't have to teach him). The original meaning of think, as noted in the OED, "may have been to cause (something) to seem or appear (to oneself)."

Various definitions—or "shades of meaning," as Simon Winchester calls them in his book on the making of the OED— include the following:

1. to conceive, feel (some emotion)
2. to meditate on, turn over in the mind
3. to exercise the mind, especially the understanding in any active way; to form connected ideas of any kind
4. to imagine, conceive, fancy, picture
5. to reflect
6. to be of opinion, deem, judge

The six definitions above tell only part of the story and the history of the word think. An Old English word, neither borrowed from another language nor coined, a root of the English language, its other definitions goes on for pages. We note here, though, that think means to imagine or fancy, aspects of thinking—and schooling—that are too often neglected, forgotten, or dismissed. And lastly, there's that word judge again. A word that defines both critical and thinking and thereby links their meanings. And we have come back to Montaigne then, for whom how to judge "is of all matters the one to which we apply our minds in the most varying degree."

What will we judge in the English classroom and how will we judge? To address these questions, we turn to a short story by Alicia Gaspar de Alba titled *American Citizen, 1921.*

A short story, *American Citizen, 1921,* is about a young high school graduate, Alberto Morales, who applies for a job as a newspaper reporter. The newspaper editors who interview Alberto show their prejudice against a young, educated, Mexican American man. They insult him, calling him "tamale."

They offer him a job, however, as an assistant reporter, not the reporter's job for which Alberto applies. As part of the job, they require Alberto to report on what's going on in his barrio—essentially, they ask Alberto to snitch on his own community.

Alberto feels pressured to take the job, even though it's not the one he applies for, nor the one he envisions for himself. His wife and his father-in-law want him to show his pride and his intelligence, as he does himself, and not condescend to take a lesser job than that of reporter. Nonetheless, when Alberto realizes that the editors have no intention of offering him the reporter's job that he seeks, he takes the job they offer, one that pays less and has less prestige than the reporter's job.

One of the questions that arises, an interpretive question, is "Why does Alberto take the job?" A second—evaluative—question asks, "Do you—we—agree with Alberto's decision to take the job?" But even before seeking critical thinking responses—judgments—of these questions, even before reading the story, we might precede the reading of *American Citizen, 1921* by asking students their views of what it means to be an American, what it means to be a citizen, and what it means to be an American citizen to provide a context for understanding themes in the story.

We don't need to look up definitions in a dictionary—OED or otherwise—for every word or concept that we teach. Before seeking dictionary definitions for the concepts of American and citizen (should we decide or judge that dictionary definitions are important here) we can draw upon students' knowledge and understanding of the concepts. Too often we assume that people—students—have shared meanings of words or concepts. Those assumptions are not always true. Meaning is more subtle and complex. In school and social settings, meaning is negotiated or defined with others.

Teachers might do a semantic web that enables students to share their ideas and compare and contrast their own understandings with those of their peers. What do students think, feel, know, imagine, and connect (all related to our definitions of think and thinking) when they think of American and citizen? Based on the ideas they generate, do they see ways in which the words used to describe American and citizen might be grouped or categorized? Students begin to make judgments, based on their own views, and in comparison and contrast with the views of others, about what it means to be an American and a citizen, and an American citizen.

This entry on critical thinking is not primarily about how to teach *American Citizen, 1921,* but rather how to think critically—judge—issues that the story raises related to pride, responsibility, citizenship, prejudice, and American, code switching. We return then to two questions that we had asked earlier: Why does Alberto take the job and does he make a good, smart, or wise decision? The first—interpretive—question asks students to seek textual support for their responses. The second—evaluative—question asks students to judge Alberto's actions. Their judgments are based on their understanding of the story and more profoundly based on their own morals, values, and beliefs.

Before students make a final judgment, if there is such a thing, of Alberto's actions and the literary merits of the story itself, we have to return to the story—its title—once more: American Citizen, two words and concepts that we have explored, but the title is *American Citizen, 1921.* We now have to provide some historical and social context, which is integral to the story.

In 1921, for example, three years after the Armistice that ended the First World War, a *New York Times* front-page article wondered about the links between genes and citizenship. Were there specific genes that made for "good" citizens? The writer of the article entertained the idea that if scientists could discover the gene(s) that determined what makes an upright citizen, then there might be ways to—well, 'make' good citizens, however that might get translated or acted upon: a frightening thought.

In 1921, Alberto could buy a pair of denim overalls on sale for sixty-nine cents a pair; Glidden house paint—all colors—for sixty-nine cents a gallon; a set of breakfast dishes for $3.19; and, a walnut dresser for $35.00.

If Alberto earns $15.00 weekly, the sum he would earn as an assistant reporter, how far would that money go in the Texas border town where he and his wife lived? How might our own deeper understanding of economic factors that influence the story inform our judgments of Alberto's decision? Was he foolish to turn down the money, if that indeed was a good paycheck to a high school graduate at the time? In Alberto's situation, better for him to keep his pride and lose the job? Or, to swallow his pride and earn a good and decent living, especially, it must be said, as a Mexican American living in the prejudiced or hostile world of 1921 Texas? And the broader questions of how our pride gets in the way of making sound decisions, sound judgments about the things in life that we do?

But that's not all that we should ask. How much has changed or remained the same in ethnic and class relations in our nation since Alberto's time? What are our judgments of where we are now? And now that we've read the story and talked about it, thought it over, what, if anything, has changed regarding our views of what it means to be an American, a citizen, an American citizen? What sense do we now make of Alberto's decision to take the job? How do we judge his actions and the story that portrays his actions?

Critical thinking, or to now say it another way, making sound judgments, which are not censorious, not carping, not fault-finding, but skillful in judging, should be an essential part of the English curriculum. We must engage students with stories, poems, plays, essays, novels, and films that stir their imaginations, thoughts, and feelings. We must encourage, promote, and teach students how to ask sound interpretive and evaluative questions. Students' creating questions based upon readings enhances their reading comprehension, so there's a practical side to it. But more than that, asking questions leads to a deeper understanding of texts and of ourselves. This entry on critical thinking, to emphasize the point, is filled with questions.

Further, writing in the mid-nineteenth century in his autobiography, Frederick Douglass asks, "Have I not as good a right to be free as you have?" And in her poem, *Wanted,* written near the end of the twentieth century, Demetria Martinez, who shares Alberto's heritage, asks, "America I'm not good enough for you?" It is the same question that Alberto might have asked in 1921 when he sought the job as reporter. Asking questions seems fundamental to our American democracy, a basic right. Maybe it's just human nature to ask.

In our discussion of critical thinking, we have suggested that defining words—etymologically, historically—and through concept development with students, conjoin to provide a broader and deeper understanding of language, the coin of the realm in the English classroom. Words. "Every word," writes Emerson, "was once a poem." And "poetry was all written before time was, and whenever we are so finely organized that we can penetrate into that region where the air is music, we hear those primal warblings and attempt to write them down . . ." (Emerson, 2003).

In critical thinking—judging—we want to encourage a close understanding of words, a close hearing of the words of others, and a close reading of texts. We want to encourage students to ask the tough questions about texts that they read, and about values and beliefs that they share or do not share with others. As students ponder their own judgments, it is critical that we—their English teachers—work with them to become finely organized. We want them to judge soundly. We want to enable them to penetrate where the air is music.

References and Further Reading

Douglass, F. (1962). *Narrative of the life of Frederick Douglass: An American slave.* New York: Collier Books.

Emerson, R. (2003). *Ralph Waldo Emerson: Essays, second series.* [On-line]. Available: http://www.literaturepage.com/read/emersonessays 2-3.htm

Manguel, A. (1997). *A history of reading.* New York: Penguin.

Martinez, D. (1997). *Breathing between the lines.* Tempe: University of Arizona Press.

Winchester, S. (1998). *The professor and the madman: A tale of murder, insanity, and the making of the Oxford English Dictionary.* New York: HarperCollins Publishers.

Literacy

Critical Multicultural Literacy: Problematizing a Multicultural Curriculum Based on Reasoning

Danny Weil

Cultural encapsulation and ethnocentricity (or the belief in the inherent superiority of one's own group or culture) are limiting factors in achieving intellectual character or human freedom in our growing pluralistic society precisely because they limit our ability to critique our own thinking and author our decisions and actions. Much of what we learn to believe uncritically is derived from social structures or the *culture of power*—television, movies, popular culture, parents, friends, teachers, and the myriad socio/political institutions that govern our lives. As associational thinking substitutes for critical reflective thinking the uncritical mind looks for stereotypes and simplistic categories in which to conveniently place people, things, and places. Unquestioned associational thinking lends itself to self-delusion, propagandistic manipulation, and authoritarian deception as uncritical associational thinkers are customary prey for political and social demagoguery (Milgram, 1974; Reich, 1946).

The reduction of prejudice and the material reality that fosters such thinking requires long-term thinking strategies and practices for developing fair and open-minded persons capable of challenging unfair and narrow-minded societal and institutional practices. To confront this challenge is a proposal for a *critical multicultural literacy* that advocates a multicultural curriculum founded on principles and strategies of critical thinking.

CRITICAL MULTICULTURAL LITERACY AS CHARACTER DEVELOPMENT

To be knowledgeable fair-minded democratic citizens in today's and tomorrow's society, students must understand the conceptions of various culturally informed points of view within American and global society. Devoid of this understanding they will be unable to participate fully and wisely in personal and democratic life and can unwittingly serve as agents for the reproduction of illegitimate cultural domination and oppression. Understanding diversity is to understand diversity of thought, action, and conditions relative to pressing social and institutional power structures. It is to understand the *logic of* thinking from the point of view of gender, gays, the aged, the disabled, newly arriving immigrants, people of color, and social class. Students need opportunities to understand the logic of thinking that fuels culturally informed points of view—the goals of their reasoning; the questions or problems that they have and continue to confront; the empirical dimensions of their thinking; the concepts they utilize; the assumptions upon which they rest their inferences, claims, and conclusions; the consequences and implications of their thinking; and their frames of reference. They need to engage in a critical historic and contemporary analysis and evaluation of culturally informed points of view with an understanding that *they too* have a logic to their thinking that is also culturally informed. Understanding the logic of their own thinking relative to the logic of other points of view helps students engage in transformative metacognition—the ability to rethink one's thinking in the interest of informed action—thus placing them in a position to become active agents in the construction of knowledge and thoughtful consumers of social, economic, political, historical, and personal life. Furthermore, in this way, the reflective examining mind can reason as to the origin and nature of its uncritical thought and, thus, more fully and wisely participate in and transform a world lived in common with others.

Reasoning multiculturally is part of a dialectical process of becoming human. It is to gain an insight into one's self and others through historical and cultural understanding, while at the same time developing an insight into history and culture through subjective self. With increased knowledge and appreciation of diversity, students have an opportunity to become not just *in* the world but *with* the world. For this reason a critical multicultural literacy is literacy for personal and social liberation and benefits both teachers and students.

CONSTRUCTING A RELEVANT CURRICULUM FOR CRITICAL MULTICULTURAL LITERACY

A *critical multicultural literacy* argues that in a pluralistic society education should affirm and encourage the quest for self-examination *through* social transformation by creating relevant problem-posing activities that allow students to confront, through reasoning, the challenges offered by the diversity of the reality of everyday life. According to Banks,

Citizenship education in a multicultural society must have as an important goal helping all students, including white mainstream students, to develop the knowledge, attitudes, and skills needed not only to participate in, but also to help transform and reconstruct, society. Problems such as racism, sexism, poverty, and inequality are widespread within U.S. society and permeate many of the nation's institutions, such as the workforce, the courts, and the schools. To educate future citizens to fit into and not to transform society will result in the perpetuation and escalation of these problems, including the widening gap between the rich and the poor, racial conflict and tension, and the growing number of people who are victims of poverty and homelessness. (Banks, 1990)

The development of critical consciousness on the part of our students promises opportunities for social praxis and transformation that challenge the social structures from which many, if not all, internalized associational assumptions and myths derive their origins. Without ample opportunities for students of all colors, genders, social classes, and races to participate in a meaningful environment of inquiry and critical thinking these citizenship skills will not grow and flourish. This is also why the subjects Banks calls attention to—subjects such as homelessness, poverty, racism, and to which I would add issues of physical disability, gender inequality, homophobia, and social and economic class—should constitute the object of a critical multicultural education. Furthermore, students need critical opportunities to begin to see their cultures as others see them—thereby allowing them to reflectively rethink their own cultural beliefs, decisions, and actions in the interest not of blind and uncritical allegiance to one cultural group or another, but for purposes of insightful reasoning that goes beyond narrowly defined self-interests.

Students at Sarah J. Hale High School in Brooklyn, New York, are pursuing precisely these kinds of inquiries. In 1988, students at the public high school founded *The Society for Social Analysis* dedicated, in their words—

to construct the foundation of a splendid journal covering the whole field of civic affairs, drawing on free, responsible, and committed students in charge of their destinies, in touch with their cultures and moved to spread the message of their love and their aspirations by the device of literary articulation. (*Crossing Swords*, 1988)

The society's journal entitled *Crossing Swords* promotes critical dialogue and discovery by "encouraging critical analysis of political, social, and cultural issues" (*Crossing Swords,* 1988). Within the journal, students engage in critical writing about issues such as multicultural education, schools for black males, police abuse,

socialization practices, abortion, teenage pregnancies, drugs, international affairs, power, authority, neighborhood, child abuse, parenting, school life, colonialism, popular culture, art, music, freedom, history, and street life to name just a few topics.

In an introduction to the third section of their summer/fall journal *Crossing Swords,* student editors introduce themselves in the following manner:

Within our mind lies the blueprint for the world. In this section of the third issue of our journal you will experience concerned young minds inflamed at injustices in society. You will also see creative minds engaged with each other. If my opening statement holds true, then our society rests on well defined grounds. Some students asks questions and others provide answers. In this section, as in the entire journal, these young thinkers acknowledge the past and give credibility and hope to the future. (*Crossing Swords,* 1990)

These voices from just a few of the urban city high school students from Brooklyn, New York, display and maintain a keen sense of critical spirit. Confronting issues of multicultural concern, they utilize critical thinking and writing to problematize contemporary and historical situations for dialogical analysis and evaluation. Although they are the general exception to current educational reality, these students and their talented instructor/facilitator Winthrop Holder provide a legacy and an excellent example of the enormous possibilities all students are able to achieve when presented with a worthy educational project.

By reasoning critically within different points of view on historical or contemporary issues, students such as those at Sarah J. Hale High School come to see the construction of knowledge and how history can become revised and institutionalized in a manner that both justifies exploitation and subjugation while idealizing and romanticizing particular historical points of view. Reasoning within culturally diverse informed points of view also allows students an opportunity to develop insights into empathetic reasoning and reciprocity, which they will be able to transfer into other personal and social domains of their lives.

FORGING A CURRICULUM FOR UNITY

Because valuing diversity is learning to reason within and about different cultural, social, historical, and economic points of view, a critical multicultural literacy that recognizes, promotes, and excels diversity appreciation through reasoning must also value what unites us as human beings in the common quest for humanity. Unfortunately, because we often do not see or appreciate our common historical struggles for humanity, it is difficult, if not impossible, to imagine or create a unified future on the same earth among diverse lifestyles, points of view, or frames of reference. Helping students examine and analyze critically the differences and similarities in the historical and contemporary struggle for self-determination, personal freedom, and social justice should be a fundamental component of a critical multicultural curriculum. Students and teachers should not only embark on the quest for unmasking the common human struggle for authenticity and validity, but also engage in a critical analysis of exploitation, oppression, authority, power, homophobia, sexism, racism, classism, and domination so evident in the lives of many students and throughout history as a whole.

Multicultural literacy is not teaching *us* about *them* or teaching others to be like us. On the contrary, to fully comprehend the American or global experience, it is necessary to reason within multiple perspectives informed by culture, gender, race, and socioeconomic class. In this way all students profit from a rich, unique multicultural curriculum precisely because they are encouraged to see the world, its history, and contemporary reality from diverse cultural perspectives. They learn to develop a social discourse that embraces critical self-inventory and historical sensibility. Furthermore, they come to see the commonalities and differences in the forces of oppression that have helped shaped both historical and contemporary reality, affording them an opportunity to develop a capacity to engage in a praxis that challenges this oppression.

Arguing that students need countless examples for reasoning within different cultural points of view is not to dismiss the necessity for students to study their own particular culture—a study often foreign to classroom life. The idea being proposed is that purely having knowledge about one's own cultural group is insufficient to understand the enormous diversity of American social life. Moreover, knowledge about one's culture of necessity requires an understanding of other cultures, as no culture exists in a vacuum. As students begin to reason about this historical cultural point of view or that contemporary sociocultural issue, they begin to see parallels in history between common economic and cultural struggles and are better able to transfer intercultural insights into everyday life.

The historical period during the Seminole wars is one example of a multicultural inquiry that would encourage historical reasoning within diverse cultural points of view in the interest of unity. In her book, *The Seminole Wars,* Henrietta

Buckmaster depicts the relationship between the Seminole Indians and black slaves and how they joined forces against oppression during the wars. Unearthing important historical examples and disenfranchised narratives of unified struggle and resistance between cultures against a common oppressor is paramount for providing students with authentic multicultural reasoning opportunities that foster a sense of human unity. Teachers might have students research this historical period paying particular attention to the common struggle, the historical identities, and the questions that faced both cultures. They could work cooperatively in groups researching and analyzing the historical period, eventually role-playing historical voices or even scripting dramatic narratives.

To create similar opportunities for critical approaches to cultural learning, teachers might have their students look at life in Los Angeles in the 1940s from the point of view of the *Pachucos*. They might interview parents and community members as a way to elicit culturally informed points of view from their communities and their interactions with daily life. Contributions made by various cultural groups in the labor movement during the early part of this century and continuing until the 1950s could be an object of inquiry. Students could analyze different points of view regarding the labor movement among whites, blacks, and Asians in the early part of the century. For example, Chinese coolies were paid slave wages to build the railroads of the West in the late 1900s, driving down the pay of native whites and creating anti-Asian riots all over the West, including California. Blacks looked at organized labor with distrust especially in light of the eurocentricity and sociocentricity of Samuel Gompers who founded the American

Federation of Labor (AF of L). Students might identify and analyze critically the different points of view of many blacks, women, and newly arrived immigrants who were barred from the AF of L in the early 1900s.

CONCLUSION

The sentiment and purpose behind reasoning multiculturally is to understand diversity for the sake of humanity *not* at humanity's expense. Furthermore, when students consider the common struggle for human dignity and the logic of oppression, they are considering their own behavior—the decisions they have made and continue to make, and the actions they choose to engage in. Insights into the connection between history and contemporary reality—between the choices the actors of history made and those we make today, and between the assumptions that guided past choices and claims and those that guide them today—place students in a better position to see how inhumanity impacts their lives and how they might be acting humanely or inhumanely toward others.

In cultivating an awareness and appreciation for and of others and their differences—gender, class, ethnic, or cultural—we as educators should strive to create relevant, meaningful opportunities for students to gain an insight into not simply the differences between people that often lead to separation and distancing, but an understanding of the historical and global nature of human relations and the interconnectedness and interrelatedness of all of us as human beings. Although this interconnectedness does not transcend our diversity, it certainly provides opportunities for creating and developing more inclusive relationships that confront racial hatred and intolerance and thus serves to unite us in the common struggle for human dignity, justice, critical self-evaluation, and freedom.

References

Banks, J. A. (1990). Citizen education for a pluralistic democratic society. *Social Studies, 81,* 210–214.

Buckmaster, H. (1966). *The Seminole wars.* New York: Collier Books.

Milgram, S. (1974). *Obedience to authority: An experimental view.* New York: Harper and Row.

Reich, W. (1946). *The mass psychology of fascism.* New York: Farrar, Strauss, and Giroux.

The Society for Social Analysis. (1988/1990). *Crossing swords.* Brooklyn, New York: Sarah J. Hale High School.

Further Reading

Lankshear, C., & McLaren, P. (1993). *Critical literacy: Politics, praxis and the postmodern.* New York: State University of New York Press.

McLaren, P. (1995). *Critical pedagogy and predatory culture.* New York: Routledge.

Weil, D. (1998). *Towards a critical multicultural literacy: Theory and practice for education for liberation.* New York: Peter Lang.

Gaining Access to Critical Literacy: Rethinking the Role of Reading Programs

Hermán S. García and Teresa Valenzuela

The important role of critical literacy in developing new ideas about reading has been extracted from the critical pedagogy literature and measured against the framework of traditional literacy views. The theoretical constructs promulgated by Paulo Freire and other criticalists impel us to move toward an education for critical consciousness in the struggle for social justice and a radical democracy.

Freire's conceptualization of literacy strongly implicates a process that involves a language of politics and pedagogy, thus providing a notion for consciousness liberation that rejects literacy as the sum part of skills learned in reading. Freire's work on reading the word and the world helps educators develop a view of literacy as a form of cultural politics. The themes that relate to the concept of cultural politics run throughout his works. Those themes view literacy as the act of individuals mediating

their world through seeing, feeling, touching, hearing, and smelling, which rely on personalized experiences that, in turn, lead to a very personalized form of meaning-making. School life should not be thought of as the only way to gain knowledge and an understanding of the world. The iron-clad rules and regulations schools operate by should not prevent students from maintaining and developing their cultural and linguistic diversity. Schools need to be a more inclusive cultural terrain in which the production of knowledge is negotiated rather than handed out as singular truth.

Literacy is an imaginative concept that goes beyond written meaning. That is, literacy cannot be reduced to viewing letters and words as a purely mechanical and skill-driven activity. The definition of literacy must go beyond this rigid meaning to include a relationship in which learners can mediate the struggle for emancipation, democracy, social justice, and transformative practices.

An emancipatory archetype for literacy presents the opportunity for us to examine schooling within a specific context. In this way educators become mindful about curriculum from a critical perspective. This entails analyses of how the selection, formulation, organization, and delivery of knowledge, social relations, values, and forms of assessment have been developed. Positions of power among school administrators, teachers, and learners can be analyzed within a broader context of schooling. To become truly emancipatory, the formulation of knowledge must be organized and earnestly orchestrated for delivery among administrators, teachers, and learners.

A major issue echoed among critical educators addressing reading programs in schools is language. Learning to read as an act of engaging the world has to start from a comprehensive understanding of reading the world. This has a powerful impact on our understanding of literacy. This implies that, as humans, we should attempt to derive meaning from the multitude of impressions about things, people, places, spaces, and ideas before we can know them in their transcendent form. It is through language that we can rethink ideas related to ourselves and build ideological constructs that will assist in developing a cultural foundation for self. It is not surprising that children who are silenced are denied the opportunity to know themselves as cultural beings.

An additional feature in the issue of language is its power of imagination. For example, liberatory actions are practiced when people reclaim their language and imagination for building a healthy world of coexistence. Consequently, the idea that reading is a dynamic and transformative process is different than those presented in traditional schooling practices.

A second issue that emerges from Freire's literacy views is "education for critical consciousness." This notion at once rejects education as a banking process— that is, where the teacher makes deposits that fill the students with the knowledge of cultural interest and values of the majority. Instead, critical consciousness education expounds on the principle that reading plays an important role in the development of language. In this view, language can become a vehicle for entering into a dialectical exchange with learners. Reading is a dynamic action that must reflect aspects of all we do in making sense of the world. Learning about the world and the word, then, is highly contextual and intricately tied to the learner's lived experiences. Recognition and intervention, both of which are important in theory and practice, are constantly at work as the learner goes through the process of meaning-making.

In both recognition and intervention, a critical consciousness is required for parallel acts of thinking, and thus naming and defining for meaning-making. What is said and then read is interpreted concurrently and given meaning in the context of its action both politically and pedagogically. This is praxis. Meaning is provided from the start and never in isolation. Another path to praxis involves helping teachers and learners to become reflective and evaluative. Recognition and intervention require an imaginative quality that permits teachers and learners to act in the world in new and exciting ways.

A third issue is the idea that learning is contextual. Freire asks us to indulge in a reflective process regarding our own education and our development of understanding of the world. We must go back to our childhood and youth to reflect on our personal development or lack thereof. Memory plays an important inner role in literacy. Images that we conjure from our pasts have a subtle, aesthetic quality. At our disposal are many metaphors to help us revisit our life, which includes homes, pets, family members, natural surroundings, and other senses. Our cultural contexts are more clearly elaborated as we link to a wider world whose existence helps recapture our truer identities.

Ultimately, however, we must critically look at the literacy programs in which we work: Do they empower or disempower? More broadly, is literacy analyzed according to whether it serves to reproduce an existing social order? Does literacy serve cultural practices that promote democratic and emancipatory transformation? As such, the idea of literacy for meaning has to be located within a theory of cultural production and understood as an integral part of what communities produce and reproduce as meaning. Learners can then be seen as subjects capable of constructing and reconstructing meaning in the process of literacy acquisition. In contrast, traditional educators have approached literacy quite literally through abstract methodological issues as opposed to ideological contexts, consequently ignoring the cross-relationship between sociopolitical structures in society.

Conservative educators want to reduce learning to read as a set of prescribed practices that are decontextualized and, for the most part, meaningless. The failure of these practices is that for learners to be able to understand themselves in the context of the broader society they must understand the meaning of their immediate social reality. On the other hand, we need to understand that learning to read should never be limited to a process of simply appreciating oneself. Empowerment should also be a means to enable students to come to a clear understanding and approve those aspects of the dominant culture that will provide a basis for transforming the wider social order. It is important to master the dominant language for accessing the wider world, but not at the expense of damaging individual's identities. Also important are literacy efforts that have been undertaken as part of broader family empowerment issues and, to some degree, that espouse the principles presented from Freire's perspectives of literacy. One of the striking features in family literacy is the emphasis given to its sociohistorical context in the acquisition of literacy. Many educators have striven to connect the fabric of family life to the rich acquisition of literacy for all families. Yet, many of these families continue to struggle in the margins of American society.

Reading practices that have been examined report the stagnating and meaninglessness reading programs in which children and their families are forced to participate. Families' adamant claims for contextualization of the curriculum and inclusiveness of their daily lives and voice are ever present. The question that emerges is whether educators can expect children who arrive with different experiences that support literacy development to be successfully connected to practices found in schools.

Several critical literacy educators have adopted an empowerment philosophy and have demonstrated, through their work in public school systems, that it is possible when done through a participatory process. Organizing conversations in their community of learners—similar to the "culture circles" offered in Brazil—is helpful. Educators need to understand the important task of reading the word and the world of families, while adopting the concept of ethnography for empowerment.

Much work is needed in the ever-changing field of critical literacy. Educators need to pursue research studies that will broaden the knowledge base of systems that are needed to assist struggling families and their children gain access to critical literacy via progressive reading programs. Much more must be done in the areas of dual language literacy, family literacy in marginalized communities, and parental involvement that is empowering. Freire's works gives us a strong theoretical base from which to spring.

Further Reading

Fehring, H., & Green, P. (Eds.). (2001). *Critical literacy: A collection of articles from the Australian Literacy Educators' Association.* Norwood, Australia: Australian Association for the Teaching of English.

Freire, P., & Macedo, D. (1987). *Literacy: Reading the word and the world.* South Hadley, MA: Bergin & Garvey.

Gallego, M. A., & Hollingsworth, S. (Eds.). (2000). *What counts as lit-er-a-cy: Challenging the school standard.* New York: Teachers College Press.

Shor, I., & Pari, C. (Eds.). (1999). *Critical literacy in action: Writing words, changing worlds.* Portsmouth, NH: Boynton/Cook.

Infusing Critical Thinking into the Sociocultural View of Literacy

Colin Lankshear and Michele Knobel

For many people, literacy is quite separate from applying critical processes to what is read or written. To them literacy is simply a neutral tool or a basic skill concerned with encoding and decoding alphabetic text. Viewed as a *tool,* literacy consists of the technology of alphabetic code. As a basic *skill,* literacy is the ability to operate this tool—to decode and encode text—above some agreed level of competence.

From this perspective literacy can be used in all sorts of different ways for all sorts of purposes. Once someone *has* literacy they can put it to all sorts of uses. One such use *might* be some form of critical thinking. But it need not be. According to this view, people can practice literacy without bringing any critical orientation or purposes to bear on the act of reading and writing or on the objects about which they are reading or writing.

This is implied in speaking of literacy as a *basic* skill. To say something is basic is to say it serves as a base for *going on* to do other things that are not integral to it. Hence, literacy is often seen as basic to learning curriculum content. Once one has literacy, one can use it to learn things via the medium of texts. One can (if one wishes) use it to critique what is expressed through texts. Equally, one may use it for purposes like reading the Bible, sharing recipes, following instructions on fixing an engine, or for writing propaganda supporting the U.S. wars on Islamic peoples. So far as this view of literacy is concerned, if someone never used their literacy to apply critical judgment to the texts they read, or to analyze and evaluate aspects of the world they experience, this would not mean they were not literate.

The opposing position—a *sociocultural* perspective—maintains that literacy is inseparable from processes of critical reflection, judgment, and evaluation. According to its advocates, this is because literacy cannot be sensibly thought of as a tool or basic skill concerned simply with encoding or decoding printed text. To see what this means, let's decode the following stretches of alphabetic code.

1. Acksa binga rezid wonkas.
2. Can you find the joint?
3. The physical problems faced by a UTM are partially solved in a VNM by implementing the most basal operations in the hardware.

It is a safe bet that anybody reading this article can decode all of these sentences. The following are also safe bets:

(a) No reader can make any sense of the first sentence (it was purposefully constructed as a readable but meaningless text);
(b) Different readers will produce different meanings and ranges of meanings for the second sentence; and
(c) Many readers would not consider they could say with any precision what the third sentence means.

If literacy were simply about decoding or encoding text more or less fluently, we could all be said to read (or write) these sentences to the same extent. Moreover, there would be no qualitative difference between "reading" the first sentence and reading the other two. Neither of these points holds, however. Unless we invent some secret code, none of us can make any sense of the first sentence, although we can all "read" it. We can all make (varying) sense of the second. And we can all recognize a qualitative difference between the first and third sentences, although many of us will be unable to make any useful sense of the third.

While we may say we can all read (i.e., follow what they inscribe) these three sentences, none of us can *read* (make meaning from) the first. We will *read* the second differently (i.e., make varying meanings of it). Many of us will be quite unable to *read* the third sentence. Some of us will be able to read the three sentences only more or less. This is because literacy is always part of some larger social practice other than just literacy itself. We never just *read* or *write* per se. Instead, we read or write within some kind of social practice. This is why we would have to invent a practical context, such as a spy game with secret codes, for the first sentence to be *readable*. From a sociocultural perspective, we can only *read* a text if it is housed within a social practice that gives it meaning, and within which we participate more or less effectively.

The same theory applies to the third sentence. Anyone who does not participate in social practices that involve dealing with and understanding the operating systems and hardware components of computers cannot *read* this sentence. Those who know a little about computers and computing jargon will likely understand that the sentence is talking about problems associated with different kinds of computers, but they will not make any more detailed meaning from it. They cannot really *read* it. It would be like picking up *enough* words in a foreign language conversation to get a sense of the topic, but not enough to *understand* what is being said about it.

The second sentence is especially interesting because it will mean different things to different people depending on their experiences of different contexts of social practice. The sentence could mean at least four different things. In the context of a text about finding leaks in a system of pipes, we would read it in terms of looking for a point where two or more pipes have been connected. In the context of preparing a roast dinner in, say, New Zealand, we would read it in terms of looking for the cut of meat to be cooked. In the context of a group of crooks looking for the building they are supposed to "case" or "rob," we would understand "joint" to mean a physical location or property. In the context of a narcotics subculture, we would read the sentence in terms of someone looking for a marijuana cigarette.

Someone without awareness of all four contexts of social practice would not be able to *read* this sentence in the way or ways that certain other people can. To be able to *read* (and write), then, means being able to locate or situate a text within a social practice and to read or write it "out of" that practice. If we do not or cannot read it out of the practice within which it has been written, we are unlikely to understand it properly. The same holds for writing.

This sociocultural view of literacy, which we accept, has important implications for the relationship between literacy and critical thinking. We will consider two implications here.

First, another way to state our recent points is to say that literacies are always embedded in discourses (Gee, 1996). These are regulated practices involving beliefs, values, concepts, goals, ways of thinking and acting, norms and standards, codes of dress, gestures, and so on. People speak and act and think and read and write and *be* in quite different ways from one discourse to another. Who we are and what we are like as individuals is a function of the discourses in which we actively participate. These vary considerably from person to person. Just as "joint" has different meanings across the discourses of

plumbing, cooking, robbing, and doping, so are persons (identities) different to the extent that they participate in different discourses or discourse combinations, as are the texts they create and share with other members of their discourses.

This leads to a second implication. We never just "read and write" or "learn to read and write" pure and simple. By learning to read and write—and subsequently engaging in reading and writing within social contexts—we are initiated into and further affirmed as members of particular discourses. Because all discourses involve particular goals, purposes, values, beliefs, and ways of doing things and of being some kind of person (*as opposed to other ones*) acquiring and practicing literacy can *never* be neutral processes. They are always part of larger processes of becoming some kind or person or other. How we do life, what we believe and value, how we approach the world, how we are related to others, and so on, have consequences for other people and other things and their interests and well-being.

This raises important questions relevant to critical forms of practice. It is never a matter of having a choice whether the ways we learn to read and write, and how we subsequently read and write, have such consequences or not. They *do,* whether we like it or not, and whether or not we are aware of it. Hence, a crucial question is, "What do we become committed to or involved in, whether consciously or not, when we become literate in a particular way and when we practice literacies associated with the various discourses we have been initiated into?"

If we just think of literacy as being a neutral basic skill, it is impossible to conceive such questions. At most we can defer these questions to a point further along a chain. For example, we might think a person is accountable for how their actions affect others when we think they had a choice. But, we are unable to get at the very roots of socialization in processes like learning to read and write that shape our orientations toward action from the outset. We are unable to recognize some of the most important places where group or national psyches originate and to take steps at *that* point to imagine and pursue better ways to build our selves and our lives. The fact is that *all* forms of literacy are ideological. They help initiate us into worldviews and value systems that have consequences for people's interests and well-being. In doing so, they make these worldviews and value systems seem like the only ones available, and make them seem natural. In fact they are neither.

The questions are as follows: What kinds of ideological beings do particular literacies and texts encourage us to become (or remain)? How would we feel about this if we were to become aware of it and see what it may involve in particular cases? How can we get some critical distance between ourselves and the literacies and texts we engage in, so that we can identify and evaluate the ideological views and positions that come with them and consider their material effects on others and ourselves?

Some simple but effective activities can be used to get students thinking about how texts encode particular assumptions about the world, constructions of the world, and orientations toward the world, which impact on how we live and act, and the consequences of how we live and act. These consequences may involve human interests and well-being. Alternatively, they may involve environmental or ecological well-being, animal well-being, and so on. Doing this kind of work on texts can be an important step toward imagining other constructions, representations, and

orientations that we believe might have better (e.g., social, moral, environmental) consequences. Let's consider two straightforward activities here.

ANALYSIS OF PARTICIPANTS AND MATERIAL PROCESSES IN AN ELEMENTARY SCHOOL HISTORY TEXT

Consider the following account of how America was colonized.

Columbus' Journeys

On his first journey, Columbus left Puerto de Palos on August 3, 1492, and after two months of traveling, on October 12, 1492, he arrived on an American island, the island of Guanahani, which he named San Salvador.

Christopher Columbus made three more journeys, during which he reached lands of the Caribbean Sea, Central American lands, and arrived at what is today known as Venezuela—but he never knew that he was dealing with a new continent.

The New World

After Christopher Columbus many Europeans adventured to cross the Atlantic Ocean.

Another Italian sailor, Amerigo Vespucio, was the one to discover that the lands Columbus had reached were a continent.

Hence, the new continent was given the name of America, in memory of that Italian explorer.

Who Traveled to the New World?

Many men set out from Spain to go to the recently discovered islands to settle them. These men were monks, who set about converting the indigenous people to Christianity and teaching them the Spanish alphabet.

Many poor peasants, whose lands did not yield them sufficient crops for living, and many men without work or who were seeking justice, also journeyed to the American world.

How They Lived in the New World

The Spanish who arrived at the islands were called colonists, because they arrived to found colonies dependent on the Spanish crown.

The Spanish royals named a government in the new lands.

The colonists exploited the mines and lands of the new possessions, using the labor of the indigenous peoples and bringing African slaves to America.

This text is typical of many recent efforts to avoid forms of racism, celebration of imperialism, and beliefs in the superiority of Western ways evident in history texts of past decades. But like any text, this one represents the world in a particular way. One way to explore this is by drawing on aspects of systemic functional linguistics to see how *participants* (e.g., human and nonhuman actors) in a text are handled in terms of *material processes* (roughly equivalent to *verbs* in conventional grammar). In the Columbus text, we can focus on the human participants (individual persons, social groups, etc.) and address the text as follows:

1. Identify the main human actors (e.g., Columbus, monks, indigenous people).
2. Identify the material processes (verbs) associated with the different actors (e.g., Columbus left, arrived, reached).
3. Draw a table with columns and enter the verbs associated with each of the different groups under the appropriate headings.
4. See what kinds of patterns emerge in the columns. For example, who does more? Who does least or nothing? Who does to others? Who has done to them?
5. How are the groups represented in terms of being social actors?
6. What does this representation *exclude* (gaps and silences)? Is it a plausible account? What alternative accounts are possible?

These questions would quickly reveal that in the Columbus text the indigenous people are represented as essentially passive. They get converted to Christianity and have their labor exploited. Yet did they not resist? Did they not have their own distinctive routines and customs? Did they do *nothing else* except become Christians and work for others?

Such simple means give us objective distance from texts. We can consider what kind of ideological position someone would be adopting if they simply went along with such texts and regarded them as natural and as portraying the way things are. Such a person is referred to as the "ideal reader" of a text. They feel no dissonance with a text because it fits smoothly with their general view of the world. Were we in fact an ideal reader of the Columbus text? Did it seem like a natural viewpoint when we first read it? Now that we have explored it more critically, do we feel the same way? Do we want to maintain the text's view? What might the implications be for social groups like the indigenous people in this text if most people thought of them like this?

USING GENERAL QUESTIONS TO EXAMINE THE IDEOLOGICAL CONSTRUCTION OF TEXTS AND THE TEXTUAL CONSTRUCTION OF IDEOLOGIES

A complementary activity involves using a set of questions as an approach to critical reading with a view to identifying assumptions and worldviews that inform texts and that readers of these texts are invited to share or adopt. The following questions, based on the work by Catherine Wallace (1988) and Gunther Kress (1994), can be applied to a wide range of texts and text types.

- What is the topic of this text?
- Why might the author have written about this topic?
- Who is the ideal reader for this text? Who is the intended audience?
- What worldview and values is the reader assumed to have?
- What knowledge must readers bring to the text to understand it?
- Who might feel left out in this text, and why? Is this problematic?
- Who might find that their values, beliefs, or experiences clash with this text?
- How is the reader positioned by the text in relation to the author (e.g., a friend, as someone to be persuaded, as someone presumed to hold similar views, etc.)?

These questions can provide interesting and unsettling outcomes when applied to everyday texts like the following mail order catalog. Readers are invited to read this text, to apply the questions to it, and then consider the extent to which they feel differently about the text (and their initial reading of it) after addressing the questions.

Sometimes in the thrill of the chase we forget the first rule of smart shopping. Just because something is cheap doesn't mean it's a great bargain. Before buying we should ask ourselves—Is it well made? Does it fit my lifestyle? Will it go with anything in my wardrobe? All these considerations add real value to every dollar we spend.

MONEY ISN'T EVERYTHING

For many of us, suits are a daily necessity, not a luxury. Value is a must. With this in mind, we've put together a fantastic range of interchangeable suit separates that feature classic, quality tailoring. A suit for under $140 definitely deserves a look, see pages 6 and 7. And when it comes to venturing outdoors, you can't go past genuine Shetland knits. We offer a range of styles for both men and women. But good value isn't just restricted to the wardrobe. This month we feature a big section devoted to the home. Starting on page 54, we provide lots of ways to keep warm this winter without breaking the budget. (cited with permission in Knobel, 1998, p. 93)

Members of modern societies regularly encounter texts like those we have presented here. They are integral to everyday discourses and play important roles in shaping who and what we become, what the world becomes, and how the world works for different peoples, groups, individuals, environments, and so on. For this reason it is important that literacy be seen as intimately linked to critical practices of reflection, analysis, and evaluation.

References

Gee, J. (1996). *Social linguistics and literacies: Ideology in discourses.* London: Falmer Press.

Knobel, M. (1998). Critical literacies in teacher education. In M. Knobel, & A. Healy (Eds.), *Critical literacies in the primary classroom* (pp. 89–111). Marrickville, NSW: Primary English Teaching Association.

Kress, G. (1994). *Learning to write*. New York: Routledge.

Wallace, C. (1988). *Learning to read in a multicultural society*. New York: Prentice-Hall.

Media Literacy

William A. Kealy

Essentially, media literacy deals with the ability to interpret, create, and analyze messages delivered by some means of communication. The medium used for conveying these messages may be nonelectronic (e.g., text, photography, drawings, diagrams, maps) or electronic (e.g., audiotape, video, CD-ROM). Although media literacy involves all kinds of media, it has traditionally emphasized mass media such as newspapers, radio, television, and, most recently, the World Wide Web. Media literacy also emphasizes the importance of being able to view media critically. Media literate persons, for example, are able to identify misinformation and propaganda where it occurs. They can distinguish between a commercial made to look deceptively like the report of a scientific breakthrough (i.e., an infomercial) and bona fide television news reporting.

Why should we attempt to make students, in particular, more media literate? Historically, a primary goal of the K-12 curriculum has been to help students to read and write. By comparison, schools have placed much less emphasis on "visual literacy" and the ability to understand and create nonverbal communications. Yet visual literacy skills are vitally important—especially in a society such as ours that is increasingly being bombarded by images on television and other media. Furthermore, students spend an enormous amount of time watching television, making little

or no judgment about what is being communicated or the person doing the communicating.

How can we assist students in becoming media literate? As a foundation for media literacy, students should have the basic visual literacy of being able to draw meaning from graphic communications. This is relatively easy to do when the graphics involved are photographs and paintings of real objects that are meant to be interpreted literally. However, understanding nonverbal communications becomes much more difficult when the message is symbolic—such as the representation of "justice" as a picture of a blindfolded woman with a sword in one hand and a pair of scales in the other. Visual messages may also be difficult to interpret when the displays themselves are rendered abstractly. For example, some students may not be able to perceive and comprehend the wartime tragedy portrayed in Picasso's famous cubist painting, *Guenrica*, because of its visual abstraction.

Some visuals—like maps, charts, and diagrams—are abstract by nature, because they communicate things like quantities, distance, and space that are difficult to put into words. Also, there are special conventions and rules that one typically needs to know about these types of displays before they can be understood. Using a map, for example, requires orienting it in a particular way and being able to use its scale and legend to interpret, respectively, the distances and features shown. Maps, charts, and diagrams cannot be understood intuitively. Rather students must be taught how to read these media to get the messages they contain. This is an extremely important literacy skill for students to acquire because such media are encountered daily in newspapers, magazines, books, and even Web sites.

As mentioned earlier, media literacy involves not only being able to decode a message but also having the ability to make judgments about the worth and validity of the message itself. When people are verbally literate they can tell when a writer is trying to trick them with double-talk or other attempts at manipulating language. In the same way, a media literate person can tell when a graphic display is attempting to deceive viewers by visually distorting information. Imagine, for example, a chart used by a company to show a 50 percent increase in sales from one year to the next. A commonly used and straightforward way to show this is with a bar chart that uses, say, a two-inch bar to indicate the first year and a three-inch bar to represent the second year. But suppose instead, that the display uses two side-by-side images of dollar bills: one that is two inches high and the other three inches high. Because the bars in this case are dollar bills with a standard proportion, the taller one is also much wider. As a result, the difference in the overall sizes of the two rectangles formed gives the illusion that the increase was not 50 percent but 125 percent. This is an example of what Edward Tufte calls the "lie factor" that exists in many information displays. Tufte's book, *Envisioning Information,* extends this criticism of graphics by also looking at the degree of information value they provide. Specifically, Tufte criticizes graphics that "dumb-down" information and then compensate for this by adding decorative "chartjunk" to increase the visual appeal of otherwise worthless displays.

When a message and its meaning is distorted, it is not always because the sender is trying to be deceptive. Sometimes the particular medium chosen to deliver a message changes how it is interpreted. For instance, people may interpret a message heard on the radio differently than when the same information is presented as text. The radio message is heard once and it is gone forever; the text, by contrast, can be reviewed and closely examined over time. This is one reason why radio is considered "information poor" compared with text. Just as in a conversation, radio listeners must add meaning to what they hear by using both context and what they expect to hear to fill in the information gaps. Therefore, to be understood well, messages over the radio need to take the prior knowledge of the listener into account. From a classroom perspective, this is important to keep in mind when choosing radio over text for delivery of lesson content. Additionally, to maximize the benefits of a medium like radio, your students will need to be taught how to be active listeners rather than passively letting the sounds of the radio wash over them. What is the speaker's purpose? What does the speaker assume about the audience? Does the speaker have a particular point of view or bias?

There are some other important differences between information-rich media, like text, and information-poor media, like radio, that were pointed out by Marshall McLuhan more than three decades ago in his book *Understanding Media.* With radio and, to an even greater extent, television, which he called "cool" media, people are more actively involved in creating meaning by adding to what is not being said or shown. To illustrate, we may see separate video clips that alternate between a woman talking and a man talking, but what we experience is a couple having a conversation. Much of what we consider "reality" in a television show is what we construct with our understanding. This active participation absorbs our attention, giving radio and television a seductive quality that is hard to ignore. Notice, for example, how much more difficult it is to turn off the television in the middle of a news program than it is to stop reading a newspaper in the middle of an news article.

Ironically, because it is so easy to become involved in a television or radio program, we tend to tune out our critical judgment about the messages being sent. We can become so caught up in the show that we fail to question the motives, biases, and messages of the sender. Compared with an information-rich and "hot" medium like a textbook, cool media, such as radio and television, are highly interpretive and impressionable, making them ideal for drama, advertising, and propaganda. An important goal of media literacy, therefore, is to make our students aware that, as Mc-Luhan said, "the medium is the message" and to develop a healthy skepticism for what they see and hear on television. Media literate students who are aware of the effects that media can have on messages are more likely to scrutinize television programs for hidden meanings.

Another aspect of mass media, which media literacy addresses, is the kind of reality that media portrays. Like other aspects of society—government, religion, big business—that loom over our lives, mass media shapes both our identity and what we think constitutes life in twenty-first century America. Media literacy challenges this status quo by asking, "who is being represented in the mass media and who is being excluded?" This facet of media literacy that Kellner (2002) calls "critical visual literacy" also examines how people are being represented in the media. One way to help students achieve critical visual literacy is to have them reflect on how, for instance, the characters in the television programs they watch are portrayed. By asking themselves questions like, "Is one group or class of people being routinely depicted in a certain way?" students will develop an increased ability to detect the presence of stereotypes in the media.

Critical visual literacy also involves asking questions about who controls the media. Access to the means to both send and receive information is a vital element of a democracy; if the media are controlled by just a powerful few, then everyone else is reduced to being merely a passive listener. Some theorists, such as Daniel Chandler (2000), offer a Marxian point of view that media are a "means of production" used to "disseminate the ideas and worldviews of the ruling class, and deny or defuse alternative ideas." When working classes have no access to media—especially mass media—they have no chance to present an alternative to the values and reality imposed by the ruling class. By contrast, when people have the opportunity to express themselves through the media, they become contributors to a more culturally diverse society.

Almost overnight, the Internet has radically changed this situation by, for the first time, putting the power of mass media in the hands of anyone who can create a Web page. Besides democratizing the media, this also provides students with an authentic opportunity to experience and practice social responsibility. The Web sites that students create are not just arts-and-crafts exercises that will never be seen outside the classroom. Rather, their Web creations are adult mass multimedia with the potential of reaching an international audience. Through their Web sites, students can express their own ideas about important global issues such as pollution, hunger, and political oppression. In doing so, they experience being citizens of the "global village" that McLuhan spoke of years ago.

When students become media producers, their media literacy improves in two important ways. First, they become consciously aware of media as a force in their lives. Among schoolchildren who lack media literacy, media is an abstract concept that, like water to a fish, is an invisible part of their surrounding environment. However, media becomes a reality for students once they engage in the concrete experience of media production. This activity also strips the media of its mystery, thereby reducing the likelihood that media literate persons will be entranced and influenced by the bells and whistles of high-tech multimedia.

As they work together to build a Web page or shoot a video, students are also confronted by the politics of media production—who decides what is going to be communicated and how it will be done? Once students are faced with these sorts of issues, they inevitably begin to ask similar questions about the media produced by others, such as the television programming they watch at home: "Is my own race, class, or gender being represented in the mass media and, if so, is the representation accurate, fair, and free of stereotyping?"

A second way that media production promotes media literacy is by making students more mindful about the message content in the media they experience. As mentioned earlier, students start to recognize their social responsibility when entrusted with the power of Web-based mass communications. Whether building a Web site or shooting a video, students will need to clarify the purpose of the media they are creating and the message they intend for it to deliver. This should lead them to ask questions about their Web site that deal with social and ethical values such as, "Can this information be accessed by people with impaired vision or hearing?" and "Is the information presented truthful and of benefit to others?" In the process of wrestling with these matters, students increase their ability to critically judge the media around them and ask, for example, whether the Web sites of others are being used for socially useful, trivial, self-serving, or evil purposes.

Traditionally, it is the school system in a society that carries the responsible of ensuring that its citizens can read and write. Therefore, it is logical to also look to the elementary and secondary classroom as the best place to foster media literacy. Recall the earlier suggestion that a potentially effective strategy for doing this is to have students collaboratively produce media as part of classroom instruction. Interestingly, as students start to develop media literacy, the classroom environment itself changes. Consider, for example, the different kinds of instructional media—videos, computer-based training, PowerPoint shows, posters, and CD-ROMs—used in the classroom. When such media are shown to the class, media literate students are more unlikely to practice active learning, questioning both the content and design of what they see and hear compared with students with poor media literacy. It is doubtful that students with media literacy will be content to sit passively, allowing themselves to be spoon fed by whatever information appears on the screen. On the contrary, learners who have produced media in the past will, in all likelihood, want to be part of the show and collaborate with the teacher to produce their own instructional media. In theory, media literacy has the potential to transform the classroom from a setting where students are passive, uninvolved, and isolated to a learner-centered and collaborative environment where active learning occurs.

Society greatly benefits from having citizens who are media literate, because they are able to make critical judgments about the information contained in newspapers and on radio, television, and the Web. In the *Wizard of Oz,* Dorothy and her companions were, at first, awed by the media trickery of the wizard—the gigantic spectacle and booming voice, the billows of smoke and the flashing lights, all designed to scare and intimidate visitors. Eventually, however, they grew skeptical of the media razzle-dazzle and looked behind the curtain to reveal the wizard's real nature. This is precisely the point of media literacy: To empower students and others to critically "look behind the curtain" of the mass media they encounter every day and, by doing so, reveal the truth.

References

Chandler, D. (2000). *Marxist media theory*. Retrieved April 22, 2002, from University of Wales, Media and Communications Studies Web site. Available: http://www.aber.ac.uk/media/Documents/marxism/marxism.html

Kellner, D. (2002). Critical perspectives on visual imagery in media and cyberculture. *Journal of Visual Literacy, 22*(1), 81–90.

McLuhan, H. M. (1994). *Understanding media: The extensions of man*. Cambridge, MA: The MIT Press.

Further Reading

The Media Literacy Review. A biannual online publication of the University of Oregon. Retrieved April 22, 2002, from http://interact.uoregon.edu/MediaLit/mlr/home

Tufte, E. R. (1990). *Envisioning information*. Cheshire, CT: Graphics Press.

Visual Literacy: Critical Thinking with the Visual Image

Roymieco A. Carter

Literacy is the ability to comprehend and create messages that convey intentions and concepts. The process of recognizing visual information, understanding that information, and then taking the appropriate actions based on the representation is a normal part of our everyday lives. Being able to receive visual information, comprehend its intentions then respond visually reflects the competencies of a visually literate person.

Children will observe adult interactions sometimes emulating what they see. They are demonstrating a level of visual literacy through their actions. In the act of emulation or play the child perceives the event or action, makes an attempt to understand the action, and then responds by becoming the new transmitter of the absorbed content. It is important to understand that even though this is a simplistic representation its relevance is based on its familiarity. How are these skills nurtured and made more acute in the comprehension of the multimedia interactions of our everyday lives? What happens when we use this skill set as a method of critical inquiry?

PRINCIPLES OF VISUAL PERCEPTION

The skills needed to become visually literate are rooted in the means of expression and the structure of the visual composition. Expression comprises eight main components:

- Subject Matter
- Content
- Author
- Context
- Form
- Audience
- Technique
- Message

The question "What is this about?" centers on the visual composition's theme. What is the person, object, place, or event that is the purpose of the visual representation? When asking the student to identify the subject matter of a visual representation, it is important to inform the student that the subject matter may or may not be visible in the visual field. The subject may also be represented by a substituted object or element in the visual field. The subject matter may be intentionally omitted from the composition. When the subject is not visible or substituted the key is to look at the objects that are present and ask the questions "What is missing?" and "Why is it not here?" This seemingly simple exercise

is at the foundation for discussions about visual literacy and critical thinking. This level of inquiry will open the doors to the other components. Following the discussions of subject matter is the need to discuss visual content.

Content is often confused with the subject. The content is the emotional, philosophical, or intellectual message embodied in the visual representation, not simply a description of the subject. When the question "What does it mean?" is asked, it is important to reflect on the question "What is it?" These questions are not the same; however, the subject matter and the content may be the same element. This is true of some popular or commercial imagery. Contemporary commercials rely on the montage or the visual story as a subject of not as a particular element in the composition. This practice is understood as high concept. The term high, however, does not denote exclusive or overly intellectual. It does mean centralized or thematic. Film will use high concept because it is an easy sell. The public is quickly able to comprehend and respond to the movie trailers or the 30 second television commercial. In the genre of high concept representations, the essential meaning, significance, and/or aesthetic value are important but not pushed to the forefront of the composition. Understanding the content of a visual means that the viewer is relying on the sensory perception, psychological affect, and emotional properties called to the consciousness of the viewer. Some examples of the visual uses of high concept are as follows:

- *The Matrix:* A movie where the main character discovers his perception of the world is not real and that we are simply a fuel source for existence: http://what isthematrix.warnerbros.com

- *12 Monkeys:* A man is sent back from the future to save the earth only to be thrown into a mental institution in the past: http://movieweb.com/movie/12monkeys

- *Toyota Commercial:* A stereotypical car salesman teaches "real" people about the skills needed for selling great cars (five-spot series)

- *Volkswagen:* Two people ride around town in their Volkswagen and discover the rhythm to living

The emotional and/or psychological qualities of a composition can be a product of the techniques utilized by the developer of the visual message.

Technique can be understood as the manner, skill, or craftsmanship the developer demonstrates in using their tools to represent the content. The developer of the visual field is utilizing the tools to maximize the desired influence of the author's message. The recognition of technique will demonstrate the variation of aesthetic quality. This will, in turn, clarify the viewer's perception of the author's intended concept. When we are asked to understand an idea, we often times look at the person expressing the idea. This source is the author, or represents the author, of the message being communicated. Why are we looking at the source? Also, what do we hope to gain by looking at the author? The author will provide the viewing audience with visual cues. The visual message is formatted and structured by the author. The author is staging the representation. In the process of an exercise, the teacher can focus the students attention and inquiry on the source/author, subject, and content as perhaps the initial steps to acquiring a visual literacy and skills necessary for critical thinking.

The visual may be nonobjective, abstract, or representational. The nonobjective visual will tell the viewer that the author is not attempting to transfer information about the look of an object. The visual is a coded message reflecting the author's attention to character, function, and/or mood. The visual is not intended to be a one-to-one representation. The use of abstraction by the author is intended to operate similarly to the nonobjective visual, but the visual elements within the composition can be understood through the association to the object in the real world. Abstraction is positioned for the analysis and critique that needs to be done for comprehension. It is a mode of representation that de-emphasizes the hierarchy and removes the focus of the archetypal truth. The archetypal truth is held and gains much of its visual strength from purely representational information. It happens to be the most familiar visual form of the three types. The author is the regulator of the representational image. The author utilizing this image is building a detailed record of an object, person, or event. The information presented visually offers an imitation of the real world. The usage is so accessible that the receivers of the visual information may take the presented message for granted and not comprehend its complexity. Visual messages come first, primarily leading the composition, making it easy for the author to hide in plain sight of the receiver of the visual information.

There are many layers to the visual interaction, none as easy to misinterpret as the author. The author is most often assumed to be the mode of delivery. It is important to note that this may be true but not evident in all cases. To identify, therefore, means we are no longer allowed the stability of status quo thinking. The information being represented is accepted as a complex, layered interaction that will not reveal its multiplicity of meaning until it is filtered for the author's intent. It is essential to capture, in the depths of the presentation, the relationship between the surface visual elements and those whose existence and hidden forms perform the essential functions. Given this concept, what do we see when we watch Primedia's ChannelOne Network provider of television educational programming for the classroom? It claims to be a learning community of 12,000 schools. These 12,000 schools comprise 8 million students and 400,000 educators. The merit of such a structure and representation is clear in its ability to generate interest and gather more than 150 awards, one such award being the George Foster Peabody Award (ChannelOne Network). This award is in recognition of distinguished achievement and meritorious service by a radio or television organization (Peabody Awards). The surface visual of ChannelOne is its delivery of news material to students in an environment that supports dialogue and inquiry. The reason for placing the television programming in the classroom is that the information reaches students who may not otherwise watch news programming. The method is sound: Why not expose students to world events in an atmosphere where they are encouraged to ask questions and can have those questions answered by a trained educator? The implementation of the information may lead the students and the parents to think that the school, or an academically driven source, authors this information. Primedia, Inc. is actually a target media company. It operates in the commercial arena of publishing (Active Media Guide). It is functioning as a provider of specialized information in the consumer, business-to-business, and education markets. The hidden forms embed-

ded, in the visual interaction, are the commercial spaces sold and integrated with the educational content. Two minutes of commercial space is presented with every 10 minutes of educational material (ChannelOne Overview). Understanding this about the author allows the viewer to be critical of the information being presented. It makes sense then to ask why Primedia, the publisher of periodical such as *Seventeen* and *Soap Opera Digest,* provides students with news paired with popular movie trailers, commercials for teen-driven television shows, soft drinks, junk food, and credit cards (Ruskin, 2000). What are the lessons surrounding the presentation of these commercial advertisements? When attempting to comprehend a visual message, determine whether the author is a part of the delivery or a distant component of the interaction.

As a matter of practice, when attempting to uncover the author, the viewer of the complex visual should make himself or herself aware of the context. Visuals have a location and time that reflect their context. We need to consider the temporal and regional effects contributing to the representation. When confronted with a visual narrative or still image that was created outside of the current frame of reference, we must locate the necessary information that will make known the important social norms and behavioral conditions relevant to the image. The same is true when decoding a visual from an unfamiliar region. The viewer should make a focused effort to uncover the social norms and dominant behaviors indicative to the region of the image's creation. Given this, it is important to uncover answers to such questions as follow: Are the current social issues different or similar to those current to the time in which the visual is attempting the to be comprehended? Is the region for which this visual was made, different from the audience currently viewing it? Does the viewer of a particular time and region, comprehend the representation, based on another time and region? If the viewer tries to comprehend the visual and finds the context inaccessible, it will be difficult to obtain an accurate read of the visual. The reason for this is that the viewer then relies on "a kernel of truth" to comprehend and respond and not on a contextualized, informed read and response. If we are to embrace the idea that we can encode images as well as actions, the practice of critical inquiry becomes a sister conversation to discussions of form. Why use this image and not that image? Why include these objects, while being fully aware that we are making choices to leave other items out of the visual space? When the conversations spiral around the image as a lifeless object, arranged without intent or meaning, we are reducing the conversation to one of form.

Equal interest must be given to the visual aspects of the composition and the way they are interrelating on the visual plane. Visual elements are the formal components, often referred to as the building blocks of the visual composition. Presented below are brief descriptions of the visual elements.

- Point—the location or area of focus within the composition
- Line—the direction of vision created by the arrangement of objects.
- Value—the lightness and darkness of a composition
- Shape—the two-dimensional representation of length and width, enclosing a space
- Color—the recognition of reflected light, expresses mood or time

- Texture—the representation of how things might feel, optical or tactile
- Scale—the relative size relationship among the visual elements

Using these elements as filters for understanding the structure of the visual composition, the viewer decodes the arrangement of the composition. The ability to read complex arrangements will guide the viewer toward analytic relationships that are reflected through choice and position of elements. Asking questions, such as How large is it? How wide is it? and How deep is it? is crucial to the comprehension of a complex concept. Form is found in both the two-dimensional and three-dimensional spaces. The square is easily understood as a two-dimensional shape if it is never looked at from the other angles. The complexity involved with repositioning the object to reveal the other sides allows the viewer a greater understanding of the object as a three-dimensional object. We should understand that, although the elements are basic units of composition, the decoding of these units might be reflections of culture, gender, location, age, and experience. This, however, cannot be treated lightly because information apprehended from the interaction, with attention to the cultural background, gender, location, age, and experience, will open key doors of inquiry. These identity components will also help the viewer construct or write an informed visual to extend the potential dialogue. The opposite is true if we only receive our life information and experience from one source or perspective. In doing so, we limit our ability to see the complexity of the conditions that we hope to understand and then formulate a response.

As we have seen, the layered intricacy of the visual message leads to conversations of complexity. The formal traditional approaches to inquiry would be placed most often opposite the literacy of abstraction and inclusion. Teachers need to study visual literacy to capitalize on its potential for critical thinking. As educators, we must be open to the multiple interpretations visual literacy offers. Our worlds are inundated with visual imagery and it is crucial that students and teachers become critically visually literate. At the intersection of visual literacy and critical thinking are discovery and inquiry, particularly questioning and a reclaiming of curiosity for the sake of learning about our world and ourselves. The process of discovery and inquiry are natural acts. We are made aware of spaces, objects, and elements. We then set out to test the limitations of our new assumptions and interactions. The variety of everyday life sets new constraints on visual literacy. What we understand today, we may find unsettling tomorrow. Becoming visually literate means that we will not only be unsettled in our desire to understand, but we will also have to find resolve to take action.

References

Active Media Guide. Available: http://www.activemedia-guide.com/profile_primedia.htm

ChannelOne Network. Available: http://www.channelone.com

ChannelOne Overview. Available: http://www.commercialalert.org/channel_one

The Peabody Awards. Available: http:.www.peabody.uga.edu/about/index.html

Ruskin, G. (2000, April 18). Guest viewpoint: Let's keep advertising—and market research—out of the classroom. *School Board News.* Available: http://www.nsba.org/site/doc_sbn.asp

Further Reading

Arnheim, R. (1974). *Art and visual perception.* Berkeley: University of California Press.

McCloud, S. (1994). *Understanding comics: The invisible art.* New York: Harper Perennial.

Rand, P. (1985). *A designer's art.* New Haven, CT: Yale University Press.

Mass Media

Mass Media and Communication

Christine M. Quail

This article consists of a critical look at communication systems (which include the media) and the impact of communication on the development of economic and political systems, or processes of social production. A student or teacher of complex critical thinking needs to understand how different processes in society are interlinked and that this interlinkage is what we, in effect, call society. When a complex critical thinker looks at these processes over the span of time, one uncovers a complex critical view of history. Knowledge production and consciousness occur within and between the intersections of the economic, political, and communicative practices of society and society's interactions with the natural world.

To explore this topic, I shall first introduce what complex critical thinking about communication entails. Then I will provide a whirlwind tour through human history describing the communication and social organization of different stages of civilization. I shall then dwell on the formation of industrial culture and the implications of an industrialized communication system. The purpose of this piece is two-fold. The first is to describe an epis-temological and ontological position of a complex critical thinker who wishes to pursue an inquiry into the subject of communication and the processes of knowledge, consciousness, and ideology formation. And second, to turn the process of complex critical thinking to the subject itself and develop a historiography of communication in human society.

YOU AND I ARE IN DIFFERENT WORLDS

To discuss the roles of the communication system in the formation of cognition and the challenges it poses for complex critical thinking, we need to understand a few basic concepts about how communication and language operate in the formation of personal and collective consciousness. First, since the adoption of language, all people in all societies have existed simultaneously in two different, but symbiotic, worlds—the physical world of material relations and a symbolic world of discursive relations. The physical world is the world that would be regarded by typical Western science as the "real world"—one that is objectified and quantifiable. The symbolic world is the realm of ideas and language.

The second notion that lays the foundation for critical thinking about communication is that the material and symbolic worlds are, at the same time, both individual and collective experiences. You experience an immediate physical reality as you live your life and move through space. Likewise, on any level of social division, from the global down to the local or familial level, people share a physical reality and exist in certain places during specific times in history. The symbolic world of a single person is the private world of that individual's thoughts and beliefs, their methods of interpretation and response. All methods of communication and interpretation depend on the trust that others have access to the same repository of concepts, that is, that others share a similar symbolic universe.

The third basic concept underlying critical thinking about communication is that the physical and symbolic worlds are not discrete and mutually exclusive but are, in fact, mutually constitutive. Simply put, the physical world shapes the symbolic world, while, at the same time, the symbolic world gives definition to the physical world. It is very important to point out that this relationship is not causal or linear. A complex critical thinker would acknowledge that mutually constitutive processes are perpetually changing processes that interact with each other and that these interactions give form and definition to the process itself. In other words, the symbolic world describes the physical world so that people can understand and interact with their surroundings. But through the observation, interaction and utilization of the physical world, people developed language and different systems of communication.

Complex critical thinking about the mass media, or communication in general, involves the practice of uncovering and describing the ways that people negotiate their existence within and between the symbolic and physical world, while at the same time recognizes how this negotiation changes the nature of both the physical and symbolic worlds. In pursuing this mode of critical inquiry, it is important to explore how these negotiations are individual and collective experiences of cognition formation. Through the practice of critically articulating these relationships, it is possible to conceptualize and critically assess the formation and deployment of power through mass media and the resulting implications for cognition. At different stages of history and in different geographical locations, a complex critical thinker can uncover and reflect on these negotiations, and utilize complex critical thinking to discuss the deployment of power in the shaping of these worlds and to think about how power is implicated in the formation of economic and political systems.

HISTORICAL RELATIONSHIPS AMONG ECONOMIC, POLITICAL, AND COMMUNICATIONS SYSTEMS

Complex critical thinking about media and communication considers these processes in historical context or historical specificity. Critical thinkers have pointed to an observable transhistoric trend in the relationship between those who control economic and political systems and those in charge of communication systems. The elite class has the dominant influence in all these areas of society, and they use their power to maintain their eliteness. Those who are economically powerful are influential in government policymaking and in the content of media. Those who control the government pass laws that are in the economic interest of themselves and the other elites. The elite media controllers create ideology and control knowledge production to complement their control of power and wealth. These relationships are seen through different eras of human life, as various modes of production have evolved along with the social systems that govern the distribution of wealth, power, and knowledge. Despite the changing forms of social institutions and organizations, the symbiotic relationship that perpetuates the rule of an elite class remains. Critical thinking about different historical eras and the dominant mode of production during that time examines the ways that material and discursive (or linguistic) life are experienced and expressed.

HUNTING AND GATHERING SOCIETY

Critical thinking about hunting and gathering links material and communicative life. Hunting and gathering is arguably the earliest human mode of production. Ironically, contrary to the assumptions of "civilization," some historians refer to society of this time period as the original affluent society. Lasting from about 2.5 million years b.c. to about 3000 b.c., hunting and gathering society was based on kinship and divided into small nomadic tribes, with the eldest, most experienced, usually in charge. The tribes consumed what was immediately available through hunting animals or finding edible plants. All work was done in a collective and what was produced was shared with the collective community. When the local food supply became exhausted, they moved. This need for constant travel made portability the prime requisite and therefore they owned no ma-

terial possessions except for the minimal tools necessary for survival. People, too, were left behind when they could no longer travel, having grown too old or sick. Hunting and gathering societies did not produce any surplus.

In thinking critically about this mode of production, it stands to reason that these societies relied on an oral culture. The tribe's history and culture was passed from generation to generation through storytelling, songs, and poetry. These mnemonic devices codified the aggregate knowledge and understanding that helped perpetuate the survival of the tribe. The eldest member of the tribe was usually in charge of retelling the stories and leading the singing. Having no permanent record, the knowledge was dynamic and changed with different contexts or landscapes. The human voice, therefore, was the main means of communication and interaction, and it involved only those who were within the immediate range of the speaker. Being exclusively personal, the hunting and gathering communication system involved a lot of feedback and was extremely interactive. Every member of the society literally had a voice and, thus, it was impossible for the communication system to be monopolized. The local scale of the communication system was effective for small and isolated groups.

In hunting and gathering tribes, the only people who existed were those who worked to support the tribe, so one could say that they were their own elite class. This is the only mode of production in human history that was able to support the entire need of the community. The only time a tribe member went hungry would be when there was no food, and in this case the entire community was starving. The hunting and gathering stage was inherently more egalitarian than any other. The political goal was one of group survival, and food and work had to be shared if everyone was going to survive. Likewise, the communication system, the system of knowledge production, was organized to include everyone and support the group survival. Hunting rites, fertility rites, communal sing-alongs around campfires, and funeral and birth rites were all community efforts to deal with different aspects of life as a collective. Thus, by thinking critically about the relationship between the mode of material production and the mode of communication, we can understand this type of social organization to be what might be considered to be democratic today.

TRIBUTARY/SLAVE SOCIETY

Critical thinking about the historical specificity of communication and media and larger processes of social production leads us to think about the impact of agriculture on social relationships. The discovery of agriculture brought about the tributary/slave era, which lasted from about 3000 b.c. to the fall of Rome in 790 a.d. Agriculture created surplus in society. With the extra food, social division of labor and permanent settlements evolved. Because it was no longer required for all people to engage in working to provide food, some could use their time to develop new skills–such as professional ruling and knowledge production. These individuals became more adept at extracting the extra produce from others and started hording what they did not immediately consume. They could then use their horde—their wealth—to hire mercenaries who would ensure that they could continue to extract wealth from the workers. Thus, society became stratified—a working class was formed that was expected to support the elite class.

People in the working class during the tributary/slave stage were either slaves (as in ancient Egypt, Greece, and Rome) or else they were serfs and paid tribute (as in India and China). The workers were allowed to retain the bare minimum that kept them alive and the elites took the entire surplus. Like the hunting and gathering tribes coming up with a community-oriented ideology, the tributary/slave system had to come up with its own set of social beliefs that would keep the system stable. Therefore, within the elite class there developed a group of professional ideology makers whose task was to convince the people that their role in society was "natural."

Critical thinking about historical specificity suggests that it was during the transition from the hunting and gathering mode of production to the tributary/slave mode of production that writing first emerged. The initial use of writing was economic, to keep track of the wealth being extracted from the slaves and titles of ownership. Soon, however, writing was utilized by the professional ideologues to create belief systems and religious texts. Be it the priesthood doctrine of Isis and Osiris or else the writings of Plato and Aristotle, the ideologues and their writings— which were ordained as truth from the gods—maintained and promoted the social order as just and the only "rational" way for society to exist. The physical writing down of philosophy and religious doctrine added extra weight and credibility to the ideas being described. The writing of these beliefs gave them permanence and thus could be past on to future generations in a constant, more static form—unlike the dynamism of oral tradition. The tributary/ slave media system created a belief that slavery was the only possible mode of production and would exist forever. Furthermore, these beliefs contended that some people were born to be slaves and were inherently inferior, while others were born superior and were meant to be the slave owners. It is important to remember when thinking critically about this era that the people who had the privilege to be born as slave owners were the only ones who had the opportunity to learn how to write and read. Their social status was invested in the maintenance of a communication system and system of social knowledge production that created a collective consciousness that supported their class privileges.

Slave-based economies were essentially stagnant. The workers had no incentive to work harder than the level at which they were driven, that is, coerced. In addition, technological advancement was extremely limited for fear that the slaves might use the new devices to revolt. These factors led to the downfall of this mode of production's dominance (although slavery continues in many forms today). Critical thinking about tributary/slave society, then, suggests an historical link between differentiation of power in terms of material and communicative processes. The end of the tributary/slave society in the West was precipitated by the destruction of the Roman Empire at the hands of Germanic and Slavic tribes. The tribal chiefs became a new elite class and the feudal system grew out of the vacuum left by the Romans. The feudal system was the basic social system of Europe during the Middle Ages.

WESTERN FEUDAL SOCIETY

Critical thinking about feudal society and its relationship to communication, as noted, sees this period in relation to earlier eras. Western feudal society begins with the social divisions outlined above. The lawless state of Europe made protection from bandits extremely important. A feudal system based on a hierarchy of allegiances, oaths of military protection, and economic support evolved in the place of a strong state presence. Serfs were protected by the local lord of the manor, who in turn held allegiance to a stronger overlord, and so on, each tier subservient to the next step up the feudal ladder to the king. The majority of people belonged to the serf class and paid tribute, either in money or in kind, for their protection. Adherence to the traditions and customs of this system of mutual obligations and services held the feudal system together.

Critical thinking about feudalism suggests that the ideological basis for the feudal system came from the notion of the Christian paternalist ethic. This Judeo-Christian moral code can be understood by comparing the organization of society to that of the organization of a patriarchal family. The poor serfs were seen as the "children" of the benevolent father-figure master. It is the lord's responsibility to take care of the "flock." To do this, he must be rich, and to be rich, he must extract the surplus wealth from the "children." The Christian religion's ideology was extremely instrumental in fostering the Christian paternalist ethic. The Judeo-Christian concept of an all-powerful heavenly father that watches and cares for his children was a central tenet to the patriarchal system.

Complex critical thinking about this era links the mode of production, the mode of knowledge production, and the communication system. The early Christian authors wrote extensively on the responsibilities of being rich; as a result, the Christian paternalist ethic was firmly entrenched in social consciousness early in the feudal stage. In a similar fashion to the writings of Plato and Aristotle, the Church tendered the notion that the social relations of the feudal society were natural and eternal, having been ordained by God. Thus, the Christian paternalist ethic was used to defend the inequalities and intense exploitation that were a result of the concentration of wealth and power in the elite classes of the Church and nobility.

In review, complex critical thinking about the historical specificity of communication systems takes the time to explore a social milieu; political and economic constructs; and the ways that knowledge is produced, reproduced, disseminated, and changed. The three modes of production and social organization I just outlined all share a common characteristic—a communication system that developed in a mutually constitutive relationship with the political and economic processes that maintained the status quo. The oral culture of the hunting and gathering tribes complemented the group effort to survive. Ironically, although many times viewed as primitive and uncivilized, this mode of production had the greatest success in providing for all members of the society with the least expenditure of labor. It is also the longest lasting mode—today, remote and isolated tribes still retain this existence. The tributary/slave cultures used literate ideologists to explain the natural way of life, which just happened to benefit the elite class of the same ideologists. Similarly, the ideology of the feudal system's Christian paternalist ethic codified a stratified society as "God's plan." Complex critical thinking about the historical development of communication systems and society reveals a transhistoric relationship between the deployment of discursive power and the maintenance of economic and political systems that support the elite status of a privileged few over the working masses.

Before the invention of the printing press, publication was a long and arduous task. Monks and priests painstakingly recopied religious and historical tracts in devotion to their god and for the preservation of ancient writings. As mentioned previously, writing was also used to keep track of financial matters (i.e., state taxes, population censuses, property ownership, business receipts, and church tithes). Hand copying was much too time consuming to allow for a wider dissemination of written information. Literacy was extremely rare and almost entirely exclusive to the clergy. It was their job to provide spiritual guidance to the illiterate masses, which included many of the feudal lords. Critical thinking about print culture suggests that the monopoly over knowledge held by the ecclesiastical class led to substantial control over the notions and common beliefs people held. The more modern forms of industrial and postindustrial society are not an exception to this trend, which I shall discuss in the next section of this article.

THE INDUSTRIALIZATION OF CULTURE

Complex critical thinking about media also involves looking at key factors in the construction of contemporary communication: industrialization and mass production. During the middle of the fifteenth century when the first printing press was put to use, the monopoly of knowledge held by the Church was suddenly broken. This momentous occasion set into motion processes that changed the human world in nearly every aspect.

One particular result of the printing press was to turn published writing—and eventually culture—into a commodity. Books, prior to the creation of the printing press, were extremely rare and were available only to the richest of the elite or to the clergy. Critical thinking about the printing press suggests that the first form of mass-mediated culture developed as books and other printed materials became available to a much larger audience. The dissemination of ideas, via a route alternate to one dependent on the Church, began public questioning of the Church's monopoly over knowledge production and thus raised public consciousness. A demand for the production of secular knowledge developed. Centuries after the invention of the printing press industrial culture immerged as the technologies of industrial production were put to the task of creating cultural commodities. From the presses that produced the daily newspaper and the development of cinemas and film to the utilization of airwaves to transmit radio and television signals, mass-mediated forms of communication utilize the technologies that are the legacy of the industrial revolution.

Thinking critically about the social implications of the industrial revolution, we see that as a result of the changing technological, economic, and political systems the process of producing culture was turned over to the rules governing the marketplace. "Culture here becomes a part of material production . . . and is subject to the same laws of economic production as other industrial spheres. This leads to what is called the industrialization of culture." Rather than the written word and other forms of cultural work being subsidized by the surplus of other economic sectors (as in previous stages of history), the culture industry sells cultural commodities to support itself. This process of commodification has a fundamental impact on the content, form, and distribution of what is produced (Jhally, 1989, p. 73).

The implications of this content can be thought about critically. We can start by acknowledging that the content of culture produced by a culture industry is designed to appeal to the largest possible audience. For example, the more readers a newspaper garners, the higher a price it can charge for ad space and the greater the revenue generated from sales. An increased emphasis on sensationalism, especially in regard to sex and violence, can also be expected. The ideology of the culture industry usually mirrors the socially constructed normalities of its audience. The fear of losing readers if a news outlet strays too far into a particular political camp is a constant editorial concern. Thus, critical thinking leads us to conclude that the content of culture industry is one of "ruthless unity" and a recombinant mentality: if a certain item was a hit, then spin-off products are inevitable. This imitation phenomenon is based on a risk-reduction strategy, where content already proven to be successful is guaranteed to be recycled (Jhally, 1989, pp. 73–77).

Further critical thinking about the industrialization of communication, or the culture industry, allows us to analyze another aspect that shapes cultural/media content: the effect of advertising. Not only do the editors of a magazine or newspaper have to worry about readers canceling subscriptions, but the threat of advertisers pulling their accounts influences editorial policy. Thinking critically through the implications of this type of policy, we understand that there is a chilling effect on criticism of the advertiser and its products. The culture industry also has the responsibility of creating a "buying mood" in the audience. Taking this line of critical thinking to the next level, we see that this can lead to many ramifications: avoiding reporting about consumer debt; a plot line or dialogue revolving around a specific consumer product; and the use of fluff, soft news, and human interest stories rather than hard news (Bagdikian, 1992, p. 201; Jhally, 1989, pp. 74–75).

Complex critical thinking about industrialized communication also must understand the place of a particular cultural producer in a larger corporate context. As a profitable economic sector, a media/communication producer in the culture industry is often owned by a larger corporation with a diversity of interests to protect. A journalist would be very hesitant to write a story that conflicted with the desires of the parent company if he or she faced the possibility of losing his or her job. Ownership, through stock options and profit gleaning, is extremely profitable in the capitalist system and therefore elite owners have a high stake in maintaining the status quo of society to protect their unequal share of holdings. Therefore, thinking critically about the link between material goods and the values/ideologies produced and circulated in the media, we can easily say that the culture industry is also a consciousness industry. In the consciousness industry, media content is crafted to perpetuate and legitimize the capitalist mode of production, as well as to support ideologies, such as consumerism (Bagdikian, 1992, p. 205; Jhally, 1989, p. 68).

The result of a market economy on the form and production of communication and culture is mainly that of increasing advertisement space and the escalation of fixed and marginal costs. Complex critical thinking about this process asks us to again historicize, and we can choose a complementary example in nineteenth-century British press. This was the heyday of the radical, worker-oriented press. During the first half of the century, the fixed costs of setting up a newspaper press were low, and the content was provided by unprofessional and part-time publishers. They had

little or no advertising and made all revenue from sales of the newspaper. The most popular of these papers had circulations that almost doubled those of the conservative papers. However, at this time with the low fixed costs and the low marginal costs, a paper didn't have to have massive circulation to be successful. The change occurred when the newspaper began to rely on advertising for revenue. The prices of the mainstream papers dropped. To reach wider audiences the mainstream paper invested more capital in getting larger and more expensive presses. The professional news staff developed. The radical presses were not appealing to the advertisers—they had the "wrong demographics," and did not get advertising revenue. The few that did survive had to move up in the class system, tempering their political stance to target a more generalized audience, thus losing the original working-class audience. The radical presses could not afford the higher fixed costs, even if they weren't losing their audience and revenue to the cheaper mainstream papers. The form of the newspapers became much slicker and attractive to the consumer. They also became thicker, with more ads, and used the improved technology to print larger, higher-quantity runs (Bagdikian, 1992; see also Curran & Seaton, 1988).

Using critical thinking about the media industries, we can argue that, in the U.S. market system, the reliance on advertising and the tendency of capitalism toward concentration has created a very select oligopoly of cultural producers. There was a trend throughout this century that led to the establishment of one-newspaper towns and, then, one-newspaper regions with many newspapers owned by a single larger firm. Advertisers saw that the most reasonable course of action would be to place their ads in the papers with the highest circulation. The competing papers, even if they had hundreds of thousands of subscribers, did not get the advertisement revenue and went bankrupt. This left a single monopoly paper, which saved advertisers money, even though they were forced to pay monopoly prices, by eliminating duplicating ads in different newspapers. As newspapers pushed out their circulation to reach more distant audiences, they became even more attractive to advertisers and, therefore, received more capital to continue the expansion. A newspaper cannot be started without huge fixed costs, and even if it did manage to start printing, the trend to one-paper towns would put it out of business (Bagdikian, 1992, pp. 196–199; Jhally, 1989, p. 68).

The complex critical question of who is targeted by the culture industry can be raised at this point. We see that the presumed consumer is also dictated by market concerns. Naturally, the industry wants to target the "best" group of people with the "right demographics" for the advertisers. These are usually young to middle-age adults with spending power, either middle or upper class. Therefore, the culture industry tends to focus less on minorities, the elderly, and the working class. This has the result of media emphasizing values that appeal to the targeted demographic (i.e., white, heterosexual, consumer-minded), increasing their visibility and also their perceived importance to the mass media audience (Bagdikian, 1992, p. 199).

Although thinking critically about communication across historical contexts may seem to indicate the futility and ultimate oppression of our communication processes, this is not the case. Because media and communication processes are human constructs, created by human actors in historical specificity, changing those systems is also possible through human struggle. The challenge of democratizing the media involves complex critical thinking, nullifying the excesses of capitalism, critical enlightenment, and reclaiming the right to participate. These goals are interrelated with complementary functions.

For example, complex critical thinking about media questions what actions can be taken to curb the power of corporate media. Controlling the power of the dominant few allows more people to participate; this participation leads to an enlightenment that will institute democratic ideologies to maintain the system. Criticism leads to political involvement—enough political involvement would create stronger antitrust enforcement. Participation provides understanding of media power, and thus an active, media-producing citizenry is an alternative to the culture industry.

For Ben Bagdikian, legislative reform and antitrust law enforcement is the solution. To bring competition back into the marketplace, the playing field must be leveled. Critical diversity of media production is the key to bringing back a media that serves the people, "for it is in diversity and openness that the genius of the United States can flower" (1992, p. 237). Ownership of media companies should be restricted and the acquisition of established firms could be made illegal. Cross-ownership of media needs to be limited. Advertising needs to be taxed progressively to reduce its presence. Complex critical thinking about media and communications might conceive of ways to implement these types of changes through policy initiatives.

Finally, complex critical thinking about media suggests that critical media literacy is a vital element in democratizing the media. There should be lifelong media education to counter the unawareness about media that perpetuates the system. Children need to be taught how to produce media to demystify the system, and how to become critical thinkers about the media. This will instill a higher demand, and subsequent responsibility, on the media to supply content that satisfies an audience with a better understanding of the media. Media literacy education can take many forms and be taught in many different contexts. If video production is not possible, magazines, newsletters, or graphic design can be used to help children think critically about the production of media. Furthermore, popular television, film, and advertising texts can be used in English and social studies classrooms to discuss themes and cultural values.

References

Bagdikian, B. H. (1992). *The media monopoly* (4th ed.). Boston: Beacon Press.

Jhally, S. (1989). The political economy of culture. In I. Angus, & S. Jhally (Eds.), *The political economy of culture* (pp. 65–81). New York: Routledge.

Further Reading

Adams, D., & Goldbard, A. (1989). Public policy and media literacy. *The Independent,* Aug/Sep.

Curran, J., & Seaton, J. (1988). *Power without responsibility* (3rd ed.). New York: Routledge.

Naureckas, J. (1995, April 17). We want the airwaves. *In These Times,* pp. 19–20.

Mathematics

Mathematics Education

Peter Appelbaum

Teachers of mathematics have been searching for ways to describe and enact critical thinking in their classrooms for a very long time. On the one hand, mathematics itself is often held up as the model of a discipline based on rational thought, clear, concise language, and attention to the assumptions and decision-making techniques that are used to draw conclusions. In the nineteenth century, a view of the mind as a muscle that could be trained and strengthened in particular skills (this has come to be called "faculty psychology") led many people to justify a central place for mathematics in the school curriculum, simply based on the belief that mathematics would train the mind in clear, logical thinking. To this day, employers often hire mathematics majors fresh out of college under the presumption that they have been trained to "think." On the other hand, teachers of mathematics have always been disappointed in the critical thinking that their students demonstrate. And there have been many research studies that point to a dismal chance of any sort of transfer of learning of critical thinking from the mathematics classroom into other realms of intellectual effort. Indeed, research has

failed to document any consistent transfer of what might be called "critical thinking skills" from even one branch of mathematical inquiry to another.

Back in 1938, Harold Fawcett was asked to publish his work with geometry students as the yearbook of the National Council of Teachers of Mathematics. This book introduced the idea that students could learn mathematics *through* experiences of critical thinking. This was a big leap from older ideas that promoted specific ideas about how to teach the skills of critical thinking. Fawcett wrote that there had never been a time in the history of education when the development of critical and reflective thought was not thought of as an important outcome of school; but he thought that this particular outcome had assumed increasing importance in the 1930s, and, further, that this importance held strong implications for the nature of the school curriculum itself.

The point Fawcett made was that it was pointless to try to teach critical thinking skills (e.g., comparing, contrasting, conjecturing, inducing, generalizing, specializing, classifying, categorizing, deducing, visualizing, sequencing, ordering, predicting, validating, proving, relating, analyzing, evaluating, and patterning; see O'Daffer & Thomquist, 1993). To learn mathematics, it would be better to take advantage of the critical thinking skills that students bring with them to school mathematics. His goals included the following ways that students could demonstrate that they were, in fact, thinking critically, as they participated in the experiences of the classroom. By

1. Selecting the significant words and phrases in any statement that are important, and asking that they be carefully defined.
2. Requiring evidence to support conclusions they are pressed to accept.
3. Analyzing that evidence and distinguishing fact from assumption.
4. Recognizing stated and unstated assumptions essential to the conclusion.
5. Evaluating these assumptions, accepting some and rejecting others.
6. Evaluating the argument, accepting or rejecting the conclusion.
7. Constantly reexamining the assumptions that are behind their beliefs and actions (Fawcett, 1938/1995, pp. 11–12, paraphrased).

Years later, in 1989, the National Council echoed this earlier call for critical thinking in its *Curriculum and Evaluation Standards*. Calling for classrooms that place critical thinking at the heart of instruction, the new *Standards* stated clearly that a pervasive emphasis on reasoning would be an essential aspect of all mathematical activity.

Presumably, more than a half century after Fawcett's lovely yearbook, thanks to years of research and accumulated teacher-lore, the Council had a clear set of ideas for how to accomplish this. Perhaps more interesting is the lack of any direct atten-

tion to critical thinking in the more recent *Principles and Standards,* published in 2000. Critical thinking is still present in the goals, but it has been subsumed by more holistic notions of what it means to teach, do, and understand mathematics. For example, in a discussion of *communication* in any K-12 mathematics classroom, we are urged to design experiences that enable students to do the following:

• Organize and consolidate their mathematical thinking through communication;
• Communicate their mathematical thinking coherently and clearly to peers, teachers, and others;
• Analyze and evaluate the mathematical thinking and strategies of others; and
• Use the language of mathematics to express mathematical ideas precisely.

How similar these ideas are to those promoted by Fawcett so many years earlier. We can see that little has changed in the mainstream ways that people tend to define critical thinking in the context of mathematics education. Yet careful attention to the details in the *Standards* does reveal increased sophistication in what the Council means by these goals. For example, there is increased interest in the idea that students must truly understand the strategies and mathematical thinking of others in the classroom community. Students are expected to search for the strengths and weaknesses of each and every strategy offered. It is no longer good enough to reach an answer to a problem that was posed. Now, students are cajoled into communicating their own ideas *well,* and to demand the same communication from others. A shift has occurred from listing skills to be learned toward attributes of classrooms that promote critical thinking as part of the experience of that classroom.

One way in which teachers can create such a classroom is by designing good ways for students to communicate with each other. More specifically, it is now recognized that reflection and communication are intertwined processes in mathematics learning. The Council recommends explicit attention and planning by teachers, so that communication for the purposes of reflection can become a natural part of mathematics learning. And the Council further urges that teachers focus on the building of a classroom community in which students feel free to express ideas. Additionally, teachers are asked to look for evidence that the students understand that contributions to this community include the skills of listening and developing an interest in the thoughts of others. It seems that the Council is asking teachers to spend more time on developing mathematics as an evolving literacy, rather than as a set of conventions and techniques to be mastered. Rather than rush to formal mathematical language, mathematics teachers should recognize mathematics as a group experience that requires reading, writing, listening, speaking, and the use of various modes of representation.

Students who have opportunities, encouragement, and support for speaking, writing, reading, and listening in mathematics classes reap dual benefits: they communicate to learn mathematics, and they learn to communicate mathematically (National Council of Teachers of Mathematics [NCTM], 2000, p. 60).

Nevertheless, from Fawcett in 1938 to the Council in 2000, we can identify a strand of undeveloped theory: Students are supposed to be communicating freely in some form of ideal democratic environment. They not only have freedom of speech but, indeed, are guaranteed an audience from the other members of their community. In this perfect democracy, students know that when they talk, people listen to them. And they grow to understand that it is this sort of communication that leads mutually to richer understanding of the material and increased sophistication in talking about mathematics. What is undeveloped, however, is a critical consideration of the context in which this perfect democracy is supposed to take place: The classroom is embedded in a society that determines a wide range of ways that students do not come to the same table with equal opportunities and resources at their disposal. Political theorists have noted that ideal speech communities require as much attention to these contextual realities, and to responses to them, as they require the generation of ways to organize democratic participation.

For the last century, teachers of mathematics have been figuring out how to drop the teaching of critical thinking in favor of establishing environments that allow for the critical thinking that is possible through discussion and interaction. This has meant abandoning long-cherished notions about what mathematics classrooms look like and what the products of such classrooms should be. Instead of timed tests with the number correct circled at the top, students now bring home portfolios of material amassed over time, or complex reports on open-ended investigations. Yet in the new millennium, teachers of mathematics are now beginning to realize that this can only go so far. They are likely to *still* be disappointed in the ways some of their students participate or contribute. The response to this current malaise, growing out of the more nuanced political awareness, is a movement called Critical Mathematics Education.

Critical Mathematics Education demands a critical perspective on both mathematics and the teaching/learning of mathematics. In doing so, it goes one step further in questioning our assumptions about what critical thinking could mean and what democratic participation should mean. As Ole Skovsmose (1994) describes, in a critical mathematics classroom the students (and teachers) are attributed a "critical competence." A century ago, we moved from teaching critical thinking skills to using the skills that students bring with them. We accepted that students, as human beings, *are* critical thinkers, and would display these skills if the classroom allowed such behavior. It seemed that we were not seeing critical thinking simply because we were preventing it from happening; through years of schooling, students were unwittingly trained *not* to think critically in order to succeed in school mathematics. So we found ways to lessen this "dumbing-down of thinking through school experiences." Now we understand human beings more richly as exhibiting a *critical competence,* and because of this realization, we recognize that decisive and prescribing roles must be abandoned in favor of all participants having control of the educational process. In this process, instead of merely forming a classroom community for discussion, Skovsmose suggests that the students and teachers together must establish a "critical distance." He explains that seemingly objective and value-free principles for the structure of the curriculum are put into a new perspective, in which such principles are revealed as value-loaded, necessitating critical consideration of contents and other subject-matter aspects as part of the educational process itself.

Keitel, Klotzmann, and Skovsmose (1993) together offer a new way for teachers to think about the mathematics that is being taught. New ideas for lessons and units emerge when teachers describe mathematics as a technology with the potential to work for democratic goals, and when they make a distinction between different types of knowledge based on the object of the knowledge. The first level of mathematical work, they write, presumes a true-false ideology and corresponds to much of what we witness in current school curricula. The second level directs students and teachers to ask about right method: Are there other algorithms? Which are valued for our need? The third level emphasizes the appropriateness and reliability of the mathematics for its context. This level raises the particularly technological aspect of mathematics by specifically investigating the relationship between means and ends. The fourth level requires participants to interrogate the appropriateness of formalizing the problem for solution—a mathematical/technological approach is not always wise and participants would consider this issue as a form of reflective mathematics. In the fifth level, a critical mathematics education studies the implications of pursuing special formal means: It asks how particular algorithms affect our perceptions of (a part of) reality, and how we conceive mathematical tools when we use them universally. Thus, the role of mathematics in society becomes a component of reflective mathematical knowledge. Finally, the sixth level examines reflective thinking itself as an evaluative process, comparing levels 1 and 2 as essential mathematical tools, levels 3 and 4 as the relationship between means and ends, and level 5 as the global impact of using formal techniques. In this final level, reflective evaluation as a process is noted as a tool itself and, as such, becomes an object of reflection. When teachers and students plan their classroom experiences by making sure that all of these levels are represented in the group's activities, it is more likely that students, and teachers, can be attributed the critical competence that we envision as a more general goal of mathematics education.

In formulating a democratic, critical mathematics education, it is also essential that teachers grapple with the serious multicultural indictments of mathematics as a tool of postcolonial and imperial authority. What we once accepted as pure, wholesome truth is now understood as culturally specific and tied to particular interests. Philip Davis and Reuben Hersh (1987) and David Berliner (2000), for instance, have described some aspects of mathematics as a tool in accomplishing a fantasy of control over human experience. They use the examples of math-military connections, math-business connections, and others.

Critical mathematics educators ask why students, in general, do *not* see mathematics as helping them to interpret events in their lives, or gain control over human experience. They search for ways to help students appreciate the marvelous qualities of mathematics without adopting its historic roots in militarism and other fantasies of control over human experience. Arthur Powell and Marilyn Frankenstein (1997) have collected valuable essays in *ethnomathematics* and the ethnomathematical responses that educators can make to contemporary mathematics curricula. Ethnomathematics makes it clear that mathematics and mathematical reasoning are cultural constructions. This raises the challenge to embrace the global variety of cultures of mathematical activity and to confront the politics that would be unleashed by such attention in a typical North American school. That is, ethnomathematics demands most clearly that critical thinking in a mathematics classroom is a seriously political act.

One important direction for critical mathematics education is in the examination of the authority to phrase the questions for discussion. Who sets the agenda in a critical thinking classroom? Stephen Brown and Marion Walter (1999) lay out a variety of powerful ways to rethink mathematics investigations in their book, *The Art of Problem Posing,* and, in doing so, they give us a number of ideas for enabling students to "talk back" to mathematics and to use their problem-solving and problem-posing experiences to learn about themselves as problem solvers and problem posers. In the process, they help us to frame yet another dilemma for future research in mathematics education: Is it always more democratic if students pose the problem? The kinds of questions that are possible, and the ways that we expect to phrase them, are to be examined by a critical thinker. Susan Gerofsky (2001) has recently noted that the questions themselves reveal more about our fantasies and desires than about the mathematics involved. Critical mathematics education has much to gain from her analysis of mathematics problems as examples of literary genre.

And finally, it becomes crucial to examine the discourses of mathematics and mathematics education in and out of school and popular culture (Appelbaum, 1995). Critical thinking in mathematics education asks how and why the split between popular culture and school mathematics is evident in mathematical discourse, and why such a strange dichotomy must be resolved between mathematics as a commodity and as a cultural resource. Mathematics is a commodity in our consumer culture because it has been turned into stuff (knowledge) that people collect to spend later (on the job market, to get into college, etc.). But it is also a cultural resource, because it is a world of metaphors and ways of making meaning through which people can interpret their world and describe it in new ways. Critical mathematics educators recognize the role of mathematics as a commodity in our society; but they search for ways to effectively emphasize the meaning-making aspects of mathematics as part of the variety of cultures. In doing so, they make it possible for mathematics to be a resource for political action.

The history of critical thinking in mathematics is a story of expanding contexts. Early reformers recognized that training in skills could not lead to the behaviors they associated with someone who is a critical thinker. Mathematics education has adopted the model of enculturation into a community of critical thinkers. By participating in a democratic community of inquiry, it is imagined, students are allowed to demonstrate the critical thinking skills they posses as human beings and to refine and examine these skills in meaningful situations. Current efforts recognize the limitations of mathematical enculturation as inadequately addressing the politics of this enculturation. Critical mathematics educators us the term "critical competence" to subsume earlier notions of critical thinking skills and propensities. A politically concerned examination of the specific processes of participation and the role of mathematics in supporting a democratic society enhances the likelihood of critical thinking in mathematics.

References

Appelbaum, P. (1995). *Popular culture, educational discourse, and mathematics.* Albany: State University of New York Press.

Berliner, D. (2000). *The advent of the algorithm: The idea that rules the world.* New York: Harcourt Brace.

Brown, S., & Walter, M. (1999). *The art of problem posing.* Mahwah, NJ: Lawrence Erlbaum.

Davis, P., & Hersh, R. (1987). *Descartes' dream: The world according to mathematics.* San Diego: Harcourt, Brace, Jovanovich.

Fawcett, H. (1938/1995). *The nature of proof* (National Council of Teachers of Mathematics [NCTM] 1938 Yearbook). Reston, VA: NCTM.

Gerofsky, S. (2001). Genre analysis as a way of understanding pedagogy in mathematics education. In J. Weaver, M. Morris, & P. Appelbaum (Eds.), *(Post) modern science (education): Propositions and alternative paths* (pp. 147–176). New York: Peter Lang.

Keitel, C., Klotzmann, E., & Skovsmose, O. (1993). Beyond the tunnel vision: Analyzing the relationship between mathematics, society and technology. In C. Keitel, & K. Ruthven (Eds.), *Learning from computers: Mathematics education and technology* (pp. 243–279). New York: Springer-Verlag.

National Council of Teachers of Mathematics (NCTM). (1989). *Curriculum and evaluation standards for school mathematics.* Reston, VA: NCTM.

National Council of Teachers of Mathematics (NCTM). (2000). *Principles and standards for school mathematics.* Reston, VA: NCTM. Available: http://standards.nctm.org/

O'Daffer, P. G., & Thomquist, B. (1993). Critical thinking, mathematical reasoning, and proof. In P. S. Wilson (Ed.), *Research ideas for the classroom: High school mathematics* (pp. 39–56). New York: Macmillan/NCTM.

Powell, A., & Frankenstein, M. (1997). *Ethnomathematics: Challenging eurocentrism in mathematics education.* Albany: State University of New York Press.

Skovsmose, O. (1994). *Toward a philosophy of critical mathematics education.* Dordrecht, Netherlands: D. Reidel.

Further Reading

Brown, S. I. (2001). *Reconstructing school mathematics: Problems with problems and the real world.* New York: Peter Lang.

Glazer, E. (2001). *Using internet primary sources to teach critical thinking skills in mathematics.* Westport, CT: Greenwood Publishing Group.

Skovsmose, O. (2000). Aphorism and critical mathematical education. *For the Learning of Mathematics, 20*(1), 2–8.

Organizational Change

Organizational Change in Public Education: From Crucial to Critical Leadership

Erik Malewski

What do critically conscious educators need to know about educational leadership? Organizational worlds are moving in new directions that dissolve traditional conceptions of how humans move through time and space. We have the *ability* to send electronic messages across the world in seconds; the *possibility* that simulations in video games and movies look so realistic that we no longer differentiate between realism, imagination, and replication; and the *opportunity* to observe a population of organizations as they change the character of consumption, the process of economic distribution, and the physical character of a region only to vanish before our eyes. The rise and fall of dot-com corporations is just one of many social phenomena that suggest the properties of leadership have changed in ways we have yet to understand. One can only imagine the impact the collapse of these corporations had on northwest public school systems. Education is intricately linked to larger societal events.

Critically conscious thinkers recognize that we live in a brave new organizational world where nation-state borders carry less meaning as multinational corporations, terrorist guerilla networks, and global injustices grow in strength; news media images become evermore disconnected from the context of their occurrence; and virtual worlds open youth to communities of possibility beyond parent and teacher control. Such radical departures from traditional community practices are compounded by the inability to conceive of and redefine our approaches to leadership. I contend that organizational lives and the ways in which we conceive of them in educational leadership theory no longer match in any significant way. More than ever we need critically conscious leaders to help guide educational futures toward emancipation, justice, and equity even as confusion exists over how it might be carried out.

In my estimation, critically conscious educational leaders can clarify pathways toward effective organizations by recasting leadership theories and practices in more complex and paradoxical ways. The idea that clarity can come from complexity might seem contradictory, but I suggest it is necessary to open leadership theory to the idea of difference. Critically conscious leaders question investment in complete and whole truths. Critique, as the process of being critical, opens leadership to healthy skepticism. Successful educational leaders will need to embrace high-level, critical thought when expectations from others are characterized more by contradiction than continuity and circuitous pathways than linear progression. The critically conscious leader weaves together multiple styles where actions reflect an acute awareness of expectations, a quest for more just and equitable social organizing, and the realization that with so many variables present in any organizational decision it is difficult to assess the impact of any one intervention.

Consider that the contemporary approach to the complexity of organizational problems in education has been to add more staff, more funds, and more technology to the analysis of crises. We are only just beginning to understand that the dilemmas of organizational life are never so easily solved as they have never been so intricately woven throughout the fabric of the personal and public sphere. Educational problems will be easier to solve when we acknowledge and work with the relationships between our organization and the social, political, and economic worlds that are both external and internal to the institution. In practice, however, we seem to believe that education will improve with better computer software programs, more professional development for teachers, a larger budget, and more systems of accountability. Are some of the problems of education, however, less easily resolved? I wonder, how do these aforementioned solutions address the dissolution of economically poor families where both parents must work fifty hours a week to make ends meet? How can we expect students to plan for a bright and promising future when their most pressing concern is the daily negotiation of a local community that is figuratively and literally under siege? The problems that plague our educational systems will not be resolved by educational standards, teacher development, or any other myopic program that neglects the contexts of schools, curriculums, and pedagogies. The critically conscious educational leader understands the complexity of public life where social organizations are as much the source of social ills as they are the source of their resolution.

With this in mind, it is my contention that we need critically conscious educational leaders in the new millennium who are able to meet the emotional, spiritual, political, structural, and social aspects of organizational members in ways that move beyond simplistic leadership models. To address each of these divergent elements it might be important to realize that historical events set the context for future leadership. Too often educational leaders move toward the future without a contextualized understanding of how past events and experiences shape leadership opportunities. Historically based expectations will haunt unwitting leaders as they mix discordance and contentiousness with the new ways people think, act, communicate, and work. If the blending of past, present, and future leadership styles and expectations sounds confusing, and I would agree that it is, that is my point. As we consider organizational change and leadership, critical thought is needed if we are to understand that, as leaders, we are caught between a series of expectations that often fall outside of the ability of single perspective theories. At its most basic, this entry attempts to loosely outline critically conscious leadership while suggesting such ideas are open to continuous revision and recasting. While I write from a position of humility as well as authority, I freely admit I do not hold the market on leadership theory. It seems, nevertheless, that for the sake of direction it is important to set a context for critically conscious educational leadership. To do so, I employ a semichronological approach here with the hope that it is more beneficial than misleading. I outline two dominant perspectives on organizational leadership from different eras followed by a call for critically conscious understandings of leadership that defy one-dimensional approaches. Critically conscious leadership, by resisting dualistic thinking and naturalized truths, illustrates that leadership, at its most effective, involves the sedimentation of historical expectations blended with new desires born of a complex social world—all set in context with the need to pursue social equity. Let us begin by outlining two historical perspectives on leadership that are still shaping us in the present day.

INNATE LEADERSHIP

I begin with the claim that, in the premodern era, educational leaders were typically conceived of as born with inherent virtues that were nurtured, developed, and refined in the creation of civil servants who dedicated their lives to improving society. These select educational leaders were called to the profession not out of a materialist desire but a drive to lead others out of ignorance and toward salvation through the creation of an erudite society.

From within the innate leadership perspective, educators are not only responsible for raising tomorrow's leaders but also for setting community standards and values and acting in loco parentis—a form of parental responsibility over younger individuals in absence of family members. These leaders were more than instrumental teachers; they set criterion for judging morality, ethical conduct, and foundations for an ethic of care and concern. These historical expectations are still with us as educational administrators and teachers are often expected to develop moral character as well as teach the content areas of each of the disciplines.

Critically conscious educators understand that leadership expectations, which are embedded in the organizational conscious, impact contemporary leaders in subtle and covert ways. Leaders are expected to be visionaries that direct teachers, students, and community members toward the creation of more responsive organizational systems and to assist with the actualization of a better community, society, and world. Leaders within the innate perspective are in their positions because they are deemed extraordinary, or so it is believed. Because of their position of authority, they are expected to emulate the best practices of material, spiritual, and emotional refinement; the innate leader is a role model for all the happiness and prosperity that exists in the world. The layperson, from an innate perspective, is heavily invested in role models as they symbolize hope and a better future for those who occupy less fortunate circumstances. As problematic as this scenario might be for some readers, innate leadership is often assumed to provide role models of refinement for lower-status individuals marginalized by racism and class bias. The assumption is that those who are uncultured might emulate in their daily practices some of the characteristics of leaders. The critically conscious educator realizes through the innate lens that leadership justifies the unexplained assertion of authority. If this perspective is the dominate paradigm in a community, it often ends in a belief that leaders have the right to control the behaviors of others as their wisdom justifies the unchecked use of power.

Critical thinkers can detect the autocratic nature of the innate perspective embedded in various dimensions of educational organizations, from regimented class periods and breaks to strict policies and single-file rows of students marching down hallways. Most important for understanding the innate leadership perspective is the assumption that individuals are born leaders or, at minimum, are provided with an exceptional education that instills the importance of setting high moral standards and ethical codes of conduct. Consider the language used by schools of high repute that explicitly state their responsibility to build the character and wisdom of individuals who will assume community leadership roles. It is important to note beliefs regarding innate leadership continue to inform present policies, such as family legacy and provisional admissions policies for our magnet and private schools. These practices stem from a belief that inherited traits and exact preparation are as important to leadership as anything that might be learned through general life experiences. Critically conscious educational leaders understand they are often believed to possess extraordinary power and ability, as innate leadership assumes the presence of a form of knowledge and skill in the leader that the requestor does not possess.

Critically conscious leaders understand that the context of human experience shapes perception. Innate leadership beliefs are prevalent in much of U.S. culture, from television to magazines and journals. Established leaders in our society are depicted as having lives destined for greatness despite hardship or struggle. Madonna broke from her Catholic roots and left The University of Michigan to play out her singing and acting career, because she *followed the dreams that lived within her,* just as Steve Jobs returned as chief executive officer to save Apple Computer, because he *possessed the vision and insight* only a born leader could hold. Innate leadership discourse provides (as well as becomes) the foundation and justification for the rich and famous, after whom millions of people in the United States model themselves in their everyday lives.

Critically conscious educators, as context detectors, understand the ways in which social norms shape leadership expectations and negotiate such terrain with the understanding that perceptions and beliefs can often extend beyond human intervention. Martin Luther King Jr., Rosa Parks, Malcolm X, and a host of others, regardless of their desires, were cast and recast as innate leaders. Revisionist history, narrative life, and myth creation worked together in serendipitous ways to create iconographic figures that are both distant from and compressed in relation to the full and contradictory experience of the individual's life. Annually we celebrate Martin Luther King Jr. with his "I Have a Dream" speech because it fits nicely with the innate perspective on leadership. What we choose not to explore and consider are many of his other works, including pieces that describe in detail King's attempts to remove himself from the Civil Rights Movement and his own prophetic fears for his own safety. Critically conscious educators recognize that in times of honor notions of trepidation, human error, and self-centered concerns are incompatible with the human desire to characterize historical leadership figures as brave and fearless warriors. Under such conditions, the breadth and complexity of leadership is masked and historical figures are recast as divine human beings. Innate leaders, under such circumstances, provide direction and purpose to the general community and society.

Evidence of individual investment in innate leadership is prevalent throughout our educational organizations. Whenever we suggest that a teacher was *born to teach* or a *natural* teacher we are referring to qualities and dispositions that we believe one possesses but not necessarily learns. As critically conscious leaders, exploration of the past is crucial for understanding future possibilities as various dimensions of leadership weave a tapestry of expectations and constraints that shape the contours of the pathways that educators blaze. The innate perspective suggests that, as humans, we desire leaders who will care for us in place of parents or in a way that is similar to parents' concern for children. In much the same way that youth often idolize their mothers and fathers, innate leadership is an extension of this parental concern over the welfare of others. There is, however, a downside. Paternalism can often go unchecked and be used as a tool to coerce others who possess less power within the arrangement and this seems to be the reason that innate leadership receded in dominance as a form of leadership within our social organizations.

EDUCRATIC LEADERSHIP

Educratic leadership is another prevalent leadership form that suggests individuals are not so much endowed with innate traits as they are trained in organizational mechanics. Critical thinkers understand that the rise of modernist thought was, in part, a response to the whimsical and subjective character of decision making conjoined with the failure of innate leadership to create more equitable social life. From the ashes of injustice and power struggles over unchecked systemic practices came that educrat who emphasized formal frameworks, measured working arrangements, systems of checks and balances, and heightened emphasis on policy and procedure. The educrat, unlike the innate leader, emphasized his or her allegiance to formality and empirical processes with the belief that such a focus displaced the arbitrary character of innate leadership. The reader must remember that, along with Martin Luther King Jr., Rosa Parks, and Malcolm X, other less amicable characters such as Saddam Hussein and Osama Bin Laden could also be characterized as innate leaders as the perspective resists an explication of ethical leadership conduct.

Critically conscious leaders understand that shifts in consciousness bring new leadership perspectives, affective investments, and approaches to organizational life. The educrat assumes that long-term planning, objective implementation strategies, and hierarchical command structures will allow organizations to rid themselves of the arbitrary nature of innate leadership and the flighty decision making associated with its institutional presence. Educrats assume standards for interaction that rational instrumental judgment and emotionally detached processes will allow for a well functioning bureaucracy unbiased in practice. The key effect of such an approach is a shift in the relationship between leadership and human life, as we no longer idolize individuals but institutions. The critical thinker understands that within such a paradigm shift humans celebrate great events and triumphs in our social worlds, from advances in technology to the greater height of our buildings. Gone with investment in educratic leadership is belief in the need for paternalism, as we embrace organizations and their provision of services over the extraordinary attributes of individuals. In the educratic world, organizations are characterized by attributes that historically were used to describe human life and, in this process, organizations are reborn metaphorical animate beings; they begin to live. Contrary to innate leaders, the educrat embraces the elevation of organizations, and celebrates his or her nominal role in institutional life and the ease with which he or she can be substituted. Individual concerns and interactions are subordinated to management through policy and procedure that allow for infinite organizational existence. The critically conscious leader understands that the educrat is heavily invested in the belief that abstract and universal rules, regardless of context, are best for fair and just operation.

It is my contention that we can best understand the popularity of the educratic perspective by looking at images of leadership in the world around us. Rational educational administrators spend their time planning, organizing, coordinating, and overseeing organizational activities. From movies to advertisements and situation comedies, we are presented with images of organizational leaders who are calm, well reasoned, and finely dressed in three-piece suits with offices that hold large desks cleared of any papers or clutter that would indicate disarray. In the ideal educratic world, mountains of data and its analysis provide the context for informed decision making. The critically conscious educator understands that leadership expectations consist of more than charisma and paternalism highlighted in innate leadership; they also involve formal authority among other elements. The effective leader, from the educratic perspective, knows how to enforce policy and procedure as a method of ensuring fair treatment for all.

The critical conscious educator detects the instrumental properties of educratic leaders who conceptualize themselves as mechanics, fine-tuning a machine to the point of optimal efficiency. The belief is that through Fordist approaches, which include the right tweaking, harmonious and effective organizational production can ensue. Labor is divided into smaller and smaller fragments until individuals can be inserted and trained on a small element of work within a larger organization they might know little about. Through the efficiency of specialization only a few individuals at the highest levels grasp the broad significance of the organization and its impact on individual human and social life. The problem with such a perspective is that an assembly line approach to organizational leadership often leads to myopic authority disconnected from human welfare—ironically, the problem educratic leadership was supposed to remedy becomes its own weakness.

Consider the 2001 Phillip Morris "Czech Report" that suggested the company should receive additional tax breaks and less regulation because more than 80 percent of Czechs use their tobacco products and, as a result, the government experienced the "indirect positive effects" of reduced health care and housing costs due to premature deaths. Most readers I am sure are appalled by such logic and yet this report illustrates the limits of educratic leadership perspectives—because of the lack of affect, formal organizational structures, policy, and procedures can be implemented without regard for context or impact. It becomes easy to justify troubling acts when cost-effectiveness is the form of rationality around which organizations take action. Invested in an educratic position and blind to the implications of such a perspective, Perni Calvet, director for Phillip Morris at its European headquarters in Lausanne, Switzerland, justified the report even among outrage from people around the world, "tobacco is a controversial industry, but still an industry and sometimes we need economic data on our industry." The critically conscious educator recognizes that the educrat, steeped in the logic of formal bureaucracy and profit, can easily sidestep issues of morality and ethical conduct in the formation of policy and procedure just as the innate leader offered whimsical justifications for their decisions that sidestepped issues of equity and justice.

Let me take a moment to tie this example more directly to public education and educratic leadership. Consider the national push for state standards and testing that mask the economic, social, and political differences among various communities and the highly inequitable funding distribution that plagues much of our public education system. The rationale behind empirical measurement and performance testing is that it is fair because the same test is administered across groups. Again, procedure and policy become synonymous with equality and act as a mask that covers up the need for an exploration of social differences and inequities. The educratic leader, through an emphasis on similarity and monoculturalism, can easily mask the power differentials and cultural differences that exist across class differences and communities and how these differences play out in the lives and leadership of people involved in public education.

The critical thinker understands that context, relativism, complexity, and tenuous relations better characterize leadership than simple dualistic ways of thinking that end in static and partial understandings of the needs of organizational members and society. Educrats, caught in a narrow-minded decontextualized mind-set, find it acceptable to engage in instrumental tactics that increase profits, decrease spending, and re-regulate or deregulate organizations, even if these actions consciously or unconsciously damage the larger social good. We find educratic leadership fails on some of the same fronts as innate leadership. Just as organizational life suffers under the personal whims of leaders who emphasize subjectivity, it can also suffer under the rule of formal policy and procedure that function without regard for the effects of its implementation on human life.

It is my sense that to become a critically conscious leader one must understand the history of leadership paradigms and how perspectives shift and change over time. It is not as if the shift away from innate leadership means it dissolves from human consciousness. One might think of it metaphorically as a shift in focus or the dominant perspective in society rather than linear stages in leadership development. Such descriptions neglect the existence of multiple competing viewpoints. Other perspectives still have influence and might be more seductive as they often reside out of sight. Certainly in the modern period organizational members have invested in the growth of the educrat with the belief that objectivity reduced the arbitrary and provisional nature of authority by placing it outside personal bias. The results, however, have been mixed at best as humans develop policies and direct their application and, at both these points, personal bias intercedes. Nevertheless, educratic perspectives have their place. Clear policy and procedure has been used to set in place measurable indicators in the process of retribution for oppressed peoples. Affirmative action policies, at their most influential, have required women and people of color at least to be interviewed for positions for which they qualify. The outcomes of affirmative action programs illustrate the limits of the educratic perspective. At many educational institutions, there have been nominal changes in the demographic make-up of employees at high levels of the organization, suggesting other factors must be at play.

Educratic leadership approaches, in addition to the limits in the realm of policy and procedure already noted, have made it difficult for organizational members to comprehend the implications of their actions. Division of work and specialization often results in deep knowledge of a selected slice of an organization with little knowledge of how the different elements tie together across units. Any educator that has attempted to coordinate curriculum across grades or courses knows the difficulty of bringing specialists together who commonly lack a broad understandings of the implications of their work. The Czech Report horrified employees of Phillip Morris even as they worked within the same organization. The hierarchy embraced by educrats, who assume that chain of command is necessary for effective organizations, often fail to realize the secondary effects segmentation and stratification have on broad-based knowledge production, the ability to understand the spaces of interaction between boundaries, and the impact on one's work. Teachers who only know their discipline might find organizational rewards for their expertise while there is little incentive within edu-

cratic leadership to understand the implications of their curriculum and pedagogy. Within such frameworks, teachers resemble middle-level corporate managers who possess working knowledge of only a small segment of the organization. It is assumed that conversations about the broad implications of teaching, learning, and leadership are most appropriate at the highest levels of the organization. The critically conscious leader recognizes that, within educratic leadership, problems arise when few members within or related to the organization gain inordinate amounts of power and use it to justify unethical activities.

At this point, the reader might wonder where we go from here. Clearly both innate and educratic leadership perspectives have failed to guarantee pathways toward more emancipatory educational organizations. It is important, however, not to disregard their significance. While we might have explored their positive and negative attributes, as well as their failure to make significant contributions to emancipatory social organizations, they still impact expectations of leadership in very real and significant ways. Theorizing future directions for educational leadership and organizational change does not negate the need to recognize the contexts in which one must operate to survive and succeed. A critically conscious leader, after review of these two perspectives, might begin to understand that investing in a single leadership lens is part of the problem as opposed to the solution. There should be skepticism toward theories that suggest they are beholden to a solution or new direction that will antiquate previous perspectives. Organizations continuously lay claim to finding a cure, a progressive resolution to a problem that is instituted through policy and procedure, only to find later it has become the source of illness that holds the organization from instituting yet another solution. In essence, what was once a progressive solution becomes through successive adaptation a hollow set of policies and procedures that are deemed part of the problem. My questions, given this realization, are as follows: Is it possible to open leadership to play without locking solutions into universal theories that neglect the dynamics of our social organizations and organizational change? Can critically conscious leadership help balance the need for institutionalization with the need to retain open-ended flexibility as a way of continuously addressing social equity within education?

OF CRUCIAL IMPORTANCE: CRITICALLY CONSCIOUS LEADERSHIP

Critically conscious leaders invest in multiple perspectives and have self-conceptions that extend beyond paternal authority figures and bureaucrats who enforce policy and procedure. In short, the critical thinker knows there are no rules to good leadership. When applied at the right moment, in the right way, to the right problem, leadership—with a small amount of luck—can be effective and influential. The critically conscious educator, aware of context and situation, knows that single perspective theories do not offer the direction needed for organizational members in an increasingly complex world.

Critical thought becomes crucial to leadership because, at its foundation, conflict and paradox are accepted and valued as fundamental to complex educational organizations. There will be moments when leaders will need to provide parental-like guidance and support to others and moments when it will be necessary to refer to formal policies and procedures in pursuit of fairness. At some moments, leaders might support students, teachers, and staff as if they were closest of kin, while other moments will call for conflict resolution and mediation that can only be performed with the application of policy. The critically conscious leader takes seriously the need for a high level of acceptance for context and ambiguity while also retaining a high level of humility. Critically conscious leaders recognize we are all in positions of learning from birth to death and, accordingly, admit to and discuss mistakes. At this level of heightened awareness, leaders are capable of blending the secular and the spiritual in ways that uplift affect and open procedures and policies to revision and interrogation by all members of an organization and the people with which it has relations. The critically conscious leader recognizes that organizational life is dynamic and intractable; at the moment a policy is established, it concurrently sets into motion an open-ended process of critique and revision so inequity is never firmly cemented within the organization. Critique becomes central to the critical educational leader who seeks out evaluation and detects injustices with the understanding that to resist inequities they must never become a naturalized part of the organization. Critical thought includes an open-ended reflexivity where educational leaders disengage from imposing their own perspectives without reflection, embrace conflict as central to negotiating healthy democracies, and recognize their own influence in the negotiation of organizational decision making. Critically conscious leaders understand power particularly at the points of its application and detect its circulation throughout the organization. They recognize its character as well as its limitations, as many organizational events are outside of the control of a single individual.

The critically conscious leader realizes that his or her impact is much like the "butterfly effect" as it was first imagined in weather prediction. Meteorologists have for many years attempted to develop more complex and intricate models of weather patterns and found, at a certain point, they could no longer improve predictability. What they concluded was that the most insignificant activity in one area of the world influenced the weather patterns in an entire region elsewhere on the globe through a series of interactions. The origins could only be traced within such patterns to a certain point at which the cause-and-effect pattern turned to chaos. It was hypothesized that weather patterns are so fragile, complex, and unpredictable that change could begin with the something as small as the flitter of a butterfly's wings.

With these ideas in mind the work of a critically conscious leader is more likely to resemble an orchestra conductor than either a spiritual sage or bureaucratic administrator. As Drucker (1989) notes,

There are probably few orchestra conductors who could coax even one note out of a French horn, let alone show the horn player how to do it. But the conductor knows how to focus the horn player's skill and knowledge of the orchestra's joint performance. This focus is the model for the leader of an information-based organization . . . Another requirement of an information-based organization is that everyone take information responsibility. The bassoonist in the orchestra does so every time she plays a note . . . The key to such a system is that everyone asks: Who in the organization depends on me for what information? And on whom, in turn, do I depend? (p. 27)

The critically conscious leader recognizes the interdependent relationships that exist between organizational members as well

as between the organization and the external world. Interactions between entities are believed to be as important as the individuals and organizations themselves and the educational institution is understood as not separate from, but intricately tied to, the surrounding community, the nation, and the world. The butterfly effect reminds us that critical leadership involves seeking out those connections so that the full range of implications are considered in decision making. For the sake of clarity, let us consider an example. At many different ages educators teach children math and accounting skills. At more basic levels we teach children how to use currency to make purchases; while in advanced accounting, we instruct on management of complicated accounts receivable and payable records and might even discuss the importance of maintaining a profit. For the critical conscious leader who is aware of the butterfly effect, this is only the beginning of an accounting lesson or an administrative decision. Math and accounting skills are tied to larger concerns about the interactions of individuals and organizations. Critical leaders discuss and contemplate the implications of purchasing decisions on the economy, the community, and the quality of human life. Critical leaders are more than problem solvers; they are problem detectors. Connections are made between the money spent and the true cost of the product purchased to the community and society in general. Critically conscious leaders see the web of connections between the inception of a product to its end in a recycling plant or landfill. With an emphasis on interactions, math and accounting and administrative decision making become a way of entering into a discussion of the true cost of a product, from the environmental burdens of its creation and disposal to its benefits to the consumer. A broadened perspective means the critically conscious leader always makes connections between the individual acts of administrating, teaching, and learning and the broader implications of decisions on society.

Educators and administrators need to be aware that there are multiple lenses through which to view and assess administrative and curricular activity for effective leadership and organizational change. As a leader in the new millennium there will be multiple expectations to act in sometimes seemingly contradictory ways. From an innate perspective, organizational members want leaders who are compassionate and paternalistic and who will take care of emotional and educational needs. Organizational members want to know that students, teachers, and staff are more than numbers and will demand leaders who know names and remember life stories. Paradoxically, organizational members also desire formal and objective measures and standards that lessen the arbitrary nature of life dominated by innate leaders. They want some form of educratic leadership that appears, at least on the surface, to offer objectivity. They want to take and pass a certain number of classes and know they will receive a degree. Within the educratic leadership perspective, individuals reject caring and compassion for empirical policies and procedures by which we can make comparisons and judgments that rely less on the arbitrariness of affective emotion. They get upset at bias activities of innate leaders and demand fair trials and arbitration boards or file complaints with union representatives. The educratic leader eschews compassion and caring for impartiality.

Critically conscious leaders, however, are skeptical of modern leadership's claims of objectivity with a belief that these declarations cover up power relationships and interactions as the space where connections are made that allow for broader understandings of organizational life. It is important to note, with the advent of a critical leadership perspective, organizational members sometimes relish in exposing the mistakes of leaders. Unlike innate leadership where organizational members might cover up mistakes to create an image of divinity, the organizational members within a critical leadership perspective might feel closer to a leader that willingly exposes his or her faults. Within a critically conscious perspective, organizational members eschew leaders who, in the process of leading, deny their humanness. Critical thinkers also recognize the limits of leadership and, like the butterfly effect, know that the sphere of influence only reaches so far. Every decision and every activity of an organizational leader can have unintentional effects and take place in the context of a community of diverse individuals that have different standards for assessing decisions. Critical leaders understand that context shapes the perspectives of organizational members.

The critically conscious organizational leader recognizes the paradox that exists between these perspectives and the complexity they bring to organizational change. There will be expectations to act with compassion and caring while, at other times, there will be expectations to implement policy from a seemingly unbiased perspective. Most importantly, a critically conscious outlook demands leadership beyond the mundane as it embraces human subjectivity and validates emotional and spiritual life as central to social organizing. Through a focus on interactions, connections can be drawn that illuminate the relationship between seemingly disparate elements. Educational leaders of the new millennium balance a multitude of expectations and utilize their talents to open organizations to changes that maximize institutional equity. As a rigorous problem detector, critically conscious leadership, at its most basic, involves compassion and policy in a nexus with attempts to build connections across diverse groups, broaden each organizational member's perspective, and eradicate institutionalized oppression.

Further Reading

Bellah, R. N. (1985). *Habits of the heart.* Berkeley: University of California Press.

Drucker, P. (1989). *The new realities.* New York: HarperCollins Press.

Sehr, D. T. (1997). *Education for a public democracy.* Albany: State University of New York Press.

Shapiro, E. (2000). *Designing democratic institutions.* New York: New York University Press.

Philosophy

Philosophical Instruction

John F. Covaleskie

With reference to critical thinking, the term "philosophical instruction" is nicely ambiguous. It might mean, on the one hand, instruction in philosophy—teaching the student to be a philosopher or, at least, to be philosophical. However, and, with no contradiction to this first meaning, it might mean that one teaches, not philosophy, but philosophically—thoughtfully and reflectively. Let us first consider what sort of instruction we might call philosophical. After we have done that, we can consider the ambiguity of philosophical instruction.

To be philosophical is to be thoughtful, to be reflective. The word philosophy simply means love of wisdom. Today, philosophy has acquired a reputation for being both difficult and useless. Useless, at least in part, because professional philosophers often address issues increasingly disconnected from what the general public understands to be relevant to ordinary life; difficult, because the professional conversation is often conducted in increasingly more jargon-laden prose. In this regard, a major contribution of the critical thinking movement has been to return philosophical activity to the realm of the everyday, especially the classroom. The critical thinking movement has helped teachers understand that their job includes modeling and teaching to their children the process and importance of clear, goal-directed thinking.

One might argue that "critical" adds little to "thinking." That is, when one is engaged in what we normally think of as thinking, that it is generally critical thinking. We do sometimes talk of thinking that is not goal directed. Consider the statement: "I am thinking of her." In this case, the thinking has no goal beyond itself; thinking of her gives me such pleasure that the thinking is its own goal. However, after thinking of her, I realize that I want to be with her. Now my thinking changes; no longer am I merely thinking of her. I am thinking of ways that we can be together. My thinking has turned purposeful; it is goal directed. I am engaged in critical thinking; I am trying to solve a problem. When we say, "I'm thinking," we are usually trying to solve a problem and/or reach a goal.

Such thinking is what Dewey (1916/ 1944/1966) refers to as "intelligence": goal-directed mental activity aimed at identifying a course of action that will move me closer to my goals. Many recent writers on critical thinking explicitly require that critical thinking not only be goal oriented, but also that it effectively motivate actions; these authors would not call thinking "critical" unless the thinker followed through on the solution arrived at. This goes beyond what is normally required of thinking, and presents a problem for the ordinary use of the word. We all know that, sometimes, critical thought brings us to understand what we should do to reach a goal, but we fail to do so because we just do not want to at that time. A dieter may arrive at the correct conclusion that the best thing to do would be to skip dessert, but then will have the chocolate cake anyway. This is the problem the Greeks referred to as *akrasia*, often translated as "weakness of will." To so label it points to the Greek's understanding that there is a difference between making a mistake about what to do (Plato's explanation of the phenomenon) and simply not having the will or perseverance (or something) to act toward carrying out one's well-conceived plan (Aristotle's explanation).

Other current writers, particularly feminists, draw on Dewey's vision of critical thinking as social in its essence; Dewey argues forcefully that democracy is a communal commitment to the communal exercise of intelligence (in effect, critical thinking) as a means to solve social problems to the advantage of all. In this conception of critical thinking, the emphasis is very much on thinking together rather than separately. The implications of this for classroom practice can hardly be underestimated. Thinking of critical thinking as a collective activity would require classrooms steeped much more in conversation and collaboration, and much less in competition and individual achievement.

Turning to the ambiguity of "philosophical instruction," then, we see that it refers to a style of teaching in which reflection is a central activity to the teaching itself. In this sense, it is a species of what Donald Schon (1983) refers to as "reflective practice." At the same time, it involves helping students become reflective and critical thinkers themselves. We can, in short, instruct philosophically and/or instruct for philosophical living. It is interesting to note that we can do the first without the second, but not vice versa (that is, the teacher can philosophically—thoughtfully—decide to teach so that children become receptive rather than reflective). However, the best instruction is philosophical in both senses.

How can instruction be philosophical in the first sense without also being so in the second? We can (and those who design instructional programs often do) reflectively and philosophically decide that we want children to be receptive and obedient (as in Plato's *Republic* or Skinner's *Walden II*). The belief that people are mostly not capable of self-governance (Plato) or that freedom is an illusion (Skinner) leads to philosophical instruction that is not designed to produce that capacity in students. However, a pedagogy that commits to making children receptive and docile is also one that denies human dignity and freedom. One of the strong complaints about "classroom management" programs, which are applications of behaviorist theories, is that such programs treat children like laboratory animals and deprive them of agency. This is only a problem, of course, if one believes that agency is a human potentiality, which is not a belief shared by behaviorists.

On the other hand, one cannot hope to produce reflective, philosophical individuals unless one sets out to do so. This goal, of helping children become reflective and thoughtful (user-friendly ways of saying philosophical), can only be reached if the teacher's own practice is committed to doing so; it will not happen by accident.

This sort of thoughtful reflection illustrates what is typically referred to as critical thinking. Instruction aimed at developing this capacity gives students practice at solving problems, which first requires problem understanding. It makes explicit and specific the process by which solutions to problems can be discovered—not by random actions, but by intelligence, by mindful action. We can discover our ability to change the world, says Dewey, by acting in a planned manner so that our actions bring about desired changes in the world.

Nor should we let the perceived difficulty of doing "philosophy" cause us to miss the fact that, in a very simple and yet profound way, *all* instruction is philosophical. This is simply to point out the obvious (if often overlooked) fact that teaching requires that we make some assumptions about the nature of the world ("metaphysics" or "ontology"); some assumptions about the nature of human learner and, therefore, what is of value in human terms ("axiology"); and some assumptions about the nature of knowledge itself ("epistemology").

This does not mean that teachers teach according to their beliefs. Far too often, teachers' practice is shaped by *other people's* beliefs about the world, humanity, value, and knowledge. These beliefs are embodied in curriculum design and/or textbook content given to teachers. Teaching is an activity-oriented profession where the ability to deal with problems of practice swiftly is highly valued; "too phil-

osophical" is a condemnation in a profession where problems come at a fast and furious pace, and teachers must react automatically, not having the luxury of time to reflect and/or consult. This often leads to an instruction that is based in technique rather than philosophy, technique that is often the reflection of someone's philosophy of education, not the teacher's. The techniques prescribed for instruction are often rooted in behaviorism, an approach that assumes that teaching a child mathematics or history is not significantly different from teaching a dog to fetch.

Ideally, then, "philosophical instruction" resolves its ambiguity by embracing both senses of the term in one practice: teachers teaching thoughtfully and reflectively in such a way as to foster the same qualities in their students. Only by being so themselves can teachers create the sort of professional practice that will foster these capabilities in their students. Only by fostering these capabilities in their students can teachers be said to be preparing their students for the demands of democratic citizenship. Philosophical instruction requires that the context for education requires opportunities for students to solve real problems in the real world that are connected to the learning in which they are expected to engage. They must allowed the opportunity and the freedom to explore the world and to change it. As Dewey pointed out, this is not an easy task, but it is one that democratic forms of life require be done well.

References

Dewey, J. (1916/1944/1966). *Democracy and education: An introduction to the philosophy of education*. New York: The Free Press.

Schon, D. A. (1983). *The reflective practitioner: How professionals think in action.* New York: Basic Books.

Further Reading

Ennis, R. (1962). A conception of rational thinking. In J. R. Coombs (Ed.), *Philosophy of education 1979: Proceedings of the Thirty-Fifth Annual Meeting of the Philosophy of Education Society.* Bloomington, IL: Philosophy of Education Society.

Siegel, H. (1988). *Educating reason: Rationality, critical thinking, and education.* New York: Routledge.

Thayer-Bacon, B. (2000). *Transforming critical thinking: Thinking constructively.* New York: Teachers College Press.

Queer Studies

Queer Studies: Banished to the Bedroom

Erik Malewski

INTRODUCTION

A couple of years ago our university was shaken up over flyers posted on campus that proclaimed, "See Live Homosexual Acts Performed," followed by the date, location, and a time for the event. The first time I had heard of it I had a week to assess the reactions of the campus community. For about six days I studied the perceptions of students, faculty, and staff as they contemplated the possible meaning behind the flyers. The reactions varied from "what flyer?" to laughter to anger and disgust. I have to believe the flyers made a strong impact on campus because, with every passing day, speculation grew regarding exactly what "acts" were going to be performed. Where the students going to have sex on the campus lawn? Was this going to be an orgy? Do we need to call any lawyers? How many legislatures have heard about this? At the height of discussions, I even heard rumor that a history professor removed them from the classroom before the start of his course because he believed they might distract students during his lectures. Evidently there was a fear that contemplating homosexual acts would be more interesting for many undergraduates than the history of Western civilization.

Figuring I had never attended a student event that started on time, on the day of the live homosexual acts, I walked over toward the designated lawn area five minutes after the act was supposed to begin. I was intrigued, although not as worried as many other administrators. Interestingly, or maybe not so interestingly, there was a group of about twelve students studying on a plot of grass that they had encircled with signs that read, "Action! Live Homosexual Acts Currently in Progress" and "Shh, Homosexuals Performing. Please Be QUIET." I laughed and thought to myself, "How brilliant. The gay and lesbian students have put themselves on display studying . . . this is a true homosexual act that we need to find ways to replicate more often on this campus." The message they offered was a simple one, while gays and lesbians might have sex and that sex might take place between individuals of the same gender, they are also students of compulsory and postcompulsory education who study, worry about exams, and, at their best, leave the university with a degree that opens doors to viable personal and professional opportunities. I wondered, however, if there was a more important and transformative message lurking beneath the surface.

CRITICAL CONSCIOUSNESS: THE POTENTIAL OF QUEER

As I reflected on this event, I realized how queer it really was. Well, at least how potentially queer it was. Knowingly or unknowingly, the students transposed the one-dimensional characterization of gay males and lesbians identified by their presumed or actual sex acts with everyday nonsexual acts that students engaged in regardless of sexual orientation. Even though these happened to be self-defined lesbian, gay, bisexual, and/or queer (LGBQ) students who were studying, there activity was one that was shared across the student body. In this way, it seemed a transgressive moment if analyzed from the right perspective: These were students, whose self-identification as same-gender loving placed them in the margins, highlighting ways they occupied the center. What a powerful way to illustrate to other students that they also engage in activities that mark the overall goals of the undergraduate student body: the pursuit of a degree. In short, LGBQ students occupy all aspects of everyday life whether or not it is acknowledged by the majority of students.

Reflecting on the approach these students took toward queering the notion of gay acts, I began to wonder, what if the transgression were queered in the opposite direction? What if I changed the focus from studying as an everyday act in which gay and straight students engage to the passion and eroticism shared between individuals of the same gender as a common everyday occurrence? In other words,

what if live homosexual acts take place throughout various communities on a regular basis that have not been displayed? For example, when men share personal stories or intimate details of their lives with other men, whether in a bar or at a conference, are these queer moments? When two faculty coauthor an article on a topic for which they have both passion and expertise, is it possible that they have partaken in a form of deep intimacy? In my estimation, critical thought begs us to consider what defines a gay act. It is at this point we can begin to understand the focus of this entry: critical thought wedded with queer theory suggests that we must come to understand what characterizes a gay act from a straight one.

CRITICAL CONSCIOUSNESS: WHAT MAKES SOMETHING QUEER?

I want to begin to address this question by asking what does critical consciousness tell us about what it means to be queer, to study queer, and to think queer? The answer to this question demands that we uncover the interrelationships that unite intellect with the erotic and disrupt reasoning that relegates passion to the bedroom alone. To undergo this process consider the question, what does it mean to be gay? Within this seemingly simple request lays a host of common assumptions. If a man has one same-gender sexual experience in high school or college, is he forever gay or bisexual? If it were one instance of same-gender sex, would you call him gay? If he is currently married, would you still define him as bisexual or would you possibly redefine him as heterosexual after his wedding day? Critical consciousness wed with queer theory challenges the metanarratives that constrain sexuality and the erotic to private, physical, and ephemeral [inter]actions behind bedroom doors. By arguing that knowledge production must expose the devices that separate passion from public life, queer theory at its most basic is a quest for finding the sexual dimensions (and those pleasurable [and painful] feelings most often associated with sexual acts) in a myriad of life activities. When we realize that reasoning is inseparable from emotion, questions are brought to bear on the separation that has developed in formal cognition where rationality is devoid of eroticism.

A critical thinker uses queer theory to examine the differences among human development, traditional notions of sexuality, and static labels that are based on limited identity frameworks, such as gay and straight, and the uncontainable character of passion, love, and the erotic that simply transcends gender and sex acts. Queer theory suggests that a critical consciousness develops when we search for erotic possibilities in all aspects of our lives and reminds the reader that heterosexual intimate relationships in traditional cognitive theory have represented the "proper" endpoint of the pathway for emotional maturation when they include same-gender sexual activity. In its most accepted form, same-gender love has been described as a phase through which some children pass on their way to maturity and, as a part of adulthood, heterosexuality. Critical educators use queer theory to transpose such beliefs with the assertion that intellectual thought on the erotic and passionate be reconceptualized to make use of anomalous ways of thinking about the emotion and reason nexus. Abnormalities and aberrations become a pedagogical and curricular tool for recasting intelligence not as an innate quality held by a particular individual but as the wedding of erotic, passion, and emotion with knowledge production. When these relationships are created, it be-

comes easier to understand that moods are a part of theoretical tapestries, just as a passionate embrace of another human being is theory in all that it is as an act and all that it becomes through interpretation. When critical consciousness develops through the queering of passion and eroticism, we begin to critique dominant reasoning that subjugates the role of fears and emotion in decision making with false claims to objectivity.

CRITICAL CONSCIOUSNESS: ACTIVISM, HIV, AND THE ORIGINS OF QUEER

Consider the role that fear played in the construction of thought on the HIV epidemic where Cardinal O'Connor chastised gay males who had contracted HIV and President Reagan refused to mention the virus in any of his addresses to the public. It took critically conscious activists to illuminate the ways in which fear (not in opposition to but as a central component of reasoning) became the impetus for tooling theories of the disease that cordoned off straight acts from gay acts with only the latter—at least in theory—becoming susceptible to the "gay disease." Out of such "emotional theorizing" by public leaders the gay disease, as it was called then, was linked to gay acts and packaged and sold to the public as the rationality of HIV: The virus became associated with a generalized social group tangible not through certain bodily characteristics but through self-definition and, as a result, certain physical spaces. Try as many officials and medical researchers might, gay and bisexual men could not be found to have certain characteristics, although they did possibly occupy certain establishments. With this in mind, it seemed conceivable in the beginnings of the epidemic to associate the disease with effeminate gay urban males who were often portrayed as immoral sex addicts, but such frameworks were filled with contradiction. For even the most novice citizen, it took constant buttressing to uphold the belief that "gay acts" transmit the disease. Stories of heterosexually defined women and men testing positive for the HIV resulted in the need to repetitiously remind the public that these were exceptions to a disease of the gay male urban community. To offer images of gay urban centers, as the spaces that were primarily impacted, left the rest of the United States, by default, safe from infection (in perception, that is). A different reality, however, kept rearing its ugly head. Many who defined themselves as heterosexual were only doing so to the extent that it allowed for a socially acceptable public identity. Membership has its privileges.

Sexual attraction, interaction, and practice do not always parallel the lines of gender and the conventions of dating and marriage. At no time was this problematic rationality of what constitutes gay acts and gay spaces of more consequence than during the illness of Rock Hudson, a Hollywood icon that represented the pinnacle of American masculinity and heterosexuality—or so America thought. His illness brought HIV to the forefront of the American mind and all of his life that had remained hidden from the public (even while it was known by much of Hollywood) became fodder for the paparazzi. People began to ask, "What happened to Rock Hudson and who is this man?" "How could this masculine icon have a disease associated with effeminate gay males?" Critical thinking provides the lens for understanding these were queer moments that needed reinterpretation to maintain the separation between gay and straight acts: Only when Rock Hudson was recast repetitiously as a

deviate could the separation between gay and straight be maintained.

Officials could not initially contain the psychological rupture Rock Hudson caused as millions of Americans panicked at the realization that this disease could some how impact their lives. For a short period, body and identity became permeable membranes of the surrounding social fabric and for many Americans there were questions about who might be gay or lesbian and who carried the disease. There was also talk about the possible ways Rock Hudson contracted HIV and the nation sat in waiting, both metaphorically as they replayed their own transgressions and literally as they sat in their doctor's office waiting for their own test results. Momentarily the infection of a movie star brought the dissolution of a divide between gay and straight acts as people began to speculate about the circles in which (and through which) this disease would travel. It was not too long, however, before the divide was reestablished through exposés of Rock Hudson's wild lifestyle, sexual promiscuity, and penchant for risk-taking with multiple partners. Once again, in the public mind, the disease had been contained within the margins of those who engaged in sexually coded gay acts, which were interpreted as the immoral deeds of sodomites that brought a need for heavenly acts of retribution. For many, Hudson had been caught doing wrong and was experiencing the wrath of a higher being and so HIV was contained, at least spiritually and mentally, within the plane of wrongdoers caught in the so-called act. Outside of the radar of middle-class America and much more interesting, however, were the practices of many U.S. males that defied the gay/straight divide and made the disease intractable in relation to containment tactics that focused on social group identity and not sexual practice. While the majority of Americans breathed a sigh of relief, many health care and social workers had the insight to foresee that the epidemic was in its infancy. Those who studied social sexual practices knew that dissonance between societal expectations and actual sexual events would bring the disease into the everyday life of most Americans within a matter of a decade.

CRITICAL CONSCIOUSNESS: TEACHING AND LEARNING AND THE ROOTS OF QUEER THEORY

Critical educators can gain a multitude of insights from the above explication of HIV as the foundation in which queer theory has its roots. Indeed, what the first lesson might involve is simply unearthing complexities that are often erased by restrictive labels that involve the power to name what are appropriate and inappropriate displays—not just in sexual practice—but also public demonstration of emotion and eroticism. Rock Hudson on camera was the All-American womanizer, while off camera he was living the life of a gay man. Critical consciousness involves the realization that projected illusions are often taken as a reality more real than the origins from which they came. Rock Hudson's intimate personal relations as a gay male were only known by a select few Hollywood friends, while the media conveyed images of him as heterosexual bachelor to millions of Americans who took these portrayals as truth. I ask the reader which is more real: the life lived or the image projected when the latter is believed by most of the population? Critical thinking realizes that labeling (such as gay or straight)

and imagery (such as that of Rock Hudson) often presume a static character that can mask the complexity of human lives that can only be understood in context. Only through critical thought wedded with queer interrogation can the dynamic and fluid nature of life supercede the context of categories ready made for television.

Critically conscious educators recognize the illusive divides that, in practice, often mask the emotions that drive decisions and the expansive possibilities of the erotic when it is understood as both an element of our lives and a potential power source for moving humans toward work for equity and emancipation. Just as Rock Hudson was shamed into hiding behind media fabricated identities that upheld stereotypes of masculinity and heterosexuality, critical educators have understood how educational standards can act as an accountability system that squelches questions of social change and democratic practice. By queering the concept of standards, just as Rock Hudson queered the concept of gayness, we can transform the debates and ask for new benchmarks upon which to reform public education. I ask, how might we have a standard of passion interwoven with curriculum and pedagogy where students are expected to "feel" emotions and energy in the classroom? In what ways can the erotic be understood not as the contained energies of the bedroom but as transferable energies that direct our projects, enabling educators to feel that "high" when they are at their best? The critical educator realizes that there are only nuanced differences in the origins of the type of care and concern lovers have for their partner's health and well-being in a strong relationship and the type of community that comes from a classroom that believes in a feminist ethic of care and concern. By queering the standards debate, a critical dimension is added to the discussion on what education should be. Within a critically aware domain, the question becomes, what sort of benchmark is there for the role of passion and emotion in our educational lives as well as the body and erotic in our pedagogy and curriculum? How can self-actualization transcend the bounds of careerist motivations to include a discussion of the risks, commitments, and emotions that come with engaging in creating and maintaining a participatory democracy?

CRITICAL CONSCIOUSNESS: FROM EXTERNAL DIRECTIVES TO SELF-ACTUALIZATION

From this exploration, I hope you begin to understand that critical thinking is a tool that queer theory utilizes to illuminate the tremendous pressure that exists on individuals to conform to current social expectations and embrace categories traditionally considered appropriate for respectable public presentation. Critical thinkers realize that one of the most important lessons of the HIV epidemic is that people often present themselves in ways that are socially acceptable while practicing quite differently either privately or in social situations that will allow for deviation. Educators need to realize the repercussions of social conventions that act as external directives that constrain the possibilities to self-actualize and explore all of life's options. Queer theory seeks to make society conscious of the social forces that shape human life with the belief that disruption of common assumptions allow for the exploration of one of queer theory's central questions: How might we, as a society, adapt to the gifts individuals have to

offer as complex, multidimensional human beings rather than constrain people within societal roles and expectations? Critical thinking demands queering commonsense assumptions regarding attraction, emotion, and even the notion of what is erotic with the belief that social change happens when people break though the logic that structures inequity by making the normal seem strange and the peculiar uncomfortably familiar.

Critical thought recognizes that queer theory is a tool that helps people explore the power relations behind the labels humans create for the sake of convenience and order. It is easier to move through life when individuals classify people, objects, and interactions in particular ways. Indeed, failure to classify people, objects, interactions, and events—in ways that they receive our attention or dismissal—would clearly result in inordinate amounts of information requiring our utmost attention. The ability to categorize and filter information allows humans to function—it might even allow us to remain sane. Yet, it has secondary repercussions. Let me offer an example. In many African countries, HIV has taken a devastating toll with as many as 2 in 10 people carrying the disease. With this level of infection, however, we in the United States are strangely unalarmed and justify our disinterest with statements that suggest because the epidemic is outside our country it should not receive our attention. Yet, the disease has impacted human life and U.S. policies have a role in creating the conditions for the ease of its transmission. Whether or not these are U.S. citizens, people living with HIV are human—they are life—and it is here that queer theory moves us toward critical consciousness by using the erotic to highlight the peculiar actions taken by humans and how they impact the lives of others. I suggest that the value of queer theory can be found in the emancipatory possibilities emanating from the belief that to categorize is innate to human life while how we categorize is learned. Through the process of queering customs, traditions, and assumptions, we can unlearn that which has created inequities. Truths are dislodged from their anchors and are set into play in ways that expose the character of power and we begin to question what we know to be true.

When critical thought is wed to queer theory, we understand that the classification of sexual identities utilized to negotiate the world has repercussions because it creates narrow frameworks for interpretation of self and the representations we present to others. Critical thought recognizes the power of classification systems and the ways in which they effectively legitimate or erase conceptions of life. Those who enter the margins or live there with more permanence know that social conventions rarely allow one to admit to socially subjugated desires. Queer theory, in an effort to illuminate the ways in which attractions, desire, and eroticism circulate throughout society, illustrates how rigid and static labels can result in flattened images of human life and its possibilities. Consider, if you will, pornography. Many social conventions, and even educational standards models, are like the pornographic in that they are strict classification systems that allow for the objectification of human activity through the disconnection of feeling and emotion from human practice. Just as it is possible to view pornographic material and objectify human bodies with little understanding of those involved, educational standards often drive a wedge between health and wellness and the pursuit of learning as fundamental to maintaining a zest for life. Standards, in their historical conception, have successfully diverted discussions of educational worth away from passionate and engaged citizenship.

Now that we have briefly explored critical thought and queer theory, let me make a few connections back to the students who engaged in live homosexual acts on the university lawn. To the extent LGBT students are defined and constrained by their pride and embracement of their same-gender affections, the equation of live homosexual acts with studying queers perceptions and opens the possibility for critical consciousness. My concern, however, is that it queers thought and is potentially critical only to the point at which the observer must be reflective not about the lives of others, but his or her own life. To become critically conscious, it is important not only to queer gay acts but also to find queer moments in all human activities. When we begin to see the erotic, emotional, and peculiar character of all human activity, the concept of live homosexual acts will not conjure notions of male-on-male sexual acts but of a full range of human actions that brings with them all the passions, emotions, and feelings that drive the work to make a better humankind.

CRITICAL CONSCIOUSNESS: QUEER THEORY AS EROTIC PLAY

If current events are any indication, we are far from a queer articulation of critical consciousness in many educational communities. In many school districts, the attempt to provide gay, lesbian, bisexual, questioning, and queer students with a safe space in which to come into a healthy understanding of self has brought substantial opposition and backlash. In 2000, the California Orange County Unified School District attempted to ban a straight/gay student alliance from meeting and only revised their positions when faced with a lawsuit. During the same year, a similar position was taken by the Salt Lake City School District when they voted to ban all nonacademic clubs from meeting on school grounds rather than allow for a gay/straight alliance to meet on school grounds. It was only when the case went to the state courts that the decision was reversed and the school was forced to again open its facilities for nonacademic meetings.

The strong reaction to students' desire to discuss sexual orientation issues in a public forum only suggests the pornographic character of everyday school life, where emotion and passion are severed from public education in such a way that the possibility of understanding the erotic properties of our lives brings outrage. To understand commitment, dedication, attraction, and love in holistic ways is essential for vibrant human endeavors where each action is judged by its ability to improve the individual, the school, and the community in ways that allow each student to make contributions based on their unique gifts. Queering external directives that constrain self-actualization becomes possible only when we begin to understand that the suppression of same-gender attractions, sexual and nonsexual, results in static and one-dimensional understandings of human interrelations that fail to blur the differentiations between dominant and oppressed human activities. Queer theory, when wed with critical consciousness, demands that thought be given to passion as innate to all the potential found in students who dare to actualize change in the world,

as measured by that sense of accomplishment that comes from building a more democratic society. The feeling of contortion that emanates out of queering the world is an intellectual endeavor that cannot be severed from the body and the material world in which we live. As people living with HIV and their friends watched as bodies wasted away, queer activists used critical thought as a theoretical catapult for justifying social change activities to the public understood as "live homosexual acts" that brought attention to the disease and the silence of the civic and medical community.

Queer theory, like critical thought, was borne of activism. Theorizing without action is the privilege of intellectuals who are not immediately threatened with life or death consequences, while queer theory drew correlations between radical transformations in perceptions of sexuality, passion, and human intimacy and the types of acceptance and support that were necessary for the survival of self, friends, colleagues, and lovers. In this way queer theory differed from some strands of critical thought that emanated from speculation and imagination apart from rebellion and practice. Queer theory utilizes critical consciousness to demand reinvention of sexuality and emotion but in ways that relate directly to tangible social policies and practices. HIV has never been a gay disease but rather a disease transmitted through particular practices made worse by poor social policy regardless of sexual partners. Queer activists were decidedly bent on upholding the right to same-gender attractions and the right to health care when struck down with chronic illness, not regardless of their sexual orientation, but precisely because like all humans they were erotically oriented beings.

CRITICAL CONSCIOUSNESS: DYNAMIC LINGUISTICS AND NEW PROGRESSIVE FRONTS

Critical thinkers realize that, to gain acceptance, gay acts have been defined in narrow ways with the belief that social change was most possible through the projection of unified and easily understood identities. Differences within the nonheterosexual communities were suppressed and certain images of gayness were advanced that would allow for mainstream acceptance of a same-gender-loving lifestyle. Gays, as it has been more recently portrayed, just want what mainstream heterosexual people want: a house with a white picket fence, two cars, and a dog. In short, it just happens to be two men or two women, but they share in a desire to fulfill the American dream. Critical consciousness comes, in part, from an understanding of the relationship between historical shifts in meaning and the power to define, as the word gay has not always had mainstream connotations. As a term that was originally used to describe both high levels of happiness and women of high morality, it was utilized in the 1960s as an alternative to the term homosexuality, which carried with it negative clinical connotations, and reinforced heterosexuality as the preferred and normal lifestyle. The term gay during this time period was considered by the same-gender-loving community as a political break from binaries that privileged heterosexuality and drew objection from social critics who were upset with its new usage. As Keith Thomas (1980) noted in his opposition to the use of the term gay to designate same-gender loving,

The first objection [to the use of gay] is political. A minority is doubtless entitled to rebaptise itself with a term carrying more favorable connotations so as to validate its own behavior and free itself from scandal. But it is scarcely entitled to expect those who do not belong to this community to observe this new usage . . . The second objection to gay is linguistic. For centuries the word has meant "blithe," "lighthearted," or "exuberantly cheerful." (p. 26)

We might find these objections humorous today as gay has been accepted as a more mainstream, positive term free of the clinical connotations of homosexuality. Yet, it no longer carries with it the progressive political possibilities as its acceptability has dislodged it from its original links to edgy political and social change. Critical consciousness is fluid and seeks new frontiers and queer has taken the place of gay as the new marker for those who break from narrow labels regarding gender and sexuality in an attempt to advance interrogation of oppositions, such as gay/straight, masculine/feminine, and other dualistic ways of thinking. In short, queer has taken over where the term gay left unfinished business. As such, queer alludes to decidedly more slippery and open-ended concepts that often defy easy definition and cooptation. Critical thought wedded to queer theory marks playfulness but not necessarily shapelessness; just as you think you have caught it and figured out its meaning, queer slips away from you again as another activist poet shows you a new angle or dimension you had never seen. It is, however, decidedly less an assimilationist strategy that focuses on the mainstreaming of same-gender loving than a form of open-ended critique of narrow definitions of sexuality and attraction. Queer attempts to highlight the absurdity of labels that constrain human life when living might be more appropriately understood as marked by dynamic changes and abrupt shifts in thought and perspective. A man who was once married with a mortgage, two children, and a suburban life might call himself queer if he decides to leave such a lifestyle in pursuit of something less socially acceptable.

CRITICAL CONSCIOUSNESS: DISRUPTING INDIVIDUALITY, REMEMBERING PERMEABILITY

Queer theory and critical thought act as reminders that while people tend to think of themselves as existing outside of images and representations that surround them we actually exist less as individuals and more as individuals-in-interactions. In other words, every human is made up of or constituted by the beliefs and values of their historical experience and, as a result, belief systems that exist around the individual not only situate people in society but also provide them with a sense of identity. The circulation and flow of ideas and beliefs around humans in the form of commercials, television shows, formal education, work expectations, conversations, life activities, religious beliefs, and local community values provide the context for sexual identity. In this way humans are less individuals than permeable membranes and queer theory was born out of a consciousness that came from interrogating and defying notions of acceptability by social and civic leaders who tried to psychologically distance themselves from those who admitted to engaging in socially unacceptable acts. While we often define individuals as existing separate from their surroundings, we are reminded by the term queer that environments constitute people; we live and think in our surroundings as much as our surroundings live and grow inside us. The critically conscious individual realizes the permeable membranes of an ameba or jellyfish might be more appropriate metaphors for human experience than ideas of the internal world of the mind and an external empirical reality.

With such fragmentation, queer attempts to disrupt the binaries that frame our lives by illuminating what is strange about seemingly ordinary human practices. Work performed within the queer rubric is decidedly, shamelessly, and overtly political. In the face of AIDS, activists utilized queer thought to assert that HIV was not a gay disease but a disease related to biology and sexual practices, which had the potential to impact people across sexual identities if social definitions were not recognized and contended with in prevention and treatment. No matter how intent President Reagan and other political leaders were on ignoring this disease, it changed the sexual psyche of Americans and the ramifications of illusions of its containment within the gay male community are still felt today. Studies have shown a significant number of individuals believe they will not contract the disease regardless of sexual practices as long as they avoid a gay identity. Queer activists asserted the need for a new consciousness that could only exist when social groups drop their separatist identities and utilized queer as an all-encompassing term that elevated political identities over old social group memberships. Within the AIDS epidemic, queer thought became a critical tool for unearthing the ways in which discrimination and power shaped education, treatment, and prevention. In this sense, queer allowed for a critical consciousness that invited the odd, strange, or marginalized to join those who were somehow outside of the mainstream and to build coalitions around political agendas. While retaining our unique identities, we can also disrupt accepted assumptions that marginalize all of us.

CONCLUSION

If you find queer theory and critical consciousness to be complex and hard to define, you are on the right track. As concepts they are more of a commitment to critique and denaturalizing assumptions than the provision of a particular logic or set of characteristics. With this in mind, queer theory and critical thought are often tools deployed against ingrained assumptions and their ambiguity is cited as the reason for their usefulness. Queer theory is a tool of critical thought that calls into question conventional conceptions of sexual identities and the dualities and oppositions that sustain them in everyday life. Consider one final example: When lesbians talk about their lives among largely heterosexually defined audiences, they are often asked how they have sex. Lesbian responses typically queer sexual activity for many people when their descriptions allude to the belief that penetration is not necessary for physical gratification. Progressive lesbians, however, often take the discussion further and make links to patriarchy and the ways in which a masculinized society overemphasizes the phallus as central to sexual pleasure and the emancipation that comes for women who explore sexuality on their own terms. These are queer moments to the extent that they breakdown norms regarding sexual activity but not necessarily because lesbians provide the stories and interpretations. Queer theory wed to critical thought can and will exclude those whose identification notes the recent legitimacy and mainstreaming of gay and lesbian life, while it works to include the lives of peoples whose actions and identities remain on the margins of what is sanctioned as normal. In short, sexual orientation does not always define who is queer or what is queered. Instead, queer is defined by an attempt to expose interlocking social practices that result in structure inequity often related to passion, eroticism, and loving.

If queer theory has any themes, it is the strategic focus on denaturalizing what seems normal within an overtly political and sexual context so that a critical consciousness can develop. It interrogates the distinctions between what is sane and pathological, normal and perverse, straight and gay, and masculine and feminine. It moves wherever it is needed as a tool to dissolve particular coagulations of community, identity, and politics that form definitions of normalcy and, consequently, it is critical of all interpretations of sexual attraction and gender definitions that emanate out of such characterizations. Critical thought wed with queer theory successively dissolves customs and traditions until a day comes when an event that advertises "See Live Homosexual Acts Performed" no longer conjures stereotypical and pornographic images of same-gender sex. Rather, it brings together students, faculty, and staff to read, study, and converse on campus lawns as they explore how eroticism brings them to engage the world in ways that help actualize a healthy and vibrant participatory democracy. In such a queer world where critical consciousness is set in play with queer theory, we acknowledge power differentials and recognize that difference is the organizing principle around which we can begin to build community that is dynamic, fluid, ever-changing and full of eroticism.

Further Reading

Jagose, A. (1996). *Queer theory: An introduction.* New York: New York University Press.

Pinar, W. (1998). *Queer theory in education.* Mahwah, NJ: Lawrence Erlbaum.

Roscoe, W. (1998). *Changing ones: Third and fourth genders in native North America.* New York: St. Martin's Press.

Talbert, S., & Steinberg, S. R. (2000). *Thinking queer: Sexuality, culture, and education.* New York: Peter Lang.

Thomas, K. (1980, July 4). Rescuing homosexual history. *New York Review of Books,* pp. 26–29.

Race and Racism

Institutional Racism

Zeus Leonardo

Institutional racism in the United States is a debilitating force in many people's lives. Critical thinking about its features is crucial if educators are going to counteract its effects in the form of discrimination or structural inequality. As such, the structural features of society are a main target of a social analysis of racism, rather than a more psychologized analysis of individual racist actions. Individual pieces of the racial puzzle do not produce a coherent understanding. Rather than being concerned with details, critical thinking brings to focus the total picture of a racialized society. A critical theory of institutional racism turns on two important premises. One, institutional racism is part of the basic fabric of society and saturates its processes. Two, institutional racism is durable, which means that it has historical roots and an objective presence. These starting points help educators understand that institutional racism is about social patterns, not random acts of hatred.

In a speech, former Black Panthers leader, Elaine Brown, noted that it took black people one hundred years to drink out of the same water fountains as whites. She is referring to the period between the official end of slavery and the 1960s Civil Rights Movement, which brought about social changes in the institutional and legal landscape of the United States. In addition to sharing water fountains, blacks can now ride in the front of the bus and enjoy access to most schools across the nation. Yet, racial integration is still a future projection and not an accomplishment of the present. Rather than emphasizing details about institutional racism, like interpersonal dynamics, critical thinking comes to grips with its structural features in society at large. Although it may be tempting to suggest that it is a thing of the past, institutional racism has taken on different forms, mutating from overt policies, like slavery and forced segregation, to euphemized social policies, like school tracking practices or de facto segregation. In all, while the United States has abolished slavery and other coercive forms of racism, we live with its structural form, or racism in our social institutions.

Critical thinking begins with the assertion that interpersonal relations do not explain the institutional basis of racism. The critical thinker problematizes the popular belief that racism is a problem between individuals. Rather, she helps students gain a proper understanding of history and the way that institutions—like schools, the workplace, or the law—are structured by racism. For example, when whites speak demeaningly about minorities, there are institutional consequences for such statements over and beyond their hurtful consequences. These statements have institutions that support them, which give them their force. In this manner, we can say that they are not only hurtful, but institutionally oppressive. When Asian Americans are called "Chinamen" or "Japs," we are reminded of the exploitation of young Chinese railroad workers and Japanese internment camps. When schools use Indian mascots and appropriate Indian culture, this is not interpreted as an innocent gesture of openness toward indigenous people. These actions are supported by hundreds of years of white cooptation of their culture, of the government's ability to subvert their self-determination, and the cultural conversion policies of the United States. Critical thinking confronts the ties between the present and the historical past.

Although they may be hurtful or stereotypic, and hence should never be encouraged, bigoted statements about whites rarely carry institutional weight. Critical thinking must make this basic distinction to avoid characterizing all racially motivated statements as having equal institutional consequences. When minorities call whites "honkeys," there is little history to suggest that it has been used to oppress whites, or that it has institutional consequences for them. In some cases, it may have damaging effects on an individual's psyche, but it lacks structural effects. Critical thinkers understand that there are important differences between misconceptions about a race and institutional ar-

rangements among the races. Misconceptions about whites can be addressed through mediation, whereas a statement like "Mexicans are beaners" is symptomatic of institutionalized immigration policies impacting Mexicans who are perceived as illegal aliens and whose rights should be curtailed.

A critical educator can teach about California as a case study. Here, Mexicans were the largest target of Proposition 187, an initiative limiting social services, like education and health care, to undocumented immigrants. Although undocumented immigrants may sound like a catch-all phrase to include many groups, its popular image in California is a brown face. White faces, like Canadians, are rarely accused of illegal immigrant status. Moreover, the recent passing of Proposition 227, which challenged the legitimacy of bilingual education, should be linked to 187 as a package that is racially motivated against Latino interests. Although they certainly represent error, misconceptions about whites can be mediated by the astute teacher. The institutionalized form of misconceptions is more durable, has material consequences, and thus requires a different analysis from the critical thinker.

Critical thinking recognizes that institutional racism ultimately reflects relations of power between groups. When whites segregated blacks into ghettos at the beginning of the twentieth century, it was made possible by white institutional power (Massey & Denton, 1993). Otherwise, it would not stick. It was supported by the courts, local and federal government, and politics in general. The historical record makes it clear that whites controlled these public spheres. In addition, critical educators remind students that housing segregation reinforces school and job discrimination, again bringing to focus a complete, rather than fragmented, picture of institutional racism. For racism to become a pervasive force in society, it must saturate every sector, soak every institution. Critical thinking engages the big picture of racism; otherwise, it is not a structural feature, but rather a background annoyance. Today, on almost every social indicator from wealth to health, minorities register less gains and more pains compared with whites. With the nation's two hundred fifty years of slavery, one hundred years of Jim Crow, and forty years of ambivalent action, a critical teacher is warranted to say that the United States was founded on the principles of institutional racism.

At the turn of the second millennium, we witness the backlash of affirmative action. How do educators make sense of affirmative action? As a policy designed to ameliorate present racial disparities and as historical compensation for the legacy of black and Indian oppression, affirmative action provided a sense of mobility for minorities. However, with concerns about falling academic rigor and perceived white disadvantage, the discourse of reverse discrimination has surfaced. The argument is premised on the belief that affirmative action discriminates against whites. Although white institutional disadvantage under affirmative action utterly lacks empirical support, it behooves the critical thinker to analyze the assumptions of such a charge from an ideological vantage point. Often, ideological statements do not rely on evidence, yet are still effective as claims about reality. Hence, critical thinkers must not dismiss them simply as examples of irrational thinking.

Critical thinking may proceed in the following manner concerning affirmative action. First, we recognize that the charge betrays a lack of understanding for the institutional basis of discrimination. Discrimination may be defined as the process whereby a group creates policies to maintain its power by oppressing other groups. Such has been the case with white ghettoization of blacks or men's disenfranchisement of women from the vote. Thus, a critical educator understands that affirmative action does not equate with discrimination in reverse because it is not a policy that minorities use to maintain their power over whites, a power that they do not possess in the first place and, therefore, cannot enforce.

Second, to name affirmative action as reverse discrimination individualizes what is otherwise an institutional arrangement. As already suggested, the charge lacks empirical support so that it becomes fairly obvious that people making it consider themselves personally victimized, which is the first mistake in our understanding of racism. Institutional racism is not explainable through the psychological or subjective dimensions of our lives. It is not a feeling absent of structural origins. Institutional racism is anchored in real things, material resources that then affect one's subjectivity or self-perception. Racism is objective of our desires and wishes in the sense that it is autonomous of them, existing independently of them, as an institutional force.

Third, critical thinking reminds us that, despite the lack of empirical support for "reverse discrimination," the ideology is enough to trigger policies. In California, Proposition 209 struck a blow to affirmative action based on the premise that it helps no group. It does not help whites because of the perceptions already stated and it cripples the legitimacy of minorities, particularly in university settings. Soon, minority students start to believe that they do not belong there either. The reaction has been to dismantle the policy rather than address the institutional climate of the universities, one which is inhospitable to minority students. In exchange for institutional intervention, the belief in rugged individualism is reasserted. Minorities should gain entrance into institutions based on their merit, thus deracinating the concept of meritocracy and leaving it unproblematized.

Critical thinking makes a fourth distinction. If segregation represents institutional attempts to maintain power relations, then attempts by racial minorities to address their own community issues through self-separation cannot be called "self-segregation" or "reverse segregation." For instance, when blacks establish Afrocentric schools, they do not promote the same segregation we saw earlier when whites segregated blacks into their ghettoized neighborhoods and prevented them from integrating into the nation's schools. If segregation is an "action perpetrated by a group on another," then it is difficult to claim that blacks are segregating whites through Afrocentric schools. In the same light, critical thinkers understand that Native American nations, Latino-based organizations, or Asian American ethnic enclaves do not represent attempts by these communities to segregate whites into their own sectors, let alone ghettoizing them. In fact, one could argue that these examples are reactions to segregation policies.

Widespread minority separatism would not be necessary in a fully integrated nation, where every child felt reflected in society at large. Afrocentric schools represent the black community's ability to organize schools addressing their particular needs, which mainstream schools have failed to incorporate into the official curriculum. Native American nations have opted for self-determination in a country where institutional genocide of

their people threatens their very existence. Finally, Asian American enclaves, like Chinatown, remind us of the difference in power between Western and Eastern cultures in mainstream society.

A popular, but problematic response to the status of race is that it is natural. Critical thinking about race understands that is a socially constructed concept; thus, any reference to naturalized racial characteristics must be questioned. For example, the eugenics movement was an attempt to determine the relationship between intelligence and race. If we understand racism to be a sociopolitical relation, then eugenics institutionalizes the relation through an apparently objective detour, like science. Although it would be tempting to discredit eugenics based on its bogus status as a pseudoscience, it was common sense in that era, not to mention its reappearance in the recent literature on intelligence. One of the lessons we learned from eugenics is, "What aspects of our society naturalize race today?" An educator can invoke the following examples.

It is now common sense to refer to Asian American students as the "model minority." Dubbed as "whiz kids," Asian Americans are touted as naturally proficient at math and science. It is assumed that, as a race, they have natural dispositions toward these disciplines. Another explanation goes through the cultural route and suggests that Asian Americans are culturally predisposed to education. These comments must be taken in relation with Latinos and blacks, who provide the backdrop as the "bad minorities." Both explanations mystify the racialized and institutional basis for Asian American choices.

It has been argued that Asian Americans suffer from institutional racism as immigrant, English language learners. Recognizing that other roads to success, such as entertainment and politics, are relatively blocked, Asian Americans choose the educational path for mobility (Sue & Okazaki, 1994). This is an institutional response as opposed to a racial or cultural characteristic of Asians. Also, experiencing discrimination as English language learners, Asian Americans opt for academic fields, such as math and science, and careers that do not depend solely on the ability to speak and write in the English language. Again, this is a rational response to the opportunity structure in light of their specific racial experience. One might wonder why Latinos, who also face linguistic racism, lag behind Asian Americans in education. Critical thinking must intervene here. An educator notes that, as a group, Asian Americans immigrate to the United States with a higher class status than most Latinos, with the exception of Cubans. Our racial comparisons are confounded by economic class considerations. In light of what we know about the positive correlation between class status and educational attainment, this fact weakens the naturalized racial explanation for Asian American educational ascendancy. Moreover, it points to the nation's selective policies for immigration, another racialized institution.

As educators discuss with their students the institutional policies that affect minority immigrants, it is important to note the comparisons students may use to frame the issue. For instance, the critical teacher may confront the justification that many immigrant groups have suffered discrimination, such as the Irish, Jews, or Eastern Europeans. Picking up speed, a student may even suggest that, whereas these groups have transcended their historical condition, blacks and Latinos have not. Thus, the problems that blacks and Latinos face are internal to their group

rather than inherent features of U.S. institutions. Critical race thinking problematizes the response by noting that the immigrant experience of minority groups is subjected to the standards of white ethnic assimilation. However, the two processes are not the same. European immigrants eventually became part of the white race, whereas Latinos, blacks, and Asians remain non-white. In addition, the response rationalizes the oppression white ethnics suffered as immigrants and portrays the experience as a process that other groups must also bear. A bit like hazing. When Irish native language practically disappeared in exchange for English, the gains could not compensate for the loss, nor could the ends justify the means. Critical thinking does not justify bad treatment of a group because of another group's suffering.

When teaching about institutional racism, educators use critical thinking to relate their different forms. First, the prison industrial complex and criminal justice system have been a concern of race activists, such as Angela Davis. The rate of incarceration for blacks in the United States is disproportionate in light of their population at large. The nation builds jails at a faster rate than it erects new schools. And when former President Clinton signed the "three strikes" law, he put minorities even more at risk. Second, the practical demise of the welfare system under President Clinton has racial consequences in light of the disproportionate number of blacks, especially women, who rely on such services. Critical thinking reminds us that both the prison and welfare systems are institutions perpetuated by longstanding racist beliefs about minorities. Although it should not end there, critical thinking can begin in our schools. For example, students benefit from a broader understanding of racial images and the institutions that support them. By studying our society's ideological representations in the media, deficit thinking about minorities, and presumptions about racially neutral policies, like the law, critical race educators fight against the daily evasions of race so common in our schools.

Critical thinking incorporates explanations about the maintenance of institutional racism. In particular, it is helpful to examine the ways that classroom discussions evade critical thinking about institutional racism. When discussing modern racism, a popular refrain suggests that groups have always oppressed each other, with Japan's imperialist history posing as a non-white example. A critical educator uses this opportunity to question the normalization of white racism, that is, its apparent banal nature. She can contextualize white global power as unmatched by Japanese imperialism, which is more regional to Asia. White racial power is different both in terms of scope and scale from other forms of group power.

Here is another scenario. When discussing black slavery and its legacy, students may respond that slavery has existed throughout history, with every conceivable group enslaving another. In attempts to deracinate the issue even further, some students may offer Egyptian enslavement of Hebrews as a case where a darker skinned people enslaved a lighter group. The critical thinker may approach the discussion by suggesting that, first, describing the specificities of black enslavement does not equate with supporting Jewish enslavement. That is, both are forms of institutionalized oppression. Second, the former example is more accurately used as evidence for religious oppression rather than racial oppression based on skin color. Third, black enslavement ended fairly recently. The critical pedagogue understands that invoking the reality of institutional racism produces evasive responses. Rather than evade the situation, the critical thinker turns it into a teaching moment.

Finally, critical thinking examines how whiteness becomes encoded as normal in everyday life. Institutions are material places and maintain a certain objectivity to them. They are durable and exist independently of our individual will. However, we maintain them through our daily belief systems and perceptions. So far, the discussion has centered around the experiences of minorities with institutional racism. As we turn to the experiences of whites, we notice that the world looks different. For example, critical thinking interrogates the ability of white consciousness to define itself as the marker for universal humanity by downplaying its own racialization process. It is not uncommon for whites to refer to themselves as individuals or just human. For educators to achieve a sense of clarity about institutions, they recognize that this form of race thinking obfuscates the role of whites in society, as racialized subjects. It is a perspective that masks white participation as color-blind, value-neutral, and racially unmotivated. Therefore, it clouds our ability to ask certain questions about group power because color-blind perspectives attempt to make whites, as a race, invisible. In the end, detecting white visibility may represent the first and final act of critical race thinking. By demystifying whiteness, the critical thinker is on her way to a more complete understanding of institutional racism.

References

Massey, D., & Denton, N. (1993). *American apartheid*. Cambridge, MA: Harvard University Press.

Sue, S., & Okazaki, S. (1995). Asian American educational achievements: A phenomenon in search of an explanation. In D. Nakanishi, & T. Nishida (Eds.), *The Asian American educational experience* (pp. 133–145). New York: Routledge.

Further Reading

Fanon, F. (1967). *Black skin white masks.* New York: Grove Weidenfeld.

Spring, J. (2000*). Deculturalization and the struggle for equality* (3rd ed.). New York: McGraw-Hill.

Wah, L. M. (Producer/Director). (1994). *The color of fear* (Video). Oakland, CA: Stir-fry Productions.

Race

Zeus Leonardo

Critical thinking about race is necessary in today's world because it is a pervasive concept that structures daily experiences in schools. Race is a relatively *modern* concept, the origin of which can be traced to the centuries of European expansion and colonization. Critical thinking about race begins with the understanding that it is defined as a social relation based on skin color and other related physical attributes. Moreover, these attributes represent the outward appearance of race, the essential issue being that race is a relation of power. A critical theory of race makes the concept of power central to any discussion about the concept of race.

To the extent that race represents a form of grouping, it is a social construction. It is the attempt to create social groups out of individuals who did not originally see one another as belonging to the same group. We construct such groups as "races" for purposes of stratifying them in society. Critical thinking on race asserts that, although genetics is partly responsible for the kind of skin color a person is born with, the notion that we should then stratify society on the basis of skin color is evidence of a social, as opposed to genetic, phenomenon. Furthermore, to the extent that students invest in the meanings they create out of the concept of race, it becomes a real part of the way they see themselves and those around them. Because people create institutions based on racialized meanings, race, a socially constructed concept, becomes real in our everyday lives.

To begin, race is not just a synonym for group. Critical thinking recognizes that, in everyday language, people tend to assume that the concept of race has always existed, even in biblical times. A common example is that the images of black and white were used in the Scriptures. One may assume that lighter or darker people were organized into their appropriate groups. But a critical teacher understands that ancient societies were organized less on the basis of skin color and more on religious principles. She teaches students the point that Egyptians enslaved Hebrews not because of their skin color, but because of their religious beliefs. By contrast, North and South American enslavement of Africans occurred through modern beliefs about race as understood through discourses about skin color, with black being inferior to white. So, to the critical teacher, any talk about a human race outside of skin color does not invoke the modern notion of race as an organizing concept. For it is quite easy to notice that whites and blacks experience the human race in different ways. Thus, the first point of critical thinking is that race does not represent a mere synonym for group because, if this were the case, women and men would represent different races because they constitute different social groups. For that matter, poor and wealthy people would also belong to different races; but we know this to be false because many races comprise economic classes, though not proportionately. Race is a *particular* grouping of people, usually and primarily based on skin color, which is then related to other physical attributes, like hair, eyes, nose, and lips. Ultimately, race is a construct used to distinguish the master race from the subordinate races.

To understand race, critical thinking must be able to distinguish between several concepts. For example, critical teachers distinguish between race and ethnicity, despite the fact that many people use them interchangeably. Whereas race is a way of organizing society into ostensibly discreet groups based on physical traits, ethnicity signifies the cultural group to which a person belongs. It may be the case that we use the same term for both a racial and an ethnic group, such as black or white designating a race and culture. To the extent that whites represent a physical group to which we attach racial meanings, they constitute a race. But to the extent that they share a culture and participate in its practices, we may call them an ethnic group. The same can be said for blacks, who comprise a race and culture group. Both white and black races are multicultural because multiple ethnic groups make up their identity.

The same term, black or white, is used to signify two concepts—race and culture—which is the crucial difference between a term and a concept. With the former, critical thinking is concerned with the process of naming a group; with the latter, it is concerned with the meaning of that group. In the case of the Asian American race, one can belong to an ethnic group, such as Japanese or Thai. Here the distinction between term and concept is easier to note.

A related concept is nationality, sometimes used interchangeably with race or ethnicity. A critical thinker notes that nationality invokes the concept of nation, one which may be geographically real, as in the United States, or imagined, as in the Filipino nationalist movement that far beyond the Philippines. Living in a national context or place represents the more general use of nationality, with the politicized form of nationality seen in recent examples like the black power or Chicano movement. The first definition of nation is tied to the idea of a State, as in the struggle for an independent Palestinian nation, whereas the second definition is sociological and refers to a group of people, like the many indigenous nations in the United States. Race is related to ethnicity and nationality in these subtle ways, but critical thinking distinguishes it from the other concepts to maintain its specific meaning and preserve its utility as an analytic tool.

With the event of European colonization of Africa, North America, South America, Australia, and other parts of the world, the birth of the modern races began. In short, the critical teacher imparts the knowledge that organizing people and society into races became meaningful, although not necessarily in its positive sense. During this period, a history teacher finds justifications for mistreating the darker others because of their assumed incivility, savagery, or subhumanity (Takaki, 1993). In general, the contact between European and non-European worlds was not innocent and occurred through the racialized justifications about the inferior other and the superior Westerner (Mills, 1997). The upshot of the relationship is that the white and black races were co-created, much like the horizon needs the curvature of the land for its identity. Again critical thinking notes that this relationship is not one based on equality. Rather, the creation of the white race represents the domination of other races. The Western world conceptually created the darker races to understand itself as a relatively cohesive group, previously made up of diverse ethnic and national identities, like Germans, British, or French. The beginning of the darker races was also the beginning of the white race.

A critical thinker can interpret the example of slavery in several ways. On one hand, it represents an economic phenomenon made possible by early capitalism and the use of human labor for profit. On the other hand, modern slavery is undeniably racial in the way it was made possible by Westerners' assumptions about their superiority over darker peoples. It was logically easier to enslave people throughout the Americas when the victims were considered savages, less human, and uncivilized. It is true that Africans also enslaved each other but none so pervasive and enduring as their enslavement under the white race. White enslavement of Africans also took on a different form, where people were sold as property or chattel, rather than as payment for a debt or as spoils of war. In this sense, critical thinking arrives at the conclusion that modern slavery was more extensive and justified through racial meanings. Lastly, the legacy of slavery centuries later in the form of Apartheid, housing and school segregation, and job discrimination makes race a structuring principle in everyone's lives today.

Currently, American mainstream discussions and images around race revolve around a crude black-white ideology. As a result, Asian Americans and Latinos are asked to choose a pole with which to associate. Critical thinking must disrupt this tendency. In a country where the history of tensions between races has been apparently fixed by a black-white discourse, other races are limited to affiliation status. It suggests that we locate Asian American, Native American, and Latino racial experience in an arbitrary place between the black and white experience. The black-white divide places these experiences in no-man's land because "yellow" or "brown" are presumably colors somewhere between white and black. In some official documents, such as the U.S. census, Latino is recognized both as a race and descent; thus, Latinos are asked to denote both heritage and racial affiliation. Critical thinking must question the simplistic versions of the black-white dichotomy in favor of a more complex engagement with multiracial experiences.

When analyzing race talk, critical thinking appreciates the way that people use language to signify or refer to race. For instance, the phrase "people of color" is often opposed to the term "white." This commonsense usage serves to delay a more critical understanding of race because it suggests that white is *not* a color, thereby mystifying the racialization process for whites. Also, the distinction between *minority* (i.e., people of color) and *majority* (i.e., whites) fails to deal with race in a specific way because, depending on the geographic location, whites do not represent the majority, such as the case of future projections for California. It is more accurate to think of minority in terms of power relations, such as minority substituting for subordinate races, rather than minority as a numerical count. A critical thinker only has to invoke the example of former South Africa where Africans were the majority in numbers and the minority in power. For similar reasons, although many people still use the descriptor Caucasian for certain phenotypes, the preference for the term white is gaining currency because it more accurately reflects a group in its social relation to power.

The point of critical thinking about race is to suggest that no element of a racialized society remains untouched by the concept of race. Either a society is completely racialized or it is not. Either one is alive or dead; there is no such thing as being a little dead. The critical thinker understands that, despite one's inability to explain the racial element of every occurrence or event in one's life, this does not mean that it is not racial in nature or has no racial consequences. The goal of critical thinking is to develop a sophisticated racial analysis that is convincing and compelling. Let us take the O. J. Simpson case. The concept of miscegenation, or interracial marriage, remains a charged issue and one did not have to use the race card to make the Simpson case racial. It already was.

The challenge of critical race thinking for educators is twofold: to unmask race and to avoid reifying it. Unmasking race requires that the critical thinker understand the innerworkings of race in our everyday lives. From the television shows that we watch, to the neighborhoods in which we live, and to the knowledge that we possess about the world, race frames both the content of the message and the way we interpret its meaning. One, television sit-coms and dramas consistently mask the reality of race in exchange for a distorted representation of the world. The series *Friends* takes place in New York, one of the most diverse cities in the world, with a primary and secondary cast that is all but absent of people of color. In the United States, network prime time shows consist of mainly white actors and actresses; when people of color are portrayed, they are cast in stereotypical representations.

Two, neighborhoods are the lynchpin of a racially segregated society. Ghettos are almost exclusively populated with blacks, which affects black children's educational experience because school funding is directly related to property values. For Latinos, barrios represent paltry housing conditions and the low-status schools into which they feed. Three, our knowledge about the world has racial origins because our experience with the world is segregated and truncated. Hence, when we see an overwhelming number of blacks in the sports industry, our knowledge about them becomes limited within this sphere of public life and "all" blacks begin to take on the appearance of an athlete, especially males. When, as in southern California, you see a disproportionate amount of Latinos mowing lawns, then that is the image you cultivate about them. This is not merely a statement about stereotypes, but the structured knowledge we have about the world, so that the act of knowing becomes a racialized moment. To counteract this situation, the critical teacher problematizes her own racial position in and knowledge of the world.

Critical thinking about race must also avoid reifying it. That is, we must risk making distinctions without naturalizing them. The possible danger for educators is that we make race even *more real,* and in the process turn wood into stone. The reification of race occurs through a long process of telling stories and at some point believing in them, of a story told one too many times. So, the critical teacher must search for a nonreifying way to talk about race, a perspective that unmasks its structures without investing them with more power than they already possess. Otherwise, we reach the point wherein a social construction graduates and becomes real. Stories about monsters may not be based initially on anything real, but when retold with compelling force, we surely create our own.

Critical thinking understands that although the concept of race is a social construction the racial experience of people, white and non-white, is real. It is real because it is lived and has material consequences. When European colonists acted on their racial beliefs by exploiting the inferiorized and infantilized other, they made the concept of race come alive. Critical race educators avoid the problematic suggestion that anything associated with race is unreal. Making this claim is tantamount to devaluing the reality of some of the hurtful interactions people have on a daily basis, especially those moments experienced by people of color. This does not suggest that our interpretation of racial experiences is always correct, which is a function of our ability to analyze them. After validating racial experiences as real, the critical educator works with students to arrive at critical understandings of race. Finally, critical race thinking is always self-reflective because racialization is present in any discussion about race.

References

Mills, C. (1997). *The racial contract.* Ithaca, NY: Cornell University Press.

Takaki, R. (1993). *A different mirror.* Boston: Little, Brown, and Co.

Further Reading

Bernasconi, R., & Lott, T. (Eds.). (2000). *The idea of race.* Indianapolis, IN: Hackett Publishing.

Du Bois, W. E. B. (1989). *The souls of black folk.* New York: Penguin Books.

Omi, M., & Winant, H. (1994). *Racial formation in the United States: From the 1960s to the 1990s* (2nd ed.). New York: Routledge.

Scholar Practitioners

Scholar Practitioners As Classroom Teachers

Carol A. Mullen

What does *scholar practitioner* mean? Imagine a teacher who thinks and acts like a detective—searching for clues to a complex problem. This individual strives to become as informed as possible about the contexts that inform her daily work. She functions above and beyond her roles as educator, curriculum developer, and concerned citizen. She is always developing her capacities for critical thought and action, and stimulating those of others. This critical thinker is not satisfied with posing superficial questions or generating obvious, accepted answers.

For the teacher who is a scholar practitioner, significant questions are highly complex. They require thoughtful analysis that leads to a variety of possible solutions. The question that puzzles her takes on a life of its own, revealing itself from various perspectives that alter from one situation to another. This teacher, who is curious by nature, feels driven to explore a problem that is messy and unresolved. Her decision-making abilities, interpersonal strengths, and research skills are all put to the test. This teacher may want to learn more about some aspect of the educational enterprise that affects the work of teachers. Or, she may want to study how one problem affects another, as in the case of mandatory testing and its affect on student learning and motivation.

THE LIGHT OF CRITICAL THINKING

Any significant issue on which the scholar practitioner sets her mind, requires critical judgment; insight, truth, and meaning are pursued for the greater good. This is a description of critical thinking itself, one that reflects Joe Kincheloe's writing in the introduction to this encyclopedia. In this essay, I translate their definition of *critical thinking* into the capacity of being able to pursue the "light" of change, while asking uncomfortable questions about the "dark."

The scholar practitioner who develops reasoned judgment combined with informed action embodies the "light" of critical thinking. Issues in the professional arena not only require attention but also educated activism, or "intelligent action" as Lortie (1998) refers to it. Teachers who work to better their school communities envision "the light" even where public opinion—fuelled by politicians to make themselves look good—offers facile solutions to misapprehended problems (Kochan & Mullen, 2001).

Centrally imposed curricula, built upon performance and assessment measures, affect teachers' work today, calling for a creative and principled response. For example, a teacher might be concerned with how degrees of freedom can be maximized within her classroom while preparing her students for success in a high-stakes testing environment. Or, if she is a teacher leader, her attention might be on how to best motivate teachers feeling discouraged over a poor school grade that fails to represent their dedication to student learning.

If obstacles to teaching such as these are to be overcome, a grassroots movement is needed that is led by teachers. The lynchpin is that those teachers who lead will need to know how to investigate issues of value and effectively communicate their results with the public. Teachers who are scholar practitioners will be tomorrow's leaders.

WHO IS THE SCHOLAR PRACTITIONER?

The scholar practitioner is a classroom teacher (or another professional) who studies a significant problem that has arisen. This individual puts theory to the test as she focuses on a problem of concern or interest. For example, she might turn to Carol Gilligan's theory of female adolescent development for learning how imposed curricula may be forcing girls into a competitive mode that works against the cooperative learning style that they value. Or, this teacher could instead generate theory out of practice by studying a selected problem: A theoretical understanding may evolve as she investigates how forced-modalities of testing relate to female values of learning.

Regardless of the approach taken, this teacher performs the scholarly role of teacher and the pedagogical role of scholar. This individual does not ignore the relevance of theory in looking at a practical issue; instead, she will use theory and combine it with practice in such a way as to produce meaningful results about a question that concerns her classroom, school, or even country. Furthermore, she will have the responsibility of disseminating her results to others while inviting their input for enriching her perspectives. All this can lead to informed activism for change at both the micro and macro level of education.

In contrast with this picture, the "armchair theorist" is divorced from practice and action. She eloquently philosophizes about what tomorrow may bring, but she does so without becoming personally involved in the problem that occupies her mind. Certainly she avoids taking any of the action or risks involved in introducing change. The "action practitioner" part of her identity is lying dormant.

Right next door, so to speak, there could be a different kind of pedagogue, one who exerts her critical thinking skills to investigate concerns and dreams shared with the theorist. Practitioners who lead by expressing their visions of the future must excel in the ability to communicate their curiosity and learning, and thus stimulate others to think and act.

In this essay, educators that function reflectively and proactively are considered knowledge-building activists. Scholar practitioners who are self-actualized care about making a difference. This value runs contrary to the myth that scholars can't be practitioners, and that practitioners can't be scholars. There needs to be a reflective part of action, and an action part of reflection, in teachers' work. While the term *scholar practitioner* may seem oxymoronic (because it combines two opposites), it is a promising vehicle for promoting school and societal change; synergism joins vision with action. This formula creates the conditions for acquiring wisdom so that the door to constructive change can be opened.

Who are those scholar practitioner activists working in today's school systems? Can they be identified? If so, using what criteria? Change agents can have very different personalities—some may be assertive or even at center-stage, while others seem shy or even withdrawn. Also, those at an earlier stage in their career tend to focus on issues related less to the whole school-community and more to their immediate context. Yet, despite these variances, teacher activists all share a deep commitment to improving schools and the quality of student learning as well as the education profession itself.

Despite their efforts to reform the educational system, these teachers' ideas and concerns are not heeded because they get drowned out at the macro level. However, the dominant voices of those in positions of power can be loudly heard: Teachers are being held firmly accountable for responding to government reform programs that mandate how schools will be restructured and to what effect. More than ever, while teachers' professional decision making about educational matters is being dictated to, the spirit of many is dissipating. This crisis of national proportion remains invisible to the public at large. For a break-through to occur in the nation's consciousness, these tensions must remain alive as the fight for voice and selfhood continues.

In some public schools, teachers have assumed ownership for making significant changes, even where they have been excluded as decision makers and where and when their freedom is limited. Such teachers function as role models because their decision-making processes are informed and not simply the resonance of a reflex nature. For example, many collect and analyze data from different stakeholder groups as part of a larger campaign that supports whole-school change. Such teachers voice their concerns, assert their opinions on power issues, and make intelligent decisions upon which change is based. They seek avenues to participate in or lead heated debates to tackle, head-on, the crucial issue of control over quality education today.

In a situation that illustrates these various elements, teachers at a public middle school in Alabama reflected on and assessed their own improvement program. The challenges that this school team experienced during its improvement planning shed light on accountability issues in standards-led education. The accreditation team, while successfully coordinating a self-study reform project, encountered tensions between state control and teacher empowerment that emerged during the school's restructuring program. The article that resulted, with feedback from the scholar practitioners involved, concludes that the informed perspectives of teachers are valuable for policy formulation and critique (Mullen with Stover & Corley, 2001). More such investigations are needed to build knowledge of how teachers actually spearhead school improvement efforts within the contradictory context of national policies that oversee site-based, decentralized efforts.

CASE STUDY TOOL

Scholar practitioners can develop research that tells their story in a way that speaks directly to the public. *Case studies* are a reflective tool for critical inquiry that address complex questions. And, they are an informed act of storytelling. The case method, a mainstay in many scholarly-practitioner fields (such as law) is now being used in educational circles. Higher education courses that encourage graduate students (in teaching) to develop case studies understand that story and science overlap—a study and its results can be shared in narrative form. Because teachers are often natural storytellers and conversationalists, this medium of research tends to work well for them. Case studies can help education students (preservice teachers) and leadership students (inservice teachers) to conduct research that leads to intelligent action.

I consider my own graduate students in educational leadership at the University of South Florida to be "thought detectives." They grapple with unresolved questions that influence their daily work in school environments, and they study problems with the open mind of a researcher. This means that they expose their personal biases, look at various influences that affect a situation that is being studied, talk in-depth with others or survey groups of people, analyze the different types of data collected, generate possible explanations for what they have found, and keep solutions open. No prescriptions for action are forced upon the reader of their reports, only suggestions for consideration. They come to understand that the problem studied will be far more complex than any single case study can hope to capture—context matters greatly. Committed to critical inquiry, some of my students have established focus groups to tackle deeply entrenched problems in their particular environments.

There are many reasons why the frequent use of case studies by teachers is worth considering. Skills development is only one benefit. Practitioners must learn how to collect and analyze data, and write up their discoveries in a convincing way—these activities are increasingly required of schools (Lortie, 1998). Results that provide insight into such difficult issues as student learning and organizational change can be useful. As informed researchers who are knowledge managers, practitioners benefit by being able to influence the culture of their workplaces and beyond.

A second benefit for case writers is that they will be placed in situations where they will need to interact with others. This activity enables them to collect data and to build interpersonal skills as well as observational and networking skills. Importantly, the self-image of the researcher (she often feels awkward at first) improves.

As a third benefit, students learn how to view problems from multiple angles and myriad points of view. This way they practice suspending judgments—withholding premature judgments while taking the time to explore an issue beyond its surface. Suspending judgment is, ironically, an important activity that supports the development of critical judgment. The gathering of different points of views on a subject is essential to becoming as informed as possible. A related benefit for students using the case study method is that they "test" the taken-for-granted notions about school culture that have shaped their own practice. Additionally, case study writers fill many gaps (and discover new ones too) in their ever-changing puzzle of knowledge and experience; in this way learning can be an exciting adventure into exploration.

In one of my courses, the graduate students chose to explore issues of diversity in their schools. Inadvertently, their topics mirrored problems currently represented in the literature, such as the inequitable distribution of support structures for at-risk schools and non-white populations. My students cared so much about making a difference for disenfranchised children that they quickly broke past fears of writing. Their protestations of "I'm not a writer!" rapidly faded. Issues concerned with children, learning, and poverty are highly relevant to teachers' work. Scholarship takes on value for my student groups once they have decided on the target population they want to study—the students for whom they want to make a difference.

When teachers develop as scholar practitioners, a new self bursts forth. As action researchers, my students set high standards for themselves, as their scholarship must come from theory and be applied to practice for it to have any value. It matters to them that someone should act on the proposals for change they endorse. They seek discoveries that can offer new directions for the children's lives they long to uplift. Teachers can become researchers of consequence whose reform work can make a difference.

CHANNELS FOR TEACHER ACTIVISM

Teacher leaders of educational reform sponsor grassroots initiatives that organize networks and campaigns around educational problems. Some of these efforts focus on standards and control, other issues confront social justice. Such sociopolitical agendas are centered on issues of power, spurring on new forms of teacher professionalism. Alliances for collective action can improve all aspects of the educational enterprise, particularly concerning the quality of student learning, as well as teachers' status.

More information is needed regarding channels for professional action in education. Noteworthy school-based initiatives do not generally become widely known. Teacher professionalism has traditionally been focused on the areas of expertise, altruism, and autonomy—not activism. Public and bureaucratic discourses continue to overwhelm teachers' discourses about vision and concerns. Teacher activism built upon collective action by school practitioners is crucial. Wherever possible, school-based activism will, paradoxically, need to be aligned with cooperative action that enlists the support of stakeholders and community leaders. How else can large-scale improvements be fostered in today's tough accountability climate?

To help propel change, teachers' visions can serve as a starting point for reform at the local school level and for the educational system as a whole. Teacher unions, as one form of grassroots organization, can help promote teacher activism by guiding pedagogical, curricular, and organizational change—not simply concentrating on only bread-and-butter issues. However, the controlling role of governments in the United States, the United Kingdom, and elsewhere imposes a non-liberatory, mechanistic view of teaching. This worldview of education limits the potency of teacher unions and other viable agents to influence substantive issues in education. As a result, the strain of trends, such as high-stakes testing on teacher unions and the decision by some to ignore social justice, become topics of fervent discussion. These are all issues that dot the landscape of scholar practitioner activism today.

FINAL THOUGHTS

Because of their commitment to student learning and their deeply rooted visions, who better than teachers can evaluate the impact, and thus the validity of state-imposed standards? Teacher activism confronts national control in the areas of performance measures, accreditation, school inspection, and school improvement plans. Teachers are, in all ways imaginable, crucial to the success of school reform. While practitioners are responsible for carrying out school improvement initiatives, they are seldom viewed as curriculum designers, and even less often as partners or co-collaborators in policy development. Teacher reformers come in many guises—some without leadership titles, and these are often unassuming and unacknowledged.

Readers, let's attend to our own role as social-scholar activists for identifying potential teacher activists who could use the support of outsiders in fulfilling their role as scholar practitioners. The benefits of such a practice will enhance both the education of the teacher and the students they serve.

References

Kochan, F. K., & Mullen, C. A. (Eds.). (2001). Probing accountability in educational leadership: For whom and for what? *Journal of School Leadership, 11*(3), 158–257.

Lortie, D. C. (1998). Teaching educational administration: Reflections on our craft. *The Journal of Cases in Educational Leadership, 1*(1), 1–12. Retrieved November 28, 2001, from http://www.ucea.org/cases

Mullen, C. A. (with Stover, L., & Corley, B.). (2001). School accreditation and teacher empowerment: An Alabama case. *Teacher Development: An International Journal of Teachers' Professional Development, 5*(1), 121–137.

Further Reading

Kincheloe, J. L., & Weil, D. (Eds.). (2001). *Standards and schooling in the United States: An encyclopedia.* Santa Barbara, CA: ABC-CLIO.

Merriam, S. B. (1998). *Qualitative research and case study applications in education.* San Francisco: Jossey-Bass.

Mullen, C. A. (2002). Mentoring aspiring school leaders in scholarly writing through case studies of diversity. In F. K. Kochan (Ed.), *Organizational and human dimensions of successful mentoring programs and relationships: No. 1. Perspectives on mentoring 1* (pp. 83–102). Greenwich, CT: Information Age Publishing.

Mullen, C. A., & Lick, D. W. (Eds.). (1999). *New directions in mentoring: Creating a culture of synergy.* London: Falmer Press.

Students As Scholar Practitioners

Nancy Kraft

When we think of the term scholar practitioner, we often think of persons who are considered to be learned individuals, not only conversant in the theory underlying practice, but also adept in applying theory, research, and knowledge in new and innovative ways to practice or through real-world applications. Being a scholar practitioner is the ultimate connection between thinking and doing, which in the field of education are often seen as dichotomous terms. We have scholars at the university level who are perceived to be involved in scholarly work (i.e., research and thinking), while practitioners are generally thought to be K-12 teachers in schools, whose role is to teach or to be the doer. The end result of such thinking is a disconnect between thinking and doing, or scholarly and practical work, thus implying that these are not synonymous functions and that K-12 teachers are certainly not capable of being both scholarly and practical at the same time.

While there has been a movement in the field of education during the last decade to acknowledge K-12 teachers as intellectuals who are engaged in thinking about their practice and to bridge the gap between scholar and practitioner, what about students? Do these terms apply to students who are perceived to be at the receiving end of the educational process? It would seem logical that a primary goal of education should be to develop persons who can engage in critical thinking and turn around and be able to apply that thinking to practical settings and situations. This, however, requires a process of education that involves students in inquiry-based approaches where they have the opportunity to develop "the attitudes and skills of social, political, and cultural criticism" as articulated by Neil Postman and Charles Weingartner in their famous 1969 book, *Teaching as a Subversive Activity.* Postman and Weingartner believe the primary goal of education should be to engage students in critical thinking processes and inquiry-based learning experiences. Yet, with the increasing accountability requirements being mandated by federal legislation since the early 1990s, many teachers are instead opting to teach students via methods of "drill and kill," where teachers feel the goal of education, and their only option, is to pour knowledge into students'

heads so that they will be able to parrot back that knowledge on standardized multiple choice tests. Such testing practices increasingly do not require students to apply knowledge in a practical setting, but rather to select the "right" answer from a list of four or five choices. Consequently, students themselves are disengaging in the teaching/learning process, becoming more apathetic about school, and often query whether "this will be on the test," suggesting that if it is, then they will store bits and pieces of information in their heads only to be retrieved later for testing purposes and then forgotten. So the process of creating students as scholar practitioners or connecting the thinking and doing part of education seems to have little relevance in today's world of high-stakes testing and accountability measures.

If we were to disregard the current testing craze and instead consider developing students to become scholar practitioners, what kinds of qualities would we expect to engender in students and what kinds of teaching practices would ensure students as scholar practitioners? There are several qualities of being a scholar practitioner, of which the foremost is being a critical thinker. In the context of examining students as scholar practitioners, critical thinking is much more than logical reasoning or a mere intellectual exercise that involves processes of conceptualizing, analyzing, synthesizing, and/or evaluating information. Rather, it entails a process of helping students to think "outside the box" and to challenge their thinking from the perspective of assumptions underlying their beliefs and behaviors. And then based on that thinking, to be ready to think and act differently in the world, to make a difference in applying that thinking to concrete settings. Another characteristic of scholar practitioners is possessing intellectual curiosity—wanting to know and having a willingness to engage in inquiry. It also involves the capacity to exercise a high degree of reflective judgment—to be able to understand and accept uncertainty and the realization that there are not necessarily absolute truths, but rather that one's understanding of the world must be actively constructed. A final necessary characteristic is having a strong sense of self and a sense that one has the individual capacity to effect change—to apply knowledge in a practical sense to make a difference in this world.

So what kinds of teaching practices are needed to enable students to become scholar practitioners? The best way to assist students in this is to democratize schooling and to give them a sense of voice and ownership in the educational process. In a Deweyan sense, classrooms would be restructured as "living democracies" that would model and prepare students for participation in public life and community activism. Learning would involve consciousness-raising—assisting students to see that they can make a difference in the world—enabling them to become more adept at reading the "world" rather than merely reading the "word." Teaching practices would be characterized as being learner-centered, participative, and focused on, and responsive to real problems. Course work would be integrated and thematic, while assessment would be performance-based and would have value beyond school. Learning would be multidisciplinary and would develop students' capacities for taking action on societal and community issues. Teaching would be characterized by methods that instill in students intellectual habits—or as Deborah Meier (1995) refers to these as "habits of mind"—and would consist of teaching in such a manner that outcomes

include (1) concern for evidence (how do you know that); (2) viewpoint (who said it and why); (3) cause and effect (what led to it, what else happened); (4) hypothesizing (what if, supposing that); and (5) who cares (does it make a difference?).

One of the most effective methods or strategies of teaching to develop students as scholar practitioners is service-learning, which is an approach to education that integrates community service with academic study to enrich learning, teach civic responsibility, and strengthen communities. Students reinforce and apply academic skills and knowledge in real-life situations while addressing authentic school and community needs. To qualify as service-learning, the following components need to be present: (1) service needs to address a genuine or authentic community need; (2) there needs to be a clear connection between the academic curriculum and the service experience; (3) student reflection, to process and learn from the service experience is central; (4) student voice is present in identifying, planning, and implementing service activities; and (5) evaluation is continuous of both service and learning outcomes. Service-learning gives schoolwork intrinsic value beyond achieving success in school, because there is a connection between the knowledge acquired and the larger social context in which students live. Service-learning can be the vehicle through which students begin to understand concepts such as community revitalization and economic development and learn how they can use their skills and education for social action to better the community (and eventually the world) in which they live, thus enabling them to become scholar practitioners in a true sense of the word.

The following is an example of what this would look like in a classroom setting that involved fifth grade students from a suburban and predominantly middleclass neighborhood who participated in a thematic unit, integrating social studies, science, math, and language arts into an intergenerational project. Every other week, over the course of a semester, students visited a nearby nursing home spending an hour reading to residents and listening to them share stories of their past and childhood experiences. To prepare the students for this experience and to integrate this into a curriculum unit that focused on the relationship between elderly and the impact of economics on lifestyles, the teacher asked his student to reflect on several questions: "what is old; how are elderly treated in this society; and what is the relationship between one's financial status and growing old?" Listing students' responses to these questions on the blackboard gave the teacher many ideas of ways he could address their responses and underlying beliefs and stereotypes they had about elderly and the elderly poor through the science, social studies, math, and language arts curriculum.

As the fifth grade science curriculum focused on nutrition, living systems, and physical change, students researched caloric needs of individuals at different stages of life and how body systems change during the aging process, looking specifically at common ailments creating physical challenges for elderly person. In social studies, which included an economics focus, students studied the relationship between income level and access to quality medical services and nutrition programs. They also compared and contrasted perceptions of elderly persons across several cultures, both represented by the student make-up of the school and those of elderly residents living in the adjacent inner city. In addition to these perceptions, students

studied social issues such as loss of autonomy, independence, and the impact of limited incomes. They also researched how government programs and policies impacted elderly in different social strata and the effects these policies had on elderly who were poor. Another assignment had students critically view television programs to assess how popular culture and the media represented elderly and the poor. Based on all their research, the students developed a survey to assess the prevalence of these issues among elderly persons in their own neighborhoods. The resulting data were tabulated and aggregated by ethnicity categories and then represented and interpreted through a variety of means such as pie charts, bar graphs, and narrative analysis. Survey results indicated differentials in access to health care and a quality of life for elderly residents dependent on a person' socioeconomic status.

This portion of the unit, about the effects of economics on elderly lifestyles, culminated with student's writing papers that illustrated their own understandings of the impact of economic conditions on lifestyles, especially those of the elderly. Students brainstormed ways to counter negative portrayals of elderly in this society and how to raise others' social and critical consciousness concerning the issues they had uncovered through their own investigations. Several students chose to submit these to the local paper where they were published in the editorial section. While the original intent of the project was for students to be involved in service to elderly citizens, the way their teacher structured learning and reflection resulted in a transformative experience for students. Their involvement in this project helped students come to view elderly from a more compassionate and respectful perspective now that they realized the breadth and depth of physical, emotional, and economic challenges confronting many elderly citizens. Students also took an active interest in supporting and advocating for social issues that impacted the lives of elderly in their own community, becoming activists themselves and further applying what they had learned in a practical and authentic setting.

As shown in this example, effective instruction in schools, using a service-learning approach, can enable students to apply academic theory to real-world practice and to assume the role of scholar practitioner. Service-learning that is coupled with critical thinking recognizes that what students learn in school does not take place in a vacuum and is not something that is learned only to be later "spit back" on a test, but rather it is learning that includes the entire social, economic, cultural, political, and historical context that shapes one's position and existence in the world. It is learning that combines community needs with students' interests and learning needs, and gives them opportunities to learn new roles, think more critically and analytically, and apply knowledge and skills in a systematic way. In the process students become more effective problem solvers, engage in higher level thinking, apply academic skills, and learn lifelong skills that increase their sense of personal power, helping them realize that through schooling and learning they are scholar practitioners and can make a difference in this world.

Further Reading

Claus, J., & Ogden, C. (1999). *Service learning for youth empowerment and social change.* New York: Peter Lang.

Meier, D. (1995). *The power of their ideas: Lessons for America from a small school in Harlem.* Boston: Beacon Press.

Postman, N., & Weingartner, C. (1969). *Teaching as a subversive activity.* New York: Dell Publishing Company.

Shor, I. (1992). *Empowering education: Critical teaching for social change.* Chicago: University of Chicago Press.

Science

Critical Thinking and the Teaching of Science

Koshi Dhingra

A critical thinker in science sees herself as a scientist. She recognizes the science she does and the scientific decisions she makes in her everyday life, be it at the workplace, home, grocery store, doctor's office, or elsewhere. Whether or not she practices science professionally, she recognizes the significance of the role played by such issues as human cloning, abortion rights, stem-cell research, and so forth and of her own role in voting on these issues. She is aware that her increased access to a vast array of information, with the development of new technologies over recent years, puts her in a position to evaluate statements and ideas with much more insight than in the past. However, at the same time, she knows that she needs to continuously question her own assumptions as well as those of others. Her understanding of the nature of science involves the myriad sociocultural forces responsible for shaping scientific progress affecting a wide range of human activity. She recognizes that science, like all other fields of work, is a human endeavor affected by many of the same errors, inconsistencies, and politics as any other social activity.

WHAT IS SCIENCE? EPISTEMOLOGICAL PLURALISM AND MULTICULTURAL PERSPECTIVES

Different, often competing, ways of accounting for natural phenomena exist. Science, therefore, encompasses a range of accounts and explanations for universal experiences (Cobern & Loving, 2001). Which accounts are accepted by the scientific community and where they come from therefore shape the nature of science. When considering what is to be classified as science, one is faced with a wide range of knowledge claims—from creation science to indigenous, local knowledge of various populations such as the First Nations people in Canada and the Yupiaq people of southwestern Alaska (Kawagley, Norris-Tull, & Norris-Tull, in Cobern, 2000). Much work is done by legitimating institutions that operate in the culture, such as family, school, religion, mass media, and so on, in determining what counts as science. As critical thinkers, we need to be mindful of the processes at play that validate some knowledge claims while disconfirming others. The notion of a singular nature of science is thus challenged by the notion of epistemological pluralism and the significance of multicultural perspectives on science.

Is science a collection of facts or truths, or is science a dynamic body of tentative knowledge claims that depend on social negotiation and that may change depending on the operating research paradigm and the sociopolitical climate under which science works? The former depiction is in keeping with positivist notions of science in which knowable truths about the world are directly accessed by our senses. The latter depiction is in keeping with a range of postpositivist philosophies of science, all of which have in common the notion that knowledge is constructed by people, whose interpretations are affected by their situations. I propose that this latter, more complex set of perspectives is the vantage point of the critical thinker. What implications does such a position have on one's views on the nature of scientific theories, scientific laws and the so-called scientific method?

THEORIES, LAWS, AND THE SCIENTIFIC METHOD

To the extent that explanatory power is the hallmark of science, theories and laws are integral to a science's ability to explain the world. However, according to many philosophers of science, neither theories nor laws are absolute truths. Pragmatic views of science depict knowledge as an instrument to deal with the world. To use an analogy, theories are the maps, which help tourists find their way. A tourist can, of course, still manage to get lost even while using a map. How one uses a map is up to the individual; the theory, like the map, is application-neutral. Pursuit of scientific knowledge then becomes the

travels through a region using a variety of possible routes and perhaps involves the discovery of some new routes along the way. A law, to continue with the analogy, is like a runabout railway ticket, which is valid for unlimited journeys within a given region. The law is thus the inference ticket for the region; the ticket itself contains no directions or specifications. The scope of the law is not apparent. Only with experience can the ticket be used with greater confidence. By such a scheme, the relationship between law and truth is not direct. Knowledge is dependent upon the route that was traveled. That which is perceived as truth is therefore relative to the method used.

Ideas in science occupy different levels depending on the degree of acceptance by the mainstream scientific community. Scientific theories evolve and have a developmental history. Understanding the history of a scientific idea adds depth and dimension to our conception of the idea while also allowing us to evaluate the explanatory power of the idea. As critical thinkers, we are aware of the significance of the effects of such contextual factors as language, political forces, social needs and values, and so forth on scientific progress.

The kind of reasoning employed by scientists and travelers alike involves logic-in-use—decisions are made on the spot and involve detours and alterations. A reformulated logic is made visible in formal scientific reports and has contributed to the notions of objectivity and the scientific method. However, the state of conceptual neutrality required by objectivity is not possible given the undeniable sociological dimension of science. Science is a human endeavor involving the interpretation of data. These do not speak for themselves; however, the power of science stems from its self-maintenance within the limits of intersubjectivity. The community structure of the sciences does much to limit solely value-directed change. As such, the social dimension of science deserves a closer look.

SCIENCE AS A SOCIAL ACTIVITY

The social nature of scientific practice works toward the maintenance of the scientific method on a group, rather than individual, level. Three aspects of the social character of science are distinctive. First, members of the various scientific disciplines depend on each other for the conditions (ideas, instruments, etc.) under which they practice. Second, initiation into scientific inquiry requires education from those who already practice it. Third, scientific practitioners are part of a society and the sciences depend on that society's valuing what they do for their survival.

Kuhn (1970) writes of the central role of the science community's current paradigm in determining what counts as legitimate scientific activity. Thus, he sees scientific progress as consisting of revolutionary science—in which new paradigms replace old ones—as well as normal science—in which work is done to build on an existing paradigm. Kuhn's revolutionary science implies a community with common language seeing and living in the same world. As Kuhn wrote in the postscript to his work (1970), such deep-rooted change in worldview takes a long time and more than a single individual to achieve. The occurrence of conflict between judgments is seen as being key to the development of science. However, in describing revolutionary change in the sciences, Kuhn makes a limited inquiry into the social arrangements of scientific practice so that the question, to him, is which scientific community will legitimately exercise

cognitive authority. He does not consider the ways in which cognitive authority extends beyond these expert cultures. Acknowledgment of the interactions between the cognitive authority of the scientific method (and those who practice it) and the rest of society is an important factor in the acknowledgment of science as social knowledge. The line distinguishing between scientist and non-scientist becomes unclear from this perspective. The existence of a singular scientific community that is distinct, by implication, from a nonscientific community is similarly thrown into question.

The transformation of an idea into scientific knowledge results in an impersonal knowledge construction, often misinterpreted as objectivity. It is important to note that it is not this impersonality but the collaborative, social dimension of scientific practice that makes a knowledge claim objective or intersubjective. However, feminist writers point to the value of developing more intimate relationships between researcher and subject in scientific study. Such a view of science further expands our notion of activities that we can classify as being scientific.

FEMINIST PERSPECTIVES ON THE NATURE OF SCIENCE

Keller's description, in *A Feeling for the Organism,* of Barbara McClintock's scientific practice in coming up with the idea of 'jumping genes', for which she was awarded the Nobel Prize in Medicine and Physiology in 1983, presents the notion of a nonscientific approach. The goal is not to reduce the complexity of nature to simplistic models but to develop a relationship with the subjects in which the goal is to understand the complexity of systems involved as far as possible. Kirkup and Keller's account of McClintock's work is also her proposal of a science that is an alternative to the rational masculine version that has dominated Western scientific practice under logical empiricism. McClintock's feeling for her study organisms, developed over time, is described by Keller as having everything to do with the emergence of her insights about transposons or "jumping genes." Science and technology as spaces for the not-impersonal exploration of subjects are called for by a range of feminist science critiques; the notion that developing a personal relationship with study subjects is not only a natural outcome but also a strength of scientific inquiry is highlighted by various feminist science thinkers.

CRITICAL THINKING AND SCIENCE IN THE MEDIA

Science learning and critical thinking in science take place in a wide variety of venues; the blurring of the lines between formal and free-choice science educational resources points to the need for critical thinkers in science to assess knowledge claims emerging from such diverse science educational sources as film, television, the Internet, museums, and print media. Given the breadth of scientific information sources, it becomes important when considering critical thinking in science to recognize that popular media, or the "edutainment" industry, represents a powerful educational agent.

High school student participants in an ethnographic study I conducted in 1999 referred to *The X Files* as being one of five television programs in which they saw the most science. This study explored the extent to which student viewers think critically about the multiple natures of science they view on television and how they as-

sess the science they viewed. The relevance and necessity of imagination and daring to question the established to science is a significant aspect of science. In response to an article in the British newspaper, *The Independent*, by John Durant, professor of the public understanding of science at Imperial College, London, an article in *Nature* cautions against dismissing the science fiction viewed on Fox Television Network's *The X Files*. The writer states, "the interaction of Mulder and Scully is as scientific as you please. They look at the evidence, they come up with hypotheses, they test them, and most are found wanting. Any truth that they think they find is soon undermined by new evidence that their preferred hypothesis cannot explain, and so they are forced to move on" ("How not to respond," p. 815). *The X Files*, an immensely popular television program, is attacked by Durant and others as promoting belief in pseudoscience. However, in that the program rejects the idea of scientists as "custodians of truth" ("How not to respond," p. 815), *The X Files* is seen to promote several important aspects of science: uncertainty combined with the absence of clearly defined answers, the possibility of multiple interpretations, and the notion that progress is often through blind alleys and false trails.

J.T. is an independent producer of science-related, nonfiction television programming who I interviewed as part of my study. He spoke to the importance of developing critical thinking in science when he conceptualized a television production. He described his area of interest as policy issues. Citizens in a mature democracy, he felt, can no longer rely on an expert's choice and, therefore, need to know how scientists make choices. In other words, he tries to show viewers how scientists know things in his programs. He describes the underlying tension in science as existing between consensus and uncertainty. In a policy debate, the focus is on uncertainty. He was recently working on a joint *Frontline* and *Nova* production on climate change. The subject matter, he felt, is fraught with uncertainty in terms of when will change happen and what should we do about it. The time scale over which this issue tracks is tremendous, given that our entire civilization is based on the use of fossil fuels. To further complicate things, the problem looks different depending on which part of the world you live in. Carbon dioxide levels are considered a mark of prosperity. India and China are at the early stages of their industrial revolutions and the idea that they should forgo increasing economic prosperity because of carbon dioxide levels is not part of their current agendas. J.T. felt that the public tends either to be uninterested in the issue of climate change or to respond uncritically to positions ranging from conservative viewpoints or "greenfears." His hope was to raise the consciousness of his viewers on two levels—first, on the level of increasing awareness of the issue itself and, second, on the level of increasing awareness of the sociohistorical complexities that bear upon this issue. In other words, his goal for this production centered around developing critical thinking about the issue of climate change.

Interestingly, as part of the same larger study, Michael, a sophomore at high school, said in an interview with me, "I haven't seen anything like *Crossfire* (on scientific issues). If you had both sides of the issue . . . I think it would be really interesting and I would watch it." Michael reacts strongly against being provided with a single perspective on information. His recommendation is for science programming to learn from political reports on news programs in which the focus, like J.T.'s focus, is on uncertainty and the opinions of a range of experts and community members.

The direction to take, as critical thinkers in science, may be the one that Michael points to. Let us recognize the need for multiple sources of information, let us understand the uncertain and dynamic nature of science, and let us know that our role is to continuously assess and evaluate scientific information from a wide variety of sources.

References

Cobern, W. W., & Loving, C. C. (2001). Defining "science" in a multicultural world: Implications for science education. *Science Education, 85*(1), 50–67.

How not to respond to *The X-Files*. (1998). *Nature, 394,* p. 815.

Kirkup, G., & Keller, L. S. (1992). A feeling for the organism: Fox Keller's life of Barbara McClintock. In G. Kirkup, & L. S. Keller (Eds.), *Inventing women—science, technology and gender* (pp. 188–195). Cambridge, U.K.: Polity Press.

Kuhn, T. S. (1970). *The structure of scientific revolutions* (2nd ed.). Chicago: University of Chicago Press.

Further Reading

Longino, H. E. (1990). *Science as social knowledge.* Princeton, NJ: Princeton University Press.

Toulmin, S. (1960). *The philosophy of science.* New York: Harper and Row.

Science Education

C. Sheldon Woods

Science has and is viewed by many youth and teachers alike as the domain of white "nerdy" males. Over the last seven years, I have asked preservice science teachers to draw images of scientist doing science. The results have been staggering. The majority draws an image of a white male (very often middle aged) wearing glasses or goggles and a white lab coat. He has bad hair or no hair. This scientist is typically indoors, working alone with chemicals, beakers, test tubes, and Bunsen burner at a lab bench. This is a very narrow view of what science is and what scientists actually do. This image mirrors the one typically drawn by students asked to complete the same task. How many children aspire to grow up and be this individual? Not many. This is a problem that sheds light on some of the problems with science education.

This image of science and scientist arises from a science education system that, in the past, has been driven by national interest with little regard for students or teachers. Science has been taught as a cold body of facts to be memorized and regurgitated on tests. Science has also been taught as a separate isolated "other" subject that focuses on reading thick texts and repeating cook book style lab activities. All the student has to do is follow the directions to achieve a known outcome. This technocratic approach deprives students of the richness and potential that the study of science has to offer and it deprives teachers of creativity and curricular input.

How did we get here? The launch of Sputnik in 1957 by the Russians served as a catalyst for major change for science education in the United States. This event challenged the national notion that the United States was the most technically superior country in the world. The result was a plethora of science curriculum that were designed by scientist and university-level science educators. The main goal of these curriculum projects was to produce future scientists and mathematicians that would help the United States win the Cold War and reclaim its position as the most technically superior country. The major problem with this approach was that very little consideration, if any, was given to student's interest nor was there much teacher input. There was unprecedented money spent and to be made, which lead to competing curriculum being pushed by powerful groups, which focused on single aspects or approaches such as textbooks, assessments, curriculum frameworks, peer learning, and technological innovation. Many of these approaches were untested or were driven by economic factors instead of the best interest of students. This resulted in a meritocracy where students with a strong desire to study science and those already with a strong science proficiency excelled while others floundered and gradually opted out of science study. In addition, teachers with a strong science background excelled and those with weak science backgrounds avoided the subject, reinforcing the notion that science education was for an elite or select group.

This approach to science education developed in the 1960s survived and flourished. Textbook companies competed with each other for the lucrative contracts offered by states, districts, and schools. In this milieu it was just assumed that students were getting a superior science education and this was evident by the numerous technological advances being made in the United States. This was all about to change.

In 1983, *A Nation at Risk* was published. This document called for educational reform of the U.S. school system. It also presented information comparing students in the United States to those in other industrialized countries, showing that the students in the United States were behind in math and science. This lead to more cries for reform.

In 1985, as Halley's Comet neared earth, scientists attending the meeting of the American Association for the Advancement of Science (AAAS) developed a definition of scientific literacy for all high school graduates. This document was entitled *Science for All Americans* and was part of Project 2061. The year 2061 would be the next appearance of Halley's comet near earth and the goal year for all Americans to be scientifically literate. Project 2061 also gave rise to *Benchmarks for Science Literacy*. This document further expands the definition for science literacy, defined in *Science for All Americans*, and provides developing hierarchy of benchmarks to be met by students in grades two, five, eight, and twelve.

The current science classroom is a far cry from what is possible and what is desired. Imagine a science classroom where students regardless of their gender, race, ethnicity, socioeconomic status, sexual orientation, or region of origin are excited about learning science because it is presented as a field of study that is open to all and has relevance to their everyday lives. It is not merely an exercise in memorizing facts or doing prepackaged unimaginative activities, but it produces scientifically literate students by developing critical thinking skills while providing students with inquiry-based activities that lead to discovery. In addition, it is a science classroom that acknowledges the many contributions of women and people of color to science and one that begins to expose students to the more than 200,000 branches of science.

The National Science Education Standards (NSES), developed in 1994 by the National Research Council, provide science standards for K-12 grades, with the main goal being scientific literacy for all students. The NSE standards content is defined to include inquiry; the traditional subject areas of physical, life, and earth and space sciences; connections between science and technology; science in personal and social perspectives; and the history and nature of science. This information on content is supplemented with information that develops student understanding. The standards also address assessment, program standards for schools and districts, education professionals, and the broader community that supports schools.

The NSES were developed in part to change the emphasis of science education. There is less emphasis on knowing facts, studying subject disciplines for their own sake, separating science knowledge and science process, covering many science topics, and implementing inquiry as a set of processes. There is greater emphasis on understanding concepts and developing abilities of inquiry; learning subject-matter disciplines in the context of technology, science in personal and social perspectives, and history and nature of science; integrating all aspects of science content; studying a few fundamental science concepts; and implementing inquiry as instructional strategies, abilities, and ideas to be learned.

Despite the best intentions of the recent science standards, many classroom teachers are still supplied with curricular materials that do not present a diverse history of science, nor do they present science in an integrated fashion while focusing on fewer concepts. The standards aim at being a catalyst for change but, unless a critical examination of the practice of science education occurs, the view and practice of science being the domain of a certain few will continue.

By critically examining curricular materials, educators can use inadequate materials to empower students by giving them voice, so that they can question the absence of people of color and women in text or question why they must learn some of the esoteric information presented in text. Teachers should reflect on such questions as "Does this text reflect the experiences of my students?" "How can I use this text to empower and motivate my students?" "What do I need to do to supplement the text?" "What does the community offer that can be a concrete example for topics covered?" Students should also be encouraged to reflect focusing on such questions as "How does this information effect me?" "How does it relate to my everyday life?" "Are there examples of this in my own community?"

Many individuals will argue that science and math are objective areas of study and that it is difficult to address issues of social justice and multiculturalism and still cover the content. This attitude ignores that fact that science and math are products of the dominant history and culture. It is critical that teachers work to present a wider view of science then the typical Western male view that is the norm. This

process does not need to take away from the content, but instead, can be used to enhance the content. One such way is to name student groups in science after individuals that reflect the cultural and ethnic background of the students and that enable students to know who the person is and what they contributed the field of science. This process does take some work on the teacher's part, but as time goes on it becomes part of the process of undoing some of the harm done by textbooks. Many textbooks marginalize women and people of color.

It is also important to realize that not every student has a desire to learn science for the sake of learning science. Teachers must be aware of what skills each student has and in which area each student excels. By so doing, they can adapt the science education curriculum to meet the needs of the students. This process may also lead to natural integration of science with other areas of study. For example, for the student who loves art, music, or poetry, designing activities that relate the topic to these areas may be the catalyst to encourage the student to want to learn more. This type of interdisciplinary or holistic approach illustrates for students that science is not a separated independent subject but, rather, that it is integrated with other areas and is all around them. Typically, the holistic dimensions of science education are empirical, technological, futuristic, philosophical, aesthetic, and historical. This approach works best with older students, but it is designed to best match the interest of individual students and acts as a point of departure or motivation to more intensive involvement with the subject area until all aspects of the content merge. For younger students, more traditional interdisciplinary approaches work. For example, using activities in math, reading, social studies, music, or physical education that reinforce the concepts learned or studied in science.

Schools and districts must be open to true science education reform and be willing to provide curricular materials that empower students instead of sustaining the status quo. Teachers need to critically examine their own attitudes and beliefs, practices, and ability with respect to science. They must challenge their own weaknesses and work to overcome them so that they can design appropriate activities for their students. Teachers play a vital role in science education and, as such, they have the potential to be agents of change or roadblocks to success.

Further Reading

American Association for the Advancement of Science. (1989). *Science for all Americans.* New York: Oxford University Press.

American Association for the Advancement of Science. (1993). *Benchmarks for science literacy.* New York: Oxford University Press.

National Research Council. (1996). *National science education standards.* Washington, DC: National Academy Press.

Sexism

Sexism: Is Critical Thinking Theory Sexist?

Barbara J. Thayer-Bacon

Sexism is the belief that one "sex" is superior to another. In most cultures throughout time sexism has favored men over women, boys over girls. Examples of sexism can be found in the desire of parents to have male children over female children, and in deciding to invest in giving males a better education in schools than girls, or denying females an education altogether. In schools, as part of the hidden curriculum, sexism teaches that girls are not as important as boys by making men more visible in the texts than women and by giving boys more attention in class than girls.

What does critical thinking have to do with sexism? Well, in fact, feminists have argued that critical thinking is based on a way of describing thinking that favors a male approach to thinking. They have argued that the paradigm of thinking, which can be traced back to ancient Greece, favors reason over emotions; privileges rational, linear, deductive thinking over intuition; is aggressive and confrontational rather than collegial and collaborative; is individualistic and privileges personal autonomy over communities and relation-ships; is abstract and disfavors lived experiences and concrete particularity; and that it presupposes the possibility of objectivity and therefore does not recognize one's situatedness (Bailin, 1995, pp. 191–192).

For example, in 1992, I wrote an essay by the same title as above in which I looked particularly at the last point: that critical thinking presupposes the possibility of objectivity and therefore does not recognize one's situatedness. I framed this problem in terms of the dualism of subjectivity/objectivity. I argued that critical thinking and what is considered intelligent thought is based on a paradigm of thinking that can be traced back to ancient Greece. It is a paradigm that stresses that critical thinking is a process based on logic where the goal is to separate facts from opinions. In this process, the critical thinker seeks to remain objective and distanced from what is being examined so he does not influence the thinking with his own biases. The critical thinker tries to separate himself from the object of his thinking in the hopes that critical thinking will help him arrive at an answer to his problems that is objective and neutral.

My focus in that essay was on the impossibility of the critical thinker separating herself from the outside world; I was pointing at an artificial split between the subject and the object, as well as between personal subjectivity and impersonal objectivity. I argued that we can never sever ourselves from ourselves, we cannot jump out of our skins to gain this illusionary objective view, and that thinking we could do so is a core problem for the traditional paradigm of critical thinking. Our fingerprints are always all over our problem solving, for we decide what problems to look at, what questions to ask about that problem, and what methodology to use in trying to answer our questions. I described four current influential philosophers contributing to discussions on critical thinking—Robert Ennis, John McPeck, Harvey Siegel, and Richard Paul—and I showed how all four of them include within their theories an effort to achieve this objectified illusion.

I argued that a paradigm of critical thinking that tries to separate the subjective voice of the knower from what is known not only sets us up for an impossibility, but believing it is possible to sever oneself from the objects of study is sexist as well. The reason for the charge of sexism is that, historically, in the Euro-Western world, men have been judged to be more capable of separating themselves from their objects of study than women. Women have been judged throughout time to be more emotional and intuitive, maybe even more imaginative, but not more rational. Women have been taught to listen to their own subjective voices and follow their "gut feeling" (maybe as a way of compensating for their lack of educational access), and yet those who do try to listen to their own subjective voices have been judged to be inferior thinkers. Many feminists have argued that philosophy's traditional critical thinking paradigm is a form of patriarchy that leads to control of knowledge and the ways of knowing by men, and it leads to the silencing and devaluing/subordinating of women's ways of knowing. Indeed, Belenky and colleagues (1986) famous study of women's ways of knowing models what has happened to women's thinking under the traditional patriarchal model: They have been silenced, or taught to refer to other, male authorities; maybe they have learned to rely on their own "women's intuition" (which has been devalued by men as "magic" or "nonsense"); or they have, if given enough opportunity for education, learned to defer to the male voice of reason. Very few have learned to be constructive thinkers, able to listen to their own inner voice, as well as their expert, authority voice, with the confidence that they, as thinkers, are able to construct knowledge.

The basic insight concerning critical thinking that I was working with was the idea that we cannot separate ourselves from our objects of inquiry, that it is an impossible goal that is very dangerous because it leaves people feeling severed and distant from each other as well as from their ideas. I recommended that we need to reclaim the self and attempt to integrate personal knowledge and expert knowledge. My sources for this insight came from feminist scholars who were emphasizing interrelationships and connections in their descriptions of knowledge, and were arguing that all methods we have for obtaining knowledge are human constructions (e.g., Keller, Harding, and Spender). I was also inspired by classic and present day American pragmatists, who also emphasize that we, as knowers, are participating in the construction of truths (e.g., Peirce, Dewey, and Rorty).

This 1992 essay, "Is Modern Critical Thinking Theory Sexist?" along with others that feminists were writing at the time, triggered many heated discussions and debates. It was a shocking claim to charge that the tool that everyone thought was neutral and unbiased, critical thinking, was not neutral after all, but in fact favored a male approach to knowledge that was possibly dangerous and destructive, as well as devaluing of other approaches to knowledge. Critical thinking scholars scrambled to try to defend themselves against charges of sexism by feminists, as well as charges of other forms of bias by other minority groups such as indigenous people. In general, their responses to these charges of bias have been to criticize the claims and show, for example, how they confuse the concept of critical thinking with the practices of thinking critically. They pointed out that the claim that critical thinking is aggressive is aimed at the practice of critical thinking, whereas the claim that critical thinking neglects emotions and intuition is aimed at current conceptions of critical thinking. Critical thinking scholars have also responded by arguing that some of the examples used to show that critical thinking theory is amiss are examples that do not fulfill criteria used to define critical thinking (such as Ennis's list, which includes taking the whole situation into account, being sensitive to others' feelings, understanding others' perspectives, and demonstrating a critical spirit).

It is a mistake to think that feminist charges that critical thinking is sexist are based on thinking that there has simply been an uneven application of existing standards. It is certainly the case that many feminists have worked to demonstrate that existing standards have not been applied

evenly. However, for some feminists, the charges run deeper than that. The charges are concerned with the standards themselves—what is used to define what gets to count as critical thinking. Some feminist scholars, such as myself, are not just suggesting that critical thinking is somehow deficient in neglecting to include the emotions and intuition, or that if critical thinkers would just try to be less confrontational and combative, a kinder and gentler form of critical thinking would end the charge of sexism. It is not going to be enough to improve the descriptions of what critical thinking entails and to improve upon the practices of thinking critically by incorporating neglected dimensions and adjusting the ways that we practice critical thinking to remove the charge of bias. Some feminists claim that *all* conceptions of critical thinking, and *all* ways of practicing critical thinking are necessarily biased for they all come from partial and limited perspectives. They claim that there is "No God's eye view of truth," that all views are from a particular, situated perspective that is limited and partial. They also claim that there is no universal method for evaluating the different ways of thinking critically, for all criteria are biased too. Any criteria that is used to justify the privileged place of critical thinking as a way of understanding and interacting with the world over other less-privileged but equally valid ways, such as intuition, will assume the legitimacy of the very enterprise it is trying to justify. You cannot use criteria that assume the value of critical thinking to try to evaluate critical thinking. In the world of philosophy that kind of circular argument is called "begging the question."

In fact, this is exactly what has happened in responses by critical thinking scholars to the charges that critical thinking is sexist. They have begged the question. They have either taken a defensive stand and used their critical thinking skills to attack the charges, or they have taken a more gracious approach and conceded that there is an alternative way of knowing that is primarily female. Either way of addressing the charge of sexism allows them to get away with not really having to look at how critical thinking is embedded within a whole philosophical paradigm that needs to be transformed. Both approaches allow critical thinking scholars to let critical thinking maintain its scope and importance when the feminist charge of sexism is actually insisting that critical thinking move out of its time-honored position of authority. Critical thinking scholars such as Bailin worry that transformative proposals must face the possibility that, in devaluing critical thinking's status, we will undercut any possibility of rational discussion. Feminists such as myself, however, argue that if one attempts to redescribe critical thinking without making problematic critical thinking's high status in Euro-Western philosophy, what one ends up doing is recapitulating and reformulating critical thinking within its given structure. Attempting to redescribe critical thinking as a concept without addressing the valued status of the practice of thinking critically separates ideas from experiences and reaffirms the very separation I started out trying to deny back in 1992—between knowers and the known, between subjectivity and objectivity.

So what does this mean for teachers? Does this mean that teachers should stop trying to teach their students to be critical thinkers? No, it does not, although it does mean that teachers need to acknowledge that, while critical thinking is a tool that has a great deal of value and use in helping us solve our problems and untangle the knots in our reasoning, it is not the only

tool available to help us, nor is it infallible (unbiased). This does not mean critical thinking is necessarily harmful or false, but that it always has the potential of being so. This is why we have the responsibility of continually reexamining "it" and continually striving to redescribe "it." We have the same responsibility with all the tools we use to help us inquire. It is dangerous to lose sight of the fact that critical thinking does not have a life of its own. Fallible human beings are those who bring critical thinking to life through their use of it as a reasoning tool.

I have presented the position here that, to address concerns of strong biases regarding critical thinking, we must begin by being willing to problematize critical thinking and displace it from its esteemed, self-legitimized status. We move discussions of critical thinking bias to a new level by continually reexamining critical thinking as a concept in relation to the practice of thinking critically. When we realize how interrelated and interconnected concepts and practices are, then we begin to understand that we cannot separate ideas from experiences without losing ideas' (such as critical thinking) contextuality. It is through the contextuality of what we experience that ideas derive their meaning. Not only does contextuality help concepts derive their meaning, but contextuality is needed to help limit the powers of ideas from going beyond their intended scope and significance.

Believing that critical thinking is biased does not mean we have to embrace all theories as being true, or that we have no way of measuring one theory against another to determine which one is better (depending on one's criteria). What it does mean is that we must acknowledge that we do not know the absolute truth, what is right. We continue to inquire, and we try to support our understandings with as much "evidence" as we can socially construct, qualified by the best criteria upon which we can agree. With a more humble view of critical thinking, we realize that that is all any of us can do.

References

Bailin, S. (1995). Is critical thinking biased? Clarifications and implications (pp. 191–197). In Symposium: Is critical thinking biased. *Educational Theory*, 45 (2), 191–233.

Belenky, M. F., Clinchy, B. M., Goldberger, N. R., & Tarule, J. M. (1986). *Women's ways of knowing: The development of self, voice, and mind.* New York: Basic Books, Harper Collins Publishers.

Thayer-Bacon, B. (1992, September). Is modern critical thinking sexist? *Inquiry: Critical Thinking Across the Disciplines,* 3–7.

Further Reading

Bunch, C., & Pollack, S. (Eds.). (1983). *Learning our way: Essays in feminist education.* Trumansburg, NY: The Crossing Press.

Spender, D. (1982). *Women of ideas and what men have done to them.* Winchester, MA: Pandora Press.

Social Studies

History Instruction and Critical Thinking

Kevin D. Vinson

In recent years, history and social studies educators have increasingly advocated instructional approaches that embrace (or are grounded in) an assortment of "critical thinking" orientations. Although the foundations of such perspectives vary and go back (in the United States) at least as far as the work of John Dewey, contemporary views claim roots in such diverse pedagogical outlooks as constructivism, reflective teaching/thinking, multicultural education, Barry Beyer's inquiry-based learning, and even the "new" social studies that dominated North America in the 1960s and 1970s. Its current leaders include scholars such as Peter Seixas of the University of British Columbia, Bruce VanSledright of the University of Maryland, and Samuel S. Wineburg of the University of Washington (among many others), educators who have brought new and sophisticated methods of research and theory to the understanding of how schoolchildren learn and come to make sense of historical subject matter.

WHAT IS CRITICAL THINKING AND WHY IS IT IMPORTANT TO HISTORY INSTRUCTION?

Critical thinking is not merely another word for deep thinking or hard thinking, or even for reflective thinking or simply thinking itself, although it encompasses, of course, aspects of each of these. It is associated, in part, with problem solving, whole language, evidence-based decision making, and authentic teaching and learning. According to noted social studies educator and scholar John J. Patrick (1986), definitions of critical thinking range from the fundamentally "broad" to the fundamentally "narrow." *Broad* definitions interpret critical thinking as related to, if not synonymous with, "cognitive processes" and "strategies" relevant to making decisions and solving meaningful problems. *Narrow* definitions define it in terms principally of "evaluation or appraisal," as in the "use of criteria to make warranted judgments about . . . some object of concern." Moreover, according to Patrick, critical thinking—whether broadly or narrowly construed—generally implies some sense of "curiosity, skepticism, reflection, and rationality . . . [and] the propensity to raise and explore questions about beliefs, claims, evidence, definitions, conclusions, and actions." For Patrick, "[a] more profound view" of critical thinking, however, "encourages appraisal of frameworks or sets of criteria by which judgments are made" *and* "counteracts egocentric, ethnocentric, or doctrinaire judgments, which result when thinkers fail to appraise fundamental assumptions or standards." In other words, for Patrick, *critical thinking* requires not only *thinking* per se, but *also* an inclination toward *being critical.* It asks for *both.*

In history education, as in social studies education more broadly, the significance of critical thinking rests first with its connection to—and meaning for—the development within students of those ideals and actions specific to *democratic citizenship.* This idea, in part, stems from Thomas Jefferson's view that a representative form of government necessitates a well-educated citizenry, one able to weigh arguments and to consider values and beliefs (such as justice, freedom, and equality) when making important decisions relative to voting and public policy. From this viewpoint, a populace empowered by its collective ability to think critically presents the best defense against the potential abuses (by an authoritarian minority) of formal institutional (political, economic, and social) power.

A second reason for the renewed commitment to critical thinking in history education is *philosophical,* and relates to post–*A Nation at Risk* perspectives that deemphasize the traditional status of memorizing names, places, and dates (yet still recognizing that these do have a place), while reemphasizing history as interpretive, subjective, multiperspectival, contested, and contextual. Much of this reconceptualization evolved in response to a range of multicultural, neo-Marxist, and feminist critiques of dominant "textbook history" (and its dominant readings) as sexist, racist, and classist—as elitist and one-sided, too often favoring the majority while silencing, stereotyping, marginalizing, and/or seeking to erase divergent or minority groups and individuals from historical study and memory.

A third justification for further incorporating critical thinking into history instruction is both *pedagogical* and *psychological,* and draws from newer conceptions of effective teaching as well as from constructivist outlooks toward learning and comprehension. Here, critical thinking is seen as more consistent with contemporary notions of "best practice" than are, say, the older and more didactic, teacher-centered, and/or lecture-driven methodologies of the past. Good teaching from this view works to counter the weaknesses of what author Alfie Kohn calls "bunch o'facts" pedagogy (see, for example, *The Schools Our Children Deserve*) and what radical educator Paulo Freire referred to as "banking education" (see, for example, his *Pedagogy of the Oppressed*). This newer instructional practice supports techniques such as cooperative learning, discussion, projects, student-centeredness, interdisciplinarity, and authentic assessment and learning. It opposes the essentialized, objectivist, homogenizing, and fact-based thinking as advocated by such scholars as E. D. Hirsch, Jr. (for example, in *Cultural Literacy: What Every American Needs to Know*) and Diane Ravitch (for example, in *What Do Our Seventeen-Year-Olds Know?*, written with Chester Finn), who assert that the United States faces severe cultural, economic, and international dangers if schools do not focus on successfully teaching an identical and limited set of basics regarding history (and also geography, literature, and so on) to *all* of its students. Consequently, advocates of critical thinking in history (and other content areas) are frequently critical of standards-based educational reforms, especially those rooted in standardized testing (especially high-stakes testing).

HOW CAN CRITICAL THINKING BE INCORPORATED INTO HISTORY CLASSROOMS?

The principles and goals of critical thinking are consistent with a number of skills, values, dispositions, and understandings generally deemed important in history education. Among these are the following:

- Confirming conclusions with facts;
- Identifying bias, stereotypes, clichés, and propaganda;
- Identifying unstated assumptions;
- Recognizing overgeneralizations and undergeneralizations;
- Identifying relevant and irrelevant information;
- Tolerating ambiguity;
- Desiring to be informed and to look for evidence;
- Being open-minded and skeptical;
- Reserving judgment; and
- Respecting others' opinions (adapted from Eggen & Kauchak, 2001, pp. 48 & 50).

Arguably, these are crucial to many of the major goals of history teaching and learning, including, most basically, discerning what happened and understanding or interpreting what it meant or means.

One place, then, for critical thinking might be those activities, procedures, and aims surrounding "primary document analysis," a set of processes in which historians (and history students) seek to authenticate and to assess the validity and reliability of specific historical writings and to make sense of their meanings or relevances vis-à-vis particular historical events and actors. Teachers and students might engage in the following types of questions: Who wrote this document? How do we know? How can we be sure? Is the document "true?" What makes anyone think so? What might have been the author's purposes in creating this piece of evidence? Is the author trustworthy? What might be (or are) his or her biases? How dependable is the work with respect to our trying to "discover" or "reconstruct" what happened, why it happened, and what it meant or means? Why? Might others who were there at the same time have felt differently? Why? How might we effectively use competing stories of some past time period? How and why is some historical evidence better than other historical evidence? And so on.

A second opportunity for critical thinking in history education might involve historical decision making, that is having students place themselves in the roles of particular historical figures (perhaps figures typically "left out") and to consider what they would have thought and done in similar or identical situations. As U.S. antebellum Southerners, for example, would they have been pro- or antislavery? Why? And what if they were Northerners? What factors would have influenced (or, in fact, influence now) their decisions? Why? Would they have signed the Declaration of Independence? As Supreme Court justices, how would they have voted on particular cases (say *Roe v. Wade* or the recent appellate decision on the Pledge of Allegiance)? How would an unemployed factory worker interpret the Great Depression differently from William Randolph Hearst? How would members of the various Estates have made sense of the French Revolution? Why? What evidence, values, knowledges, and beliefs would have made a difference (or, indeed, make a difference now)? What these questions demonstrate are (1) the importance of *setting*—that is, historical time, place, location, and status; (2) that groups and individuals *make a difference*—although not necessarily in a deterministic sense; and (3) that even in "simply" living through their everyday lives, all human beings are important historical persons and take part in major historical movements.

A third application involves asking students to consider their places in their own histories—not only in terms of their pasts, their ancestors, and their backgrounds, but also in terms of their impact on today, on what will be "tomorrow's history." What roles do—and will—they play? How do/can they make a difference and/or contribute to public debate? What elements go into (or should go into), for example, positions on significant issues and/or voting decisions? How do/should they know what to do? How do/can/should they evaluate governmental policy? What insights on contemporary life might be culled from a substantive understanding of history?

All in all, students should learn to view history as complex and evolving, as real, and as something that their existence contributes to (and has been affected by) in multiple and incisive ways. They should, that is, think critically, so that they know that the way things are (and/or were) are not necessarily the way they have (or had) to be, and that legitimate disagreements exist over both what, in fact, actu-

ally happened, and what, in fact, such contested historical happenings could ultimately represent.

CONCLUSIONS

History instruction that embraces critical thinking demands its inclusion in the curriculum as a central feature of in-school learning. It necessitates as well taking students seriously *as thinkers* and *as critical,* as individuals whose unique levels of cognitive and social development, and whose special and distinctive personal backgrounds, are important. It compels (1) a continuous and holistic approach to teaching and learning, where children can pursue connections between courses that generally are presented as discrete and between the curriculum and their own life experiences; (2) a classroom organized around democracy and exploration and questioning; (3) practice; and (4) the freedom to create, make mistakes, and reconsider prevailing, controlling, and/or standardized answers and interpretations.

Lastly, critical thinking in the history classroom obligates teachers to model critical historical scholarship themselves (not always easy in a standards-based environment or within a regime of high-stakes and/or standardized testing) and to consider its imperatives in their techniques of classroom management. As Patrick (1986) points out:

There is a strong relationship between an open, supportive, and structured classroom climate, where opinions on issues may be explored and expressed in a free and disciplined manner, and development of critical thinking and attitudes supportive of it. Effective teachers challenge students to examine alternative positions on controversial topics or public issues, require justification for beliefs about what is true or good, and insist on orderly classroom discourse. In this manner, they provide powerful lessons on responsible scholarship and citizenship in a free society. (p. 1)

For ideally, history instruction *is* critical thinking, and critical thinking *is* history instruction, and high-quality teaching and learning—as well as the success of a democratically inclined society—can settle for nothing less.

References

Eggen, P. D., & Kauchak, D. P. (2001). *Strategies for teachers: Teaching content and thinking skills* (4th ed.). Boston: Allyn & Bacon.

Patrick, J. J. (1986). *Critical thinking in the social studies* (ERIC Digest No. 30). Retrieved in 2002 from ERIC database http://ericae.net/edo/ED272 432.htm (ERIC Document Reproduction Service No. ED 272 432)

Further Reading

Cantu, D. A. (2002). *Take five minutes: American history class openers: Reflective and critical thinking activities.* Westminster, CA: Teacher Created Materials.

Freire, P. (1970). *Pedagogy of the oppressed.* New York: Continuum.

Hirsch, E. D. (1987). *Cultural literacy: What every American needs to know.* New York: Houghton Mifflin.

Kohn, A. (2000). *The schools our children deserve.* New York: Mariner Books.

Levstik, L. S., & Barton, K. C. (2000). *Doing history: Investigating with children in elementary and middle schools.* Mahwah, NJ: Lawrence Erlbaum.

Ravitch, D., & Finn, C. (1987). *What do our seventeen-year-olds know?* New York: HarperCollins.

Wineburg, S. S. (2002). *Historical thinking and other unnatural acts: Charting the future of teaching the past.* Philadelphia: Temple University Press.

Social Studies and Critical Thinking

E. Wayne Ross

Critical thinking has been a central focus of social studies education since it was first conceived as a school subject in the early part of the twentieth century. Critical thinking is generally considered an essential element of "civic competence"—the ability of people to confront persistent and complex social problems—which is the goal of social studies education that distinguishes it from the disciplinary study of history and the social sciences.

Despite a rhetorical emphasis on critical thinking in social studies, researchers have found very little teaching for critical thinking in classrooms. The dominant pattern of classroom social studies pedagogy is characterized by text-oriented, whole-group, teacher-centered instruction, with an emphasis on memorization of factual information. There have been widespread criticisms of traditional patterns of social studies instruction and numerous alternatives presented, yet these decidedly uncritical approaches to social studies teaching and learning persist (Stanley, 1991).

The gap between the rhetoric and reality of critical thinking in social studies can be explained, in part, by a number of factors, including the powerful influences of the organization, culture, and architecture of schools; assumptions about the purposes of schools; and the increasing emphasis on test scores as opposed to more authentic representations of student learning. The most fundamental obstacle in efforts to promote critical thinking in social studies, however, is the actual conception of what critical thinking means. In what follows, I will briefly outline deficiencies in our current thinking about critical thinking and offer a radical alternative.

THE PROBLEM: "NONDIALECTICAL" THINKING

Most social studies educators turn to John Dewey for their definition of what constitutes critical (or what he termed "reflective") thinking. In *How We Think* (1933), Dewey described what has since become the rhetorical holy grail of social studies instruction:

Active, persistent, and careful consideration of any belief or supposed form of knowledge in the light of the grounds that support and the further conclusions to which it tends . . . (p. 8).

There are two principle obstacles to achieving this kind of thinking in social studies classrooms. First, Dewey's holistic conception of thinking—which does not separate knowing from doing—tends to be treated as a series of mechanical steps for students to follow. Dewey lays out the elements of critical thinking as follows:

(1) *suggestions,* in which the mind leaps forward to a possible solution; (2) an intellectualization of the difficulty or perplexity that has been *felt* (directly experienced) into a *problem* to be solved, a question for which the answer must be sought; (3) the use of one suggestion after another as a leading idea, or *hypothesis,* to initiate and guide observation and other operations in collection of factual material; (4) the mental elaboration of the idea or supposition as an idea or supposition (*reasoning,*

in the sense in which reasoning is a part, not the whole, of inference); and (5) testing the hypothesis by overt or imaginative action. (Dewey, 1933, p. 106, emphasis in original)

Although Dewey never suggested that critical thinking occurs in mechanically consecutive stages or is the consequence applying discrete cognitive skills to solve a problem, social studies educators often interpret him in this way. Over the years many teacher educators have encouraged teachers to take a skills-based approach to teaching critical thinking is social studies. The basic tenet being that teachers must use direct instruction to teach discrete critical thinking skills, giving students many opportunities to practice application of thinking skills and assisting students in transferring critical thinking skills from one context to another.

As a result, exercising critical judgment in social studies is often reduced to simplistic yardsticks for evaluating discrete bits of information. For example, social studies teachers often employ schemes that identify cognitive skills or aspects of critical thinking that are linked to the notion of logical argument:

- Grasping the meaning of a statement.
- Distinguishing between verifiable facts and value statements.
- Distinguishing relevant from irrelevant observations or reasons.
- Determining the factual accuracy of a statement.
- Determining the credibility of a source.
- Identifying ambiguous statements.
- Identifying unstated assumptions.
- Detecting bias.
- Recognizing logical inconsistencies in a line of reasoning.

- Judging whether there is ambiguity in a line of reasoning.
- Judging whether certain statements contradict each other.
- Judging whether a conclusion follows necessarily.
- Judging whether a statement is specific enough.
- Judging whether a statement is actually the application of a certain principle.
- Judging whether an observation statement is reliable.
- Judging whether an inductive conclusion is warranted.
- Judging whether the problem has been identified.
- Judging whether something is an assumption.
- Judging whether a definition is adequate.
- Judging whether a statement made by an alleged authority is acceptable.[1]

The problem with critical thinking schemes that focus on the development of transferable generic skills is that the key element in the development of students' critical thinking is left out—knowledge. In a review of research on critical thinking in social studies, Stanley (1991) concludes that "attempts to teaching generic thinking skills or models without adequate attention to content are unlikely to have any impact on student performance in subject areas" (p. 255). Recent studies indicate students most skilled in using critical thinking to solve problems had both a detailed knowledge of the relevant subject matter and a good understanding of problem-solving strategies.

The fundamental problem with traditional approaches to critical thinking in social studies is its "nondialectical" nature, that is, the separation of what cannot be separated with distortion. Students should be presented with opportunities to make connections between prior knowledge and various elements of new knowledge, rather than learning skills in isolation or examining only oddments of information. As Bertell Ollman has pointed out, most people see the parts well enough, but not the connections and the overall patterns of human existence.

CRITICAL THINKING AS DIALECTICAL THINKING

Inadequacy of nondialectical thinking—unconnected thinking—is particularly evident in social studies education where students are expected to confront persistent and complex social problems. If we define civic competence as the ability to understand the world and act on it, then it is crucial that we understand the differences among getting the facts right, explaining the facts, and constructing prescriptive actions.

For example, many people of various political persuasions have pointed out the paradox of the growing wealth of the few and the increasing poverty of the many, as well as connections between the interests of corporations and the actions of governments and of being powerless and poor. As Ollman (1993) points out, despite awareness of these relations, most people do not take such observations seriously. Lacking a theory to make sense of what they are seeing, people don't know what importance to give it; forget what they have just seen, or exorcise the contradictions by labeling them a paradox. The problem is that the socialization we undergo (in and out of school) encourages us to focus on the particulars of our circumstances and to ignore interconnections. Thus, we miss the patterns that emerge from relations. Social studies education plays an important role in reinforcing this tendency. The social sciences break up the human knowledge into various disciplines (history, anthropology, sociology, geography, etc.) each with its own distinctive language and ways of knowing, which encourages concentrating on bits and pieces of human experience. What existed before is usually taken as given and unchanging. As a result, political and economic upheavals (such as the revolutions of 1789, 1848, 1917, and 1989) are treated as anomalous events that need explanation.

Dialectical thinking, on the other hand, is an effort to understand the world in terms of interconnections—the ties among things as they are right now, their own preconditions, and future possibilities. The dialectical method takes change as the given and treats apparent stability as that which needs to be explained (and provides specialized concepts and frameworks to explain it). Dialectical thinking is an approach to understanding the world that requires not only a lot of facts that are usually hidden from view, but a more interconnected grasp of the facts we already know.

The problem is that reality is more than appearances and focusing exclusively on appearances—on the evidence that strikes us immediately and directly—can be misleading. Basing an understanding of ourselves and our world on what we see, hear, or touch in our immediate surroundings can lead us to conclusions that are distorted or false.

Understanding anything in our everyday experience requires that we know something about how it arose and developed and how it fits into the larger context or system of which it is a part. Just recognizing this, however, is not enough . . . After all, few would deny that everything in the world is changing and interacting at some pace and in one way or another, that history and systemic connections belong to the real world. The difficulty has always been how to think adequately about them, how not to distort them and how to give them the attention and weight that they deserve. (Ollman, 1993, p. 11)

Dialectics, Ollman explains, is an attempt to resolve this difficulty by expanding the notion of "anything" to include (as aspects of what is) both the process by which it has become that thing and the broader interactive context in which it is found. Dialectics restructures thinking about reality by replacing the common-sense notion of "thing," as something that *has* a history and *has* external connections to other things, with notions of "process" (which *contains* its history and possible futures) and "relation" (which *contains* as part of what it is its ties with other relations).

Unlike nondialectical thinking, where one starts with some small part and through establishing connections tries to reconstruct the larger whole, dialectical thinking begins with the whole (or as much as one understands of it) and then examines the part to see where it fits and how it functions—eventually leading to a fuller understanding of the whole. The quintessential example of this kind of thinking is the work of Karl Marx; for Marx, capitalism was the beginning point for an examination of anything that takes place within it. (Although it should be noted that most of Marx's dialectic was taken from Georg Wilhelm Friedrich Hegel, who systematized a way of thinking that goes back to the ancient Greeks. Additionally, non-Marxist thinkers like Alfred North Whitehead and F. H. Bradely developed their own versions of dialectics.)

Dialectical investigations proceed from whole to part (from the system inward) and are primarily aimed at examining four kinds of relations. The first relation is *identity/difference*—how things are either the same/identical or different, not both. For example, there are differences among profit, rent, and interest; however, dialectical analysis brings out the identity of each as forms of surplus-value, that is, wealth created by workers that is not returned to them in the form of wages.

The second relation is *interpretation of opposites,* which is based on the recognition that, to a large degree, how anything appears and functions is due to its surrounding conditions. For example, a capitalist sees a machine as a commodity, bought on the market and that is something that will bring her a profit. While, a worker looks at the same machine and sees an instrument that will determine her movements in the production process.

The third relation is *quantity/quality.* Quantity becomes quality and qualities become quantities. The motive force of change is the addition of specific quantities that cause change. For example, reducing the temperature of water creates a new quality—ice. Adding years to life creates a new quality. Adding salt to food, nearness to friendship, velocity to a bullet, instruments to a band, all make something new. Incremental change, then, is accompanied by qualitative—revolutionary change—an apparently sudden leap.

Lastly, and most important, is *contradiction.* Contradiction is the incompatible development of different elements within the same relation (the unity and struggle of opposites). All things are composed of contradictions. Simple examples of unified polarity include:

- Anatomy: the thumb and forefinger

- Mathematics: addition/subtraction; multiply/divide
- Education: nature and nurture
- Music: major/minor keys; sound/silence
- Literature: the best of times, the worst of times
- Mechanics: every action has a reaction

Ollman explains that "nondialectical thinkers in every sphere of scholarship are involved in nonstop search for the 'outside-agitator,' for something or someone that comes form outside the problem under examination that is the cause for whatever occurs, dialectical thinkers attribute the main responsibility for all change to the inner contradictions of the system or systems in which it occurs" (1993, p. 16).

Without a conception of things as relations, it is difficult to focus on the different sides of a contradiction at the same time. As a result, even if all the sides of a contradiction are examined, they do not receive the same level of attention and their mutual interaction is often mistaken for causality. For nondialectical thinkers, real contradictions—such as the fact that during the "economic boom" of the 1980s and 1990s, when the Gross Domestic Product of the United States increased 25%, the poverty rate among workers increased 7.4% or that while the rich have gotten substantially richer, four out of five households in the United States take home a thinner slice of the economic pie since 1977—can only be understood as differences, paradox, opposition, imbalance, while the underlying forces responsible for these appearances remain invisible and unrecognized.

Dialectical thinking is no simple matter and like nondialectical thinking there are distortions associated with this way of thinking. If nondialectical thinkers miss the forest for trees, dialectical thinkers often do the opposite, de-emphasizing details in favor of generalizations.

Dialectical thinking, however, is a way to understand the full range of changes and interactions that occur in the world. If we want our students to be able to understand and act on the world, dialectics helps us to pose questions that make effective action possible: What kind of changes are already occurring? What kinds of changes are possible? The only thing that cannot be chosen is what we already have. Dialectics is both critical and radical. It helps us to understand the present as a moment through which we are passing. Dialectics forces us to examine where we have come from and where we are heading as part of learning what our world is about. It enables us to understand that everyone and everything are connected, and that we have the power to change our world.

Note

1. The single best source on traditional conceptions of critical thinking in social studies education is the work of Barry K. Beyer: see, for example, *Developing thinking skills programs* (Boston: Allyn and Bacon, 1988). See also the work of Benjamin Bloom, Robert Ennis, and Shirley Engle.

References

Dewey, J. (1933). *How we think.* Lexington, MA: Heath.

Ollman, B. (1993). *Dialectical investigations.* New York: Routledge.

Ollman, B. (2001). *How to take an exam and remake the world.* Montreal: Black Rose.

Stanley, W. B. (1991). Teacher competence in social studies. In J. P. Shaver (Ed.), *Handbook of social studies teaching and learning* (pp. 249–262). New York: Macmillan.

Further Reading

Hursh, D. W., & Ross, E. W. (Eds.). (2000). *Democratic social education: Social studies for social change.* New York: Falmer Press.

Ross, E. W. (Ed.). (2001). *The social studies curriculum: Purposes, problems, and possibilities* (Rev. ed.). Albany: State University of New York Press.

Standards

Standards and Critical Thinking

Valerie J. Janesick

STANDARDS, ASSESSMENT, AND CRITICAL THINKING

I would like to begin this article with the following three questions:

1. What would critical thinking standards look like if we created them?
2. How can we teach students to evaluate themselves using critical thinking standards and principles?
3. If we don't create such critical thinking standards, who might construct them?

Although these questions are challenging, they resonate with the current interest in education about standards and assessment, and ultimately to critical thinking. I want to begin this discussion with the notion that we are at an exciting moment in our history in terms of deciding on the importance of critical thinking. It is now or never. If we look at the root of the words standards and critical, we have a good beginning for understanding. The word standards comes from the idea of a rallying point or yardstick. The word critical is from the Greek *kritikos* or discerning judgment. One could also apply the word *kriterion* or standard here. Let me explain

by looking back at the history of the standards movement, to deal with these three questions. The standards movement is often linked to the educational reform movement sparked by the report *A Nation at Risk*, but we can easily claim that educational reform has been a pastime for more than a century. We can all recall the buzz words over the years, such as whole language, technology reforms, school within a school, math their way, and the list can go on for pages. However, more recently, individual educators and professional organizations have demanded standards as a remedy to almost every educational problem. In fact, my students who are teachers in the K-12 schools often remark that the reforms are usually politically inspired, and always revolve around getting those test scores higher and higher. Not only that, if scores don't go up, lower scoring schools are listed in newspapers, reports, and so on. As a result, children in these schools often internalize the lower rating. In fact many states, like Florida and Illinois, for example, are currently threatening to remove funds from lower scoring schools altogether. As a result, control of education has shifted from local control to the national and state levels. To develop a critical thinking approach to standards and assessment, we need to begin challenging prevailing policies that work against the critical thinking approach. Testing and publishing test scores will not get very many people to become critical thinkers.

The time has come to challenge the premise that massive funding, written standards, and a firm resolve to create reform will cause students to achieve at higher levels, because there are developmental limits to student achievement. Furthermore, research and intuitive practice show us, clearly, that all children need to learn to be critical thinkers, problem posers, and problem solvers. Other writers have argued that the notion of setting high standards for all students is hard to resist. For example, it is difficult to argue against high standards. Yet, if we go deeply into this complex issues related to standards, this house of cards may easily crumble. To address the question what would standards look like for critical thinking, at the very least we would have to include something like this—

1. Learners and teachers determine the extent of information needed
2. Access this information effectively
3. Evaluate information and sources critically

Through the use of rubrics, portfolios, and print and nonprint media

4. Incorporate selected information into one's knowledge base
5. Understand the complexity of any given topic area.

If we take a developmental view of standards, at first, learners use a set of foundational skills and move onto higher order thinking skills. When I talk about critical thinking, I refer to the classic text by Richard Paul, *Critical Thinking: How to Prepare Students for a Rapidly Changing World*. It is almost impossible to discuss critical thinking without talking about authentic assessment. Authentic assessment is an approach that allows learners to show what they "can do" and is most often identified with the work of Grant Wiggins and his text, *Educative Assessment*. Authentic assessment is the antidote to overtesting and high-stakes testing. In addition to that, ethical questions are addressed and taken seriously by learners and teachers when using authentic assessment techniques.

ASSESSMENT TECHNIQUES FOR A CRITICAL APPROACH TO STANDARDS: PORTFOLIOS FOR THE CRITICAL THINKER

In the past twenty years, portfolios have emerged as one the finest techniques for authentic assessment. It is also one of the most dependable ways for students to monitor their own critical thinking skills and progress. A portfolio is a work in progress and is the historical record of a learner's progress. Usually the tasks performed by a student fall in the following areas:

1. The tasks performed were done over time and in a variety of ways.
2. The tasks show evidence of learning, growth, and development and sample a wide spectrum of tasks.
3. The task performed show many levels of understanding.
4. The tasks are tailored to the individual learner to show what the learner can do. Thus, the teacher's role is adjusted to the role of facilitator.

Types of Portfolios

There is no model carved in stone in terms of portfolios, however, there are at least three categories of portfolios:

1. The working portfolio
2. The record-keeping portfolio
3. The showcase portfolio

All three models may involve the student, the teacher, and the parents in the development of the portfolio. Portfolios allow for the display of the learner's progress in thought and action. The level of critical thinking of the learner can be traced through the portfolio process. Portfolios are a natural evolution from constructivist approaches to curriculum, Socratic dialogue, collaboration, hands-on activities in learning, and multidisciplinary approaches. Over all, portfolios offer us hope. They offer students the hands-on ability to evaluate their work, their critical thinking skills, and their progress on the journey of their education. Portfolios are a dependable mechanism for showing what students can do.

ETHICAL PROBLEMS WITH THE STANDARDS MOVEMENT

Think about the standards movement framed with the following questions:

1. Who benefits from setting standards?
2. Whose voice is taken into account when the standards are formulated?
3. Are we creating new inequalities, by advocating standards?

As you can see, the problems created by setting standards are complex. Let's look at the first problem—who benefits from setting standards. Can we all admit that educational accountability is in its infancy and most often relies on the single measure of test scores? The extremely high monetary cost of the tests themselves, the upkeep of all the prep materials, and the like illustrate the very high cost of testing. Clearly, the testing industry benefits from encouraging testing. In addition, those of us with a life in education realize that testing is often handled questionably. Some educational leaders suggest that some teachers actually teach for the test alone, thereby casting teaching as test preparation. In fact, the standards movement was initiated with grandiose aims such as world class high standards. Yet in actual cases, like the State of Texas for example, the standards movement has become distorted by politics and expedience. Let's look at this more closely as we examine this case study of Texas, for it illustrates the political and economic consequences of the push for standards. Note that while emphasis is on testing and standards, a good deal of class time is lost for critical thinking activities. This time might better be used to allow students to become critical thinkers, practice critical thinking activities, and evaluate their own work against the standards that should include the complexity of the learning process.

The Texas School Reform Case

The well-known researcher Linda McNeil (2000) has done a thorough analysis of the Contradictions of School Reform, in a book by that title, and particularly examines this reform movement in Texas from the mid-1980s to the present time. She completed the first study to document and track standardized reforms from their beginnings in the state legislature to their effects on the curriculum in schools, teacher reactions, and, subsequently, student achievement. The "reform" in Texas was begun by Ross Perot, who basically took local control of schools away from the public and professional teachers, into the arms of business-controlled external management and accountability systems. This major shift from public to private is a key underlying and barely examined reality. The accountability system in Texas is called the Texas Assessment of Academic Skills, or TAAS. TAAS is basically promoted for the following reasons:

1. It has shaped up the schools.
2. Teachers and principals are held accountable for test scores.
3. "Performance contracts" are used for evaluating principals based on test scores.
4. Test results are used for decisions about school practice.

Mr. Perot was very articulate about how to improve schools through testing and basically argued that, if its good enough for business, its good enough for schools. Thus the injection of a business orientation, as well as a political one, complicates matters even further. But McNeil (2000) looks closely at this situation and points out the flaws in this simplistic approach to education.

For one thing, she raises the issues of historical inequities in funding schools, staff allocation, investment in materials, and support from the broader community. In fact, many writers point out that what drives the standards movement in general can be distilled into two assumptions, both based on fear:

1. Our nation is losing its competitive edge and is falling behind other countries and, to compete in the global marketplace, we must push students to learn more and learn faster. We can do this by raising standards.

2. If we raise standards for all students, we automatically address the disparity between high and low achievers.

Oddly enough, earlier in our history, John Dewey argued for a child-centered, critical thinking approach to education rather than test-centered curriculum in the attempt to address some of the key points on inequality. In our present day, we are listening to test makers who obviously argue for more tests as the way to resolve the serious complexities of standards. By raising standards, and using an appropriate test to measure achievement, we automatically improve education, and our place in a competitive global economy. If only it were that simple. Let's look again at the Texas case. McNeil reports on various teachers' reactions and changed behavior when a mandated curriculum driven by testing is in place. Basically, teachers explained that the TAAS prep component of curriculum totally recast the teachers' and principals' role. Teachers were silenced and marginalized. They had little voice in the matter. Likewise, principals also lost a voice in the matter. But what is the cost of standardization and compliance? Where is the space for the "public" in public schools? As we increase standardization, will we eliminate the voice of parents, teachers, and other community members? Likewise, who benefits most from the noise about raising standards? In the highly politicized milieu of an election year, politicians especially love the opportunity to get tough with standards and provide less in terms of resources. Does that make any sense?

Basically, mandatory typical tests will be used as the means for implementing state standards. By aggregating test scores, the inequity within and between schools is masked. For example, a suburban school may do well in preparing college-bound students. At the same time, they may not do well at all in preparing non-college-bound students. Yet, by aggregating all the scores, someone looking at the test data may see the school as excellent. Thus, the way data is reported is a problem and has political, racial, and economic overtones. In addition, many ethical issues pop up, including the time taken from actual class work for content mastery.

Teaching for the Test

In Texas, McNeil (2000) reported that many of the schools she studied used large amounts of time practicing for tests. Students practiced "bubbling" in answers, learned to recognize that test makers never have the same letter choice for a correct answer three times in a row. In fact, to help students remember this, a catchy phrase was repeated. They said, "Three in a row, no, no, no." What are we to make of this? Still further, principals who participated in the study reported using the lion's share of the budget to purchase expensive study materials. Again we return to the question, who benefits from all this? Do children benefit from this or do test makers? What would the state of the art look like if we were to make standards for critical thinking in classrooms? Or, alternately, at least incorporate into testing, and into the written standards, a space for emphasizing critical thinking activities such as journal writing, reflective essays, and critical reasoning. What this case shows us is that teaching toward the test alone, diminishes the student's ability to practice critical thinking skills. Do we really want to go that route?

Alternatives to Teaching for the Test

Critical thinking techniques offer an alternative to the drill-and-kill model of teaching to the test. If students learn the basics of the following, we will be light years ahead:

1. Learn to examine assumptions and premises
2. Learn to examine others' positions
3. Learn to gather evidence and data to support positions
4. Address conclusions

Likewise, in today's world, students have the opportunity to access all types of databases and information on the Web. In fact, a quick check of the Web recently resulted in the following Web sites on critical thinking, all of which offer advice and examples of good critical thinking models to maintain high standards in the disciplines. Here are a few:

http://www.criticalthinking.org

http://www.Utc.edu/teaching

http://www.Wannalearn.com

In addition to the Web, any number of texts may be valuable tools for enabling students and teachers to practice critical thinking approaches. For example, the use of portfolios of all types may be one of the best techniques to enhance critical thinking.

A Major Contradiction: The New Discrimination

What is the most distressing about centralized, standardized testing is how this masks ongoing inequality. As McNeil (2000) and others (Horn & Kincheloe, 2001) point out, minority students, who may be disadvantaged to begin with, are now thrown into the pool of the entire school. As the curriculum narrows to a focus on test preparation, a new kind of discrimination emerges. Instead of outright tracking and stratification, the new discrimination uses the *appearance of same-*

ness to cover up inequalities. Most of the "basics" or a "back to basic's" mantra is historically rooted in the mistaken notion that sameness produces equity. Nothing could be further from the truth. Is there any evidence that standardization brings up the bottom scoring students? Given McNeil's (2000) text, one would have to look very far and wide to find evidence for this. In fact, she argues persuasively, based on the Texas case, that the TAAS system is actually harming students, teaching, curriculum development, and the faith and trust in public schooling. This makes sense given the almost unquestioned faith in the business model so prominent in states like Texas. McNeil (2000) argue that substituting a rich curriculum in poor and minority population schools with drill and repetition exercises is the new discrimination. Even if standardization and drill-and-kill exercises raise scores in the present moment, children's learning is not often enhanced or enriched.

HOPE FOR THE FUTURE

All of us as educators struggle with issues about standards, testing, assessment, and evaluation. There is a grassroots movement of parents, educators, and students concerned about these issues, and the organization responsible for this is Fairtest. This groups has raised these serious questions to a wide audience by their Web site, http://www.fairtest.org. This Web site offers the history of the standards movement, reform movement, and testing movement, and criticism of those movements. States are listed and evaluated as to what level of high-stakes testing is being done, and how citizens have organized to fight this mindless and rampant testing. For example, in California, Ohio, and Iowa, citizens fight high-stakes testing by removing students from the classroom on those high-stakes testing days, writing letters to the editor, and holding meetings in public places to confront administrators about the ethics of standards and testing. In fact Fairtest, lists samples of letters to editors, descriptions and accounts of meetings, and how to get organized in your state. This Web site offers all of us examples of actual citizens coming together to build community through showing their deep concern for education. By doing so, critical thinking is not just critical thinking but also critical action.

References and Further Reading

Horn, R., & Kincheloe, J. L. (2001). *American standards: Quality education in a complex world—the Texas case.* New York: Peter Lang.

McNeil, L. (2000). *Contradictions of school reform: Educational costs of standardized testing.* New York: Routledge.

Paul, R. (1993). *Critical thinking: How to prepare students for a rapidly changing world.* Santa Rosa, CA: Foundation for Critical Thinking.

Weil, D., & Anderson, H. K. (Eds.). (2000). *Perspectives in critical thinking: Essays by teachers in theory and practice.* New York: Peter Lang.

Wiggins, G. (1998). *Educative Assessment*: Designing assessments to inform and improve student performance. San Francisco: Jossey-Bass.

Teaching and Learning

Becoming a "Good Teacher": Thinking Critically about Teaching

Paul Brawdy and Juan-Miguel Fernández-Balboa

Critical thinking, in the way we use it here, focuses on the identification of limiting ideologies and the analysis of unquestioned assumptions that support such ideologies. The identification and analysis of beliefs, practices, structures, and other manifestations of an ideology does not occur through a value-free lens. Rather, this type of critical analysis requires a value-laden position from which critical reflection is possible. The reflective lens shared by the authors of this paper is shaped by their appreciation for learning experiences that support a vital and renewable democracy. Basic to such learning experiences is an emancipatory interest that operates on the premise that education, in support of democracy, not only leads toward personal edification as an articulation of one's essential freedom, but also leads toward the awareness of that same essential freedom found within the other.

In this article, we will think critically about some commonly held assumptions associated with good teaching. To critically analyze what constitutes good teaching, it is important to first examine some

of the commonly held assumptions associated with the term teacher and how teachers participate in the schooling of children.

Interestingly, the term teacher is used on a day-by-day basis without really giving it much thought. *Merriam-Webster's Dictionary* defines *teacher* as, "one that teaches; *especially*: one whose occupation is to instruct." And yet, when we plug the word teacher into any one of several search engines available on the Internet we see that teacher is not only popularly constructed as an occupation, but one that is almost exclusively conducted in our public schools. In effect, teaching in our culture is largely defined in vocational terms and maintains its legitimacy through an institutional affiliation with our public schools. Based on these embedded assumptions, teachers are thought of not so much in terms of their relationships with students but, instead, in reference to the places where they work and the kinds of things they do at these places of work. As such, the role of the teacher is closely tied to, and largely defined by, the process of schooling students (i.e., transmitting and upholding certain institutional rules, regulations, and content) at the expense of educating them (i.e., empowering students to be free, intelligent, and active citizens). In this regard, from a democratic perspective, the conventional modes of teaching (and schooling) are limiting, constraining, and may be viewed as oppressive.

This idea may seem uncomfortable, ludicrous, and even threatening to some. After all, we have been taught to think of schooling as a good thing. Besides, most teachers enter the so-called profession with the admirable and honest intention to help their students become "all they can be." We, the authors, want to acknowledge those intentions from the outset and want to make clear that our analysis is not meant as a personal attack on the hundreds of thousands of dedicated and well-intentioned teachers. What we want to do here is to critically examine some of the embedded assumptions that support the prevailing *ideology* (i.e., the dominant worldview) that dominates the thinking and practice regarding the meanings of good teaching and schooling. Put another way, we know that most teachers do try to help and make a difference in their students. On the other hand, we also want to call attention to the fact that, once new teachers enter the context of schools, their socialization as new employees begins almost immediately to focus on work demands that often have very little to do with educating students for participation in a democratic society.

Actually, it can also be said that such socialization starts in teacher education programs. After all, teacher-training programs at the university borrow much from public school culture. In this regard, these programs are often characterized by conservative models of professional training

that, in turn, are based on courses and curricula designed to prepare young teachers to fit into, not to reform, public schools. Hence, in many instances would-be teachers are trained to reproduce behaviors and attitudes that support and perpetuate the existing, however dysfunctional, system of public education in this country. To be sure, would-be teachers are coached on various strategies for dealing with today's overcrowded, underfunded classrooms. They learn about the importance of being open-minded when working with diverse populations of learners and implement various instructional technologies. Yet, the bulk of their training continues to focus on command-style and other direct methods of teaching (modeled, by and large, by their teacher educators). Toward this end, coursework and practice are integrated into four- to five-year curricula in ways that emphasize practical solutions to the practical problems encountered by public school teachers. Of course, all of this could be beneficial (i.e., personally empowering and socially democratizing) if the focus also included the detection, deconstruction, and remediation of ideological contradictions that functionally constrain and limit their development, as well as that of their students, toward participation in a free and democratic society. Yet, this is too often not the case, and the main emphasis remains on carrying out preestablished policy that supports and perpetuates the culture of schooling. Thus a vicious cycle is created.

When we reflect on basic embedded assumptions suggesting that teaching is a job legitimized by institutional authority, it is easy to see that what often passes for good teaching, both in teacher education programs and in schools, is basically reduced to a set of vocational skills and workplace attitudes (e.g., the more-or-less efficient passing on of information; the monitoring, managing, and disciplining of bodies; and the following of top-down evaluative and administrative procedures). Put another way, instead of being defined in terms of personal and political empowerment of students toward democratic practice, good teaching is characterized by the exercise of control that is experienced by teachers and students alike, especially in the circles of our culture's working class.

Still, this ought not to come as a surprise. After all, public schools, as well as teacher education programs, were specifically designed to promote and assimilate working class values and dispositions, their goal being *not* to promote individual curiosity, critical thought, and open-mindedness—traits so crucial for democratic ethics and politics. Rather, schools and teacher training programs were designed to trade on decontextualized curricula, apolitical objective attitudes, and the unquestioning acceptance of institutional authority that fosters an anemic standard of good teaching. This culture of control is easy to perpetuate insofar as the concept of good teaching continues to have this false meaning.

One of the consequences, of course, is that teachers often find themselves caught in a painful contradiction. On the one hand, they want to be good teachers; on the other hand, they act misleadingly under the prevailing false ideology of good teaching in the service of the school. Furthermore, even when teachers become aware of this false ideology, they have a great deal of difficulty overcoming it because they are dependent on the institution. It is no secret that public school teachers achieve their professional status according to the degree to which they contribute to the stability of the institution that

pays them. In addition, this dependence is not only economic (in as much as they draw their livelihood from their institutional salary) but also ideological (because they have spent a great deal of their life within the institutional context and seldom have been exposed to other alternatives). No wonder that, under these circumstances, many teachers tend to promote routine and orderly behavior among their students, while presenting content often imposed on them by top-down policy. It goes without saying that exceptional (i.e., outside the lines) teaching does occur; yet, it must also be acknowledged that, in those cases, teachers take great risks, jeopardizing their careers and facing negative pressure from parents, peers, and administrators alike. In other words, good teaching, within the institutional context, means compliant and controlling teaching. That is why it is forever challenging to reconcile the dynamism that is implied in true education and learning with the stabilizing *inertia* of schooling and the practice of good teaching.

In view of this, we may consider that, with very few exceptions, good teaching is still the equivalent of demonstrating good work deportment and compliance with institutional policy. Put another way, the conventional way of perceiving good teaching has become a force that *conserves* rather than *transforms*. This, of course, has dreadful consequences for democracy. Schooling, both as a purpose and as a process, promotes a very particular form of learning about the world that has very little to do with democratic values and student empowerment.

The ideology behind the concept of good teaching is extremely difficult to see because it is deeply embedded in the institutional *modus operandi,* that is, it is everywhere. Therefore, because this ideology is ubiquitous it becomes hidden from consciousness because it is simply taken for granted. What adds to the confusion, and to its strength, is that its pernicious essence is couched in positive language (i.e., good teaching) suggesting that it is something to aspire. Hence it becomes even more difficult to argue against.

Let us see how this ideology works through two practical examples. The first example is related to the broadly accepted belief that schools where good teaching takes place promote social mobility. This assumption is easy to accept because without education it is extremely hard to access economic power in our society. Yet, good teaching helps little in this regard because schools are not places where one actually learns to transcend his/her social class. More likely, because of a larger institutional mandate to provide stability within the culture, schools actually tend to preserve the integrity of a social class' structure and any stratifying differences that tend to make social classes distinct. Moreover, teachers themselves tend not to be very good models of social mobility. Teachers, in essence, are often members of either a working or middle class and, lacking the essential knowledge, strategies, and so, to transcend it, they tend to remain in this social stratum for life. Therefore, it might be argued that one of the life lessons that good teachers actually pass onto students is how not to succeed at gaining upward social mobility.

Perhaps a more practical example of how the ideology of good teaching manifests itself concerns the teacher-dominated dialogue in the classroom. It is well known that democracy requires degrees of freedom and equity in the use of one's voice in the public sphere; yet, teachers are typically the ones who ask most of the questions and dominate the discourse in the classroom. By contrast, student voices are reduced to pseudodeclarative statements that either respond exclusively to teacher-posed questions or are designed to gain insight into the teacher's intentions. Frequently, the questions students do ask are usually posed to explore the teacher's expectations for their behavior and performance. This is not at all consistent with the way we use language outside the school walls when attempting to learn. Imagine finding yourself lost on a trip and trying to obtain directions from a stranger using a similar strategy to that employed in the classroom. With such a method, your chances of ever finding your way back home would be quite slim. But beyond such examples, where do such forms of classroom discourse leave our students upon graduation? Of what practical use are such compliant response-providers in a vital democracy? As one can see, the dominant ideology of good teaching has a tendency to obscure the lived experience of both teachers and their students with beliefs and practices that are inconsistent with widely-held outcomes associated with public education and sound instruction.

A critical analysis of issues such as these can uncover the unequal dynamics of power where the teacher, while being controlled by administrative policy and top-down impositions, is forced in turn to gain control over students. So, what passes for good teaching is bound by a culture of schooling that is typically hierarchical, power-laden, and inconsistent with the interests of a vital democracy.

Many are the issues one could critically examine concerning the ideology of good teaching (e.g., the use of space and time; the traditional assessment practices; the dynamics of curriculum development, selection, and instruction; the type of language that is used; the system of rewards and punishments; the evaluation procedures and justifications; the impact of prevailing public policy). By asking questions such as, who does really benefit from all this? or, in what ways does this promote or hinder democracy? we can begin to gain awareness of limiting oppressive ideologies and their effects, begin to tear down the walls of institutional control, and promote educational practice that is truly democratic. Emancipatory critical thinking (see Fernández-Balboa's entry in this encyclopedia) can help teachers and students in this regard.

In summary, teaching as it is practiced may be quite different from how it is idealized in a vital democracy. While democracy depends on the cultivation of thoughtful voices of conscience and the continued critical examination of our social power structure, good teaching in the service of schooling is often an unwitting practice through which institutional authority acts to preserve the status quo. Consequently, good teaching, in this sense, is neither transformative nor relational, but rather exists as an institutionally-legitimized set of work practices characterized by conservatism and control.

Further Reading

Bell, I. (1991). *This book is not required. Wisdom and knowledge*. Fort Bragg, CA: The Small Press.

Merriam-Webster's Collegiate Dictionary (11th ed.). (2003). Springfield, MA: Merriam Webster.

Palmer, P. (1998). *The courage to teach: Exploring the inner landscape of a teacher's life*. San Francisco: Jossey-Bass.

Spring, J. (2002). *American education* (10th ed.). New York: McGraw-Hill.

Critical Cooperative Learning

Nell B. Cobb

The competency requirements for productive citizenship in the twenty-first century dictate that individuals must have qualitative, quantitative, and technological literacy. The catalyst for acquiring and strengthening these competencies is understanding how to build collaborative relationships and knowing how to foster critical thinking. Teachers must understand that when students develop collaborative and critical thinking competencies in educational arenas these competent individuals successfully transition to job sites and prevail in society. A concerted effort must be made by teachers to help students develop these skills.

So what exactly is cooperative learning? "Cooperation is working together to accomplished shared goals. Within cooperative activities individuals seek outcomes that are beneficial to all other group members. Cooperative learning is the instructional use of small groups so that students work together to maximize their own and each other's learning" (Johnson & Johnson, 2002, p. 1). When small groups are used in cooperative ways, students learn to listen to other students, expect to be heard by other students, learn to come to consensus about decisions, and expect to take responsibility for some aspect of the task. These expectations are not evident in all small group configurations. Examples of listening to others, ways of reaching consensus, and ways to divide and define necessary tasks must be explored before groups can become cooperative entities. Specifically, Johnson and colleagues (1993) describe five components of cooperative learning: positive interdependence, interaction, accountability, interpersonal skills, and group processing. These are also skill-building tasks that teachers can practice with students as prework for cooperative learning. This prework involves critical thinking skill development and reinforcement.

Interdependent relationships can take many forms. Positive interdependence among cooperative group members provides the glue that holds the group together. Group members get the sense that more can be learned or accomplished by working together than by working individually. Positive interdependence is found in many sports situations. The football players on the defensive line have a sense that they can accomplish more by working together to keep the opposing team from advancing toward the touch down goal. The goal or task of the group must be clearly defined by the coach or teacher. Examples of division of labor and how these tasks are interrelated must be explored and clarified until interdependence is realized. The question becomes what can I do to contribute to the good of the group? It is also important that group members have positive expectations of each other. This is an underling belief or faith that others are capable of uniquely contributing to the group. Interdependent relationships can be established by engaging students in solving logic puzzles that contain multiple clues. Individual members can use these clues to contribute to a common solution. Students are critically creating solutions by identifying and grouping common information and patterns. They must explore by asking questions, collecting data, and organizing data from other group members. Teachers can design group problem-solving activities by identifying a rich problem and separating the components into several parts or clues. Positive interdependence leads to effective interaction.

Traditionally, the most effective interaction has been face-to-face. Members of the group will have a shared experience that includes listening to others and being listened to. These communication skills provide a means for the group members to use examples, support a statement, and use appropriate reasoning. Students can also analyze a situation by breaking an item into its components and describing each part. Teachers can also give students two or more items to compare and contrast to find similarities and differences. Accountability can follow these tasks.

Accountability is key for individual growth. Each member of the group is accountable for knowing the task, identifying strategies for addressing the task, providing information concerning the implementation of the task, and completing the task. Collective knowledge must become individual knowledge. Therefore, all students should be able to pass tests and report on any aspect of the group task. It is the responsibility of the group to prepare members for success. Students can assess themselves and the group by taking a quiz or test together and agreeing on the answers. Teachers can also provide group assessment opportunities. This group experience can set the stage for individual success.

Interpersonal skills require that students must assume leadership, decision making, trust building, communication, and conflict management roles. Teachers must establish a safe classroom environment where students mutually respect each other. For example, students can define interaction expectations by using letters from any word. If the word rope is used, students might offer the following expectations: R—respect all group members, O—open your mind to the ideas of others, P—positive responses for all members, and E—examine your ideas and the ideas of others. Teachers should model giving and getting attention, asking questions of clarification, criticizing ideas not people, asking for justification, and debriefing methods.

Group processing is the assessment of the shared experience. The effectiveness of the group can be measured by content and process. Some questions the group could address are as follows: Do we all know the required content? Did we all contribute to the task? What are some things that we could do differently if we had this task again? Did each individual feel included in the task? Did you feel that the other group members listened to you? Did you listen to other group members? How could you change your behavior to better enhance the group process? and Did you always direct your attention to the speaker? Group processing should provide information for future long-term group interactions.

Once the five components of cooperative learning are addressed and practiced frequently, there are many different strategies that can be used. In every component, it is the job of the teacher to design ways for students to practice these components by serving as a coach, resource person, questioner, and critical thinking advocate. How can teachers transition their competitive classrooms into effective learning group communities? Three good transitioning strategies are the Think-Pair-Share Model, Problem-Solving Partnerships, and Student Teams Achievement Divisions.

The Think-Pair-Share Model prepares students to work with at least one other person. Individuals have an opportunity to discuss their strategy with another person, get feedback from that person, come to agreement with that person, and share a common solution with the class. Opportunities for learning can occur during the individual, pair, and whole class sessions. The role of the teacher is provide a cue for students to enter the think mode, establish the length of the activity, make the transition to the pair-and-share mode, and help students extend their thinking during all modes. Think-Pair-Share is an excellent strategy for teachers to introduce students to each other and discover students' past experiences with a topic or concept.

Problem-solving partnerships can have up to three students per group and are formed to solve a specific problem. Students are encouraged to identify a strategy for approaching the task, helping to implement the strategy, reaching a conclusion or solution, and examining and possibly extending the conclusion. Learning is achieved on both the individual and whole class level. This partnership can be used in any subject area. In mathematics, students can find multiple approaches to a problem and possible multiple solutions to an open-ended problem. In language arts, students can read a story and brainstorm to create alternative endings or other parts of the story. Students can make an account of a historical event from the perspective of different groups of people in a social studies class.

A popular cooperative learning strategy is the Student Teams Achievement Divisions (STAD). This strategy is most effective when convergent answers are required. Groups consist of four or five members with high, average, and low achievers. The teacher would introduce a lesson to the whole group, team members work on a group task sheet, and individuals are tested on the material without group help. A team score could be derived from the difference between the individual scores on a previous test and current test. Each group member can contribute a maximum of 10 points. The team score is found by averaging the improvement points for the team. No matter how the team score is derived, less able students and high-achieving students are motivated to perform better on assessments as a way to increase the team score. Teachers can help students transition into the work site by structuring learning experiences that use these introductions and other cooperative learning structures.

On the job site, workers are collaboratively problem solving, communicating, and consensus seeking. Bankers no longer simply quote interest rates to customers; they must understand and communicate information about sophisticated accounts, credit profiles, and stock market activities. These banking tasks are completed more effectively and efficiently in collaboration with others. Factory workers have expanded their role of simply handling tools. These workers exercise collaborative problem-solving skills that include quality control, trouble shooting, equipment repairs, and design procedures. Office workers need to know how to use advanced technology, how to process an enormous amount of information, and how to be productive team members. Employers look to schools and the education process to prepare their employees with appropriate competencies for success in job settings. Critical and collaborative workers become productive members of society.

References and Further Reading

Johnson, D., & Johnson, R. (2002). Cooperative learning at University of Minnesota. Retrieved April 2002 from http://www.clcrc.com/pages/cl.html

Johnson, D., Johnson, R., & Holubec, E. J. (1993). *Cooperation in the classroom* (6th ed.). Edina, MN: Interaction Book Company.

Johnson, P. A. (2000). *Up and out: Using creative and critical thinking skills to enhance learning.* Boston: Allyn and Bacon.

Critical Dialogue: The Learning Conversation and Learning to Suspend Judgment

Danny Weil

We use the word dialogue often in conversation. But just what does the term mean? The term dialogue is an old term that has its meaning within Greek origin. *Dia* means "through or with each other" while *logos* means "the word." The purpose of a critical dialogue, or what has been referred to elsewhere as a "learning conversation," is to advocate critical inquiry into our everyday experience and what we take for granted, or assume, in our thinking. Thus, a critical dialogue is both one of advocacy and inquiry. Advocacy lets us put forth our ideas and reasoning so that we might convince others of the truth and veracity of our position on issues. Inquiry is both an internal and external process that helps us see the ideas of others by drawing out their reasoning through questioning as well as by developing an insight into our own thinking through critical dialogical reflection. Dialogue helps build shared understanding, vision, and aspirations, as well as sets forth the principle differences or contradictions between multiple lines reasoning.

To dialogue critically and effectively it is essential that we develop a repertoire of tools that allows us to compassionately inquire and advocate within the context of collaboration and critical reflection. These skills, or techniques, allow for skillful Socratic discussion that seeks to elicit reasoning as it may apply to problem solving or decision making within specific contexts. One of the most important skills in developing effective and critical dialogue opportunities is to appreciate the necessity to suspend judgment when reasoning within different points of view. The ability to suspend judgment allows for critical listening and empathic understanding—and critical listening is the key to critical dialogue.

LEARNING TO SUSPEND JUDGMENT

Although we would like to think we should be nonjudgmental, the fact is that there rarely is a moment when we are not engaged in some type of sort-and-judge process. After all, that's what makes us human. Consider the following: You take an idea or ideas; talk to people about them; gather data and facts about them; sort, classify, and evaluate the data and facts; make decisions and solve problems, right? Throughout your development as a person, the process accelerates and you come to learn to make more effective judgments. Or do you? All judgments are the product of a mental process in which you are engaged and how well you understand your mental processes and the manner in which you reason your way toward judgments within specific contexts will allow you to become a better decision maker and problem solver, that is, a better critical thinker. After all, good decisions and well-crafted solutions to problems require that we form critical judgments, not uncritical judgments. But what's the difference?

Judgment differs from opinion in one very important way: Judgment requires that we consider different points of view, evaluate reasons and evidence that may not agree with us, and learn the process of reasoning so that we can look at our thinking and develop more sound and cogent judgments. Opinions, on the other hand, can be accomplished without considering different points of view and multiple perspectives; opinions require a different reasoning process than judgment making. Opinions are fine and judgments certainly are not bad; in fact, you couldn't live your life without making either of them. However, judgments and opinions are very different and the processes we use to make them are equally as disparate.

Suspension of judgment is all about developing the ability to develop critical judgment—to learn to visualize our judgments and the processes we use to attain them while we consider fairly the points of view and perspectives of others. It requires not that we give up cherished opinions or thoughts on matters we feel are important, but that we try to maintain a critically reflective position when considering multiple perspectives. Suspension of judgment asks that we recognize the importance of listening critically to others not in the interest of defeating their ideas, but to truly understand how they might come to arrive at judgments that may be different than ours. To develop learning conversations that allow for creative thinking, suspension of judgment and the development of critical judgment is crucial, for uncritical judgmental thinking can serve to shut down listening, hijack conversations, and therefore suffocate the consideration of other points of view. Learning to suspend judgment is not based simply on courtesy and benign respect for another's points of view, although that too is required. It is also grounded on the need for all of us to hear and see how others arrive at different judgments than we might arrive at, enabling us to fine-tune our own thinking and oxygenate our own thought-manufacturing process. Learning to listen to others and learning to effectively dialogue and develop learning conversations enriches personal effectiveness and the development of critical judgment processes, which are aware of the practice of reasoning.

The automatic paths that our judgments often lead us down can be both functional and dysfunctional. Take the following example: If I am driving a car or performing some other fairly complex process, I want to be able to do all of it without the need for too much conscious effort. Therefore, I will automatically collect information and make choices and drive along without much endeavor at all. On the other hand, if I am trying to critically think

and find some creative solution to a problem at work or in my personal life, judgment manufacturing—or the habitual uncritical judgment process—can limit my ability to move in new directions or discover new and creative alternatives to problems because I will suffer from complacency in my thinking and might not entertain or generate alternative creative solutions to social and personal problems.

The automatic judgments we make can certainly help us by reducing the mental labor we must engage and put into service. This whole process of observing, interpreting, and then making judgments can happen so rapidly that we are usually not aware of it; becoming aware of the process we use to arrive at our judgments, learning to slow down our thinking, can make the thinking process more responsible, mindful, and effectual. However, the downside of judgment manufacturing is that we can pigeonhole ourselves with old thoughts and thereby limit our ability to understand other people and grow as human beings precisely because we become prisoners of our perceptions. Judgments help us develop unconscious filters that we use to interpret the world and to decide what information, what assumptions and perspectives, and what evidence we wish to consider, collect, and utilize to live our lives. At some time, we have all become aware that our judgments might have been limiting our ability to expand in new directions, find more satisfying learning conversations, and encourage a new-borne sense of wonderment about the world. When this happens, we either shut down or we are forced to make conscious our judgment-manufacturing process and examine the assumptions that have led us to the judgments we have. At this point, we begin to notice and consider new data;

look for diverse perspectives on issues; develop an appreciation for evidence; explore unchartered possibilities that we might never have considered before; enhance our listening and dialogue skills; learn to examine our own assumptions and the reasons and origins for them; and develop new, refreshing relationships with people and the world—in short, we develop critical judgment.

UNCRITICAL JUDGMENT IS AN ECHO CHAMBER FOR ITSELF

The inability to suspend judgment limits our ability to listen and, as a result, reduces our emotional intelligence by affecting our ability to empathize as well as by depriving us of opportunities to learn and grow through and with others. Limiting listening opportunities means that people are not able to develop a critical understanding of information within their environment because judgment will often operate to fail to see that which disagrees with it; this is the notion of the halo affect. When the mind has formed an uncritical judgment that will often listen only to what reinforces its own judgment, what we call a confirmation bias in logic, the inability to critically reflect and examine assumptions one has through the assumptions of others becomes compromised. This limits the ability of the mind to give other points of view a fair hearing in decision-making and problem-solving processes and can assure that impulsivity in thinking or group think can become an unfortunate yet dominant mode of mental activity. In fact, the inability to suspend judgment until all views are fair-mindedly expressed can lead to what is referred to as a process of confirmation bias, whereby judgment seeks only to consider evidence that confirms itself: It listens to corroborate its worldview, it collects and selects only the information that substantiates its worldview, it will bend evidence to fit within its worldview, and, as a result, it reduces other points of view and information and data about the world to preordained judgments that have often not been subjected to rigorous critical thinking. Creating collaborative partnerships at work, in neighborhoods, and in families signifies that critical thinking must be utilized to explore alternative ways of thinking and acting to avoid the pitfalls associated with the psychological barriers to thinking critically. This requires that the human mind value and encourage diversity of thinking and engagement with multiple perspectives—that the mind understand the need for and the processes necessary for suspending judgment in the interest of creating critical judgment.

To be able to suspend judgment when necessary, critical thinking asks that we do a number of things. One, control our impulsivity in thinking. The mind wants to take shortcuts, jump from what it thinks is the problem to the solution, move fast and quickly and, as a result, we often shoot from the hip making rapid-fire judgments that do not allow us to consider all sides of an issue. This can lead to our inability to listen to others and personally profit from multiple perspectives, as well as to our misinterpreting data and facts and failing to take charge of our thinking. This is the essence of uncritical judgment; the propensity to act, then think, and then act again as opposed to think, then act, and then rethink.

Suspension of judgment asks that we give a fair hearing to ideas when we are engaged in the process of forming reasoned judgment; it asks that we see the whole picture when we are problem solving and engaged in decision making; it asks us to look at how the parts relate to the whole and vice versa. Arriving at what can be called critical judgment is a process that requires not only the ability to suspend judgment but also a conception of what we do when we think and what others do; it asks us to consider that we might not have the best idea, the best way of proceeding, or that perhaps we might have overlooked something in our reasoning process. It calls upon us to embrace constructive doubt for it is only through constructive doubt and critique that we are able and willing to look at other points of view regarding personal and social life.

We all can learn the art of suspension of judgment and thereby increase our ability to listen and dialogue with other people who hold a diverse collection of points of view. To do this, it is not necessary to stop our judgments but to learn the process of forming critical judgment—to be aware of the origins of our judgments and how we have derived them, to become sensitive to the reasons and evidence we use or do not use to support our positions, to be sensitive to the fact that our judgments might not be the judgments others have and thus learn to reason within the points of view of others, and to become aware of our process for thinking about how we have been manufacturing the judgments we have made and will continue to make all of our lives. It requires that we be willing to release, at least for some period of time, our time-held certainties, the arrogance that often accompanies these certainties, and

our egocentric attachments to our assumptions and our worldview, as well as that we become aware of how our feelings arise and their origin—especially when engaged in dialogue or listening. Being detached from our judgments does not imply that we have to abandon what we feel is right or in our best interests. On the contrary, it is about creating critical opportunities to become more aware of our neutrality regarding our thinking, and to become aware of the reasons others may give for their conclusions and the assumptions they might make regarding issues of complexity and controversy. We all have the ability to learn to suspend judgment in the interest of entering into more caring relationships and in the interest of advancing our abilities to dialogue and listen to others so that we might form processes for maturing our critical judgment. For critical thinking advocates, we must take the time to copiously examine our thinking through internal and external questioning opportunities. In this way we may find that narrow-mindedness and limited growth are replaced with empathy and unlimited potential.

Further Reading

Brookfield, S. (1987). *Developing critical thinkers: Challenging adults to explore alternative ways of thinking and acting.* San Francisco: Jossey-Bass.

Freire, P. (1970). *Pedagogy of the oppressed.* New York: Continuum.

Phillips, C. (2001). *Socrates café.* New York: Norton.

Formulating Best Practices for Teaching and Learning

Thomas Nelson

Any attempt to reformulate the role of educators has to begin with the broader question of how to view the purpose of schooling. I believe that central to a realizable critical pedagogy is the need to view schools as democratic spheres. This means regarding schools as democratic sites dedicated to forms of self and social empowerment. In these terms, schools are public places where students learn the knowledge and skills necessary to live in an authentic democracy. Instead of defining schools as extensions of the workplace or as front-line institutions in the battle of international markets and foreign competition, schools as democratic public spheres are constructed around forms of critical inquiry that dignify meaningful dialogue and human agency.

Henry A. Giroux

TEACHERS AS INTELLECTUALS: TOWARD A CRITICAL PEDAGOGY OF LEARNING

Influencing the formulation of best practices in teaching and learning has long been perceived as one of the goals of educational research. Much has been learned about the nature of teaching and learning and the results indicate that formulating best practices requires an intellectually complex set of constructs challenging the reflective nature of both the teacher and the learner. Critical thinking is believed to be among the goals of education and directly related to meaningful educational experiences, however, much of what continues to take place in classrooms is more closely associated with knowledge acqui-

sition for the primary purpose of preparing students for taking tests. The assumption here is that answers are much more important than the questions that drive a deeper understanding of human experience. Teachers ask questions, primarily derived from textbooks and prepackaged curricula. Students are determined successful or not based on their ability to recall a memorized set of decontextualized material, most often limited to lower-level understandings. In classrooms, it is rare to see teachers and students engaged in more complex levels of understanding, such as application, analysis, synthesis, and evaluation of content. This requires a deeper sense of context in which the knowledge is generated.

Many questions, issues, and competing ideas about effective teaching and learning have been debated in both educational and political circles for decades. Today's educational climate is dominated by legislated accountability resulting in clearly prescriptive standards-based curricula and accompanying high-stakes testing regimens. In recent years, state legislation throughout the nation has focused on the development and implementation of both standardized testing for students as well as on highly accountable expectations of teachers. This has been based on the overwhelming assumption that good teaching can be both prescribed in specific terms and easily measured, that teaching and learning are rooted in technical skill acquisition rather than being recognized as a complex human activity deserving of intellectual inquiry and reflective practice. In the current era of standardized testing and increasing political pressure toward the nationalization of curricula, efforts to advance critical thinking within classrooms have received little attention. The emphasis in schools remains focused on knowledge acquisition and test-taking skills at the expense of a more collaborative, problem-based approach utilizing critical thinking skills. Curricula continue to be viewed as something that needs to be covered and ruled by routine tasks, which are usually determined by policymakers and curriculum leaders rather than by teachers themselves. When subject matter content is perceived in this lower order manner, there lacks a basis for intellectually challenging exploration of deeper meanings of knowledge, as well as minimizing the importance of long-term understanding.

Much has been learned over the past twenty years about the ways in which learning occurs. A good deal of research has been conducted on the ways in which teaching and learning are manifested in classrooms that suggests that these activities are tied inextricably to interactive processes associated with critical thinking, revolving around inquiry and discovery approaches to teaching and learning. Much of this research has important implications for viewing teaching as a co-constructive experience, actively engaged teachers and students collaborating toward deep and meaningful understanding of content. Theories associated with constructivist approaches to teaching and learning have gained attention, primarily among educators; however, they have yet to be embraced in educational policymaking arenas. The idea that making sense of the world is a socially constructed phenomena flies in the face of traditional forms of top-down teaching that continue to dominate contemporary classroom processes.

How can we think productively about incorporating critical thinking into the ways in which we perceive the activities of teaching and learning? And, how can critical thinking positively influence our notions of formulating best practices in both teaching and learning?

First, what does critical thinking mean and what does it look like in educational settings? Several definitions of critical thinking are posed.

According to Michael Scriven and Richard Paul, "Critical thinking is the intellectually disciplined process of actively and skillfully conceptualizing, applying, analyzing, synthesizing, and/or evaluating information gathered from, or generated by, observation, experience, reflection, reasoning, or communication, as a guide to belief and action." Richard Paul further states, "Critical thinking . . . approaches all content explicitly as thinking. It takes thinking apart. It weaves new thinking into old. It assesses thinking. It applies thinking. It is thinking about thinking while thinking to make thinking better, more clear, more accurate, more relevant, more deep, more broad, and more effective."

Actively engaging students in critical thinking about content requires a set of strategies that aim to challenge teachers' curriculum decision-making processes. Potts (1994) has identified a list of discrete skills related to an overall ability for critical thinking. These are as follows:

- Finding analogies and other kinds of relationships between pieces of information.
- Determining the relevance and validity of information that could be used for structuring and solving problems.

- Finding and evaluating solutions or alternative ways of treating problems.

Just as there are similarities among the definitions of critical thinking across subject areas and levels, there are several generally recognized hallmarks of teaching for critical thinking. These include the following:

- Promoting interaction among students as they learn—Learning in a group setting often helps each member achieve more.
- Asking open-ended questions that do not assume the one right answer. Critical thinking is often exemplified best when the problems are inherently ill-defined and do not have a right answer. Open-ended questions also encourage students to think and respond creatively, without fear of giving the wrong answer.
- Allowing sufficient time for students to reflect on the questions asked or problems posed—Critical thinking seldom involves snap judgments; therefore, posing questions and allowing adequate time before soliciting responses helps students understand that they are expected to deliberate and to ponder, and that the immediate response is not always the best response.
- Teaching for transfer—The skills for critical thinking should travel well. They generally will do so only if teachers provide opportunities for students to see how a newly acquired skill can apply to other situations and to the student's own experience.

Based on these views, in what ways does critical thinking express itself through curriculum enactment in classrooms? First, both teachers and students engage in inquiry approaches to content where generating questions is more important than recalling answers. All fields of study, from the sciences, to history, mathematics, and literature, are based on the development of well-crafted questions that push the limits of existing content knowledge and posit new views and conceptual understandings. In other words, content knowledge is never static, but rather it flows in a fluid-like state of dynamic evolution. For example, scientists are continually redefining their understanding of the cosmos—it's age and behavior—furthering their understanding through questioning and then questioning again. Questions drive knowledge production. Answers are merely fleeting and most often lead to further questions and, hence, the evolving nature of knowledge production and application. Rarely, does this kind of understanding of knowledge and evolving understanding manifest itself in classroom practices. However, when it does, it reflects a much deeper view of teaching and learning than normally expected. We have all been students in classrooms, and have some well-conceived notions about good teaching and meaningful learning. We can remember our best teachers, usually by counting them on one hand. What was it that those teachers did to inspire us, to beckon our investigative selves, to invite us into a world rich with exploration, intellectual analysis, and knowledge production? Clearly, the best of teachers view their work with students as an intellectually challenging, inquiry-based approach wherein critical thought is central to academic outcomes.

So, the question arises, how best to promote critical thinking within teacher preparation programs, helping ensure a more meaningful, and less formula-driven and rote learning experience for students in classroom environments? Unfortunately, current policies governing the preparation of teachers are focused on an accountability system wherein emphasis is placed on highly prescriptive content standards and student outcomes are measured by standardized tests. The assumption is rather simplistic. Impart factual information to students and expect them to commit to memorization and become efficient multiple-choice item test takers. In other words, more testing will result in a better education for our children. Inadequate legislative attention has been paid to discovery-based learning, exploratory inquiry, critical analysis, and creative expression of contextually based content understanding, in part due to the complexities inherent in standardizing a valid assessment system, and to the political stance taken that the education of students is best done in a mechanized, normalized, assembly line fashion.

In affecting the formulation of best practices in teaching and learning, the ways in which we perceive the work of teachers need to be reconsidered from both theoretical and political viewpoints. Classroom practice is generally based on routines developed for controlling student behavior rather than on notions of liberation, the exploration of ideas and critical thought associated with adventurous and powerful learning. The goal of teaching then becomes something quite different than the acquisition of skills and dispositions outlined in learning-to-teach textbooks. It becomes alive with curiosity and questioning. It becomes the basis for a rich and deep engagement into what it means to be human. How is it that we can make sense of ourselves and the world around us without employing critical thinking as a tool for understanding that very interconnectedness? A critical pedagogy is a liberating pedagogy and critical thinking becomes the method by which a powerful education is enacted.

As Elliot Eisner once asked, is what you do as a teacher "liberating or limiting?" We must challenge ourselves with the question of what it means to be an educated person and what it means to engage in critical thinking throughout the educational experiences of both teachers and students. The development of critical thinking skills is directly related to the essential responsibility of formulating best practices for teaching and learning. In as much as critical thinking is overlooked in school systems, clearly it is those teachers who challenge students in powerful ways, operating from a critical pedagogical perspective, who are the beacons of the teaching profession.

References

Giroux, H. (1988). *Teachers as intellectuals: Toward a critical pedagogy of learning*. New York: Bergin & Garvey.

Potts, B. (1994). *Strategies for teaching critical thinking* (ERIC/AE Digest No. 73). Washington, DC.: ERIC Clearinghouse on Assessment and Evaluation. (ERIC Document Reproduction Service No. ED 385 606).

Scriven, M., & Paul, R. (1996). Defining critical thinking. A draft statement for the National Council for Excellence in Critical Thinking. Retrieved from http://www.criticalthinking.org/University/univclass/Defining.html

Further Reading

Ennis, R. H. (1991). *Critical thinking*. Upper Saddle River, NJ: Prentice-Hall.

Halpern, D. F. (1996). *Thought and knowledge: An introduction to critical thinking*. Mahwah, NJ: Lawrence Erlbaum.

Norris, S. P. (1985). Synthesis of research on critical thinking. *Educational Leadership, 42*(8). 40–46.

Siegel, H. (1988). *Educating reason: Rationality, critical thinking, and education*. New York: Routledge.

Weil, D., & Anderson, H. K. (Eds.). (2000). *Perspectives in critical thinking: Essays by teachers in theory and practice*. New York. Peter Lang.

Knowledge Acquisition

Charles Bingham

Recent research into critical thinking is changing the way educators think about how knowledge acquisition can be achieved. Yet, there are age-old, Western assumptions about knowledge acquisition that remain steadfast in educational practices, creating quite a conflict between how teachers and students teach and learn at present, and how they might do so in the future. The aim of this entry is first to lay out a brief description of the ways knowledge acquisition has been considered in the past. Then, it will further describe, how, informed by more recent educational investigations into critical thinking, knowledge acquisition might be understood differently in the future.

Traditionally, knowledge acquisition has been considered along the following model. Knowledge is considered to be like an entity that is *deposited* into the brains of individuals. Paulo Freire, well-known Brazilian educator and an advocate of anti-oppressive, critical thinking, has objected to this model of depositing, naming it "the banking model" in his book, *Pedagogy of the Oppressed*. Following this traditional model, teachers are said to deposit knowledge into the heads of their students so that it will be available for use in the future. Students are said to have acquired knowledge after it has been deposited. Many of us are familiar with this model because we were educated this way. Guided by the banking model, teachers have given us information that we are required to memorize. Then, when it is time to be assessed over this information, we are given a test so that the knowledge can be withdrawn. The banking version of knowledge acquisition lends itself to a teacher-student relationship where the teacher gives the student the cash (the knowledge) and the student stows the cash away (acquires the knowledge). Freire notes that teaching based on such a version of knowledge acquisition, however prevalent it may be, puts the student in a passive, even submissive role as learner.

To further understand this traditional model of knowledge acquisition, the model upon which so much teaching and learning has been based but that needs to be replaced by a more critical model, it is useful to look at the assumptions it holds about knowledge and about human beings who acquire knowledge. About knowledge, this tradition model takes an objective standpoint. To say that knowledge is objective is to say that it is something different, something out there, something separate from the human being who acquires that piece of knowledge. For example, the fact that the United States Civil War ended in 1864 is a piece of knowledge, and that fact is treated as objective in the banking system because knowledge is unchangeable. Anyone could learn that the Civil War ended in 1864 because knowledge stands by itself and does not depend on the one who acquires it. And this traditional, objective understanding of knowledge applies even to knowledge that is less concrete than something such as a date. Even when knowledge is an ability, as in the ability to play the guitar, it is assumed by this traditional model that *anyone* could acquire such an ability, such knowledge. Even if such knowledge is acquired by different people in different ways, it is assumed that the knowledge itself (the how to play) does not change. Thus in the traditional, noncritical model, knowledge can be deposited into anyone as long as that person is willing to make the necessary effort to learn the material.

About human beings, the noncritical model of knowledge acquisition assumes that they are atomistic. In other words, it is assumed that people do not depend on interaction with one another for knowledge acquisition to occur. The idea that the self is atomistic can be traced to influential psychological theories such a Jean Piaget's. In Piaget's view, the self is most fully a self once it has reached a point where it does not depend on another person. This atomistic perspective has been prevalent among experts who assume that technology can teach human beings just as well as other people might teach them. When the television was first mass produced, it was assumed that televisions would replace teachers. Currently, there are similar claims being made about personal computers. Such claims are based on the belief that people are atomistic and that the process of knowledge acquisition is also atomistic. Following this logic, people do not need other people to gain knowledge; they just need the knowledge itself.

Recent research on knowledge acquisition and critical thinking suggests, however, that knowledge is not objective and that human beings are not atomistic. Once objectivity and atomism are put into question, the traditional assumptions governing the banking system must also be put into question. To move to a more critical stance on objectivity, it is important to look to feminist understandings of knowledge. Sandra Harding's book, *Is Science Multicultural?*, is a good example of critical research proving that knowledge is not merely objective. Any given piece of knowledge is instead dependent on the person who is acquiring that knowledge. Instead of being thought of as something different, something out there, knowledge needs to be considered to be something that is intimately linked to the identity of the person who is acquiring knowledge. For example, it is possible that even knowledge that seems to be straightforward, say, a fact like "The Civil War ended in 1864," is dependent on the orientation of the person who is acquiring such a piece of knowledge. For some, the end of the Civil War may have been a bad thing; for some a good thing. For some, the Civil War's end is a meaningless, unimportant description of events. And for some, the same event is central to family and cultural history. In short, even a seemingly factual piece of knowledge such as when the Civil War ended is not the same piece of knowledge for all people. Knowledge depends on people's societal positions and is thus not objective.

The assumption that individuals are atomistic, that they do not depend upon one another to be who they are, has also been critically challenged as of late. A book by the educator Alexander Sidorkin called *Beyond Discourse* is important in this regard. Instead of being closed off to others, people are being redescribed as living on the boundary between self and other. Following this more recent view, the equation for existence is not Descartes's "I think; therefore I exist." It is instead "You exist; therefore, I exist." Thus, when it comes to knowledge acquisition, it cannot be said that people learn knowledge individually. It cannot be said that knowledge is acquired solely by personal effort, or that technology is just as good a medium for the distribution of knowledge as people are. Knowledge is not acquired by individuals. It is rather acquired at the borderline between individuals. Because people are relational, knowledge acquisition is also relational.

Given these critical understandings of knowledge as nonobjective and human beings as relational, educators are being called to rethink knowledge acquisition. These two major assumptions about how human beings acquire knowledge must be critically examined and challenged. Critical thinking thus calls for reformulating teaching and learning. Knowledge acquisition can no longer be considered a transfer of facts and abilities from one source (say the teacher) to another (say the student). Because knowledge is not a standalone, and because a person is not a standalone, this model of knowledge transfer does not make sense. And, the banking method of education, the method of depositing information and then withdrawing it, is not suitable because it still treats knowledge as objective and students as atomistic. For example, when knowledge is considered to be personal, it is not actually possible for students to learn information and then give it back in its same form. Instead, students must make sense of knowledge in personal and culturally specific ways. When a student learns about the ending date of the Civil War, it is unrealistic to think that such an ending date has the same meaning for each student. And, it is quite uneducative to create a system of withdrawal that forces each student to give one piece of knowledge back in the same form that every other student gives it back. Because knowledge acquisition happens in very personal ways, classroom techniques of assessment cannot be objective, cannot require identical outcomes for each student. Because knowledge acquisition depends on personal meaning-making, students must be able to show what they know in personally meaningful ways.

Moreover, because knowledge acquisition depends on the relation that is established between the learner and others in his or her life, more critical thought must be given to the social surroundings in classrooms and schools. Because people are relational rather than atomistic, knowledge acquisition will differ according to the people among whom learning takes place. Learning that happens with computers will not be the same as learning that happens with teachers. Learning that happens within a culturally diverse group of students will not be the same as learning that happens within a more homogeneous group. Learning that happens only between boys will not be the same as learning that happens only between girls. Learning is a shared practice of meaning-making, a practice taking place between people. And so, the particular people with whom education takes place are just as important as the knowledge that is taught and tested. Honoring the complex process of knowledge acquisition demands a more critically informed practice than the banking system has to offer. Through critical examination of knowledge acquisition, the banking system is exposed as the oppressive force that it is.

Further Reading

Freire, P. (1970). *Pedagogy of the oppressed.* New York: Continuum.

Harding, S. (1998). *Is science multicultural?* Bloomington: Indiana University Press.

Sidorkin, A. (1999). *Beyond discourse: Education, the self, and dialogue.* New York: State University of New York Press.

Socratic Questioning: Helping Students Figure Out What They Don't Know

Danny Weil

Socratic questioning is a process whereby reasoning and thinking is elicited and probed based on a commitment to an authentic philosophical journey of leaning and individual and social development. The power of Socratic questioning lies in its ability to allow people to explicate their ideas, to slow down in their thinking and learn the process of evaluating their thinking and elaborate on it—to develop tortoise thinking in a hare world. Not only does this allow individuals to test their ideas relative to others, but it also enables them to develop a more cohesive and well-reasoned perspective as to what they are studying or thinking. In many ways, it is crucial in helping both oneself and others develop empathic critical thinking in the interest of building communities of learning.

For the person not accustomed to Socratic questioning, it is necessary to develop an inner-Socratic spirit, to take seriously the voices of others, what they think, how they form their beliefs, and how their ideas might be tested relative to what they are thinking. Thus, Socratic questioning must begin with the understanding that what people think is important, something to be respected, and something to be harvested for greater understanding. What Socratic questioning seeks to encourage is that people abandon what might be termed "vagrant chatter" and develop the reasoning and dispositions to engage in a learning conversation where argumentation is redefined as an admission to humility, a serious dialogical and dialectical journey toward the unknown in the interest of understanding and learning.

Socratic questioning rests on the assumption that everything has a logic that can be uncovered by use of questioning and thinking. It is also an effective habit of mind for helping people gain an insight into how they might be relating to people by asking them to think critically, to respect the ideas of others, and to critically and actively listen to points of view they might not agree with, and therefore it serves to promote humility and independent thinking and living.

Through Socratic questioning people are asked to clarify the purpose of what they are thinking or studying, to identify key concepts in what they are studying, and are asked to work to clarify what they mean, to distinguish relevant from irrelevant information and then test its reliability and sources, to question the assumptions inherent in what they are saying and what others might be saying, to reason within different points of view in the spirit of cooperation not competition, to probe the consequences or implications of what they and others are thinking, and to marshal reasons and evidence for what they know or think they know as well as be sensitive to evidence and reasons that are presented to them.

Because it is so poorly understood, one of the most common errors associated with an understanding of Socratic questioning is that it is a free-for-all discussion with no apparent end—a chaotic brainstorming without direction. Yet nothing could be further from the truth. In fact, Socratic questioning has a logic that can be used effectively within any domain of human thinking. Learning to participate well within a Socratic discussion requires copious critical listening skills, something foreign to most people, and thus directly teaches the power of both listening and questioning. It is a directed format for questioning that takes people from what they don't know or what they think they know, to clarity as to what they know and how they came to know it. It works to penetrate the structure of appearance and cast sunlight on actual reality and, as such, must admit to a redefinition of learning as that being "the more one learns, the less one knows." This is true because, as students and teachers discover the power of questioning for wonderment and inquiry, they see that one question leads to two, two to four, and on and on. Students and teachers begin to question answers as opposed to simply answering questions.

The forum for Socratic questioning may either be participant generated, that is, in collaborative problem-solving groups of students or with group leaders questioning within group processes. These discussions can be spontaneous and unrehearsed, probative and exploratory, or specific-issue or subject related. Furthermore, they can also be "silent dialogue" activities where people generate questions about material they are thinking about for both internalized learning and later use in larger Socratic discussions. I often ask students to generate a list of questions they would need to have answered to understand the problems they are trying to solve or the decisions they have to make within a given domain or subject area. This helps them discover the art of internal questioning, while at the same time providing a platform for future external Socratic questioning. Socratic questioning helps students figure out what they don't know, not what they do know, and thus serves to cultivate the humility necessary for learning.

It is important that teachers understand that there is no formula or step-by-step procedure to follow; we are talking about developing a mind-set that thinks in questions not in answers. Following are tactics to keep in mind when questioning people and when having them question themselves and what they might be thinking.

- You must understand that people confuse interrogation with questioning so preface your questions with empathy, which shows you have heard the person with whom you are speaking

- Ask people for their reasons and evidence for what they believe

- Respect and listen to what people say

- Have confidence in their ability to discover good thinking through the art of questioning

- Don't worry if some of your questions misfire

- Be willing to take risks with your questions

- Ask questions that help people distinguish between what they know and what they merely believe
- Go slowly and gently with people who have not been exposed to this method of learning
- Ask questions that require people to reason within different points of view
- Ask questions that elicit examples, analogies, or metaphors
- Help people reflect on the information they have or need to get
- Ask people to clarify key concepts and use them in other contexts
- Ask them questions that require them to reflect upon their assumptions and conclusions
- Don't give up when people are not responding
- Make your questioning relevant to peoples' lives, helping them transfer insights into ordinary experience
- Be willing to take the devil's advocate role
- Give people opportunities to generate questions about what they are thinking about, remembering that Socratic questioning can be done silently without conversation
- Allow for enough wait time for people to answer
- Remember, it is an artful process in which ones' strengths and effectiveness develop over time
- Ask people for examples of what they mean
- Sum up what people say and then ask them if this is what they mean or meant

It is essential to embrace the understanding that the notion of Socratic questioning is based on the idea that all thinking has a logic that can be elicited and assessed by the human mind. Contrary to a chaotic free-for-all where students assert mindlessly formulated questions and amorphous discussions based on unsystematic thinking, Socratic questioning is thoughtful systematic probing of students' thinking, both with the teacher and among students. Structured Socratic thinking helps take student thinking from the unclear or ambiguous to the clear and unambiguous. It is a clarification process whereby language is probed for assumptions. It is a commitment to guided questioning that probes beneath the surface of thought, raises essential issues, helps students arrive at their own well-reasoned judgments and perspectives through conscientious reasoning, and helps them gain an insight into their thinking and how their thinking pertains to controversies and issues that confront them as well as human reality. In short, it is a structure of thinking and questioning that is unequivocally committed to helping students and teachers discover the construction of their own thought and the thought of others in the interest of transformative metacognition. Furthermore, it requires that all involved listen critically, not selectively, to what others say; take what they say seriously; recognize and reflect on their assumptions and the assumptions of others; seek explanatory power through requirements of examples, analogies, metaphors, and objections; endeavor to distinguish what one believes and what one actually knows; and be willing to play the role of devil's advocate with the interest of helping students marshal evidence for what they think relative to what others think, while encouraging them to maintain a healthy sense of critical self-skepticism.

The following Socratic discussion represents an attempt to get students, in this case blue-collar workers, to think critically about what they perceived as labor relations and why. I have selected it as an example because it shows that Socratic questioning goes beyond schooling and is really an approach to life and the process of becoming.

In her article "Union Maid," which appeared in *Monthly Review,* February 1993, Aleine Austin described her work for the National Maritime Union. Working with the Union's Educational Director, Leo Huberman, Austin had been selected to be his assistant as the River Ports Education Director. Working to provide educational instruction on trade unionism in the major ports along the Mississippi and Ohio Rivers during 1944, Austin describes Huberman's philosophy and method of teaching. The small exchange that follows underlies Huberman's understanding of critical thinking and the art of Socratic questioning. Coupling his technique of questioning with a greater understanding of the role of education and politics, Huberman was an astute educator as exemplified in the following exchange: "Don't lecture!" was his number one lesson. "The first thing a good teacher wants to do is get the students involved," he explained. "A lecturer usually is more concerned about teaching the subject matter than he is about teaching people. Lecturing turns a student into a passive recipient. The trick is to stimulate students to become active thinkers."

"How do you do that?" marveled Austin. "By involving their experience. Start where they are. Ask them questions that draw on their own knowledge. Do you know Latin?" When she nodded, he broke down the word *education* into its Latin roots and asked her to analyze them. She did as follows:

E-duc-ation
out from—lead—the act of

"You see," he pointed excitedly to her translated syllables. "Lead out from" or "draw out from"—that's the original meaning of education. You draw on what your students know—the seeds of their understanding are in their old experiences. You draw out from them what they already know."

From there they prepared a lesson plan for the first class. Even the topic started with a question: "Why Unions?" The following is a sample of the kind of dialogue that took place in Leo's introductory class the next day:

Leo: Who is stronger, you or the employer?

Boatman I: My employer, of course.

Leo: How do you know that?

Boatman I: I have to go to him to get my job.

Leo: What enables him to give you the job?

Boatman I: He owns the boat.

Leo: Why don't you own the boat?

Boatman I: Me? Where would I get that kind of money?

Leo: So you need money, or capital, to own a boat. The same holds true for a factory, or restaurant, or any kind of enterprise that employs others to make a product or provide a service. But why does that make an employer stronger than a worker—doesn't he need workers to operate the boat? (He points to another boatman to answer his question.)

Boatman II: Sure, he can't run the boat without us.

Leo: Then you can decide what wages you'll work for, can't you?

Boatman II: I can decide what wages I'd *like* to work for—but that doesn't mean I'll get them.

Leo: Why not? (Points to another Boatman.)

Boatman III: Because some other bloke can come along and accept less.

Leo: But aren't you free to refuse to work for a wage you feel is too low?

Boatman III: Sure, and I'm free to starve, too—But if I want to eat, I have to take the wage the employer offers, no matter how low because if I don't, someone else will. I'm powerless, that's all.

Leo: Isn't there anything you can do to get some power?

Boatman III: Well, I could try to talk that other bloke out of working for so low a wage.

Leo: (Addressing the whole class.) Would that work?

Boatman IV: Naw—What good would one other worker do? You'd have to get all the boatman in the port to refuse to work below a certain rate before the employer would pay any attention.

Boatman V: That wouldn't work—he'd just go to another port and hire his boatmen there.

Boatman VI: Suppose you get all the boatmen in all the ports to refuse to work, say, below $5.00 an hour—then you'd have some power, wouldn't you?

Boatman II: You'd have a union!

Leo: What do you mean by a union?

Boatman II: You know! A union is when workers unite.

Leo: For what purpose?

Boatman II: To control their wages.

Leo: Control? Can they get any wage they want?

Boatman V: Sure. They're in the drivers (*sic*) seat now?

Boatman II: Yeah. They could drive the employer right out of business by demanding to high wages.

Leo: What would the employer do then, if the union demanded, say, $10.00 an hour and he felt that he'd lose money or his business would go broke?

Boatman I: Maybe he'd compromise—maybe he'd offer $7.00 or $8.00.

Leo: You mean he'd start bargaining with the boatmen?

Boatman I: Yeah, I guess that's what you call it.

Leo: Well, didn't you say before you'd have to take what the owner offered—or starve? Now you're saying he'd bargain with you. What's different now from before?

Boatman I: Before I was just one person—acting alone. I didn't have any bargaining power. Now—with all the other workers united in a union, I've got real bargaining power by joining together with the rest of the boatmen.

Leo: You sound like you're quoting from the Supreme Court. Let me read a section from a decision made in 1937. "Long ago we stated the reason for labor organizations. We said they were organized out of the necessities of the situation: that a single employee was helpless in dealing with an employer . . . that union was essential to give laborers an opportunity to deal on *an equality with their employer*." That's what unions do. They don't make workers stronger than employers; they make workers "more equal" to employers, by giving them a voice in determining their wages and working conditions. Does anybody know what kind of bargaining that is called?"

Boatman I: Isn't that called Collective Bargaining?

Leo: "Right." (Affirmed with a broad smile.)

I smiled, too. "Someday, I will teach like that," I promised myself . . . (Austin, 1993, pp. 40–43).

Austin demonstrates unequivocally that, without a doubt, Socratic questioning is at the heart of critical thinking. It is a thinking disposition, both cognitive and affective, that fuels students' thought, elicits and probes their thinking, and allows them to develop and evaluate their thinking and the thinking of others by forcing them to make what is unconscious conscious so that it might be visualized and pronounced. Thus, it must be understood as more than just a pedagogical gimmick or technique; it is a habit of mind and value that must be cultivated and nurtured in the interest of formulating a new way of learning, living, and thinking.

Students need educational opportunities to develop and examine their thinking and the thinking of others in an atmosphere of civility and inquiry that affords them the opportunity to slow their thinking down, to express it patiently and with clarity, and to put a premium on the process of questioning as opposed to the tyranny of obsessively searching for the "right" answer. Furthermore, Socratic questioning helps students unmask authority and dominion while it heralds taking a reflective critical self-inventory.

For the teacher as facilitator, a requisite for fair-minded and critically constructed Socratic questioning is a serious and deep compassion for and commitment to the students' thinking on the part of both students and those who instruct them. Without a commitment to compassionate discourse with students, Socratic questioning turns out to be yet another inefficient technique and becomes pseudo-educational gimmickry. Helping students approach problem solving and decision making with the idea that they need to figure out what they don't know, as opposed to confirm what they think they know, will allow students to develop the values and dispositions that encourage creativity, discovery, forceful imagination, curiosity, the necessity to embrace doubt and question, and the development of an investigative orientation as well as a deep-seated empathy for the lives of others. In short, Socratic questioning is a process of becoming.

References

Austin, A. (1993). Union maid. *Monthly Review, 44* 40–44.

O'Sullivan, E. (1999). *Transformative Learning: Educational vision for the twenty-first century.* London: Zed.

Steinberg, S. R., & Kincheloe, J. L. (1998). *Students as researchers: Creating classrooms that matter.* New York: Falmer Press.

Teaching Current Events Using a Constructivist Critical Thinking Paradigm: A Model for Teachers

Judi Hirsch

Teaching critical thinking is intimately tied to helping students understand the world and their relationship to it. Before we delve more deeply into this concept, here is a list of teaching strategies designed to help teachers promote critical thinking:

- Ask more questions; answer fewer
- Use alternative textbook sources

- Don't avoid controversial issues
- Question everyone's assumptions
- Give students more responsibility
- Check out alternative media
- Provide a safe environment
- Let your imagination go; brainstorm
- Construct tentative hypotheses
- Share unfamiliar perspectives
- Encourage group collaboration
- Consider ethical solutions
- Evaluate the credibility of sources
- Identify inherent biases
- Explore consequences
- Teach students, not concepts
- Don't have ready answers
- Focus on process not product
- Give students tools, not answers
- Encourage inquiry
- Support student exploration
- Listen to students
- Respect all points of view
- Focus on learning, not teaching

Our world is changing rapidly. Each day, as we take in new information, there seems to be almost as much to unlearn, as there is to learn. To deal intelligently with current events requires critical thinking. As teachers, we have the unique responsibility of preparing the next generation for participation in the creation of a more just and democratic society. It is our challenge to help students do this job well. We need to help them learn—and model for them—that asking questions is at least as important as finding answers. As Einstein said, "Imagination is more important than knowledge."

Headlines and news broadcasts assail us daily about escalating violence at home and abroad. Neither we, nor our students, are immune to the media's frightening words and images. Textbooks, which are supposed to provide accurate, objective, and current information suited to the learning needs of students, are woefully inadequate. This is due both to the rapidity with which information becomes obsolete and to the inherent bias of sources. The same is true of mass media and the Internet. Given the current information glut, it is important that young people have the tools to recognize the subtle yet ubiquitous presence of corporate influence in public and civic arenas. What tools can help our students sort through the daily barrage of data and propaganda and learn to make well-informed, well-reasoned, just decisions? What is the role of schools? Consider the following:

I am a survivor of a concentration camp. My eyes saw what no man should witness: Gas chambers built by learned engineers, children poisoned by educated physicians, infants killed by trained nurses, so I am suspicious of education. My request is: Help your students become human. Your efforts must never produce learned monsters, skilled psychopaths, educated Eichmans. Reading, writing, and arithmetic are important only if they serve to make our children more human. (Ginnot, 1972, p. 72)

Teachers are responsible for guiding student activity, modeling appropriate behavior, and providing the examples—and counter examples—that can turn student conversations into meaningful dialogue. Student-centered learning requires active participation, not passive reception. Young people learn by experimenting with ideas and by thinking about what they see; then, by comparing new experiences with what they already know, they construct hypotheses about how the world works. Critical thinking is a major component of such learning. It is the polar opposite of rote memorization, whereby one might be able to recall many facts, but explain few. Constructivist critical thinking is an ongoing process that seeks to help students transform society by searching for solutions that solve social problems and improve people's lives (Freire, 1970).

The future of civilization as we know it may depend on our ability to sort through increasingly complex and often one-sided news bulletins without being swayed by patriotism, greed, or emotion. We are facing ideological conflicts over diminishing natural resources, overpopulation, and the increasing disparity between north and south, east and west, haves and have-nots. Our students need to figure out what lies behind the news stories they see and hear, and become aware that most of our media is owned by a few global megacorporations with ties to the movies we see, the food we eat, and the clothes we wear.

Since September 11, the need for citizens to be able to apply the principles of critical thinking to current events is more crucial than ever. In the fall of 2002, the President of the United States described the current fight against terrorism as a fight of "good" versus "evil"; you are either "with us or against us." In 2003, he ordered a preemptive invasion if Iraq that resulted in a quagmire of terrorist guerrilla attacks on U.S. interests. He even listed seven "rogue" states that the United States might decide to nuke. How can we help our students figure out whether there are circumstances under which it might be okay to nuke a country? What is acceptable collateral damage? How many lives lost is too many? Are all lives equal? How can we help them know what is true and who is good? Students might gain some insight by reading about the controversy that surrounded the atomic bombing of Hiroshima and Nagasaki by the United States in 1945.

U.S. citizens need to distinguish between "terrorists" and "freedom fighters" and then decide whether there is a better way to fight terrorism than the current approach of our government. We need to figure out whether a military solution is the best way to provide security. For fiscal year 2003, President Bush asked to increase military spending by 65 times the amount allocated for humanitarian aid; this would bring the military budget to nearly $800 billion, making up 46% of the federal budget, while funds for health, education, and housing are cut (Center for Defense Information, 2003). As of spring 2003, school districts throughout the United States are laying off teachers; cutting services to the neediest students; closing schools; and reducing teachers' salaries, pensions, and health care benefits. One wonders whether this will make us more secure.

Current social, economic, and political conditions are too unstable and too critical for educators to lecture without student input. This is not the time for business as usual. If we don't get our young people into the habit of asking questions while they are still in school, it will be too late once they graduate. How can we persuade our students to act out of compassion and resist the material temptations surrounding them? We might teach them to listen to the voices of the marginalized and the downtrodden, and hear their cries for help. Heeding the words of Martin Luther King, we can help them see that "Peace is not the absence of war, but the presence of justice."

The news we hear and the history we read is always recorded from the point of view of those who have the time and means to report it. Is it possible to see the world from outside of one's ethnocentric position? Is it possible that the content and process of our teaching affects *how* and *what* students learn? What can we do to share an unfamiliar perspective with our students? The author, Howard Zinn, tries to do just that:

I prefer to tell the story of the discovery of America from the point of view of the Arawaks, of the Constitution from the standpoint of the slaves, of Andrew Jackson as seen by the Cherokees, of the Civil War as seen by the New York Irish, of the Mexican War as seen by the deserting soldiers of the Scott's army, of the rise of industrialism as seen by the young women in the Lowell textile mills, . . . of the First World War as seen by socialists, the Second World War as seen by pacifists, the New Deal as seen by blacks in Harlem, the postwar American empire as seen by peons in Latin America, etc. (1995, p. 10)

Following this approach, some U.S. history teachers have used England's high school history textbooks' version of our Revolutionary War. We might use a similar technique to help our students learn about current events. We could accompany them as they work their way through a complicated issue, and support them as they try to develop reasoned positions. Teachers might ask their students what they'd like to learn about and encourage their inquiry. Because we are trying to get them used to a process-based paradigm, the actual topic is somewhat irrelevant. It would be best if we could discipline ourselves *not* to give them too many answers or opinions, for teachers, too, are biased, and it's important that this be acknowledged. In fact, it might be a good idea for us *not* to know too much about the chosen topic. We need not be experts, but only know enough to keep our students engaged in the process of inquiry. Giving them practice in explaining their thinking to each other before sharing it with the group can help them become

adept at thinking more clearly and speaking more confidently.

Some teachers might be tempted to avoid a particular issue, thus leaving students at the mercy of fear, ignorance, and bias. Perhaps we agree with those who say an issue is too complicated for us to even think about. So what can teachers do? How can students learn to question the next time they're confused if we stop them from asking now? Learning to ask is an essential learning technique. Suppose there was a fight at school. What's the best way to handle it? We would want to know what happened, how it happened, if there were any witnesses, and if there was a history of trouble between the two sides. (A good introduction to multiple perspectives in the retelling of an incident might be the film "Roshomon" by Kurosawa. It is the story of a rape and murder from the point of view of the woman, her husband, the other man, and a witness.)

Teachers can learn to reframe the curriculum so that classrooms focus on the learner's experience rather than on what the teacher knows or what the textbook says. As hard as it is to do, *it is far more important that students explain their thinking to us than we explain our thinking to them.* Students who construct knowledge for themselves are in a much more powerful position than those who simply go through school memorizing what their books and teachers say, trusting that it is correct. These students, many of whom have 4.0 grade point averages, are not the kind of people I'd want on my jury, deciding my fate, for they have relinquished their critical thinking skills for the lure of getting the "right answer."

From the moment they enter school, children are told what to do and how and when to do it. They are told when their time is up and then are graded on their efforts and rewarded for their compliance. Students treated this way resist making independent investigations and defending their conclusions, just as teachers who are used to being in charge have a hard time being quiet and supporting students' process. This is our pedagogical challenge. As we shift from the traditional didactic paradigm of instruction to a more constructivist approach, we must pique our students' interest and then support their intellectual exploration.

For example, rather than teaching the formula for the circumference of a circle, and then asking the students to practice plugging different numbers into the formula, we might ask them to experiment with various sized circles and pieces of string to try to figure out whether there's a relationship between the diameter and circumference of a circle, and, if so, what that relationship is. Once they find that the relationship is constant, we can praise them for their diligence, let them know about *pi,* and *then* introduce the formula. They will probably never forget it. More importantly, they will never forget that they arrived at the formula by trying to figure it out. Which approach would be more empowering to them as learners? How many people who aren't math teachers still remember that formula?

The above example relates to the current national obsession with testing. Recently, there has been much criticism regarding the ability of high school students to reason well and be prepared to enter the workforce; pressure is being put on legislatures and schools to come up with standards whose attainment can be measured. This has given rise to widespread use of norm referenced, standardized, high-stakes tests. Teaching to the test is now commonplace, with art and music, science and social studies, recess and constructivist criti-

cal thinking relegated to the past. One wonders if this trend will help our students to become more thoughtful citizens.

Teachers should not be cowed or motivated by standardized tests that call for a regurgitation of isolated, trivial, contextless bits of information. Instead, we must teach our students to always evaluate the credibility of sources, ask for evidence, and insist upon rigorous examination of claims. Rather than depending on ready-made simplistic sound bites, we must allow our students the time to consider all points of view. We can no longer rely on teachers' editions and publishers' guides when teaching about controversial issues. Instead we must encourage our students to figure things out for themselves. We must be prepared *not* to have answers for our students and, instead, support their forays into confusion and contradiction. We must focus on the journey rather than the destination, on students learning rather than on teachers teaching. When we emphasize thinking rather than facts, our students not only learn more, but also perform better on standardized tests (Hirsch, 1987).

Using a constructivist critical thinking paradigm can help keep our students focused and clear-headed while negotiating the quagmire of emotion-laden and multifaceted political situations; it can provide a protective coating of confidence that can help make one immune to baseless claims made by all sides in a dispute. Using a constructivist critical thinking paradigm, our students would be encouraged to do the following:

1. *Ask about the issues:* question assumptions; identify and acknowledge biases, myths, and prejudices on all sides, including the questioner's.
2. *Gather relevant background information* by searching for and listening to diverse voices that represent all parties.

3. Evaluate what has been accumulated using rational criteria.
4. *Consider moral and ethical solutions* using social justice and fair-mindedness as guidelines.
5. Explore the consequences and implications of any decisions to see whether they are both just and compassionate.

We can teach current events using a constructivist critical thinking paradigm. Consider the conflict in Israel/Palestine, one of the many confusing, emotional, and contentious issues of our day. The media tempts us into simplistically thinking there are two sides—victim and oppressor—and tries to force us to support one; however, it's more complicated than that. What exactly is the conflict? What do we know about it? Who is involved? How do we know? What are our sources? Should a people aspiring to be a country have the same status as a "real" country? What is a country? What is a people? How long must a country be in existence to have credibility? Do we know that most of the countries of the region were created by European colonial powers at the end of World War I for their own benefit? Does this matter? How does a people become a country? How did Israel become a country? What's an Israeli? What's a Jew? Are all Israelis Jews? Who are the Israeli Arabs? What's an Arab? What's a Moslem? What's a Palestinian? Are they Arabs? Should the Palestinians have a country? Why do they need one? Do they deserve one? Do the Jews? Who decides? These questions could go on *ad infinitum;* just listing them would make a good beginning exercise in constructivist critical thinking. Lists could be created by students, posted, and amended daily for the duration of the course.

Critically analyzing current events requires access to alternative sources that do not represent the bias of the mainstream media and textbooks. Students should be encouraged to check out the Web, watch videos, and conduct interviews to learn about history from a variety of perspectives. By constantly asking, "What do you mean?" "Why do you think that?" and "How do you know?" we can help students clarify their thinking and construct their own knowledge. Isn't this a better way of teaching the importance of citing one's sources than completing exercises in a grammar book?

We want to support our students as they learn to think critically about current events. Perhaps they will find just and humane solutions to some of the social, political, and economic issues facing the world today. As teachers, we can remember that young people are fully capable of using constructivist critical thinking. To get them started, all we need to do is let them ask questions; they will do the rest. This may be difficult for those teachers who have only experienced the teacher-as-the-authority model, but it is possible to learn to ask more than we answer. Children do not learn as well by being told, as they do by continuing to think about something. "It is the child's own efforts to resolve a conflict that takes him or her on to another level" (Duckworth, 1987, p. 39).

The constructivist critical thinking paradigm is a messy process, which requires constant practice and vigilance in order to remain viable. We must continually reexamine our prejudices and biases and listen to people who hold views that are different from our own. We can make this can happen in our classrooms if they become places where the process is one of supporting inquiry and learning rather than memorization and regurgitation. We can do this. More than that, we must. *It is our duty as teachers to provide the environment in which real thinking and learning occurs.*

References

Center for Defense Information. (2003). Budget of the U.S. Government, fiscal year 2003. Washington, DC: Center for Defense Information.

Duckworth, E. (1987). *The having of wonderful ideas.* New York: Teachers College Press.

Freire, P. (1970). *Pedagogy of the oppressed,* New York: Continuum.

Ginnot, H. (1972). *Teacher and child: A book for parents and teachers.* New York: Macmillan.

Hirsch, J. (1987). *A study of a program based on Feuerstein's theories intended to teach high-level cognitive skills to African-American and Mexican-American junior high school students identified as learning disabled.* Unpublished manuscript.

Zinn, H. (1995). *A people's history of the United States.* New York: Harper.

Further Reading

Kincheloe, J. L. (2001). *Getting beyond the facts: Teaching social studies/social sciences in the twenty-first century.* New York: Peter Lang.

Kincheloe, J. L., & Steinberg, S. R. (Eds.). (2004). *The miseducation of the West: Constructing Islam.* Westport, CT: Greenwood Publishing Group.

Lowen, J. (1992). *Lies my teacher told me: Everything your American history textbook got wrong.* New York: Simon and Schuster.

Terrorism

Terrorism: Western Definitions Since 9/11

Yusef Progler

We have wondered why it was that Dr. Savimbi's Unita in Angola and the Contras in Nicaragua were "freedom fighters," lionized especially by President Reagan's White House and the conservative right wing of the United States of America, whereas our liberation movements such as the Pan-African Congress were invariably castigated as "terrorist movements."

Archbishop Desmond Tutu

Dr. Savimbi is a freedom fighter and Nelson Mandela is a terrorist. Yasser Arafat's Palestine Liberation Organization (PLO) is a terrorist movement, while the Shah of Iran is a statesman. Mandela is a statesman, but so is Saddam Hussein. Hezbollah is a terrorist movement, and Iran supports terrorism, but Arafat is a statesman. The Contras are freedom fighters, and Syria is on the list of states supporting terrorism. Osama Bin Laden is a freedom fighter, but Arafat is a terrorist, again. General Musharraf is a statesman, but Saddam now supports terrorist movements. The Irish Republican Army is a terrorist movement, the Taliban are statesmen, but Bin Laden is a terrorist. Syria is back on the list of terrorist states and Arafat is a statesman, again, but the Taliban are now terrorists. Ariel Sharon is a statesman, while Hezbollah is still a terrorist movement. For those of us who get our news from the mainstream media like Cable News Network (CNN) and British Broadcasting Company (BBC), it is difficult enough to keep track of the shifting and often contradictory images and sound bites used to describe complex political events, so how, in such a climate, can we ever learn to think critically about "terrorism"?

One way is to engage in a closer, comparative study of events. In my secondary social studies methods courses, I do a unit about primary sources that emphasizes critical thinking. We begin by reading several news reports about a botched Israeli commando raid in southern Lebanon on February 23, 1999, which resulted in several Israeli casualties. Using the Nexis/Lexis database, we found four different reports filed within hours of the initial incident, and we studied the language each used to describe the incident. Israeli radio reported that its soldiers were on an "initiated operational activity," and that they were killed "in exchanges of fire with terrorists." Radio Lebanon reported that "Islamic Resistance units" had "intercepted" an "Israeli commando force" inside southern Lebanon. The Chinese state news service described the incident as an "Israeli commando unit" trying to "penetrate the areas" in southern Lebanon, but that they were met by "strong resistance" from "Lebanese guerillas." *The Boston Globe* reported that the Israeli casualties resulted from "clashes" with "pro-Iranian Hezbollah guerillas." Through further research we learn that Hezbollah was indeed resisting an illegal military occupation of southern Lebanon, from which the Israelis pulled out in May 2000.

Each time I teach this lesson, it leads us in many interesting directions, some times to discussions about the foundation of Israel and the question of Palestine, and other times about the reliability of various news media. But one discussion that consistently returns each time is the vocabulary and imagery used by state power to describe resistance to military aggression. Although Israel is consistently condemned by the United Nations for its illegal occupation of Lebanese and Palestinian territories, the Israeli state defines the actions of anyone who resists that occupation as "terrorism." Whatever the circumstances, by definition, the Lebanese and Palestinian resistance are invariably termed "terrorist movements." This is partly to dehumanize them, but also to justify the arbitrary use of state power. That train of thought usually leads us to further investigations of similar ways that state power defines how we understand the world, and students begin to unravel the legacy of "terrorism" as a highly politicized term in public discourse, whether in the context of the Cold War or various national liberation movements.

Palestine is an important case study for critical thinking about terrorism. The Israelis consistently depict as "terrorism" all Palestinian resistance to an illegal military occupation. The use of the word "terrorism" to describe a bombing of a cafe in an Israeli town may be accurate, but it gets more difficult to apply the term when the targets of such attacks are military, and it is even less credible to describe as terrorism the Palestinian resistance of Israeli tanks and bulldozers rolling over their homes. The Palestinians have an internationally recognized right to resist the Israeli occupation of their land and the destruction of their homes, as well as Israeli attacks upon ambulances and journalists, the massacres of families, and the arresting of men without charges. In this context, Israel is practicing "state terrorism," although the news media never make that distinction. But unqualified in this way, terrorism becomes a politically charged term. When the American media use this term to portray opponents of American allies, they do a grave injustice to the English language, and a greater injustice to the cause of diplomacy, including any measures that can be enacted to end ongoing conflict in Palestine.

We need to think critically about how it is, for example, that Israel, which has a history of aggression against Palestine, has come to be seen as the main victim of terrorism. Critical thinking can involve the need to look at the purposes served by such reversals, and who gets to define terrorism and what is left out of that definition. Terrorism is often a self-serving intellectual construct that is hidden from view by its politicized use. Most recently, its meaning has been hijacked by the United States, which began to use the word regularly in the 1970s to describe various forms of nationalism in developing countries, and Israel, which has insisted on defining Palestinians as terrorists for resisting occupation. In the information age, power is in words and images. What we are seeing in the world now are aggressors framing their victims as "terrorists." But for the purposes of critical thinking, we need to sometimes separate the realities on the ground from the way we talk about things, otherwise we may contribute to propagandizing ourselves by normalizing definitions and concepts that actually have no agreed upon meaning.

Because it has no agreed upon public definition, terrorism can be used for a variety of purposes and the meaning can change as needed. Sometimes it means anybody who gets in our way, and other times it means somebody who resists colonization or other forms of invasion. A good example is the image of Yasser Arafat. For years, the Americans and the Israelis refused to call him anything but a terrorist. After Oslo, he became a "statesman." However, his new title was contingent upon him terrorizing Islamic and leftist activists, which is why the Israelis gave the PLO guns and allowed them to build prisons and bunkers. But that plan did not work, because it is hard to shoot your brothers and cousins when the real enemy is the occupation and its injustice, so then we see Arafat stripped of the robes of a statesman and unceremoniously returned to his previous garb as a terrorist, with some calling for his elimination. However, when Arafat's services as a policeman were needed, the media once again dropped the terrorist appellation. In this context, then, what is a terrorist? It is what Israel and America say it is.

Since September 11, the naming and blaming game has gotten quite absurd. After President Bush declared a "war on terrorism," every two-bit dictator and repressive regime around the world wanted to reign in its opposition under the rubric of "fighting terrorism." Anything that goes on in the world that is against the United States or its allies is now termed an act of terrorism. Various governments are taking advantage of this to disguise their own agendas of violating the human rights of people within their borders. In China, for example, the government now describes nationalists in its centuries-old ethnic and religious conflicts in the north as terrorists, allied with Osama Bin Laden. The Philippine government, which has long been struggling with religious and ethnic nationalism in its southern islands, has now joined the "war on terrorism" by bringing in U.S. commandos into a region that has seen American imperial intervention since the nineteenth century. Regional geopolitical problems become linked to a global threat of terrorism. We could extend this discussion back to the Cold War, when any form of nationalism in less-developed countries promoting a leftist agenda was termed terrorism by the Americans, and the Soviet Union was the main sponsor of terrorism. Meanwhile, American-backed terrorists became freedom fighters. Further back, we could trace a legacy of bandits and pirates, the nineteenth century terrorists.

In addition to justifying self-serving policies and explaining the aggressive actions of state power, terrorism serves other purposes. America has always needed an "evil other" in opposition to its good self. The evil other in history has taken on many names and shapes, from despots, pirates, and bandits to communists and terrorists. In Western civilization, which is ferociously dichotomous, there has always been a necessity to define through opposition, and, therefore, a terrorist or some other nefarious character—real or imagined—has actually become necessary for the maintenance of a Western self-image.

This can be traced back to the Crusades, and carried forward through the Enlightenment and the Age of Imperialism and into the twentieth century. In this framework, Muslims are not singled out as terrorists, because other peoples at other times have suffered the same labeling, which always serves the power interest of the time. Of course, the question can be asked as to why people so readily accept an image of Muslim terrorists. This has a lot to do with the legacy of the Crusades in the Christian West and several decades of anti-Arab propaganda on behalf of Israel in America.

In a bid for unipolar world domination after the fall of communism, America has been trying to bring various sorts of stubborn holdouts into its sphere of influence. This is what the World Trade Organization and other big financial entities are trying to do, much like the Marshall Plan did after World War II. Islam is feared not so much for things like terrorism and fundamentalism, because the West has always had much more virulent strains of both; what is feared is that Islam has its own epistemology, its own way of seeing the world, its own outlook that differs in many fundamental ways from the liberal Western outlook being propagated by America. Islam is not alone in this; there are other alternative visions out there too. Some coming from large states like China, but others from various indigenous peoples. The West is now insecure of itself, its institutions, its military tactics, its self-image, its education, its economy, and many other areas. There is a profound insecurity in the Western world—a fear that the rest of the world is waking up to modernity as a destructive and unsustainable event in human history, soon to pass away of its own accord. This is the real fear, fear of self-destruction, implosion, but it is much easier to try and blame these essentially internal problems on some external enemy. Enter the terrorists, or the anarchists, or the communists, or whatever other heinous monster one can possibly imagine.

What is really going on, then, is a form of self-definition by using the other as a proxy. So, for instance, with Machiavelli the image of "oriental despotism" was central to the method in his celebrated treatise on politics. The Medieval Catholic Church used images of "Muslim depravity" as a way to define the purity of Christianity. Enlightenment secularists like Voltaire used negative constructs of Islam as a way to discredit religion in general. During the Victorian era, when Europeans were uptight about sexuality, artists and painters discovered the Turkish harem and the seraglio as an imaginary place of desire and lust that they could portray in paintings. The distance of the "other" allowed a certain degree of acceptance toward public nudity in those times, since it was not "our" nudity, it was those barbarous and depraved Turks. In this and other ways, Islam has real utility. The list is long and interesting, but the theme remains the same: Western civilization, in the foundational moments of modernity, constructed its self-image in the opposing mirror of Islam. This was not based on any reality of Islam or the way Muslims lived it at the time, which didn't matter. What mattered was that there was this other civilization out there of which most people were aware, but which few really took the time to learn about, and that this mysterious other could be pressed into service toward many cultural and political ends. Once you begin to think critically about Western history, you find Islam everywhere as a proxy to work out internal dilemmas. Violence plays a central role in this self-definition.

The West has had an unbelievably violent heritage, one hundred million people killed in the twentieth century alone, but it cannot come to grips with that legacy. So, instead, we see a projecting of Western guilt and insecurity about violence onto others, who in many cases turn out to be Muslim "terrorists."

Of course, some people have tried to offer definitions of terrorism that are more substantive or definitive. One potential definition centers around the deceptively simple idea of "killing or intimidating civilians for some political or military gain." However, that definition is dangerous, because one could then point to the "terror" bombing of civilians in Hiroshima and Nagasaki, or the "terror" bombing of Dresden, or the "terror" bombing of Vietnam and Cambodia. One could also mention the American sponsorship of various torture regimes in the Third World, which terrorize their own people to make way for things like progress and development. Thus, that definition is not pursued in the mainstream media, and it is more useful to those in power to keep a fuzzy, unclear, ever-shifting definition and sell it daily via the media, from which most alternative voices are excluded.

Further Reading

Abukhattala, I. (2004). The new bogeyman under the bed: Image formation of Islam in the Western school curriculum and media. In J. L. Kincheloe, & S. R. Steinberg (Eds.), *The miseducation of the West: Constructing Islam*. Westport, CT: Greenwood Publishing Group.

Furedi, F. (1994). *The new ideology of imperialism: Renewing the moral imperative*. London: Pluto Press.

Hentsch, T. (1992). *Imagining the Middle East*. Montreal: Black Rose Books.

Herman, E., & O'Sullivan, G. (1989). *The "terrorism" industry: The experts and institutions that shape our view of terror*. New York: Pantheon Books.

Kincheloe, J. L. (2004). Iran and American miseducation: Cover-ups, distortions, and omissions. In J. L. Kincheloe, & S. R. Steinberg (Eds.), *The miseducation of the West: Constructing Islam*. Westport, CT: Greenwood Publishing Group.

Textbooks

The Anti-Textbook Textbook: Critical Thinking and Politics in the Apolitical Classroom

Marjorie Mayers and James C. Field

I was recently reading an article by Perlmutter (1997) about textbooks and the sociopolitical climate in which they are imbedded with a class of becoming teachers. To enliven the discussion about textbooks, the students facilitating the class brought in a few examples of high school social studies texts for the perusal of the class. The students asked us to examine a number of designated pages in the books. We turned to the pages and were directed to think about what we were seeing and reading. We were being asked to consider, carefully and thoughtfully, the kinds of messages that are conveyed through the textbook medium. The class was divided into small groups and immediately after instructions were given there was a loud din in the room. The guiding question for the day was: What and whose values are imbedded in the curriculum? Off to work we went. In my group, we began by scrutinizing everything we were seeing in the text—the knowledge given, the pictures, the layout, and so on. All of a sudden,

looking at the textbooks seemed strange to me. I stared at the pages of the textbook upon which the class discussion was focused but was unable to put my finger on exactly what I was *reading* from the text—something was definitely bugging me.

The article about textbooks that we read in preparation for this class explored the significance of textbook construction, marketing, and knowledge-production as a deeply value-laden and highly mediated process. This seemed obvious to me. Of course, textbooks are, after all, big business. For example, Perlmutter (1997) reports that in 1995 the elementary through high school "market generated almost $2 billion in sales" and "textbooks comprised 30% of the entire market for books in the U.S." (p. 69). The direct involvement of corporations in textbook construction, production, and marketing is in itself a cause of great concern—that is, that textbooks are "media product[s] [which are] influenced by a complex amalgam of industrial, commercial, and social domains of control related to the particular qualities and complexities of the targeted audience" (Perlmutter, 1997, p. 70)—but perhaps even more troubling to me is the seamlessness and noneventness of textbook adoption and utilization. That is, "whatever is printed in a book [seems to be taken] as authoritative, and whatever is pictured [seems to be accepted] as incontrovertible" (Perlmutter, 1997, p. 70), not to mention (and this is an understatement) that textbooks are, in large measure, *the* knowledge medium of schools. That understood, I wondered about the political ends that are being shaped by these educational means and questioned whether discussions about the politics of the books themselves were ever topics of conversation in the classroom. I wondered what kinds of knowledges are shaped, opened, or inspired by the texts and whether the content and context of those books are ever challenged.

I recognized, in those moments in the classroom with my students, that the seemingly innocuous, inoffensive textbook is itself a harbinger of a particular canon of knowledge—sanctioned by the higher-ups who order them, deemed *official* in the *unofficial* spaces that they occupy, and meticulously crafted to invigorate swift and ever-increasing sales. Perlmutter (1997) comments that the visual and print "content [of textbooks] is selected, created, and displayed . . . with purposive, communicative intent [and that these methods of textbook production are to] encode certain meanings" about what is deemed to be knowledge-worthy (p. 70). Furthermore, he suggests that given that half of U.S. children do not go to college, high school social studies textbooks "are the last officially endorsed guides to the ordering and meaning of U.S. and world history and society" (p. 68). Textbooks, it seems to me,

are pretty important and powerful knowledge-shapers. I wonder, though, how many of us have considered what kinds of knowledge we participate in shaping and who is privileged to partake in those kinds of decisions.

I stared at the pages, reading and understanding the industry behind the production of the pictures and print of the textbook, and also learning something new about the extent to which photographs and other pictorial information is carefully staged and set for textbook production (Perlmutter, 1997), but something else continued to tug at me. Something else was beckoning my attention, but what? I was looking at a timeline of Canadian history spread over two pages in the text. The paper glossy, the photos slick, I read a tiny little blurb about the events of 1942. It read as follows:

Japanese Canadians were interned in camps in the British Columbia interior. Their property was confiscated, and their lives totally disrupted. Some German and Italian Canadians, also suspected of sympathy with the Germans, were interned as well.

On a different page, the students had us look at another glossy insert describing the Canadian government's relocation of Inuit tribes from one part of Northern Quebec to the Arctic Circle in the years between 1953 and 1955. Again, the text began, "Between 1953 and 1955, the Inuit communities in Northern Quebec were facing starvation."

These two examples highlight the politics of the classroom, and specifically the politics of the textbook, which I believe, are, for the most part, overlooked. I suddenly heard/read the text in a new way, calling into question the authoritative voice of the third-person persona delivering the lesson, the knowledge, the history, the content, and the context of these events. The language of the text, it dawned on me, is what codifies a certain dominant-culture read of the text's substance. Put another way, when a text reads, "The Japanese" or "The Inuit," I hear the distinctions between other and the dominant voice of the dominant-culture author (read white, middle class, capitalist, colonialist). I wonder out loud with my students about who the voice is—obviously not Japanese or Inuit. I muse about how the third-person voice suggests a neutral place from whence the information of the text is being offered and question how this othering embodies a particular politic. Who gets to other whom? I think about the experience of high school students reading this text who hear/learn, as a normal course of events, and as a regular part of their pedagogic diet, that there is indeed an apolitical, neutral, and value-free read of the world and it is delivered to them in the authority of the textbook. I know this is subtle; I wrestle in class to bring to bear that which strikes me about the language of the text as both political and purposeful. I try to name the textbook's othering in a way that highlights the safe neutrality that insures the textbook's widespread adoption. I struggle to articulate what seems to me to be so taken for granted and so normal that rendering it visible, audible, graspable is nearly impossible.

It is noteworthy for me to mention the great difficulty I am having here in exposing the kind of innocuous, subtle, and sustained political power that is levied by textbooks in classrooms and the ways in which we are numb to how they lull and teach us. I believe that this difficulty is testimony to the ways in which textbooks (and knowledge) are positioned in school culture. The discourse seems so tightly tied up that there is hardly any room to interrupt it—

to open it up, to shake it loose of the power and position it holds. Perlmutter (1997) acknowledges this by explaining that textbook construction is all about the middle-of-the-road, no controversy or conflict to disenfranchise anybody, just even-keeled neutrality that masquerades as the truth.

Another way to talk about the kinds of things that we take for granted in our everyday lives, that wash over us without our knowing or paying attention to them, that are so familiar to us that we cannot even see them or recognize them, really, is called *everyday consciousness*.[1] Perhaps we might think of the textbook as a kind of *educational everyday consciousness* that washes over us without controversy or concern. Michael Apple's (1990) explication of *everyday consciousness,* called *hegemony,*[2] compels us to look at the structural and ideological *givens* that frame our lives together—in schools and elsewhere. Apple (1990) asks us to " . . . [think] about the relationships between the overt and covert knowledge taught in school, the principles of selection and organization of that knowledge, and the criteria and modes of evaluation used to 'measure success' in teaching" (p. 2). It is to this problematic that I have turned my attention in terms of trying to make visible that which seems invisible vis-à-vis textbooks and their political ramifications in the classroom. I do this to open up critical opportunities in classrooms, to bring attention to the *pedagogic everyday consciousnesses* that slip over, by, and through us by foregrounding here the long-held belief[3] that schools and schooling are apolitical educational spaces (particularly public schools). I submit that classrooms, and the instruments used therein, are neither apolitical nor value-neutral and that these myths are but constructions of the *everyday consciousness* that we have become blinded by and beyond which we struggle to see. Apple (1990) suggests that "the issues surrounding the knowledge that is actually taught in schools, surrounding what is considered socially legitimate knowledge [e.g., the contexts and contents of textbooks], are of no small moment in becoming aware of the school's cultural, economic, and political position. Here, the basic act involves making the curriculum forms found in schools problematic so that their latent ideological context can be uncovered" (pp. 6–7). I also believe that it is from these myths that great opportunities arise for critical thought and dialogue, inviting conversations about the process and substance of learning and teaching (normally concealed and/or passed over) to emerge in ever more critical and meaningful ways.

THE ANTI-TEXTBOOK TEXTBOOK

The idea for the anti-textbook textbook emerged from the same classroom experience I described above. My students wrote responsive texts to the readings and class discussions on a weekly basis, and I responded accordingly. Commenting on Perlmutter's (1997) assertion that the aim of the editorial process of textbook construction is "not to offend anyone . . . [and knowing] that adoption board people have very little time, so look is vital and the main way a book is judged" (p. 76), a student of mine[4] wrote, " . . . it could be more interesting to construct a textbook out of material not included." This inspired me to think about the critical thinking possibilities that would be enlivened if a course of study was undertaken to examine the political, economic, social, and other considerations that are invested in textbook construction. Whereas textbooks might

constrain broader knowledge positions and compromise more inclusive and diverse perspectives on that which is *given,* the anti-textbook textbook would serve as the companion antidote to the apolitical veneer of *textbook knowledge* in schools. In response to my student, I wrote, "maybe it would be interesting if students, while working through a textbook, created a textbook of their own called, 'What they didn't want to tell you,' or 'Alternatives to one view.'"

It seems to me that if students were engaged in both reading the *officially sanctioned* textbook as well as invested in a process of creating their own companion textbook—a textbook challenging and investigating the authority, voice, perspective, purpose, and context of the school textbook—a more critical and deep understanding of world events and ideas would be/could be rendered. What would it be like for students to read of "Inuit relocation" and then to explore the meaning of that experience of Inuit culture by interviewing a member of the Inuit community or by looking to Inuit artifacts and literature to gain insight into their lived experience? What might it look like if students had an opportunity to question why a Canadian social studies textbook glosses over, in a timeline, the racist and brutal treatment of Japanese in 1942? What would learning look like if students were able to and were invited to ask, "Whose knowledge is this?" "What purpose does it serve?" "Who wants me to know?" "What social and political ends am I being invited into here?" What might classrooms be like with critical questions inspiring debate, controversy, and curiosity? It is to these questions that the anti-textbook textbook is directed. It is to disrupt the *everyday consciousness* that prevails as textbooks occupy the authoritative power of knowledge producer and arbiter. I'm convinced that a more critical approach would inspire engaged learning and active sociopolitical participation in our young. Or is that what we're trying to avoid?

To my mind, the standard textbook stands as an example of how *hegemonic truths* are perpetuated in classrooms as *official knowledge,* often without the slightest interruption or contention. As an apparatus of the institution designed to make its readers into *good citizens* and as the product of a constellation of industries invested in similar ends, the appearances and perceived political neutrality of textbooks perpetuate myths that prevent us from more critical (read informed, broadened, and aware) ways of understanding and acting in the world. The authoritative voice of the textbook does not seem to invite us to question the status quo, never mind contest it. I offer the anti-textbook textbook as a way to challenge the hegemonic technology of the official textbook and as an antidote to the fixed, neutral, and politically covert knowledges that are delivered in textbooks. Similarly, I offer the anti-textbook textbook as a pedagogic invitation to take up more critical questions about the ways, purposes, and instruments of our teaching and learning, and as a way to begin to see the political, social, and economic values that undergird our educational practices.

To that end, the following questions are offered for your consideration and as a practical way to begin to engage in a critical dialogue about what and whose knowledge counts in classrooms:

1. How many of us have thought about the textbook as a technology of truth delivery, oppression, and/or politics?

2. How many teachers and students are inclined to disbelieve or challenge information gleaned from textbooks? How do we encourage our students to do just that?

3. Whose position and/or politics does this middle-of-the-road approach, non-controversial read of the world serve? Whose knowledge? For whom? For what purpose?

4. What kinds of critical practices are in place regarding the politically charged spaces of the classroom and the textbooks used therein?

5. What opportunities are there to challenge the given knowledge that is presented in the officially sanctioned texts of the school?

Notes

1. Used in an article by Marjorie Devault (1990) to bring attention to the sociocultural significance of language and talk.

2. Apple (1990) suggests that hegemony "refers to an organized assemblage of meanings and practices, the central effective dominant system of meanings, values, and actions which are lived" (p. 5) Hegemony or hegemonic practices "act to saturate our very consciousness, so that the educational, economic, and social world we see and interact with, and the commonsense interpretations we put on it, becomes the only world" (p. 5) we can see or know or deal with. In other words, hegemony signifies the predominant, given, and taken-for-granted assumptions of the dominant culture. And more, hegemony also pertains to the pervasiveness and absolute acceptance of these assumptions, givens, and taken-for-grantednesses as normal or, put another way "as the *way things are.*"

3. This belief may overstate the political naiveté that I am attributing to teachers and other people connected to schools and be-

yond. It is indeed possible that teachers, administrators, and citizens in general are more savvy about the politicized nature of schools, schooling, and the artifacts of teaching. The point I am trying to raise here, however, is that in our pedagogic aim for inclusivity and diversity, which manifests in our wholesale adoption of textbooks, we simultaneously perpetuate the illusion of political fairness, neutrality, and balance. I submit that even this well-intentioned, middle-of-the-road pedagogic space is itself political, serving some and excluding others.

4. A note of thanks to this student for allowing me to share the anti-textbook textbook idea and for providing me with a copy of his response to reconnect me with the inspiration for the idea.

References

Apple, M. (1990). *Ideology and curriculum.* New York: Routledge.

Devault, M. (1990). Talking and listening from women's standpoint: Feminist strategies for interviewing and analysis. *Social Problems, 37*(1), 96–116.

Perlmutter, D. (1997). Manufacturing visions of society and history in textbooks. *Journal of Communication, 47*(3), 68–81.

Further Reading

Apple, M. (2001). *Educating the 'right way': Markets, standards, god, and inequality.* New York: Routledge Falmer.

Freire, P. (1998). *Pedagogy of freedom: Ethics, democracy, and civic courage.* Lanham, MD: Rowman & Littlefield.

Theory

Critical Theory

David W. Hursh

As educators, our conception of how the society works guides our thinking and actions. We are all, as sociologist Charles Lemert suggests, social theorists. Furthermore, as our social theories inform our actions and the results of our actions lead us to revise our theories, we are engaged, says Lemert, in "practical sociology." It is especially useful, writes C. Wright Mills, to investigate the relationship between the practical questions we face in our daily lives as educators with such larger questions as who holds power and for what purpose, the relationship between school and society, and the causes and consequences of inequality. By connecting our personal troubles to public issues we learn that it is not enough to change ourselves but that we must work to understand and reform educational and social structures.

Our social theories evolve as we interact with others. For example, in asking colleagues why they incorporate their students' experiences into their classroom, they may respond that their social theory suggests that including students' experiences assists those students whose culture is not reflected in the curriculum. Or, we may explicitly refine our social theories as

we engage in formal analysis of social and educational issues either through group discussions or individual readings. We might reflect on the social theories implied in literature, such as George Bernard Shaw's critique of capitalist oppression in *Major Barbara* or Pablo Neruda's critique of colonialism in his poem *The United Fruit Company*. Or our social theories may be challenged by the explicit political and social analysis provided in Karl Marx's *The Communist Manifesto* or Michael Apple's *Official Knowledge: Democratic Education in a Conservative Age*. Because our social theories guide our everyday actions, reflecting on and refining our theories is crucial to becoming an ethical and informed educator.

In education, a particular form of social theory—critical theory—has been useful in analyzing a range of educational questions, such as the purpose and organization of schools, the nature of curriculum, and the relationship between schools and society. Critical theory is characterized by an emphasis on how social groups attain and retain power and other groups resist. Critical theory has evolved, as I will describe, over the last 150 years along three central characteristics. First, how inequality is conceptualized has progressed from a focus on economic inequalities, as represented by economic classes, to include disparities by race, gender, sexual orientation, and culture. Second, as critical theorists have progressed beyond analyzing economic inequality, they have examined not only how economic inequality creates disparities in power but also how cultural and linguistic processes create inequality as well. The third and last characteristic builds on the first two. Critical theorists have reconceptualized how we have come to understand the world from one where knowledge is objective to one that combines the subjective and objective. As I describe the evolving characteristics of critical theory, I will also suggest some of the ways in which critical theory has led us to rethink educational issues.

In this essay I have adopted a broad definition of critical theory that includes a range of social theorists and educators. The distinction I make between critical theory and social theory is that critical theory assumes that different social groups—whether they are distinguished by class, race, gender, culture, or other feature—have competing interests and that particular groups are able to obtain power that places their interests above others. Critical theory focuses on ways in which individuals and groups obtain and retain power and how other groups resist power. Additionally, critical theory examines the implications that this power struggle has for social structures, organizations, and individuals. However, I should note that critical theory is often more narrowly defined to focus on the theorists who were associated with the Institute for Social Research or "Frankfurt School," a Marxist-oriented research institute that existed in Germany between the World Wars. These theorists included T. S. Adorno, Max Horkheimer, and Herbert Marcuse. While the theorists associated with the Institute rarely shared identifiable positions and did much of their work in exile in the United States, they did share the goal of developing a critical theory of society, critiquing domination and developing a theory of liberation. While I will not explicitly refer to the Frankfurt School theorists, their ideas influenced many of others who followed. My overview of critical theory will span the range of work from Karl Marx in the mid-1800s to contemporary theorists.

CHANGING CONCEPTIONS OF INEQUALITY: FROM CLASS TO GENDER, RACE, AND CULTURE

As stated above, critical theory grew out of Marx's and Marxist descriptions of the conflicting interests of the social classes, in particular, the conflict between the ruling class—or capitalists who owned the factories and businesses—and workers who produced goods and services. For Marx and critical theorists, a class analysis required examining the *conflicting* interests between the classes; capitalists desire to increase profits while workers desire to increase their pay. The two classes have conflicting, incompatible goals. This kind of analysis differs from that of mainstream social theorists who describe people as belonging to differing socioeconomic statuses, where it is assumed that people differ by income and educational level but that they have the same interests. That the opposing interests of capitalists and workers are obscured by mainstream socioeconomic status descriptions is, for critical theorists, a good example of the way in which ideology works. Ideology, or the masking of the interests of the ruling class, results from the ability of the ruling class to use the media, government, and education to portray their interests as the interests of all. In the following quote from the conservative Heritage Foundation, women and people of color are identified as special interest groups, while it is implied that the corporate and political elite act in the best interests of all. "By catering to the demands of special interest groups—racial minorities, the handicapped, women, and non-English speaking students—America's public schools have successfully competed for government funds, but have done so at the expense of education as a whole." Furthermore, current neoliberal economic policies that promote privatizing or reducing spending on education, health, and other social services and facilitating investment across national borders are presented as being in the interests of all, even as economic disparity increases. Such policies, it can be argued, benefit the wealthy more than the poor. The ability to mask the interests of the ruling-class by presenting their interests as the interests of all is one of the meanings that Marx gave to ideology. Ideology prevents those outside the ruling classes from seeing clearly which societal decisions promote *their* interests.

Those adopting a Marxist analysis of education looked to see how education, while seeming to promote everyone's welfare, might primarily benefit those already in power. While not a Marxist but someone who understood Marxist ideas, John Dewey understood how schools undermined democracy and perpetuated inequality. In 1915, for example, Dewey and David Snedden debated the merits of developing vocational tracks in schools and preparing students for either college or work. Snedden's view was that schools needed to develop a few people to lead and many who would know their place and be willing to follow. Snedden was confident that testing students in the early grades would reveal who was capable of becoming society's leaders and that they would primarily be white, upper-class males. Dewey was appalled by such elitist views. He argued that tracking preserved the status quo by placing those already advantaged in the upper track and by undermining the possibility for everyone to participate in democratic decision making. In the 1930s, Dewey joined with other critics of the educational status quo to write for the journal *The Social Frontier*. There John Dewey, George Counts, and others explicitly criticized schools for perpetuating the myth that everyone had an equal chance to succeed in schools and that the subsequent social inequality was the result of a fair meritocratic system. They argued against the individualistic and competitive ethos of capitalism and urged that schools be used to develop a more compassionate, egalitarian system.

In the 1970s, Herb Gintis and Sam Bowles, in *Schooling in Capitalist America: Educational Reform and the Contradictions of Economic Life,* undertook an explicitly Marxist class analysis of the educational system to argue that schools maintain inequality by preparing students for the same occupational and class positions as their families. Historically, they argued, the goal of education has been to preserve and extend the capitalist order by preparing workers for the expanding capitalist economy. Further, they cited empirical evidence that the school system (as, indeed, Snedden pressed for) prepared students, who it is assumed varied by class or race, to occupy the varied economic levels of the class structure. Students from wealthier homes were prepared for leadership positions while students from middle and working-class homes were prepared to be compliant, dependable, and punctual rather than creative and independent. However, because Bowles and Gintis' conclusions were based on statistical correlations, it was not clear how the process actually occurred in schools. Consequently, other researchers undertook ethnographic investigations into the students' school experiences. In England, Paul Willis explicitly asked how it is that working-class males resign themselves to working-class futures. By following a group of working-class "lads," Willis learned how they came to reject the school's middle-class culture, thereby failing school and facing a lifetime of bleak economic prospects.

These initial studies were criticized by some for comparing only the educational and career trajectories of sons and their fathers and ignoring issues of gender and class. Subsequent critical theorists and educational researchers argued that inequality was not only a result of economic processes but social structures and experiences that promoted gender and race inequalities. In the 1970s, Dorothy Smith, building on the critique of patriarchy by feminists such as Simone de Beauvoir in *The Second Sex,* argued that as social theorists (and as educators) we cannot claim to have an objective view of society as if we are standing outside of society looking in. Instead, Smith argued, our viewpoint arises from our experiences as (in her case) a woman. Smith's argument can be broadened to make the case that, for each of us, our viewpoint arises from our experiences in society as males or females, or as white Europeans, African Americans, Latinos/as, Asians, or other groups.

Researching education from, as Smith described, a woman's standpoint, led to research on the educational experiences of females. Educational researchers began an-

alyzing how girls made sense of age, class, and gender in the context of their own experience inside and outside of schools. For example, Angela McRobbie, in *Feminism and Youth Culture,* began researching working-class girls' experiences of gender inequality in their everyday lives, including the pressure to achieve idealized forms of femininity and the minimal economic support for teenage mothers.

In the same way that those examining gender inequality situated gender within the context of class and age, those examining issues of racial inequality and identity broadened their analysis. Educational researchers soon found themselves studying race within the variables of class, gender, sexuality, nation, and culture. Furthermore, the study of race also began to include "whiteness" as a constructed identity.

CHANGING CONCEPTIONS OF THE FOCUS OF ANALYSIS: FROM THE ECONOMIC TO THE CULTURAL AND DISCURSIVE

The examples above in which researchers began to analyze the gendered and racial dimensions of schools, including school and student culture, are central to the second evolving characteristic of critical theory: the evolving analysis beyond economics to the cultural and discursive. No longer were researchers satisfied in examining the relationship between the student and economic structures and whether schools reduced or reproduced economic inequality. Instead researchers began to investigate how students experienced culture—whether that be the school curriculum or teenage magazines or films—and how they transformed it. Furthermore, critical theorists were investigating the way in which capitalism promoted a discourse of rationality and, as reflected in the recent movement to hold teachers and schools accountable through high-stakes standardized exams, a discourse in which everything is calculable.

By adopting a cultural perspective, theorists and educators have developed a less deterministic understanding of the relationship between individuals and society in which individuals do not simply reproduce society but reshape it. Individuals are both constrained by the culture and actively modify it. However, critical theorists, such as Pierre Bourdieu, point out that it is by adopting the dominant class's culture that one gains power. In examining the relationship between the student's culture and school's culture, Bourdieu developed the notions of cultural and social capital. Bourdieu explained that, because schools embody the culture of the upper classes, students who grew up in families in which that culture could be passed on through conversation and cultural pursuits, such as concerts, museums, and bookstores, were the students most likely to succeed. Those working-class students who entered school without the necessary cultural capital were at a disadvantage. Consequently, while academic success appears to be a result of students' effort and intelligence—their merit—academic success is partly a result of which students arrive at school with the necessary cultural capital. Furthermore, Bourdieu showed how educational success is also a consequence of students' social capital, or the knowledge they gain from peers and adults who know how to negotiate the educational and vocational systems and facilitate achieving educational and vocational success. In sum, Bourdieu argues that the educational system, while appearing to be fair, favors those whose home culture most closely matches the school culture and who know successful people. School success is, to a large degree, a result of what you learned and whom you know outside of school.

Critical theorists have increasingly sounded an alarm over the increasing emphasis in capitalism on rationality. Max Weber warned in 1920 that modern Western capitalism, or what he described as "sober bourgeois capitalism," represented the rationalization of all aspects of society, including ethics, politics, art, and religion. In the current movement toward standards, standardized testing and accountability, we see an outcome of this movement to make everything calculable, predictable, and, therefore, controllable. Critical theorists have pointed out how the discourses of rationality, calculability, and accountability are being used to develop standardized curriculum in which curriculum development and pedagogical practices are being removed from teachers' control.

CHANGING CONCEPTIONS OF KNOWLEDGE: FROM OBJECTIVITY TO SUBJECTIVITY AND BEYOND

From its beginnings in the 1800s, social theorists emulated scientific research, particularly physics, with its aim of developing objective knowledge about the world. The aim was to understand the world without distortion by human preconceptions. But the goal of objectivity has slowly unraveled as unattainable as social theorists have acknowledged and welcomed the idea that our experiences shape the questions we ask and the interpretations we make.

Marx began with the goal of developing an objective critique of economics and history. He proposed that it was the working class, the proletariat, who, in their position as the oppressed, would have the incentive and ability to counter the false ideologies promulgated by the capitalist class and develop an objective social analysis. However, as described above, our understanding of the world is shaped by our experiences based on our class, gender, race, culture, ability/disability, and sexual orientation/identity. Furthermore, our interpretation of society is influenced by normative, and therefore subjective, descriptions of what is desirable. We cannot, therefore, hope for an objective description of society. Our understanding is necessarily subjective.

However, incorporating our own subjective experience into our analysis does not require adopting a relativistic view of the world. Bourdieu reminds us that much of what we know about the world is a consequence of the kinds of questions we ask and the way in which we interpret those questions. While there is no one right answer or explanation in attempting to develop an understanding of the world we live in, there are criteria regarding what kinds of explanations make sense. We, therefore, continually combine objective and subjective criteria to much that we say and do.

Acknowledgment that the goal of developing an objective description of the world must be abandoned has implications for how we think about teaching in curriculum. For example, we can no longer think of historical research as the process of carefully deepening and refining history until we develop the one unbiased narrative of events. Rather, what events we choose to recount and what meaning we give to them depends on which subjective viewpoint we choose for our analysis. For instance, European exploration of the Western Hemisphere, as typically presented in schools, has been criticized by critical theorists. Most textbooks portray Columbus as a brave explorer who opened up the Western Hemisphere to Europe. Historians and educators, however, desiring to include the viewpoint of the indigenous people, have included Columbus' genocidal treatment of the Caribbean people when they could not meet his demand for gold. Furthermore, the treatment of Native Americans by European explorers can be cast in new light given recent research by anthropologists and historians. Rather than describing the European explorers as bringing civilization to the West, many anthropologists and historians now describe pre-Columbian Native American culture as rivaling that of Europe.

While it might be evident that subjectivity enters into all historical and political analyses, it may be less evident that supposedly objective subjects, such as science, are also subjective. Whereas textbooks often portray science as an ongoing accumulation of facts to which students rarely can add, scientific research and its interpretation is often subjective and political. For example, analyses of the relationship between our health and pollutants or toxins in our environment, such as lead or polychlorinated byphenyls (PCBs), reveals the constructed and problematic nature of scientific research and the difficulty of determining risk levels and environmental solutions.

The purposes of schooling and what and how we teach are not questions to which objective answers can be provided. Critical theory provides us with ways to analyze educational institutions and practices. Critical theorists remind us that there are conflicting interests regarding education. Corporate and governmental representatives, under our current neoliberal policies, propose that schools should meet the needs of a globalized, capitalist economy. Many educators counter that schools should develop critical thinkers who uncover ways in which interests are masked; acknowledge that our gendered, raced, and classed experiences influence our understanding; and critique assertions that claim a false rationality and objectivity.

References

Kellner, D. (1989). *Critical theory, Marxism and modernity,* Baltimore, MD: Johns Hopkins University Press.

Lemert, C. (1997). *Social things: An introduction to the sociological life.* Lanham, MD: Rowman and Littlefield.

Webb, J., Schirato, T., & Danaher, G. (2002). *Understanding Bourdieu.* Thousand Oaks, CA: Sage.

Thinking Skills

Dialectical Thinking

Dialectics is a philosophical theory and tool of critical inquiry and examination used to understand the way things are and the way personal life, social phenomenon, human history and culture, and, in fact, everything in general changes. It is a form of critical thinking that is based on the understanding of three fundamental principles explicated by the philosopher Frederick Engels, a revolutionary thinker and partner of Karl Marx, who elaborated on these principles in the 1870s in his book *Dialectics of Nature*. Engels (1968) believed that dialectics was "A very simple process which is taking place everywhere and every day, which any child can understand" (p. 211). The three principles which Engels elaborated are as follows:

1. Everything is composed of opposites.
2. Gradual changes lead to qualitative transformations.
3. Change moves in spirals, not circles.

The first principle of dialectical awareness recognizes that every thing (every object and every subjective process) is made of opposing forces or opposing sides. As an illustration of this, for example, no object could hold itself together without an opposing force to keep it from flying apart. We see planets try to fly away from the sun, but gravity holds them in orbit. Scientists see electrons try to disperse from the nucleus of an atom, but electromagnetism holds the atom together; and physiologists are aware that ligaments provide the tie that holds muscles to bones (*Dialectics for Kids*, 2002).

Much like material objects, the process of social and personal change needs a driving force to push it forward, otherwise everything would remain static and inert. So, for example, a billiard ball only moves when hit with a pool cue or another ball; we eat when our hunger tells us to; a car won't move if its engine won't start; and to be victorious in fair elections, candidates need more votes than their opponents. These are just some simple examples for viewing the embodiment of the dialectical principle developed by Engels. Working from the theoretical positions of the philosopher G. W. F. Hegel, Engels referred to this law as the "interpenetration of opposites." The philosopher Hegel often referred to what he called the "unity of opposites" to explain this phenomenon (Hegel, 1830/1975, p. 117).

The notion of the inpenetration of opposites may appear contradictory, but it is fairly simple to understand. There is no baseball game if one side quits; there is no atom if the electrons fly away. Dialectical awareness and thinking demand we understand that the whole needs all of its parts to be a whole and vice versa. Thus, we can understand no particular without reference to the logic of the system within which it operates.

With this in mind, it becomes easy to see how we might encourage this understanding in young children through education. For example, in attempting to understand the development of unions within the United States, history students would need to study the historical development of unions within an interdisciplinary context. They would need to understand the development of unions within specific historical circumstances and examine the changing development of these institutions over time, especially in relationship to historical forces such as economics, politics, sociology, and culture that affect unions' characteristics and development.

In working with students to develop critical dialectical awareness, teachers might set up activities that encourage students to see the dialectics of opposing sides in their everyday lives. They could be asked to generate analogies, examples, or metaphors that would illustrate the dialectical principle and then go on to explain their reasoning in either groups or individually in speech or writing.

The second principle of dialectics asserts that gradual quantitative changes lead to eventual qualitative transformations. The principle is based on the theory that qualitative changes result because of a gradual buildup of one opposing force, or forces, that becomes dominant over time. According to dialectics, this principle is powerful in describing the historical stages of development of virtually anything and enhances critical methodological analysis of phenomenon. For example, boiling water transforms into steam when the heat gradually overcomes the water. And, according to dialectical theory, a person's life is said to follow these quantitative/qualitative changes as well and can only be understood using a method of dialectical analysis. One needs only to look at their own aging progression to see the dialectical process in motion. Likewise, human history, or the history of a particular geographical location, has also gone through many stages of quantitative development and qualitative transformation that can be studied using dialectical thinking.

Young children in elementary schools can, of course, use science as a vehicle to understand the dialectical principle by seeing the transformations inherent in the growth of tomato seeds on vines as the fruit goes through its dialectical development and transformatory journey.

Finally, the third principle of dialectics posits that change moves in spirals, not in circles. Many changes are cyclical, that is to say that, at first, one side dominates and, after time, the other side. Take for example the notion of day and night or breathing in and breathing out; these all reveal the existence of one opposite and then another. What dialectics argues is that these cycles do not return to exactly where they started; that is, they don't come to form a perfect circle. Instead, change is seen as constantly evolutionary and de-evolutionary, moving in and out as a spiral would. Perhaps the changes are tiny, so we think nothing has really changed—that nothing is really different. We often do not notice the incremental quantitative changes and leaps in our lives and social reality that occur over time. This might be called the phenomenon of "gradualism"—the notion that quantitative change is often so gradual, so incremental, that it cannot be seen until a qualitative transformation has taken place. Perhaps it might be best summed up by the dialectical phrase, "The straw that broke the camel's back."

One can imagine this principle when considering the development of a rural town in America into a suburb. As commercial and residential development grows within and around the once rural town, traffic increases; however, the increase in traffic is so gradual it is often undetectable at first. Yet slowly and slowly the development proceeds until one day residents notice crowded freeways, long commutes, and bumper-to-bumper traffic. A spiral, evolutionary transformation has occurred—a rural town is now transformed into a suburb. Yet the change did not happen overnight, as it might appear.

With dialectical awareness, one can see that many cycles do result in unique transformations. Take, for example, children. They are not the same as their parents, even if they are a lot alike; similarly, people go to school and learn and, when they return home, they are no longer the same; and, like it or not, you are a bit older with every breath.

Engels called this spiraling change the law of the "negation of negation." This sounds complicated but, as Engels noted, it is going on all the time and in all contexts. What happens is that first one side overcomes its opposite; this is the first negation. This marks a turning point. Next, the first side once again overcomes the new side. This is negation of negation, and what results, is qualitative transformation.

Consider for example a normal conversation regarding a matter that requires reasoned judgment or engagement with multiple points of view. The conversation requires the negation of negation to move ahead or the conversation would die. To start with, one person begins speaking and soon the other; the second is said to "negate" the first. As the conversation proceeds, however, the first person begins talking again. The conversation obviously would make no sense if the first person simply repeated what they said the first time. Instead, the first person now has listened to the second person talk, so the negation of negation returns to a different mental location as a result of listening to the opposing point of view.

Encouraging students to develop the ability to engage in learning conversations with others—whereby they exercise suspension of judgment in the interest of understanding multiple points of view—would be paramount to engage students in developing dialectical thinking. Dialogue is essential for dialectical awareness because it is through communication that we convey our point of view and engage in the negation of the negation for more understanding. Students can learn the power of dialectical and dialogical thinking by learning to engage in an argument or learning conversation and then, consequently, assessing whether and how they may have changed their thinking as a result of hearing another point of view.

THE HISTORY OF DIALECTICS

The ideas inherent in dialectics are historical and found in multiple cultures. In Asia, the idea that everything is made of opposites—yin and yang—dates back to the I Ching around 3,000 years ago and the Taoist master Lao Tzu around 2,500 years ago. Taoism holds that change is the only constant—that the only thing that does not change is change itself. Taoist philosophy also understood that "gradual change leads to a sudden change of form (hua)" (Karcher, 2000, p. 53). Also, around 2,500 years ago in ancient Greece, Heraclitus advanced the idea that all change comes through the struggle of opposites. Similarly, the Aztecs acknowledged the idea of nature being made of opposites, as did the Lakotas in North America. In their view of nature and human existence in Africa, the Dogon people of Mali hold the concept of "twin-ness"—such as the idea of perfection/imperfection and disorder/order as dialectical truths.

The idea of everything being made of opposites disappeared from Western thought some hundreds of years ago, perhaps as a result of the advent of scientific objectivism, reductionism, and determinism. Yet by failing to recognize that change comes through the conflict between opposing forces, Western philosophy has mystified, misunderstood, or even denied change.

The great European philosophers Immanuel Kant and Hegel reintroduced the idea of dialectics just as the first industrial revolution was beginning. Their starting point was ancient Greek philosophy, from which they took the word, dialectics. Hegel writes, "Dialectic . . . is no novelty in philosophy. Among the ancients Plato is termed the inventor of Dialectic; and his right to the name rests on the fact that the Platonic philosophy first gave the free scientific, and thus at the same time the objective form to Dialectic." Hegel also went on to describe Socrates' use of, "the dialectical element in a predominantly subjective shape, that of Irony" (Hegel, 1830/ 1975, p. 117).

Two young followers of Hegel, Marx and Engels, took Hegel's ideas in the 1800s and transformed them into a philo-sophical tool for analyzing history and nature and for creating social change. They kept the idea of dialectics, motion and change coming about through opposing forces, but turned Hegel "upside down." They argued that thought is a manifestation of the natural world. The world is not a manifestation of our thoughts, as Hegel believed, and they argued that our thoughts flow from our experiences and from the specific historical and material conditions of the world within which we live. This is the theory of "dialectical materialism" and most of the credit for popularizing the idea that this dialectical material process is based in nature and human affairs goes to Marx's colleague, Engels. He took the voluminous and obscure writings of Hegel and divided them into the three "laws" we have been discussing.

THE PRINCIPAL CONTRADICTION

Dialectics utilizes a concept called the "principal contradiction," a phrase coined by Mao Zedong, in its theory. This concept is used to distinguish nonpressing issues from the not-so-pressing ones that need to be addressed within any given problem-solving situation. One way of expressing this is the phrase, "first things first." Identifying the key task—the goal we are pursuing—helps us focus on and set our top priority; this, in turn, allows us to focus on the most essential element of the process we are employing, rather than trying to accomplish too many things at once or getting distracted by unimportant and irrelevant matters. We isolate the principle contradiction so that we might organize our reality for purposes of study and examination.

The idea of a principal contradiction is primarily a human concept because it is based on a teleological understanding. Most of nature—for example, the sun, an ocean, or a leaf—does not appear to have any goal; it just exists. Life, of course, has the conscious goal of survival, or more importantly, the continued survival of future generations.

It is true that cats can figure out very clever ways to get into a garbage can, and dogs and cats do learn how to get what they want from their owners. However, it is only we as humans who must constantly make complex choices through reason and, thus, we employ processes of reasoning. While genetics is undoubtedly important in human behavior and reasoning, humans must make critical decisions that require judgment and planning. Such questions as "Should we build a highway or invest in public transportation like light rail?" "Should we develop our cities based on the automobile or based on other modes of transportation?" "Should our city develop housing and educational centers or should it concentrate on encouraging business and commercial development?" "Should we buy organic food or nonorganic food?" "Should we pass this law or another law?" require judgment and are often complex and necessitate an exchange of points of view in an atmosphere of civility and inquiry. There is no evidence that our primate DNA and our instincts are any help in making such decisions—decisions that involve many contradictions and involve the analysis of complex situations. Critically recognizing and trying to precisely be aware of and identify contradictions, and then deciding which is the principal contradiction, is essential for humans to make sense of their reality and the rapidity of change.

IDENTIFYING THE PRINCIPAL CONTRADICTION

The principal contradiction depends on what the goal or objective of an overall process is. When one identifies an explicit objective or purpose, one can then begin to identify the steps needed to achieve it and the mind can begin to prioritize what is essential for the task based on what is perceived as the principal contradiction.

For example, if your goal is to live a physically active life, you will need to eat properly, exercise, and get enough sleep. On the other hand, if your goal is to relax and you really don't care, then these healthy habits would not be as important to you—they would not be the principle contradictions. If you want good grades as a student, you would need to do your homework, study, and prepare for examinations. On the other hand, if your goal is to simply pass the course or get by you may do the minimum amount of work, do term papers at the last minute, and put off studying until the night before exams. If you are on a sports team, and you want to win, you have to practice, learn teamwork, study your opponent, and work out. On the other hand, if you would like to win, but don't care too much, you can go through the motions of practice and hope everything works out.

Sometimes we can't decide what to do next in a particular circumstance or context, that is, we can't decide what is the principal contradiction and how to resolve it. Often times this is because we may have conflicting goals. For example, we may want to write a letter, but we may also want to relax and watch a ball game. What we do depends on what we think our main goal and objective is within a certain context. Examining and listening to what people do and say provides the mind with the ability to infer what these people might see as the principal contradiction within any context in which they may be operating. This is true even if the goal is subconscious, as advertisers and marketers are keenly aware of.

Sometimes we might misjudge what the principal contradiction is, even if we know what we want. For example, if a car has a problem with its brake pads, it will not do any good to fix the ignition system. In such a case we may replace one part, then another, and still not get the car to run. Fixing a car requires diagnosing and clearly identifying the real problem or the principal contradiction preventing the car from running. Finding the real problem with the car may require a process called troubleshooting, whereby we deductively eliminate the irrelevant. Without a process for determining the principle contradiction affecting the car's performance, we would be engaging in simple guesswork as opposed to troubleshooting to solve the problem and we are not likely to be very successful in repairing the vehicle.

THE CONSEQUENCES OF NOT ADDRESSING THE PRINCIPAL CONTRADICTION

The principal contradiction in a process must be resolved or the process will not move forward. There may be several problems blocking the process, but resolving the principal contradiction allows other ancillary problems to be illuminated, expressed, and then addressed. Of course, there's nothing that says you have to move a process along at all. Maybe you never will get around to reading that book on your coffee table, seeing that movie, going on that trip, or inviting your friends over for dinner. If this is a *conscious* decision,

it may be fine. However, some times, people maintain a state of denial about a problem because they really don't want to acknowledge it. In these cases, a serious contradiction can be allowed to fester—like not seeking therapy for a problem or chemical dependency—and consequently the problem only gets worse.

One of the strengths of dialectical thinking, in terms of social reality, is that it is a critical analytical tool that helps clarify and identify political forces and the need for alliances and broad strategies to achieve more freedom and better survival for human beings. If our goal is to improve the human condition, we should use every methodological tool available. So let's see where a dialectical analysis of the contradictions facing humanity might lead us.

CRITICAL THINKING AND THE PRINCIPAL CONTRADICTION

Trying to identify a principal contradiction within any context requires that we specifically define a goal or an objective. When working with students, for example in a sociology or social studies class, we might ask them, "What should our goals as a society be? Should we first address basic human needs such as health needs, jobs, housing, and social services like educational, transportation, water, and sanitation needs or should we concern ourselves with prioritizing the creation of other goods and services? Why? Is that going on now? Why or why not?" Students can then work in groups to prioritize goals and objectives for what they feel should be a society's priorities—that is, the principle contradiction. Students can become enamored to see that meeting these human needs takes a lot of hard work, human ingenuity, and the organization of people and tasks. For example, providing clean water is a huge issue all around the world that involves scientists, engineers, technicians, construction and maintenance workers, politicians, and the cooperation of all the citizenry of a region. Students could be asked to work together to come up with plans that would help them carry out the purposes and goals they identified as important for the sustenance and growth of a society and then to formulate the questions at issue—the principle contradictions—that they feel would be necessary to answer to meet the goals and objectives they thought were a priority. Because there are difficult issues of overpopulation, racism, sexism, classism, homophobia, urbanization, inadequate education, and poor public health and disease control, which have to be figured into the solutions, students would need to study how the goal of meeting basic human needs has often been outweighed by powerful competing goals, such as accumulating wealth and power by elite individuals and the historical use of racism and sexism to divide people. Through research, they could examine historically how countries have gone about defining goals and then look at some of the principle contradictions, such as imperialism, through institutions such as the World Bank, that these countries confront and continue to face in attempting to meet their basic needs.

Critical dialectical awareness reorganizes our thinking about reality by replacing the commonsense notion of a something in isolation as not something separate, in and of itself, but on the contrary, something that has a history and external connections with other things (Ollman, 1993). As a form of thinking, it emphasizes the notion of process and the idea of relations that can be understood by the human mind.

Perhaps this notion can best be explained by the Roman Myth of Cacus, which was retold by Marx in his book *Capital* (Ollman, 1993). Cacus lived in a cave but came out during the night to steal oxen. In an attempt to fool those who pursued him for his crime, Cacus forced the oxen to walk backwards into the den of his cave so that their footprints might appear to have led from the cave to the outside. When the next morning arrived and people came looking for their stolen oxen, they found only footprints. Based on their interpretation of the evidence of these prints, the concluded that the oxen had left the cave and wandered out into the field and disappeared.

What this story tells us is that by focusing on appearances the evidence that immediately pronounces itself on us may be misleading. According to dialectics, if the people in Cacus's story really wanted to find out what happened to their oxen, they would not have been fooled by mere appearances but would have had to critically investigate what had transpired the night before the oxen were stolen, what was going on in the cave before they came and after.

For dialectical thinkers, critical awareness of the dialectical process is necessary to make intelligible any aspect of our experiences our human endeavors—from our personal lives to our social lives. Yet, unfortunately, for many, life is a often a mere accident and many people base their understanding of the world on what appears to them without dialectically analyzing the reality behind it. Dialectics argues that understanding anything requires that we know about its history, how it arose and developed, and how it fits into a larger context of contradictions. Equipped with dialectical thinking, all of us can make better sense of ourselves and the world within which we live.

References

Dialectics for Kids. (2002). Retrieved November 2002 from http://home.igc.org/~venceremos/whatheck.htm

Engels, F. (1968). *Dialectics of nature.* New York: International Publishers.

Hegel, G.F.W. (1830/1975). *Hegel's logic, part one of the Encyclopedia of the Philosophical Sciences* (J. N. Findlay, Trans.). Oxford: Clarendon Press.

Karcher, S. (2000). *Ta Chuan, The great treatise.* New York: St. Martins Press.

Ollman, B. (1993). *Dialectical investigations.* New York: Routledge Publishers.

Emancipatory Critical Thinking

Juan-Miguel Fernández-Balboa

INTRODUCTION

Critical thinking is now part of the official discourse in education. Nonetheless, the phrase critical thinking (CT) is not understood in the same way by all those who use it. Here, I will argue that the mainstream interpretations of this term represent very particular positions and forms of knowledge that, in turn, help legitimize certain sociopolitical interests while excluding others. In its present condition, CT is intimately tied to a capitalistic political economy. Moreover, the prevailing interpretation of CT determines the path and value of one's inquiry and pedagogy in ways that reinforce and justify neoliberalism (i.e., the ideology of the free market). That is why in those educational contexts where it is taught (not all educational contexts teach critical thinking) CT is framed in technical, not in political, terms. By not questioning its purposes, these terms are taken for granted and become part of the agenda of the privileged groups of society. In this regard, the assumed purpose of CT is to maximize efficiency in business, factories, and offices, thus multiplying profits for the powerful, while increasing accountability for—and disem-

powering—the working class (namely, most human beings). My argument is that such an approximation to CT is not only limited and limiting but also often detrimental and dehumanizing for the vast majority of the people.

To make my point, I must first start with the premise that the educational reality of CT is socially constructed, that is, legitimized and perpetuated in many different ways through institutions and organizations such as schools and universities, research bodies, think tanks, policy agencies, scholarly journals, and the like. Given that educators are embedded in, and affected by, these institutions and organizations, their perception of CT is reduced to a repertoire of skills on how to think that, oddly enough, is accepted uncritically. Under such circumstances, it is little wonder that CT is perceived to be the sole prerogative of so-called experts rather than an ability that everyone can possess. What is more, understood in this vein, CT becomes merely a technical skill, not a political one, and, therefore, is seldom seen in the context of promoting social justice.

Hence, to make critical thinking *really* critical (i.e., critical of the reality in which we live and the system that constrains and conditions our lives as educators and citizens) we must problematize this concept, transgress its technical approach, and realize its political nature. Put another way, CT can be a very viable means to foster people's politics so as to struggle for personal dignity and social justice.

CRITICAL THINKING AS A PROBLEM: WHAT HUMAN INTERESTS DOES IT SERVE?

To problematize critical thinking is to make it a topic for inquiry; to investigate it; and to dialogue about its principles, processes, and purposes in relation to human interests. For example, Kurfiss (1988) defined critical thinking as "an investigation whose purpose is to explore a situation, phenomenon, question, or problem to arrive at a hypothesis or conclusion about it that integrates all available information and that can therefore be convincingly justified" (p. 2). This definition can be either accepted at face value or made suspect. By accepting it at face value, this definition would seem neutral and apolitical, leading one to operate within its technical parameters which, in turn, would be presumed to be good for everyone. On the other hand, if one sees it as suspect, then one would begin to ask poignant questions about it. For instance, what types of phenomena, problems, and questions are we talking about here? Who determines these phenomena, problems, and questions? What other phenomena, problems, and questions are there? Who would benefit from examining one set of phenomena *versus* another? Who would suffer as a result of such examinations? Whose information is one referring to? When one says, "convincingly justified," whose criteria are we applying? Who are those who are supposed to be convinced by the justification?

Where does their power to pass judgment over these justifications come from? All these questions would unpack this seemingly simple definition of CT and take it out of its supposed neutrality. In fact, this type of unrelenting examination would help one realize that the term critical thinking is loaded with ethical and political implications intimately related to the nature of both knowledge and human interests.

According to Habermas (1972), knowledge is organized by virtue of three types of human interests: (1) technical, (2) practical, and (3) emancipatory. The first type refers to certain interests that prompt humans to gather or create instrumental knowledge so as to, in turn, enable them to gain control over natural and artificial objects. The second type of human interest (i.e., the practical) is served by knowledge that enables humans to interpret their environment for them to adjust or modify it according to the needs of the moment. Yet, given that most interpretations of the world are limited by one's cultural and contextual circumstances, and given that those interpretations are usually approached in uncritical ways, people's ability to modify their environment is very restricted. Therefore, in many cases, all people can do is to adjust. The third type of human interest is concerned with the actual transformation of one's environment and circumstances because emancipatory interests are closely related to the struggle for freedom and justice in the world. In turn, emancipatory interests aim at, and depend on, the establishment of a system of human and civil rights and responsibilities that will enhance people's living and working conditions as well as their personal and political power.

As a norm, the vast majority of definitions of CT revolve around the first two sets of human interests and are designed to improve current practices. In this regard, CT is applied under the assumption that these practices are legitimate and beneficial for all. In other words, conventional CT is mostly framed in terms "how" (i.e., how to solve a particular problem) and seldom in terms of "why" (i.e., for what reasons should one solve a particular problem or why is it considered a problem to begin with). The "why" and the "what for" are taken for granted and seldom questioned. In the same vein, and for the most part, the prevailing pedagogical interpretations of CT not only fall under these first two categories but also are viewed as value-free and objective, thus contributing to the universalization of the dominant norms, relationships of power, values, and practices. Thus, the technical and practical forms of CT tend to perpetuate the status quo, while showing little concern with people's emancipatory interests and social justice.

Given that most teachers have been trained to think within the frame of the first two sets of human interests, they themselves are bound by the dominant conceptualizations of CT and, hence, act as mere transmitters and perpetuators of the status quo instead of acting as transformative intellectuals. Under these circumstances, no one ought to be surprised that students do not learn the emancipatory meanings of CT. It is little wonder, then, that—when it comes to political decision making and action—apathy and ignorance are the norm. To reverse this trend, it is crucial to foster an emancipatory form of CT.

TOWARD EMANCIPATORY CRITICAL THINKING

The type of critical thinking I am advocating here serves the emancipatory interests of human beings, both in essence and intent.

The Purposes of Emancipatory Critical Thinking

The ultimate goal of emancipatory critical thinking (ECT) is to create a better (i.e., more dignified and just) society. To this end, ECT is rooted in community and is concerned with the analysis and reconstruction of particular ethical, educational, political, and sociocultural discourses, ideologies, and practices. In this regard, ECT is a means to learning how to denounce the inhuman conditions in which many human beings are forced to live. Moreover, ECT provides people with the necessary intellectual, ethical-moral, and political foundations and resources to be able to both identify and act on problems that negatively affect their lives. As such, ECT also focuses on developing alternative beliefs and dynamics that challenge the dominant ways of thinking and acting.

The Process of Emancipatory Critical Thinking

Emancipatory critical thinking is an ongoing process, not just a momentary happening. The way I see it, ECT can be presented in four stages that are not necessarily linear; each stage can inform the other three. The first state is to develop awareness about both people's circumstances and the causes of those circumstances. For instance, one of the first steps in the empowerment of people is to help them realize that their status is, to a great extent, due to systemic forces (e.g., institutional meritocracy) designed to keep them ignorant and resigned. The second stage of ECT consists of providing the oppressed with the necessary tools for their emancipation. Two of the most important tools in this regard are literacy (numerical, linguistic, political, etc.) and dialogical skills. Through these, people learn to regain their voice, pose and understand problems, and articulate possibilities. Another important tool is alliance formation—realizing that action will be easier and more successful if undertaken with the support of others. Alliance formation also counters the dominant ideology of individualism, which is so detrimental to both social activism and the politics of liberation. It is through literacy campaigns, democratic dialogue, and the development of groups and alliances that the peasants, miners, and social activists lead by Paulo Freire in Brazil, Orlando Fals Borda in Colombia, and Miles Horton in the United States (to name a few) have been able to claim their rights and struggle for dignifying working and living conditions. In short, these tools are essential for raising consciousness and starting transformative action. Engaging in transformative action is the third stage of ECT. The previous stages would be of little use without the actual implementation of what is learned. Action, in turn, necessitates careful planning, conviction, and courage. ECT can help develop these as well. The fourth stage is critical reflection. This is a crucial element of the whole process, for it enables one to regroup, analyze, and redirect one's efforts. Needless to say, this type of reflection must be done at all stages of the process, not only at the end.

The Content of Emancipatory Critical Thinking

As the reader can see, ECT is a process whereby people learn to become suspicious of what is thought of as important and to deconstruct reality as it is given to them. In addition, ECT helps them "sniff" the ideological and systemic tricks and traps (e.g., ulterior motives, hidden agendas, top-down policies, folly rhetoric,

sham rewards, unjust punishments) designed to keep people in their place and to take their power away. More concretely, through ECT, people can learn to question policy and practice based on, and geared to, capital accumulation and marketplace profits at the expense of the less powerful and disenfranchised groups of society.

ECT also serves as the basis for a *critical pedagogy* (see recommended readings) whose purposes are also to make learners (both the teacher and the student alike) more fully human and to create a better and more egalitarian society. Through ECT, within the framework of a politics of liberation, persons can learn to (1) assume the roles of creative, reflective, and transformative subjects; (2) discover new ways of looking at things; (3) defamiliarize common experience and link their life conditions, contradictions, and injustices with their own history(ies) and contexts; (4) begin to intentionally investigate the origins and implications of their thoughts and actions; (5) link their personhood to social, economic, cultural, and political conditions; (6) gain the courage to challenge rules that are irrelevant and dehumanizing; (7) regain their voice (especially those who have been traditionally and systematically silenced); (8) ask meaningful and empowering questions and challenge oppressive relations, ideologies, and practices; (9) establish conditions and relations that are dignified as well as dignifying for themselves and others; and (10) create alternative social and political possibilities and visions to transform the structures and dynamics (institutional and otherwise) that render them oppressed and powerless. A good example of the practice of ECT can be found in Bill Bigelow's entry in this encyclopedia.

CLOSING REMARKS

As one can see, ECT not only constitutes an act of thinking but also a means for cyclical, intentional, and purposeful action. With that in mind, it is important to point out that ECT does not automatically guarantee personal, social, political, or economic emancipation. Still, it provides an essential precondition for that to occur. This is why it is utterly important that those of us who teach ask ourselves two fundamental questions. First, what type of human interests am I serving through my pedagogical practices? Second, in what ways can I endeavor to serve the needs, and enhance the futures, of my students, especially those whose life is characterized by oppression and despair? In short, ECT is about justice and freedom, courage and struggle. It is also about hope, for it helps one realize that, even in the most dreaded of conditions, dignified and dignifying action is possible. After all, nothing is so hopeless for us not to combat it.

References

Habermas, J. (1972). *Knowledge and human interests.* Boston: Beacon.

Kurfiss, J. C. (1988). *Critical thinking: Theory, research, practice, and possibilities* (ASHE-ERIC Higher Education Report No. 2). Washington, DC: Association for the Study of Higher Education. (ERIC Document Reproduction Service No. ED 304 401).

Further Reading

Adorno. T. W. (1998). *Critical models: Interventions and catchwords.* New York: Columbia University Press.

Freire, P. (1970). *Pedagogy of the oppressed.* New York: Continuum.

Horton, M. (1997). *The long haul: An autobiography.* New York: Doubleday.

Kincheloe, J. L. (2001). *Getting beyond the facts: Teaching social studies/social sciences in the twenty-first century.* New York: Peter Lang.

Higher Order Thinking Skills

Tanya Brown

While Bloom's Taxonomy is an attempt to order and structure critical thinking, the higher order thinking skills are an attempt to make them even more accessible—critical thinking that is *ready for Monday.* Specifically, the higher order thinking skills are the skills, activities, and questions that evolve out of Bloom's Taxonomy. The terms higher order thinking skills and critical thinking skills are sometimes used interchangeably, and certainly, they are not exclusive of one another. The term critical thinking skills may refer to the levels included in Bloom's Taxonomy, but there also may be references to the ideas of *reasoning* and *logic.* These terms are not exclusive to Bloom, but they also are not direct references. The term higher order thinking skills generally refers to the skills that come directly from Bloom. There have been some adaptations to the structure of Bloom's Taxonomy. Another commonly used structure is the *Quellmalz Framework of Thinking Skills* (Ellmann &

O'Clair, 1989). This system, which was developed by Edys Quellmalz, has fewer levels so some teachers may find it easier than Bloom to manage in the classroom. This system folds the *knowledge* level and the *comprehension* levels into one level: *recall*. The *analysis* level of Bloom's is divided into two levels: *analysis* and *comparison*. The application level and the synthesis level of Bloom's are folded in to one level: *inference*. The last level of this framework is also called *evaluation,* but this level incorporates both the *synthesis* and *evaluation* levels of Bloom's Taxonomy.

Both of the systems attempt to fill out the principles of critical thinking. It may be difficult to imagine ways to promote critical thinking, especially in an environment where the teacher is accountable to a particular curriculum. The higher order thinking skills are not so much about content. They are not about what the students learn and think, but, rather, they are about how they learn and think. In some cases, there may be a question of *whether* our students learn and think. The higher order thinking skills can help to move us a little closer to that goal every day. The good news is that this system of question and activities can be applied to any content. The more difficult news is that really making them work requires shifting our views about what knowledge is and how it is created. It requires changing both our habits and the habits of our students, too. But, if we keep an open mind, these skills can be one tool in our collection that will help us override a curriculum that does more to shut down our students than it does to uncover their ability to question and examine. If our students learn to practice these thinking skills, they can become active, responsive, and critical thinkers, not just passive receptors of information. It can

also help us to nurture our students' innate ability to learn because they are aware of and care about the process itself. This awareness is what helps to establish critical thinking.

Remember, this is a tool to help construct learning, not evaluate it. The purpose is to provide the structure and organization necessary to making critical thinking possible in our classrooms. Every student thinks and evolves differently—keep this in mind as we investigate the higher order thinking skills as well.

Making a commitment to promoting critical thinking in our classrooms is hard work. It helps to have a variety of tools at our disposal so we are always ready—no matter what the subject or situation. Higher order thinking skills are very useful tools that can help to make critical thinking accessible and natural to any grade level and with any discipline.

WHAT HAPPENS AT EACH LEVEL?

Each level of Bloom's Taxonomy of the Cognitive Domain represents a certain thinking skill. The higher order thinking skills (HOTS) system includes the thinking skill as well as the questions and activities that support the development of that skill. Critical thinking is a process that involves a disciplined questioning and interrogation of the subject at hand. The goal of the HOTS system is to provide structure and substance to this process.

The *knowledge* level concerns itself with the recall and memorization of facts. At this level, the student should be able to list, define, show, name, describe, and identify. If the student is able to do these things with accuracy, then it can be assumed he or she has mastered this level. Questions that would promote the development of this level are as follows: Who, what, when, where . . .? How many . . .? What is . . .? What does _____ mean? These questions assess factual knowledge and don't require any other skill but knowing and understanding the facts. To reinforce mastery on this level, one might ask students to memorize and recite a poem, or to list all of the major plot twists in a story.

The *comprehension* level involves the translation of knowledge and the interpretation of information. At this level, the student should be able to explain, discuss, restate, outline, paraphrase, and summarize. Questions that promote this level of thinking are as follows: What is the main idea? Can you give an example? Can you restate it in your own words? At this level, a teacher could ask his or her students to outline a chapter or draw a picture of a scene in a story.

These are the two levels concerned with convergent thinking. At these levels, the outcome of the student learning will already be determined because it is based in the facts. There should only be one correct answer. The next levels are representative of divergent thinking, so the outcomes will vary depending on how the student processes the information at each level.

The *application* level includes the ability to use information and apply it to a new context. At this level, the student should be able to classify, demonstrate, illustrate, and solve. Questions that support development at this level are as follows: Can you apply this to a different situation? Can you write instructions for____? To reinforce this level of thinking, one could ask a student to make a diorama or a map, or to apply a given set of skills—the steps involved in long division, for instance—to a new problem.

The skills demonstrated at the analysis level are the ability to reorganize and restructure information. At this level, we are looking for students to be able to separate, connect, compare contrast, classify, order, and infer. At this level, we might ask a student to make inferences about a character's motive or to imagine other, alternative outcomes to a series of actions. We may ask a student to think about how one set of information is similar to another and then to draw conclusions about their findings. Here, we might ask a student to construct a graph or a chart that makes information available visually, or to write a letter as a character in a book.

The next level, the *synthesis* level, is concerned with the ability to make sense of a group of different facts and to use the gained skills and ideas to create new ones. Questions that support this level would be as follows: How many different ways are there to ____? How would you design a _____? What could be a new and different use for____? Activities that support this level require the student to create something new and of their own design that demonstrates understanding on the previous levels. The student might be asked to write a poem or paint a picture that utilizes a particular set of skills or elements.

The final level, the *evaluative* level, requires that the student assess value and make judgments. At this level, we may ask a student questions such as the following: Which is the best or most effective? Or, what do you believe about_____? We may reinforce these skills by asking the student to hold a debate or come up with criteria for judging another student's work. At this level, we want to make sure the student can defend his or her own opinions with strong, thoughtful arguments. This is one of the most crucial elements of critical thinking.

WHAT DOES THIS LOOK LIKE AT WORK?

Let's take a closer look at a piece of literature. We will use the poem "maggie and milly and molly and may" by ee cummings to better understand what the HOTS system looks like at work. Let's assume the students have read the poem and are somewhat familiar with the work of ee cummings. If we wanted to pose a question on the knowledge level, we might ask this question: Who are the characters in the poem? We could even pose this as a multiple choice question: In the poem, which of the following girls is *not* a character?

A. Molly
B. Milly
C. Mara
D. May

This question could easily be answered by referring to the title of the poem.

If we wanted to move on to the comprehension level, we could ask about the tenth line and the phrase *as small as a world and as big as alone.* Asking students to identify whether this is a simile or a metaphor would require knowledge of the definition of both simile and metaphor, but it also would require the ability to apply this knowledge to a new context. We could ask the students to explain what exactly chased Molly in the eighth line. To tell us that this thing was a crab, the students would have to interpret the line, relying on the information that it ran sideways and blew bubbles. At this level, we could also ask the students to interpret what Maggie felt after listening to the *star that sang.*

To demonstrate understanding at the application level, the students might pose questions that they would ask the characters about their day at the beach, or they might translate the poem into a short story. This would show that they have grasped

the basic facts and that they are able to apply those facts to a different context. Here we see the necessary emergence of metacognition. To make an application, or to proceed into any of the higher levels, the student must be aware of his or her own thinking. This requires a pedagogy that also places faith in the student and what he or she brings to the table. A student who is nurtured in this faith is an empowered student. Empowering our students is one of the most crucial elements to creating critical thinkers.

Asking the students to make an analysis of the poem would involve questions such as the following: What does the author mean by *five languid fingers* in line five? To answer this, the student would have to make an inference based on the knowledge that he or she has acquired at the previous levels as well as an educated guess as to the meaning of the word *languid,* if it wasn't already known. We might ask the student to compare and contrast the four girls and their different experiences, or even to talk about how a day at the beach is different than a day spent playing in the snow. Again, this privileges the individual experience of the student over the accuracy of information. Not only does every student learn differently, even more so, every student brings a remarkably different realm of experience and prior knowledge to the classroom. Validating each child's knowledge and experience can be very empowering for our students, but requires risk and effort on the part of the teacher. It also requires a fundamental reorganization of what we ordinarily assume to be knowledge and truth.

Writing a poem of their own with the similar structure, but different content, would be one way students could demonstrate knowledge at the synthesis level. We could ask them to imagine new titles for the poem. This would be a good place to attend to cummings' unconventional use of grammar and syntax. Students could write a poem of their own using the same method, or rewrite another poem that uses conventional rules of grammar.

At the evaluation level, students would have a chance to explain and defend their own opinions about the poem. We could ask them to speak to cummings' use of unconventional methods, employing what they have learned about poetry to defend or attack it. This level is somewhat tricky. It is easy to develop an opinion about something. However, what is entailed in this level is not just the establishing of an opinion, but the ability to defend and justify it. This is at the root of empowering our students and building and shaping identity as well. Beyond this, if a student can evaluate, he or she can also disseminate and scrutinize information. Our students are bombarded every day with a tremendous amount of information about how the world works and their role within it. Students deserve, *it is their right to have,* strategies to weed out and reject information that is harmful to their own emerging identities or that conflicts with their values and beliefs. It is our job to prevent them from becoming compliant consumers of information and ideas. Therefore, an evaluative thinker is much more than just the holder of an opinion. This is the heart of, as well as one of the nobler goals of, critical thinking.

WHAT ARE THE BENEFITS TO USING THE HIGHER ORDER THINKING SKILLS?

Clearly, this system provides myriad ways to approach and unpack any object that one may wish to study. This approach, which gives attention to both breadth and depth, is a useful antidote to the overgeneralized curriculum in place in many of our schools today. This system, as well as the others that are modeled after it, are useful and dexterous tools to have in any classroom, which can promote discussion and inquiry and even serve as a reminder for the many ways there may be to skin a cat.

The HOTS system can be very useful when it comes to approaching subject matter that may be somewhat unconventional or uncanonical in nature, especially subject matter that emerges out of our students' culture. One could use the HOTS system as a tool to provide a point of entry or to reveal meaning that might otherwise be obscured.

When a teacher is planning, it can only be helpful to have an awareness of what happens as a student moves through different stages of his or her own learning process, as well as questions and activities that will foster growth at each level.

WHAT ARE THE PROBLEMS TO USING THE HIGHER ORDER THINKING SKILLS?

As with Bloom's Taxonomy, the inflexibility of the structure presents some problems. Each learner has a different process and may not proceed linearly through the model, but instead make loops or zigzags. The responsible teacher must understand that this is perfectly all right. Because the activities and questions provide such a range of material to work with, there should be something here for everyone, but don't assume that it will work the same for each student, or that if one individual doesn't catch on at a particular level, that he or she won't at a different level.

HOW DO WE USE THE HIGHER ORDER THINKING SKILLS?

Have fun with them; use them as a way to discover unexpected things about your subject matter and your students. Returning to Bloom's Taxonomy of the Cognitive Domain, we are reminded that learning should be enjoyable and ongoing. We want our students to be receptive and responsive to learning. Use the HOTS system to make learning about the students. Use it as a tool to elicit their thoughts and perceptions. Use it as a way to gain knowledge and understanding about who they are and how they can best integrate what they learn into how they live. Part of the process of teaching students to think critically is giving them a host of skills and strategies with which they can confront the world. Use and practice of the HOTS system should give our students a sturdy, working set of tools.

Reference

Ellmann, R., & O'Clair, R. (1989). *Modern poems.* New York: W.W. Norton & Company.

Further Reading

Bransford, J., Brown, A. L., & Cocking, R. (Eds.). (2000). *How people learn: Brain, mind, experience and school* (Expanded ed.). Washington, DC: National Academy Press.
Davis, B., Sumara, D., & Luce-Kapler, R. (2000). *Engaging minds.* Mahwah, NJ: Lawrence Erlbaum.
Stiggins, R. J., Rubel, E., & Quellmalz, E. (1988). *Measuring thinking skills in the classroom.* Washington, DC: National Education Association.

Radical Critical Thinking: Part 1: Theoretical Background

Kathleen S. Berry

INTRODUCTION

Many democracies are falling short in their initial promises of providing basic human needs and rights within their borders. What does this mean in the context of critical thinking in schools? This question is the focus of radical critical thinking.

Which of the following best suits the meaning of critical: Critical thinking? Critical care? Critical studies? Critical reading? Critical writing? Critical literacy? Critical mass? Critical moments? Critical times? Critical actions? Critical policies? Critical theory? Critical look? Critical area? Critical decision? Critical process? Critical questioning? Critical relationships?

Whichever term is chosen to apply to everyday life, the meaning and actual application is problematic and complex. Currently, the term is being appropriated by government and corporate agendas as an answer to globalization and capitalist economies. Critical is being confiscated as a means to manage thinking as systemic and thus manage society and organize institutional practices. In business, systemic thinking—classified under categories such as open systems theory—organizational cybernetics, and interactive planning are gaining prominence. In educational circles, the major use of the word critical is attached to thinking, an assumption that that's what education is about. Most areas of education policies and studies, curriculum, academic disciplines, and practices seem to coopt the term critical thinking without questioning its assumptions and foundations. On the one hand, the practices seem consistent over the range of its use. The most consistently applied practice is derived from Bloom's Taxonomy, a series of levels of thinking that are arranged hierarchically and have served educational circles for decades. In fact, as education moves into the twenty-first century, I still hear university students and teacher educators insist on the value and need for Bloom's Taxonomy with the footnoted comment, "it's essential." In turn, the levels are used with public school students to teach them to read the texts of a particular subject discipline. The levels of thinking are arranged from low-level to higher-level thinking, knowledge (information) to evaluation (judging), each with a specific definition and a set of verbs that directs the students' thinking. These categories, which are hierarchical in nature, provide a convenient ordering of knowledge based on an authority's notion of what it means to think. I remember many times that I was at a loss for questions to ask students when faced with a new piece of knowledge, wondering how to teach a lesson, or asking how to get the students thinking. Models such as Bloom's Taxonomy, and many others, offered the answer. Convenient, quick, efficient, testable, measurable, and accountable, they worked for everybody from self to students, principals, educational administrators, and parents. On the other hand, regardless of the institution coopting these frameworks, questions about what counts as knowledge, who produced the knowledge, and for whose benefit are never asked.

Rethinking what is meant by critical thinking *expands* taxonomies such as Bloom's. Hierarchical levels and categorical reductions of knowledge production and thinking fade into a mass of complexity and seemingly uncontrollable chaos. No longer can teachers' and students' depend solely on taxonomies or models of critical thinking. In a postmodern, poststructural, postcolonial world of education, these prescriptive, convenient models of thinking cannot prepare the users for the authentic, complex, and chaotic process of (what I call) radical critical thinking. The frightening aspect of all this is that, as educators, we short change our students by believing in these reductionistic models as gateways to knowledge; knowledge that when connected to a world within and outside the immediate text impacts not only how we think but also how we are to be in and act in the world. Thus, for the sake of our students and the pursuit of democracy, inclusivity, equity, and social justice, it is necessary to disrupt what we mean by critical thinking.

What is involved in radical critical thinking is very complex compared to the linear, hierarchical, methodological rationality modeled by Bloom's Taxonomy and most modernist uses of the concept. Disruption does not mean, however, an abandonment of the categories and vocabulary of critical thinking used by Bloom and others. An expanded notion of critical thinking, in contemporary contexts, includes not merely thinking as a set of isolated skills, hierarchical taxonomies, or vocabulary lists but also as the production of knowledge and values. In addition, the skills are activated and connected to a multitude of historical, sociocultural, personal, institutional, economic, and civilizational contexts and, thus, political contexts. Radical critical thinking is about power, not just to think but to think about the world and its inequities, injustices, and exclusions by and against people. Radical critical thinking is about why, what, and how to question the world as problematic; how those questions challenge the inequities; and how the critical thinker can transform self and the world. Radical critical thinking is thinking about the equal distribution of power, whether economic, social, political, intellectual, physical, medical, or historical and whether gender, race, class, spirituality, sexuality, age, ethic, local, national, or global. Most importantly, an expanded notion of critical thinking is about practicing democracy, thinking that requires conditions of complexity and participation. These ideals and principles, however, are slippery and can be confiscated by many factions of right- and left-wing politics. Thus, it is imperative to describe practices that not only contextualize traditional critical thinking but positions it in the radical pedagogy of left-wing politics. With these issues in mind, what do they mean for practice?

CHALLENGING TRADITIONAL NOTIONS OF CRITICAL THINKING

Getting started is the easy part. Many models and vocabulary are available to initiate teachers and students into the process of traditional critical thinking. Given a text in any subject discipline, the series of hierarchical levels as categorized by authors such as Bloom are applied to the text along with a list of certain verbs that create a particular thinking skill, such as follows:

- for knowledge (as information, facts)—tell, define, repeat, identify

- for comprehension (understanding as singular)—explain, translate, demonstrate, interpret
- for application (using as problem solving)—solve novel problems, use information, construct, report
- for analysis (a neutral taking apart of information)—discuss, list, examine, survey, compare, contrast, categorize, classify
- for synthesis (creating new)—generalize, modify, ask what if
- for evaluation (judging)—judge, dispute, form opinions debate, critique, assess, verify

There are many other lists and vocabulary, however, it is Bloom's Taxonomy that is one of the more recognized because of its compatibility with Western thought. that is, how it organizes thinking to appear logical, rational, objective, scientific, and thus measurable and accountable. Therein lies its seductiveness. Therein lies the illusion.

What it means to *think* logically, rationally, objectively, and scientifically has been created by particular people, in a particular space and time, and for particular reasons. What counts as thinking in Western culture has a history beginning as early as the Greek pedagogues. The most famous of these, Socrates, Plato, and Aristotle, developed a philosophy about what it means to think, to learn, and to teach. At the time, what counted as knowledge and how it was produced and taught was contextualized in particular historical, political, economic, and social conditions. Meanings of democracy were constructed to suit the times and certain people. Thinking as a political (polis) and democratic practice was limited to the upper-class, male, white Greek members of the elite.

Today, those philosophies and the practices that defined and structured what thinking, whose thinking, and how to think have been formalized by systemic, hierarchical models and legitimized by curriculum documents and dominant pedagogical practices. For example, the most prevalent evidence of this can be seen in the form of (what has become known as) the triad. The teacher asks a question and waits, for about three seconds, for a response to which she or he already has an expected correct answer. Then, a student (usually the same few) responds with a yes/no answer or another very short answer. The teacher, in turn, acknowledges with a nod or by saying, "that's right," and moves on to the next question or skill (discuss, analyze, compare, etc.). This triadic mode of thinking usually occurs within thirty seconds and has become so systematically entrenched that practitioners assume this is what critical thinking is, should be, and has to be. Examination and critique of this model will demonstrate that this is a very limited notion of critical thinking and is actually saturated with discursive practices that create conditions of inequity, social injustice, exclusiveness, and partisan democracy for many students.

When we, as critical theorists, examine the ideology of the hierarchical taxonomy and triadic model, we are left with a very limited notion of critical thinking. Upon further examination we find issues of knowledge and power, thus a Foucaultian haven for critique. Whether the question is working from the knowledge (information) level or any other level; whether the skill of discussing, debating, synthesizing, surveying, or even examining is applied; whether the content is established as valuable and testable by government policies; whether corporate agendas are infiltrating educational pedagogy; or whether positivistic research convinces the profession and public that there are declining standards (read as not teaching status quo thinking/knowledge), traditional practices of critical thinking are apolitical, limited, decontextualized, and dominated by particular notions of knowledge and controlled by particular players. To rethink these assumptions means to challenge and change the foundations of critical thinking.

ENTERING COMPLEXITY

Both the triadic and the hierarchical model of critical thinking represent a linear or back-and-forth interaction with limited to nil feedback except from the teacher. The feedback is in response to an answer to a pseudoquestion where the teacher already has an expected answer. In addition, the feedback is singular, one way, and controlled by the teacher who acts hegemonically to also control the knowledge produced by the students. Locked in by these linear and triadic models, the students are only regurgitating knowledge they assume to be true and accept as legitimate (to please the authority/teacher or to pass the standard knowledge asked on a test or examination). Even the structure of the knowledge produced is organized by textbooks or the imposition of a formal structure on the process. No new knowledge is produced by the students nor do the students take personal or social ownership. In essence, the students are forced into a totalitarian mode of thinking, without freedom or creative spaces for them to participate as in a deliberative democracy. Over the years, the students are trained to accept the format, the linearity, and the authority of institutionalized and formalized knowledge. In other words, what it means to *be* a critical thinker and *do* critical thinking is really defined by institutional, state, and corporate knowledge, which are not really favorable conditions for producing citizens ready to enter and shape democratic societies.

Resistance, however, to the dominant hegemonic forces at work in traditional theories and practices of critical thinking is entering the discussions and critiques of modern, structuralist, and Western modes of thinking. Spawned by the early Greek philosophers and formalized over centuries by institutional policies and practices, challenges to the dominance and assumptions of Western thought, discourses, and practices are infiltrating the field of critical thinking. Critical thinking is collapsing the rigidity of its positivistic borders in such areas as postmodernism, poststructuralism, and postcolonialism; marginalized voices of women, people of color, and colonized nations; economically and politically oppressed people; Internet and the World Wide Web; corporate agendas and Western globalization; and the host of disruptive questions from postformal critical studies. Once teachers and students recognize the changes and understand the why of radical critical thinking, they are compelled to enter a field of complexity and self-organization, admittedly with hesitation, fear, anxiety, frustration, baggage of the past, and, lastly, the mild and severe political consequences of challenging the status quo.

Earlier I discussed how the easy part of getting started in postformal radical critical thinking was to operate from a traditional framework and vocabulary such as Bloom's Taxonomy. The path of complexity, however, begins many times with the familiar and, like any adventure, heads into

the unknown. For many teachers, the initial task is to create a safe environment for themselves and the students without falling back on the familiar. Because most teachers and students were raised on a fodder of knowledge production established by modernist, structuralist, and formalized textbook and examination devices, any disruption in these century old traditions can be dangerous to the point of losing jobs and failing exams.

DELIBERATIVE DEMOCRACY

What keeps the participants engaged in complexity is the moral and ethical directives of freedom, equity, social justice, and deliberative democracy. I use deliberative democracy as initiated (but with flexible interpretations) by Habermas in response to the limitations and inequities cultivated by Western civilization's practice of democracy as plebiscite, that is, majority rule. Deliberative democracy requires a moral and ethical space for the diversity and plurality of difference. It is a process of negotiation, resistance, and controversy. In an educational environment, radical critical thinking changes the relationship between teacher and student, between the knower and the known, between knowledge production and knowledge consumption.

As humans, we have the gift of language to use for personal and social justice. Thus it is necessary to perform as radical critical thinkers, to use language in its many functions, forms, content, and contexts. Participants ask certain questions and collaborate in the construction of personal and social practices—what I am calling radical critical thinking. They create educational environments, knowledge and values, conditions, skills, and thinking that are antifoundational in respect to the dominance of Western civilization's notions of critical thinking.

Further Reading

Tyson, L. (1999). *Critical theory today: A user-friendly guide.* New York: Garland Publishing Group.

Young, I. M. (2000). *Inclusion and democracy.* Oxford: Oxford University Press.

Radical Critical Thinking: Part 2: The Practice

Kathleen S. Berry

TEACHING IN TURBULENCE

What happens when radical critical thinking is applied to a taxonomy such as Bloom's or the triadic model mentioned in the theory of Part I? Radical critical thinking attempts to avoid binarisms, that is, thinking that works on polarities where one side of the binary construction belongs in large part to the dominant knowledge, players, and practices (such as in the triad or exams) of good/bad, positive/negative, true/false, right/wrong, smart/stupid, yours/theirs, included/excluded, and so forth. Radical critical thinking questions assumptions that are encoded in the knowledge. In addition, it works into the mainstream center to disrupt the power assigned both to the knowledge content and the process of production. But there are ways to counter these extremes, push forward, and enter the complexity of postformal critical thinking and still be safe. There is a conservative approach with intentions to subvert yet engage radical critical thinking as the norm. In so doing, a climate of turbulence results and features of complexity emerge. There is no need for

fear or hesitation as we enter into the turbulence of radical critical thinking. I think of it as a courageous and heroic adventure; a mythological quest for social justice and the pursuit of democracy.

To eliminate the linearity and formalism of taxonomies, teachers stretch the categories of questions and generate interactions as fields of complexity. Thus, radical critical thinking *dares* teachers and students to do the following:

- *Articulate* new ways for producing knowledge as practice not merely as abstracted and reduced from the world but as knowledge that creates practices for social and personal change. Knowledge is seen as process and practice that can be applied not as an object that creates a binarism of right/wrong or for testing as in modern examination practices. Teachers and students engage new and traditional discourses as poetic playfulness. Vocabulary, sentence, and narrative structures interact to produce new articulations of knowledge and understandings. Evaluation and examinations are measures of the creative processes of language use and projects for social justice.

- *Avoid* essentializing, generalizing, and universalizing. Most of the knowledge and values that are generated in textbooks, canons, testing (standardized), media, and so forth work from a positivist perspective. That is, knowledge is abstracted from the world through symbols systems (print, visual, oral) and reduced to knowledge that over time and space becomes accepted as applicable to all people, all places, and for all times. Universalizing and generalizing, either through quantitative (such as statistics or charts) or qualitative (literature, ethnographic, biography, history, etc.) texts reduces the complexity of human experience. When essentializing, a person speaks as if they are speaking for the other, which is problematic to the inclusionary practices of radical critical thinking.

- *Blur* the boundaries between traditional academic disciplines not merely as intra- or interdisciplinary but as complex interweavings and threads of discourses and ideologies that produce new knowledge with flexible and constantly shifting borders. Thus, a rigor is required that foregoes mere memorization and consumption of traditional subject area knowledge. Teachers and students identify with multiple fields and discourses of study. Expertise and experience is defined by the ability to work in the field of complexity and provide applications that contribute to conditions of diversity, equity, inclusion, social justice, and deliberative democracy.

- *Borrow* from any area, source, discipline, discourse, history, and ideologies. Important, however, is to recognize, for example, the cultural, historical, gendered, racial, religious, and national frameworks from which the borrowing takes place. The purpose is not to appropriate the works of the other or set up cultural/historical relativism but to include side-by-side, and equally, the range of possibilities available for thinking about the world and changing it. Different cultural and historical texts spoken/written by others, but marginalized by the dominant powers, contain different ideas and ways of living in this world, different ways of thinking about the same event, issue, or topic. Maybe borrowing and sharing will create an atmosphere of deliberative democracy and social justice both at the micro level (classroom) and the macro level (national and global).

- *Challenge* the authority of textbooks, prepackaged sources of knowledge, peers, and teachers. In traditional beliefs of critical thinking, that which appears as valuable and legitimized knowledge and truths is organized in a manner that rejects challenges by its consumers, especially students. Modernist knowledge and values are circulated as representative and necessary for success in academic and life circles. Because of the power assigned to certain knowledge and values, radical critical thinking demands that teachers and students question the author's production and the context, purposes, and structures in which the knowledge is presented.

- *Check and recheck* assumptions about what counts as knowledge. Accepted and dominant knowledge and practices, resulting from centuries of formal and institutional conventions, carry with them taken-for-granted meanings and apparatus that needs to be checked and rechecked for the assumptions that reproduce inequities, exclusions, and social injustice. A teacher and the students may be required to trace where certain ideas, concepts, and words (etymology) originated; what assumptions are embedded within the ideas and words; why and how did the ideas, concepts, and words enter the lexicon as valuable and powerful; how did the ideas, concepts, and words enter the lexicon; whose concepts are they; and why do we work with certain ideas, words, and concepts and not others?

- *Confront* the self in the unfolding revelations and discussions. Traditional critical thinking worked from an objective standpoint that considered the subjectivity of self as contaminating the knowledge. Persons engaged in radical critical thinking are obligated to include their understandings, beliefs, opinions, personal responses, histories and connections, vocabularies, and implications for the knowledge produced.

- *Confuse* the dominant players and practices with questions and answers of subversion, ludic complicity, conflicted subjectivities, and irony. Questions, discussions, teachings, and writings that appear to accept the status quo, but instead confuse typical responses and structures, perform as devices of disordering and disequilibrium, essential strategies in poststructural, postmodern, postcolonial, and postformal readings of the world.

- *Connect* the pieces and fragments of knowledge without ever completing the puzzle. Radical critical thinkers show the relationships between seemingly unconnected fragments of knowledge. Like people who connect their history through the family tree, genealogical connections untangle the web of complexity in how and why life has come to be like it is. In conjunction with the thinking skill of excavation, a radical critical thinker is an archeological genealogist in the manner intended by Michael Foucault. Archeological genealogists excavate and connect disparate bodies of knowledge and societal/institutional practices and structures to disclose power inequities and social injustices (a basic practice of radical critical thinking).

- *Critique* everything and everyone (including self) to the point of limitations and exhaustion until the transformation of self, society, institutions, and the world is reached. This is not a process that evolves as a positive/negative binary statement, as many people tend to feel when first confronted with the principles, discourse, and practices of radical critical thinking. Binary thinking breeds polarity and reproduces dominance when practices are set up as positive or negative (who decides?). Critique is for change in the unequal, undemocratic, exclusionary, homogeneous, and social injustices that exist in the discursive texts and practices that have come to be accepted as the norm and natural. Critique is meant to study and expose power that reproduces inequities, not as a binarism of positive/negative, but along a continuum that is constantly shifting, blurred, complex, chaotic, and infinite.

- *Decenter* canons and positions of privilege (such as based on dominant gender, race, class, religion, sexuality, ethnicity, nationality, etc.). For example, texts of literature, philosophy, and grand narratives of Western civilization (e.g., liberal-humanism, existentialism, capitalism, Freudian psychoanalysis, Euro-American documents, Christianity) have created the canons that privilege certain knowledge, values, and discourses to the exclusion, marginalization, and oppression of other discourses and texts. Postcolonial voices, for example, are decentering the Euro-American canons by writing back to the colonizers. Feminists of color are writing back to the dominance of canons produced by males and white feminists. From early years of schooling onward, the literature of British white male writers is being challenged and supplemented with literature of the other, including women, South Americans, aboriginals, Asians, Muslims, and gays and lesbians (and the multiple voices with each of these arenas).

- *Deconstruct* the logic of Western civilization and the institutional research, structures, and policies that harbor sexism, racism, classism, and other monological ways of thinking. A plethora of strategies exist that examine the thinking that is constructed as rational, logical, scientific, objective, legitimate, and universal. Deconstruction dismantles, not destroys, the Western-centered constructs that have, over time, neglected the multiplicity, diversity, and potential of human rationalities and differently constructed logic. The troublesome aspect of deconstruction for teachers and students seems to be the lack of closure that was so normal for conventional critical thinking.

- *Distribute* power equally—power as freedom and human rights, not the accumulation of power as the rights and privileges of a few. Power is everywhere: in knowledge, in texts, and in political, economic, historical, national, and cultural locations and interactions within a classroom setting. Democracy promises the equal distribution of power to all. However, as stated at the beginning of the theoretical chapter on radical critical

thinking, many democracies (meaning the macro level of nations) are "falling short of their initial promises of providing basic human needs and rights within their borders." And partisan democracy strays from this promise at the micro level of classrooms that purport to be doing critical thinking. Deliberative democracy shuns the distribution of power by partisan politics and practices, even for the young students in a classroom. Students are awarded an equal share of the power to be included, diverse, and taken seriously, and an equal share of the material wealth to construct knowledge. In addition, distribution of power, combined with the practices of complexity and chaos, expects students to engage in apparently random behavior; unstable, aperiodic behavior; thinking as nonlinearity, feedback looping with others and texts; fractal dimensionality; cultural and identity attractors; turbulence; bifurcations; dissipative systems; self-organization; interrelatedness; and states near and far from equilibrium. These features of chaos and complexity are being employed in many areas, including the classroom, as major features of such processes as radical critical thinking.

- *Employ* the diverse and multiple artifacts of society. Where print has occupied a privileged position in the knowledge-based thinking of Western civilization and institutional practices, radical critical thinkers employ every possible cultural and historical artifact available with each one possessing equal value. The eclectic sources of artifacts from the past—such as oral, dramatic, musical, and visual along with the current technologies of computers, e-mails and hypertexts, film, television, popular culture, music, and magazines—maximize the opportunities and necessity for radical critical thinking.

- *Engage* the oppressor as well as the oppressed. Critical thinking in the past has spoken on behalf of the oppressors without questioning their assumptions. To be a thinker, the oppressor assumed that the path of critical thinking (as designed by them) was also the way for the oppressed. Radical critical thinking engages the diversity, language, knowledge, and experiences of both oppressor and oppressed. In addition, radical critical thinking assigns agency to the oppressed to avoid missionary tactics on the part of the oppressors and democratic rights of self-organization and self-determination for the oppressed.

- *Examine* everything with the discourses, skills, strategies, principles, and practices of radical critical thinking. The idea here is that an unexamined world/life provides spaces for totalitarianism, poverty, dominance, inequalities, and social injustices to develop and remain as if natural, normal, and unchangeable. An examined life is inclusive and democratic.

- *Excavate,* with the tools of radical critical thinking, the layers of knowledge and meanings produced, circulated, and maintained as if logical, legitimate, rational, true, ethical, normal, natural, and so forth. Like the archaeologist who carefully uncovers the history of artifacts and events contained in the layers of soil, radical critical thinkers unearth the multiplicity of thinking rigorously and deeply. In addition, they place the knowledge in the political, social, and historical contexts in which it was produced. The process of interpretation is similar to the archeologist who interprets the meanings of the uncovered artifacts according to the historical and cultural layer in which it is located.

- *Expose* contradictions, complicity, consent, conflicts, and conformity within the status quo, mainstream thinking, and practices. Once the hegemony is exposed at the personal, societal, institutional, and civilizational levels, as archeological genealogists do, radical critical thinkers do not rest here. They articulate and invent counterhegemonic practices that challenge the status quo and produce practices and discourses for social justice and a deliberative democracy where differences (of ideas, knowledge, values, people, etc.) are included.

- *Locate* the knowledge in a cultural, historical, political, and economic context. Identify the creators (Western, gender, class, race, sexuality, religion, nationality, etc.) of the knowledge and for whose purpose and what benefit. Locate the knower also and how each is influenced, privileged, or oppressed by the knowledge and the actions, structures, institutions, practices, and policies that are produced by that knowledge.

- *Position* alternative and even oppositional identities within a conflicted social arena.

- *Reread and rewrite* and discuss against the grain.

- *Reclaim* that which has been lost to dominant, status-quo thinking and practices. Most of what has been produced and valued at the personal and local levels has been erased by the dominant powers' telling of history and production of texts. Reclaiming lost histories, knowledge, values, experiences, structures, and languages is possible, perhaps, only in the imagination and through artifacts and elders that in themselves have suffered centuries of neglect and silence.

- *Resist* that which positions self and others in conditions of poverty (economic, social, individual, material, intellectual, physical, spiritual, political, participation, historical, agency, local, national, global). If any one thinking skill is needed in schools and other institutions it is the freedom and power to resist the positioning of self and others in any condition of poverty. The intention of radical critical thinking is to supply the principles, discourses, vocabularies, spaces, safety, and time to do so. Poverty is not a promise of democracy and is not deserving but, rather, a social construct that continually reproduces itself in many ways.

- *Rethink* means to think again and again and differently each time. Once accorded this expectation, radical critical thinkers act as re-ers: that is reject, resist, reclaim, re-see, re-search, rediscover, re-invent, and so on.

- *Search* for multiple truths, knowledge, and values while rejecting the absolute, fixed, and final conclusions of modernist and colonial thinking.

- *Theorize* by challenging the grand theories/narratives of Western civilization and also valuing local/personal narratives. Radical critical thinking uses the discourses and devices of different theories to push the borders of categorical, provincial, and personal thinking. In conjunction with the language provided by the grand narratives, no one theory takes hold of society to establish homogenous ways of thinking and being. And theorizing is an ongoing process, never fixed or concluded, only temporarily put in place for actions that tomorrow could shift if inequities are recognized and reproduced.

- *Track* as in archeological genealogy. Radical critical thinkers track how daily practices move into formalized and institutional political processes, thus possibly reproducing sexism, racism, classism, and other social injustices. Tracking is difficult as the footprints of the dominant have and can cover the tracks with discursive discourses, positivistic policies, and hegemonic practices that smokescreen and even eliminate democratic processes, certain knowledge, values, and truths. Tracking is also dangerous for radical critical thinkers—the landscape on which they tread is paved with traditions, rituals, procedures, methods, and beliefs that are held by and privilege the dominant.

- *Value* personal and local knowledge in institutional contexts (from family to school, from government to corporation) as well as global and disciplinary knowledge.

This is just a preliminary list for shifting radical critical thinking into everyday practice. Many more possibilities exist and can be added as the complexity increases or apathy creeps in: *contest* the status quo/norms, the sites where inequities thrive; *deliberate* openly; *dismantle* not destroy or destruct (radical critical thinking does not censor, it critiques and transforms); *disrupt* not interrupt; *emplace* cultural artifacts (literary, visual, etc.) in sociohistorical contexts; *foreground* that which has been backgrounded by the dominant power(s); *include* ethical and moral imperatives; *interrelate* the past and present to remake identities long constructed as pathological; *interrogate; investigate; recognize* before judging; *recover* that which has been erased by dominance throughout time and space and by gender, race, class, and so on; *relate and interrelate* features, discourses, ideologies, policies, and structures that produce certain practices; *research; situate* yourself, knowledge, ideas, actions, language, others, and institutions in the relationships of power; *unmask* that which is hidden behind the norm (including radical critical thinking) and has been taken for granted.

As you might realize, none of these skills acts singularly or hierarchically or is used without interconnectedness to one another and to cultural, sociohistorical, political, spatial, and temporal contexts. In no way are the questions meant to be asked in any taxonomic, formalist, procedural, or linear method. Once the questions have been asked, or the skills of radical critical thinking have been modeled by teacher and/or students, there is no procedural method or hierarchical level that guides the participants through the process. They act in accordance with the principles of radical critical thinking. Each one acts as an entry point into the complexity and turbulence of radical critical thinking. Used singularly, or in combination, the journey through radical critical thinking engages teacher and students in a field of possibilities but always with the intention of excavating the hidden ideologies and messages that, without challenge, would continue to legitimate practices that reproduced inequities, exclusions, and so forth. When deliberative democracy; the multiplicity of postmodern, poststructural, postcolonial, and postformal knowledge; support for self-organization of knowledge and the conditions of chaos and complexity are present during the interactions, radical critical thinking is easily introduced into the everyday practices of education, in schools and elsewhere.

Further Reading

Appleman, D. (2000). *Critical encounters in high school English: Teaching literary theory to adolescents.* New York: Teachers College Press.

Lynn, S. (2001). *Texts and contexts: Writing about literature with critical theory* (3rd ed.). New York: Longman.

Reasoning Readiness for Primary School Students: Critical Thinking As Developmentally Appropriate

Danny Weil

This article argues that the debate on relevant and meaningful education has not focused on some of the crucial questions that need to be asked when looking to devise methods and calibration mechanisms to promote and assess learning and teaching. Some of these questions would include the following:

- What should we be teaching students in the elementary grades and what should they be learning?
- What are the roles of standards and assessment in the conception of being educated and how can we use evaluation and valid assessment to further authentic instruction for primary students?

- What should we be assessing and why?

- What about emotional intelligences? Should we be teaching that as well?

- What about multiple intelligences and testing?

- What does it mean to be intelligent and how would this impact on how we teach and measure student performance in the early grades?

- What is a problem-based curriculum and how can we teach the skills students need and wed them to critical thinking?

- Should we be relying solely on one test to test elementary students, or should we be developing methods and mechanisms of assessment on a weekly or monthly basis that are more holistic?

These important questions, and countless others, represent just some of the inquiry that should be undertaken to begin to rationally think about and consequently construct an authentically designed critical thinking curriculum that furthers the mission of education.

As a former bilingual kindergarten, first grade, second grade, and junior high school and high school teacher, I have unfortunately heard from colleagues and administrators alike that primary school students need first to be taught skills and information before they can engage in reasoning activities that call upon them to develop their critical thinking capacities. Thus, elementary teaching, these colleagues contend, should be designed to teach students the skills they need to know and test them on the skills they have acquired. In fact, when it comes to teaching students to think critically, I often hear the argument that children are not developmentally ready for critical thinking, that critical thinking in the early elementary grades simply is not developmentally appropriate.

The argument assumes that students need an information base before they can think critically and that elementary schools should be a place where this informational base is constructed and important skills acquired. The reasoning surreptitiously maintains that students really need to be taught *what to think* not how to think. What's needed, argue those that take this position, is to concentrate on teaching students in early primary grades the myriad skills associated with reading, writing, listening, mathematics, and so on—a skill-based curriculum. The argument contends that these students will have plenty of time to think critically in the higher grades. Other teachers have maintained that primary grades should be affective centers of learning where students play, learn to feel good about themselves, and socialize. Thinking critically, maintain some teachers, can be uncomfortable and students in early grades should be protected from it, not exposed to it.

With these arguments in mind, learning becomes reduced to teaching skills and giving information, usually divorced from context, while knowing something is equated with having information about it. Protecting students from reasoning, as opposed to engaging them in it, becomes accepted as the norm. I believe that what we should be asking is, "Where do these assumptions about early childhood education derive their origin? What assumptions underlie these perspectives regarding learning and teaching?"

For teachers interested in developing the critical capacities of their students, this theoretical conceptualization of education for primary students is unsound and unsuitable—in fact, it is downright dangerous as thinking becomes thought of as a subversive activity as opposed to a necessity. Teachers truly concerned with developing the critical capabilities of their students would argue that knowledge is not equated with having a lot of information. Similarly, having students engage in activities to simply show what skills they are able to execute is not equated to having and executing specific skills in the interests of developing critical consciousness. The linear step-by-step process, whereby disciplines are broken into fragments and skills into isolated subparts taught outside the context of thinking, is challenged. Furthermore, although students obviously need information, it is the manner within which they uncover it, interpret it, as well as use it to solve problems, make decisions, and otherwise develop a critical understanding of daily life that is of interest to those who advocate critical instruction. Will they collect information based on a problem-posing curriculum that asks them to construct knowledge in the interest of inquiry and discovery? Or will they be forced to memorize and uncritically accept information without learning to categorize it, verify its sources, classify it, form it into patterns from which they might make plausible inferences, and otherwise use it critically? How students get the information they need, how they assemble it, interpret it, and what they do with it is the real issue that faces educators and the field of education today.

In terms of actual skills, it is inarguable that students need to learn specific skills called for in various elementary school curriculums. For example, not being able to regroup numbers would seriously impact on a child's ability to understand and perform mathematical manipulations. What *is* arguable is how they learn these skills, how they orchestrate these skills in the interest of con-

structing knowledge, and how these skills are employed in a self-conscious, metacognitive manner.

While reductionist learning argues that elementary school skills can and often should be taught in rote isolation, advocates of critical thinking would claim that the obsession with teaching skills isolated from thinking is actually the problem. The modernistic elementary school, with its necessity to teach fourteen disciplines, has created a factory orientation toward teaching and learning. Take your spelling book out; put your spelling book away. Take your math book out; put your math book away. Take your science book out; put your science book away—this obsession with systematically deconstructing disciplines into subparts represents an attempt to teach pieces of subjects in isolation with no interdisciplinary connections. It presents knowledge unsystematically and consequently and simultaneously teaches unsystematic, convergent thinking in a world of holistic thought and divergent realities. For many students, the parts never fit into the whole and they learn skills, but the skills cannot be harnessed to critical thinking; they never truly become educated in the sense critical thinking demands.

Take the skill of reading, for example. Reading critically and reading uncritically are simply not the same processes. To read critically implies thinking critically—a process whereby the reader actively engages in a silent dialogue with the author as an attentive, questioning participant in the process of interpretation. To simply read without comprehension represents little more than the act of decoding—what Donaldo Macedo has aptly called, "barking at print" (Macedo, 1994, p. 7). Yet reading is usually broken up as a discipline and taught as phonics, comprehension, language, and so on. So, when doing phonics, the student is not concerned with comprehension. And understanding vocabulary is divorced from both as lists of vocabulary words are constructed for memorization purposes. Spelling is taught as a separate subject again, usually relying on assembled lists to be memorized.

By taking a subject like reading and breaking it down into component parts taught as separate entities, students never see the interdisciplinary connections and processes necessary to comprehend what they read. They do not get a feel for how the parts make up the whole and the subjects and skills taught within them become so many bee in a bag. Reading becomes a chore as opposed to an exciting adventure into imagination and thought.

Traditional notions of childhood education have reduced early elementary school experiences, for both teachers and students, to the act of teaching and learning rudimentary skills so that students can simply memorize and recite information. This form of anorexic-bulimic learning has established the content and borders for teaching and learning and left a ruinous educational wake in its stead. Regrouping, decoding, sentence diagramming, grammatical certainty, spelling, memorizing, following formulas, and the like have all been equated with developmental appropriateness and being intelligent in elementary school. And this has not only resulted in conducting and directing the methods of teaching, but also has provided a structural foundation. Upon this house of cards is built the multimillion dollar assessment, or standards, industry.

The debate between those who advocate knowing as a process of learning basic skills and using these skills for information gathering and retention and those who perceive of knowing as an interdisciplinary process of developing skills in the interest of constructing meaning out of a given situation or a given set of facts continues unabated. Knowledge, according to the latter view, is socially constructed. This means that the knower is implicated in the act of knowing and brings to the interpretative knowledge process both her historical reality, class, gender location, race, and set of values and personal assumptions and experiences to the process of knowing. Joe Kincheloe speaks to this as he attempts to help us redefine intelligence:

The point of intelligence, therefore, is not to just gather thoughts from memory but to find patterns in those ideas one has collected—i.e., to gather and choose apart. The process of pattern detection is not simple, however, as it involves the detection of multiple patterns depending on the context in which particular concepts are viewed. Thus the pattern that memory imposes on thoughts must be transcended, as the thinker gains the imaginative ability to see events in ways not necessarily his or her own. (Kincheloe, 1999, pp. 12–13)

Frankly stated, we don't memorize what we learn and we don't learn what we memorize. We see the logic of what we are attempting to understand and through abstract, systematic thinking, we arrive at decisions, make inferences, come to conclusions, and detect solutions to problems. Committing something to memory, obviously a necessary ingredient in forming a reservoir of knowledge, is quite a different process than memorization, per se.

In harmony with this awareness is the understanding that one can have specific skills but not know how to execute them in the interest of the construction of a given project, set of ideas, or creation. For example, knowing how to use a hammer does not mean that one has the intelligence to build a house. And this is especially true if the instruction in learning how to use a hammer is broken down into its fragmentary parts and practiced in rote isolation from the construction of the house itself. These insights seem to be lost on modernistic educational approaches that continue to conceive of formal thinking in elementary schools as the most valued form of thinking—a thinking that must be learned in fragmented, linear stages.

There are many reasons for conceiving of learning and education as mere information gathering and rote, skill acquisition. The purpose of this entry is not to discuss the myriad political, economic, racial, psychological, and sexually based topics that contribute to a specific modernistic, technical understanding of knowing as staged skill development and information gathering and retention. However, when attempting to analyze the relationship between standardized tests in elementary schools and what they purport to assess, the psychological assumption upon which these tests rely must be scrutinized. By tying standardized tests in primary school to staged developmental readiness, specific skill acquisition, and rote memorization, these tests have been designed to assess knowledge as information retention and competency as specific skill acquisition.

On the other hand, if we change our assumptions about learning and knowing in the primary grades and conceive of knowing as a holistic, interdisciplinary process—which relies upon academic skills and their acquisition as tools for inquiry, discovery, problem solving, critical thinking, and the construction of knowledge—standardized tests would, of necessity, concentrate on assessing what students can do with what they think they know and how they think they came to know it. These tests would be one of many powerful tools for helping our students develop thinking processes that they might use to make sense out of their daily lives. Unfortunately, as we shall see, this is not the case.

Perhaps the most important guiding psychological philosophy still dominant in educational circles today, and specifically within elementary education, is the work of Jean Piaget. Piaget's writings in the area of educational psychology have appeared for more than half a century but, until recently, have received little critical scrutiny. Although Piaget formulated many theoretical positions regarding behavior and learning, it is his notion of developmental stages of cognitive growth that has had the largest impact on early childhood education and the notion that deserves intense scrutiny and critique.

According to Piaget, a child goes through cognitive developmental stages that occur as a result of a combination of maturation, physical and logical mathematical levels, social experience, and equilibration. These developmental stages were important for Piaget for they implied what was developmentally appropriate at specific ages in terms of providing learning opportunities and developmentally appropriate subject-matter content.

For Piaget, the process of knowing was not one that was constructed by the learner. On the contrary, Piaget psychologized the study of cognition outside of a child's particular experience of life. He observed learning as a psychological process—learning decontextualized from gender, sociological, political, economic, and other individual and social phenomenon. By psychologizing learning divorced from social and personal context, Piaget effectively removed cultural, racial, gender, and class conditions from his formulation of learning and subjective formation. The Piagetian formulation of developmental stages removed social interaction, diversity, gender, culture, race, and socioeconomic class from the intelligent equation as it manifested itself as a mechanized and formulaic approach to teaching and learning. Coupled with this was Piaget's belief that the highest order of intelligence was that found in formal mathematical-scientific reasoning. The entire affective dimension of learning was marginalized in favor of purely rational thought formations.

Accepting Piaget's theories of intelligence and learning, designed around cognitive developmental stages, afforded modernistic educators a structural approach to defining and measuring intelligence. It also allowed the system to develop calibrating mechanisms called standardized tests, to decide which students would succeed and which students would not. These tests became technologies of power that operate to include and exclude.

Schools and standardized test designers consequently focused their attention on measuring what they saw as the highest order of intelligence. This one-dimensional definition of intelligence has formed the basis and rational for the standardized tests given to elementary school students and, in so doing, has defined the method and theory behind instruction—the tests drive the teaching. Piaget's theories rationalized early childhood learning; teaching elementary school students was now thought of as purely a linear process that was to be undertaken in specific stages, based on what was defined as developmentally appropriate—even though this appropriateness was defined generically and outside the realm of cultural context and individual understanding.

However Piaget's theories have not been without its critics. In 1983, Harvard psychologist Howard Gardner startled the educational field by publishing his book *Frames of Mind: The Theory of Multiple Intelligences.* Gardner's contribution to the field of cognitive psychology cannot be underestimated. His work, for the first time, specifically challenged Western societal assumptions underlying the definition of intelligence and forcefully argued that the conception of intelligence used to construct teaching practices and the assessment of learning were narrow and theoretically shortsighted. Gardner understood that intelligence could not be reduced to measurement by some short objective test and, thus, educational instruction must be re-thought and removed from the domain of inauthentic measurement tools. And Gardner was not convinced by the Piagetian notions of intelligence that measured verbal, mathematical, and scientific reasoning at the exclusion of what he called "multiple intelligences." He seemed to be aware of the social construction of knowledge and his work challenged the linear, one-dimensional conception of knowledge. Gardner posited not only multiple intelligences but also *multiple* ways of knowing. His work postulated that rational, Cartesian ways of knowing were not the beginning and end of intelligence but represented simply one form of intelligence. By expanding the notion of intelligence to embrace multiplicity in thought, Gardner both democratized it as a concept and theoretically challenged the preconceptions that marked both the theory and its application to assessment and learning practices. Human potential, argued Gardner, was developed by paying attention to the multiplicity of intelligences and designing educational opportunities that would help tease out these intelligences and allow them to flourish while consequently assessing their development in the interests of personal growth and self-improvement.

Gardner's notion of multiple intelligences, and his attempt to formulate a neo-Piagetian conceptual understanding of intelligence, has more than mere academic implications. Gardner and others who have attempted to push the cognitive psychological envelope have argued that a new understanding of intelligence would, of necessity, require a new form of teaching and learning, especially for primary students and the teachers that teach them. This, of course, would spark the need for new and different forms of assessment—from standardized test to daily teacher assessments in the classroom. Adopting a theory of multiple intelligences would force teaching to examine itself and theorize about its activities and assumptions. Such an examination may open the door for powerful reasoning opportunities for our primary students whereby instructors of these students become animated with the knowledge that teaching is an act of love, not a linear tool for mere preparation and skill instruction. This would revolutionize the entire educational endeavors of primary school teachers—from how they are taught to teach to how they collaborate on designing and implementing instruction. In closing, it would allow developmental appropriateness to be tied to critical thinking as opposed to holding critical thinking hostage to stages of development.

References

Gardner, H. (1983). *Frames of mind: The theory of multiple intelligences.* New York: Basic Books.

Kincheloe, J. L. (1999). Trouble ahead, trouble behind: Grounding the post-formal critique of educational psychology. In J. L. Kincheloe, S. R. Steinberg, & P. H. Hinchey (Eds.), *The postformal reader: Cognition and education.* New York: Falmer Press.

Macedo, D. (1994). *Literacies of power: What Americans are not allowed to know.* Boulder, CO: Westview Press.

Reflective Practitioner

Brenda Edgerton Conley

Improving professional practice is a major concern of all professional groups and finding effective mechanisms for this improvement is a critical task for teachers and other educators. How do teachers become better at their craft? Do they learn the practice of effective teaching by observing others in action? Do they do it under the supervision of a guide or a mentor? Or, are good teachers just born, not made? How do teachers engage in the process of professional learning? How do they go about upgrading their skills? What actions do they take to ensure that they are effective in today's classrooms?

Answers to these questions lie in the basic assumptions we hold about teaching and learning. Unearthing and scrutinizing these assumptions is the core process of reflective practice. Studying the theory and concepts of reflective practice gave me an opportunity to step back in time and reflect on my personal experience as a teacher in training. I can remember spending an inordinate amount of time on the development of lesson plans. Page after page of content was developed that simply outlined, in a mechanical sort of way, all of the directed teaching activities that would be done to achieve learning in the classroom. While the lesson plan did include assessment procedures, I would use them to evaluate the achievement of the objectives for the lesson. There was no mechanism for me, the teacher, to reflect on what I had done in a structured way and organized as part of the lesson planning process. I have watched for many years that very narrowly focused process repeat itself over and over again in teacher development activities. This lack of knowledge about the importance and value of reflective practice ultimately leads to a repetition of mistakes. Learning cannot take place without reflection.

Even today when you ask teachers what they do to improve their practice, the answer usually includes some process outside of themselves. For example, the answer simply might be, "I attend workshops to obtain new information about a program or teaching methods." It might be important to note that many of these inquiries are made of seasoned teachers. The research suggests that those most resistant to critical reflection are those with thirty years or more of experience, who have built careers on a set of unquestioned assumptions about good practice. Michael Eraut (1994) characterizes this kind of knowledge as unorganized experiential knowledge, which is usually drawn on without people realizing they are using it. He describes it as embedded in habits, procedures, decision making, and ways of thinking. He also states that it is never scrutinized or brought under "critical control." Teachers, in other words, are controlled by their own unknown knowledge. Donald Schon (1983) would explain this behavior by saying that reflective practice

is not only a time-consuming process but also that it involves personal risk, because the questioning of practice requires practitioners to be open to examination of beliefs, values, and feelings about which there is great sensitivity.

Most would agree that teaching is a very complex process and that the development of competence and expertise in this profession is tied to learning. In this instance it is teacher learning, not student learning, that is the primary area of focus. In recent years, research on learning has significantly altered fundamental understandings of how and why people learn. One of the learner-centered principles described by Alexander and Murphy (1997) is that "the ability to reflect upon and regulate one's thoughts and behaviors is essential to learning and developing."

A theory of how professionals learn can be drawn from reflective practice and critical reflection. Reflective practice is a beneficial process for teachers to engage in to improve professional practice. Reflective practice, coupled with critical reflection, is a powerful adult learning model. Reflective practice links thought and action with reflection. It involves thinking about and critically analyzing one's actions with the goal of improving practice. It further requires individuals to assume the perspective of external observer to identify assumptions and feelings underlying practice and speculate how assumptions and feelings affect practice. Reflective practice has historical roots in the work of John Dewey and Jean Piaget. Each of them recognized learning as dependent upon the integration of experience with reflection and theory and practice.

Critically reflective teaching, according to Brookfield (1995), happens when we identify and scrutinize the assumptions that undergird how we work. Seeing how we think and work through different lenses is the core process of reflective practice. What turns this into critical reflection is a consistent focus on unearthing and scrutinizing two kinds of assumptions: (1) those that masks the ways in which power affects and often distorts educational interactions; and (2) those that seem congenial but that actually work against our own best interest.

To effectively serve today's complex school environment, teachers must continually make changes in their practice that preserve and advance their abilities to bring about student learning. The work of a teacher is complicated by criticisms of failure and inefficiency and by the complexity of problems associated with the changing context of families, communities, and schools and the social, political, sociological, and economic needs of the community. Additionally, many urban schools are characterized by discipline problems, low academic achievement, and disaffected students.

The difficulty that exists for teachers is that they are attempting to work and bring about change in very turbulent times. Peter Vaill (1996) describes the turbulence as "permanent white water" and suggests that it consists of events that are "surprising, novel, messy, costly, and unpreventable" (p. 10). This description seems to reflect appropriately the life and practice of a teacher. Vaill says further that this permanent white water puts organizations and their members in the position of continually doing things with which they have little experience or doing things that they have never done before. This means, "that beyond all of the other new skills and attitudes that permanent white water requires, people have to be (or to become) extremely effective learners" (p. 42). Many researchers stress the im-

portance of learning as a way of increasing individual capacity to deal effectively with change and the permanent white water demands that make even planned change complex, dilemma-ridden, and hard to predict.

Schon (1983) has written several texts that provide insightful and thought-provoking notions about reflective practice and defines reflective practice as the process by which we thoughtfully consider our own experiences in applying knowledge to practice while being coached by professionals in the discipline. Reflective practice is used at all levels of teaching. He uses three different but significantly integrated phases in the cycle of reflective practice. The terms knowing-is-action, reflection-on-action, and reflection-in-action describe these phases. Knowing-in-action describes that body of knowledge that goes beyond "facts, procedures, rules, and theories" (Schon, 1987/1990, p. 26). It is that body of knowledge that provides adjustment and decision making on the spot.

Reflection-on-action refers to " . . . thinking back to what we have done to discover how our knowing-in-action may have contributed to an unexpected outcome" (Schon, 1987/1990, p. 26). Quite often, when the term reflection is used, the reference is to what has already happened. In Schon's three-pronged concept, it is vital to use the term reflection-on-action as separate from reflection-in-action. To reinforce the point, Kottkamp (1990) uses the terms "offline" and "online" to distinguish between reflection-on-action and reflection-in-action.

Reflection-in-action describes the point at which " . . . our thinking serves to reshape what we are doing while we are doing it" (Schon, 1987/1990, p. 26). Killion and Todnem took Schon's cycle one step further in their description of reflection-for-action. Reflection-for-action is believed to be the ultimate goal of all forms of reflection.

Through reflection-for-action, educators broaden their understanding of what skills are necessary to accommodate a variety of circumstances in order to develop a vision of what could be, and to seek ongoing opportunities in which they can talk about how they carry out their work.

Reflection-for-action invites a disposition that allows educators to adjust the plan at the moment the need presents itself, to justify that adjustment, and to begin to wonder about the implications of their adjustment. Kenneth Zeichner uses the terms technical reflection, practical reflection, and critical reflection to describe the three phases. Technical reflection describes "the best way to get somewhere, when the somewhere is already determined" (Zeichner, 1989, p, 15). Practical reflection requires "deliberation both about the means and about the purposes" (Zeichner, 1989, p. 15). Critical reflection "happens when educators raise issues that have to do with ethical and moral dimensions of their practice that are not explicit with other forms of reflection" (Zeichner, 1989, p. 16).

Schon (1983) presents several techniques for investing teaching practice with reflection. He suggests that critically reflective teaching happens when we identify and scrutinize the assumptions that undergird how we work. It happens when we are able to view our practice from different perspectives. There are four lenses through which practice can be viewed.

- Autobiographical experiences represent a rich source of information.
- Students' eyes tell us how our actions are perceived, whether they are affirming or inhibiting.

- Colleagues and their perspectives are defined as mirrors, mentors, and critical friends.
- Literature from inside and outside of our area of practice helps us locate what we do in alternative theoretical frames.

Seeing how we think and work through different lenses is the core process of reflective practice. What turns this process into critical reflection is a consistent focus on two kinds of assumptions: (1) those that mask the ways in which power affects and often distorts educational interactions, and (2) those that seem congenial but that actually work against our own best interest.

Critical reflection reinforces the theme, "teacher as learner." Reflection is important for teachers because change is inevitable and the ongoing process of reflection and revision is what allows change to occur in a way that reduces chaos and ambiguity.

When we hear teachers make statements like, "Hindsight is 20/20. If I had it to do over again, I would," we know that they are engaging in the reflective process at some level. We known from Schon's research that "professionals learn to reflect in action by first learning to recognize and apply standard practice rules and techniques then to reason from general rules to problematic cases characteristic of professions then develop and test new forms of understanding and action when familiar patterns of doing things fails" (1983, p. 107). The Deweyan philosophy tells us, "adults don't learn from experience, they learn from the processing of experience" (*Education and experience*, 1939), Knowledge of the DATA process developed by J. M. Peters (1991) is a tool that could be used to help teachers reveal discrepancies between espoused theories (what they say they do) and theories in use (what they actually do). The process consists of four steps:

1. Describe: The teacher describes the practice he or she desires to change.
2. Analyze: The teacher analyzes the factors that contribute to the current situation and then reviews the theory associated with the practice.
3. Theorize: The teacher theorizes alternative ways of approaching the development of new theory.
4. Act: The teacher takes action by trying out the new theory.

Other strategies that support the development of reflective practice include coaching and peer involvement, and having teachers use their personal histories, dialogue, journals, and small and large-group discussion about their experiences to help preservice and inservice teacher reflect upon and improve their practices.

Reflective practice is a beneficial process for teachers to engage in to improve professional practice. Reflective practice coupled with critical reflection is a powerful adult learning process. Research on effective teaching shows that effective practice is linked to learning, inquiry, and reflection. Reflective practice can provide teachers with a mechanism to better understand their own individual teaching styles and thereby improve their effectiveness in the classroom.

Strategies like the DATA process developed by Peters (1991) provides a focused structured way for teachers to learn from their experiences, improve themselves, and thus improve schools and education. If Stephen Covey ever considers adding an eighth habit to his "Seven Habits of High Effective People," it would surely have to be "reflective practice."

References

Alexander, P. A., & Murphy, P. K. (1997). The research based for APA's learner-centered psychological principles. In N. L. Lambert, & B. L. McCombs (Eds.), *Issues in school reform: A sample of psychological perspectives on learner centered schools* (pp. 120–134). New York: APA Books.

Brookfield, S. (1995). *Becoming a critically reflective teacher.* San Francisco: Jossey-Bass.

Dewey, J. (1939). *Education and experience.* New York: Collier.

Eraut, M. (1994). *Developing professional knowledge and competence.* Washington, DC: Falmer Press.

Killion, J. P., & Todnem, G. R. (1991). A process for personal theory building. *Educational leadership, 48*(6), 14–16.

Kottkamp, R. B. (1990). Means for facilitating reflection. *Education and Urban Society, 22* (2), 182–203.

Peters, J. (1991). Strategies for reflective practice. In R. Brockett (Ed.), *Professional development for educators of adults. New directions for adult and continuing education:* Vol. 51 (pp. 89–96). San Francisco: Jossey-Bass.

Schon, D. A. (1983). *The reflective practitioner: How professionals think in action.* New York: Basic Books.

Schon, D. A. (1987/1990). *Educating the reflective practitioner.* San Francisco: Jossey-Bass.

Vaill, P. (1996). *Learning as a way of being.* San Francisco: Jossey-Bass.

Zeichner, K. M. (1989). Reflecting on reflection. *Colloquy 2,* 15–21.

Further Reading

Clift, R. (Ed.) (1990). *Encouraging reflective practice in education: an analysis of issues and programs.* New York: Teachers College Press.

Osterman, K. (1993). *Reflective practice for educators.* Newbury Park, CA: Corwin Press.

Values

Values and Dispositions of Critical Thinking: Developing Habits of Mind As Moral Commitments to Thought

Danny Weil

Much of critical thinking asks us to focus our attention on identifying the cognitive nature of learning—how we might foster in others and ourselves the art of self-directed, self-disciplined reasoning as we learn to understand the deeper logic of what others are attempting to solve or decide. Yet critical thinking is more than simply a set of cognitive skills or logical thinking abilities. It is artful reasoning coupled with human values and dispositions of the mind that help us decide what to believe, what to do, and/or how to act with and for ourself and others. These values and dispositions have been referred to as the *affective dimension* of thinking, or helping people develop an *emotional intelligence* that is indispensable for open-minded critical thinking. Before we look at some of these values or habits of mind, it is important to note that these values are learned, not gifted as in an inheritance estate. Furthermore, they are values that go beyond the classroom or workplace and are essential for a lifetime of productive living and the achievement of a more equitable and just society.

It is significant to note that one can learn to be bigoted, biased, arrogant, hypocritical, cowardly, undirected, or irresponsible. This is learning, but obviously not of the variety that critical thinking advocates. Similarly, empathy, courage, faith in one's ability to solve problems, self-authored thinking, responsibility, and perseverance also can be learned. It is important to recognize that one cannot engage in open-minded reasoning if one has no empathy. Human beings cannot solve problems collectively or individually if they do not know how to cooperate civilly. We cannot expect that students come to our classrooms or learning centers with the values and dispositions that will help them reason more effectively and beneficially in the interest of self-reflection and socioeconomic and racial/gender equality. Again, these values of mind are learned, and critically reflective teachers interested in fostering a culture of thinking and learning know that learning opportunities must be created that allow students to understand when they are engaging in egocentric thinking or when, for example, they might be unaccepting of other viewpoints, cultures, racial outlooks, or varied perspectives. We can't simply put our students in collaborative problem-solving groups and *hope* they will cooperate. Many students don't know what cooperation is and why it might be valuable; many of them have existed in the battleground of win-lose situations where individualistic competition works to vitiate the healthy exchange of perspectives and rationalizations. Similarly, we cannot hope that students will be compassionate, open-minded, and civil when engaging in collaborative problem solving or working with others that have backgrounds and perspectives different than their own. Students must be exposed to meaningful cooperative reasoning opportunities that allow them to develop an insight into valuing thinking and the dispositions and habits of minds that accompany it.

VALUES AND DISPOSITIONS OF A REASONING MIND

The following represent the values and dispositions of a reasoning mind or what can be characterized as an emotional intelligence that is necessary to thinking critically.

Self-Authored Thinking: Developing an Investigative Orientation

Self-authored thinking, as opposed to authored and dependent thinking, calls upon us to come to our own conclusions as to what to believe, how to act, and what to decide to believe and do. Developing a passion for independent thinking and problem solving, or figuring things out for yourself, is an essential value for knowledge acquisition, problem solving and decision making, and character development. Independent thinking is essential to avoid manipulation of thought and the management of perceptions by others.

Empathy

Empathy asks us to exercise reciprocity or put ourselves in the shoes of others who might not see the world the way we do. It is particularly difficult in light of our tendency to wed ourselves to our own self-justifying belief systems and perspectives, which we have often gained and accommodated because of habit, custom, and an uncritical lack of self-reflection. Reasoning within diverse points of view, often not in keeping with our own, is essential for higher-order thinking. We discover ourselves through relationships with others, not in rote isolation from the world and others who inhabit it. Both students and teachers should develop the ability to actively, precisely, specifically, and fairly recognize a point of view and articulate it, reason from its assumptions, and encapsulate its conclusions. Often the human tendency is to judge and dismiss the positions and points of view of others without the ability to concretely, precisely, and accurately represent this view first. The opposite of empathy is narrow-mindedness and the tendency to see the world from one's own self-serving point of view—a trait that destroys the ability to think critically for it aggressively prevents the ability to dialogue and develop learning conversations with others.

Humility

Humility asks us to honor the fact that we have not figured everything out—that there is a limit to our knowledge and that we are in the process of intellectual, social, and personal transformation. It is a consciousness of the limits or parameters of one's own knowledge and the recognition that inherent self-vested interests often operate to deceive, delude, or otherwise limit critical thinking. Humility, or not claiming more than one knows, contrasts with intellectual arrogance. Humility asks us to substitute self-righteousness with self-questioning. One cannot figure out what one does not know through questioning, if one believes that he or she already has encapsulated truth.

Courage

Developing the courage to examine our beliefs, in light of what others believe, is often a difficult process for all of us. The courage to confront one's own irrational thinking becomes paramount and requires fortitude and strength. Similarly, having the courage to give a fair hearing to the assumptions, conclusions, claims, and beliefs of others is of paramount importance in assessing our own thinking. As we develop the courage to confront ideas fair-mindedly and squarely based on critical thinking, we may come to find that we adopt thinking that deviates drastically from the norm. The courage to stand by one's convictions and thinking, with the knowledge and understanding that "we have not figured it all out," is often deemed nonconformist and subversive.

Yet, without this courage, it is impossible to develop self-authored thinking. As much as independent thinking requires courage, dependent thinking requires a sense of cowardice.

Integrity

Holding ourselves up to the same standards that we hold others up to is reminiscent of the Golden Rule. Yet for most individuals it is difficult, if not impossible, to judge the thinking of others as they would their own and to honestly admit when they are reasoning irrationally or sophistically. Maintaining a healthy sense of honesty and integrity is essential for good dialogue and good thinking. Contrasted to integrity in thinking is hypocrisy in thinking, a trait that allows us to judge others and their thinking differently than we would ourselves for the sake of our own self-interests.

Perseverance and Discipline

To persevere in any pursuit requires the discipline and diligence to pursue one's goals despite the obstacles one might confront or the frustrations one might encounter. It is a commitment to forging ahead despite seeming confusion, ambiguity, or downright appearances of impossibility. The persevering mind understands that there are no quick fixes to complicated problems and seeks to accomplish goals and objectives despite the odds. In a rapidly changing global society, the ability to persevere will become—and is a necessity for all—good judgment. Taken from the famous legend of the tortoise and the hare, we must learn to develop turtle thinking in a hare's world.

Curiosity

Creative critical thought requires a curious mind that seeks questions and answers to complex problems. Armed with curiosity, human beings can begin to go beyond what is expected of them and look for new and innovative ways to extend their feedback and inquiry into all areas of learning. This quickly translates into curiosity about better ways to relate to oneself and others, better ways to solve problems, and better ways to work and dialogue with others, because the curious mind looks for novel answers to difficult questions as well as novel questions to discover difficult answers.

Civility

Reasonable minds may disagree, but it is the form of disagreement that remains salient. Learning how to agree to disagree in face of lack of consensus is paramount. It is not enough to ask students to work in collaboration if they do not have the ability to act and behave civilly toward those whom hold ideas with which they disagree. Helping students gain an insight into how we as human beings behave civilly in light of controversy is essential if we are to learn to cooperate in a learning environment and develop the learning conversations necessary to probe critical reflection and critical thinking.

Imagination

Developing the ability to imagine how things might be or what questions and answers might exist is an essential component of good thinking. Having the courage to dream and imagine carries with it both the cognitive benefit of developing an insight into further exploration, as well as the emotional intelligence to cultivate hope and possibility in face of dystopia and despair. Helping students develop an insight into imaginative thinking equips them with the understanding that there are many solutions to problems and many possibilities for rational learning and living.

Responsibility

Responsibility asks us to take command of our own learning, problem solving, and decision making. It asks that we understand that commitment and enthusiasm are important components of all successful thinking and learning. Too often students believe that teachers have the responsibility to solve their problems as opposed to understanding that it is their responsibility. Fostering a classroom for the mind by building curriculum and instructional methods based on critical thinking can serve to help students gain an insight into the role of responsibility and how this transfers into work plans, roles, and responsibilities for collaborative problem solving and discovery. This, in turn, teaches how we can delegate opportunities to begin to develop self-motivating approaches to advancing our own thinking.

Developing an Insight into the Nature of Ego and Sociocentric Thinking

Egocentricity is a natural tendency in both adults and children. It is confusing reality with what one thinks is owed to a belief in the inherent superiority of one's point of view, beliefs, and conclusions. The egocentric mind sees reality one way and any discourse aimed at questioning this picture of reality is seen as a threat or an obtrusive excursion into one's self. We are all too familiar with the egocentric person who is always right even when confronted with the best evidence against what they believe. As egocentricity advances much as a disease would, it often evolves into sociocentricity, or the inherent belief in the superiority of one's culture, society, and/or way of perceiving and living life. We see the egocentric mind go from "I am right and you are wrong" to "We are right, our group is right, our country is right, etc." Because egocentricity and sociocentricity are blocks to empathic reasoning and open-minded thinking, we must help learners recognize when they might be reasoning in this manner.

Developing a Tolerance for Ambiguity

Ambiguity is a state of affairs that connotes unclarity. Developing a tolerance for ambiguity or situations that are not clear, that do not have black and white answers, is essential in a world that is increasingly subject to rapid global changes and cataclysmic shifts in thought. Becoming comfortable with unresolved situations, with uncertainty, and with unfamiliar situations and complex questions of values is an essential attitude for critical thinking. Many people have developed rigid ways of looking at the world and, when faced with uncertainty and unclarity, they often become immobilized as they attempt to search through the past for answers to the future. Confronting ambiguous relationships and situations with a sense of confidence and critical thinking is paramount if we are to sort through tremendous change and complex fluctuations of global reality.

Achieving Self-Esteem through Faith and Confidence in the Ability to Develop Critical Reasoning

Helping people develop a confidence in the fact that human reason will advance both personal and social interests rests its premise on the notion of competence. Students must come to understand that developing a faith in their ability to effectively problem solve and critically think about their own lives, the problems and decisions they confront, as well as the lives and perspectives of others, will greatly increase their sense of confidence and self-worth as they feel more comfortable with grasping the process of thinking. This is paramount for lifelong learning and effective problem solving. There is no substitute for belief in one's self, in the effectiveness of one's mind, and in the ability to govern one's life as opposed to having one's life governed, to manage ones' existence as opposed to having it managed, to lead as opposed to having to be lead, and to dream as opposed to having to rely on the imagineering of others. Self-esteem is based on competence and developing confidence in thinking translates into developing self-esteem in one's life, a healthy acknowledgment of self worth.

When keeping in mind the need to create valuable educational opportunities whereby students can learn what it means to value thinking and innovative problem-solving techniques, we as critical thinking facilitators cannot help but take note that many of the values of the reasoning mind that I will explicate are not rewarded values in society. Popular culture, friends, media, the consumer society, and other cultural diversions operate to increase individualistic frames of looking at the world and operate to heighten uncritical acceptance of racism, sexism, and homophobia and, thus, vitiate much of the affective dimension needed to reason within the points of views of others. For this reason, educators must become living models for students, advocating and modeling the thinking they are encouraging. We must, in the words of Mahatma Ghandi, "become the change we seek." For if we, as teachers and human beings, are not empathic and do not listen to the voices of our students and others, if we do not have the confidence in our students' ability to reason and solve problems, if we do not think out loud in front of our students and model self-authored thinking and a commitment to understanding the parameters of our own thinking, if we do not engage our daily life in the classroom in ways that promote and encourage civility and respect for diverse points of view, if we do not put a premium on humility in thinking and seek to substitute self-righteousness with self-questioning and to be aware of (and admit to) when we might be reasoning egocentrically or sociocentrically, then why should students?

Critical thinking has often falsely been accused of separating cognition from emotion. This conception of critical thinking removes our emotional selves from our rational lives and creates false bifurcations that obscure and prevent critical thinking. Understanding that critical thinking involves the development of a moral commitment to an emotional intelligence can only serve to advance the course of critical thinking and enhance the way teachers and students think about what it means to think critically in a world shared with others.

Further Reading

Ellinor, L., & Gerard, G. (1998). *Dialogue: Rediscover the transforming power of conversation.* New York: John Wiley and Sons.

Freire, A. M., & Macedo, D. (Eds.). (1998). *The Paulo Freire reader.* New York: Continuum.

Paul, R. (1992). *Critical thinking.* Sonoma County, CA: The Center for Critical Thinking and Moral Critique.

Work

Critical Thinking, Power, and the Workplace

Vicki K. Carter

We talk about work every day, but rarely do we analyze exactly what that means. We say we are overworked or working hard. We may discuss working in our gardens or on our relationships. Much of our education is focused on preparing us for the workforce. Once we have become a part of the workforce, ongoing education typically involves maintaining or enhancing skills and knowledge for purposes of obtaining, keeping, or getting a better job. However, although we are surrounded by different aspects of work, we seldom think deeply and critically about what work is and what it means to work.

I suggest that a critical analysis about work means that workers consciously think beyond the series of tasks and assignments they perform at work. To think critically about work is to look at work from various perspectives and to ask why work is constructed the way it is. We might decide to consider, for example, why certain policies exist, or why an organization chooses to offer certain training courses. In meetings, we may listen carefully to whose ideas are valued and whose are not.

When a new memo is issued, we can use what we know about thinking critically to analyze what purposes management had in mind when they encourage certain practices and behaviors and discourage others. We can listen carefully to conversations, examine the language of policies, and look at the components of a training program to determine how our actions, and our thoughts, can be imperceptibly controlled and shaped. As we learn to analyze our contexts in this way, we enter a more sophisticated and complex dimension of thinking about work and the workplace. We can think about the experience of work from different vantage points and understand how those in power construct work. Then, after learning to think critically about work, we are able to act intelligently within that construction.

For whom do we really work? Who really benefits from our work? And, what is the purpose of our work? To think critically about work is to see these questions as complex and difficult, and to answer them in a way that goes beyond stating we work to make money or to improve our lives and surroundings. In short, to think critically about work is to become a smart worker who understands the connection between the context of one's own work and how this context affects circumstances surrounding all the workers of the world.

More often than not, we define work in economic terms. We think about work in terms of being paid, while unpaid work is invisible to us. Recognizing that there is such a thing as unpaid work is an example of what an act of critical thinking really means. Paid work is regarded as an economic transaction, while unpaid work that supports the market economy goes unrecognized. The very existence of unpaid work is an example of a nearly invisible force that affects the lives of people everywhere. Therefore, we will take this first critical observation—our notion that there are paid and unpaid forms of work—and continue the process of looking at work from these two angles to explore how work is defined and constructed by society.

Paid work primarily involves the practices of organizations. Modern corporations are the dominant institutional form, an effective system of control affecting everything from what is distributed and consumed to personal identities and values. Yet, sheltered from public control, corporations often operate outside democratic and ethical principles. Business and industry function in ways that appear neutral and empowering but are often, in reality, disciplinary. Overtly or subtly, modern organizations of all varieties define and constrain feelings, thoughts, sense making, perceptions, and actions. Organizations structure time, influence education, train, lobby governments, and have leverage with the media.

At the time this encyclopedia was being written, the biggest corporate scandal in recent history was unfolding. Enron, an international energy conglomerate, collapsed among charges of fraud, environmental and human rights abuses, and the loss of billions of taxpayer dollars. Corporate executives escaped unscathed, while employees lost life savings because they were prevented from selling Enron stock that made up the bulk of their pension plans. Before the Enron debacle, however, its employees, like most other corporate workers, undoubtedly experienced an organizational culture that talked about empowerment, quality, shared decision making, continuous improvement, and teams. According to news reports, Enron workers believed they were part of "something special." Encapsulated in the Enron episode are paradoxes that help lead us to think critically about paid work. For example, we might question expectations of loyalty and commitment to job, employer, and institution. In light of what happened to Enron employees, are these expectations not lip service? Are high-level corporate leaders exempt from loyalty and commitment to employees, while employees are expected to believe benevolent rhetoric about leadership, trust, teams, commitment, quality, and empowerment?

The situation with Enron, and the actions of its executives, makes it imperative for workers to carefully untangle whose interests are being secured via corporate rhetoric and management strategies. A critical inquiry into most workers' lives reveals how work is shaped by organizational culture, organizational priorities, and the notion that corporations and organizations own the minds, bodies, and hearts of workers. These expectations of workers are all the more powerful in their formlessness because the employees immersed in typical work environments easily internalize unexamined values and goals. These corporate "entitlements," however, can be barely discernable without learning to have at least a healthy skepticism (i.e., to think critically) about work.

Organizations tend to see people as a form of capital—possessions that have skills and economic value. People have become human resources or commodities that, when combined with other forms of capital, produce increased wealth for owners and shareholders (remember the critical question "who benefits from my work?"). Furthermore, business operates beyond most humans' power to affect it, increasingly controlling what workers think and do. One of the characteristics of today's work environments is that institutions no longer want workers, or the public, to feel employees are forced to comply; instead, they cultivate workers who *want* to obey. Managers are trained to restructure work to achieve the goal of having a workforce that is happy to serve.

If we take another step and think critically about language, the words and phrases used at work, what emerges? Institutional jargon is compelling and carefully coded by organizations to create specific meanings. Language, terminology, and concepts deployed in the workplace often appear to be logical and harmless, but particular beliefs about, and expectations of, workers are inherent in them. For instance, perfection becomes a standard; change is the normal way of life. Empowerment, trust, collaboration, teams, self-directed learning, and quality are all used to mold workers into desirable forms. While purporting to place trust in workers and give them real control, in fact, institutions rarely allow workers to change corporate goals or create more power for themselves. Just imagine the difference if workers *were* empowered to make decisions about downsizing, or moving the company to a location where there was

cheaper labor. Too few of us spend time honing the kind of literacy skills that adequately pull apart this kind of language manipulation. If we were to examine corporate jargon, critically thinking workers may actually reveal oppositional definitions of management terms, such as "cultivating appropriate work habits," "improving human efficiency," "staff empowerment," "upgrading morale," and "conflict resolution," and expose layers of meanings that respond to the question "for what purpose do I work?"

Taking a concrete example for illustrative purposes, how might we go about thinking critically about Total Quality Management (TQM), one of many strategies employed in today's workplaces? Imagine you are working for an organization that produces pacemakers, and you are about to be educated about the TQM process. Recall our three critical questions: For whom are we learning about TQM? Who benefits from it? And, what is its purpose? Now consider the following ideas as one process that critically examines alternative ideological dimensions of this management strategy.

First, anything that is described as "total" erases perspectives that are less powerful or speak with less authority and legitimacy. In a totalized environment, people are simply elements of the production process. Second, the idea of quality focuses specifically on processes, services, and products; it is unconcerned about qualities of democracy, humanity, or the outcomes of TQM methodology on the quality of *workers'* lives (e.g., effects such as less job security, higher stress levels, dehumanizing standardization practices, work speed-ups, self- and group-surveillance, the health and well-being of workers in developing countries, or the ecological balance of the planet). TQM targets processes, expecting workers to attend to those processes, uncover defects, and monitor their own and their fellow workers' performance. If this sounds esoteric, imagine Lucy and Ethel, scrutinized by their boss, trying to box chocolates as the conveyor belt goes faster and faster. Now, picture these two women attending a team meeting at which they are to propose ways to continuously improve the chocolate-boxing process.

TQM is supposed to provide continuous quality improvement, but the question of quality and improvement for whom and for what purpose is seldom interrogated. Neither are questions of scale where disparate items such as muffins, baggage, prescriptions, pacemakers, and even deaths can be equated. TQM is attractive to business as it affords the appearance of "niceness," of ceding control to employees, and of fostering a democratic environment. But, in fact, if interrogated critically, TQM can be seen from alternate vantage points—no longer as a benign, straightforward, neutral, or simple technique to improve products and services—because, through TQM, management gains added control. Continuous quality emerges as a strategy full of elements of power, affecting the everyday experience of millions of workers who cannot effectively resist it, particularly in the face of outsourcing, reengineering, and downsizing.

Carrying critical thinking even further, workplace devices such as TQM do not remain confined to business practices. The meanings constructed at work permeate other aspects of life as well. Families hear real descriptions of work around the dinner table. What do children (i.e., future workers) learn to expect from their jobs when parents come home and describe their day? If parents are role models who influence children's beliefs and values, what messages seep into family members' consciousness? What do children internalize from the descriptions of work brought home by parents? What may be absorbed depends on whether workers are apathetic or cynical, or cultivate that healthy skepticism about work.

Thoughts of home and family lead us to the second kind of work we identified—unpaid work. Standard measures of economic activity do not include allowances for production from unpaid labor. This labor is in the form of childcare, elder care, or youth's work around the farm. Given these configurations of work, we may also ask critical questions such as the following: Who cares for our children and our elders? What is a productive citizen? How do we build community? How do we sustain and enhance the safety and beauty of our neighborhoods? How does work contribute to a democratic society? These kinds questions suggest forms of work that are not market oriented but that allow the market economy to function, because the economy depends on unpaid underappreciated work. Similar to job classifications that refer to farming as *unskilled* labor, we tend to talk about this kind of work in a way that cheapens it and fails to recognize its importance. Therefore, our critical thought has uncovered a highly important yet unacknowledged form of work.

In the same way we analyzed TQM, let us think about the concept of "motherwork" as one of the ingredients in the many formulas for unpaid work. Motherwork is all of the crucial but unnoticed responsibilities that mother's accept, and these responsibilities are exploited by a market-oriented economy. The economy depends on the unpaid labor of mothers to reproduce to replenish the labor force. Mothers' caring for home and children does not show up in the adjusted gross income column of an annual tax return. The work of mothers and other unpaid community and civic workers is not, for instance, calculated in the Gross National Product. Women, particularly single mothers, increasingly occupy the lowest spots on the poverty scale. Unpaid work is labeled family work, exists in the private sphere of life, and is seen as gendered. This definitional process then positions women in the private sphere, reserving the public sphere for men. In other words, through the concept of motherwork, we ultimately sustain a sexist system of values that describes family issues as problems for women. By thinking critically, however, we can learn a lot about how unpaid work operates as well as determine for whom and against whom it operates.

As we have seen, work's hidden agenda favors corporate interests and objectives. Workers, both paid and unpaid, are caught between work that, on one hand, purports to value fundamental freedoms but, in reality, consists of suppression, constraint, and invisibility. For paid workers, participatory initiatives such as empowerment, teams, and distributed decision making are powerful weapons in the hands of management, but they may also create a kind of paradox for workers who understand how commitment to so-called core values is, in reality, an economic strategy for the benefit of business. Equally paradoxical is the economy's dependence on, yet total neglect of, the recognition of the implications of unpaid work. What would happen economically if there were no motherwork or other kinds of labor that augment and develop our lives? How much does the elderly population contribute to our churches, hospitals, and charities and as aides to family, friends, and neighbors? Critical thinking about work questions the assumption that everyone who works for pay is productive and those who do not are a burden. Critical thinking reveals that unpaid activities are not part of the economic equation for measuring contributions to society.

A closer link between paid and unpaid work, long established as central to understanding gender issues and equitable policy development, helps us to identify opportunities for critical thinking that can be turned in favor of all workers. For example, workers who think deeply about their jobs may be able to redefine corporate jargon to create worker-centered definitions of quality, empowerment, commitment, participation, trust, collaboration, and teams. Strategies for critical thinking about work privilege all forms of labor and value unpaid work at least as much as the kind that produces commodities. Recognizing unpaid work done by women in our society is an emancipatory act that, in turn, would spawn new policies and tactics to support people in paid, as well as unpaid, roles. Critical thinking and learning change our ideas about what productivity really means by moving beyond the current, generally accepted market-oriented definition.

Fundamentally, worker critique of the bottom line—the maximization of profit and valuing of acquisitive materialism—is lacking. Although economic endeavors are central and integral to society, we often forget that the very nature of those endeavors can be questioned. To be socially aware and to become responsible citizens, we must see beyond goals of maximizing profit and think critically about the values and social policies of our organizations and our very definitions of work. Critical thinking and learning at work shifts our concerns from the organizationally defined tasks and goals of one individual to how individual workers connect to one another across society.

The following kinds of critical questions would help us to examine both the paid and unpaid work all of us perform: Is corporate economic activity ecologically sound? Is gender discrimination in the workplace addressed? Is the corporation socially responsible? Do workers share benefits from their labor? Is free female labor acknowledged as work? Do corporations produce products or services we can believe in? Is a materialistic society suited to human needs? What is the connection among the interests of economic experts, their political counterparts, and the business elite (especially regarding productivity, quality, and certification)? Are business and industry helping to create a sustainable society? And, finally, does our society fulfill its needs without diminishing the prospects of future generations? Critical thinking, as illustrated via the critical questioning above, offers us, as workers, an orientation and an opportunity to create new futures and to transform society.

Further Reading

Hart, M. (1995). Motherwork: A radical proposal to rethink work and education. In M. Welton (Ed.), *In defense of the lifeworld: Critical perspectives on adult learning.* New York: State University of New York Press.

Hayden, A. (1999). *Sharing the work, sparing the planet: Work time, consumption and ecology.* London: Zed Books.

Kincheloe, J. L. (1999). *Who will tell the workers? The socioeconomic foundations of work and vocational education.* Boulder, CO: Westview Press.

Xenophobia

Fear and the Construction of the "Foreigner"

Stephen M. Fain and Mary Anne Ullery

Xenophobia, the fear of *foreigners* or *strangers,* describes a disposition grounded in a perceived threat for which there is no basis in fact. When we fear the *stranger* simply because she is different from us, we are victims of xenophobia. Every culture has a way in which it deals with *strangers* in its homeland. Some cultures set up special political programs to deal with them; some employ violence. For thousands of years, societies have addressed the question of how to deal with *others;* in some cases, societies were wiped out completely by outsiders, while other societies cast the *strangers* out. Today, virtually every country in the world must confront the issue of the outsider. The critical educator especially must confront xenophobia in the classroom and encourage students to think critically about the implications of active xenophobic sentiments in the United States as well as globally. Educators must share with students examples of xenophobia and allow students to consider these sentiments from various historical perspectives as well as encourage students to look introspectively

at their own xenophobic tendencies. This may be a daunting task for teachers, but students, for example, could read articles written by the Ku Klux Klan or Morris Dees as a way of noting this phenomenon in contemporary America.

How can teachers present such material in the wake of incidents such as school violence and domestic terrorism rooted in xenophobia or prejudice? Clearly, educators need to have a keen grasp of the historical context to think critically about xenophobia. Teachers must also take care to ensure that the information presented encourages open and thorough discussion of such sensitive issues.

Although there is a close relationship between racism and xenophobia it is important that the difference between the two be understood. Whereas racism tends to reflect prejudice and bigotry directed at specific groups of people who can be distinguished by physical characteristics, such as color, xenophobia tends to reflect a fear of the individual or group based on nationality or ethnicity. Whereas racism tends to be focused on social, economic, and political oppression, xenophobia tends to be focused on the elimination or expulsion of the *stranger* (the foreigner). Xenophobic sentiments are most often exhibited in societies with strong national identities. Students may consider their feelings regarding Arabs and Muslims in the wake of September 11. Teachers may ask students whether they see evidence of xenophobia in the thinking of the terrorists or in themselves.

Scholars and social scientists distinguish between xenophobia and racism. One might ask why this distinction is significant. If this distinction is important, and we are looking at the issue of xenophobia critically, we might also wonder why, on the popular level and on political fronts, discussions about race prejudice are so much more prevalent than are conversations about xenophobia? Teachers may ask students to consider the possibility that, simply because of fear, they may feel that their negative feelings about the people they fear are well grounded. Once students understand their own vulnerability to xenophobia, they may begin to experience the transformation that often comes with realization.

XENOPHOBIA AS PUBLIC POLICY

Examples of xenophobia are often found in public policy that reflects the fears of the general society. It would appear that, although these policies seem to originate with political leaders, it is more reasonable to assume that political figures often use the xenophobic disposition of those they lead, or wish to lead, as a rallying point or political focus. In other words, leaders of xenophobic movements are more likely to represent the disposition of their constituents then to be the source

of the xenophobia. What societal issues might breed xenophobic sentiments? What are some of the underlying reasons why xenophobic sentiments manifest themselves in some societies more than others? Allowing students to critically think about xenophobia will open the doors for dialogue in the classroom. Teachers can ask if anyone knows of a political figure who uses xenophobia to garner support from their constituents.

Some general strategies that xenophobic societies employ that may be explored further in the critical classroom include categorization, national identity preservation (nativism), and genocide.

CATEGORIZATION

Phenotypic differences have historically been the easiest way to distinguish between the *in group* and the *others*. In the 1800s and early 1900s, investigations in racial categorization resulted in the generation of xenophobic sentiments in both Europe and in the United States. Joseph Artur Comet de Gobineau began his study of humanity by dividing the people into two categories: white and colored. He broadened his conception in 1853 by classifying Jews as a subcategory of the white race. From scientific studies of race and intelligence, came the idea that members of the white European race were more intelligent as well as morally superior to those of any other race. This scientific quest to prove this true involved studies in Craniology (a corrupt and ridiculous effort appreciated as *scientism* rather than science). This work was closely followed by Alfred Binet's IQ test and the work of Henry Herbert Goddard, Robert M. Yerkes, Lewis M. Terman, and Sir Cyril Burt who sought scientific evidence to determine an individual's worth. Building on the work of these men of influence and during a huge wave of immigration into the United States, the Immigration Restriction Act of 1924 was passed. This Act legitimized the xenophobic concern that feebleminded immigrants would bring down the nation. The result was the exclusion of thousands of Eastern Europeans who were seen as swarthy, slow to learn English, and lacking in basic Anglo-Teutonic values.

Through the establishment of quotas in the 1920s, a total of 154,000 individuals were to be admitted to the United States. Almost 84,000 of these quota slots were filled with immigrants who were British and Irish. In fact, 82% of the quota was set aside for Northern and Western Europeans.

Through the systematic classification of immigrants, and others who look different, societies justify and legitimize their xenophobic policies and actions. Such was the case in the United States with the Chinese Exclusion Act of 1882, the treatment of Jews and Gypsies in Europe during World War II, and apartheid in South Africa. At the onset of the twenty-first century, the United States still classifies Cubans (generally considered white) as refugees and grants them entry, while classifying Haitians and Mexicans (generally considered people of color) as illegal residents who must be repatriated.

These are but a few examples of classifications systems that reflect and foster the xenophobic dispositions of societies. Critical educators can encourage students to investigate the societal forces that encourage these classification systems and encourage critical thinking among students about classification systems. Once students have focused on these examples

of classification systems, it would be effective to discuss the implications growing from the classification of persons or groups as vital in maintaining the resulting xenophobic policy. Today, public policies often require that we classify individuals according to criteria such as race, gender, national identity, and/or disability. Critical educators could discuss these classifications and examine the potential in this practice for engendering xenophobia.

NATIONAL IDENTITY PRESERVATION (NATIVISM)

Nationalist doctrine is based on the premise that the world is broken into different nations, thus declaring who is a *national* and who is a *foreigner*. Those who fear the foreigner and find security within the boarders of their nation often find it easy to see the world in terms of *us* and *them*. National identity results from two considerations: one is the perception of *belonging* to a national group with all of its cultural and ideological values, and the *other* is the is phenomena of *exclusion* that justifies the perception of the outsider as *other*. Fundamentalist national identity provides an easy breeding ground for xenophobic sentiments and often manifests itself in public policy regarding immigration.

The prevailing centers of national identity tend to be grounded in far-right ideology articulated by groups such as the Ku Klux Klan, National Socialist (NAZI) parties, and skinheads, as well as organizations such as the Edmund Burke Society in Canada or the John Birch Society in the United States. These groups are commonly anti-Semitic, antiblack, anticommunist, anti-immigration, anti–foreign aid, anti–world government, antihomosexual, antifeminist, and antiabortion. They tend to support nuclear arms and violence and most believe that there is a worldwide Jewish conspiracy. In the aftermath of the events of September 11, many also now believe in a worldwide Islamic conspiracy.

Nationalists and xenophobic sentiments run high in multi-ethnic countries such as Greece, Italy, and Spain. Building on chauvinistic ideologies of identity, political opportunists make effective use of *ethnicity* as a tool for rallying groups of people. In the case of minorities, the call is for the establishment of a state of their own and, in the case of the majority, the call is for hegemony. This is evident in the break up of Yugoslavia that began with the Croatians seeking independence in 1991 and Serbia resisting the secession. Slovenia and Croatia declared independence one year later. The rivalries between Croats, Serbs, and Muslims dates back centuries and the ensuing wars stand as evidence of the potential force of nativist movements that generally combine nationalism and xenophobia.

The critical educator can ask students to interview members of their community regarding issues of immigration to determine whether they can identify a xenophobic potential within their own community. Interviews could focus on the events of September 11 and the suggested policies to control the entry of foreign students into United States colleges. Researching the historical xenophobic predisposition of the examples above can also give students an opportunity to ask questions and formulate their understanding of xenophobia. Providing opportunities for students to think critically about the historical foundations of xenophobia is crucial for further exploration of their own biases and can open the doors for personal change.

POLITICAL/ECONOMIC JUSTIFICATION

In many cases, the fear of *strangers* is based on the feeling that the *others* are usurping political power or economic opportunity. In a democracy this can easily happen as the number of *strangers* among *us* increases in proportion to the general population, thus gaining strength in numbers at the ballot box. Feeling threatened by this potential shift in power, laws and policies are sometimes enacted to limit or reduce the power potential of the stranger. In cases where the *stranger* among us is willing to work for the lowest wages, we find our livelihood threatened and we feel resentment toward and fear of the *foreigner.* If we allow these individuals to cluster in voting districts, *they* may become a powerful political force against *us.* These conditions are sometimes used by individuals and societies to justify oppressive policies directed at the *outsider.* Teachers could present the examples below and then challenge students to find other examples.

Beginning with an economic boom in the 1960s, a steady stream of migrants from Southern Europe, North African, Asia, and the Caribbean came to Northern Europe in search of work. Most of the guest workers were people of color. As the boom began to turn toward recession, xenophobic reactions became evident. In 1992, Sweden, a country that had not only provided asylum for draft evaders from other countries, welcomed in more than 84,000 foreigners (80% were from Yugoslavia). Three years later a Parliamentary committee recommended that Sweden restrict immigration and no longer accept draft evaders. Finally, the committee recommended that state support for refugees cease after two years. Similar events have occurred across Europe and all of them are justified on political and economic grounds.

GENOCIDE

The United Nations Convention on Genocide defines genocide as acts committed with the intent to destroy, in whole or in part, a national, ethnic, racial, or religious group. History is filled with examples of acts conceived with the intent to destroy specific groups of people who were different. It should be clear that this type of extreme action is often motivated by fear. Some of the more obvious examples of genocide include the Ottoman Empire's genocide against the Armenians (1915–1923), which took the lives of 1.5 million; the Holocaust (1939–1945) in which about six million Jews were killed (another six million were also put to death); the Rwanda genocide (1994); and the war in Bosnia (1995). In each of these examples those in power took actions intended to completely eliminate specific groups of people they feared. Analysis of these atrocities reveals that the leaders could not have launched any of these events without popular support and it is clear that the support comes from the fear the general public has of the target group.

Teachers may find it helpful to make students aware of the fact that in all cases of genocide the dominant group expends a great deal of energy justifying the elimination of the target group. Common themes include a belief in racial purity and a concern for the potential contamination of the race by the target group. Students will have little difficulty finding evidence of this by researching media archives now easily accessible via the Internet. Teachers can invite students to seek out evidence of the propaganda usually disseminated among the people to justify actions intended to cleanse the population.

CRITICALLY TEACHING TO REDUCE XENOPHOBIA

Persons of good will, especially the critical educator, will instinctively move to teach to reduce xenophobia. Because fear of the unknown is quite natural, it is not surprising that the potential for xenophobia is within all of us. Teachers would do well to begin to combat tendencies toward xenophobia by engaging their students in critical thinking activities around xenophobia and prejudice reduction. Teachers can facilitate the shaping of the belief system of students by providing opportunities for them to think critically about sensitive topics such as xenophobia. Understanding the many faces of xenophobia from different angles can provide students with the opportunity to reflect on their own assumptions regarding the *other*. Utilizing such resources as Facing History and Ourselves National Foundation, Inc. and the Anti-Defamation League (see addresses below), teachers can secure classroom materials and information that will provide their students with an effective focus on different aspects of xenophobia. Many groups promoting xenophobia (especially those in the United States) have become quite computer savvy and their Web sites are available for critical analysis (Dees & Corcoran, 1996). Finally, teachers might want to consider allowing their students to create a mock television news and commentary show. In this format, the students can share research and raise appropriate questions for classmates, and perhaps schoolmates, to discuss. To this end, a few resources are recommended below.

Further Reading

Dees, M., & Corcoran, J. (1996). *Gathering storm: America's militia threat.* New York: Harper Perennials.

Smelser, N., Wilson, W., & Mitchell, F. (Eds.). (2001). *America becoming: Racial trends and their consequences* (Vols. 1–2). Washington, DC: National Academy Press.

Triandafyllidou, A. (2001). *Immigrants and national identify in Europe.* New York: Routledge.

Support Services

Facing History and Ourselves National Foundation, Inc.
16 Hurd Road Brookline, MA 02146-6919
(617) 232-1595
(617) 232-0281 (fax)
http://www.facing.org

Anti-Defamation League (ADL)
A World of Difference Institute
823 United Nations Plaza
New York, NY 10017
(212) 885-7800
(212) 490-0187 (fax)
http://www.adl.org

Bibliography

Adorno, T. W. (1998). *Critical models: Interventions and catchwords*. New York: Columbia University Press.

Anderson, L. W., & Krathwohl, D. R. (2000). *A taxonomy for learning, teaching, and assessing: A revision of Bloom's taxonomy of educational objectives*. Boston: Longman Press.

Apple, M. (1990). *Ideology and curriculum*. New York: Routledge.

Apple, M. (2001). *Educating the 'right way': Markets, standards, god, and inequality*. New York: Routledge Falmer.

Appleman, D. (2000). *Critical encounters in high school English: Teaching literary theory to adolescents*. New York: Teachers College Press.

Arnheim, R. (1974). *Art and visual perception*. Berkeley: University of California Press.

Atwell, N. (1998). *In the middle*. Portsmouth, NH: Heinemann.

Baldwin, J. (1988). A talk to teachers. In R. Simonson, & S. Walker (Eds.), *The Graywolf annual five: Multi-cultural literacy*. St. Paul, MN: Graywolf Press.

Bandura, A. (Ed.). (1995). *Self-efficacy in changing societies*. Cambridge: Cambridge University Press.

Banks, J. A., & Banks, C. A. M. (1999). *Multicultural education issues and perspectives* (4th ed.). New York: John Wiley & Sons.

Barell, J. (1995). *Teaching for thoughtfulness: Classroom strategies to enhance intellectual development* (2nd ed.). White Plains, NY: Longman.

Barrett, T. (2000). *Criticizing art: Understanding the contemporary* (2nd ed.). Mountain View, CA: Mayfield.

Bell, I. (1991). *This book is not required. Wisdom and knowledge*. Fort Bragg, CA: The Small Press.

Benne, K. D. (1990). *The task of post-contemporary education: Essays in behalf of a human future*. New York: Teachers College Press.

Bernasconi, R., & Lott, T. (Eds.). (2000). *The idea of race*. Indianapolis, IN: Hackett Publishing.

Best, S., & Kellner, D. (1999). Rap, black rage, and racial difference. *Enculturation, 2*(2), 1–20.

Beyer, L., & Apple, M. W. (Eds.). (1998). *The curriculum: Problems, politics, and possibilities*. Albany: State University of New York Press.

Bingham, C. (2001). *Schools of recognition*. New York: Rowman & Littlefield.

Bloom, B. S. (Ed.). (1956). *Taxonomy of educational objectives. Handbook one: Cognitive domain*. New York: David McCay.

Bolotin, J., Luster-Bravmann, S., Windschitl, M. A., Mikel, E. R., & Stewart-Green, N.

(2000). *Cultures of curriculum*. Mahwah, NJ: Lawrence Erlbaum.

Bransford, J., Brown, A. L., & Cocking, R. (Eds.). (2000). *How people learn: Brain, mind, experience and school* (Expanded ed.). Washington, DC: National Academy Press.

Brookfield, S. (1987). *Developing critical thinkers: Challenging adults to explore alternative ways of thinking and acting*. San Francisco: Jossey-Bass.

Brookfield, S. (1995). *Becoming a critically reflective teacher*. San Francisco: Jossey-Bass.

Brooks, K. (1995). *Cultural diversity without prejudice: A guide for critical thinking in the 21st century*. Vallejo, CA: Amper Publishing.

Brown, S. I. (2001). *Reconstructing school mathematics: Problems with problems and the real world*. New York: Peter Lang.

Bruner, J. (1995). *The Culture of education*. Cambridge, MA: Harvard University Press.

Bunch, C., & Pollack, S. (Eds.). (1983). *Learning our way: Essays in feminist education*. Trumansburg, NY: The Crossing Press.

Burman, E. (1995). *Deconstructing developmental psychology*. New York: Routledge.

Calkins, L. (1993). *The art of teaching writing*. Portsmouth, NH: Heinemann.

Campbell, J. (1995). *Understanding John Dewey: Nature and cooperative intelligence*. Chicago: Open Court.

Cannella, G. S. (1997). *Deconstructing early childhood education*. New York: Peter Lang.

Cannella, G., & Kincheloe, J. L. (Eds.). (2002). *Kidworld: Childhood studies, global perspectives, and education*. New York: Peter Lang.

Cantu, D. A. (2002). *Take five minutes: American history class openers: Reflective and critical thinking activities*. Westminster, CA: Teacher Created Materials.

Cary, R. (1998). *Critical art pedagogy: Foundations for postmodern art education*. New York: Garland.

Chuck, D., & Jah, Y. (1998). *Fight the power: Rap, race, and reality*. New York: Dell.

Clift, R. (Ed.). (1990). *Encouraging reflective practice in education: An analysis of issues and programs*. New York: Teachers College Press.

Cuban, L. (1993). The lure of curricular reform and its pitiful history. *Phi Delta Kappan 75*, 182–185.

Cullinan, C. (2000). *Institute for diversity trainers Resource manual*. The 13th Annual National Conference on Race and Ethnicity in Higher Education. Santa Fe, NM.

Dahlberg, G., Moss, P., & Pence, A. (1999). *Beyond quality in early childhood education and care: Postmodern perspectives*. London: Falmer Press.

Darder, A., Torres, R., & Gutierrez, H. (Eds.). (1997). *Latinos and education: A critical reader*. New York: Routledge.

Davis, B., Sumara, D., & Luce-Kapler, R. (2000). *Engaging minds*. Mahwah, NJ: Lawrence Erlbaum.

Dees, M., & Corcoran, J. (1996). *Gathering storm: America's militia threat*. New York: Harper Perennials.

Dei, G., Hall, B., & Rosenberg, D. (2000). *Indigenous knowledge in global contexts*. Toronto: Toronto University Press.

Desautels, J., Garrison, J., & Fleury, S. C. (1998). Critical-constructivism and the sociopolitical agenda. In M. Larochelle, N. Bednarz, & J. Garrison (Eds.), *Constructivism and education*. New York: Cambridge University Press.

Dewey, J. (1916/1944/1966). *Democracy and education: An introduction to the philosophy of education*. New York: The Free Press.

Dewey, J. (1938/1997). *Experience and education*. New York: Touchstone.

Dilts, R. (1990). *Changing belief systems with NLP*. Cupertino, CA: Meta Publications.

Drucker, P. (1989). *The new realities*. New York: HarperCollins Press.

Du Bois, W. E. B. (1989). *The souls of black folk*. New York: Penguin Books.

Du Bois-Reymond, M., Sunker, H., & Heinz-Herman, K. (Eds.). (2001). *Childhood in Europe*. New York: Peter Lang.

Duckworth, E. (1987). *The having of wonderful ideas*. New York: Teachers College Press.

Eagleton, T. (1991). *Ideology*. New York: Routledge.

Edelsky, C. (1996). *With literacy and justice for all: Rethinking the social in language and education*. Bristol, PA: Taylor & Francis.

Eisner, E. (1985). *The educational imagination: On the design and evaluation of school programs*. New York: Macmillan.

Eisner, E. (1992). The misunderstood role of the arts in human development. *Phi Delta Kappan, 73*(8), 591–595.

Elder, L., & Paul, R. (2001). Critical thinking: Thinking to some purpose. *Journal of Developmental Education 25*, 40–41.

Ellinor, L., & Gerard, G. (1998). *Dialogue: Rediscover the transforming power of conversation*. New York: John Wiley and Sons.

Emerson, R. (2003). *Ralph Waldo Emerson: Essays, second series*. [On-line]. Available: http://www.literaturepage.com/read/emersonessays2-3.htm

Engels, F. (1968). *Dialectics of nature*. New York: International Publishers.

Ennis, R. (1962). A conception of rational thinking. In J. R. Coombs (Ed.), *Philosophy of Education 1979: Proceedings of the Thirty-fifth Annual Meeting of the Philosophy of Education Society*. Bloomington, IL: Philosophy of Education Society.

Ennis, R. H. (1991). *Critical thinking*. Upper Saddle River, NJ: Prentice-Hall.

Fanon, F. (1967). *Black skin white masks*. New York: Grove Weidenfeld.

Feuerverger, G. (2001). *Oasis of dreams: Teaching and learning peace in a Jewish-Palestinian village in Israel*. New York: Routledge-Falmer.

Fine, M. (1989). Silencing and nurturing voice in an improbable context: Urban adolescents in public school. In H. Giroux, & P. McLaren (Eds.), *Critical pedagogy, the state, and cultural power*. New York: State University of New York Press.

Fishman, S. M., & McCarthy, L. (1998). *John Dewey and the challenge of classroom practice*. New York: Teachers College Press.

Flinders, D., & Thornton, S. (Eds.). (1997). *The curriculum studies reader*. New York: Routledge.

Fraser, N. (1997). *Justice interruptus: Critical reflections on the "postsocialist" condition*. New York: Routledge.

Freire, A. M., & Macedo, D. (Eds.). (1998). *The Paulo Freire reader*. New York: Continuum.

Freire, P. (1970). *Pedagogy of the oppressed*. New York: Continuum.

Freire, P. (1985). *The politics of education. Culture, power, and liberation*. South Hadley, MA: Bergin & Garvey.

Freire, P. (1998). *Pedagogy of freedom: Ethics, democracy, and civic courage*. Lanham, MD: Rowman & Littlefield.

Freire, P., & Macedo, D. (1987). *Literacy: Reading the word and the world*. South Hadley, MA: Bergin & Garvey.

Furedi, F. (1994). *The new ideology of imperialism: Renewing the moral imperative*. London: Pluto Press.

Gardner, H. (1991). *The unschooled mind: How children think and how schools should teach*. New York: Basic Books.

Gee, J. (1996). *Social linguistics and literacies: Ideology in discourses*. London: Falmer Press.

Giroux, H. (1981). *Ideology, culture, and the process of schooling*. Philadelphia: Temple University Press.

Giroux, H. (1988). *Teachers as intellectuals: Toward a critical pedagogy of learning*. New York: Bergin & Garvey.

Giroux, H. (1993). *Living dangerously: Multiculturalism and the politics of difference*. New York: Peter Lang.

Giroux, H., & Shannon, P. (Eds.). (1997). *Education and cultural studies: Toward a performative practice*. New York: Routledge.

Glazer, E. (2001). *Using Internet primary sources to teach critical thinking skills in mathematics*. Westport, CT: Greenwood Publishing Group.

Gordon, L. R. (2000). *Existentia Africana: Understanding Africana existential thought*. New York: Routledge.

Gray, A., & McGuigan, J. (Eds.). (1993). *Studying culture: An introductory reader*. London: Edward Arnold.

Grimshaw, J. (1986). *Philosophy and feminist thinking*. Minneapolis, MN: University of Minnesota Press.

Hahn, T. N. (1992). *Peace is every step*. New York: Bantam Books.

Hale, J. B. (1982). *Black children: Their roots, culture, and learning style*. Baltimore: Johns Hopkins University Press.

Halpern, D. F. (1996). *Thought and knowledge: An introduction to critical thinking*. Mahwah, NJ: Lawrence Erlbaum.

Harding, S. (1998). *Is science multicultural?* Bloomington: Indiana University Press.

Hart, M. (1995). Motherwork: A radical proposal to rethink work and education. In M. Welton (Ed.), *In defense of the lifeworld: Critical perspectives on adult learning*. New York: State University of New York Press.

Harwayne, S. (2001). *Writing through childhood*. Portsmouth, NH: Heinemann.

Harwood, A. C. (1958). *The recovery of man in childhood*. New York: Myrin Books.

Hayden, A. (1999). *Sharing the work, sparing the planet: Work time, consumption and ecology*. London: Zed Books, Ltd.

Hentsch, T. (1992). *Imagining the Middle East*. Montreal: Black Rose Books.

Herman, E., & O'Sullivan, G. (1989). *The "terrorism" industry: The experts and institutions that shape our view of terror*. New York: Pantheon Books.

Horn, R. A. (2002). *Understanding educational reform: A reference handbook*. Santa Barbara, CA: ABC-CLIO.

Horton, M. (1997). *The long haul: An autobiography*. New York: Doubleday.

Hursh, D. W., & Ross, E. W. (Eds.). (2000). *Democratic social education: Social studies for social change*. New York: Falmer Press.

Jagla, V. M. (1994). *Teachers' everyday use of imagination and intuition: In pursuit of the elusive image*. Albany: State University of New York Press.

Jhally, S. (1990). *The codes of advertising*. New York: Routledge.

Johnson, D., Johnson, R., & Holubec, E. J. (1993). *Cooperation in the classroom* (6th ed.). Edina, MN: Interaction Book Company.

Johnson, P. A. (2000). *Up and out: Using creative and critical thinking skills to enhance learning*. Boston: Allyn and Bacon.

Keating, D. (1988). *Adolescents' ability to engage in critical thinking*. Madison, WI: National Center for Effective Secondary Schools.

Kellner, D. (1989). *Critical theory, Marxism and modernity*. Baltimore, MD: Johns Hopkins University Press.

Kincheloe, J. L. (1999). Trouble ahead, trouble behind: Grounding the post-formal critique of educational psychology. In J. L. Kincheloe, S. R. Steinberg, & P. H. Hinchey (Eds.) *The postformal reader: Cognition and education*. New York: Falmer Press.

Kincheloe, J. L. (1999). *Who will tell the workers? The socioeconomic foundations of work and vocational education*. Boulder, CO: Westview Press.

Kincheloe, J. L. (2003). *Teachers as researchers: Qualitative paths to empowerment* (2nd ed.). London: Falmer Press.

Kincheloe, J. L. (Ed.). (2004). *Multiple intelligences reconsidered: An expanded vision*. New York: Peter Lang.

Kincheloe, J. L., & Steinberg, S. R. (1997). *Changing multiculturalism*. London: Open University Press.

Kincheloe, J. L., & Steinberg, S. R. (Eds.). (1998). *Unauthorized methods: Strategies for critical teaching*. New York: Routledge.

Kincheloe, J. L., and Steinberg, S. R. (1999). A tentative description of post-formal thinking: The critical confrontation with cognitive theory. In J. L. Kincheloe, S. R. Steinberg, & P. H. Hinchey (Eds.), *The postformal reader: Cognition and education.* New York: Falmer Press.

Kincheloe, J. L., Steinberg, S. R., & Hinchey, P. H. (Eds.). (1999). *The postformal reader: Cognition and education.* New York: Falmer Press.

Kincheloe, J. L., Steinberg, S. R., & Villaverde, L. (1999). *Rethinking intelligence: Confronting psychological assumptions about teaching and learning.* New York: Routledge.

King, P. M., & Kitchener, K. S. (1994). *Developing reflective judgment: Understanding and promoting intellectual growth and critical thinking in adolescents and adults.* San Francisco: Jossey-Bass.

Kirkup, G., & Keller, L. S. (1992). A feeling for the organism: Fox Keller's life of Barbara McClintock. In G. Kirkup, & L. S. Keller (Eds.), *Inventing women—science, technology and gender* (pp. 188–195). Cambridge, U.K.: Polity Press.

Knobel, M. (1998). Critical literacies in teacher education. In M. Knobel, & A. Healy (Eds.), *Critical literacies in the primary classroom.* Marrickville, NSW: Primary English Teaching Association.

Kochan, F. K., & Mullen, C. A. (Eds.). (2001). Probing accountability in educational leadership: For whom and for what? *Journal of School Leadership, 11*(3), 158–257.

Kozol, J. (1991). *Savage inequalities: Children in America's schools.* New York: HarperCollins.

Kuhn, T. (1970). *The structure of scientific revolutions* (2nd ed.). Chicago: University of Chicago Press.

Lankshear, C., & McLaren, P. (1993). *Critical literacy: Politics, praxis and the postmodern.* New York: State University of New York Press.

Larochelle, M., Bednarz, N., & Garrison, J. (Eds.). (1998). *Constructivism and education.* New York: Cambridge University Press.

Leistyna, P., & Woodrum, A. (1996). Context and culture: What is critical pedagogy? In P. Leistyna, A. Woodrum, & S. A. Sherblom (Eds.), *Breaking free: The transfor-*

mative power of critical pedagogy. Cambridge, MA: Harvard Educational Review.

Lemert, C. (1997). *Social things: An introduction to the sociological life.* Lanham, MD: Rowman and Littlefield.

Levstik, L. S., & Barton, K. C. (2000). *Doing history: Investigating with children in elementary and middle schools.* Mahwah, NJ: Lawrence Erlbaum.

Longino, H. E. (1990). *Science as social knowledge.* Princeton, NJ: Princeton University Press.

Longman-Costa, A. (Ed.). (2001). *Developing minds: A resource book for teaching thinking.* Arlington, VA: Association for Supervision and Curriculum Development.

Lortie, D. C. (1998). Teaching educational administration: Reflections on our craft. *The Journal of Cases in Educational Leadership 1*(1), 1–12.

Lowen, J. (1992). *Lies my teacher told me: Everything your American history textbook got wrong.* New York: Simon & Schuster.

Lynch, C. L., Kitchener, K. S., & King, P. M. (1994). *Developing reflective judgment in the classroom: A manual for faculty.* New Concord, KY: Lynch.

Lynn, S. (2001). *Texts and contexts: Writing about literature with critical theory* (3rd ed.). New York: Longman.

Manguel, A. (1997). *A history of reading.* New York: Penguin.

Marx, K., & Engels, F. (1947). *The German ideology.* New York: International Publishers.

McCloud, S. (1994). *Understanding comics: The invisible art.* New York: Harper Perennial.

McLaren, P. (1995). *Critical pedagogy and predatory culture.* New York: Routledge.

McLuhan, H. M. (1994). *Understanding media: The extensions of man.* Cambridge, MA: The MIT Press.

Merriam-Webster's Collegiate Dictionary (10th ed.). (1993). Springfield, MA: Merriam-Webster.

Morrison, T. (1987). *Beloved.* New York: Knopf.

Norris, S. P. (1985). Synthesis of research on critical thinking. *Educational Leadership, 42*(8), 40–46.

Ocvirk, O. G., Stinson, R. E., Wigg, P. R., Bone, R. O., & Cayton, D. L. (1998). *Art fundamentals: Theory and practice.* New York: McGraw-Hill.

Okin, S. M. (1979). *Women in Western political thought.* Princeton, NJ: Princeton University Press.

Ollman, B. (1993). *Dialectical investigations.* New York: Routledge.

Omi, M., & Winant, H. (1994). *Racial formation in the United States: From the 1960s to the 1990s* (2nd ed.). New York: Routledge.

Osterman, K. (1993). *Reflective practice for educators.* Newbury Park, CA: Corwin Press.

Palmer, P. (1998). *The courage to teach: Exploring the inner landscape of a teacher's life.* San Francisco: Jossey-Bass.

Paul, R. (1992). *Critical thinking.* Sonoma County, CA: The Center for Critical Thinking and Moral Critique.

Paul, R. (1993). *Critical thinking: How to prepare students for a rapidly changing world.* Santa Rosa, CA: Foundation for Critical Thinking.

Paul, R., & Elder, L. (2001). Critical thinking: Inert information, activated ignorance, and activated knowledge. *Journal of Developmental Education, 25,* 36–37.

Phillips, C. (2001). *Socrates café.* New York: Norton.

Pinar, W., Reynolds, W., Slattery, P., & Taubman, P. (1995). *Understanding curriculum: An introduction to the study of historical and contemporary curriculum discourses.* New York: Peter Lang.

Rand, P. (1985). *A designer's art.* New Haven, CT: Yale University Press.

Rappaport, J. (1987). Terms of empowerment/exemplars of prevention: Toward a theory for community psychology. *American Journal of Community Psychology, 9,* 1–25.

Robertson, S. (2000). *A class act: Changing teachers' work, the state and globalisation.* New York: Falmer Press.

Rose, T. (1994). *Black noise: Rap music and black culture in contemporary America.* Hanover, NH: University Press of New England.

Ross, E. W. (Ed.). (2001). *The social studies curriculum: Purposes, problems, and possibilities* (Rev. ed.). Albany: State University of New York Press.

Sambuli-Mosha, R. (2000). *The heartbeat of indigenous Africa: A study of the Chagga educational system.* New York: Falmer Press.

Sarason, S. (1990). *The challenge of art to psychology.* New Haven, CT: Yale University Press.

Schiller, H. (1989). *Culture, inc.: The corporate takeover of public expression.* New York: Oxford University Press.

Schon, D. A. (1983). *The reflective practitioner: How professionals think in action.* New York: Basic Books.

Schwartz, E. (1999). *Millennial child: Transforming education in the twenty-first century.* Hudson, NY: Anthroposophic Press.

Sehr, D. T. (1997). *Education for a public democracy.* Albany: State University of New York Press.

Shapiro, E. (2000). *Designing democratic institutions.* New York: New York University Press.

Shor, I. (1992). *Empowering education: Critical teaching for social change.* Chicago: University of Chicago Press.

Sidorkin, A. (1999). *Beyond discourse: Education, the self, and dialogue.* New York: State University of New York Press.

Siegel, H. (1988). *Educating reason: Rationality, critical thinking, and education.* New York: Routledge.

Simon, K. (2001). *Moral questions in the classroom: How to get kids to think deeply about real life and their schoolwork.* New Haven, CT: Yale University Press.

Skovsmose, O. (2000). Aphorism and critical mathematical education. *For the Learning of Mathematics, 20*(1), 2–8.

Sleeter, C., & Grant, C. A. (1999). *Making choices for multicultural education. Five approaches to race, class, and gender* (3rd ed.). New York: John Wiley & Sons.

Sloan, D. (1983). *Insight-imagination: The emancipation of thought and the modern world.* Westport, CT: Greenwood Publishing Group.

Smelser, N., Wilson, W., & Mitchell, F. (Eds.). (2001). *America becoming: Racial trends and their consequences* (Vols. 1–2). Washington, DC: National Academy Press.

Smyth, J. (2000). Reclaiming social capital through critical teaching. *The Elementary School Journal, 100* (5), 491–511.

Smyth, J. (2001). *Critical politics of teachers' work: An Australian perspective.* New York: Peter Lang.

Soto, L. D. (2002). *Making a difference in the lives of bilingual/bicultural children.* New York: Peter Lang.

Spender, D. (1982). *Women of ideas and what men have done to them.* Winchester, MA: Pandora Press.

Splitter, L., & Sharp, A. (1995). *Teaching for better thinking: The classroom community of inquiry.* Melbourne: Australian Council for Educational Research.

Spring, J. (2000). *Deculturalization and the struggle for equality* (3rd ed.). New York: McGraw-Hill.

Spring, J. (2002). *American education* (10th ed.). New York: McGraw-Hill.

Steinberg, S. R., & Kincheloe, J. L. (Eds.). (1997). *Kinderculture: The corporate construction of childhood.* Boulder, CO: Westview Press.

Stiggins, R. J., Rubel, E., & Quellmalz, E. (1988). *Measuring thinking skills in the classroom.* Washington, DC: National Education Association.

Storey, J. (Ed.). (1996). *What is cultural studies: A reader.* London: Edward Arnold.

Thayer-Bacon, B. (2000). *Transforming critical thinking: Thinking constructively.* New York: Teachers College Press.

Thompson, J. (1984). *Studies in the theory of ideology.* Berkeley: University of California Press.

Tishman, S., Perkins, D. N., & Jay, E. S. (1995). *The thinking classroom: Learning and teaching in the culture of thinking.* Boston: Allyn & Bacon.

Toulmin, S. (1960). *The philosophy of science.* New York: Harper and Row.

Triandafyllidou, A. (2001). *Immigrants and national identity in Europe.* New York: Routledge.

Tufte, E. R. (1990). *Envisioning information.* Cheshire, CT: Graphics Press.

Wah, L. M. (Producer/Director). (1994). *The color of fear* (Video). Oakland, CA: Stir-fry Productions.

Webb, J., Schirato, T., & Danaher, G. (2002). *Understanding Bourdieu.* Thousand Oaks, CA: Sage.

Weil, D. (1998). *Towards a critical multicultural literacy: Theory and practice for education for liberation.* New York: Peter Lang.

Weil, D., & Anderson, H. K. (Eds.). (2000). *Perspectives in critical thinking: Essays by teachers in theory and practice.* New York: Peter Lang.

Wiggins, G. (1998). *Educative assessment: Designing assessments to inform and improve student performance.* San Francisco: Jossey-Bass.

Wigginton, E. (1985). *Sometimes a shining moment.* New York: Anchor Press/Doubleday.

Winchester, S. (1998). *The professor and the madman: A tale of murder, insanity, and the making of the Oxford English Dictionary.* New York: HarperCollins Publishers.

Wineburg, S. S. (2002). *Historical thinking and other unnatural acts: Charting the future of teaching the past.* Philadelphia: Temple University Press.

Woods, P., Jeffrey, B., Troman, G., & Boyle, M. (1997). *Restructuring schools, reconstructing teachers: Responding to change in the primary school*. London: Open University Press.

Wright, H. (2000). "Pressing, promising, and paradoxical": Larry Grossberg on the relationship between cultural studies and education. *Review of Education/Pedagogy/Cultural Studies, 22*(1), 1–25.

Zinn, H. (1995) *A people's history of the United States*. New York: Harper.

Index

About the Editors and Contributors

PETER APPELBAUM is an associate professor and coordinator of mathematics education programs at Arcadia University, where he teaches curriculum theory, cultural foundations, and critical perspectives on mathematics education. He is the author of *Embracing Mathematics: On Becoming a Teacher and Changing with Mathematics*; *Popular Culture; Educational Discourse and Mathematics*; and *Multicultural and Diversity Education,* and co-editor of *(Post) Modern Science (Education)*. His research interests range from youth's perspectives on technoculture and popular culture to the critique of conceptual discourses in curriculum theorizing. He can be contacted at appelbaum@arcadia.edu.

KATHLEEN S. BERRY is a professor of education at the University of New Brunswick in Canada. She has presented keynote addressees and published several articles and chapters on critical studies in education, including using critical multiculturalism in drama and literature. With her graduate students in critical studies, she is publishing work on bricolage as research with Joe Kincheloe. Recently she received the Allan P. Stuart Award for Excellence in Teaching, which is her favorite part of being a professor. She can be contacted at kberry@unb.ca.

BILL BIGELOW teaches at Franklin High School in Portland, Oregon, and is an editor of *Rethinking Schools*. He has written extensively on school reform.

CHARLES BINGHAM is an assistant professor of curriculum at Simon Fraser University in Vancouver, British Columbia. He is the author of *Schools of Recognition: Identity Politics and Classroom Practices,* 2001.

PAUL BRAWDY is an assistant professor of physical education at Saint Bonaventure University. A former national-level weightlifting coach and avid outdoorsperson, Dr. Brawdy draws upon a wide range of traditional and nontraditional movement-based learning experiences in his teaching. His research interests include the phenomenology of learning through movement and the impact of public policy and institutional politics on teach identity. He can be contacted at pbrawdy@sbu.edu.

TANYA BROWN is a writer and an educator. She has taught for several years at both the primary and seconary levels. She holds an MAT from the School of Education at Columbia College and is anticipating a doctorate in education from DePaul University. She lives on the south side of Chicago with her family.

ALBERTO M. BURSZTYN is an associate professor of special education and school psychology. His writing focuses on how schools and education professionals address issues of disability, cultural diversity, and linguistic competence. He has worked as a teacher, school psychologist, and administrator in the New York City public schools; and as program head of special education and assistant dean at the School of Education at Brooklyn College—CUNY. His most recent publication, *Rethinking Multicultural Education: Case Studies in Cultural Transition* (2002), was co-edited with Dr. Carol Korn. Alberto is also an artist who works in a variety of media. He can be contacted at Abursxtyn@brooklyn.cuny.edu.

GAILE S. CANNELLA is a professor in childhood studies in the College of Education at Texas A&M University. She is the author of *Deconstructing Early Childhood Education: Social Justice and Revolution,* co-editor with Joe Kincheloe of *Kidworld: Childhood Studies, Global Perspectives, and Education,* and many other books and articles.

ROYMIECO A. CARTER is a visiting assistant professor in the School of Computer Science, Technology, and Information Systems at De Paul University. He is also a graphic designer and lectures on design, multimedia, web design, and social criticism.

VICKI K. CARTER holds a doctorate in adult education from Pennsylvania State University, where she works as a senior instructional designer. Her research interests include critically examining workplace learning through a cultural studies lens.

RICHARD CARY is an artist, educator, and scholar who lives in Asheville, North Carolina. He holds a Ph.D. in aesthetics from the University of Tennessee and an M.F.A. in photography from Goddard College. Cary published *Critical Art Pedagogy: Foundations for Postmodern Art Education* in 1998. He writes and speaks on the critical theory perspective on art and visual culture, and is a professor of art at Mars Hill College. He can be contacted at rcary@mhc.edu.

NELL B. COBB is an associate professor at DePaul University School of Education, where she teaches mathematics education courses on the elementary and secondary levels. Dr. Cobb also teaches the elementary mathematics content courses for education majors and mathematics courses for first year students in the university's Bridge Program. Her research interests include the Algebra Project's Model of Excellence, the Algebra Project's Young People's Project, Complexities of Collaborations, San Miguel Christen Brothers School, and preservice students' electronic portfolios.

BRENDA EDGERTON CONLEY is chair of Teacher Education Programs and an associate professor in the graduate school at the University of Maryland's University College. Prior to her university appointment, Dr. Conley was employed by the Baltimore City Public School System for 29 years. In addition to spending ten years as a classroom teacher, she served as the Assistant Superintendent for Professional Development, Organizational Development, and Attitudinal Reform; Director of Policy Development and Leadership Support; Director of Human Resources, and director of the Performance-Based Teacher Evaluation Project. She was also employed by Johns Hopkins University School of Business and Professional Studies, where she directed Project

SITE SUPPORT, a partnership of three universities (Johns Hopkins University, Morgan State University, and the University of Maryland Baltimore County). SITE SUPPORT was funded by a $12.8 million United States Department of Education Title II Grant. Dr. Conley earned both a bachelor's and a master's degree at Morgan State University in Baltimore, Maryland, and received her doctorate in education from The George Washington University in Washington, D.C.

JOHN F. COVALESKIE is a professor of education at Northern Michigan University. His interests include issues of social morality, moral education, and character formation. He can be contacted at jcovales@nmu.edu.

KOSHI DHINGRA, a science educator, has an Ed.D. from Teachers College, Columbia University. She taught middle and high school in New York City for seven years and then taught undergraduate teachers at Brooklyn College of the City University of New York. She is currently on leave of absence with her husband, Arun, and son, Ronak, as she waits for the arrival of twins in May. She can be contacted at kdhingra@brooklyn.cuny.edu.

LOURDES DIAZ SOTO is a professor of education at Penn State University. She has authored numerous articles and chapters in books. Her books include *Language, Culture, and Power: Bilingual Families and the Struggle for Quality Education, The Politics of Early Childhood Education,* and *Making a Difference in the Lives of Bilingual/ Bicultural Children.*

MICHAEL J. DUMAS is a graduate student in the Ph.D. program in Urban Education/ Educational Policy Studies at The Graduate Center of the City University of New York. His research interests include Black education, urban development policy, globalization and Africana existential thought. He can be contacted at Mduma@gc.cuny.edu.

STEPHEN M. FAIN is a professor in the College of Education and a fellow in the Honors College at Florida International University, Miami, Florida, where he teaches curriculum theory, curriculum history, the social foundations of education, and courses that examine the American experience. Professor Fain has taught at both the elementary and secondary levels and has served as an elementary school principal. He holds an Ed.D. in curriculum development from Teachers College, Columbia and a B.S. from Rutgers University. Professor Fain is the co-author of three books as well as contributing author to numerous collections of essays on curriculum. He is past president of the American Association for Teaching and Curriculum. He can be contacted at fains@fiu.edu.

JUAN-MIGUEL FERNÁNDEZ-BALBOA is a professor of education in the Department of Curriculum and Teaching at Montclair State University (New Jersey). He received his doctorate in education from the University of Massachusetts at Amherst in 1998. His scholarship interests center around the practice of critical pedagogy in teacher education. He is a frequent speaker at national and international conferences, and his work has been published in the *Journal of Teacher Education, Teaching and Teacher Education,* and *Quest,* among other reputable journals. He has co-authored and edited *Critical Postmodernism in Human Movement, Physical Education and Sport,* published by SUNY Press in 1977. He can be contacted at fernandezj@mail.montclair.edu.

JAMES C. FIELD is an associate professor on the faculty of education at the University of Calgary. His interests include alternative assessment, qualitative research methods, adolescents in schools, and teacher education. He is currently researching adolescents' experiences of learning in the junior and senior high school. He can be contacted at jfield@ucalgary.ca.

STEPHEN C. FLEURY is currently a professor of education at Le Moyne University and director of the Syracuse Center for Urban Education. He has taught social studies education for 20 years in middle school, high school, and in an alternative program for pregnant teens. During an internship with the New York State Bureau of Social Studies, he was involved in constructing statewide Regents examinations in his field and teaching social studies content, methods, and curriculum at the undergraduate and graduate level. His teaching and research focus is on the relationship between knowledge and power, and includes the areas of educational policy studies, the philosophy and use of science as public knowledge, and educational constructivism as a philosophical and cognitive theory in a democratic society.

JOHN GABRIEL is an associate professor in the Department of Language, Literacy, and Culture at California State University at San Bernadino. His research interests are in secondary literacy, especially English education, democratic classrooms, and action research in teacher education.

HERMÁN S. GARCÍA received his doctorate in curriculum and instruction from New Mexico State University in 1982. He joined the College of Education at NMSU in the fall of 1991, and currently serves as a professor and Head of the Department of Curriculum and Instruction. Before coming to New Mexico State, Dr. García taught at Texas Tech University and Texas A&M University, and completed postdoctoral studies at Harvard University in higher education administration in management and leadership. He is a nationally recognized critical bilingual educator and has authored and co-authored numerous articles, chapters, and books in critical bilingual education. Dr. García is a member of the editorial boards and field editor of several journals and book publishing companies. He has traveled throughout Latin America and currently has a teacher education program that offers a Master of Arts in Teaching TESOL to Brazilian educators at the University of Southern Brazil in Tubarão, Santa Catarina. He also serves on several state and national boards and committees and speaks at local, national, and international meetings and conferences.

JAIME GRINBERG is an associate professor of educational foundations at Montclair State University and the codirector of the New Jersey Network for Educational Renewal. His research has been published in journals such as *Review of Educational Research, Teachers College Record, Educational Administration Quarterly, School Leadership,* and *Theory Into Practice* among others. He has two forthcoming books to be published by Peter Lang Publications.

PATRICIA H. HINCHEY holds a doctorate in English education from Teachers College, Columbia University, and is an associate professor of education at Penn State University. In addition to professional development offerings for K–12 and college faculty, she teaches undergraduate and graduate courses in educational theory, media literacy, and methods for the language arts classroom. She has published a wide variety of journal articles and is the author of *Finding Freedom in the Classroom: A Practical Introduction to Critical Theory* (1998) and *Student Rights: A Reference Handbook* (2001); she is also co-author, with Isabel Kimmel, of *The Graduate Grind: A Critical Look at Graduate Education* (2000).

JUDI HIRSCH has been a public school teacher for more than 30 years, half of which have also been spent supporting teachers through workshops, college courses, and on-the-job mentoring. She has worked in New York, Jerusalem, and California, and studied with Paulo Freire and Reuven Feuerstein. Her doctorate is in multicultural education. Her research demonstrated that when African American and Mexican American students labeled learning disabled were taught high level thinking skills, they improved in both academic achievement and school adjustment. Many of her special education students have gone on to complete college. Judi Hirsch lives and works in Oakland, California. She can be contacted at judih@ousd.k12.ca.us.

RAYMOND A. HORN, JR. is an assistant professor of education at Penn State, Harrisburg and was a public school teacher for 30 years. His most recent book is *Understanding Educational Reform: A Reference Handbook*. He can be contacted at rah175@email.psu.edu.

DAVID W. HURSH is an associate professor in the Teaching and Curriculum Program in the Warner Graduate School of Education and Human Development at the University of Rochester. His writings focus on the prospect of democratic education in conservative times, including critiquing the rise of testing and accountability within the current neoliberal era. His book, co-edited with E. Wayne Ross, is *Democratic Social Education: Social Studies for Social Change*. He can be contacted at dhrh@troi.cc.rochester.edu.

KATHY HYTTEN is an associate professor of education in the Department of Educational Administration and Higher Education at Southern Illinois University, Carbondale. Her primary areas of scholarship are the philosophy of education, social theory, and cultural studies. She can be contacted at kyytten@siu.edu.

VALERIE J. JANESICK is a professor, chair of the Department of Educational Leadership and Organizational Change, and Doctoral Program Director at Roosevelt University. She teaches courses in qualitative research methods, program evaluation, curriculum theory, development, and assessment. She has written books and articles in these areas and her most recent text is *The Assessment Debate: A Reference Handbook* (2001). She recently participated in the Oxford Roundtable, 2002 at Lincoln College, University of Oxford. Her text, *Stretching Exercises for Qualitative Researchers* uses the metaphor of dance and the arts to teach interviewing, observation, and archival techniques, Her articles and book chapters on qualitative research methods argue for understanding the value of aesthetics in the research process.

WILLIAM A. KEALY has taught the design and development of video, multi-image, and graphics of print and Web delivery since 1989 at Ithaca College, Texas A&M University, Florida State University, and the University of South Florida, where he is currently an associate professor of instructional technology. His research on ways to improve the effectiveness of instructional media has appeared in such journals as *Contemporary Educational Psychology,* the *Journal of Educational Psychology,* the *British Journal of Educational Psychology, Reading Psychology,* and *Educational Technology Research and Development.* Prior to obtaining his Ph.D. in learning and instructional technology at Arizona State University, Dr. Kealy served as art director for a Honolulu-based advertising agency. He can be contacted at wkealy@coedu.usf.edu.

JOE L. KINCHELOE is a professor of education at the City University of New York Graduate Center and Brooklyn College where he has served as the Belle Zeller Chair of Public Policy and Administration. He is the author of numerous books and articles about pedagogy, education and social justice, racism, class bias, and sexism, issues of cognition and cultural context, and educational reform. His books include *Teachers as Researchers, Toil and Trouble, Getting Beyond the Facts: Teaching Social Studies/Social Sciences in the Twenty-first Century, The Sign of the Burger: McDonald's and the Culture of Power,* and *Changing Multiculturalism* (with Shirley Steinberg). His co-edited works include *White Reign: Deploying Whiteness in America*, the Gustavus Myers Human Rights award winner *Measured Lies: The Bell Curve Examined,* and *The Postformal Reader* (with Shirley Steinberg and Patricia Hinchey). He can be contacted at Jkincheloe@aol.com.

MICHELE KNOBEL is an adjunct professor at Central Queensland University, Australia, and is an associate professor at Monclair State University in New Jersey. She also lives and works as a university teacher, researcher, and writer in Mexico. Her recent books include *New Literacies* (with Colin Lankshear), *Cyber Spaces/Social Spaces: Culture Clash in Computerized Classrooms* (with Colin Lankshear, Ivor Goodson and Marshall Mangan), and *Ways of Knowing: Researching Literacy* (with Colin Lankshear). She can be contacted at michele@coatepec.net.

CAROL KORN is a psychologist and associate professor of early childhood education at Brooklyn College. She worked as a school psychologist in the New York City public schools and in clinical settings prior to earning a Psy.D. in Professional Child/School Psychology from New York University in 1990. Dr. Korn is currently pursuing postdoctoral work in psychoanalysis at New York University. Her research interests include the role of the arts in early education, the experience of cultural transitions, and the development of narrative in childhood. She can be contacted at CarolKB@brooklyn.cuny.edu.

NANCY KRAFT has been an educator for 24 years and has focused on enabling critical reflection in students and teachers for much of her career. She has taught at the high school, community college, and university levels, and has been involved in developing a public charter school for at-risk high school youth in Kansas where students develop the skills of scholar-practitioners through authentic, context-based, service learning. She is currently the director of the Kansas Parent Information Resource Center. She can be contacted at nkraft@nekesc.org.

COLIN LANKSHEAR is currently a part-time professional research fellow at the University of Ballarat in Australia. He is also an educational researcher and writer based in Mexico, where he has lived since 1999. Formerly a professor of education and research director, his current academic interests lie in exploring the emerging literacies and cultural practices associated with new information and communications technologies, and the research methods of qualitative inquiry. His recent books include *Ways of Knowing, Maneras de Ver,* and *New Literacies* (all with Michele Knobel), *Teachers and Technoliteracy* (with Ilana Snyder), and *Boys, Literacy and Schooling* (with Leonie Rowan, Michele Knobel, and Chris Bigum). He can be contacted at c.lankshear@yahoo.com.

ZEUS LEONARDO has published articles and book chapters on critical education and social theory with special attention to issues of race, class, and gender. He is the author of *Ideology, Discourse, and School Reform* (2003, Praeger) and co-editor (with Tejeda and Martinez) of *Charting New Terrains in Chicana(o).Latina(o) Education* (2000). His work can best be described as the political integration of ideology critique and discourse analysis. Dr. Leonardo is currently an assistant professor in the College of Education at California State, Long Beach. He can be contacted at zleonard@sulb.edu.

ERIK MALEWSKI is a visiting professor of curriculum studies at Purdue University. He was previously Diversity Advocate for Penn State University where he developed a network of faculty, staff, and students dedicated to creating organizational cultures that embraced notions of difference. His research interests include the role of affect in the revitalization of education, participatory democracy as the production of knowledge, and critical perspectives on organizations as social life and canonical bodies.

MARJORIE MAYERS received her Ph.D. in counseling/educational psychology from the University of Calgary, where she is currently teaching. Her interests include the political topography of youth and youth culture, the political and social context of schooling, and interpretive inquiry. Her first book, *Street Kids and Streetscapes: Panhandling, Politics, and Prophecies* (2001).

CYNTHIA McCALLISTER is an assistant professor of literacy education at New York University's Steinhardt School of Education. She is a former elementary school teacher and staff developer, and currently does research on issues relating to literacy education and school reform. She can be contacted at cynthia.mccallister@nyu.edu.

CAROL A. MULLEN, assistant professor, teaches in the Department of Educational Leadership and Policy Studies at the University of South Florida. She specializes in collaborative mentoring development for groups within schools and universities. Dr. Mullen has published five books. *Breaking the Circle of One* (2000, 2nd edition) received the Exemplary Research in Teacher Education Award for AERA (Division K) in 1998. Forthcoming is *Backpacking with New Administrators Across the Himalayas of School Leadership*. Dr. Mullen is also editor of the journal *Mentoring & Tutoring*. She has published many referenced journal articles and, as guest editor, 11 special issues of academic journals, including *Teacher Development*, the *Journal of Curriculum Theorizing,* and *Qualitative Inquiry*. She can be contacted at cmullen@coedu.usf.edu.

THOMAS NELSON is a professor in the Benerd School of Education at the University of the Pacific. He specializes in secondary school teacher education, curriculum theory, educational policy, and qualitative research methods. He is also the editor of *Teacher Education Quarterly,* one of the most widely recognized research journals in the field. He can be contacted at tnelson@uop.edu.

PRIYA PARMAR is an assistant professor of education at Brooklyn College. Her work in urban education involves the study of hip-hop and its multidimensional relationship to education.

YUSEF PROGLER is coordinator of the General Education Program at Zayed University in Dubai. He teaches interdisciplinary social science and comparative education. He has written extensively on Muslim education, social studies, and the social-cultural politics of education.

CHRISTINE M. QUAIL is a doctoral candidate at the University of Oregon. She studies the political economy of communications and the politics of knowledge production in the mass media. She is currently on the steering committee of the Union for Democratic

Communications, an international organization of scholars, activists, and media producers.

WAYNE A. REED is an assistant professor of education at Brooklyn College. He has published numerous articles in urban pedogy.

E. WAYNE ROSS is a Distinguished University Scholar and chair of the Department of Teaching and Learning at the University of Louisville. He has published numerous books and articles on social studies education, curriculum studies, and the politics of education, and is a founding member of the Rouge Forum (www.rougeforum.org). Ross is co-editor of the journals *Cultural Logic: Marxist Theory and Practice* and *Workplace: The Journal of Academic Labor*. His latest book, *Image and Education: Teaching in the Age of the New Diciplinarity*, was co-authored with Kevin D. Vinson. He can be contacted at wross@louisville.edu.

LADISLAUS M. SEMALI is an associate professor of education in the Department of Curriculum and Instruction at Pennsylvania State University, specializing in language, media, and literacy education. His work has been published in the *International Review of Education* and *Comparative Education Review*. He is author of *Literacy in Multimedia America: Integrating Media Education Across the Curriculum* (Routledge/Falmer, 2000), *Postliteracy in the Age of Democracy* (1996), and editor of *Intermediality: The Teacher's Handbook of Critical Media Literacy* with Ann Pailliotet. He can be contacted at Lms11@psu.edu.

KAIA SKAGGS is an assistant professor of education in the Department of Teacher Education at Eastern Michigan University. Her scholarly work involves issues of educational assessment and multiple intelligences.

JUDITH J. SLATER is an associate professor at Florida International University, Miami, and is involved with curriculum theory, evaluation, organizational analysis, and women in higher education. Her books include *Anatomy of a Collaboration*, *Acts of Alignment*, *The Freirean Legacy: Educating for Social Justice*, and the forthcoming *Teen Life in Asia* (Greenwood) and *A Pedagogy of Place*. She can be contacted at slaterj@fiu.edu.

JOHN SMYTH is professor emeritus and was foundation professor of teacher education at Flinders University of South Australia and director of the Flinders Institute for the Study of Teaching. He is a former Fulbright Senior Research Scholar; Lansdowne Fellow at University of Victoria, British Columbia; a Distinguished Visiting Scholar at the University of British Columbia; and a recipient of the Palmer O. Johnson Award from the American Educational Research Association. His areas of research interest are the sociocritical policy analyses of education and the sociology and politics of teachers' work. He is the author/editor of fifteen books, the most recent being *A Critical Politics of Teachers' Work* (2001).

TIMOTHY SPRAGGINS is associate vice president for diversity education at DePaul University, Chicago, where he is also a doctoral candidate in curriculum studies. He received his undergraduate and graduate degrees in education from the University of Alabama, Alabama State University, the University of Dayton, and Auburn University in Montgomery. He can be contacted at tspraggi@depaul.edu.

IAN STEINBERG is a production editor at an academic press in New York City. He is also a documentary filmmaker currently working on a television series that explores the phenomena of high modernity and late capitalism.

SHIRLEY R. STEINBERG is the chair of Graduate Literacy at Brooklyn College. The author and editor of many books and articles on education, popular culture, and consumerism, Steinberg's most recent book is *Multi/intercultural Conversations: A Reader*.

LAYLA P. SULEIMAN GONZALEZ is an assistant professor in the Education Policy Studies and Research Department of the School of Education at DePaul University in Chicago. For over 15 years, she has served as a research, policy, and evaluation consultant to various public, NGO, and foundation entities in the area of youth development and social services.

KENNETH TEITELBAUM is a professor and chair of the Department of Teaching, Leadership and Curriculum Studies at Kent State University in Ohio. He has taught courses on curriculum theory and history, elementary and secondary curriculum, multicultural education, social studies education, and educational foundations, His scholarly interests focus on schooling, school reform, and issues of power, equality, and justice; school knowledge within current and historical contexts; and critical reflection in teacher education and teachers' work. He can be contacted at kteitelb@kent.edu.

BARBARA J. THAYER-BACON teaches undergraduate and graduate courses on the philosophy and history of education, social philosophy, and cultural diversity at the University of Indiana at Bloomington. Her primary research areas are the philosophy of education, pragmatism, feminist theory and pedagogy, and cultural studies in education. She is an active member of numerous professional organizations, including the American Educational Research Association, the American Educational Studies Association, and the Philosophy of Education Society, and presents papers regularly at their annual conferences. She is past president of the Ohio Valley Philosophy of Education Society, and president-elect of the Philosophical Studies in Education and the Research of Women and Education groups, which are special interest groups within AERA. She is the author of several chapters in essay collections and over fifty journals, such as *The Journal of Thought, Educational Theory, Studies in Philosophy and Education, Inquiry, Educational Foundations*, and *Educational Studies*. She has written several books: *Philosophy Applied to Education: Nurturing a Democratic Community in the Classroom* with Dr. Charles S. Bacon as contributing author (1998), and *Transforming Critical Thinking: Constructive Thinking* (2000). Her third book, *Relational "(e)pistemologies*," was recently published. She can be contacted at bthayer@utk.edu.

MARY ANNE ULLERY works at Florida International University as a research assistant and studies full-time in the Ed.D. program for curriculum and instruction, instructional leadership. She has coordinated grant-funded ESOL programs and taught adult education. Mary Anne served for two years in the Peace Corps in Kenya where she taught high school English. She has a B.A. in English from East Carolina University and an M.A.T. in Secondary English from SUNY Cortland. She can be contacted at maullery@msn.com.

TERESA VALENZUELA is a doctoral candidate in the Department of Curriculum and Instruction at New Mexico State University. She has been a bilingual educator for over 10 years and has always worked in schools with high Latino enrollments. She specializes in working with Latino parents, and serves on several boards, committees, and organizations that directly and indirectly serve children and adults.

LEILA E. VILLAVERDE is an assistant professor in cultural foundations in the School of Education at the University of North Carolina at Greensboro. She also lectures on feminist theory, curriculum studies, critical pedagogy, and aesthetics.

KEVIN D. VINSON is an assistant professor in the Department of Teaching and Teacher Education in the College of Education at the University of Arizona. His work in social studies education, critical educational theory, and educational philosophy has appeared in numerous books and journals.

DANNY WEIL is the in-service specialist and director of the Critical Thinking Institute, which serves educators, organizations, and businesses throughout the United States, Mexico, Canada, and Puerto Rico. In 1997, Dr. Weil authored the critical thinking course for the American Management Association and was for more than four years a presenter for the American Management Association in the areas of critical thinking, collaborative problem solving, organizational development, and problem solving and decision making. He holds a Ph.D. in critical thinking and education as well as a Juris Doctorate in law and is the author of many books on critical thinking and education. He is currently the editor of *Taboo,* an educational journal for teachers. Dr. Weil has coauthored a PBS series on critical thinking, been published in various national and international magazines and journals, and written many books on critical thinking, education, and educational public policy. He currently works as a philosophy instructor at Hancock Junior College in Santa Maria, California.

PAT WILLIAMS-BOYD is an associate professor of education and director of Middle Vision: Associates for Dynamic Middle Levels Education at Eastern Michigan University. During her 28 years in the public school system she won numerous awards, including Teacher of the Year, Outstanding Young Educator from the Jaycees, and the Governor's Award for Exceptional Service to Kansas Public Education. She holds two doctoral degrees, one in ethnomusicology and the other in curriculum and instruction. Williams-Boyd has written books and articles and received numerous grants for projects on middle-grades reform, and presents her work at workshops and conferences throughout the United States and Europe. She can be contacted at Pwilliamboyd@aol.com.

C. SHELDON WOODS is an assistant professor of science education in the Department of Teaching and Learning at Northern Illinois University. For the last decade he has focused on hands-on, inquiry-based learning, evolution education, and educational technology. He can be contacted at cwoods@depaul.edu.

HANDEL KASHOPE WRIGHT is an associate professor of cultural studies at the University of Tennessee. His research interests include cultural studies in education, continental and diasporic African cultural studies, curriculum theorizing, multiculturalism, and qualitative research. He has published widely on variety of issues, including African cultural studies, the transition from literature to cultural studies, the status quo of curriculum theorizing, drama studies in Africa, an endarkened feminist epistemology in qualitative research, and pedagogy as cultural praxis. His forthcoming book is titled *A Prescience of African Cultural Studies.* He can be contacted at hwright@utk.edu.

111005